Age of Rogues
Rebels, Revolutionaries
and Racketeers at the
Frontiers of Empires

Edited by
Ramazan Hakkı Öztan and Alp Yenen

EDINBURGH
University Press

Edinburgh University Press is one of the leading university presses in the UK. We publish academic books and journals in our selected subject areas across the humanities and social sciences, combining cutting-edge scholarship with high editorial and production values to produce academic works of lasting importance. For more information visit our website: edinburghuniversitypress.com

© editorial matter and organisation Ramazan Hakkı Öztan and Alp Yenen, 2021, 2023
© the chapters their several authors, 2021, 2023
Chapter 12, *The Last Ottoman Rogues*, is published under a Creative Commons Attribution-NonCommercial licence

Edinburgh University Press Ltd
The Tun – Holyrood Road
12 (2f) Jackson's Entry
Edinburgh EH8 8PJ

First published in hardback by Edinburgh University Press 2021

Typeset in 11/15 Adobe Garamond by
Servis Filmsetting Ltd, Stockport, Cheshire

A CIP record for this book is available from the British Library

ISBN 978 1 4744 6262 4 (hardback)
ISBN 978 1 4744 6263 1 (paperback)
ISBN 978 1 4744 6264 8 (webready PDF)
ISBN 978 1 4744 6265 5 (epub)

The right of the contributors to be identified as authors of this work has been asserted in accordance with the Copyright, Designs and Patents Act 1988 and the Copyright and Related Rights Regulations 2003 (SI No. 2498).

'Ramazan Hakkı Öztan and Alp Yenen have assembled a wonderful gallery of rebels, revolutionaries and racketeers – extraordinary characters located at the margins of imperial power. The stories presented here, of colourful personalities operating in dramatic contexts, make fascinating reading while the scholarship is of the highest quality. A fine book.'

Stephanie Cronin, Elahé Omidyar Mir-Djalali Research Fellow,
St Antony's College, University of Oxford

'*Age of Rogues* is a rich and original work dedicated to one of the most compelling issues within late imperial history: how did outlaws and rebels reflect and influence the development of modern states and society? Through a rich of array of case studies spanning the Caucasus, Balkans and Middle East, this volume offers important insights into how would-be revolutionaries and common brigands helped shape the nature of borders, governments, and provincial communities between the nineteenth and twentieth centuries. Each chapter of this work exemplifies the most current research into the global and local factors that gave birth to this period of violence and upheaval. As a study dedicated to a bottom-up understanding of the late Ottoman and Russian empires, *Age of Rogues* clearly sets new benchmarks for students and scholars alike.'

Ryan Gingeras, Professor in the Department of National Security Affairs,
Naval Postgraduate School

'This fascinating volume brings together a wide range of case studies of ground-level political violence in the frontier zones of the Balkans, the Caucasus, and the Middle East in an era of imperial disintegration. The collection's detailed exploration of the multifarious figures – brought together here under the label of "rogues" – engaged in an often-violent politics of transgression offers a new and compelling case for the importance of apparently marginal actors, acting outside the state, to the process of imperial disintegration. Further, it traces how such "rogues" gradually made their way into the structures of nationalism emerging before and after the First World War and eventually came to constitute central figures in institutions of postwar governance, installing their often-anarchic sense of political strategy into structures of statehood and nationalism from Macedonia to Iran. In its timely analysis of the politics of transgression, then, this volume is a crucial addition not just to the conversation about how these empires disintegrated but also to the analysis of the fractured and violent nation-states that replaced them.'

Laura Robson, Oliver-McCourtney Professor of History,
The Pennsylvania State University

'In a stunning collection, the editors Öztan and Yenen not only expertly steer an otherwise disparate set of authors writing on seemingly very different themes, historic trajectories, and locales, they also masterfully conjoin this volume to serve as one of our generation's best exemplars of scholarship on the late Ottoman Empire. A highly readable collection of cutting-edge research on agents of change along the fringes of both the Ottoman and larger modern world, this book must be considered an addition to the library of all serious scholars, and a candidate for their graduate seminars. I most enthusiastically recommend this invaluable new addition to the scholarship.'

Isa Blumi, Professor of Turkish and Middle Eastern Studies,
Stockholm University

Contents

List of Figures vii
Notes on Contributors viii
About this Book xiv

    Foreword xviii
    Jack A. Goldstone

Part I Rogues in History

1 Age of Rogues: Transgressive Politics at the Frontiers of the Ottoman Empire 3
   Alp Yenen and Ramazan Hakkı Öztan

2 Gendered Narratives of Transgressive Politics: Recovering Revolutionary Rubina 53
   Houri Berberian

3 Caucasian Banditry in Late Imperial Russia: The Case of *Abrek* Zelimkhan 83
   Jeronim Perović

4 Racketeers in Politics: Theoretical Reflections on Strong-man Performances in Late Qajar Iran 120
   Olmo Gölz

Part II Rogues and Regimes

5 Conspiracy under Trial: Christian Brigands, Rebels and Activists in Bosnia during the Tanzimat   151
Anna Vakali

6 The Abode of Sedition: Resistance, Repression and Revolution in Sasun, 1891–1904   178
Toygun Altıntaş

7 Conspiracy, International Police Cooperation and the Fight against Anarchism in the Late Ottoman Empire, 1878–1908   208
İlkay Yılmaz

8 Between Ruler and Rogue: Sayyid Talib al-Naqib and the British in Early Twentieth-century Basra   235
Aline Schlaepfer

Part III Rogue Trajectories

9 Chemistry of Revolution: Naum Tyufekchiev and the Trajectories of Revolutionary Violence in Late Ottoman Europe   261
Ramazan Hakkı Öztan

10 Late-Ottoman 'Rogues' and their Paths to Power: A Prosopographic Study   302
Benjamin C. Fortna

11 A Man of the Frontier: Ramadan Shallash and the Making the Post-Ottoman Arab East   333
Michael Provence

12 The Last Ottoman Rogues: The Kurdish–Armenian Alliance in Syria and the New State System in the Interwar Middle East   355
Jordi Tejel

Afterword   383
Erik Jan Zürcher

Index   390

Figures

1.1	Enver Bey as a counterinsurgency officer in Ottoman Macedonia, 1903–8	22
1.2	Locating transgressive politics	32
2.1	Rubina (Areshian) and Kristapor (Mikayelian), *c.* 1904	82
3.1	Map of the Caucasus in the Russian Empire, 1903–14	89
3.2	Photograph on the front page of the Russian weekly magazine *Iskry*, No. 40, 13 October 1913	114
5.1	Example of an Ottoman interrogation protocol. BOA, I.MVL. 459 20664, 30 December 1861	168
9.1	Naum Tyufekchiev, *Servet-i Fünun*, 17 Eylül 1331, 309	264
9.2	Naum Tyufekchiev in the Ottoman Ministry of War	295
9.3	Tyufekchiev together with the members of the CUP and select journalists from Constantinople	296
11.1	Ramadan Shallash at the Arab Officer's Club Damascus, *c.* 1920	346

Notes on Contributors

Toygun Altıntaş works on the social and political history of minoritisation, supremacism and inequality in the late Ottoman Empire. He received his PhD in Near Eastern Languages and Civilizations from the University of Chicago in 2018. Altıntaş worked as an MA Preceptor at the University of Chicago (2017–18). He taught courses on Middle Eastern history and Ottoman language and palaeography at Bilgi and Boğaziçi universities (2018–2020). Currently, he is a Humboldt fellow at the Forum Transregionale Studien in Berlin (2020–2). He has published articles in the *Journal of the Ottoman and Turkish Studies Association* and in the edited volume *To Kill a Sultan: A Transnational History of the Attempt on Abdülhamid II (1905)* (2018). He is currently preparing a book on the making of the 'Armenian Question' in the second half of the nineteenth century.

Houri Berberian is Professor of History, Meghrouni Family Presidential Chair in Armenian Studies and Director of the Center for Armenian Studies at the University of California, Irvine. Her research interests include revolutionary movements, women and gender, and identity and diaspora. She is the author of *Armenians and the Iranian Constitutional Revolution of 1905–1911: 'The Love for Freedom Has No Fatherland'* (2001) and, most recently, the award-winning *Roving Revolutionaries: Armenians and the Connected Revolutions in the Russian, Iranian, and Ottoman Worlds* (2019), as well as the co-editor of *Reflections of Armenian Identity in History and Historiography* (2018).

Benjamin C. Fortna is Professor and Director of the School of Middle Eastern and North African Studies at the University of Arizona and formerly Professor of the History of the Middle East, SOAS, University of London. His research focuses on the history of the late Ottoman Empire and the early Turkish Republic. He received his degrees from Yale, Columbia and the University of Chicago. His publications include *The Circassian: A Life of Eşref Bey, Late Ottoman Insurgent and Special Agent* (2016), *Childhood in the Late Ottoman Empire and After* (2016), *Learning to Read in the Late Ottoman Empire and the Early Turkish Republic* (2010) and *Imperial Classroom: Islam, Education and the State in the Late Ottoman Empire* (2002).

Jack A. Goldstone is the Virginia E. and John T. Hazel Jr, Chair Professor of Public Policy and Director of the Center for the Study of Social Change, Institutions and Policy at George Mason University. He is also a Senior Fellow at the Mercatus Center and a member of the Council on Foreign Relations. His books and edited volumes include *Revolution and Rebellion in the Early Modern World: Population Change and State Breakdown in England, France, Turkey, and China, 1600–1850* (1991; 25th anniversary edition 2016), *The Encyclopedia of Political Revolutions* (1998), *Why Europe: The Rise of the West in World History, 1500–1850* (2008), *Political Demography: How Population Changes are Shaping International Security and National Politics* (2012) and *Revolutions: A Very Short Introduction* (2014).

Olmo Gölz is a research fellow in Islamic and Iranian Studies and a primary investigator within the Collaborative Research Centre 'Heroes – Heroizations – Heroisms' at the University of Freiburg, Germany. He received his PhD with a thesis on rackets and racketeers in Pahlavi Iran, 1941–63, published by the University of Freiburg. His research and teaching focus on the history and culture of modern Iran, and the sociology of revolution, violence, gender, heroism and martyrdom in the Middle East. His publications, including both theoretical and historical studies, have appeared in edited volumes and journals like *Die Welt des Islams: International Journal for the Study of Modern*

Islam, *Behemoth – A Journal on Civilisation* and *Thesis Eleven*. Currently, he is preparing an edited volume on violence and heroism as well as a second book on the dynamics of the heroic in the Iran–Iraq War.

Ramazan Hakkı Öztan teaches history at the Atatürk Institute for Modern Turkish History at Boğaziçi University, Istanbul. He completed his PhD in May 2016 under the supervision of Peter Sluglett at the University of Utah. He was a postdoctoral researcher at the University of Neuchâtel, where he worked for an ERC project led by Jordi Tejel on the borders of the interwar Middle East. He has published articles in *Past and Present, International Journal of Middle East Studies, Journal of Contemporary History* and *Journal of Migration History*. Currently, he is working on two separate book projects: a monograph on illicit economy and violence in the late Ottoman Balkans; and a history of Turkish–Syrian border (1921–46). He is also co-editing a volume titled *Regimes of Mobility: Borders and State Formation in the Middle East, 1918–1946*.

Jeronim Perović is Professor of Eastern European History at the University of Zurich. He specialises in the history of Russia and the Soviet Union, as well as the history of the Balkans. He has previously held scholarships at the Woodrow Wilson International Center for Scholars, the Davis Center for Russian and Eurasian Studies at Harvard University, and the Center for Russian, East European and Eurasian Studies at Stanford University. He is the author of several monographs, including *From Conquest to Deportation: The North Caucasus under Russian Rule* (2018), and the editor of several books, including *Cold War Energy: A Transnational History of Soviet Oil and Gas* (2017).

Michael Provence is Professor, Department of History, University of California, San Diego. He earned a PhD in Modern Middle Eastern History from the University of Chicago. He has lived and studied in Syria, Lebanon, Egypt, Turkey, Germany and France. He is the author of *The Last Ottoman Generation and the Making of the Modern Middle East* (2017) and *The Great Syrian Revolt and the Rise of Arab Nationalism* (2005), also in Arabic and Turkish translation and many articles on the late Ottoman and colonial

Middle East of the early twentieth century, including 'Ottoman Modernity, Colonialism and Insurgency in the Interwar Arab East', *International Journal of Middle East Studies* (2011).

Aline Schlaepfer is assistant professor at the Department of Near and Middle Eastern Studies, University of Basel, with the Swiss National Science Foundation's Eccellenza Professorial Fellowship. She was a postdoctoral fellow at the American University of Beirut and Princeton University, as well as a research associate and senior resident at the University of Geneva. She is the author of *Les intellectuels juifs de Bagdad: Discours et allégeances (1908–1951)* (2016) and a number of articles dealing with the history of Jews in Arab lands, nationalism, history of minorities and the study of the Ottoman imprint in Arab spaces.

Jordi Tejel is a research professor in the History Department at the University of Neuchâtel. Since 2017, he has led a research programme funded by the European Research Council (ERC) on borderlands, border-making and state-formation processes in the interwar Middle East. He is the author of *Syria's Kurds: History, Politics and Society* (2009), *La Question kurde: Passé et présent* (2014) and co-authored *Les Kurdes en 100 questions* (2018). He has also published many articles in journals such as *Journal of Borderlands Studies, 20&21: Revue d'histoire, Middle Eastern Studies, Iranian Studies, British Journal of Middle Eastern Studies, European Journal of Turkish Studies* and *Ethnic and Racial Studies*, among others.

Anna Vakali works on the social and legal history of the Ottoman Balkans during the nineteenth century. She received her PhD in Near and Middle Eastern Studies from the University of Basel (2017). Her PhD thesis deals with the interrogations and trials of bandits and (proto-)nationalists at the newly founded *nizamiye* courts of the Balkans during the Tanzimat reform era. Between 2017 and 2019 she worked as a postdoctoral researcher of the Austrian Academy of Sciences in the framework of a project related to the diplomatic and social history of the borders between Ottomans, the Austrian Empire and Serbia during the nineteenth century. In 2020, she participated at a project affiliated with the Research Centre for the Humanities, Athens, which deals with the historical trajectories of urban space from the Ottoman Empire to the modern Greek state. Currently she works as a postdoctoral researcher at the University of Athens in a project that deals with intercommunal musical geographies of late Ottoman Istanbul. She has published in the *Turkish Historical Review* and several Turkish journals.

Alp Yenen is assistant professor of modern Turkish history and culture at the Institute for Area Studies at Leiden University. Previously, he was a research associate and senior resident at the University of Basel, where he completed his PhD in 2016. He has published in journals such as *Contemporary European History* (forthcoming), *Behemoth – A Journal on Civilisation*, *Die Welt des Islams: International Journal for the Study of Modern Islam*, *Middle Eastern Studies* on the comparative and connected history of contentious politics in the Middle East. Currently, he is finishing a book on the international history of the Young Turk movement in the aftermath of the First World War, as well as preparing a second book on the history of the Cold War and political violence in Turkey during the long 1970s.

İlkay Yılmaz is Einstein guest researcher at the Friedrich-Meinecke-Institut at the Freie Universität, Berlin, and a research fellow at 'Europe in the Middle East – The Middle East in Europe' at the Berlin-based Forum Transregionale Studien, 2020–1. She was a research fellow at the Leibniz-Zentrum Moderner Orient, Berlin, 2014–15 and 2017–19. She was a research assistant and an assistant professor at Istanbul University. She has published on passport history, inter-imperial collaboration on policing, public order, state formation and security in *Journal of Historical Sociology*, *Journal of the Ottoman and Turkish Studies Association*, *PhotoResearcher*, as well as in her book *Serseri, Anarşist ve Fesadın Peşinde: II. Abdülhamid Döneminde Güvenlik Politikaları, Mürur Tezkereleri, Pasaportlar ve Otel Kayıtları* (2014).

Erik Jan Zürcher is Emeritus Professor of Turkish Studies at Leiden University. His main research interest is the political and social history of the late Ottoman Empire and the early Turkish Republic. His books include *The Unionist Factor: The Rôle of the Committee of Union and Progress in the Turkish National Movement 1905–1926* (1984) and *Political Opposition in the Early*

Turkish Republic: The Progressive Republican Party 1924–1925 (1991), *Turkey: A Modern history* (first published 1993, substantially revised 2004 and 2017) and *The Young Turk Legacy and Nation Building: From the Ottoman Empire to Atatürk's Turkey* (2010), as well as edited volumes, including *Socialism and Nationalism in the Ottoman Empire: 1876–1923* (1994), *Fighting for a Living a Comparative History of Military Labour 1500–2000* (2013) and *Islam and Jihad in World War I* (2015).

About this Book

This book has long been in the making and therefore has a history of its own. But perhaps above all, it reflects our continued fascination with the history of rebels, revolutionaries and racketeers. As two young doctoral candidates who studied different episodes of revolutionary politics in late Ottoman history, we have collaborated at several conferences throughout the years. While searching for a common approach, we first presented our thoughts in a panel at the 2014 conference of the Association of Nationalities Studies in New York. Soon thereafter, our collaboration led to the organisation of an international conference, which took place on 22–24 January 2015, at the University of Basel.[1] Featuring more than twenty paper presentations that explored diverse aspects of insurgency and counterinsurgency in the

---

[1] The conference, titled 'The Age of the Komitadji: Entangled Histories and Political Sociology of Insurgencies in the Ottoman World (1870s–1920s)', was co-organised with Selen Etingü, Maurus Reinkowski and M. Hakan Yavuz. We are grateful to the co-organisers and contributors for this collaboration. For a conference report, see Alp Eren Topal, Conference Report, 'The Age of the Komitadji: Entangled Histories and Political Sociology of Insurgencies in the Ottoman World (1870s–1920s)', University of Basel, *H-Net*, published online 10 March 2015, available at: https://networks.h-net.org/node/11419/discussions/63624/conference-report-%E2%80%9C-age-komitadji-entangled-histories-and-political. For a Turkish translation of the report, see 'Komitaci Devri: Osmanli Dünyasında Ayaklanmaların İç İçe Geçmiş Tarihi (1870–1920): Basel Üniversitesi'nde Konferans, 22–24 Ocak 2015', *Toplumsal Tarih* 227 (2015): 80–85.

Ottoman world and beyond, the conference signalled the need to establish an analytical framework in studying this period of contentious politics.

After a long break during which both of us defended our dissertations and survived the precariousness of academia, we decided to return to this project with a new cast of contributors and a novel framework. On 31 May 2018, we had the chance to share our approach in a workshop, titled 'Relational Elites in the Early Twentieth-Century Middle East', organised by Henning Sievert at the University of Bern. This is where we coined the 'age of rogues', proposing it as a comprehensive framework to better understand what we call transgressive politics at the frontiers of empires. As it stands, this book is a collective endeavour towards this direction, bringing together recent research that addresses issues of historical legacies, regime interactions, and complex biographical trajectories during the tumultuous twilight of Ottoman, Tsarist, Habsburg and Qajar empires.

The ambitious scope of contributions required us to put the volume through an additional process of internal peer review. We would like to acknowledge the cast of experts who have agreed to extend us a helping hand. We therefore thank, in alphabetical order, Ahmet Serdar Aktürk, Aydın Babuna, Alexander Balistreri, Harun Buljina, Camille Cole, Axel Çorlu, Roger Deal, Tolga Esmer, James Gelvin, David Gutman, Kevan Harris, Barbara Henning, Michael Kemper, Varak Ketsemanian, Andreas Kosmas Lyberatos, Bedross Der Matossian, Polat Safi, Ashgar Sayed-Gohrab, Stefan Troebst and Peter Wien. We would like to thank our contributors as well for patiently going through several stages of the review process. We also thank Beyiz Karabulut for preparing the index. Finally, we owe a debt of gratitude to Nicola Ramsey from Edinburgh University Press for all her support throughout the process.

We have been fortunate to have Jack A. Goldstone and Erik Jan Zürcher write the Foreword and Afterword of this volume. Part I, titled 'Rogues in History', starts with four chapters that situate transgressive politics in history and historiography. The first contribution is our conceptualisation of the age of rogues as a historical episode of transgressive politics in the Balkans, the Middle East and the Caucasus at the turn of the century. Following a discussion of Ottoman Macedonia and the biography of Enver Paşa as a revolutionist-cum-imperialist, we will discuss the historical emergence of transgressive politics and the culture of agency in the frontiers of the Ottoman Empire. Approaching issues of gender in transgressive politics, Houri Berberian then reconstructs the contentious biography of Rubina, an Armenian revolutionary who is often silenced in the male-dominated narratives of revolution and nationalism. Up next is Jeronim Perović, who presents the life of Zelimkhan as a complex case study that sheds light on the bandits that operated across the Russian-controlled Caucasus. Part I concludes with a study by Olmo Gölz who takes readers to Qajar Iran, where he explores the social dynamics of masculinity, heroisation and protection rackets during the Constitutional Revolution of 1906–11.

In Part II, 'Rogues and Regimes', a series of contributions showcase contentious interactions between rogues and imperial regimes. The first contribution in this section is from Anna Vakali who explores the subaltern revolts in Ottoman Bosnia, which she situates within the changing nature of the Ottoman responses to dealing with subversion. Toygun Altıntaş then zooms in on the Sasun rebellion and its suppression, an important episode in the Ottoman East that illustrates the complex confrontations between the Armenian insurgency and the Hamidian counterinsurgency. İlkay Yılmaz examines the broader practices of Ottoman state surveillance, which she places in a global context by discussing international police cooperation against anarchism. The final contribution in Part II comes from Aline Schlaepfer, who focuses on an Iraqi strongman who survived under both Ottoman and British regimes in Basra, illustrating how power was actually negotiated on the ground.

In Part III, 'Rogue Trajectories', the contributions explore complex life histories and illustrate the unique political agency of individual rebels, revolutionaries and racketeers across the frontiers of empires. Ramazan Hakkı Öztan highlights the analytic significance of technological expertise and political entrepreneurship by reconstructing the biography of a Macedonian bomb-maker and uncovering his transregional revolutionary networks. Benjamin C. Fortna in turn offers a prosopographical approach by outlining the intersections of a group of Young Turk activist officers, while also examining issues of patronage and rivalry. The third contribution is by Michael Provence, who explores post-Ottoman biographical trajectories by reconstructing the life history of a frontier warrior in the Arab Middle East.

The final piece comes from Jordi Tejel who focuses on what he calls the last Ottoman rogues, examining the Khoybun League and the formation of Kurdish–Armenian alliance in the post-Ottoman Middle East.

While acknowledging that these twelve studies offer only a short glimpse into the wider age of rogues during the turn of the twentieth century, we are sure that they will inspire further studies in understanding how transgressive politics shaped the modern world.

September 2020
Ramazan Hakkı Öztan
Alp Yenen

Foreword

Jack A. Goldstone

'It was the best of times, it was the worst of times.' Charles Dickens' description of pre-revolutionary France from *A Tale of Two Cities* could also serve as a description of the late nineteenth-century Ottoman Empire. By the 1870s, the Ottoman Empire had successfully carried out three decades of reforms, modernising its army, its banking system, its schools and its laws based on Western models. Following victory in the Crimean War with British and French support, the Ottoman territories stretched from Baghdad to Bosnia, and from Kuwait to Tripoli. A more centralised Ottoman government now wielded power over its lands assisted by new railways and telegraph lines. In 1876, the Ottomans even adopted a Western-influenced constitution with a parliament.

Yet the reforms ran into two walls. First was the fact that these reforms, no matter how successful, were undeniably foreign. Foreign banks, foreign debts, foreign ideas and foreign practices now were displacing Ottoman and Muslim traditions. If all these foreign ideas and inventions and institutions were superior, why then maintain a sprawling, multinational empire under the rule of a sultan who claimed, as the caliph, to be the leader of the entire Muslim world? Would it not be better to go all the way in challenging the West by setting up a new, constitutional regime under the rule of a modernising elite of Turkish-Muslim nationalists? This in fact became the ideology of the Young Turk movement, which grew into a serious threat to the Hamidian regime in the early twentieth century. Meanwhile, nationalism spread through all the subject peoples of the Empire, spurring nationalist movements and rebellions in the Balkans, the Caucasus, Armenia and the Middle East.

Second was the resistance of the Ottoman sultan to any restraints on his power, especially as he now had to deal with extensive rebellions and domestic opposition. In 1878, Sultan Abdülhamid II, who had agreed to the constitution just two years earlier when he came to the throne, dismissed the new parliament, exiled many liberals and executed others; the parliament did not meet again for thirty years.

Meanwhile, the sultan sought to use his new army to hold on to his empire in the face of European attacks and uprisings. Defeat in the Russo-Turkish War of 1877–8 led to the loss of Bulgaria, Serbia and Montenegro to independence, and of Tunisia to France and Egypt to Great Britain. From 1880 to the First World War, the Ottomans faced repeated efforts by Greece, Bulgaria, Serbia and Macedonia to expand or throw off Ottoman rule; growing conflicts between its Muslim majority and the increasingly successful Christian, Jewish and Armenian minorities who could leverage their ties to foreign wealth and investment; and internal arguments over how to shape the Ottoman government: Ottoman or Turkish? Strongly centralised rule or decentralised governance? Embrace Westernisation or resist it? Though richer and more modern than ever, the late nineteenth- and early twentieth-century Ottoman Empire was also more afflicted by crises of legitimation, rebellion and military defeat than at any time in the previous two hundred years.

Age of Rogues provides a fresh and fascinating look at this tumultuous period. From 1880 to 1920, waves of rebellions and revolutions transformed eastern Europe and western Asia. The Austro-Hungarian Empire, the Romanov Russian Empire, the Qajar Persian Empire and the Ottoman Empire itself all broke into pieces as revolutionary movements toppled centuries-old dynasties and gave rise to new, nationalist states. It is easy to note that this was a period in which the structural flaws of unwieldy empires resulted in their demise: rapid population growth made administration difficult and birthed large generations of idealistic youth; the collision of proud but lagging empires with the newly industrialised West exposed technological weakness; and new beliefs in nationalism, secularism, anarchism and communism undercut the legitimacy of older multi-ethnic and traditional regimes.

Yet knowing that empires were likely to collapse in a certain period is far from showing how they actually failed, tracking why efforts to salvage them faltered, and understanding the history and motives of the individuals who propelled events. For these purposes, we need precisely the kind of collective biographies assembled in this volume, showing the range of men and women, from all across the Balkans, the Caucasus and the Middle East, who found opportunities and life missions in the contentious frontiers of these decaying empires.

The decay was, by the beginning of the twentieth century, quite apparent. That made it difficult for idealistic young people to simply aspire to traditional roles and envisage their future as one of upholding the institutions of the existing order. Individuals like Enver Paşa – touched on in several chapters of this volume – groomed for military or bureaucratic office, found themselves on the front lines of their disintegrating states. Enver fought, at various times, against rebels in Macedonia, Armenia and Arabia, eventually reaching the rank of Minister of War. Yet he also found himself admiring the commitment of the rebels to building new, nationalist societies, and became persuaded that only a modern nationalist state could deliver a better future for the Turkish people. This conviction led Enver to participate in rebellions and coups against the Ottoman government as well. When the new Ottoman government in which he was a senior official was defeated in the First World War, he took his revolutionary vision abroad, to Russia and Turkestan. Like an early Che Guevara, he too died while trying to spread his vision of revolution to other lands.

Sayyid Talib al-Naqib, the subject of Chapter 8 by Aline Schlaepfer, was a scion of a leading Arab family, descendants of the Prophet, who had held important positions in Iraq under the Ottomans. In 1877, he became a member of the new Ottoman parliament. Yet when parliament was dissolved, he came into conflict with the Young Turks, and was exiled to India. After the First World War, he became an advocate for Iraqi nationalism and a contender for the crown which was given to King Faisal. Although Talib became a minister in Iraq's provisional government, that too did not last, and he died after efforts to resettle in Syria and Egypt.

Naum Tyufekchiev, whose revolutionary odyssey is described by Ramazan Hakkı Öztan in Chapter 9, was a skilled chemist and merchant, who used those skills to carve out a career as an itinerant bomb-maker for a variety of turn-of-the-century revolutionary organisations. As Öztan recounts, 'Tyufekchiev had gained transnational notoriety since the early 1890s, when he began to get involved in a range of high-scale assassinations, bombing campaigns and arms transfers, all of which kept the Russian, Ottoman and Bulgarian authorities on their toes.' Thus, Tyufekchiev's biography is also 'the biography of the transgressive politics in the frontiers of empires, where business, politics, ideology, violence and diplomacy all intersected in the personalities of such rogues as Tyufekchiev'.

The 'rogues' of this volume are therefore many-sided figures. They had careers as military officers, rebels, guerrilla fighters, nationalist leaders and revolutionaries – both successful and not. They were both products of their time and shapers of it; through their lives we can much better understand how great empires fractured and a maze of new nations and societies was born.

Research on revolutions has now turned away, with good reason, from overly structural and macro-social explanations. Recent scholarship recognises that revolutions are fuelled by emotions and produced by the actions of leaders and followers, created by revolutionary entrepreneurs and the intersection of events, and are subject to contingent and conjunctural factors involving transnational communications and actors.[1] To advance this agenda, we deeply need books like this one, which tracks the complex lives and actions of rogue actors across borders, and traces their role in the waves of revolution and rebellion that crashed across multiple empires.

The period from 1870 to 1920 should be of special interest to us today, a century later, as the world is in the grip of a similar cycle of decay. At the time, the half century from the 1870s to the 1920s seemed to be a march of successful Westernisation and democracy, breaking down traditional autocracies

---

[1] George Lawson, *Anatomies of Revolution* (Cambridge: Cambridge University Press, 2019); Eric Selbin, *Revolution, Rebellion, Resistance: The Power of Story* (London: Zed Books, 2013); Jack A. Goldstone, *Revolutions: A Very Short Introduction* (New York: Oxford University Press, 2014).

and empires and producing modern national states. By the mid-1920s, the leading Western democracies were congratulating themselves on their prosperity and success in remaking the world. Yet by the mid-1930s, it had all come crashing down: the world was in a Depression, and fascism had taken over much of Europe. In another decade, the world would again be at war. In the aftermath, Britain's days as a world power ended, and democracy, far from being unquestioned, yielded to communism and later Islamism in parts of the world as unifying ideologies. Much of the failure of the post-First World War order lay in the failure to recognise the lasting power of the nationalist and revolutionary sentiments that had been developed in the 'Age of Rogues'. The presumption that democracy would 'naturally' spread and prosper was wrong; opportunists seeking power and national advantage in the wake of instability were able to flourish instead.

The period from 1970 to 2020 is eerily similar. Democracy seemed to be on a global march to success, led by Western prosperity drawing all other countries in its wake. The collapse of communism in Eastern Europe in 1989–91 seemed to herald a new era of global unity. Yet that too was an illusion. Recessions in 2001, 2008 and 2019, each one greater than the last, showed that Western democracy was not an infallible road to prosperity; China's rapid ascent surely seemed to suggest an alternative. Western efforts to establish democracies in Afghanistan and Iraq ran into the same problems of nationalist sentiments and rogues that had bedevilled the Ottoman frontier regions a century earlier. Democracy and unity are again waning in the face of nationalism and populism – the European Union has been shaken by Britain's exit; NATO is faltering under America's weakening resolve. A wave of rebellions and revolutions has occurred across the Middle East and North Africa, sending out streams of refugees, and reshaping the relations among Turkey, Syria, Iraq, and Iran. The borderlands in the Caucasus and Ukraine have seen renewed conflicts, and the withdrawal of US power in the Middle East has created new opportunities for rebels and revolutionaries. Even the pandemic of COVID-19 seems fated to repeat much of the experience of the 1918 'flu pandemic.

When looking to determine what will happen next, we would be well advised to keep in mind that situations like this do not have fixed outcomes. The power of nationalism, the appeal of transgressive politics and the opportunities for revolutionary entrepreneurs instead create tangled trajectories. In thinking about how political change and instability unfold, we need to see how they are shaped by individual actors and the intersection of events. The stories and analysis of the 'rogues' in this volume, showing how they grasped their opportunities, played out their frustrations and developed with their age, are a major advance in helping us do so.

PART I
ROGUES IN HISTORY

I

Age of Rogues: Transgressive Politics at the Frontiers of the Ottoman Empire

Alp Yenen and Ramazan Hakkı Öztan

Imagine an age of rogues marked by the clash of empires and a heightened level of interstate competition that spawns one insurgent group after another; when isolated yet authoritarian despots increasingly use coercion to contain opponents and rebels alike. Imagine an era when armed insurgents manipulate international rivalries for their own benefit, making extreme violence and irregular warfare the new routine of contentious politics – when rural insecurity and paramilitary violence, coupled with extreme demographic measures, create floods of refugees and a humanitarian crisis to which the responses of the international community of states remain fractured, reflective of their own interests that continue to fuel the conflict. Ultimately, imagine a time of contentious sociability out of which the rebels could one day emerge as rulers, while the latter might eventually turn into insurgents.

For many of us, imagining a time as such brings to mind recent images from Syria, if not from many other zones of conflict found across the global South today.[1] This timely book will take its readers to an age of rogues in

---

[1] For an earlier comparison between the developments in the Ottoman Balkans and contemporary Middle East, see Ramazan Hakkı Öztan, 'Are We Witnessing the Macedonian Question of the 21st century?' *Middle East Monitor*, 16 October 2014, available at: https://www.middleeastmonitor.com/20141016-are-we-witnessing-the-macedonian-question-of-the-21st-century. See also: Barış Çaylı, *Violence and Militants: From Ottoman Rebellions to Jihadist Organizations* (Montreal: McGill-Queen's University Press, 2019).

history that is neither near nor far – back to the turn of the twentieth century and to the frontiers of the Ottoman Empire, where, we claim, the way the contentious politics played out shaped the shaky foundations upon which the modern Balkans, Middle East and Caucasus were forged.[2] What qualifies the turn of the twentieth century as particularly transformative is that it brought with it the collapse of the long-standing Romanov, Habsburg, Ottoman and Qajar empires. It was in their contentious frontiers that a variety of new political actors had emerged, playing crucial roles in the violent undoing of empires and the making of new nation-states.

We shall define the 'age of rogues' as a particular geopolitical and historical context within which imperial rivalries gave birth to a cast of parapolitical and paramilitary agents whose violent autonomy and culture of transgression managed to transform the legitimate norms of politics and the formal institutions of state sovereignty. We conspicuously label these actors as *rogues*, for the term is less concerned with the social status of non-state actors than its alternatives in the literature, such as 'subalterns', 'subversives' and 'dangerous classes'.[3] Politically charged terms such as 'revolutionary', 'insurgent' or 'terrorist' do not fully capture the complex agency of non-state actors, either.[4] Nor does 'paramilitarism', which, even though an important feature

---

[2] For a concise but comprehensive overview of this formative period, see Isa Blumi, *Foundations of Modernity: Human Agency and the Imperial State* (New York: Routledge, 2012). For contentious politics, see Charles Tilly and Sidney G. Tarrow, *Contentious Politics* (Boulder, CO: Paradigm, 2007). On the formative role of contentious politics in the history of the modern Middle East, see John Chalcraft, *Popular Politics in the Making of the Modern Middle East* (Cambridge: Cambridge University Press, 2016).

[3] Despite our terminological differences, these collections of articles should be considered as complementary with this volume. Edmund Burke, III and David Yaghoubian (eds), *Struggle and Survival in the Modern Middle East*, 2nd edn (Berkeley, CA: University of California Press, 2005); Stephanie Cronin (ed.), *Subalterns and Social Protest: History from Below in the Middle East and North Africa* (London: Routledge, 2008); Odile Moreau and Stuart Schaar (eds), *Subversives and Mavericks in the Muslim Mediterranean: A Subaltern History* (Austin: University of Texas Press, 2016); Stephanie Cronin (ed.), *Crime, Poverty and Survival in the Middle East and North Africa: The 'Dangerous Classes' since 1800* (London: I. B. Tauris, 2019).

[4] As Jeremy Black proposes, global historians need to adopt a more fluid understanding of such categories of contentious politics and their state-led counterparts. Jeremy Black, *Insurgency and Counterinsurgency: A Global History* (Lanham, MD: Rowman & Littlefield, 2016).

of political violence, focuses on state-led armed actors alone.[5] The ideological characterisation of 'nationalist', on the other hand, embodies pre-configured historical consequence, suffering from methodological nationalism.[6] We instead call these actors 'rogues', since the term denotes agency in transgressive politics, while acknowledging multiplicity of interests – whether political, social or personal.

In designating their time as an age of rogues, however, we are not proposing yet another periodisation that may project a singular, linear and enclosed timeframe. Much to the contrary, we situate our actors within a world-historical setting of multiple and overlapping historical processes.[7] As such, we maintain that the age of rogues in fact took place along with other related ages of 'empire', 'Western domination', 'nationalism', 'steam and print', 'coexistence' and 'genocide'.[8] For us, then, the age of rogues is less a temporality than a genre of politics that very much emerged out of these entangled historical processes. As Alan Mikhail and Christine Philliou have noted, 'identifying particular ages with their own characteristics, features, and cultural attributes' has a further benefit of 'suspending the question of outcomes' and evaluates a period on its own terms.[9] We believe this is all the more necessary in late Ottoman historiography,

---

[5] Uğur Ümit Üngör, *Paramilitarism: Mass Violence in the Shadow of the State* (Oxford: Oxford University Press, 2020), 6–18.

[6] Andreas Wimmer and Nina Glick Schiller, 'Methodological Nationalism and Beyond: Nation-State Building, Migration and the Social Sciences', *Global Networks* 2(4) (2002): 301–34.

[7] Helge Jordheim, 'Against Periodization: Koselleck's Theory of Multiple Temporalities', *History and Theory* 51(2) (2012): 151–71.

[8] Eric Hobsbawm, *The Age of Empire, 1875–1914* (New York: Vintage, 1989); Francis Robinson (ed.), *Cambridge History of Islam: The Islamic World in the Age of Western Dominance* (Cambridge: Cambridge University Press, 2010); M. Brett Wilson, *Translating the Qur'an in an Age of Nationalism: Print Culture and Modern Islam in Turkey* (Oxford: Oxford University Press, 2014); James L. Gelvin and Nile Green (eds), *Global Muslims in the Age of Steam and Print* (Berkeley, CA: University of California Press, 2014); Ussama S. Makdisi, *Age of Coexistence: The Ecumenical Frame and the Making of the Modern Arab World* (Oakland, CA: University of California Press, 2019).

[9] Alan Mikhail and Christine M. Philliou, 'The Ottoman Empire and the Imperial Turn', *Comparative Studies in Society and History* 54(4) (2012): 721–45, 731.

where the benefit of hindsight continues to stand at the heart of historical meta-narratives.[10]

As a collective endeavour, *Age of Rogues* hopes to attend to this task by mapping out the connected history of transgressive actors and their shared political culture that survived the First World War, even if their empires did not. In this sense, this volume is a study of a generation, covering roughly the formative period of an adult's lifespan from the late nineteenth century to the mid-interwar years. We suggest that this was a time marked by similar, if not shared, experiences of contentious sociability as it unfolded across the connected geography of the Balkans, the Middle East and the Caucasus. As such, while chapters in this volume focus foremost on the Ottoman world, they provide a range of biographical and prosopographical studies that are rooted in imperial frontiers – contributions that are particularly attentive to the experiences of non-Muslim communities, questions of gender and agents of emerging social classes.[11]

Perhaps most critically, this volume is transregional in its outlook.[12] After

---

[10] For our own interventions against the teleological bias in Ottoman Studies, see Alp Yenen, 'Envisioning Turco-Arab Co-Existence between Empire and Nationalism', *Die Welt des Islams* 61(1) (2021): 72–112; Ramazan Hakkı Öztan, 'Point of No Return? Prospects of Empire after the Ottoman Defeat in the Balkan Wars (1912–1913)', *International Journal of Middle East Studies* 50(1) (2018): 65–84; Ramazan Hakkı Öztan, 'Nationalism in Function: "Rebellions" in the Ottoman Empire and Narratives in its Absence', in M. Hakan Yavuz and Feroz Ahmad (eds), *War and Collapse: World War I and the Ottoman State* (Salt Lake City: University of Utah Press, 2016), 161–202.

[11] In this sense, we situate our work in a burgeoning line of biographical and prosopographic approaches to contentious actors in the Ottoman Empire and the Middle East. See Michael Provence, *The Last Ottoman Generation and the Making of the Modern Middle East* (Cambridge: Cambridge University Press, 2017); Laila Parsons, *The Commander: Fawzi al-Qawuqji and the Fight for Arab Independence, 1914–1948* (New York: Hill & Wang, 2016); Benjamin C. Fortna, *The Circassian: A Life of Eşref Bey, Late Ottoman Insurgent and Special Agent* (Oxford: Oxford University Press, 2016).

[12] This connected geography roughly corresponds to what Karl Kaser coined as 'Eurasia Minor' (*Kleineurasien*), a region connecting the Balkans to the Black Sea littoral, and the Middle East to the Caucasus. Karl Kaser, *The Balkans and the Near East: Introduction to a Shared History* (Münster: LIT-Verlag, 2011). For other transregional approaches that centre around the Ottoman world, see Stefan Rohdewald, Stephan Conermann and Albrecht Fuess (eds), *Transottomanica-osteuropäisch-osmanisch-persische Mobilitätsdynamiken: Perspektiven und Forschungsstand* (Göttingen: V&R Unipress, 2019); Steffen Wippel and Andrea Fischer-Tahir (eds), *Jenseits etablierter Meta-Geographien: Der Nahe Osten und Nordafrika in tran-

all, when it comes to the study of war, violence and revolution, historians have often chosen to highlight regional exceptionalism. We hope to depart from such emphasis on distinct paths of regional development and therefore challenge the compartmentalisation of history by area studies. Inspired by the existing body of literature that explore Ottoman legacies in post-imperial spaces, *Age of Rogues* hopes to suggest shared trajectories of historical development across what many believe to be distinct regions.[13] In studying the Balkans, the Middle East and the Caucasus in an interactive framework, the volume ultimately seeks to point to commonalities in historical development, and highlight opportunities to study a cross-regional, if not a global history of transgressive politics.

We consider the connected regions of the Balkans, the Middle East and the Caucasus as frontiers of empires. In framing this vast geography as a frontier, we take both multilateral and unilateral dimensions into consideration. In their multilateral dimensions, frontiers correspond to what have been variously called 'shatterzones' and 'borderlands' of empires.[14] In the unilateral sense of the concept, frontiers are as much the sites of heightened

---

sregionaler Perspektive (Baden-Baden: Nomos, 2018); Pascal Firges, Tobias Graf, Christian Roth and Gülay Tulasoğlu (eds), *Well-Connected Domains: Towards an Entangled Ottoman History* (Leiden: Brill, 2014).

[13] For studies of the shared Ottoman legacy in the Balkans and the Middle East, see Carl L. Brown (ed.), *Imperial Legacy: The Ottoman Imprint on the Balkans and the Middle East* (New York: Columbia University Press, 1996); Christine Philliou, 'Paradox of Perceptions: Interpreting the Ottoman Past through the National Present', *Middle Eastern Studies* 44(5) (2008): 661–75; Edin Hajdarpašić, 'Out of the Ruins of the Ottoman Empire: Reflections on the Ottoman Legacy in South-Eastern Europe', *Middle Eastern Studies* 44(5) (2008): 715–34; Eyal Ginio and Karl Kaser (eds), *Ottoman Legacies in the Contemporary Mediterranean: The Balkans and the Middle East Compared* (Jerusalem: European Forum at the Hebrew University, 2013). Frederick Anscombe offers a similar shared history of the Balkans and the Middle East in his *State, Faith, and Nation in Ottoman and Post-Ottoman Lands* (Cambridge: Cambridge University Press, 2014).

[14] Omer Bartov and Eric D. Weitz (eds), *Shatterzone of Empires: Coexistence and Violence in the German, Habsburg, Russian, and Ottoman Borderlands* (Bloomington: Indiana University Press, 2013); Alfred J. Rieber, *The Struggle for the Eurasian Borderlands: From the Rise of Early Modern Empires to the End of the First World War* (Cambridge: Cambridge University Press, 2014).

civilisational and colonial encounters[15] as they are the peripheries subordinated to state formation and centralisation.[16] In the Ottoman Empire, much like elsewhere, these dimensions of frontiers were intricately linked to one another. Heightened competition in inter-imperial frontiers in the late nineteenth century, for example, drove state centralisation and civilisational missions in the empire's internal frontiers,[17] as 'the state needed the frontier . . . while the frontier might not have needed the state'.[18] At other times, the empire's internal frontiers turned inter-imperial, as was the case with Eastern Anatolia during the First World War or the Ottoman frontiers in North Africa.[19]

Taken as a whole, Ottoman frontiers had long been spaces of contention no matter which trajectory they followed. In these seemingly peripheral settings, contentious episodes, as dictated by inter-imperial competition and elite rivalries as well as demographic changes,[20] created local economies of

---

[15] Imperial and colonial encounters between the Muslim world and European empires is discussed in its regional and imperial varieties in David Motadel (ed.), *Islam and the European Empires* (Oxford: Oxford University Press, 2014).

[16] One cannot overestimate the impact of centre–periphery approaches in Ottoman Studies. For a paradigmatic essay, see Şerif Mardin, 'Center–Periphery: A Key to Turkish Politics', *Daedalus* 102 (1973): 169–90. While scholars of the early modern period stressed the break-up of the centre–periphery alliance, such as in Rifa'at Ali Abou-El-Haj, *Formation of the Modern State: The Ottoman Empire Sixteenth to Eighteenth Centuries* (Albany, NY: State University of New York Press, 1991), historians of the modern period studied the bargaining of power between the Istanbul and provincial power-holders. For a critique of centre–periphery approaches, see Cem Emrence, *Remapping the Ottoman Middle East: Modernity, Imperial Bureaucracy, and the Islamic State* (London: I. B. Tauris, 2011).

[17] Ussama Makdisi, 'Ottoman Orientalism', *American Historical Review* 107(3) (2002): 768–96; Selim Deringil, '"They Live in a State of Nomadism and Savagery": The Late Ottoman Empire and the Post-Colonial Debate', *Comparative Studies in Society and History* 45(2) (2003): 311–42; Thomas Kühn, 'Shaping and Reshaping Colonial Ottomanism: Contesting Boundaries of Difference and Integration in Ottoman Yemen, 1872–1919', *Comparative Studies of South Asia, Africa and the Middle East* 27(2) (2007): 313–29.

[18] Eugene L. Rogan, *Frontiers of the State in the Late Ottoman Empire: Transjordan, 1850–1921* (Cambridge: Cambridge University Press, 1999), 9.

[19] Michael A. Reynolds, *Shattering Empires: The Clash and Collapse of the Ottoman and Russian Empires 1908–1918* (Cambridge: Cambridge University Press, 2011); Mostafa Minawi, *The Ottoman Scramble for Africa: Empire and Diplomacy in the Sahara and the Hijaz* (Stanford, CA: Stanford University Press, 2016).

[20] Jack A. Goldstone, *Revolution and Rebellion in the Early Modern World: Population Change*

competitive violence which led to the emergence of contentious politics. As many historians have illustrated time and again, this dynamic has been the primary feature of the contested borderlands of the Ottoman Empire since the late eighteenth century.[21] Yet, only from the second half of the nineteenth century onwards, we argue, did the existing local repertoires of contention – what one may call traditional cultures of transgression – begin to adopt global models and turn into forms that could be adopted and mimicked in frontier struggles elsewhere.[22] Particularly after the first wave of globalisation started diffusing actors, ideas, tools and repertoires, as we point out, rogues began to emerge in frontiers where the local struggles could become part of the global, and the global might connect with the local.[23] These globalising processes not only enabled cooperation among transgressive actors, but also helped them to see their struggle as part of a wider script of contention that had been taking place on a more global scale.[24]

---

and *State Breakdown in England, France, Turkey, and China, 1600–1850*, 25th anniversary edn (New York: Routledge, 2016).

[21] See various contributions in A. C. S. Peacock (ed.), *The Frontiers of the Ottoman World* (Oxford: Oxford University Press, 2009). See also Khaled Fahmy, *All the Pashas Men: Mehmed Ali, His Army, and the Making of Modern Egypt* (Cairo: American University in Cairo Press, 2002); Isa Blumi, *Rethinking the Late Ottoman Empire: A Comparative Social and Political History of Albania and Yemen 1878–1918* (Istanbul: Isis Press, 2003); Ali Yaycıoğlu, *Partners of the Empire: The Crisis of the Ottoman Order in the Age of Revolutions* (Stanford, CA: Stanford University Press, 2016). How Iran's tribal frontiers shaped state formation is discussed in Firoozeh Kashani-Sabet, *Frontier Fictions: Shaping the Iranian Nation, 1804–1946* (Princeton, NJ: Princeton University Press, 1999); Stephanie Cronin, *Tribal Politics in Iran: Rural Conflict and the New State, 1921–1941* (London: Routledge, 2007); Arash Khazeni, *Tribes and Empire on the Margins of Nineteenth-Century Iran* (Seattle: University of Washington Press, 2009).

[22] For repertoires of contention, see Charles Tilly, *From Mobilization to Revolution* (Reading: Addison-Wesley, 1978), 151–9. Different types of repertoires and regimes commonly shape each other. Charles Tilly, *Contentious Performances* (Cambridge: Cambridge University Press, 2008), 146–74.

[23] For the most recent examples of this line of approach, see Houssine Alloul, Edhem Eldem and Henk de Smaele (eds), *To Kill a Sultan: A Transnational History of the Attempt on Abdülhamid II (1905)* (London: Palgrave Macmillan, 2018); Houri Berberian, *Roving Revolutionaries: Armenians and the Connected Revolutions in the Russian, Iranian, and Ottoman Worlds* (Oakland, CA: University of California Press, 2019).

[24] This is best studied in global comparisons and connections of the constitutional revolutions in the early twentieth century. Nader Sohrabi, 'Historicizing Revolutions: Constitutional

This chapter will introduce the age of rogues as a framework for studying transgressive politics at the frontiers of the Ottoman Empire. The first section will first zoom in on the turn-of-the-century Ottoman frontier in Macedonia, a historical theatre of charged interstate competition and local rivalries that gave birth to a particular brand of rogue actors. Second, by intersecting the history of the Macedonian revolutionary organisations in the early twentieth century with the biography of İsmail Enver, a prominent Ottoman counterinsurgency officer who would later become a Young Turk revolutionary, we will seek to illustrate the individual trajectory of a rogue between forces of revolution and empire. Third, by building on the example of Macedonians and Young Turks, we will explain the historical sociology of transgressive politics that led to the emergence of an age of rogues at the frontier of empires. Finally, we will stress the need to study the culture of agency that defines the historical trajectory of transgressive politics at the frontiers of the Ottoman Empire.

A Frontier of Contention: Ottoman Macedonia, 1878–1908

The Balkans has long been a frontier among empires.[25] Since the European age of revolutions, the region had encountered its own wave of revolts and crises.[26] But only by the end of the nineteenth century did Ottoman Macedonia emerge as one of the most contentious inter-imperial frontiers in world history.[27] By then, the region had become such a theatre of heightened levels of

---

Revolutions in the Ottoman Empire, Iran, and Russia, 1905–1908', *American Journal of Sociology* 100(6) (1995): 1383–447; Charles Kurzman, *Democracy Denied, 1905–1915: Intellectuals and the Fate of Democracy* (Cambridge, MA: Harvard University Press, 2008); Erik Jan Zürcher, 'The Young Turk Revolution: Comparisons and Connections', *Middle Eastern Studies* 55(4) (2019): 481–98.

[25] The region most notably functioned as the military frontier (*Militärgrenze*) between the Habsburgs and the Ottomans. See Jean Nouzille, *Histoire de frontières: l'Autriche et l'Empire ottoman* (Paris: Berg, 1991). For a recent revisiting of the military frontier, see the contributions for the forum 'The Habsburg–Ottoman Borderlands: New Insights for the Study of the Nineteenth-Century European Legal and Social Order' in *Austrian History Yearbook* 51 (2020): 15–87.

[26] Frederick F. Anscombe, 'The Balkan Revolutionary Age', *Journal of Modern History* 84(3) (2012): 572–606.

[27] While there was no such administrative unit in the empire as Macedonia, the term referred to a geography that corresponded to the Ottoman provinces of Salonica, Bitola and Kosovo,

political competition that it made a contemporary conclude that Macedonia was 'a conveniently elastic term which is made to include all the territory anyone wishes to annex'.[28] The remark was not far off the mark, capturing the essence of what came to be known in diplomatic circles as the 'Macedonian question', which had developed since the end of the Russo-Ottoman War 1877–1878.[29] This was when the sweeping Russian gains alarmed Britain, France and Austria-Hungary, who convened the Congress of Berlin (1878) to check the Russian influence in the Balkans.[30] While it restored the balance of power, the Treaty of Berlin projected the protection of minority rights in the newly independent post-Ottoman states, ensuring not only the rights of Jews and Christians, but also the continued involvement of the Great Powers in affairs of the Balkan frontier for decades to come.[31]

The treaty resulted in the independence of Montenegro, Romania and

---

situated in southeastern Europe. Yet what Macedonia is and who Macedonians are is a debate that continues to spark nationalist tensions in the Balkans to this day. See Hugh Poulton, *Who Are the Macedonians?* (Bloomington: Indiana University Press. 1995); Loring M. Danforth, *The Macedonian Conflict: Ethnic Nationalism in a Transnational World* (Princeton, NJ: Princeton University Press, 1995); James Pettifer, *The New Macedonian Question* (New York: St Martin's Press, 1999); Victor Roudometof, *Collective Memory, National Identity and Ethnic Conflict: Greece, Bulgaria and the Macedonian Question* (Westport, CT: Praeger, 2002); Basil C. Gounaris, 'Macedonian Questions', *Southeast European and Black Sea Studies* 2(3) (2002): 63–94. For a recent take on how the naming dispute was resolved, see Matthew Nimetz, 'The Macedonian "Name" Dispute: The Macedonian Question – Resolved?' *Nationalities Papers* 48(2) (2020): 205–14. Yet this seemingly narrow conflict on naming rights is indicative of the broader relevance of the past for the politics of the present – an aspect that is well studied in the critical Balkan historiographies, such as in Keith Brown, *The Past in Question: Modern Macedonia and the Uncertainties of Nation* (Princeton. NJ: Princeton University Press, 2003); Roumen Daskalov, *The Making of a Nation in the Balkans: Historiography of the Bulgarian Revival* (Budapest: Central European University Press, 2004).

[28] Mary Edith Durham, *The Burden of the Balkans* (London: Edward Arnold, 1905), 58.

[29] Fikret Adanır, *Die Makedonische Frage: Ihre Entstehung und Entwicklung bis 1908* (Wiesbaden: Steiner, 1979).

[30] M. Hakan Yavuz and Peter Sluglett (eds), *War and Diplomacy: The Russo-Turkish War of 1877–1878 and the Treaty of Berlin* (Salt Lake City: University of Utah Press, 2011).

[31] Carole Fink, *Defending the Rights of Others: The Great Powers, the Jews, and International Minority Protection, 1878–1938* (Cambridge: Cambridge University Press, 2004). For a critical take on minority rights treaties, see Laura Robson, 'Capitulations Redux: The Imperial Genealogy of the post-WWI "Minority" Regimes', *American Historical Review*, forthcoming.

Serbia, as well as the granting of autonomy to Bulgaria. The sultan's remaining territories in Europe, on the other hand, were gradually to turn into a zone of competition among these newly emerging neighbouring states and an already independent Greece, as each of them sought to cultivate irredentist aspirations and conflicting visions of cultural, religious and economic influence over Ottoman Macedonia. The region had long been home to an ethno-religiously mixed population, with a majority of Orthodox Christians comprising Bulgarians, Greeks, Serbs, Macedonians and Vlachs, as well as sizeable communities of Turkish and Albanian Muslims, and Jews. Their socio-economic cleavages would become the major currency with which the growing interstate competition was to unfold.[32] Initially, the contours of this competition followed the script inherited from the previous decade. Bulgaria and Serbia sought to increase the influence of their national churches vis-à-vis the Greek Patriarchate, while also establishing schools in order to appeal to the minds and hearts of Ottoman Macedonians whom they saw as co-patriots.[33] Revolutionary tactics did exist, but they largely remained under state control.

The status quo changed after 1885 when a secret committee of revolutionaries in Plovdiv, with links to Sofia, took control of the autonomous province of Eastern Rumelia and announced its unification with Bulgaria. Ottoman armies were mobilised and Greece threatened to annex parts of Macedonia, while the Great Powers cautioned restraint. Serbia acted on its fury and declared war, but Bulgaria emerged victorious against all odds.[34] A crucial consequence of the episode was the souring of relations between Russia and Bulgaria, due to the latter's increasing autonomy of action.[35] While St Petersburg's plots would thicken in the following years to bring

---

[32] For an excellent intervention in this regard, see Basil C. Gounaris, 'Social Cleavages and National "Awakening" in Ottoman Macedonia', *East European Quarterly* 29(4) (1996): 409–26.

[33] Dimitris Stamatopoulos, 'The Bulgarian Schism Revisited', *Modern Greek Studies Yearbook* 24/25 (2008/2009), 105–25; Dimitris Stamatopoulos, 'Orthodox Ecumenicity and the Bulgarian Schism', *Etudes Balkaniques* 51(1) (2015): 70–86.

[34] Gül Tokay, 'A Reassessment of the Macedonian Question, 1878–1908', in H. Yavuz and Peter Sluglett (eds), *War and Diplomacy: Russo-Turkish War and Berlin Treaty* (Salt Lake City: University of Utah Press, 2011), 253–69.

[35] R. J. Crampton, *Bulgaria* (Oxford: Oxford University Press, 2007), 123–32.

Bulgaria back to its orbit, the Russian withdrawal of support ultimately created a wedge between moderate and revolutionary factions in Bulgaria: as the Bulgarian prime minister Stefan Stambolov moved closer to the sultan and embraced a more restrained policy towards Macedonia, he came to estrange the revolutionary elements that had been thus far acting within the parameters defined by Sofia.[36] Organisations, such as the Young Macedonian Literary Society, were shut down and Macedonian students were kicked out of schools due to ongoing purges of 'Russophiles'. Among those forced to leave for Macedonia were individuals such as Dame Gruev, Georgi Delchev and Ivan Hadzhinikolov who met in 1893 in Salonica, where they established the Internal Macedonian Revolutionary Organisation (IMRO hereafter), which would ultimately become the model for rogue conduct in the Ottoman world.[37]

If the earlier generation of Bulgarian revolutionaries was denied access to the metropole – that is, Constantinople[38] – this newer generation of revolutionaries was barred from accessing national politics in Sofia.[39] Stambolov's bid to set Bulgaria on a course independent from Russia and the ensuing crackdowns swelled the ranks of the estranged. Soon after its inception, IMRO quickly began to expand its organisation through a string of secret cells across the region, calling for a Macedonia that was autonomous both from Constantinople and Sofia.[40] In doing so, they implemented circulating notions of revolutionary activism on the ground, which they saw as embodied

---

[36] For a biography of Stambolov, see Duncan M. Perry, *Stefan Stambolov and the Emergence of Modern Bulgaria, 1870–1895* (Durham, NC: Duke University Press, 1993).

[37] Duncan M. Perry, *The Politics of Terror: The Macedonian Liberation Movements 1893–1903* (Durham, NC: Duke University Press, 1988), 35–7.

[38] For an overview of those schooled in Istanbul, see Orlin Sabev, 'Boğaziçi Kıyılarında Hayata Hazırlanmak: Osmanlı Istanbul'unda Okumuş Bulgarlar Üzerine Bazı Gözlemler', in Feridun M. Emecen, Emrah Safa Gürkan and Ali Akyıldız (eds), *Osmanlı Istanbulu III. Uluslararası Osmanlı Istanbulu Sempozyumu Bildirileri* (Istanbul: Istanbul 29 Mayıs Üniversitesi Yayınları, 2015), 163–81.

[39] In arguing as such, we are particularly drawing upon Benedict Anderson's discussion of official nationalism and the prevented passages of creole elites to positions of power in the metropole. Benedict Anderson, *Imagined Communities: Reflections on the Origin and Spread of Nationalism* (London: Verso, 2006).

[40] Stephen Fischer-Galati, 'The Internal Macedonian Revolutionary Organization: Its Significance in "Wars of National Liberation"', *East European Quarterly* 6(4) (1973): 458–9.

in the person of Vasil Levski, who was a legendary revolutionary before being caught and hanged by the Ottoman authorities in 1873.[41] While the IMRO drew from a shared repertoire of action available across the Balkans in general and Bulgaria in particular, it continued to be cautious of external meddling although remaining open to external support for the cause. After the Supreme Macedonian Committee was founded in Sofia in 1895 – an organisation that would always be its arch rival, the IMRO developed relations with it, on the condition of keeping its own organisational independence, so that it could reach out to the Macedonian constituency in Sofia.[42]

By the end of the century, the IMRO boasted of an underground organisation, complete with its own postal system and experienced couriers and smugglers who disseminated money, weapons and propaganda to its members, while also ensuring communication among the leadership – all in all operating as a state within a state.[43] IMRO leaders travelled regularly across Macedonia to maintain the organisational networks, while local leaders – often teachers – tapped into local student bodies to expand membership. As Keith Brown noted, 'resistance to Ottoman rule was far more labor-intensive and economically integrated than national mythologies sometimes suggest'.[44] In line with the larger goal of preparing the groundwork for a peasant rebellion, the organisation propagated a message

---

[41] Vasil Levski's activities are often seen as the harbinger of the April Uprising of 1876. For a narrative of his activities, see the records of his interrogation by the Ottoman authorities, Cengiz Yolcu, '"Bulgar Fesad Komitesi Reisi" Vasil Levski'nin Eylemleri ve Mahkemede Verdiği İfade Üzerine bir Değerlendirme', *Güney-Doğu Avrupa Araştırmaları Dergisi* 27 (2015): 15–63. For later appropriations of Levski's legacy, see Maria Todorova, *Bones of Contention: The Living Archive of Vasil Levski and the Making of Bulgaria's National Hero* (Budapest: Central European University Press, 2009).

[42] Perry, *The Politics of Terror*, 47–9, 82–3.

[43] Frederick Moore, 'The Macedonian Committees and the Insurrection', in Luigi Villlari (ed.), *The Balkan Question: The Present Condition of the Balkans and of European Responsibilities* (London: John Murray, 1905), 192.

[44] See Keith Brown, *Loyal unto Death: Trust and Terror in Revolutionary Macedonia* (Bloomington: Indiana University Press, 2013), 54. For an overview of these emigration patterns, see Basil C. Gounaris, 'Emigration from Macedonia in the Early Twentieth Century', *Journal of Modern Greek Studies* 7(1) (1989): 133–53. For global and local interactions of Ottoman migration flows, see Isa Blumi, *Ottoman Refugees, 1878–1939: Migration in a Post-Imperial World* (London: Bloomsbury, 2013).

of radical land reform to a receptive audience of impoverished peasants, promising a radical re-ordering of rural society by overthrowing Muslim landowners.[45] The organisation similarly tapped into circuits of seasonal labour migration. Aware of the latter possibility, the Ottoman authorities kept a close tap on labour market dynamics, particularly attentive to inexplicable patterns in seasonal labour movement, as seemingly happened in the spring of 1903.[46]

For the IMRO, the use of violence initially served similar goals of organisational empowerment. When resorted to for strategic aims, violent acts served to achieve discipline among ranks, eliminate rivals and raise money, while also helping to consolidate popular support by highlighting the IMRO's commitment to the cause.[47] In this sense, local revolutionary committees and armed bands not only set an example of dedication, but also played an active role in drilling the peasants in how to use weapons and engage in guerrilla warfare. They even used visual aids to describe how to use bayonets, revolvers, scythes and bombs, illustrating different ways to shoot in different postures while taking cover behind trees and fences against an approaching enemy.[48] Even if the use of violence against enemies was glorified, the organisation knew the limits of its capabilities, particularly vis-à-vis regular units. From 1897 onwards, however, as Ottoman authorities slowly understood the full scale of the organisation's webs of loyalty and acted to dismantle it, the IMRO was forced to ramp up its coercive capacity and increase the number of its paramilitary bands. In principle, choosing leaders and recruiting members for each band was less of a problem than arming them. But the end of the century also saw a greater availability of second-hand weapons and hand

---

[45] Tasos Kostopoulos, '"Land to the Tiller": On the Neglected Agrarian Component of the Macedonian Revolutionary Movement, 1893–1912', *Turkish Historical Review* 7(2) (2016): 134–66.

[46] Başbakanlık Osmanlı Arşivi (Prime Ministry's Ottoman Archives, BOA hereafter), DH. TMIK. M. 140-22, lef 1, 3 and 6. This particular intelligence originated from the Third Army Headquarters in Salonica and supported by the Ministry of Public Security, but was later dismissed by the authorities.

[47] İpek K. Yosmaoğlu, *Blood Ties: Religion, Violence, and the Politics of Nationhood in Ottoman Macedonia, 1878–1908* (Ithaca, NY: Cornell University Press, 2014), 209–87.

[48] For such visual aids intercepted by the revolutionaries, see BOA. Y.MTV. 228–37, 2 Nisan 318.

bombs in the world markets, which slowly trickled into the hands of IMRO bands.[49]

The Ottoman Empire already maintained a significant military presence in the region, but the emerging demands of rural guerrilla warfare soon led to the creation of specific units that were led by officers handpicked from among the most skilful of their class from imperial staff colleges. Despite up-to-date staff education, better equipment and numerical strength, the Ottoman counterinsurgency operations remained precarious until 1905. In the end, guerrilla warfare demanded swift responses, but the Ottoman command structure did not always process intelligence fast enough to enable its units to pursue the bands.[50] Even when they could, Ottoman officers were trained in conventional warfare, not in guerrilla tactics. Lacking an officially articulated strategy, the officers learned counterinsurgency methods only through experience on the field.[51] It did not help, either, that the Ottoman officer corps was divided between the *mektepli* (schooled) and *alaylı* (commissioned) officers, which ultimately caused significant infighting that held back coordinated action.[52]

The IMRO was plagued by similar problems which, however, had broader consequences for Ottoman Macedonia. Particularly after the Salonica Affair in 1901 when most members of its central committee were arrested by the authorities, a considerable power vacuum emerged, which raised the stakes

---

[49] Ramazan Hakkı Öztan, 'Tools of Revolution: Global Military Surplus, Arms Dealers, and Smugglers in the Late Ottoman Balkans, 1878–1908', *Past & Present* 237(1) (2017): 167–95; Ramazan Hakkı Öztan, 'Commodities of Nationalism: Technologies of Rebellion and Networks of Resistance in the Late Ottoman Balkans, 1878–1912', PhD thesis, University of Utah, 2016.

[50] Gül Tokay, 'The Macedonian Question and the Origins of the Young Turk Revolution, 1903–1908', PhD thesis, University of London, 1994, 147–53.

[51] Mesut Uyar and Edward J. Erickson, *A Military History of the Ottomans: From Osman to Atatürk* (Santa Barbara, CA: Praeger, 2009), 215–16. This lack of familiarity with guerrilla warfare was not peculiar to the Ottomans. For an account of the French troubles in Algeria, see Douglas Porch, 'Bugeaud, Galliéni, Lyautey: The Development of French Colonial Warfare', in Peter Paret (ed.), *Makers of Modern Strategy from Machiavelli to the Nuclear Age* (Princeton, NJ: Princeton University Press, 1986), 376–407.

[52] While the 'schooled' designated those who became officers after a modern military education, the latter meant those who rose through the ranks thanks to their loyalty to the sultan. Feroz Ahmad, *Turkey: The Quest for Identity* (Oxford: Oneworld, 2003), 76.

considerably in leadership cadres. As Adria Lawrence argued, 'when and where nationalist movements fractured, nationalist actors had incentives to adopt violent strategies to compete with one another'.[53] Indeed, different factions operating in this increasingly competitive environment quickly began 'to outbid each other by the adoption of more radical positions or the use of more militant forms of action'.[54] Right after the Salonica arrests in 1901, the Supreme Committee in Sofia tried to take over the internal organisation – a bid that ultimately failed. A year later in 1902, the Supremacists raised the banner of revolt and sent their own *chetas* to lead the revolution in Macedonia before the IMRO could – a strategy frustrated by Ottoman units. In late 1902, Ivan Garvanov, who now controlled IMRO, responded by convening a makeshift congress which then announced the long-awaited peasant uprising to take place in spring 1903.[55] Meanwhile, a splinter, anarchist group called the Gemidzhii, with loose links both to the Supremacists and the IMRO, responded by carrying out bomb attacks in Salonica, targeting many Western-owned ships, cafes, banks and schools to attract global attention to the plight of Macedonians.[56]

These cycles of competitive escalation resulted in the Ilinden Uprising, which was the only episode of open rebellion in Ottoman Macedonia that featured the participation of around 20,000 armed rebels. The Porte responded by mobilising forces that, according to one estimate, equalled those during the Russo-Ottoman War in 1877–8.[57] The confrontation lasted from August well into the autumn and led to a death toll of thousands, while Ottoman counterinsurgency tactics rendered tens of thousands of local subjects into refugees. The uprising not only failed to attract foreign intervention, but also fractured the IMRO into multiple factions that would continue to

---

[53] Adria Lawrence, 'Triggering Nationalist Violence: Competition and Conflict in Uprisings against Colonial Rule', *International Security* 35(2) (2010): 90.
[54] Donatella della Porta, 'Radicalization: A Relational Perspective', *Annual Review of Political Science* 21 (2018): 465.
[55] Nadine Lange-Akhund, *The Macedonian Question, 1893–1908 from Western Sources* (New York: Columbia University Press, 1998), 107–18.
[56] Pınar Şenışık, 'Osmanlı Makedonyası'nda Şiddet ve Nisan 1903 Olayları', *Türkiyat Mecmuası* 27(1) (2017): 289–303.
[57] The National Archives (TNA), Foreign Office (FO), 78/5268/521, Therapia, 28 August 1903, f. 286.

compete for leadership in Macedonia, often in violent ways.[58] The situation became worse when Greece and Serbia, and to a much lesser extent Romania, responded to the 1903 uprising by forming and sending their own armed bands into Macedonia in a bid to protect the interests of those they saw as co-patriots.[59] According to this logic of competitive violence, 'every thrust had to be answered with counter-thrust, and passivity was a sign of weakness, not wisdom'.[60] The Ilinden Uprising had therefore turned Ottoman Macedonia into a frontier of rogues, where interstate competition and intra-elite rivalries began to unfold in more violent ways than ever before.

As violence engulfed Macedonia, the Ottoman security forces ramped up their counterinsurgency efforts. The Ottoman officers who took part in these operations were themselves politically alienated by the authoritarian rule of Sultan Abdülhamid II. Faced with revolutionaries in Macedonia, the empire's counterinsurgents were about to go rogue. In this sense, they displayed a political development that was similar to that of the IMRO. While the leaders of the latter were in one way or another tied to the Bulgarian high school in Salonica, the Ottoman revolutionaries were graduates of Ottoman military and medical academies in Istanbul. The origin of these Ottoman revolutionary committees went back to a secret society founded in 1889 by four students at the military school for medicine, but they and their growing supporters were soon exiled by the Hamidian regime in 1895.[61] These so-called 'Young Turk' émigrés were united under the Committee of Union and Progress (*İttihad ve Terakki Cemiyeti*, CUP hereafter) and formed the

---

[58] Ryan Gingeras, 'The Internal Macedonian Revolutionary Organization: "Oriental" Terrorism, Counterinsurgency, and the End of the Ottoman Empire', in Carola Dietze and Claudia Verhoeven (eds), *The Oxford Handbook of the History of Terrorism* (Oxford: Oxford University Press, 2014).

[59] Douglas Dakin, *The Greek Struggle in Macedonia, 1897–1913* (Thessaloniki: Institute for Balkan Studies, 1966); Dimitris Livanios, '"Conquering the Souls": Nationalism and Greek Guerilla Warfare in Ottoman Macedonia, 1904–1908', *Byzantine and Modern Greek Studies* 23(1) (1999): 195–221.

[60] Mark Mazower, *Salonica, City of Ghosts: Christians, Muslims and Jews, 1430–1950* (New York: Alfred A. Knopf, 2005), 253.

[61] M. Şükrü Hanioğlu, *The Young Turks in Opposition* (Oxford: Oxford University Press, 1995); Oya Gözel-Durmaz, 'The Rise of the Ottoman Military Medical School as the Centre of Anti-Hamidian Opposition', in Oya Gözel-Durmaz, Abidin Çevik, and Günay Gönüllü (eds), *Current Debates in History and Politics* (London: IJOPEC, 2017), 7–20.

backbone of the external committees that were established in Europe, notably in Paris, Brussels and Geneva (but also in Cairo and Tripoli).

Like the IMRO, the Young Turk movement broke into factions, largely due to disagreements over tactics and the means of revolution, but also because of personal rivalries. Ultimately, however, it was the dynamics of the competitive escalation of violence in Macedonia after 1903 that gave the upper hand to the 'activist' faction among the Young Turks which was based in Salonica.[62] Many of them had built a professional military career in counterinsurgency operations. For them, Macedonia was not only a source of existential anxiety for the viability of the Ottoman Empire, but also a laboratory where they were socialised in the tactics of conspiratorial politics and revolutionary warfare.[63] Without doubt, as Erik Jan Zürcher aptly noted, the Young Turks were the 'children of the borderlands'.[64] One of them was İsmail Enver, a young Ottoman military officer serving in the Third Army, who would have a spectacular trajectory in this age of rogues.

A Rogue between Revolution and Empire: İsmail Enver, 1881–1922

The frontier had long been important in shaping Enver's identity and worldview. Although he was born in Istanbul in 1881, Enver was a descendant of refugees from Crimea who were relocated to the Ottoman Empire after the Russian conquest.[65] Young Enver spent his school years in Bitola in

---

[62] This coming to power of the 'activist' faction is one of the main arguments of M. Şükrü Hanioğlu, *Preparation for a Revolution: The Young Turks, 1902–1908* (Oxford: Oxford University Press, 2001). For a further discussion, see also Suavi Aydın, 'İki İttihat-Terakki. İki Ayrı Zihniyet, İki Ayrı Siyaset', in Tanıl Bora and Murat Gültekingil (eds), *Modern Türkiye'de Siyasi Düşünce I: Cumhuriyet'e Devreden Düşünce Mirası: Tanzimat ve Meşrutiyet'in Birikimi* (Istanbul: İletişim Yayınları, 2004), 117–28.

[63] The centrality of Macedonian experience to the emergence of Young Turks has long been noted by a number of Turkish scholars, most notably Zafer Tarık Tunaya, *Türkiye'de Siyasal Partiler, Vol. 3: İttihat ve Terakki: Bir Çağın, Bir Kuşağın, Bir Partinin Tarihi* (Istanbul: Hürriyet Vakfı Yayınları, 1989). On the impact of the Macedonian question on the Young Turks, see Adanır, *Die Makedonische Frage*; Tokay, 'The Macedonian Question and the Origins of the Young Turk Revolution'; Mehmet Hacısalihoğlu, *Die Jungtürken und die Mazedonische Frage (1850–1918)* (Munich: Oldenbourg, 2003).

[64] Erik Jan Zürcher, 'The Young Turks – Children of the Borderlands', *International Journal of Turkish Studies* 9(1/2) (2003), 275–86.

[65] For Enver's biographies, see Murat Bardakçı, *Enver* (Istanbul: İş Bankası Yayınları, 2015);

Ottoman Macedonia, where his father served as an agricultural technician for the provincial bureaucracy. Having graduated from the Hamidian institutions of education in Macedonia, Enver enrolled at the military academy in Istanbul. Like many of his peers who received modern education, Enver, too, considered himself both a patriot and a progressive. Enver's hero in his youth was Ali Süavi (1839–78), a revolutionary of the former generation and the origin of Enver's later *nom de guerre* as a revolutionary.[66] Ali Süavi was one of the leading members of the 'Young Ottomans', an opposition movement founded in 1865 as a secret society of civil servants, but he was later killed while carrying out a coup attempt against Abdülhamid in 1878, after the latter had prorogued the constitution of 1876.[67]

Although invested in subversive political thoughts, with ready role models in front of him, young Enver had no organic connection to the CUP. Only after being arrested and interrogated by the Hamidian secret police did Enver become irreversibly embittered towards the regime's despotism.[68] After graduating from the staff college as the second in his class, Enver was assigned to the Bitola garrison of the Third Army to take part in the counterinsurgency operations in unruly Macedonia (Figure 1.1). Only a few months into his new post in the summer of 1903, Enver witnessed at first hand the Ilinden uprising and the power of revolutionary warfare. In an autobiographical sketch about his counterinsurgency experience in Macedonia, Enver noted that 'the Internal Macedonian [Revolutionary] Committee reminded him of the reserve military structure of the Ottoman army'. As he declared with envy, the Macedonian committee was recruiting young men far more efficiently than the Ottoman army. The IMRO not only mirrored the organisation of the Ottoman army, but also the Ottoman state.

M. Şükrü Hanioğlu, 'Enver Paşa', *Türkiye Diyanet Vakfı İslam Ansiklopedisi*, 44 vols (Istanbul: Türkiye Diyanet Vakfı İslam Araştırmaları Merkezi, 1988–2013), 11:261–4; Şevket Süreyya Aydemir, *Enver Paşa: Makedonya'dan Orta Asya'ya*, 3 vols (Istanbul: Remzi Kitabevi, 1972). There is still no comprehensive biography of Enver in English.

[66] Bardakçı, *Enver*, 72.

[67] Florian Riedler, *Opposition and Legitimacy in the Ottoman Empire: Conspiracies and Political Cultures* (London: Routledge, 2011), 26–70.

[68] This episode is recounted in Glen W. Swanson, 'Enver Pasha: The Formative Years', *Middle Eastern Studies* 16(3) (1980): 194–5.

'Everybody knew that in Macedonia', Enver wrote, 'there was a state within a state' which undermined the Ottoman state's own infrastructure while building up its own parallel networks.[69] While mobilising devoted supporters and training capable leaders, as Enver wrote in his memoirs, 'this Organisation had a cadre of young idealists, fearless volunteers, who were willing to give up their lives'. For Enver, these were a new type of political partisans who were shaping the course of events. These so-called *komitadjis* 'were cruel and ready for bloody sacrifice', conducting terrorist attacks and robberies and bringing out into the open the Ottoman state's inability to dispense justice.[70] 'Was it possible to establish law and order?' Or, more precisely, Enver wondered, 'how could the Sultan's Empire survive?'[71] The contemporary revolutionary wave in Russia and Persia after the Japanese victory of 1905 incited not only restive Ottoman-Muslim officers in Macedonia, like Enver, but also the wider the Young Turk movement in exile to turn to revolution in order to save the empire.[72]

In 1906, Enver was recruited by the Ottoman Liberty Society, a 'Young Turk' secret society of officers and bureaucrats in Salonika. 'We had studied other revolutions', said Enver, while 'I myself had studied very closely the Internal Organization of the Macedonian Bulgars. I admired it, and it gave us many hints.'[73] By 1907, the Ottoman Liberty Society in Macedonia merged with the Committee of Union and Progress in Parisian exile. After the merger, the CUP ended up formally adopting the organisational structure

---

[69] Here quoted from the English translation in Christ Anastasoff, 'Enver Pasha's Comments on the Work and Organization of the Macedonian Anti-Ottoman Committees', *Balkania: An International Quarterly Magazine on Balkan Affairs* 7(1) (1973): 3–8. These autobiographical sketches were penned in 1909 and were first published in Aydemir, *Enver Paşa: Makedonya'dan Orta Asya'ya*. For the full text in Turkish transliteration, please consult Halil E. Cengiz (ed.), *Enver Paşa'nın Anıları: (1881–1908)* (Istanbul: İletişim Yayınları, 1991).

[70] Anastasoff, 'Enver Pasha's Comments', 6.

[71] Ibid., 7.

[72] Nader Sohrabi, 'Global Waves, Local Actors: What the Young Turks Knew About Other Revolutions and Why It Mattered', *Comparative Studies in Society and History* 44(1) (2002): 45–79. See also Nader Sohrabi, *Revolution and Constitutionalism in the Ottoman Empire and Iran* (Cambridge: Cambridge University Press, 2011), 82–4.

[73] Quoted from an interview with Enver in Charles-Roden Buxton, *Turkey in Revolution* (London: T. Fisher Unwin, 1909), 135.

Le champion de la Liberté, Enver Bey en tenue de campagne

Figure 1.1 Enver Bey as a counterinsurgency officer in Ottoman Macedonia, 1903–8. See at: https://commons.wikimedia.org/wiki/File:Enver_Pasha_Ottoman_Postcard.jpg.

and revolutionary tactics of the Macedonian revolutionaries.[74] While the 48th article of the internal regulations of the CUP required that 'all members

[74] Hanioğlu, *Preparation for a Revolution*, 210–27.

who join the committee should sacrifice their lives for the sacred cause of the committee', there was a volunteer unit of 'those members who wish to be enlisted as self-sacrificing volunteers' (*feda'i*) for special operations.[75] The CUP adopted a statue of armed forces for the coordination of revolutionary mobilisation and the organisation of Muslim-nationalist armed vigilantism vis-à-vis Balkan revolutionaries.[76]

While Balkan revolutionaries provided an organisational model, Great Power interventions in Macedonia provided the backdrop to the CUP's revolutionary plans.[77] The Reval meeting (Tallinn in Estonia) between British King Edward VII and Russian Tsar Nicholas II in June 1908, where the Macedonian question was expected to be settled, created an immediate urgency for revolutionary action.[78] Following the executive orders of the CUP, secret committee members in the Third Army, most prominently Enver, took to mountains and started a mutiny that combined guerrilla tactics with popular mobilisation among the Muslim villages.[79] Once an unrelated Albanian uprising in Firzovik (today Ferizaj/Uroševac in Kosovo) was co-opted by the revolutionaries by performing a collective oath, the picture of an organised mass uprising in the name of constitutionalism was complete.[80] The extent

[75] Quoted in ibid., 217.
[76] Cengiz, *Enver Paşa'nın Anıları*, 111–13.
[77] Gül Tokay, 'Macedonian Reforms and Muslim Opposition during the Hamidian Era: 1878–1908', *Islam and Christian–Muslim Relations* 14(1) (2010): 51–65; Murat Kaya, 'Western Interventions and Formation of the Young Turks' Siege Mentality', *Middle East Critique* 23(2) (2014): 127–45. However, it remains doubtful how far previous tax revolts in Anatolia were part of the revolutionary moment, as argued by Aykut Kansu, *The Revolution of 1908 in Turkey* (Leiden: Brill, 1997).
[78] For an overview of the events and historiographical debates, see Erik Jan Zürcher, 'The Historiography of the Constitutional Revolution: Broad Consensus, Some Disagreement and a Missed Opportunity', in *The Young Turk Legacy and Nation Building: From the Ottoman Empire to Atatürk's Turkey* (London: I. B. Tauris, 2010), 26–40. For the revolutionary processes in the Macedonian and Albanian provinces, see Hanioğlu, *Preparation for a Revolution*, 261–78; Hacısalihoğlu, *Jungtürken und die Mazedonische Frage*, 162–205; George W. Gawrych, *The Crescent and the Eagle: Ottoman Rule Islam and the Albanians 1874–1913* (London: I. B. Tauris, 2006), 140–69; Isa Blumi, *Reinstating the Ottomans: Alternative Balkan Modernities, 1800–1912* (Basingstoke: Palgrave Macmillan, 2011), 146–8.
[79] Cengiz, *Enver Paşa'nın Anıları*, 86–125.
[80] Gawrych, *Crescent and the Eagle*, 151–2.

of the uprising was multiplied by the flood of telegrams sent to the palace from various places in Ottoman Macedonia and elsewhere. Encouraged by the developments, the revolutionaries threatened to march to the capital in order to reinstate the constitution of 1876. Fearing further chaos, Sultan Abdülhamid announced the restoration of the constitution on 24 July, which marked the Ottoman constitutional revolution of 1908.

Enver's post-revolutionary career continued to draw from his Macedonian culture of revolution. After the revolution, Macedonian and other Balkan *komitadjis* returned to towns and villages, where they were welcomed by the crowds. Enver was publicly celebrated as the 'hero of freedom'. The revolution brought certain types of transgressive actors into the fold of conventional politics.[81] Despite forming an official political party, the CUP remained a secret revolutionary committee in the footsteps of the Macedonian tradition.[82] While elbowing themselves a place in the capital, several committee leaders, including Enver, continued to associate themselves with Albanian bandits, irregular fighters and urban gangsters. In the following years, the CUP would accordingly instrumentalise its 'guerrilla spirit' to maintain its firm grip on political affairs, while also engineering consent through more formal avenues of politics.[83]

Even though Enver was promoted to the prestigious post of a military attaché in Berlin, he returned to guerrilla warfare after Italy occupied Ottoman Libya in 1911. Along with a special envoy of volunteers, Enver secretly travelled to Benghazi where he conducted skirmishes with local militias against Italian forces and strongholds.[84] As such, the Balkan-style irregular warfare was transported to North Africa and merged there with the existing local forms of tribal resistance. Rushed back to the Balkans in the midst of

---

[81] Sohrabi, *Revolution and Constitutionalism*, 24. But the dreams of an inclusive revolution were soon to be shattered. See Bedross der Matossian, *Shattered Dreams of Revolution: From Liberty to Violence in the Late Ottoman Empire* (Stanford, CA: Stanford University Press, 2014).

[82] Tunaya, *Türkiye'de Siyasal Partiler*, 3:13.

[83] On the 'guerrilla spirit' of the CUP, see George W. Gawrych, 'The Culture and Politics of Violence in Turkish Society, 1903–14', *Middle Eastern Studies* 22(3) (1986): 320. See also Sohrabi, *Revolution and Constitutionalism*, 135–88.

[84] For Enver's diary entries from this period, see Enver Pascha, *Um Tripolis*, ed. Friedrich Perzyński (Munich: Bruckmann, 1918).

the First Balkan War, Enver and fellow Young Turks were devastated by the terrible defeat and blamed the government, which had previously ousted the CUP from political offices. Enver, with the help of a group of CUP gunmen, engineered a violent coup in Istanbul, where the minister of war was killed and the government was forced to resign. In the Second Balkan War, Enver recaptured the former Ottoman capital of Edirne in a theatrical manner, adding yet another token to his official heroisation.[85] The CUP increasingly established a single-party dictatorship in the Ottoman Empire from then onwards. Already married to an Ottoman princess, Enver became the minister of war and the generalissimo, endowed with the title of Paşa at the onset of the First World War.[86] His meteoric rise was not a simple result of growing militarism in the Ottoman Empire but, instead, a manifestation of the CUP's growing transgressive capacities, in which Enver and his entourage proved to be influential in creating facts on the ground.[87]

The Ottoman war effort in the First World War was accompanied by revolutionary and paramilitary mobilisation on all frontiers, including a declaration of a jihad against the Sultan-Caliph's 'infidel' enemies at home and abroad.[88] For the purposes of unconventional warfare, Enver organised special

---

[85] Eyal Ginio, *Ottoman Culture of Defeat: The Balkan Wars and their Aftermath* (Oxford: Oxford University Press, 2015), 227–64.

[86] On Enver's role and how much he represented the *weltanschauung* of his Young Turk generation on the eve of the First World War, see Mustafa Aksakal, *The Ottoman Road to War in 1914: The Ottoman Empire and the First World War* (Cambridge: Cambridge University Press, 2008).

[87] There is a tendency in the historiography to overstate role of the military in Young Turk politics, such as in otherwise rich studies, see Handan Nezir-Akmeşe, *The Birth of Modern Turkey: The Ottoman Military and the March to World War I* (London: I. B. Tauris, 2005); M. Naim Turfan, *Rise of the Young Turks: Politics, the Military, and Ottoman Collapse* (London: I. B. Tauris, 2000). Despite the importance of the military, the CUP remained the dominant political force after 1913; see Erik Jan Zürcher, 'Young Turk Governance in the Ottoman Empire during the First World War', *Middle Eastern Studies* 55(6) (2019): 897–913; M. Şükrü Hanioğlu, 'Civil–Military Relations in the Second Constitutional Period, 1908–1918', *Turkish Studies* 12(2) (2011): 177–89.

[88] There is now a growing body of literature on the Ottoman experience in the First World War. For general overviews, see Ryan Gingeras, *Fall of the Sultanate: The Great War and the End of the Ottoman Empire, 1908–1922* (Oxford: Oxford University Press, 2016); Eugene L. Rogan, *The Fall of the Ottomans: The Great War in the Middle East* (New York: Basic Books, 2015). On military mobilisation, see Yiğit Akın, *When the War Came Home: The*

forces and secret intelligence operations under the Ottoman army's *Teşkilat-ı Mahsusa* ('Special Organisation'), which intersected with the CUP's own clandestine paramilitary bands.[89] At the most tragic intersection of imperial and revolutionary struggles was the 'Armenian question'. In the eyes of the CUP leadership, the Macedonian question was about to repeat itself in Anatolia.[90] Armenian homelands were located at the frontier of empires and were the sites of heightened inter-imperial competition and revolutionary rivalries.[91]

Before officially declaring war against Russia on the German side, the CUP made a secret offer to the Armenian Revolutionary Federation (ARF hereafter), with whom they had long had good relations until the recent Armenian reform talks.[92] '[I]f war breaks out, rebellion in the Caucasus is inevitable: highlanders [Dagestanis], Turks and the Georgians alike will stand up, let the Armenians join them', as CUP emissaries proposed to the ARF. 'In

---

Ottomans' Great War and the Devastation of an Empire (Stanford, CA: Stanford University Press, 2018); Mehmet Beşikçi, *The Ottoman Mobilization of Manpower in the First World War: Between Voluntarism and Resistance* (Leiden: Brill, 2012). On the Ottoman jihad, see Erik Jan Zürcher (ed.), *Jihad and Islam in World War I: Studies on the Ottoman Jihad at the Centenary of Snouck Hurgronje's 'Holy war Made in Germany'* (Leiden: Leiden University Press, 2015).

[89] On the contentious historiography of the *Teşkilat-ı Mahsusa*, see Polat Safi, 'History in the Trench: The Ottoman Special Organization – Teşkilat-ı Mahsusa Literature', *Middle Eastern Studies* 48(1) (2012): 89–106. For the organisational history of the *Teşkilat-ı Mahsusa*, see Polat Safi, 'The Ottoman Special Organization – Teşkilat-ı Mahsusa: An Inquiry into Its Operational and Administrative Characteristics', PhD thesis, Bilkent University, 2012. The historiography of the *Teşkilat-ı Mahsusa* is primarily complicated by the question of whether it participated in the Armenian massacres and whether it was under the command of the Ottoman army or the CUP after March 1915. See Ahmet Tetik, *Teşkilat-ı Mahsusa (Umur-ı Şarkıyye Dairesi) Tarihi*, 2 vols (Istanbul: Türkiye İş Bankası Kültür Yayınları, 2014–18); Oktay Özel, 'Tehcir ve Teşkilat-ı Mahsusa', in Fikret Adanır and Oktay Özel (eds), *1915: Siyaset, Tehcir, Soykırım* (Istanbul: Tarih Vakfı Yurt Yayınları, 2015), 377–407; Taner Akçam, 'When Was the Decision to Annihilate the Armenians Taken?' *Journal of Genocide Research* 21(4) (2019), 457–80.

[90] Erik Jan Zürcher, 'Macedonians in Anatolia: The Importance of the Macedonian Roots of the Unionists for their Policies in Anatolia after 1914', *Middle Eastern Studies* 50(6) (2014): 960–75.

[91] Onur Önol, *The Tsar's Armenians: A Minority in Late Imperial Russia* (London: I. B. Tauris, 2017); Reynolds, *Shattering Empires*, 46–81.

[92] Dikran Mesrob Kaligian, *Armenian Organization and Ideology under Ottoman Rule: 1908–1914* (New Brunswick, NJ: Transaction Publishers, 2009).

return we promise to give Armenians autonomy.'[93] Uncertain about the prospects of a war against Russia, however, Armenian revolutionaries rejected and decided to remain neutral in a war of empires.[94] Some other local Armenian committees prepared for armed defence and resistance, creating yet further suspicions in the paranoid eyes of state surveillance.[95] Even more, the formation of Armenian volunteer battalions in the Russian army connected the Armenian revolutionaries directly with the inter-imperial competition.[96] After the devastating defeat in the Caucasus campaign in the winter of 1914/15, which he had commanded personally, Enver put the blame on subversive activities of Armenians in Eastern Anatolia.[97] Insisting that the Armenian population constituted a danger, he demanded from Talat Paşa that the ministry of the interior should deport Armenians from the conflict region to the Syrian desert. The rationale of counterinsurgency aside, however, the forced deportations were accompanied by political purges, paramilitary massacres, the abduction of women and children, as well as economic confiscations that ultimately had genocidal consequences for the Armenian population of Anatolia. Indeed, the convolution of imperial and revolutionary struggles was dramatically decisive in the destruction of the Ottoman commonwealth – the CUP leaders certainly knew what they were doing.[98]

Much like Eastern Anatolia, the Arab frontier was also plagued by imperial

---

[93] Quoted in Yektan Türkyılmaz, 'Rethinking Genocide: Violence and Victimhood in Eastern Anatolia, 1913–1915', PhD thesis, Duke University, 2011, 160. See also Kaligian, *Armenian Organization and Ideology*, 220.

[94] Türkyılmaz, 'Rethinking Genocide', 163–4.

[95] Donald Bloxham, 'Terrorism and Imperial Decline: The Ottoman–Armenian Case', *European Review of History* 14(3) (2007): 301–24.

[96] Armenian volunteer battalions were soon demobilised by the Russians, precisely because of their anti-imperialist revolutionary motivation. Manoug Joseph Somakian, *Empires in Conflict: Armenia and the Great Powers, 1895–1920* (London: I. B. Tauris, 1995), 109.

[97] The evidence does not necessarily back up Enver's conclusion that there was a wide-scale Armenian revolt. Taner Akçam, *The Young Turks' Crime against Humanity: The Armenian Genocide and Ethnic Cleansing in the Ottoman Empire* (Princeton, NJ: Princeton University Press, 2012), 162–75; Edward J. Erickson, *Ottomans and Armenians: A Study in Counterinsurgency* (New York: Palgrave, 2013), 161–82.

[98] Taner Akçam, 'When Was the Decision'; Ümit Kurt, 'Theatres of Violence on the Ottoman Periphery: Exploring the Local Roots of Genocidal Policies in Antep', *Journal of Genocide Research* 20:3 (2018): 351–71.

competition and revolutionary rivalries that had significant consequences for the region's populations. Although the CUP regime had invested great efforts into its Arab provinces after the Balkan defeat, their despotic centralisation policies were responsible for the continued discourse of Turkification among the Arab elites.[99] Arab secret societies became more revolutionary with the outbreak of the First World War, even though most of them opted more for decentralism and federalism than separatism.[100] In early 1916, Enver made an official inspection tour to Syria, Palestine, Sinai and the Hijaz. A few months later, Cemal Paşa, the CUP's man on the ground, publicly executed a prominent group of Arab nationalists for alleged revolutionary conspiracy in May 1916, as Enver and other CUP leaders had given him a free hand against subversive Arab activities.[101] Although the British-sponsored Arab Revolt in Hijaz in the summer of 1916 was not a direct cause of these events, it certainly ended up increasing revolutionary rivalries and changed the course of the inter-imperial war in the Middle East.

In the end, the Ottomans lost the war. Having conquered Baku shortly before the Ottoman defeat, Enver briefly considered leading an insurgency from Eastern Anatolia and the Caucasus, where weapons were stacked and troops were deployed. A senior German official, however, advised him against becoming a 'brigand chief' out of desperation.[102] Vocal critiques of the CUP, too, were demanding that 'rogue and false attempts such as the Special Organization as well as the detrimental activities of secret and vicious committees should come to an end'.[103] Despite all the advice and critique, Enver

---

[99] Hasan Kayalı, *Arabs and Young Turks: Ottomanism, Arabism, and Islamism in the Ottoman Empire, 1908–1918* (Berkeley, CA: University of California Press, 1997), 209–10; Leila Tarazi Fawaz, *A Land of Aching Hearts: The Middle East in the Great War* (Cambridge, MA: Harvard University Press, 2014), 251–2.

[100] Eliezer Tauber, 'Secrecy in Early Arab Nationalist Organizations', *Middle Eastern Studies* 33(1) (1997): 119–27; Yenen, 'Envisioning Turco-Arab Co-Existence', 95–102.

[101] M. Talha Çiçek, *War and State Formation in Syria: Cemal Pasha's Governorate during World War I, 1914–17* (London: Routledge, 2014), 45.

[102] Hans von Seeckt, letter (Constantinople) to Dorothee von Seeckt (Germany), 20 October 1918, Bundesarchiv Militärarchiv (German Federal Archives – Military Archive, BA-MA), Freiburg im Breisgau, N247/218, 173.

[103] Cenab Şehabeddin, 'Cihad', *Hadisat*, 4 November 1918, quoted in Orhan Koloğlu, *Aydınlarımızın Bunalım Yılı 1918: Zaferi Nihai'den Tam Teslimiyete* (Istanbul: Boyut Kitaplar, 2000), 108.

decided to go rogue anyway. He and his fellow CUP leaders fled to Germany as political outcasts and internationally wanted war criminals, while the CUP's intact underground networks started to organise the armed resistance movement against the Allied occupation.[104] As a professional revolutionary promising to incite anti-colonial uprisings in the Muslim world, Enver was welcomed by Bolshevik leaders in Soviet Russia in August 1920 and founded the Union of Muslim Revolutionary Societies.[105] Similar to his revolutionary actions in Macedonia, Enver planned in detail how local revolutionary committees in Muslim lands should entertain their 'revolutionary militia organisation' against European empires.[106] After all, the whole world seemed to have resembled Macedonia in the aftermath of the First World War.

While Enver refashioned himself as a global rogue, his local supporters in Trabzon, a CUP stronghold on the Black Sea coast, had established what an intelligence officer from Ankara dismissively called 'a state within a state'.[107] After a failed bid for power in Anatolia in September 1921, however, Enver decided to seek his fortunes elsewhere and joined the *Basmachi* rebels in Turkestan. But his stint in Central Asia did not last long, as he was killed in a charge against the Red Army. 'Que voulez-vous, c'est la fin d'un révolutionnaire!' commented a fellow Young Turk to a German friend upon hearing that Enver had been killed in action.[108] Indeed, Enver's political trajectory from his Machiavellian rise as a revolutionary officer and his Macbethian transformation into an imperial generalissimo to his Quixotic fall as a professional revolutionary illustrates the complexities that characterise his transgressive agency. Even if his trajectory was most spectacular, we argue that

---

[104] Erik Jan Zürcher, *The Unionist Factor: The Role of the Committee of Union and Progress in the Turkish National Movement, 1905–1926* (Leiden: Brill, 1984); Nur Bilge Criss, *Istanbul under Allied Occupation, 1918–1923* (Leiden: Brill, 1999), 94–114.

[105] Alp Yenen, 'The Young Turk Aftermath: Making Sense of Transnational Contentious Politics at the End of the Ottoman Empire, 1918–1922', PhD thesis, University of Basel, 2016, published online 2019), at: https://doi.org/10.5451/unibas-007110817.

[106] Enver Pasha, 'Draft of the Revolutionary Organization of Autonomous Committees', n.d., Türk Tarih Kurumu Arşivi (Archive of the Turkish Historical Society, TTK), Enver Pasha Papers, 03-09.

[107] Feridun Kandemir, *Şehit Enver Paşa Türkistan'da* (Istanbul: Barıman Yayınevi, 1945), 76.

[108] Hans von Seeckt, 'Erinnerungen an Enver Pascha: Von Generaloberst von Seeckt', *Velhagen & Klasings Monatshefte* 45(1) (1931): 84.

Enver was not a singular example but, in fact, the manifestation of a new type of an actor who, like many other similar rogues of his time, emerged out of the contentious frontiers of empires and prevailed against rival rogues to have a say in the brutal making of a new political order.[109]

Transgressive Politics in a Changing World

In order to better understand rogues like Enver and organisations such as the IMRO, we need to contextualise under what conditions transgressive politics actually emerge. As an analytical category, we accordingly locate transgressive politics at the intersections of three distinct spheres of politics. First, the very notion of transgression necessitates the framing of conventional politics as routine and formal political conduct. According to Weberian political sociology, conventional politics are state-centric, whereby states are the only legitimate actors that could define the conventions of politics. Second, if we are to assume that politics have conventions, every collective claim that attempts to challenge these conventions must be considered as a contention, if not a transgression. Therefore, our understanding of transgressive politics shares a common ground with contentious politics, which refers to a variety of collective political interactions from non-violent and episodic demonstrations to violent and prolonged insurgencies.[110] While some contentious campaigns may collaborate with political institutions through conventional channels, other forms of contentious politics can become truly transgressive when contentious agency violates states' sovereignty or legitimacy. Third, transgressive politics can overlap with so-called parapolitics, particularly if

---

[109] Enver's trajectory is commonly read through ideological parameters. See, for instance: Şuhnaz Yılmaz, 'Revisiting Networks and Narratives: Enver Pasha's Pan-Islamic and Pan-Turkic Quest', in Odile Moreau and Stuart Schaar (eds), *Subversives and Mavericks in the Muslim Mediterranean: A Subaltern History* (Austin: University of Texas Press, 2016), 143–65.

[110] On the comparison of different types of contentious politics, see George Lawson, 'Reform, Rebellion, Civil War, Coup d'État and Revolution', in James Defronzo (ed.), *Revolutionary Movements in World History: From 1750 to Present*, 3 vols (Santa Barbara, CA: ABC-CLIO, 2006), III:721; Jack A. Goldstone and Daniel P. Ritter, 'Revolution and Social Movements', in David A. Snow, Sarah A. Soule, Hanspeter Kriesi and Holly McCammon (eds), *The WileyBlackwell Companion to Social Movements* (New York: John Wiley, 2019), 683–97.

they involve extra-legal (state) or illegal (non-state) agency as well as secretive structures of terrorism, paramilitarism and organised crime.[111] We therefore locate rogue conduct at the transgressions of these three spheres, where agents and structures are involved in making violent and public actions to contend (or defend) the conventions of formal politics through extraordinary and extra-legal means (Figure 1.2).

If we are to follow neo-Weberian historical sociology as a historical process, modern state-formation was a result of 'protection rackets' that tried to monopolise the means of violence in establishing legitimate coercive power.[112] In this sense, the origins of modern states can be traced back to institutions and actors that were involved in coercion, taxation and protection. Irregulars and mercenaries were as important in processes of state-formation across the frontiers as they were for conventional armies.[113] Weber's sociology of the

---

[111] Robert Cribb, 'Introduction. Parapolitics, Shadow Governance and Criminal Sovereignty', in Eric Michael Wilson (ed.), *Government of the Shadows: Parapolitics and Criminal Sovereignty* (New York: Pluto Press, 2009), 1–9; Eric Michael Wilson, 'The Concept of the Parapolitical', in Eric Michael Wilson (ed.), *The Dual State: Parapolitics, Carl Schmitt and the National Security Complex* (Farnham: Ashgate, 2012), 1–28; Üngör, *Paramilitarism*, 64–182.

[112] Charles Tilly, 'War Making and State Making as Organized Crime', in Peter B. Evans, Dietrich Rueschemeyer and Theda Skocpol (eds), *Bringing the State Back In* (Cambridge: Cambridge University Press, 1985), 169–91; Charles Tilly, *Coercion, Capital, and European States: AD 990–1990* (Cambridge, MA: Blackwell, 1990), 67–95. For a similarly 'bellicose' historical sociology of state-formation, see Michael Mann, *Sources of Social Power, Vol. 1: A History of Power from the Beginning to A.D. 1760* (Cambridge: Cambridge University Press, 1986). For a discussion of bellicose theory of state-formation, see Siniša Malešević, *The Sociology of War and Violence* (Cambridge: Cambridge University Press, 2010), 71–5.

[113] Tolga U. Esmer argues that irregulars are the byproduct of imperial governance, so much to the point that crime and governance cannot be distinguished from each other. Tolga U. Esmer, 'Economies of Violence, Banditry and Governance in the Ottoman Empire Around 1800', *Past & Present* 224(1) (2014): 163–99. On the role of irregulars in state-formation, see Diane E. Davis, 'Contemporary Challenges and Historical Reflections on the Study of Militaries, States, and Politics', in Diane E. Davis and Anthony W. Pereira (eds), *Irregular Armed Forces and Their Role in Politics and State Formation* (Cambridge: Cambridge University Press, 2003), 3–34; Klejda Mulaj, 'Violent Non-State Actors: Exploring their State Relations, Legitimation, and Operationality', in Klejda Mulaj (ed.), *Violent Non-State Actors in World Politics* (London: Hurst, 2010), 1–25. At the same time, rivalling irregular bands also constituted a challenge to state-formation in the frontiers. Oren Barak and Chanan Cohen, 'The "Modern Sherwood Forest": Theoretical and Practical Challenges', in Dan Miodownik and Oren Barak (eds), *Nonstate Actors in Intrastate Conflicts* (Philadelphia: University of Pennsylvania Press, 2013), 12–33.

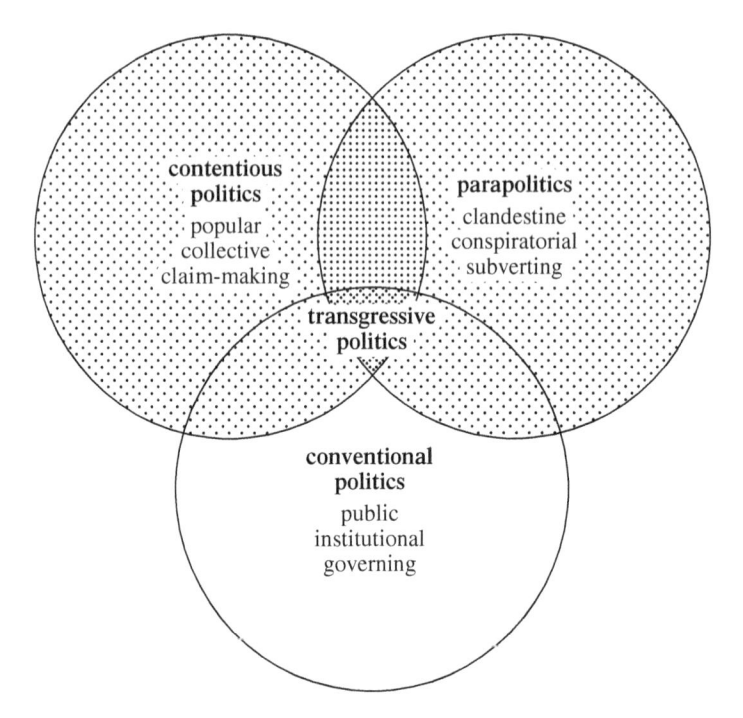

Figure 1.2 Locating transgressive politics.

state, which assumes that states are defined by the 'monopoly over legitimate means violence',[114] is certainly less accurate in displaying the historical reality of imperial sovereignty. Empires effectively administer 'states of exception' on their frontiers and tolerate (if not delegate) the use of violence by others within a flexible legal framework.[115] Both paramilitaries and partisans are

---

[114] Max Weber, *Wirtschaft und Gesellschaft* (Tübingen: Verlag von J.C.B. Mohr, 1922), 29. How far this monopoly is disregarded in imperial contexts is noted in Juan R. I. Cole, 'Of Crowds and Empires: Afro-Asian Riots and European Expansion, 1857–1882', in Fernando Coronil and Julie Skurski (eds), *States of Violence* (Ann Arbor: University of Michigan Press, 2006), 269–305, at 280; Tolga U. Esmer, 'Notes on a Scandal: Transregional Networks of Violence, Gossip, and Imperial Sovereignty in the Late Eighteenth-Century Ottoman Empire', *Comparative Studies in Society and History* 58(1) (2016): 127.

[115] This idea that sovereignty is defined by the 'state of exception' comes from Carl Schmitt, *Political Theology: Four Chapters on the Concept of Sovereignty* (Chicago, IL: University of Chicago Press, 2005). In imperial contexts, this idea is discussed in Lauren Benton, *A Search for Sovereignty: Law and Geography in European Empires, 1400–1900* (Cambridge: Cambridge University Press, 2009), 279–99.

transgressive agents who thrive in the state of exception and, in turn, define the contentious contours of state sovereignty on the ground.[116]

The Ottoman Empire is a case in point, as the use of irregulars and mercenaries in fact defined the very basis of its military and social power on the frontiers.[117] The situation was similar on the other side of the Ottoman frontier, too, where the *uskoks* were the border raiders of the Habsburg Empire, protecting and violating the contentious frontier.[118] Therefore, irregular warfare, by which we mean the decentralised organisation of small autonomous armed bands, was a formative element that sustained the autonomy of violence on imperial frontiers. As autonomous as rogues can be, however, some of them could be co-opted. In fact, empires regularly contracted such auxiliaries to perform state-sanctioned violence.[119]

The line between irregulars and mercenaries, as well as bandits and rebels, is a contentious matter of definition. The former two categorisations either depend on their eventual political trajectory or the length of service to the state, while the latter two are generally products of partisan representations. Most famously, however, Eric Hobsbawm coined the concept of social banditry by drawing attention to the example of the cult of banditry in the traditional cultures of the Balkans. Hobsbawm's social bandits were imagined as 'primitive rebels' who, due to their heroic subversion of the socio-economic coercion of the government,

---

[116] Carl Schmitt's *Theory of the Partisan* (New York: Telos Press, 2007) should be understood in terms of 'state of exception'. See Gabriella Slomp, *Carl Schmitt and the Politics of Hostility, Violence and Terror* (Basingstoke: Palgrave Macmillan, 2009), 57–78; Wilson, 'The Concept of the Parapolitical'.

[117] For the use of irregulars (*levends*) by the Ottoman military, see Uyar and Erickson, *A Military History of the Ottomans*, 91–4.

[118] Catherine Wendy Bracewell, *The Uskoks of Senj: Piracy, Banditry, and Holy War in the Sixteenth-Century Adriatic* (Ithaca, NY Cornell University Press, 1992).

[119] Tolga U. Esmer, 'War, State and the Privatisation of Violence in the Ottoman Empire', in Robert Antony, Stuart Carroll and Caroline Dodds Pennock (eds), *The Cambridge World History of Violence* (Cambridge: Cambridge University Press, 2020), vol. 3, 194–216. Such lucrative imperial practices were continued by post-Ottoman nation-states in the Balkans, which came at the detriment of state institutions and civil society. See: John Gledhill and Charles King, 'Institutions, Violence, and Captive States in Balkan History', in *Ottomans into Europeans: State and Institution-Building in South Eastern Europe*, eds Wim Van Meurs and Alina Mungiu-Pippidi (London: Hurst, 2011), 245–76.

supposedly received the support and admiration of the peasant populations.[120] Despite his obvious romantic-socialist projection, there has indeed been a tradition in the Balkans, traceable in songs and epics that celebrate the legends of famous bandits – commonly known as *hayduks* in Hungarian and Slavic dialects or *klephts* in Greek – as heroes of the people.[121] These traditional folkloric legends that celebrated hero-bandits ultimately informed nationalist (and later socialist) mythologies.[122] As a category of transgressive politics and a phenomenon of social construction, social banditry can also be observed in the Middle East, but the rarity of local folkloric sources as well as the sectarian and tribal categories readily attached to the bandits tend to undermine attempts to frame them as such.[123] After all, in colonial contexts, banditry not only needs to survive the violence of empires, but also their hegemony over the production of knowledge.[124] As such, they are subjected both to discourses of defamation and heroisation, as was the case with the north Caucasian

---

[120] For Hobsbawm's social bandit definition, see Eric J. Hobsbawm, *Primitive Rebels: Studies in Archaic Forms of Social Movement in the 19th and 20th Centuries*, 3rd edn (Manchester: Manchester University Press, 1971), 13–29; Eric J. Hobsbawm, *Bandits*, rev. edn (New York: Pantheon, 1981), 17–29. The social banditry concept unleashed a vast research wave in various disciplines. For one early but major critique, see Anton Blok, 'The Peasant and the Brigand: Social Banditry Reconsidered', *Comparative Studies in Society and History* 14(4) (1972): 494–503.

[121] For critiques of idealised histories of social banditry in the Balkans, see Fikret Adanır, 'Heiduckentum und osmanische Herrschaft. Sozialgeschichtliche Aspekte der Diskussion um das frühneuzeitliche Räuberwesen in Südosteuropa', *Südost-Forschungen* 41 (1982): 43–116; Andreas Helmedach and Markus Koller, '"Haiducken" – Gewaltgemeinschaften im westlichem Balkanraum im 17. und 18. Jahrhundert', in Winfried Speitkamp (ed.), *Gewaltgemeinschaften: Von der Spätantike bis ins 20. Jahrhundert* (Göttingen: V&R Unipress, 2013), 231–49.

[122] On the heroisation of bandits, see Alp Yenen, 'Banditen', in Ronald G. Asch, Achim Aurnhammer, Georg Feitscher and Anna Schreurs-Morét (eds), *Compendium heroicum*, issued by University of Freiburg, published online, 28 July 2020, at: https://dx.doi.org/10.6094/heroicum/bd1.0.20200728.

[123] For a comprehensive discussion, see Stephanie Cronin, 'Noble Robbers, Avengers and Entrepreneurs: Eric Hobsbawm and Banditry in Iran, the Middle East and North Africa', *Middle Eastern Studies* 52(5) (2016): 845–70.

[124] Kim A. Wagner, 'Thugee and Social Banditry Reconsidered', *The Historical Journal* 50(2) (2007): 353–76. See also Ranajit Guha, *Elementary Aspects of Peasant Insurgency in Colonial India* (Delhi: Oxford University Press, 1983).

bandits (*abrek*) in the Russian Empire and thereafter.[125] The latter-day trajectories of banditry in the Middle East are therefore indicative of how state-formation was accompanied by transgressive politics. The modern states in the region re-invented banditry as a social hazard in order to legitimise state control in distant peripheries.[126] In Turkey, for instance, the continued rogue conduct of Kurdish bandits (*eşkıyâ*) until the 1960s illustrates the interplay between state centralisation and subaltern traditions of autonomous violence.[127]

While rogue conduct could inadvertently push governments to pursue coercion, respond through counterinsurgency tactics, and initiate coalitions among local and global enemies, rogues could also utilise and co-opt the very same technologies, tactics and coalitions to increase their own subversive capacities. For centuries, the Porte effectively co-opted warlords, bandits and rebels in governing its frontiers.[128] From the late eighteenth century

---

[125] Jeronim Perović, *From Conquest to Deportation: The North Caucasus under Russian Rule* (London: Hurst, 2018), 21–52; Rebecca Gould, *Writers and Rebels: The Literature of Insurgency in the Caucasus* (New Haven, CT: Yale University Press, 2016); Vladimir Bobrovnikov, 'Bandits and the State: Designing a "Traditional" Culture of Violence in the North Caucasus', in Jane Burbank, Mark Von Hagen, and Anatolyi Remnev (eds), *Russian Empire: Space, People, Power 1700–1930* (Bloomington: Indiana University Press, 2007), 239–67.

[126] Nathan Brown, 'Brigands and State Building: The Invention of Banditry in Modern Egypt', *Comparative Studies in Society and History* 32(2) (1990): 258–81.

[127] Uğur Ümit Üngör, 'Rethinking the Violence of Pacification: State Formation and Bandits in Turkey, 1914–1937', *Comparative Studies in Society and History* 54(4) (2012): 746–69; Jordi Tejel Gorgas, 'The Shared Political Production of "the East" as a "Resistant" Territory and Cultural Sphere in the Kemalist Era, 1923–1938', *European Journal of Turkish Studies* 10 (2009), at: http://journals.openedition.org/ejts/4064. For the continued occurrence of banditry in eastern Anatolia and its depiction in popular culture, see Ahmet Özcan, 'Les derniers bandits kurdes de la Turquie moderne: Analyse des soulèvements individuels "spontanés" kurdes ou le banditisme contre l'État-nation turc', *Dans L'Homme et la Société* 1–2 (187–8) (2013): 155–81.

[128] To see how the Ottoman state interacted with and co-opted bandits in Anatolia during the early modern era, see Karen Barkey, *Bandits and Bureaucrats: The Ottoman Route to State Centralization* (Ithaca, NY: Cornell University Press, 1994). For the troublesome military history of how the Ottoman Empire settled for 'a federative, mercenary, or paramilitary force for the maintenance of its remaining territories on the Danube and in Greater Syria', see Virginia H. Aksan, 'Mobilization of Warrior Populations in the Ottoman Context, 1750–1850', in *Fighting for a Living: A Comparative Study*

onwards, as the bureaucratisation of state apparatus demanded far-reaching control and coercion, the imperial state began to challenge the autonomy of warlords on the frontiers, while also continuing to use them against the state's enemies.[129] The different types of Ottoman irregulars, for example, were all grouped together under the notorious umbrella term *başıbozuk*, which the state regularly marshalled in times of conflict throughout the nineteenth century.[130] The Ottoman state's co-optation of such indigenous militias constituted a challenge to later nationalist representations that idealised the role of warlords and brigands in their respective national spheres. In the Greek case, the Ottoman state's indigenous militias, the so-called *armolotoi*, were idealised as national heroes after Greek independence, but their rogue conduct similarly continued to be a risk to the fledgling Greek state.[131] Contrary to their projection as proto-nationalist armed forces, many of these militias had in fact a mixed ethnic–religious membership. Nevertheless, the increased recruitment of certain ethnic groups – most notably Albanians and Circassians as well as Kurds in Anatolia – as irregulars

---

    of Military Labour 1500–2000 (Amsterdam: Amsterdam University Press, 2013), 351.

[129] Frederick F. Anscombe, 'Continuities in Ottoman Centre–Periphery Relations, 1787–1915', in A. C. S. Peacock (ed.), *The Frontiers of the Ottoman World* (Oxford: Oxford University Press, 2009), 235–52.

[130] Literally meaning 'broken head' in the sense that they were unruly in their armed conduct, the term *başıbozuk* was popularised by foreign observers, such as Edward Vizetelly, *The Remininiscences of a Bashi-Bazouk* (Bristol: J. W. Arrowsmith, 1897), as well as by those who depicted Ottoman rule as alien and unjust, such as in Avetis Nazarbek, 'Zeitun', *The Contemporary Review* 69 (January 1896): 513–28. For the Ottoman military's problems with 'irregulars-cum-bandits', see Uğur Bayraktar, 'From Salary to Resistance: Mobility, Employment, and Violence in Dibra, 1792–1826', *Middle Eastern Studies* 54(6) (2018): 878–900.

[131] John S. Koliopoulos, 'Brigandage and Irredentism in Nineteenth-Century Greece', in Martin Blinkhorn and Thanos Veremis (eds), *Modern Greece: Nationalism and Nationality* (Athens: SAGE-ELIAMEP, 1990), 67–102; Achilles Batalas, 'Send a Thief to Catch a Thief: State-Building and the Employment of Irregular Military Formations in Mid-Nineteenth-Century Greece', in Diane E. Davis and Anthony W. Pereira (eds), *Irregular Armed Forces and Their Role in Politics and State Formation* (Cambridge: Cambridge University Press, 2003), 149–77; Gerassimos Karabelias, 'From National Heroes to National Villains: Bandits, Pirates and the Formation of Modern Greece', in Stephanie Cronin (ed.), *Subalterns and Social Protest: History from Below in the Middle East and North Africa* (London: Routledge, 2008), 263–83.

further sharpened identity politics across different frontiers of the Ottoman Empire.[132]

The shared organisational features of such bands of rebels and bandits became their key characteristics, blurring their categorical differences in terms of their political legitimacy. Both rebels and bandits were organised in small armed groups (*cheta* in Slavic and *çete* in Turkish) with a chain of command subordinate to a charismatic leader, navigating across a frontier territory, if not rural hinterlands. Such bands drew from an existing repertoire of rural brigandage and frontier warfare. Primarily recruiting bachelors, landless peasants, refugees and deserters to their cause, they could also attract adventurers and mercenaries. The term *çete* denoted multiple meanings over time, ranging from a band of guerrilla warriors to more contemporary usage indicating gangster violence and deep-state networks.[133] According to an Ottoman military manual for irregular warfare from 1909, there were two categories of *çete*: first, the 'roadside criminals' and, second, those 'in pursuit of national and political intentions'.[134] This differentiation between political rebels and criminal bandits is common elsewhere, too. In Russian Turkestan, for instance, Enver Paşa had joined the insurgency of the *Basmachi*, literally meaning 'raider'.[135] 'It is necessary to distinguish between two classes of Basmachis in

---

[132] Frederick F. Anscombe, 'Albanians and "Mountain Bandits"', in Frederick F. Anscombe (ed.), *The Ottoman Balkans, 1750–1830* (Princeton, NJ: Markus Wiener, 2006), 87–113; Ryan Gingeras, *Sorrowful Shores: Violence, Ethnicity, and the End of the Ottoman Empire, 1912–1923* (Oxford: Oxford University Press, 2009), 23–36; Janet Klein, *The Margins of Empire: Kurdish Militias in the Ottoman Tribal Zone* (Stanford, CA: Stanford University Press, 2011); Antonio Ferrara and Niccolò Pianciola, 'The Dark Side of Connectedness: Forced Migrations and Mass Violence between the Late Tsarist and Ottoman Empires (1853–1920)', *Historical Research* 92(257) (2019): 608–31; Caner Yelbaşı, *The Circassians of Turkey: War, Violence and Nationalism from the Ottomans to Atatürk* (London: I. B. Tauris, 2019).

[133] For an excellent conceptual history of the term, see Polat Safi, 'Üç Tarz-ı Çete', *Kebikeç* 34 (2012): 85–105.

[134] Ömer Fevzi, *Muhafâza-i Âsâyişe Me'mûr Zabitanın Vezâifi: Usûl-i Ta'kib-i Eşkiyâ' ve Çete Muhârebeleri* (Istanbul: Matbaa-i İkbal, 1325 [1909/1910]), 20–9, quoted in Safi, 'The Ottoman Special Organization', 109.

[135] On the origins of the *Basmachi* revolt, see Yulia Uryadova, 'Bandits, Terrorists, and Revolutionaries: The Breakdown of Civil Authority in the Imperial Ferghana Valley, 1905–1914', PhD thesis, University of Arkansas, 2012.

Ferghana', noted a British observer, 'The genuine political Basmachis, the original Soviet rebels against Soviet rule . . . On the other hand, there are the purely bandit Basmachis . . . who terrorise the countryside.'[136] While the shared organisation made them appear identical, the criminalising discourse also served state interests that tried to deny and delegitimise the politicisation of rebels-cum-bandits.[137]

In the late nineteenth century, however, *çete* came to describe a new form of rogue conduct, readily equated with the Ottoman term *komitadji* (in Turkish: *komitacı* or *komiteci*). Even though the term is originally an Ottoman–Turkish expression used by government officials with the literal meaning of 'committee man', the word in fact still exists in various Balkan languages, identifying either an individual partisan fighter or agency on behalf of a revolutionary committee. The term *komitadji* uniquely signifies the merging of rural and urban forms of transgressive politics into a shared repertoire of rogue conduct. On the one hand, the rural repertoire – the formation of small units of brigands and the elaboration of tactics of irregular warfare and the mobilisation strategies of peasants – were locally rooted processes that served a variety of political agendas. On the other hand, a new urban repertoire combined the organisational features of secret societies and political parties with the tactics of terrorism and 'propaganda of the deed' – complete with the political socialisation of followers through collective action among workers and youth. This led to a new type of urban warfare, whereby bomb attacks and political assassinations could generate new levels of pressure on political regimes, most notably as in the raid on the Ottoman

---

[136] Quoted in Şuhnaz Yılmaz, 'An Ottoman Warrior Abroad: Enver Paşa as an Expatriate', *Middle Eastern Studies* 35(4) (1999): 57–8. For conflicting narratives of the *Basmachi* in post-Soviet countries, see Kirill Nourzhanov, 'Bandits, Warlords, National Heroes: Interpretations of the Basmachi Movement in Tajikistan', *Central Asian Survey* 34(2) (2015): 177–89.

[137] Yenen, 'Banditen'. For instance, sabotage attacks on Ottoman railways by the Macedonian Revolutionary Committee were referred to in Ottoman bureaucratic language as conducted by 'bandits (*eşkiya*) or "trouble makers" (fesatciler)'. Peter Mentzel, 'Accidents, Sabotage, and Terrorism: Work Hazards on Ottoman Railways', in Colin Imber, Keiko Kiyotaki and Rhoads Murphey (eds), *Frontiers of Ottoman Studies: State, Province, and the West*, (London: I. B. Tauris, 2005), vol. 2, 237.

Bank in Istanbul in 1896.[138] Successful and failed assassination attempts against presidents, monarchs and ministers, including Tsar Alexander II (1881), Bulgarian prime minister Stefan Stambolov (1895), Nasser-al-Din Shah (1896), Empress Elisabeth of Austria (1898) and Sultan Abdülhamid II (1905), demonstrated the vulnerability of public rulers in the face of the new urban repertoire of transgressive politics, but also fed into bureaucratic insecurities vis-à-vis new political challenges.[139]

The emergence of this new *modus operandi*, we argue, was the product of new opportunity structures for contention that emerged out of the structural ruptures in the late nineteenth century. Increased access to military and civilian education since the mid-nineteenth century had given birth to a class of disgruntled individuals whom the Ottoman *ancien régime* was unable to absorb. Rogues were borne out of this group of individuals who were denied access to the metropole and positions of power. They would find opportunities elsewhere, particularly after the balance of power shifted in Europe thanks to the rise of Germany as a Great Power, which heralded new forms of imperialism in the last two decades of the nineteenth century.[140] In this age of territorial scramble, an increasingly competitive political climate opened up new political opportunities for transgressive actors, particularly in the frontiers of empires where interstate competition and local rivalries were at their fiercest. Their genre of transgressive politics included a particular brand of radicalism that called for land reform, social justice and protection of rights, which appealed to the disgruntled rural populations who were hard hit by the price recession due to the Long Depression (1873–1896), and to those urban workers suffering from an unstable labour market.[141] It was

---

[138] Bloxham, 'Terrorism and Imperial Decline', 309–10.
[139] Richard Bach Jensen, 'Daggers, Rifles, and Dynamite: Anarchist Terrorism in Nineteenth Century Europe', *Terrorism and Political Violence* 16(1) (2004): 116–53. On reactions of the Ottomans, see İlkay Yılmaz, *Serseri, Anarşist ve Fesadın Peşinde: II. Abdülhamid Dönemi Güvenlik Politikaları Ekseninde Mürur Tezkereleri, Pasaportlar ve Otel Kayıtları* (Istanbul: Tarih Vakfı Yurt Yayınları, 2014); İlkay Yılmaz, 'Propaganda by the Deed and Hotel Registration Regulations in the Late Ottoman Empire', *Journal of the Ottoman and Turkish Studies Association* 4(1) (2017): 137–56.
[140] Hobsbawm, *The Age of Empire*, 56–61; Benedict Anderson, *Under Three Flags: Anarchism and the Anti-Colonial Imagination* (London: Verso, 2000), 4.
[141] Linda Schatkowski Schilcher, 'The Great Depression (1873–1896) and the Rise of Syrian

the coalescence of these three interrelated ruptures in the mid-1880s that ultimately enabled transgressive action outside the routine and normativity of conventional politics.[142]

Crucially, there were many examples to follow. While the IMRO model was a source of inspiration for Enver and his fellow Ottoman-Muslim revolutionaries, the Armenian revolutionary organisations provided templates of revolutionary activism across the Balkans, Anatolia, and Russian and the Iranian Caucasus. In Qajar Iran, the Armenian revolutionaries played a prominent role in the dissemination of the revolutionary repertoire, which merged with Muslim reform policies proposed by Iranian constitutionalists after the Tobacco Revolt of 1890–2.[143] In Persian, the term *anjoman* came to denote both political organisations and secret societies during the constitutional struggle.[144] For the Young Turk volunteers who were dispatched to the Caucasus to support the Iranian constitutionalists and collaborate with

---

Arab Nationalism', *New Perspectives on Turkey* 6 (1991): 167–89; Donald Quataert, 'The Age of Reforms', in Halil İnalcik and Donald Quataert (eds), *An Economic and Social History of the Ottoman Empire, Vol. 2: 1600–1914* (Cambridge: Cambridge University Press, 1994), 856, 871; Joel Beinin, *Workers and Peasants in the Modern Middle East* (Cambridge: Cambridge University Press, 2001), 44–70; Ilham Khuri-Makdisi, *The Eastern Mediterranean and the Making of Global Radicalism* (Berkeley, CA: University of California Press, 2010); Nadir Özbek, 'The Politics of Taxation and the "Armenian Question" during the Late Ottoman Empire, 1876–1908', *Comparative Studies in Society and History* 54(34) (2012): 770–97; Kostopoulos, 'Land to the Tiller'.

[142] All the (in)famous revolutionary organisations on the frontiers of the Ottoman Empire date back to this period. The Armenian Hunchaks were founded in 1887, the Committee of Union and Progress (CUP) in 1889, Dashnaktsutyun (aka ARF) in 1890, Internal Macedonian Revolutionary Organization (IMRO) in 1893, and the External Macedonian Revolutionary Organization in 1895.

[143] Houri Berberian, 'Nest of Revolution: The Caucasus, Iran, and Armenians', in Rudi Matthee and Elena Andreeva (eds), *Russians in Iran: Diplomacy and Power in Qajar Era and Beyond* (London: I. B. Tauris, 2018), 95–121; Moritz Deutschmann, 'Cultures of Statehood, Cultures of Revolution. Caucasian Revolutionaries in the Iranian Constitutional Movement, 1906–1911', *Ab Imperio* 2 (2013): 165–90; Mangol Bayat, *Iran's First Revolution: Shi'ism and the Constitutional Revolution of 1905–1909* (Oxford: Oxford University Press, 1991), 76–105.

[144] Sohrabi, *Revolution and Constitutionalism*, 367–77; Bayat, *Iran's First Revolution*, 70–5, 111–17, 146–59, 161–8; Nezam-Mafi M. Ettchadieh, 'Origin and Development of Political Parties in Persia 1906–1911', PhD thesis, University of Edinburgh, 1979, 248–88.

Armenian revolutionaries, the terms *anjoman* and *komitadji* were understood to refer to the same type of rogues.[145] Even though methodological nationalism may portray them as the embodiments of irreconcilable nationalisms within an empire, they in fact cooperated as much as they competed with one another,[146] just as empires cooperated and competed with one other in controlling the *komitadjis*, anarchists and socialists.[147]

Not only constitutional revolutions, but also wars – especially the total war experience of the Balkan Wars and later the First World War – offered new opportunities for the *komitadjis*. True to their guerrilla culture, they participated in conventional wars and re-entered the sphere of state control and co-optation. Leon Trotsky, as a war correspondent during the Balkan Wars, revealed how '[t]he *komitadjis* were organized already before the war, in different ways in different areas . . . When war came, they were attached to particular army units for outpost duty and scouting . . .'[148] Similarly, to all intents and purposes, the Ottoman army's special operations organisation, *Teşkilat-ı Mahsusa*, was a *komitadji* organisation that grew out of the unconventional warfare experience across the Ottoman frontiers, turning into the CUP regime's paramilitary and parapolitical enforcer.[149] This convolution of rogue conduct and interstate warfare in the Balkans not only affected

---

[145] Fethi Tevetoğlu, *Ömer Naci* (Ankara: Kültür ve Turizm Bakanlığı, 1987), 105. For more background, see Farzin Vejdani, 'Crafting Constitutional Narratives. Iranian and Young Turk Solidarity 1907–09', in H. E. Chehabi and Vanessa Martin (eds), *Iran's Constitutional Revolution: Popular Politics, Cultural Transformations and Transnational Connections* (London: I. B. Tauris, 2010), 319–40.

[146] Duncan M. Perry, 'The Macedonian Revolutionary Organization's Armenian Connection', *Armenian Review* 42(5) (1989): 61–8; Garabet K. Moumdjian, 'Rebels with a Cause: Armenian–Macedonian Relations and Their Bulgarian Connection, 1895–1913', in M. Hakan Yavuz and Isa Blumi (eds), *War and Nationalism: The Balkan Wars, 1912–1913, and Their Sociopolitical Implications* (Salt Lake City, UT: University of Utah Press, 2013), 132–75; Berberian, *Roving Revolutionaries*, 131–2.

[147] Richard Bach Jensen, 'The International Campaign Against Anarchist Terrorism, 1880–1930s', *Terrorism and Political Violence* 21(1) (2009): 89–109.

[148] Leon Trotsky, *The Balkan Wars, 1912–13: The War Correspondence of Leon Trotsky*, ed. George Weissman and Duncan Williams (New York: Pathfinder Press, 1980), 120.

[149] Uğur Ümit Üngör, 'Paramilitary Violence in the Collapsing Ottoman Empire', in Robert Gerwarth and John Horne (eds), *War in Peace: Paramilitary Violence in Europe after the Great War* (Oxford: Oxford University Press, 2012), 164–83.

the making of states but also contributed to the forging of nations.[150] Even the First World War was triggered by rogue conduct in a contested frontier of empires, when a group of Bosnian-Serbian revolutionaries, who were associated with the Black Hand Society and trained by the Serbian military intelligence, assassinated the Habsburg crown prince in Sarajevo on 28 June 1914.[151] After the First World War, the contentious repertoire of rogues continued to travel from the Balkans to the Middle East. A British intelligence officer described Arab uprisings in 1920 as 'insurrections resorting to the avowed tactics of guerrilla and *cemitadji* [sic] warfare'.[152] Transgressive politics is always a product of its time and place. War and revolution conditioned the emergence of rogues across the frontiers of empires; as was the case the other way around as well.

Rogue Conduct: Search for a Culture of Agency

From frontiers of empires to the centres of power, rogues played important roles in the social construction of identities in the Balkans, the Middle East and the Caucasus. Neo-Weberian perspectives on the role of war and violence, however, fail to account for cultural and ideological dimensions.[153] While

---

[150] Mulaj Klejda, 'War and State Making at the End of Empire: Ottoman Collapse and the Formation of the Balkan States', *Peace & Change: A Journal of Peace Research* 41(4) (2016): 539–66; M. Hakan Yavuz, 'Warfare and Nationalism: The Balkan Wars as a Catalyst of Homogenization', in M. Hakan Yavuz and Isa Blumi (eds), *War and Nationalism: The Balkan Wars, 1912–1913, and Their Sociopolitical Implications* (Salt Lake City, UT: University of Utah Press, 2013), 31–84; Siniša Malešević, 'Wars that Make States and Wars that Make Nations: Organised Violence, Nationalism and State Formation in the Balkans', *European Journal of Sociology* 53 (2012): 31–63.

[151] Tetsuya Sahara, 'The Making of "Black Hand" Reconsidered', *Istorija 20. veka* 34(1) (2016): 9–29; Christopher M. Clark, *The Sleepwalkers: How Europe Went to War in 1914* (London: Penguin, 2013), 3–64. In many ways, the pre-war Balkans foreshadowed the paramilitary violence in Europe during the aftermath of the First World War. John P. Newman, 'The Origins, Attributes, and Legacies of Paramilitary Violence in the Balkans', in Robert Gerwarth and John Horne (eds), *War in Peace: Paramilitary Violence in Europe after the Great War* (Oxford: Oxford University Press, 2012), 145–62.

[152] Quoted in Isaiah Friedman, *British Miscalculations: The Rise of Muslim Nationalism, 1918–1925* (New Brunswick, NJ: Transaction, 2012), 56.

[153] Malešević, *The Sociology of War and Violence*, 79–80.

nationalism as the growing ideology of the time certainly needs attention,[154] one must be wary of methodological nationalism which often treats nationalism as less a subject of study than as a tool of analysis. In avoiding the latter, we see nationalism as part of the same dynamics of modernity that shaped the age of rogues on the frontiers of empires. This was when print media, cultural associations, secret societies and political parties created new public spheres to make collective claims on behalf of nationalist imaginations.[155] Yet nationalism is only one of several global ideologies, such as anarchism, socialism and radicalism, all of which had a considerable impact on both Muslim and non-Muslim intelligentsia in imperial frontiers.[156] Notions of radical reform, social revolution and/or territorial claims co-existed with material interests in rents derived from racketeering and brutal cultures of violence.

The historical significance of the IMRO, Enver, and many others from their creed and generation lay not in the consistency of their ideological positions or in the sharpness of their discursive articulations, but rather in their proclivity to contentious and transgressive action in pursuit of their political interests. In approaching the latter, we reject the notion of violence as a *degree* of conflict, but consider it as a *form* of contentious and formative interaction that is context-dependent.[157] It is neither the strength of

---

[154] Umut Uzer, *An Intellectual History of Turkish Nationalism: Between Turkish Ethnicity and Islamic Identity* (Salt Lake City, UT: The University of Utah Press, 2016).

[155] For a comparative approach, see Fatma Müge Göçek, 'Decline of the Ottoman Empire and the Emergence of Greek, Armenian, Turkish and Arab Nationalisms', in Fatma Müge Göçek (ed.), *Social Constructions of Nationalism in the Middle East* (Albany, NY: State University of New York Press, 2002), 15–84.

[156] Nationalism as a framework shaped the study of socialists and anarchists in the Ottoman world. For a pioneering overview, see Mete Tunçay and Erik Jan Zürcher (eds), *Socialism and Nationalism in the Ottoman Empire: 1876–1923* (London: I. B. Tauris, 1994). On the cosmopolitism of anarchism beyond nationalism, see Axel B. Çorlu, 'Anarchists and Anarchism in the Ottoman Empire, 1850–1917', in Selim Karahasanoğlu and Deniz C. Demir (eds), *History from Below: A Tribute in Memory of Donald Quataert* (Istanbul: Istanbul Bilgi Üniversitesi Yayınları, 2016), 551–81. For the Levant, see Khuri-Makdisi, *The Eastern Mediterranean*. For anarchism's global dimension, see Steven Hirsch and Lucien van der Walt (eds), *Anarchism and Syndicalism in the Colonial and Postcolonial World, 1870–1940: The Praxis of National Liberation Internationalism and Social Revolution* (Leiden: Brill, 2010).

[157] Rogers Brubaker and David D. Laitin, 'Ethnic and Nationalist Violence', *Annual Review of Sociology* 24 (1998): 426; Adria Lawrence, 'Driven to Arms? The Escalation to Violence in

nationalist convictions nor the degree of exasperation that causes violence, while the resort to violence certainly leads to both. As Tolga U. Esmer demonstrated, the transgressive politics of the Ottoman state in the co-opting of rebels and bandits affected the culture of violence on the ground.[158] Violence played into the boundary work of the construction of collective identities, too. 'Paramilitarism', noted Ryan Gingeras, 'was a political, economic, and social institution that enabled both statist and resistance factions to mobilize popular support'.[159] The experience of paramilitary violence was therefore constitutive of militant expressions of nationalism. In an often-quoted passage by a *Teşkilat-ı Mahsusa* agent, the conduct of a *komitadji* was defined as 'the most extreme form of patriotism':

> And the *komitadji* is a person who sacrifices everything, even his life, for the cause of the fatherland, who does not forsake anything, and who has renounced his whole being from head to toe. When it is necessary for the interests of this country and nation, he abandons compassion, if it is necessary to burn something, he burns, if there is a need to destroy, he destroys it all! He does not leave a stone on top of a stone or a head on top of a torso![160]

Beyond violence, romantic visions of camaraderie and adventure similarly helped to shape identities. The *komitadjis* were 'modern knights of the round table' in the imagination of contemporary European observers critical of Ottoman rule over the Balkans.[161] 'The ambition of every Macedonian boy in those days was to become a *comitadji*, to raise a beard, a mop of shaggy hair', as Ottoman–Macedonian-born American writer and US senator Stoyan Christowe remembered.[162] The cult of a charismatic leader of a *çete* was another feature of constructing a collective identity. In the Balkans,

---

Nationalist Conflicts', in Erica Chenoweth and Adria Lawrence (eds), *Rethinking Violence: States and Non-State Actors in Conflict* (Cambridge, MA: MIT Press, 2010), 145.

[158] Esmer, 'Economies of Violence'.
[159] Gingeras, *Sorrowful Shores*, 6.
[160] Fuat Balkan, *Komitacı: BJK'nin Kurucusu Fuat Balkan'ın Anıları*, ed. Turgut Gürer (Istanbul: Gürer Yayınları, 2008), 43, 45; quoted here from the English translation in Göçek, 'Decline of the Ottoman Empire', 92.
[161] Jan Gordon, *A Balkan Freebooter: Being the True Exploits of the Serbian Outlaw and Comitaj Petko Moritch* (London: Smith Elder, 1916), 243.
[162] Stoyan Christowe, *Heroes and Assassins* (New York: R. M. McBride, 1935), 15.

these leaders were called *voivode*. Popular admiration for *voivodes* and *chetas* was not restricted to the Christian population. Şevket Süreyya Aydemir, an Ottoman-Muslim born in Edirne in the Balkans in 1897, remembered from his childhood that it was their favourite game to play *çete* and *komitadji* wars with the neighbourhood children:

> First, we chose *kaptans* and *voivodas* . . . from among the strongest and bravest of the children, who then split up into groups. Those who took part in the game would turn back the edges of their fezes to make them look like the fur hats (*kalpak*) worn by Greek and Bulgarian bandits . . . Instead of knives and guns, they stuck sticks and pieces of wood into their belts, and instead of bombs, they filled their pockets and sashes with stones.[163]

A very different but similarly formative childhood memory about the *komitadji* phenomenon comes from Minas Dersakissian who, as a young twelve-year-old Armenian boy, was put under detention by Ottoman officials on his way to the Armenian seminary in Jerusalem in 1907. In an interview in 1970, he recalled the impact of his unjust encounter with Ottoman authorities:

> He tells me I am a 'Komitaji', a member of an 'Armenian terrorist group', a group I had never heard of, and, to say the least belong to. In fact, that incident sparks an interest in me to find out who those 'Komitajis' are, and later on in my life when I learned about the mission of this group, which was to fight by taking arms against all oppressive enemies of Armenia, be it Turkey or [Russia] which had occupied our motherland, Armenia, I too become a 'Komitadji', and a life-long member of the Armenian Revolutionary Federation, and actually took arms and fought against them.[164]

Under such state repression and surveillance, many *komitadjis* tapped into the cultural repertoire of Masonic secret societies that provided clandestine

---

[163] Şevket Süreyya Aydemir, *Suyu Arayan Adam*, 7th edn (Istanbul: Remzi Kitabevi, 1979), 16, quoted here from the English translation in Andrew Mango, *Atatürk* (New York: Overlook Press, 2002), 12–13.

[164] Vahak D. Sarkis, *The Odyssey of an Armenian Revolutionary Couple: How They Survived the First Genocide of the 20th Century* (Bloomington, IN: Xlibris, 2010), 26–7.

support and shelter to some revolutionary movements.[165] Masonic societies were also the context, where most *komitadji* organisations adopted the initiation and secrecy rituals, topped off with the fraternal principles drawn from the Carbonari-styled parties. In shaping identities and loyalties, transgressive politics commonly sacralised its own *raison d'être*. The CUP was vernacularly called the 'sacred society' (*cemiyet-i mukaddes*). The secret oath given to the revolutionary committee created terminal loyalty among members and commitment to political violence.[166] In their initiation oath, the CUP, in copying other Balkan revolutionary committees, put their hand on a Qur'an, a dagger and a revolver.[167] Even more, transgressive politics sacralised the violent self-sacrifice and political martyrdom. The cult of the *feda'i*, namely, the self-sacrificing volunteers, created a political culture based on killing and dying among Turks, Armenians, Iranians and Arabs.[168]

Returning to Tilly's dictum, it remains unanswered why and how subaltern forms of protection rackets continue to exist beneath and beyond state hegemony long after the formal monopolisation of legitimate means of violence – a point critically emphasised in the Frankfurt School's racket theory long before.[169] While the state cannot exist without racketeers, racketeers can

---

[165] Thierry Zarcone, 'Freemasonry and Islam', in Henrik Bogdan and J.A.M. Snoek (eds), *Handbook of Freemasonry* (Leiden: Brill, 2014), 233–57. The Young Turk networks in Salonica held their secret meetings in the Freemason lodges. M. Şükrü Hanioğlu, 'Notes on the Young Turks and the Freemasons', *Middle Eastern Studies* 25(2) (1989): 186–97.

[166] Brown, *Loyal unto Death*, 74–86.

[167] This oath ritual was later copied even by the Muslim Brotherhood in Egypt and Indian Muslims. Hanioğlu, *Preparation for a Revolution*, 218; Richard P. Mitchell, *The Society of the Muslim Brothers*, reprinted with new Introduction (New York: Oxford University Press, 1993), 206; Azmi Özcan, *Pan-Islamism: Indian Muslims, the Ottomans and Britain (1877–1924)* (Leiden: Brill, 1997), 157.

[168] Khachig Tölölyan, 'Cultural Narrative and the Motivation of the Terrorist', *Journal of Strategic Studies* 10(4) (1987): 217–33.

[169] The Frankfurt School's racket theory is based on scattered notes and references throughout Max Horkheimer's work, including Max Horkheimer, 'Theorie der Rackets', in Alfred Schmidt and Gunzelin Schmid Noerr (eds), *Gesammelte Schriften 14: Nachgelassene Schriften 1949–1972* (Frankfurt: Fischer, 1988), 340; Max Horkheimer, 'Die Rackets und der Geist', in Gunzelin Schmid Noerr (ed.), *Gesammelte Schriften 12: Nachgelassene Schriften 1931–1949* (Frankfurt: Fischer, 1985), 287–91. For a concise but illuminating reinterpretation of racket theory, see Olmo Gölz, 'The Dangerous Classes and the 1953 Coup in Iran: On the Decline of "lutigari" Masculinities', in Stephanie Cronin (ed.),

exist without the state. In addressing this discrepancy, we need to reconsider statehood as a collective performance. Every organisation or social community performs statehood in one way or another. It was no surprise that both the IMRO and later the CUP functioned like 'para-states' within states.[170]

Historical and political anthropology show that other key features of statehood besides violence, such as control over territory and people, are similarly claimed by rebels and bandits when they control passages, tax the peasants, punish traitors and recruit followers.[171] This para-state dimension of transgressive politics in rural areas and contentious frontiers was not much different in the microcosm of urban centres. Gangsters and strongmen emerged at the intersection of traditional and modern social communities in the neighbourhoods of towns and cities giving birth to the archetype of infamous gangsters across the modern Middle East (Turkish: *kabadayı*; Arabic: *qabaday*; Persian: *luti*).[172] In the absence of a formal state or extra-legally on

---

Crime, Poverty and Survival in the Middle East and North Africa: The 'Dangerous Classes' since 1800 (London: I. B. Tauris, 2019), 187–9.

[170] For 'para-statehood', see Trutz von Trotha, 'Der Aufstieg des Lokalen', *Aus Politik und Zeitgeschichte* 28/29 (2005): 32–8, at: https://www.bpb.de/apuz/28956/der-aufstieg-des-lokalen. See also Hans Joas and Wolfgang Knöbl, *War in Social Thought: Hobbes to the Present* (Princeton, NJ: Princeton University Press, 2013), 231.

[171] Brown, *Loyal unto Death*, 119–43. See also James C. Scott, *The Art of Not Being Governed: An Anarchist History of Upland Southeast Asia* (New Haven, CT: Yale University Press, 2009).

[172] On Ottoman–Turkish *kabadayı*, see Yücel Yesilgöz and Frank Bovenkerk, 'Urban Knights and Rebels in the Ottoman Empire', in Cryille Fijnaut and Letizia Paoli (eds), *Organized Crime in Europe: Concepts, Patterns and Control Policies in the European Union and Beyond* (Dordrecht: Springer, 2004), 203–24; Roger A. Deal, *Crimes of Honor, Drunken Brawls and Murder: Violence in Istanbul under Abdülhamid II* (Istanbul: Libra, 2010); Noémi Lévy-Aksu, *Ordre et désordres dans l'Istanbul ottomane (1879–1909)* (Paris: Éditions Karthala, 2013), 253–76. On *qabaday* in the Arab world, see Philip Khoury, 'Abu Ali Al-Kilawi: A Damascus Qabaday', in Edmund Burke, III and David Yaghoubian (eds), *Struggle and Survival in the Modern Middle East*, 2nd edn (Berkeley, CA: University of California Press, 2005), 152–63; Guilain Denoeux, *Urban Unrest in the Middle East: A Comparative Study of Informal Networks in Egypt, Iran, and Lebanon* (Albany, NY: State University of New York Press, 1993), 77–80. On Iranian *luti*, see Gölz, 'The Dangerous Classes and the 1953 Coup in Iran'; Sivan Balslev, *Iranian Masculinities: Gender and Sexuality in Late Qajar and Early Pahlavi Iran* (Cambridge: Cambridge University Press, 2019), 34–42; Farzin Vejdani, 'Urban Violence and Space: *Luti*s, Seminarians, and *Sayyid*s in Late Qajar Iran', *Journal of*

its behalf, racketeers performed statehood in local quarters, social communities and craft guilds. The traditional agents of urban violence – military slaves, provincial notables, religious brotherhoods and guildsmen – were increasingly joined by neighbourhood gangs and worker's unions in mobilising collective action.[173]

Due to its intimacy, transgressive politics on the micro level often involves some form of gendered violence. As much as bands of brigands and militias cultivated their own idealised notions of manhood and brotherhood, they reaffirmed the hegemonic masculinity by subaltern means. Hegemonic masculinity subordinated not only women revolutionaries and 'weaker' men, but also sanctioned a code of honour that institutionalised gendered violence for the sake of protecting values and penalising wrongdoings. All kinds of rogues in the Balkans, the Middle East and the Caucasus constructed their own codes of honour – which awkwardly resembled each other.[174] Where there is much talk about honour, sexual violence is commonly not far away. Hence, sexual violence was part of the repertoire of so many 'honourable' revolutionaries, irregulars, rebels, bandits and gangsters. Even more in episodes of demographic cleansing in the Balkans and Anatolia, sexual violence against women accompanied the brutal making of nations at the expense of others.[175]

Social History 52(4) (2019): 1185–211; Vanessa Martin, *The Qajar Pact: Bargaining Protest and the State in Nineteenth Century Persia* (London: I. B. Tauris, 2005), 113–32.

[173] Juan R. I. Cole and Moojan Momen, 'Mafia, Mob and Shiism in Iraq: The Rebellion of Ottoman Karbala 1824–1843', *Past & Present* 112 (1986): 112–43. Previous Ottoman reforms had broken with the power of many tribal and notable families in the urban towns of the Ottoman provinces. Hanna Batatu, *The Old Social Classes and the Revolutionary Movements of Iraq: A Study of Iraq's Old Landed and Commercial Classes and of its Communists, Ba'thists, and Free Officers* (Princeton, NJ: Princeton University Press, 1978), 217–20.

[174] For the continued references to this code of honour in contemporary Albanian organised crime, see Jana Arsovska, *Decoding Albanian Organized Crime: Culture, Politics, and Globalization* (Oakland, CA: University of California Press, 2015), 153–94.

[175] Cathie Carmichael, *Ethnic Cleansing in the Balkans: Nationalism and the Destruction of Tradition* (London: Routledge, 2002), 68–73; Matthias Bjørnlund, '"A Fate Worse than Dying": Sexual Violence during the Armenian Genocide', in Dagmar Herzog (ed.), *Brutality and Desire: Genders and Sexualities in History* (Basingstoke: Palgrave Macmillan, 2009), 16–58. See also Tolga U. Esmer, 'The Precarious Intimacy of Honour in Late

Rogues maintained a complex culture of agency that unfolded locally, but nevertheless maintained a capacity to interact with transnational forces and shape political affairs elsewhere. By tapping into streams of rumours, channels of public discourse and popular myths, rogues could enhance their gravitational force in the communicative field of politics.[176]

In navigating in this age of rogues, the rebels, revolutionaries and racketeers were capable of channelling popular discontent, while embracing the ideological frames of the urban intelligentsia. In doing so, rogues consolidated their culture of agency through the deliberate use of political violence, sacralisation of politics and performances of para-statehood, complete with opaque ideological messages, obscure conspiracy theories and idealised notions of masculinity and fraternal autonomy that sought to mobilise a network of fighters, if not a mass of followers.

Conclusion

Neither the dynamics of transgressive politics nor the culture of agency of this period can be wholly grasped with static, linear, binary and normative concepts, which makes it necessary to cross conceptual frontiers. We accordingly propose the term *rogue* as an inclusive concept that not only signifies capability of transgression, but also denies any pre-configured historical consequence. Rogues could be both heroes and villains, rebels and rulers, revolutionaries and counter-revolutionaries. A 'rogue' is a transgressive political actor who operated especially in rural frontiers, but also in the urban microcosms of changing societies. Commonly engaged in political violence, rogues were often organised into small bands with a chain of

---

Ottoman Accounts of Para-militarism and Banditry', *European Journal of Turkish Studies* 18 (2014), at: http://ejts.revues.org/4873.

[176] Ever since, conspiracy theories in these regions not only trace the origin of transgressive politics to the age of rogues at the turn of the century, but also enjoy a popular reception in their respective societies. Esmer, 'Notes on a Scandal'; Alp Yenen, 'Elusive Forces in Illusive Eyes: British Officialdom's Perception of the Anatolian Resistance Movement', *Middle Eastern Studies* 54(5) (2018): 788–810; Ramazan Hakkı Öztan, 'Republic of Conspiracies: Cross-Border Plots and the Making of Modern Turkey', *Journal of Contemporary History* 56(1) (2021): 55–76. See also Cornel Zwierlein and Beatrice de Graaf, 'Security and Conspiracy in Modern History', *Historical Social Research*, Special Issue 'Security and Conspiracy in History, 16th to 21st Century', 38(1) (2013): 7–45.

command subordinate to a charismatic leader. Through the propagation of ideals of masculine conduct, rogues were socialised by bonds of brotherhood and committed to codes of honour, which enabled a higher degree of group cohesion. Informed by a culture of secrecy, they gathered intelligence and operated through networks of secret cells in rural and urban areas alike. In order to access resources, rogues either tapped into existing smuggling rings or helped to create new illicit circuits, which provided them access to late nineteenth-century technologies of warfare. Equipped with such means of violence and well-versed with a repertoire of contentious politics, rogues performed acts of paramilitary and clandestine political violence against both state and non-state enemies. Through the strategic deployment of violence, rogues formed protection rackets which not only served to extract valuable economic resources outside state control, but also helped to create operational communities of solidarity vis-à-vis a world of violence that they helped to maintain. Although rogues were mostly autonomous in their local organisation and impulsive in their violent agency, they were at times dependent upon state sponsorship for the provision of precious resources and could therefore take advantage of lucrative opportunities offered by state patronage, but concomitantly they could also choose to eschew them at times.

Yet the emergence of rogues was context-specific. Their brand of transgressive politics particularly flourished on imperial frontiers whose inhabitants not only benefited from the newly opening avenues of socio-economic mobility, whether via education or emigration, but also suffered from demographic pressures and economic fluctuations in an increasingly globalised world as well as from interstate conflicts that generated successive waves of refugee crises.[177] Taken as a whole, these transformations ultimately enabled transgressive politics, challenging the normative political paths that had otherwise defined *anciens régimes*. Yet these macro-level transformations ironically took place in an era known as the *belle époque*, a nostalgic moniker often associated with peace and stability in Europe. After all, this was a time of accelerated changes and increasing opportunities when human agency, social mobilisation and cultural change were understood to be major forces in the making of future states and societies. In this sense, the age of

[177] Blumi, *Foundations of Modernity*, 78–109.

rogues corresponds to a particular conjuncture when 'the horizon of expectation' shifted considerably thanks to 'the idea that the future would not only change society at an increasing rate, but also improve it'.[178] Drawing from a reservoir of shared historical experiences, and imbued with a belief in human capacity to re-order the state of things for a better future, rogues accordingly embraced activist agendas in a bid to change the unhappy course of history that, in their experience, had been increasingly unkind to their imagined civilisational order. In stark contrast to the optimism of the *belle époque*, hapless rogues took decidedly violent paths, foreshadowing the 'dark side' of the carnage to come during remainder of the twentieth century.[179]

As the following contributions in this volume will illustrate, rebels, revolutionaries and racketeers played central roles in the violent processes of imperial disintegration as it unfolded on the frontiers of the Ottoman, Habsburg, Romanov and Qajar empires. After the collapse of these empires, rogue conduct continued to have a complex afterlife. As paramilitary violence engulfed the post-First World War spaces, many of the rogues reconfigured themselves and began to take an active part in the 'nationalist' struggles that characterised the early 1920s.[180] On an interstate level, the post-war uncertainties provided a range of opportunities to rogues who were willing to exploit them.[181] On an organisational level, too, the debacles of the First World War removed the prominent leadership of revolutionary organisations

---

[178] Reinhart Koselleck, *Futures Past: On the Semantics of Historical Time* (New York: Columbia University Press, 2004), 270.

[179] For a comparative historical project that explores this angle, see the ERC project titled 'The Dark Side of the Belle Époque: Political Violence and Armed Associations in Europe before the First World War', at: http://prewaras.eu. For the 'dark side' approach to the history of the twentieth century, see Michael Mann, *The Dark Side of Democracy: Explaining Ethnic Cleansing* (New York: Cambridge University Press, 2004); Philipp Ther, *Die dunkle Seite der Nationalstaaten: 'Ethnische Säuberungen' im modernen Europa* (Göttingen: Vandenhoeck & Ruprecht, 2011).

[180] Michael Provence, 'Ottoman Modernity, Colonialism, and Insurgency in the Interwar Arab East', *International Journal of Middle East Studies* 43(2) (2011): 205–25; Alp Yenen, 'The "Young Turk Zeitgeist" in the Middle Eastern Uprisings in the Aftermath of World War I', in M. Hakan Yavuz and Feroz Ahmad (eds), *War and Collapse: World War I and the Ottoman State* (Salt Lake City, UT: University of Utah Press, 2016), 1181–216.

[181] Alp Yenen, 'Internationalism, Diplomacy, and the Revolutionary Origins of the Middle East's "Northern Tier"', *Contemporary European History* (forthcoming 2021).

from power, such as Enver, allowing more junior and secondary figures to step in and thrive in the midst of the resistance to the Paris settlements. In places where the resistance was successful, such as Turkey, the former revolutionaries refashioned their rogue conduct into more formal forms of politics, rebranding their organisations but continuing to be rogues in essence.[182] In so doing, they institutionalised transgressive politics into the emerging structures of national governance. Elsewhere, rogues continued to operate under the same revolutionary umbrella, as in the Balkans and Caucasus where the IMRO or ARF continued to exist and operate – and do so still to this day. The political violence in late Qajar Iran, too, shaped the culture of revolutionary violence in the twentieth century.[183] As for the Middle East, the continuing territorial scramble for the region by the European powers provided opportunities to former Ottoman officers, some of whom turned rogue and thrived and criss-crossed post-Ottoman frontiers.[184]

---

[182] Öztan, 'Republic of Conspiracies'.
[183] Mansour Bonakdarian, 'A World Born through the Chamber of a Revolver: Revolutionary Violence, Culture, and Modernity in Iran, 1906–1911', *Comparative Studies of South Asia, Africa and the Middle East* 25(2) (2005): 318–40.
[184] Parsons, *The Commander*; Provence, *The Last Ottoman Generation*; Laura Robson, *The Politics of Mass Violence in the Middle East* (Oxford: Oxford University Press, 2020).

2

Gendered Narratives of Transgressive Politics: Recovering Revolutionary Rubina

Houri Berberian[1]

A 131-page report issued by the Ottoman Special Commission investigating the attempted assassination of Sultan Abdülhamid II in 1905 describes Rubina (*nom de guerre* of Sophie Areshian), who helped to plan and carry out this act of political violence, as 'Armenian, originally from the Caucasus, 32 years old, hysterical, short, skinny. Brown, large black eyes, vague look, rather pronounced and hooked nose, thin bloodless lips, oval chin, speaks Russian, Armenian and very little German.'[2] Similar depictions

---

[1] This study benefited from stimulating discussions with colleagues, especially those who participated in the Second Feminist Armenian Studies Workshop: Gendering Resistance and Revolution, which Lerna Ekmekçioğlu, Melissa Bilal and I co-organised at the University of California, Irvine, in May 2019. I am most grateful to my colleague Susan Morrissey as well as this volume's editors and peer reviewers for their insightful comments. I have followed a modified version of the romanisation system of the Library of Congress for Classical Armenian except for personal names, for which I follow the phonetic values of Western or Eastern Armenian as applicable to the individual unless the personal name is part of a publication's title.

[2] *Enquête sur l'attentat commis dans la journée du 21 juillet à l'issue de la cérémonie du Sélamlik: Travaux de la Commission Spéciale* (*Investigation into the Attack on 21 July at the end of the Selamlık Ceremony: Work of the Special Commission*) (Istanbul: F. Loeffler), 75. Also cited in Gaïdz Minassian, 'The Armenian Revolutionary Federation and Operation "Nejuik"', in Houssine Alloul, Edhem Eldem and Henk de Smaele (eds), *To Kill a Sultan: A Transnational History of the Attempt on Abdülhamid II (1905)* (London: Palgrave Macmillan, 2018), 42–3, n. 16.

of Rubina, who was only twenty-four at the time of the attack (1881–1971), as hysterical, emotional, prone to nervousness, and easily roused and distressed are echoed in contemporary accounts by her own male comrades. Some comrades even attempted to blame her for the failed assassination, citing the unsuitability of her 'crisis'-prone character and bouts of fits, which they viewed as jeopardizing the operation.[3]

Are these kinds of depictions a reflection of Rubina's actual character or state of being? Or are they a reflection of the inability to come to terms with the critical role she played in an assassination attempt that did not have its intended result? Was the falling back on old tropes of the volatility and hysteria of women a way to address a transgressive woman, a rogue, who defied and contradicted contemporary gender norms and, therefore, was viewed to be in a state of tension with the nation? Were revolutionary comrades, the Ottoman state, and contemporary and later writers merely trying to make sense of what must have challenged deeply ingrained notions of gender propriety and expectations? After all, just as Caron Gentry and Laura Sjoberg make the case for politically violent women, Rubina too acted 'outside of the ideal-typical gender role' and therefore faced critical scrutiny not only for her 'behaviour but also for the gender transgression involved in its perpetration'.[4] Thus, the gendered narrative of Rubina may be understood in the context of gendered aspects of transgressive politics and, more broadly, hegemonic masculinity.[5] Joane Nagel's argument that 'nationalist politics is a masculinist enterprise' is particularly apt here.[6] Pointing to the intimate relationship between masculinity and nationalism and the dominant role of men in nationalist movements,

---

[3] See, for example, Session 27 (10 March 1907), Fourth General Congress of the Armenian Revolutionary Federation, in *Niwt'er H. H. Dashnakts'ut'ean patmut'ean hamar* (*Materials for the history of the A. R. Federation*), vol. 3, ed. Hrach Dasnabedian (Beirut: Hamazgayin Vahē Sēt'ean Tparan, 1976 and 2007), 71.

[4] Caron E. Gentry and Laura Sjoberg, *Beyond Mothers, Monsters, Whores: Thinking about Women's Violence in Global Politics* (London: Zed Books, 1988), 6.

[5] Hegemonic masculinity, as R. W. Connell and James Messerschmidt explain, is meant as masculinity's 'ascendancy achieved through culture, institutions, and persuasion' although it may also be 'supported by force'. R. W. Connell and James W. Messerschmidt, 'Hegemonic Masculinity: Rethinking the Concept', *Gender & Society* 19(6) (2005): 832.

[6] Joane Nagel, 'Masculinity and Nationalism: Gender and Sexuality in the Making of Nations', *Ethnic and Racial Studies* 21(2) (1998): 244.

she concludes, 'it is not surprising that masculinity and nationalism seem stamped from the same mould'.[7] While women have taken part in nationalist politics, it has been largely a male-centric and male-dominated venue. They have also perpetuated a culture of 'manliness' reflected in and entwined with themes of courage, honour and patriotism.[8] Women's place in the nation or national politics, on the other hand, has for the most part been appropriated to reproducers – either biological or cultural.[9] Therefore, Rubina's act of political violence in a masculinist–nationalist setting may be viewed as a transgressive and challenging act that has been depicted in gendered terms.

The scholarship on Russian women revolutionaries and terrorists is critical to understanding Rubina, just as the context of Russian political violence – of the People's Will movement (*Narodnaia Volia*) and Socialist Revolutionaries (SR) – in the late nineteenth and early twentieth centuries is crucial to appreciating Armenian acts of terror against Ottoman and Russian authorities. As Gentry and Sjoberg point out, the narratives about women terrorists depict them 'as without the agency in violence attributed to men and without the femininity of real or regular women'.[10] Instead, women's acts of political violence are often 'stripp[ed] ... of their political content', thus women are portrayed as 'feeling' rather than 'politically motivated' actors.[11] In her study of Sofia Perovskaia, who planned the assassination of Tsar Alexander II on 1 March 1881, Anke Hilbrenner contends that because the 'violence spurred by emotion was less shocking than if it were coolly calculated, and emotionality was also a feminine trait ... women who committed a crime not out of emotion, but for allegedly rational reasons, such as politics, represented a

---

[7] Nagel, 'Masculinity and Nationalism', 251.
[8] Ibid., 251–2.
[9] See, for example, the introduction of Nira Yuval-Davis and Floya Anthias (eds), *Women, Nation, State* (New York: Palgrave Macmillan, 1989), 7–8; Nagel, 'Masculinity and Nationalism', 252–3.
[10] Gentry and Sjoberg, *Beyond Mothers, Monsters, Whores*, 11.
[11] Anke Hilbrenner, 'The Perovskaia Paradox or the Scandal of Female Terrorism in Nineteenth Century Russia', *Journal of Power Institutions in Post-Soviet Societies* 17 (2016), at: https://journals.openedition.org/pipss/4169, paragraph 1, last accessed 30 July 2019; Tatiana Borisova, 'Public Meaning of the Zasulich Trial 1878: Law, Politics and Gender', *Gender and Crime in Russian History* (Leiden: Koninklijke Brill NV, 2017), 224, 238. See also Richard Pipes, 'The Trial of Vera Z.', *Russian History* 37(1) (2010): 1–82.

much greater breach of the norm'.[12] This breach of the norm – as we shall see – also applies to Rubina and figures in her gendered portrayal.

There is little written about Rubina, a rogue in her own right who transgressed legal as well as gender boundaries. Treatment of her in scholarship is spotty. Most recently, she appears in a chapter of a collection titled *To Kill a Sultan* as Rubina Aghechian – a mangling of her family name (Areshian).[13] Other than a few minor mentions and an important several-page treatment by Sona Zeitlian, Rubina rarely receives attention in contrast to many of her male revolutionary counterparts. Rubina fled from Constantinople the very night of the failed assassination attempt. It is possible that Rubina's escape instead of her sacrifice with her life further threw her into obscurity. Perovskaia, who unlike Rubina was arrested and executed, attracted substantial public attention and press, as she became a celebrity among her contemporaries and throughout the twentieth century.[14] Fame for the assassination of the tsar extended to Perovskaia's co-conspirator, Vera Figner, a prolific author who thrived in 1920s Soviet Russia and endured much of Stalin's rule, dying of natural causes in 1942.[15] Rubina's contemporary, Maria Spiridonova, also had a markedly different path than that of Rubina. Spiridonova was found guilty of the 1906 assassination of provincial governmental councillor Gavriil Nikolaevich Luzhenovskii, served time in prison until her release in 1917, became a leader in the SR movement, only to be re-arrested by the Bolsheviks. In all, she endured thirty years of imprisonment until her execution in 1941. Spiridonova left behind a detailed account of the attack and the torture she suffered in the form of a letter to her sister, which was then published in the liberal newspaper *Rus'*.[16] The few letters we have

---

[12] Perovskaia was Andrei Zheliabov's partner in the assassination and took over once he was arrested in February 1881. Hilbrenner, 'The Perovskaia Paradox', para. 18.

[13] Minassian, 'Operation "Nejuik"'.

[14] Hilbrenner, 'The Perovskaia Paradox', paras. 10, 11, 15, 16.

[15] For a study on Figner, see Lynne Ann Hartnett, *The Defiant Life of Vera Figner: Surviving the Russian Revolution* (Bloomington: Indiana University Press, 2014).

[16] Sally A. Boniece, 'The "Shesterka" of 1905–06: Terrorist Heroines of Revolutionary Russia', *Jahrbücher für Geschichte Osteuropas, Neue Folge, Bd. 58, H. 2, Themenschwerpunkt: Modern Times? Terrorism in Late Imperial Russia*, 58(2) (2010): 172; Sally A. Boniece, 'The Spiridonova Case, 1906: Terror, Myth, and Martyrdom', *Kritika: Explorations in Russian and Eurasian History* 4(30) (2003): 606.

from Rubina were written twenty to forty years after the attack, seemingly in response to pressure from comrades. They also seem less politically motivated than that of Spiridonova who – in contrast to Rubina – through her writing tried deliberately to shape her public persona and 'participated [along with her comrades and sister] in the construction of her own myth'. Spiridonova was one of many SR women, most of whom, however – like Rubina – remain relatively unknown.[17]

In this study, I make an attempt to recover Rubina from obscurity by summoning her voice through 'bloodless lips' and turning our gaze towards her 'vague look' and into her 'black, large eyes'. I do so within the context of a male-dominated revolutionary discourse by juxtaposing her own words and positions with those of male comrades through an exploration of published and unpublished documents and correspondence from the Armenian Revolutionary Federation (ARF) archives, a French-language Ottoman report of the operation, an Armenian-language account of the act, and predominantly nationalist narratives of her role. I argue that the portrayal of Rubina by her contemporaries and others has produced a highly gendered narrative at the cost of appreciating her truly revolutionary role – not only in the conventional sense of her participation in a revolutionary act of terror, but also revolutionary and transgressive in terms of her gender. Furthermore, the aim and approach of this study focus on recovering and inserting Rubina's story into the larger Armenian revolutionary narrative as well as the broader context of the turn-of-the-twentieth-century revolutionary terror, a predominantly masculine world of revolution, and an age of rogues.

Becoming Rubina

Rubina was born in 1881 into a wealthy, landowning, Russian-speaking family in Tiflis/Tbilisi, an Armenian cultural and intellectual hub at the time.[18] By the end of the nineteenth century, the South Caucasus had become a centre of both cultural reception and transmission due in part to its geographic

---

[17] Boniece, 'The Spiridonova Case', 603.
[18] Russian SR terrorists were also often in their early twenties, and half were from the elite classes. See Amy Knight, 'Female Terrorists in the Russian Socialist Revolutionary Party', *Russian Review* 38(2) (1979): 139–59, at 144; Boniece, 'The "Shesterka" of 1905–06', 175.

location at the crossroads and contentious frontiers of three empires (Russian, Ottoman and Iranian), the influx of migrants (workers and political activists), growing urbanisation, and an increase in transportation and communication, in particular, railways, telegraph and the proliferation of print. Thus, Rubina experienced her roaring twenties in the roaring Caucasus – a playground and battleground of revolutionary ideas. She grew up and evolved in an already radically transforming frontier region that was experiencing more frequent encounters between peoples and ideas, circulation and connections before and during revolutionary struggles, a world of crisscrossing workers, intellectuals and revolutionary activists. A community of over a million Armenians existed in the Araxes valley and Ararat plain, as well as Tiflis, Yerevan, Kars, Elisavetpol, Batumi, as well as other areas. Rubina's birthplace, Tiflis, was home to the most important Armenian community in the South Caucasus. Tiflis, along with Baku and Batumi, supported an Armenian bourgeoisie whose dominant economic position was disproportionate to its population size and raised tensions with the larger communities of Georgians and, especially Muslims. Although smaller in number than Armenian communities in the Ottoman Empire, it was also the South Caucasus that produced the two most important and long-lasting Armenian political parties, the Social Democratic Hnchakian Party and the ARF, with cells, members and supporters throughout the Ottoman Empire, Caucasus, Iran and Europe, as well as the United States and beyond. Encounters with leaders of the ARF in Baku changed the course of Rubina's life.

Both Rubina's father and brother were high-ranking officers in the Russian military. Rubina herself may not have known how to communicate in Armenian until the age of eighteen.[19] She graduated from a Tiflis gymnasium at nineteen and a year later, in 1901, began teaching at a school for oilfield workers in Baku – a bustling urban environment and magnet for local

---

[19] Her comrade, Abraham Giulkhandanian, recalls Rubina beginning to learn Armenian in 1903, at about the age of twenty-two. See A[braham] Giulkhandanian, *Bagui derě mer azatagrakan sharzhman měj* (*Baku's role in our liberation movement*) (Tehran: Alik', 1981), 135. For a study on Giulkhandanian, see 'From Nationalist-Socialist to National Socialist? The Shifting Politics of Abraham Giulkhandanian', in *The First Republic of Armenia (1918–1920) on Its Centenary: Politics, Gender, and Diplomacy*, ed. Bedross Der Matossian and Barlow Der Mugrdechian (Fresno: Armenian Series of The Press at California State University, 2020).

and foreign investors, oil refiners, as well as migrant workers and revolutionaries.[20] In Baku, she lived with her sister and brother-in-law, whose neighbour was the Armenian revolutionary and ARF leader Nikol Duman (Nikoghayos Ter Hovhannisian, 1867–1914). It was in Baku that Rubina met at least two of her future comrades and co-conspirators, Kristapor Mikayelian (1857–1905) – co-founder of the ARF and the brains behind the assassination attempt – and Safo (Martiros Margarian), leader of the attempted regicide after Mikayelian's death and her neighbour. Duman's home had become the location of the first ARF regional meeting of the Caucasus in 1903.[21] It is also in the same year that she met her future husband, and the last prime minister of the First Republic of Armenia from May to November 1920, Hamo Ohanjanian (1873–1947), whom she married in 1915. Writing years later, Rubina reflected on their first meeting: 'I promise that we loved each other in silence and thus began our tragedy – after all, was he not married? (չէ՞ որ նա ամուսնացել էր/*ch'e vor na amusnats'el ēr?*)'.[22] In his somewhat sympathetic treatment of Safo, one of Rubina's detractors, Gaïdz Minassian alludes to an 'affair' between Rubina and Mikayelian: 'she expressed a fervent adoration for Mikayelian to the point of sacrificing herself to join her "father" in the pantheon of the Dashnaktsutyun [ARF], even though it was rumoured that she had an affair with Mikayelian'. Minassian does not, however, provide any evidence or references to such rumours.[23]

According to Rubina's own account, her initial meeting with Mikayelian in the latter half of 1903 was eye-opening. When the young Baku teacher asked Ohanjanian the identity of Duman's guests, she then learned for the first time about the plight of Armenians in the Ottoman Empire and the work of the ARF, which had taken up their cause. She writes, 'I was shaken;

---

[20] Giulkhandanian, *Bagui derě*, 134.
[21] Giulkhandanian, *Bagui derě*, 134.
[22] Rubina's letter to Abraham Giulkhandanian (3 March 1939) cited in Sona Zeitlian, *Hay knoj derě hay heghap'okhakan sharzhman mēj* (*The role of the Armenian woman in the Armenian revolutionary movement*) (Los Angeles: Hraztan Sarkis Zeitlian Publications, 1992), 58. According to Avo, it was Mikayelian and not Hamo Ohanjanian from whom she learned about Turkish–Armenian relations, crediting Mikayelian with giving her 'spiritual gratification and inspir[ing] the spirit of service'. See Avo, 'Rubina Ohanjanian', *Heghap'okhakan albom* (*Revolutionary album*) 9(4) (1972): 101.
[23] See Minassian, 'Operation "Nejuik"', 58.

all this was a new world for me.'²⁴ When she heard about operation Nzhuyg ('Courser') – the code name for Sultan Abdülhamid – she expressed her commitment to join the mission.²⁵ She herself must have left a lasting impression on Mikayelian, who months later took her up on her offer calling her to Athens via a telegram to Berlin where she was staying. With a newly acquired passport, she left Baku passing through several places, including Greece where apparently she became an excellent shot. In Athens, she also became Rubina Fain, daughter of Jewish merchant Samuel Fain – one of Mikayelian's pseudonyms.²⁶ From there, she went to Izmir/Smyrna and finally arrived in Constantinople in 1904. Rubina and Mikayelian used these pseudonyms throughout the operation. In fact, the Ottoman authorities did not know her real name, as indicated by the Ottoman special commission's report, which refers to her as 'Robina Fain, also known as *daughter Wolff* and *Nadejda Datalian* (fugitive), an Armenian from the Caucasus whose real name could not be established . . .'²⁷

Seeking to Stop the 'Courser' in His Tracks

The attack on Sultan Abdülhamid was the first and last such attempt of regicide by the ARF. The idea to target the sultan had been deliberated for years since the slaughter of tens of thousands of Armenians in 1894–1896, referred to as the Hamidian massacres. When Mikayelian met his ARF comrades on 16 July 1904 in Athens to begin planning, they focused their discussions on three issues: (1) avenging the Hamidian massacres, as well as other acts of state terror, including the violent quelling of the Sasun rebellion in 1904; (2) bringing down the sultan; and (3) attracting the attention of Europeans.²⁸ The act of regicide, therefore, had multiple goals, from local

---

[24] Rubina's letter to Abraham Giulkhandanian cited in Zeitlian, *Hay knoj derĕ*, 58.
[25] In all some thirty-nine people were involved but only eleven actively. See Maarten Van Ginderachter, 'Edward Joris: Caught Between Continents and Ideologies?' in Houssine Alloul, Edhem Eldem and Henk de Smaele (eds), *To Kill a Sultan: A Transnational History of the Attempt on Abdülhamid II (1905)* (London: Palgrave Macmillan, 2018), 67–97.
[26] See Rubina's letter to Abraham Giulkhandanian, 3 March 1939, in *Heghap'okhakan albom*, 108–9.
[27] *Enquête*, 121.
[28] 'Ts'uts'kan Marmni voroshumnerĕ' ('The Demonstrative Body's decisions') – 16 July 1904, in *Niwt'er H. H. Dashnakts'ut'ean patmut'ean hamar* (*Materials for the history of the*

vengeance for state-inflicted violence on the empire's Armenian subjects to the broader regional and global that sought to topple an autocrat and garner European sympathy and assistance – a long-sought goal for the Armenian revolutionary movement. The strike itself came after months of preparations. They included surveillance of the site surrounding the Yıldız mosque and the sultan's movements during the *selamlık* (Friday prayer ceremony). According to the committee responsible for the terror act, this meant dozens of visits by Rubina and a few others to the actual site. They assessed the best places from which to strike and meticulously calculated the sultan's steps and the time it took – down to the second – for him to walk from the mosque to his carriage. Preparations also involved importing explosive 'apples' (hand-thrown bombs), capsules, clocks, electrical parts, melanite (picric acid) and other components, through Varna to Constantinople often with collaboration and transactions with arms dealers and smugglers. Throughout the process, explosives and participants were at risk. Some explosives were discovered and seized by authorities. While some men were arrested and imprisoned, others suffered a worse fate. Preparations entailed experiments and trials with explosives in remote parts of Bulgaria, which took the lives of two comrades (Mikayelian and Vramshapuh Kendirian).[29] The road to the Yıldız bombing was a bumpy one for the Demonstrative Body, the group responsible for the attack (sometimes referred to as the Responsible Body in the documents): full of disagreements, difficulties and doubts, as well as changes to the original plan devised by the mastermind Mikayelian. The day of the attack itself, 21 July, was a bloody one; it took the lives of twenty-six individuals – a preponderant

---

A. R. Federation), vol. 5, ed. Yervant Pambukian (Beirut: Hamazgayin Vahē Sēt'ean Tparan, 2007), 399–400. See also 'Nakhagitz Vishapi gortsunēut'ean' ('Protocol of Vishap's activity'), Part B, Folder 215, Document 1, Armenian Revolutionary Federation Archives, Watertown, MA. Vishap refers to Yıldız. For a fascinating study on vengeance and revolutionary terrorism, see Susan Morrissey, 'Terrorism and *Ressentiment* in Revolutionary Russia', *Past and Present* 246(1) (2020): 191–226.

[29] See Demonstrative Body report for details, *Niwt'er H. H. Dashnakts'ut'ean patmut'ean hamar* (*Materials for the history of the A. R. Federation*), vol. 4, ed. Hrach Dasnabedian (Beirut: Hamazgayin, 1982), 209. For Rubina's account of that day, see her letter, 24 July 1924, Cairo, Part E, Folder 177, Document 109, ARF Archives. Russian original. Thanks to Artem Boyajyan for assistance with the Russian. See also Letter to Giulkhandanian in *Heghap'okhakan albom*, 109.

number of civilians, including many coachmen and a few journalists – and wounded fifty-eight men – mostly civilians and a few soldiers. It missed, however, its intended target.[30] What followed were the arrests, trials and sentencing (from years of imprisonment to death – some in absentia) of dozens of co-conspirators or collaborators, as well as acrimonious deliberations by the ARF to try to work out how and why things had gone wrong. Rubina, along with others, was sentenced to death in absentia and became a pawn in the hands of her detractors trying to elude blame.[31]

On the eve of the attack, Rubina along with her comrades prepared the explosives. She had in preparation taken part in experiments and in assembling bombs.[32] The next day they were loaded onto the carriage. On the morning of the 21st, Safo, Emille and Rubina stopped for flowers for Rubina, likely as a cover for the real objective that brought her to the *selamlık*.[33] They then went to the carriage. Against Safo's objections, Rubina had brought a pair of scissors with her. Her objective was to remain in the carriage and cut the conducting wires (հաղորդիչ/*haghordich'*) in order to render the explosion instantaneous in case the timer did not function and in the process sacrifice her life. Safo, however, considered it 'useless and superfluous'.[34] Zareh, a coachman, drove the carriage transporting Rubina, presumably holding a bouquet of flowers, carrying a hidden revolver in case she was stopped during the attack, and watching over a portion of the hundreds of kilos of melanite

---

[30] For a list of the names of the wounded and dead, see *Enquête*, 5–7. Safo claimed as many as 200 dead and wounded. See Demonstrative Body report, in *Niwt'er*, 4:198. For a report of preparations and activities of the Demonstrative Body, see *Niwt'er*, 4:194–220. For surveillance, see, *Niwt'er*, 4:200–1.

[31] For details, see *Enquête* as well as *Yĕltĕzi mahap'ordzĕ: yeghernakan ateani datavarut'iwnĕ teghi unets'ats Polsoy mēj, 1905 Noyemberin: Stoyg teghekut'iwnner mahap'ordzi masin* (The Yıldız attempted assassination: the criminal tribunal's trial that took place in Istanbul in November 1905: the true account of the attempted assassination) (At'ēnk': Tparan-Gratan 'Nor Ōr', 1933).

[32] See, for example, 'Ts'uts'kan Marmni ardzanagrut'iwnner' (The Demonstrative Body's registration) regarding experiments of explosives, 1 December 1904, *Niwt'er*, 5:426, 427. See also Rubina's letter to Giulkhandanian in *Heghap'okhakan albom*, 109.

[33] Emille/Emily was an auxiliary member of the Body and the pseudonym of Marie Seitz, a Russia-born German who acted as Safo's wife, Sophie Rips.

[34] Demonstrative Body report, *Niwt'er*, 4:216.

that had been smuggled into the capital.³⁵ They rode to the Yıldız mosque, parked the carriage in the visitors' parking area under the clock tower, and Rubina waited for the sultan to come out of prayers. The clock neared the fateful moment of 12:43:36. Rubina set off the timers for the explosives 1 minute 24 seconds before disembarking the carriage. That was the time – according to her and her comrades' calculations after countless visits to the *selamlık* – that it would take for the sultan to reach his own coach where he would be killed by the explosion from the 'infernal carriage' (դժոխային կարք/*dzhokhayin kaṛk'*).³⁶ Rubina and her comrades left the site believing, according to their own testimony, that their deed had the intended result and only discovered by telegram the next day – after they had already fled Constantinople by the last train at 8 pm and reached Sofia where they had sought safe haven – that while dozens of mostly civilians and some fifty horses had been killed, the 'Courser' (Nzhuyg) himself lived. The sultan had lingered in conversation with the Şeyhülislam Cemaleddin Efendi and thus had been spared.³⁷

The attempt on Sultan Abdülhamid's life must be viewed not merely within the Ottoman context and, of course, the *fin-de-siècle* global context – as it occurred during a period that saw an increase in terror acts of regicide (from Qajar Shah Naser al-Din to American President William McKinley and Empress Elizabeth of Austria) – but equally within the context of Russian revolutionary terror, especially, but not exclusively, because Rubina and the

---

[35] 'Ts'uts'kan Marmni voroshumnerě', *Niwt'er*, 5:402. Regarding the revolver, see handwritten French-language report on the attack by the investigating judge Sadreddin Ali Rıza on Ottoman Imperial Legation stationery, see Part B, Folder 215, Document 17, ARF Archives. The twelve-page report, which includes an appendix, has three dates. For the first seven pages – 11 Djmazi-el akhire 1323/31 Juillet 1321 (31 July 1905); for the next two – 21 Djemazi ul evel 1323/11 Juillet 1321 (11 July 1905); and for the appendix – Appendix 23 Djemazi ul evel 1321/13 Juillet 1321 (13 July 1905). Ashod Yeghigian identifies him as Zareh Khachigian, a native of Constantinople. See Ashod Yeghigian/Ashot Eghikean, *Ariwni chambun vray: heghap'okhakani mě hushatetrēn* (On the bloody path: the scrapbook of a revolutionary) (K. Polis: Tpagrich' Hratarakich' Vaghinak S. Biwrat, 1911), 334.

[36] For references to the 'infernal carriage', see, for example, *Niwt'er*, 3:199. For drawn maps of the site of the operation surrounding Yıldız mosque, see Part B, Folder 213, Documents 110 and 111, ARF Archives.

[37] Demonstrative Body report, *Niwt'er*, 4:217. See also, report by Sadreddin Ali Rıza, Part B, Folder 215, Document 17, ARF Archives.

leadership behind the attempt hailed from the Russian Empire. The repertoire of political violence against the state derived from the Russian example, which began with *Narodnaia Volia* – a movement that attracted the young Mikayelian as a university student – and was closely followed by the SRs. As Jocelyne Fenner points out in her study of nineteenth-century Russian terrorists, Polish, Balkan and Armenian revolutionary struggles were influenced by and employed 'Russian methods'.[38] As in other areas, the ARF closely resembled and in many ways mirrored the agenda, strategies and tactics of the SRs when it came to terror, and periodically assisted them financially and with personnel.[39] Very much like the Russian SRs, the ARF considered political violence against the agents of autocracy to be 'moral in purpose'. As Boniece explains:

> to the SRs and their supporters, 'terrorist' was a heroic label, because 'terrorism' meant a righteous violence in the cause of political change, employed against a corrupt autocracy on behalf of an oppressed and helpless people. Occurring in what one scholar has characterized as a 'blocked society', with

---

[38] Jocelyne Fenner, *Les terroristes russes* (Rennes: Editions Ouest-France, 1989), 273. See also the growing literature on anarchist movements in the Ottoman Empire, especially Toygun Altıntaş' and İlkay Yılmaz's essays on the assassination attempt. Altıntaş deftly contextualises the Yıldız bombing and the Ottoman state's response within the broader framework of European and Russian radicalism and 'anti-anarchism'. See Toygun Altıntaş, 'The Ottoman War on "Anarchism" and Revolutionary Violence', in Houssine Alloul, Edhem Eldem and Henk de Smaele (eds), *To Kill a Sultan: A Transnational History of the Attempt on Abdülhamid II (1905)* (London: Palgrave Macmillan, 2018), 99–128. Yılmaz's study centres on the period between 1876 and 1908, when new legislative and administrative security, especially hotel regulations to monitor the activities of foreign nationals were enacted in large part as a response to the anarchist 'propaganda by the deed' in Europe and its consequent anti-anarchist regulations. See İlkay Yılmaz, 'Propaganda by the Deed and Hotel Registration Regulations in the Late Ottoman Empire', *Journal of the Ottoman and Turkish Studies Association* 4(1) (2017): 137–56. See also Axel B. Çorlu, 'Anarchists and Anarchism in the Ottoman Empire, 1850–1917', in Selim Karahasanoglu (ed.), *History from Below: A Tribute in Memory of Donald Quataert* (Istanbul: Istanbul Bilgi University Press, 2016), 553–83.

[39] Manfred Hildermeier, *The Russian Socialist Revolutionary Party before the First World War*, trans. from German (Münster and New York: Lit Verlag and St Martin's Press, 2000), 52. For a discussion of ARF and SR similarities and influences, see Houri Berberian, *Roving Revolutionaries: Armenians and the Connected Revolutions in the Russian, Iranian, and Ottoman Worlds* (Oakland, CA: University of California Press, 2019), 174–7.

no national forum for political participation let alone toleration of political opposition, the SR party's assassinations of tyrannical government officials met with acclaim rather than fear from much of the Russian population.[40]

The ARF was no different from the SRs in viewing revolutionary terror as a '*legitimate* and *essential* weapon' that 'show[ed] the people the means and the objectives of the revolutionary struggle "with the *fewest possible victims* and in *the shortest possible time*"'.[41] It is very likely that just as the SRs' theoretical justification for terror came from *Narodnaia Volia*, as Hildermeier explains, so did that of the ARF, and in the same way that the SRs viewed terror as honourable and holy, so did the ARF.[42] Thus, in many ways, the attack on the sultan was very much in the vein of *Narodnaia Volia*'s *podvig* ('heroic deed'). Just as for the *Narodniks*, an attack on the Russian tsar was the 'ultimate "heroic deed"', so too was it for the ARF to strike at the Ottoman sultan.[43] It was no coincidence that Victor Chernov, one of the key figures in shaping SR approach to terror, was also read and translated by the ARF.[44]

Another, perhaps equally important, element in the mix was what Ramazan Hakkı Öztan calls 'the global marketplace of revolution, in which

---

[40] Boniece, 'The Spiridinova Case', 573, 579.

[41] Hildermeier, *Russian Socialist Revolutionary Party*, 52.

[42] Hildermeier, *Russian Socialist Revolutionary Party*, 53–4. See, for example, the poem 'P'aṛk' ahabekich'nerun' (Praise to the terrorists), *Drōshak* 8 (1905): 115–16. Among the Party of Socialist Revolutionaries' more high-profile assassinations were Minister of Interior Vyacheslavovich von Plehve (April 1904) and Governor-General of Moscow Sergei Aleksandrovich (February 1905); among the ARF's was Governor of Baku Mikhail Nakashidze (May 1905). High Commissioner in the Caucasus Grigorii Sergeyevich Golitsyn (1896–1904), who saw to the confiscation of Armenian Church properties in 1903, survived an assassination attempt by the ARF's rival Hnchakian Party in 1903. For a list of ARF victims compiled by tsarist authorities, see Document 19 in *The Armenians and the Okhrana, 1907–1915: Documents from the Russian Department of Police Archives*, ed. Vartkes Yeghiayan (Los Angeles: Center for Armenian Remembrance, 2016), 64–83. (This report attributes Golitsyn's attempted assassination to the ARF.)

[43] Boniece, 'The Spiridonova Case', 580.

[44] Such works include V. Chernov, *About the Theory of the Class Struggle*, trans. M. Har (1907); and *The Proletariat and the Hard-Working Farmers*, trans. A. Mehrabian (1907); Anahide Ter Minassian, 'Role of the Armenian Community in the Foundation and Development of the Socialist Movement in the Ottoman Empire and Turkey, 1876–1923', in Mete Tunçay and Erik J. Zürcher (eds), *Socialism and Nationalism in the Ottoman Empire and Modern Turkey* (London: I. B. Tauris, 1994), 194–6 n. 33, 200–1 n. 47.

Ottoman revolutionary actors enjoyed increasingly easier access to a range of tools of revolution thanks to globally expanding circuits of illicit exchange'. Öztan argues that factors such as 'technological shifts and international trade' in arms were instrumental in not only providing the weapons for revolutionary action but also in 'contribut[ing] to the consolidation of a particular radical revolutionary culture in the late Ottoman Balkans'. His focus on arms dealers like Tyufekchiev and the Ivanov brothers bear out not only this contention, but also speak to the connections between the ARF and Macedonian/Bulgarian revolutionaries, in particular, Tyufekchiev – himself a Macedonian radical and an arms smuggler who enabled 'heroic deeds' such as the assassination attempt on Sultan Abdülhamid.[45]

The failure of this particular 'heroic deed' set in motion several less than heroic, rather rancorous and fierce disagreements and discussions in ARF circles and official meetings and congresses about who and/or what was responsible for the botched mission. These discussions lay bare not only internal discord, but also shed light on the gendered narrative that developed around Rubina.

Gendering Rubina

Rubina's role in the attempted regicide was crucial not only to the act itself, but also to its planning, its consequent recriminations, and, more broadly, in the context of women's participation in acts of revolutionary terror.

---

[45] Ramazan Hakkı Öztan, 'Tools of Revolution: Global Military Surplus, Arms Dealers and Smugglers in the Late Ottoman Balkans, 1878–1908', *Past and Present* 237 (2017): 170, 171, 183–6. For Tyufekchiev, see Ramazan Hakkı Öztan's chapter, 'Chemistry of Revolution: Naum Tyufekchiev and the Trajectories of Revolutionary Violence in Late Ottoman Europe', Chapter 9, in this volume. For a detailed study of Armenian–Macedonian relations, see Garabet Moumdjian, 'Rebels with a Cause: Armenian–Macedonian Relations and Their Bulgarian Connection, 1895–1913', in Hakan Yavuz and Isa Blumi (eds), *War and Nationalism: The Balkan Wars, 1912–1913, and Their Sociopolitical Implications* (Salt Lake City, UT: University of Utah Press, 2013), 132–75. See also Duncan M. Perry, 'The Macedonian Revolutionary Organization's Armenian Connection', *Armenian Review* 42(1/165) (1989): 61–70. For a more recent study that has as one of its foci the ARF Military Academy in Bulgaria in the context of Armenian–Macedonian cooperation, see Varak Ketsemanian, 'Straddling Two Empires: Cross-Revolutionary Fertilization and the Armenian Revolutionary Federation's Military Academy in 1906–07', *Journal of the Ottoman and Turkish Studies Association* 4(2) (2017): 339–63.

According to the report of the Demonstrative Body, written by Safo months before the attack in December 1904, the issue of women's participation came up in two meetings. The discussion revolved around whether women should be included as a 'fresh' new force or, instead, they should be 'spared'. Safo claimed that although the decision to engage them was made in an earlier session, it was deferred because women were absent, and the men present did not want to place 'moral pressure' on them. Thus, they brought women into the discussion held on 4 December 1904 and gave them the opportunity to choose of their free own will. When the question of sparing them was put to the women present – 'Mrs Michelle', 'Miss Emille' and 'Miss Rubina' – they took offence and expressed in 'most ardent' terms their desire to participate. Apparently, the women had already on numerous occasions revealed that, if necessary, they were willing to take it upon themselves to carry out the operation.[46]

Despite these revelations, the decision, and the central role Rubina, a woman, played or perhaps because of her role in a failed mission, she was consistently portrayed by most male comrades – contemporaries and those who came after – and the Ottoman special commission not as a revolutionary equal to her male counterparts, but as a 'young woman' or 'girl' to be handled delicately or cautiously, much like the explosives she detonated. Had she been caught and tried, perhaps a question similar to that the prosecutor asked in Perovskaia's trial would have been asked of her: 'Why did the executive committee not find a stronger hand, a sharper intellect, a more experienced revolutionary when Zheliabov was arrested? How could anybody trust such a task to the delicate hands of a woman, even if this woman lived with Zheliabov?'[47] In a similar vein, during the ARF Fourth General Congress of 1907, at one of the sessions examining the Demonstrative Body's activities – in this case the questionable purity of the melanite provided by Naum Tyufekchiev for the explosion – Sargis Minasian (Aram-Ashot) suddenly

---

[46] Demonstrative Body meeting, Session on 5 December 1904, *Niwt'er*, 5:405–7. Mrs Michelle, like Ms Emille/Emily, was an auxiliary member of the Body. *Enquête*, 50, 75. Her real identity seems a mystery. She appears only as Mrs Michelle in ARF documents and does not make an appearance in the Ottoman Special Commission's report or sentencing. See *Enquête*, 103–4.

[47] Hilbrenner, 'The Perovskaia Paradox', para. 20.

blurted out, 'Who is responsible for inserting such a nervous young woman (օրիորդ/*ōriord*) into such a responsible activity?' Further adding with much alarm, 'She was a young woman with whose crisis/կրիզ/*kriz* (fit/նոպա/ *nopa*, anxiety/տագնապ/*tagnap*) she could have endangered the work at every moment'.[48] Almost immediately after this clearly gendered outburst, the discussion quickly reverted to the questionable melanite.

According to the Ottoman special commission, Rubina was guilty not only of participating 'in the preparation of the criminal enterprise . . . including taking part in all the deliberations . . . taking an effective part in the tests of explosive devices, the study and the preparation of the infernal machine' and its detonation, but also of 'lending herself as an inspired virgin to the attempts of the organisers to garner followers, to excite revolutionary ideas and to stimulate the activity of the members of the Committee'.[49] This is quite a provocative interpretation of her role, as Rubina's power was viewed to derive directly from her presumed virginity/purity which serves to inspire and 'excite' and 'stimulate' men into revolutionary action. Armenian sources, while not directly addressing her virginity, have nevertheless often referred to her as 'miss' (օրիորդ/*ōriord*) as a designation of her unmarried status during the operation and, therefore, her assumed virginity. The portrayal of Rubina as 'pure' along with delicate and nervous has dominated the discourse. Allusions to her purity are not surprising given the emphasis placed on women's honour and their place in nationalist discourse. While men 'may be defenders of the family and the nation', it is women who 'embody family and national honour'.[50] In the case of her Russian counterpart, Perovskaia, contemporaries cast her either as morally upright – becoming a martyr once executed – or 'blam[ed] her for moral depravity and promiscuity'.[51] We saw a hint of the latter in passing earlier regarding an insinuation of an unconventional relationship between Rubina and Mikayelian. Others have focused on Rubina's personal motivations for her commitment to nation and revolu-

---

[48] Session 27, *Niwt'er*, 3:71. Rostom, Safo and others believed the melanite that Tyufekchiev provided to be spoiled or impure. See Demonstrative Body report, *Niwt'er*, 4:218–19.
[49] *Enquête*, 121.
[50] Nagel, 'Masculinity and Nationalism', 254.
[51] Hilbrenner, 'The Perovskaia Paradox', paras 37 and 48.

tion. An article titled 'Rubina: The Patriotic Girl' published in 1971 after her death describes Rubina's transformation from a 'delicate' (նուրբ/*nurb*), 'delightful' (նազելի/*nazeli*), 'cheerful' (շեն/*shēn*), 'slender' (նրբակազմ/ *nrbakazm*) and 'coquettish' (պչրասէր/*pch'rasēr*) girl to a patriot who put aside her 'spoiled fancies/whims' (քմահածոյքներ/*k'mahachoyk'ner*) and committed herself to the operation with the intent of sacrificing her life in the process – but not for political or ideological reasons.[52] According to the author, who seems to take special delight in the dramatic but cannot seem to get Rubina's name right, mistakenly referring to her as Sonia, Rubina – the 'most beautiful' of five sisters – 'wants to die. She has decided to die because Kristapor [Mikayelian] is no more'. She is 'mad from grief, the poor girl' after witnessing Mikayelian die violently; with 'pieces of flesh falling from the sky', Rubina – 'tearless, hardened and revenge in her heart' – takes an 'oath to carry out the Sultan's assassination attempt personally'.[53] The ascription of a personal instead of a political reason for the choice to carry out the assassination attempt and for self-sacrifice seems to be somewhat common. In their introduction to *Women, Gender, and Terrorism*, Gentry and Sjoberg discuss such a framing in the literature on women and terror, which privileges personal factors behind women's choices – factors that are irrational, emotional, 'obsessive [and] pathological'.[54]

We encounter references to her zeal for self-sacrifice in other places, too, as part of her perceived general 'hysterical' disposition. According to one of Rubina's comrades, Ashod Yeghigian, Rubina insisted on being in the carriage and having the responsibility for detonating the explosives. She objected to drawing lots for that position. According to Yeghigian, she 'implore[ed]', 'entreated', 'cr[ied]' then 'became indignant and demand[ing]', was 'beside herself from her anger' and even 'threaten[ed]' her comrades: 'If you don't entrust it to me, I will kill myself . . .'[55] We come across the same refrain

---

[52] Avo, 'Rubina Ohanjanian', 1.
[53] Armen Nayiri, 'Rubina: hayrenasēr aghjikě' ('Rubina: The patriotic girl), *Hayrenik Amsagir* 123(17826) (1971): 1–2.
[54] Caron E. Gentry and Laura Sjoberg, 'The Gendering of Women's Terrorism', in Caron E. Gentry and Laura Sjoberg (eds), *Women, Gender, and Terrorism* (Athens, GA: University of Georgia Press, 2011), 71, 73.
[55] Yeghigian/Eghikian, *Ariwni chambun vray*, 336, 337. See also Avo, 'Rubina Ohanjanian',

during the General Congress in 1907 by Safo, who avows, 'I knew very well that she was devoted; she was prepared to die.'[56] What is puzzling, however, is not that Rubina as a revolutionary and transgressive historical actor was prepared to sacrifice herself, but that her zeal was portrayed by her male comrades as troubling and at times even irritating. Amy Knight provides a distinct perspective regarding the will to die. In her discussion of the disposition of women terrorists of *Narodnaia Volia*, she argues that the 'passionate desire to sacrifice themselves appears to result not from a disregard for their own lives, but rather from a heightened sense of their own importance as individuals within the movement . . . They saw themselves as part of an elite revolutionary group that would provide inspiration to society by their own examples . . .'[57] These kind of reflections and considerations did not seem to play a role in the narrative of Rubina's male comrades and contemporaries; and if they did, they were certainly not expressed. Instead, we are prompted to accept that despite her supposed fit and maniacal behaviour – portrayed very much like a child's temper tantrum in the sources – comrades handed this purportedly 'hysterical' woman the metaphorical keys to the carriage for what was to be one of the gravest and most consequential acts of political violence taken on by the party – the assassination of an imperial sovereign.[58]

Rubina was very much aware of these depictions of her. Safo, the leader of the operation after Mikayelian's death, seems to have been the originator of the gendered narrative about Rubina. In a report to the ARF Western Bureau, one of the party's highest bodies, as well as a letter to the same body, Safo reveals

---

104–6; S. Kirak [Ashod Yeghigian], 'Rubina Ohanjanian (1881–1971)', *Azdak Shabat'oreak-Droshak* 13(19), 30 May 1982. Safo thought Ashot's [Pakraduni/Yeghigian] presence endangered operations and, thus, he was distanced from Operation Nzhuyg. See *Niwt'er*, 5:439. The letter asking for his expulsion appears in Yeghigian/Eghikian, *Ariwni chambun vray*, 354. Yeghigian successfully contests this decision. For Yeghigian's protest letter to the Fourth General Congress of the ARF, see 355–63. For its decision in his favour, see 370.

[56] Session 74 (9 April 1907), Fourth General Congress, in *Niwt'er*, 3:199.

[57] Knight, 'Female Terrorists', 151–2. Boniece makes a similar contention regarding SR terrorists. See Boniece, 'The "Shesterka" of 1905–06', 581–2. See also Aileen Kelly, 'Self-Censorship and the Russian Intelligentsia, 1905–14', *Slavic Review* 46(2) (1987): 194–8.

[58] In a 1933 letter, she writes, 'Safo presented me to Zareh as death-seeking mad'. Rubina's letter to Giulkhandanian, 3 March 1939, in *Heghap'okhakan albom*, 110. Yeghigian, too, notes Zareh's readiness for self-sacrifice, but also his 'real heroism'. See Yeghigian/Eghikian, *Ariwni chambun vray*, 334, 335.

his assessment of Rubina.⁵⁹ The letter – written before the operation but after the explosion that killed Mikayelian and Kendirian – expresses concern about Rubina's 'nervousness' (ջղայնութիւն/*jghaynut'iwn*) and how imprudent it would be to include her in operations. Although he finds her 'fearless and selfless', he calls her unpredictable, expounding, 'one unforeseen circumstance could shake her involuntarily (ակամայից/*akamayits'*) and make her lose consciousness (or faint/ուշաղնաց/*ushagnats'*) at a critical moment'.⁶⁰ In a written response to the General Congress' investigation into the failed operation in 1907, Safo recalls not wanting to include her in the operations after Mikayelian's death because Rubina 'often faint[ed]'. Citing her 'severe nervous sickly system', he added that he did not consider her suitable but deemed her threatening to the success of the operation, an opinion he had expressed earlier in letters as well as in the Demonstrative Body's report.⁶¹ Thus, Safo claimed that her condition was so acute that 'she would faint a few times a day because of the slightest reason. It was enough for the word "Kristapor" to be uttered in her presence for her to faint, crying out.' Moreover, he added that he had agreed to have Rubina resume work on the project in June 1905 and return from recuperating in Geneva only because ARF co-founder Rostom (Stepan Zorian, 1867–1919) and other comrades implored him, claiming that she had recovered and that 'she would die' if she was not called back.⁶²

There is no doubt that Mikayelian's death shook Rubina – by her own admission – to her very core – both spiritually and physically. In a letter addressed simply to 'dear comrade', which she seems to have written after some prodding, Rubina explains that fateful day as 'the most terrible day of my life' (самый кошмарный день моей жизни/*samyi koshmarnyi den'*

---

⁵⁹ 'Ts'uts'kan Marmni ardzanagrut'iwnner', in *Niwt'er*, 5:435.

⁶⁰ For a rare and somewhat positive view where Safo expresses full confidence in Rubina, see 'Ts'uts'kan Marmni ardzanagrut'iwnner', 1 December 1904, *Niwt'er*, 5:435. For the opposite, which was much more common, see Safo's letter to the Western Bureau, undated (but likely May/June 1905), *Niwt'er*, 5:438; Safo's letter to Rostom, undated, *Niwt'er*, 5:439.

⁶¹ Report by the Investigating Committee of the Demonstrative Body's Activities (presented to the Fourth General Congress), *Niwt'er*, 5:455; Demonstrative Body report, *Niwt'er*, 4:212.

⁶² Demonstrative Body report, *Niwt'er*, 4:212. Although Rubina was the main target of charges of nervousness, Safo, too, at least on one occasion was called 'neurasthenic' (ջլախտավոր/*jlakhtavor*) by Yeghigian. See Yeghigian/Eghikian, *Ariwni chambun vray*, 288.

moeĭ zhizni). After all, she witnessed the explosion and consequent death of her comrades, especially her '*hayrik*' (papa/father) as she often referred to Mikayelian. As she recounts, she heard the explosion and 'beside the slowly rising smoke, I saw nothing and no one'. She somehow reached Mikayelian's side and, in her 'mad cry' of '*hayrik*', she saw him open and close his eyes three times. She could not see his wound and could not appreciate the gravity of his situation. It became clear later that a small piece of shrapnel had lodged in his heart and another in his hip. Fully aware of the enormity of the danger to themselves and the operation if the authorities were to find their explosive contraband, Rubina was entrusted with hastening to their hotel and, before the search by authorities could begin, cleaning out the rooms and transferring 'all the suitcases with bombs' to the residence of Macedonian revolutionary and ARF collaborator Boris Sarafov.[63] And yet, Safo and some other comrades still considered her unable to act under pressure.

Internal Rancour

The picture that emerges is that of a dysfunctional working relationship fraught with hostility, especially between Rubina and Safo, along with some others, and quite accusatory of Rubina. In his testimony in the Fourth General Congress in Vienna about the workings of the Demonstrative Body, Safo again refers to her nervousness and fits and consistently and aggressively impugns Rubina, even blaming her for having detonated the explosives before their scheduled time and thus missing the sultan.[64] Rubina, however, challenges and confronts Safo at every turn, calling him out as being mistaken, misrepresenting her words or just outright lying.[65] In a statement towards the end of the many sessions of the Fourth Congress, Rubina goes further by calling into question Safo's report on behalf of their group and his intentions. She states, 'I always referred to your report with derision because that – as I have always said – is not a report but [a mark of] Safo's character . . .'[66]

---

[63] Rubina's letter, 24 July 1924.
[64] Session 27, Fourth General Congress, *Niwt'er*, 3:69, 71.
[65] Session 74, *Niwt'er*, 3:199; Session 108 (28 April 1907), Fourth General Congress in *Niwt'er*, 3:263.
[66] They seem not to have read it and yet signed it. Session 108, *Niwt'er*, 3:264, 265

As we saw, the committee's report, written by Safo, his letters, and especially the discussions at the Fourth General Congress (March–April 1907) provide us with essential clues about not only how Rubina was perceived and branded, but also how she challenged the narrative developing about her. Therefore, it is worthwhile to delve more deeply into the bitter and often caustic disagreements and discussions, which preoccupied the sessions on Operation Nzhuyg. They revolved around three issues: the timing of the explosives set off by Rubina; the change of strategy; and the drawing of lots as a way to select a vital member of the attack unit – the latter two challenged by Rubina.

The report of the Demonstrative Body presented to the Fourth General Congress in writing and in person by Safo bears the signatures of only three committee members (Safo, Torkom and Kris).[67] Rubina had not signed the report due to numerous objections regarding Safo's account of the workings of the committee and the attack itself.[68] The five-member investigative ad-hoc subcommittee of the Congress took a few weeks to study Safo's report as well as all relevant documents, and Safo's own letters.[69] It focused its findings on three elements: technical, organizational and social (meaning, relations between comrades). Safo vehemently objected to the subcommittee's findings, constantly interrupting its reading, threatening to walk out, and calling it 'mud (գեխ/*ts'ekh*) and reproach (ամբաստանութիւն/ *ambastanut'iwn*)'.[70] His comportment became even more disquieting when Safo accused Rubina, according to her own statement he claimed, of setting off the timer for the explosives 'two minutes' (երկու րոպէ/*yerku robē*) early. Rubina disagreed strongly, stating that she had indeed set off the timer at the right time and moreover had said no such thing because it would have been 'wholly false. I had not lost my mind and my consciousness; if you are accepting such a thing, then you are cruelly mistaken.' Likely sarcastically,

---

[67] Torkom is Ardashes Seremjian (from Constantinople); Kris is Kris Fenerjian (aka Silvio Ricci).
[68] Session 26 (9 March 1907), Fourth General Congress, *Niwt'er*, 3:69. For the Demonstrative Body's report, see *Niwt'er*, 4:194–220.
[69] Members included Aram Manukian, Arshak Vramian, Yervant Topchian, Hagop Zavrian/ Zavriev, Vartan Mehrpanian. Session 74, Fourth General Congress in *Niwt'er*, 3:198
[70] Session 74, *Niwt'er*, 3:198

Safo asked for forgiveness if he was mistaken.[71] Safo's sarcasm clearly comes out in his statements during deliberations of the Congress, especially regarding Rubina. Somewhat resentfully, in his defence against the criticism of the Investigative subcommittee that spared Rubina, Safo exclaims, 'Rubina has a singular place; she is different; yes, we know . . .'[72] While Safo's claim is a denunciation of sorts, it does point to the special position Rubina occupied not only in the operation, but also as a preserver of Mikayelian's vision and legacy.

The picture becomes more evident when – in the 108th session of the 1907 General Congress – Rubina was allotted time to make a statement as a participant in the operation to explain – as she says – the change in strategy and Safo's conduct. Rubina began her narrative with her arrival in September 1904 to Constantinople. One of her first acts was to go to the *selamlık* with Mikayelian in a carriage, but being denied access, they watched from the terrace where European visitors stood. It was then that, according to Rubina, Mikayelian decided to employ small round hand-thrown bombs (precursors to the grenade), adding 'we did not think about a carriage'.[73] Safo stood against that method from the start, citing various reasons: that such bombs were 'not perfected';[74] that they did not have the 'men' – which she found surprising – and, because it was summer, bombs could not be hidden under clothes – which she considered unfounded reasoning as they had capes/cloaks (накидка/*nakidka*). Rubina was also perplexed by Safo's insistence that there should be no 'superfluous sacrifice': 'I was astonished; how could one be a revolutionary and be afraid of sacrifice and not take advantage of all the positions' available? Here, Rubina is accusing Safo of cowardice. By doing so, she is turning the tables on him and challenging his masculinity and

---

[71] Session 74, *Niwt'er*, 3:199. Rubina repeats that, despite Safo's claims to the contrary, she did push the timer's spring at the right time, that is, after the sound of the trumpet. Session 108 in *Niwt'er*, 3:264

[72] Safo's Response to the Demonstrative Committee', *Niwt'er*, 5:482. The response in full runs over several pages, 471–513.

[73] Session 108, *Niwt'er*, 3:263.

[74] In the Demonstrative Body report, Safo references Russian uses of such explosives for assassination attempts but claims a 5 per cent rate of success as some bombs would not explode after being thrown. See Demonstrative Body report, *Niwt'er*, 4:204–5, 211.

even his devotion to the Armenian nation. As Nagel argues, 'the culture of nationalism is constructed to emphasize and resonate with masculine cultural themes. Terms like honour, patriotism, cowardice, bravery and duty are hard to distinguish as either nationalistic or masculinist, since they seem so thoroughly tied both to the nation and to manliness.'[75] Comparing herself with Safo, Rubina presents herself as one 'prepared for every sacrifice'.[76] Thus, she juxtaposes her honour, patriotism and courage – read masculine – with Safo's dishonourable timidity – read feminine.

Mikayelian and Rubina's original brazen plan to kill Sultan Abdülhamid with hand-thrown bombs was modified after discussions with Safo. Because of Safo's objections, a compromise was reached that combined Mikayelian's hand-thrown bombs with explosives in a carriage. As Minassian describes, 'A terrorist commando, carrying foreign passports, would sneak into the pavilion where diplomatic delegations customarily attended the ceremony and throw bombs as soon as the Sultan arrived. If he managed to escape, one commando member would sacrifice himself by exploding a bomb placed in a carriage parked as close as possible to the mosque.'[77] After Mikayelian was killed along with Kendirian, while carrying out tests of explosives loaded with melanite, Safo took leadership of the group and – against Rubina's judgement – forsook the first part of the strategy, favouring the carriage mode instead. Rubina concluded by asserting that the original plan would have succeeded.[78]

The third point of contention between Rubina and Safo was the issue of

---

[75] Nagel, 'Masculinity and Nationalism', 251–2.
[76] Rubina recalls her comrades deriding her by calling her insistence on Mikayelian's method 'fantasy'. Rubina contends that Safo seemed to trust that the sultan would not be delayed and would arrive punctually more than he trusted a comrade who 'was prepared for every sacrifice'. See Session 108, *Niwt'er*, 3:263–4. According to Safo's report, though, when Rubina returned from Geneva where she went to recuperate after witnessing the death of Mikayelian and Kendirian, Rubina agreed with the change in strategy, expressing 'disillusion[ment] with explosives'. See Demonstrative Body report, *Niwt'er*, 4:212.
[77] Minassian, 'Operation "Nejuik"', 46.
[78] For details about preparations for the operation, individuals involved, the attempt itself and aftermath, see *Enquête* and *Yěltězi mahap'ordzě*. On the Demonstrative Body, including Rubina, see Hovik Grigoryan, 'H.H.D. Ts'uts'akan Pataskhanatu Marmni steghtsumě ew gortsuneut'iwně minj K. Poli ants'nelě' ('A.R.F. Demonstrative Body's creation and activity until its move to Constantinople'), available at: http://ysu.am/files/3_Hovik_Grigoryan.pdf, last accessed 1 May 2019.

drawing lots. The essential personnel for the operation were to be the coachman Zareh, Safo who would supervise and follow the operation to its end, and a third party to sit in the carriage and set off the timer for bombs. Safo's idea was to draw lots for that third position, which Rubina opposed.[79] Lots were drawn regardless of her opinion. The narrative by Safo and others is that Rubina became distraught when she was not selected. She 'screamed and fainted' and insisted on a second drawing, which went to Aram for the second time. Three days later she 'entreated', convincing Aram to agree to let her ride in the carriage, which he finally did.[80] In her statement, Rubina invoked the Belgian anarchist Edward Joris who helped the group in several important ways, including renting a house, storing explosives, and sheltering Mikayelian and Rubina. Joris was arrested, testified about the activities of the body, and was sentenced to death but released from prison in 1907.[81] Recalling Joris' objections to draw lots because it is 'our moral debt' to carry out the deed, she adds that Joris realised that 'I had the most moral right' to take on that role. Twice, Safo retorted with 'you're dreaming', which Rubina challenged. Torkom chimed in taking Safo's side, but Rubina quickly silenced him by questioning his honesty.[82]

The session became even more disagreeable as Safo reminded Rubina of her parting words on the night of the failed attack: 'And did you not say that I am your enemy and will always remain so . . . ?' Rubina responded with an emphatic confirmation: 'Yes! I said so and say [now]; I am your enemy and will stay [an enemy] of hayrik's [Mikayelian] murderer. You killed hayrik, you!' Rubina held Safo responsible for Mikayelian's death. As she explains in a letter to ARF comrade and later Minister of Internal Affairs and Minister of Justice of the First Armenian Republic (August 1919–January 1920) Abraham Giulkandanian, Mikayelian had gone to Bulgaria 'against his will' at Safo's insistence.[83] Safo retorted in a manner that befitted Ohanjanian's

---

[79] Demonstrative Body report, *Niwt'er*, 4:217.
[80] Demonstrative Body report, *Niwt'er*, 4:217.
[81] See Demonstrative Body report, *Niwt'er*, 4:201–2. For Joris' death sentence, see *Yĕltĕzi mahap'ordzĕ*, 103. Much of the Ottoman Special Commission's findings are based on Joris' testimony. See *Enquête*; for a study on Joris, see Van Ginderachter, 'Edward Joris'.
[82] Session 108, *Niwt'er*, 3:265
[83] See Rubina's letter in *Heghap'okhakan albom*, 109. Rubina employs the plural/formal of the second person (դուք/you).

characterisation of him as self-aggrandizing: 'I, who brought you out of nothingness and brought you here.' Rubina did not back down: 'Yes, it is because of you that I became worthy of this fortune, but I am your enemy, yes!'[84] The session (and future ones, too) then moved quickly to admonishing Safo. Ohanjanian, Topchian, Rostom and others called out Safo as 'immoral', hypocritical, lying, and 'subject to a kind of psychological illness', and determined on 'blemishing (արտավորել/*artavorel*) Kristapor's memory' and laying blame on Rubina. Ohanjanian was adamant that Rubina was the only person who stood firm against Safo and had it not been for her, the operation would not have even reached as far as it did.[85] Two points are worth mentioning here: first, ARF leaders, as well as Rubina, seemed very concerned about guarding Mikayelian's memory and legacy against what they regarded as Safo's attempts to sully it; and, second, for these leaders, both Rubina's stature and their defence of her were clearly intertwined with how Mikayelian would be remembered. Therefore, while Rubina was defended against Safo, that defence was not exclusive of her attachment to Mikayelian and the confidence and faith he had placed in her revolutionary fervour and competence. In a similar vein, Safo's venom for Rubina was not singularly for her, but may have been Safo's way of settling scores with his political rivals – other male comrades with whom he had personal or political disputes. Thus, as the discussion below demonstrates, the only other person who became Safo's target was Mikayelian, thus for Safo as for Rubina's defenders, characterisations of Rubina and Mikayelian were entangled.

The Congress' general remarks regarding the members – all but Rubina – of the Demonstrative Body under Safo's leadership charged them with being more concerned about saving themselves (լոկ իրենց գլուխն ազատել/*lok irents' glukhn azatel*) and of tarnishing the 'precious memory' of 'unforgettable comrade Ellen [Mikayelian]' by representing the 'unfortunate accident' as a 'plot' concocted by Mikayelian against young Kendirian.[86] Safo's report

---

[84] Session 108, *Niwt'er*, 3:266. For Ohanjanian's comments, see Session 114, *Niwt'er*, 278–9.
[85] Those speaking are Ohanjanian, Topchian and Rostom. See Session 108, *Niwt'er*, 3:266, 267, 278–9. See also 1904–1906 Ts'uts'akan marmni gortserĕ k'nnogh handznakhmbi koghmē – teghekagir Investigating Committee of the Demonstrative Body's activities report (presented to the Fourth General Congress), *Niwt'er*, 5:458, 462–3.
[86] Session 114, *Niwt'er*, 3:310.

about the actual day of the accident that took the lives of both men painted a disagreeable picture of Mikayelian, which ARF leaders, including Rostom and Simon Zavarian, co-founders of the party with Mikayelian, found abhorrent, objectionable and offensive. It is worth noting that Safo himself was absent from the explosive experiments that killed his comrades, although he penned the report. Safo reproached Mikayelian posthumously for entrusting Kendirian – an 'inexperienced' and 'unpractised' (խամ/*kham*) young man – with explosives and of making the 'biggest mistake' by giving him faulty advice about when to throw the bomb. He also claimed that Mikayelian was uncharacteristically and extremely nervous that day and, worst of all, that Mikayelian shamed and intimidated Kendirian into throwing the bomb. ARF leaders admonished Safo for presenting the 'calamity' as a 'horrible thing whose culpable author' was Mikayelian and thus defiling the memory of a 'martyred' comrade.[87] Accordingly, the Congress found Safo, as leader of the Demonstrative Body, preparer of its documents, and 'the author behind the amassing of doubts and slander around Ellen and Shapuh's [Kendirian] deaths and principal creator of the suffocating immoral environment dominant around that body' most blameworthy.[88] In the end, Safo was expelled from the party, three other comrades distanced (temporarily) and Rubina vindicated.[89]

We could presume from this decision that Rubina had the last word in the assignation of culpability for the failure of the assassination plot, that in a

---

[87] 'Ts'uts'kan Marmni ardzanagrut'iwnner', *Niwt'er*, 5:430; Report by the Investigating Committee of the Demonstrative Body's Activities (presented to the Fourth General Congress), *Niwt'er*, 5:462–3. The report was signed by all members of the Demonstrative Body: Safo, Ashot, Kris, Torkom and Rubina. Rubina later claimed that she signed the report knowing full well that her signature would arouse curiosity and force Safo to come to the Congress to explain himself. See Session 108, *Niwt'er*, 3:264.

[88] Minasian advances Safo's position on this issue: 'The Party needed someone to take the blame for the Yıldız fiasco and Mikayelian's death. Safo was the best scapegoat. Some even wanted him to receive the supreme punishment: death by execution'. Minassian, 'Operation "Nejuik"', 59

[89] Session 114 (30 April 1907), Fourth General Congress, *Niwt'er*, 3:281. The decision may also be found in *Niwt'er*, 5:515. Yeghigian's many written protests from 1907 to 1991 to ARF bodies did not result in the overturning of that decision despite the earlier decision in favour regarding his illegal expulsion from the Demonstrative Body. See correspondence reproduced in his memoirs, Yeghigian/Eghikian, *Ariwni chambun vray*, 371–95.

sense not only was she vindicated and her comrades distanced or expelled in Safo's case, but that Mikayelian's legacy as a founding father of the party and revolutionary idol was preserved. It is possible that her engagement with and use of masculinist and nationalistic tropes such as courage (versus cowardice), sacrifice (versus timidity), patriotism (versus fear) was itself a way to take control over the gendered constructions and narratives and itself a revolutionary and transgressive political act. Although it is difficult to ascertain without more evidence the extent to which Rubina had a role to play in the demise of her comrades and the placement of blame, it is likely that she was quite influential.

After the Fact: 'What have I done anyway . . .'

Nearly everything of the little that is known about Rubina is written or uttered either by contemporary detractors who are men or by men who have in hindsight constructed a particularly gendered narrative and national/nationalist discourse. Thus, in a sense, Rubina's involvement and leadership in the act of revolutionary terror are considered outside the conventional parameters of not only gender norms and expectations, but also of a masculine vision of a nation. Rubina's voice is somewhat muffled and only surfaces in statements during the General Congress and a few letters in which, at the behest of others, she recounts her early revolutionary days. We know that after Mikayelian's death and then again after the failed assassination attempt, she spent some time in Geneva recuperating from the trauma of the bloody violence that she witnessed and, in the case of the latter, helped to cause. In 1908, she accepted ARF leader Aknuni's (Khachatur Malumian, 1863–1915) invitation and moved to Constantinople with Ohanjanian's sister Satenik. When she received news of Ohanjanian's arrest in Tiflis by Russian authorities, she left for the South Caucasus in 1909 where other ARF activists Avetis Aharonian (1866–1948), Hovsep Arghutian (1863–1925), Abraham Giulkhandanian (1875–1946), Garegin Khazhak (1867–1915) and many more had been arrested. She followed the transfers of her imprisoned comrades and sought to assist them despite Russian intentions to imprison her.[90]

---

[90] This was a common occurrence in the Russian revolutionary movement. See Hilbrenner, 'The Perovskaia Paradox', para. 1. Regarding Ohanjanian's arrest and Rubina following him

When she was arrested herself, her brother Mikhail (Misha) Areshian, an officer in the Russian army who later became one of three commanders of the Armenian volunteer units in the Russian Empire during the First World War, intervened and succeeded in freeing her on condition that she never set foot in the Caucasus, Moscow or St Petersburg. She pursued medicine in Kharkov and, in 1912, moved to Siberia where Ohanjanian was sentenced to serve four years. They married near Irkutsk in 1915.[91] The couple then travelled to Tiflis in 1917, and Rubina served in hospitals near the battle lines and witnessed the birth of the First Republic of Armenia and her husband becoming prime minister in the last few months of the republic in 1920. After Sovietisation, they went through Iran and settled in Cairo, an important Armenian diasporan centre, where they helped to shape the Hamazgayin Armenian cultural organisation. Years after Ohanjanian's death (1947), Rubina finally settled in Montreal and lived there close to her only son and his family until her death in 1971 at the age of ninety.[92] Always modest about her revolutionary role, Rubina's response to the bestowing of the honour of Princess of Cilicia in 1968 by Catholicos Khoren of the Great House of Cilicia was 'what have I done anyway . . .? (Ես ի՞նչ եմ արել որ . . ./*es inch' em arel vor?*)'.[93]

---

prison to prison, see Part C, Folder 1749, Document 59, ARF Archives. Also in *Niwt'er H. H. Dashnakts'ut'ean patmut'ean hamar* (*Materials for the history of the A. R. Federation*), vol. 9, ed. Yervand Pampukian (Beirut: Hamazgayin Vahē Sēt'ean Tparan, 2012), 207–8.

[91] Ohanjanian's wife had already passed away. Avo, *Heghap'okhakan albom*, 114*.

[92] For Rubina's notice of death, see 'Ohanjanian, Sophie', *The Gazette* (Montreal), 22 April 1971, 37. Rubina's son, Vigen Ohanjanian, wrote about his mother in a letter (dated 11 October 1990) addressed to the Education Committee of the Armenian Relief Society Western American Regional Administration on the occasion of a 'Revolutionary Armenian Women' programme organised for the ARF's centennial. Sona Zeitlian references the letter in her *Hay knoj derě*, 60, and kindly put me in touch with the letter's current holder; however, I was not given permission to view the letter, which at the time of the writing of this study remained in private hands.

[93] Zeitlian, *Hay knoj derě*, 63. For biographical details, see also Avo, *Haghap'okhakan albom*, and excerpts from Rubina's letter to Abraham Giulkhandanian, in *Haghap'okhakan albom*, 108–10. This kind of modesty and silence about one's violent revolutionary past is also apparent with a more famous example, Soghomon Tehlirian, the assassin of Talat Paşa. For example, Tehlirian's son said his father never talked about his revolutionary past, adding 'my father never thought of himself as a hero'. See Tim Neshitov, 'Der Adler' [The Eagle], *Süddeutsche Zeitung* (19 April 2015). Despite a consensus that Rubina was modest about her role, according to Yeghigian, after fleeing to Bulgaria, Rubina 'immediately gathered

To some degree, because of her self-effacing attitude and a general distaste for talking about her activities in public, Rubina in a sense may have undermined her own role instead of creating her own narrative. Agency depends on recovering voices, and voices are best preserved in what are called 'ego documents' – that is, memoirs, journals, private papers, correspondence and so forth. These kinds of documents are rarer to come across for women and especially for revolutionary women like Rubina. Unlike some Russian women terrorists who left behind memoirs or wrote more extensive accounts of their activities, our rogue did not leave behind memoirs or journals, only a few letters.[94] Although she lived into her ninetieth year, there is not one published interview with her. It seems she did not want to relive or recount those days of terror.

Despite the presence of women in nationalist politics and active participation in political violence even in the face of prejudice and discrimination by comrades and fellow male revolutionaries, women remain primarily absent from the historiography of the Armenian revolutionary movement. Yet, as we saw with the case of Rubina (Figure 2.1), gendered narratives contain within them alternative possibilities, which in a way create a space for women to participate in revolutionary and transgressive politics and sometimes even engage masculinist and gendered terms and themes in distinctly defiant ways. Many questions remain about Rubina. This study serves as an effort to mend or at the very least patch what Ranajit Guha would call the 'torn fabric' of Rubina's history and of the revolutionary past.[95]

---

around her tens of women and boys and began to narrate her heroism'. Some young women even called out, 'Long live the Armenian Joan of Arc'. When Yeghigian, by his own account, pulled one of the young women aside and told her it was dangerous to carry on like this, Rubina got angry, asking 'Who are you to teach me sense?' See Yegheghian/Eghikian, *Ariwni chambun vray*, 347.

[94] See Barbara Alpern Engel and Clifford N. Rosenthal (eds), *Five Sisters: Women Against the Tsar* (London: Routledge, 1975).

[95] Ranajit Guha, 'Chandra's Death', *Subaltern Studies V* (New Delhi: Oxford University Press, 1987), 138–9.

Figure 2.1   Rubina (Areshian) and Kristapor (Mikayelian), *c.* 1904. *Source*: Avo, 'Rubina Ohanjanian', *Heghap'okhakan albom* (*Revolutionary album*) 9(4) (1972). Courtesy of the National Library of Armenia.

3

Caucasian Banditry in Late Imperial Russia: The Case of *Abrek* Zelimkhan

Jeronim Perović[1]

On the morning of 27 March 1910,[2] dramatic events unfolded in the small North Caucasian town of Kizlyar, located in what was then the Terek *oblast'*. A group of around sixty heavily armed riders set out in the direction of the town, at that time mainly inhabited by Cossacks. The two men riding at the head of the group were wearing trim officers' uniforms, and since the others were also dressed as Cossacks, at first they attracted little attention from the local residents. Only in the aftermath of the events did it emerge that this was a group led by none other than the most notorious bandit of the time: the Chechen *abrek* Zelimkhan Gushmazukaev, 'or a person claiming to be him'.[3]

Half of the riders advanced into the town centre, while the other half remained on guard outside the area. Without encountering any significant

---

[1] This chapter is based on my German-language chapter titled 'Banditen und Heilige: Abrek Zelimchan' ('Bandits and Saints: Abrek Zelimkhan'), in Jeronim Perović, *Der Nordkaukasus unter russischer Herrschaft: Geschichte einer Vielvölkerregion zwischen Rebellion und Anpassung* (Cologne: Böhlau, 2015), 154–89.
[2] Unless otherwise noted, the dates given correspond to the Julian calendar officially used in Russia until February 1918; the Julian calendar is thirteen days behind its corresponding Gregorian date.
[3] Cited from the letter by Count Illarion Vorontsov-Dashkov to Tsar Nicholas II, dated 29 April 1910: GARF (Gosudarstvennyi Arkhiv Rossiiskoi Federatsii), fond (f.) 543, opis' (op.) 1, delo (d.) 462, list (l.) 3ob.

resistance, Zelimkhan and some of his followers forced their way into the Kizlyar treasury office, as others took up positions in front of the building. A bloodbath then ensued, as the bandits shot down and wounded treasury employees, and also killed security guards and civilians who happened to be in the building at the time. Shots were also fired outside. Even though the bandits had the element of surprise on their side and managed to overwhelm the security officials fairly quickly, from the attackers' point of view the assault was a complete failure: Zelimkhan and his companions were unable to break their way into the locked safe where almost half a million roubles were held and had to be satisfied with a sum of just 4,124 roubles and 41 kopecks, which was all they could find in the cash registers and office desks. Still, they left a bloody trail behind them, killing a total of eighteen people, with only a small number of wounded on their side.

By the time the Cossack troops arrived on the scene, the bandits had already left. Despite having the Cossacks as well as regular Russian army units on their heels, Zelimkhan and his supporters managed to escape over the River Terek towards Khasav-Iurt, and then deep into Chechen-populated areas. The track soon went cold from that point, since the local village elders and rural inhabitants were not willing to give the military units pursuing the bandits any information about their whereabouts. After five days of searching in vain around the town of Vedeno, the army gave up the chase. The gang had dispersed, and no trace of Zelimkhan was to be found.

So ran the account in the detailed report prepared on the tsar's instructions by the viceroy (*namestnik*) of the Caucasus, Count Illarion Vorontsov-Dashkov. In his report dated 29 April 1910, and addressed directly to Tsar Nicholas II, Vorontsov-Dashkov reconstructs the sequence of events in great detail and discusses the immediate background and underlying causes that made this brazen attack possible.[4] When Tsar Nicholas II appointed Count

---

[4] Vorontsov-Dashkov's letter, which is about forty pages long (double-paged), is contained in the State Archive of the Russian Federation: GARF, f. 543, op. 1, d. 462, ll. 1–21. A largely identical letter by Vorontsov-Dashkov to Prime Minister Piotr A. Stolypin, dated 4 May 1910, is found in a shortened version in V. A. Kozlov, F. Benvenuti, M. E. Kozlova, P. M. Polian and V. I. Sheremet (eds), *Vainakhi i imperskaia vlast': Problema Chechni i Ingushetii vo vnutrennei politike Rossii i SSSR (nachalo XIX–seredina XX v.)* (Moscow: ROSSPEN, 2011), 223–36.

Vorontsov-Dashkov in 1905 as his direct representative and commander-in-chief of the Caucasus military district, he was already looking back on a long career of service to the Russian Empire. The Caucasian wars had been fought almost half a century before, and since the last major uprising of Chechens and Dagestanis in 1877, which had been put down successfully by Russian troops, there had been no serious military threat emanating from this multi-ethnic region.

Yet even in the following years and decades, the North Caucasus could not truly be described as calm from the Russian administrators' perspective. On the contrary, at the beginning of the twentieth century, reports of attacks on Cossack settlements, trains, post offices and banks became more frequent. Particularly along the Sunzha, the former Caucasian military line separating the Cossack settlements from the mountain villages (*auls*) of the Chechens and Ingush, the situation developed into a full-blown guerrilla war. Whereas the indigenous, non-Russian population of the North Caucasus had experienced discrimination under Russian and Cossack rule in the outgoing nineteenth century, now, at the beginning of the twentieth century, the Cossacks were increasingly becoming the target of raiding Chechen and Ingush bands.[5]

The reason the attack on the treasury office in Kizlyar caused such a stir in far-off St Petersburg was because the action had been carried out in broad daylight on a guarded facility in a town with military barracks and the robbers had not been caught, despite extensive efforts to do so. The detailed coverage of the events in Russian newspapers of the time had the effect of not only boosting the reputation of Zelimkhan, but also making the Russian administration in the Caucasus appear in a poor light. In fact, by the time of the Kizlyar attack, Zelimkhan and his band had been roaming the region for almost a decade, raiding Cossack farms, robbing banks, trains and post offices, and murdering local representatives of the tsarist government. All efforts to capture and liquidate this bandit had failed.

Some saw a deeper reason for the Terek region experiencing such an increase in banditry at the beginning of the twentieth century in the unduly

---

[5] On the 1877 rebellion and the subsequent developments in the North Caucasus, see Jeronim Perović, *From Conquest to Deportation: The North Caucasus under Russian Rule* (London: Hurst, 2018), 75–102.

lax attitude taken by representatives of the Russian imperial state towards the local non-Russian population. A Russian police report prepared after the Kizlyar attack, for example, puts the banditry problem down to the 'irresolute and indulgent approach' of a state that 'since the liberation movement [following the measures introduced by Tsar Nicholas II in 1905/6] . . . has lost all authority among the mountain population'. A people who had been accustomed 'to being ruled with a firm hand', the report continues, had realised that 'most of their crimes go unpunished, and that it is merely a matter of bribing the heads of the respective administrative sections, whereby the moral level [of these officials] [has] completely collapsed . . .'[6]

In fact, under the somewhat more liberal policy introduced by the tsar in reaction to the revolutionary unrest of 1905/6, the Chechens and Ingush were now taking revenge for the wrongs they had suffered during the period of Cossack rule in the late nineteenth century. In light of the abuses of the past, even Vorontsov-Dashkov was ready to admit that punitive measures on their own would not be sufficient to deal with the 'appalling evil' of banditry, which 'the Russian administration had long been [struggling] to deal with'.[7] In his report to the tsar, he cited not only the shortage of land in the mountains but also the special way of life and worldview of the indigenous population, who lived in great poverty, he said, and remained at a 'low cultural level'.[8] Vorontsov-Dashkov understood that this provided fertile soil for the growth of the banditry phenomenon and urged that these underlying causes be addressed. In the same report, however, he made it quite clear that he would not hesitate to respond with punitive action 'every time the indigenous inhabitants commit serious crimes against . . . peaceful citizens'.[9]

Following the incident in Kizlyar, the Russian authorities increased their punitive measures. As a direct consequence of this bloody incident, the tsar's administrators in the Caucasus decreed that not only the immediate members of Zelimkhan's family but also more distant relatives would be exiled to cen-

---

[6] The report was written by Colonel I. I. Pastriulin, head of the gendarmerie of the Tiflis (Tbilisi) Governorate, and dated 18 December 1910. The report is contained in Kozlov et al., *Vainakhi i imperskaia vlast'*, 236–46, at 245.

[7] GARF, f. 543, op. 1, d. 462, l. 18.

[8] GARF, f. 543, op. 1, d. 462, ll. 18–19.

[9] GARF, f. 543, op. 1, d. 462, l. 18.

tral Russia. Even the inhabitants of villages that had been guilty of assisting him were deported, with entire settlements being razed to the ground in some cases.[10] As a further punitive action, collective fines in the form of taxes were imposed on the indigenous population.[11]

At the same time, and because of the need to demonstrate his determination to take action, Vorontsov-Dashkov sought scapegoats within the imperial state apparatus: Among those dismissed from office after the Kizlyar affair were the Cossack ataman responsible for the town of Kizlyar, Lieutenant-Colonel Verbitskii; the mayor of Kizlyar, Variev; and Captain Bashkov, the commanding officer of the 15th company of the Shirvanskii regiment stationed near Kizlyar.[12] In the Vedeno district, Berzniev, the head of the 4th administrative section (*uchastok*), was forced to step down. He was accused of meeting with the fleeing bandits and allowing them to pass through the district.[13] Also punished for 'inaction in the pursuit of the bandits' and dismissed from their positions were the Chechen village elders of Gudermes, Adil-Iurt, Aksai, Kadi-Iurt and Azam-Iurt.[14] In addition, Vorontsov-Dashkov also intensified military efforts to capture Zelimkhan, which, however, did not bear fruit.

The longer the authorities failed to defeat Zelimkhan the more his popularity rose. Due also to extensive reporting in the Russian press, Zelimkhan gained legendary status already during his lifetime. At the same time, the problem of Caucasian 'banditry' was also frequently discussed in Russia's ruling political and military circles: while social-democrats tended to portray this figure as a symbol of the oppressed people and a fighter for social justice, conservatives saw in Zelimkhan the living proof that the empire's

---

[10] 'Vysylka rodstvennikov Zelim-khana', *Russkoe slovo*, 20 November 1911; 'Vysylka chechentsev', *Russkoe slovo*, 15 February 1912. All pre-1917 Russian newspapers, here and in subsequent notes, were retrieved from http://starosti.ru, last accessed 12 August 2019.

[11] 'Shtraf za Zelim-khana', *Russkoe slovo*, 3 April 1912; 'Posobie postradavshim ot Zelim-khana', *Russkoe slovo*, 16 March 1912; '100-tysiachnyi shtraf', *Russkoe slovo*, 10 November 1911; 'Shtraf za ukryvatel'stvo Zelim-khana', *Russkoe slovo*, 18 August 1911; 'Nagrada za poimku Zelim-khana', *Russkoe slovo*, 22 April 1911; 'Zelim-khan', *Russkoe slovo*, 1 March 1911.

[12] GARF, f. 543, op. 1, d. 462, l. 15ob.

[13] GARF, f. 543, op. 1, d. 462, ll. 8, 15ob.

[14] GARF, f. 543, op. 1, d. 462, l. 16ob.

modernising project in this part the Caucasus had gone terribly awry. It was only three-and-a-half years after the attack on Kizlyar, on 26 September 1913, that a special unit formed mainly of Dagestanis managed to track down and kill Zelimkhan near the Chechen *aul* of Shali.[15]

This chapter aims to give insights into the phenomenon of Caucasian 'banditry' (*abrechestvo*) in tsarist Russia at the turn of the twentieth century. By discussing various episodes from Zelimkhan's life and his actions – his development from a simple man to an outlaw, his alleged transfiguration to imam and connection to religious groups, as well as the circumstances of his death – the goal is to critically analyse prevalent conceptions about banditry and Caucasian *abrek*s, thereby providing an understanding of the complex social realities in Chechnya and the North Caucasus under Russian imperial rule (Figure 3.1). This chapter goes beyond a discussion of the more romanticising literary writings on Zelimkhan and Caucasian *abrek*s, which became vastly popular in the 1920s and have informed contemporary notions of the banditry phenomenon to a large extent; rather, this chapter investigates the narratives as they appear in lesser known publications from the time, press reporting as well as secret police reports and other documents from the Russian imperial archives. While the meanings attached to such prominent figures as Zelimkhan varied, any attempt to do justice to the concrete person of Zelimkhan and *abrechestvo* needs to take the specific historical context into account. Unravelling the 'real' Zelimkhan by analysing a wide range of contemporary accounts will show that it is necessary to revise the idea that most of the indigenous non-Russian population saw Zelimkhan as a hero, saint or freedom fighter; neither is Zelimkhan to be seen as some kind of modern 'Robin Hood', nor does he belong to the category of the 'bandit-patriot', as suggested by British historian Eric Hobsbawm.[16]

*Abrek*s and *Abrechestvo*

Zelimkhan was an *abrek*. According to Russian ethnographer Vladimir Bobrovnikov, the term *abrek* is thought to originate from the Iranian word

---

[15] D. Bagration, *Podvig Terskago Kazaka: Nyne dagestankago konnogo polka por. Kibirova, unichtivshago abreka Zelimkhana* (Petrograd: T-vo R. Golike i A. Vil'borg', 1914), 41.
[16] Eric Hobsbawm, *Bandits*, rev. edn (New York: New Press, 2000), 121.

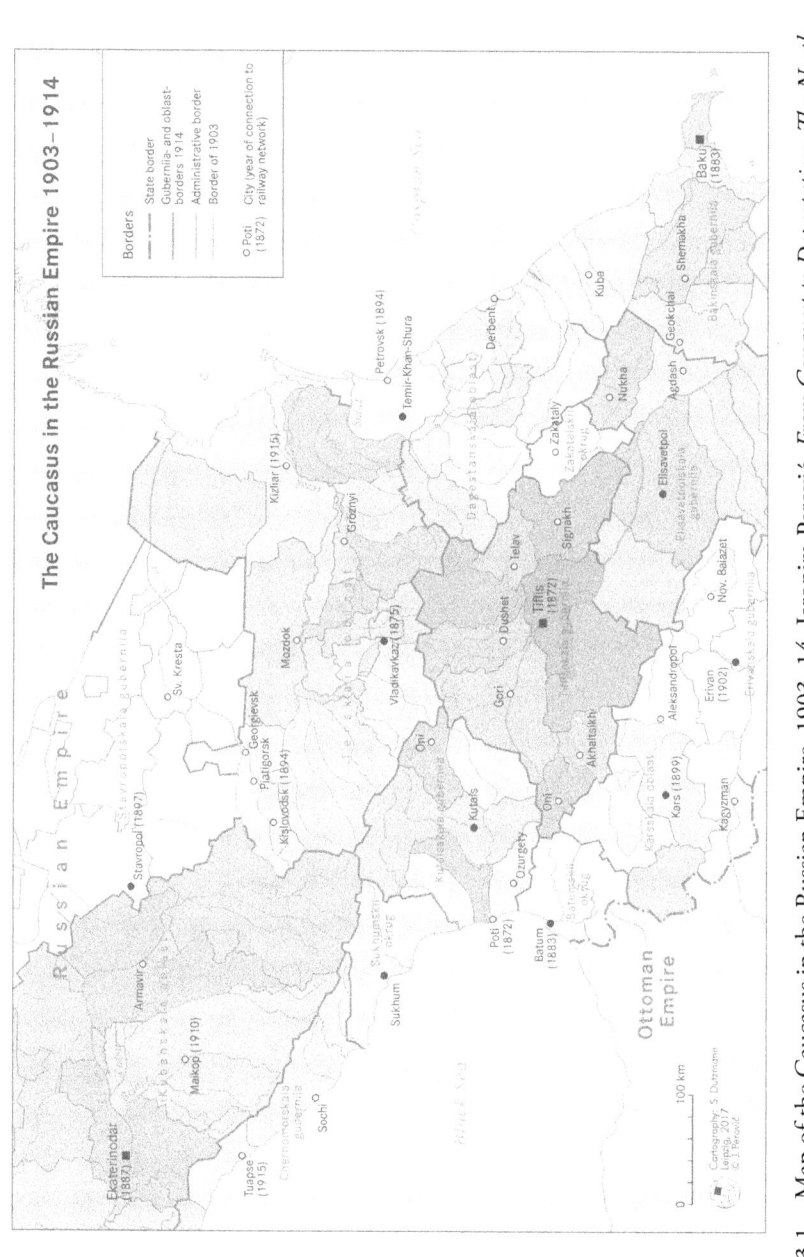

Figure 3.1 Map of the Caucasus in the Russian Empire, 1903–14. Jeronim Perović, *From Conquest to Deportation: The North Caucasus under Russian Rule* (London: Hurst, 2018).

aparak (bandit, vagrant), which long ago also found its way into the Caucasian languages.[17] In the Caucasus, the term initially had a negative connotation. An *abrek* was an exile or a migrant who hid away in the forest or in the mountains as a fugitive from captivity or servitude, or was seeking refuge from a blood feud. He lived by robbing and stealing from others, and might sometimes form small bands with other *abrek*s. An entry in Russia's *Brockhaus and Efron Encyclopedic Dictionary* (published in 1890) defines the term *abrek* as a 'person who takes a vow to avoid all pleasures of life and to be fearless in all battles and confrontations with people'. During this time of retreat, which could last 'up to five years', 'the *abrek* renounces all previous connections, relatives and friends; the *abrek* cherishes nothing, and fears nothing'.[18]

Abrek was a term with changing meanings and connotations. Already during the Russian conquest of the Caucasus in the nineteenth century, the concept had been reinterpreted when Imam Shamil (*c.* 1797–1871), who led the armed resistance against Russia until 1859, accepted many *abrek*s into the ranks of his followers as fighters. A new meaning for the concept of *abrechestvo* (living as an *abrek*) emerged after the end of the Caucasus War, since the term was now applied to individuals or groups who had retreated into the mountains to avoid capture by the state authorities. In the period after the Caucasus War, while the Russian administrators generally equated *abrechestvo* with banditry, viewing the *abrek*s as common robbers or brigands (*razboiniki*), among the peoples of the region the term took on a more positive meaning, with the *abrek*'s resistance at times being equated with the people's resistance against Russia.[19]

There were indeed some cases of individual *abrek*s being given equal status to hero figures such as Mansur or Shamil, with the hopes and desires

---

[17] Vladimir Bobrovnikov, 'Abreki i gosudarstvo: Kul'tura nasiliia na Kavkaze', *Vestnik Evrazii* 8(1) (2000): 19–46, at 24–6.

[18] *Entsiklopedicheskii slovar' Brokgauza i Efrona*, vol. 1 (St Petersburg: AO 'F. A. Brokgauz – I. A. Efron', 1890), 41.

[19] Cf. Vladimir Bobrovnikov, 'Bandits and the State: Designing a "Traditional" Culture of Violence in the North Caucasus', in Jane Burbank, Mark Von Hagen and Anatolyi Remnev (eds), *Russian Empire: Space, People, Power 1700–1930* (Bloomington: Indiana University Press, 2007), 239–67, especially 245–53; Iu. M. Botiakov, *Abreki na Kavkaze: Sotsiokul'turnyi aspekt iavleniia* (St Petersburg: Vostokovedenie, 2004).

widespread among the population being projected on to them. Some of them were elevated to the status of 'holy man', particularly (although not only) in Shiite-populated districts of Dagestan and on the territory of present-day Azerbaijan. In these parts of the Russian Empire, *abrek*s who had been killed were honoured within the context of Shiite Islam martyr worship as *shahīd*s (from the Arabic *shahīd*, 'witness') who had laid down their lives for the dissemination or defence of Islam; their graves became places of adoration for pilgrims.[20] *Abrek*s could also incur the local population's disfavour, however, if they breached the customary law of the North Caucasian peoples. In this case, their relatives would deny them protection, and the *abrek* would forfeit the right of hospitality, which was tantamount to a death sentence.[21]

The word *abrek* found its way into Russian linguistic usage, and therefore wider public discourse, via three literary works of early Russian Romanticism: Mikhail Lermontov's *Khadzhi Abrek* (1833), and two novellas by Aleksandr Bestuzhev-Marlinskii, *Ammalat Bek* (1832) and *Mullah Nur* (1836).[22] While the notion of the *abrek* was popularised essentially via the Russian language, it was not a Russian invention. The word is documented in Chechen songs from an early date, and appears in the poems of North Caucasian and Georgian poets.[23]

The *abrek* also entered the writings of Russia's evolving newspaper landscape, which became increasingly interested in this phenomenon with the marked upsurge of violence in the North Caucasus at the beginning of the twentieth century. In fact, for contemporary Russian journalists, Zelimkhan was a highly rewarding topic to write about, one that could be exploited in many different ways. For example, in the autumn of 1911, the press reported, not without a measure of admiration, that the bandit, although surrounded by some 400 soldiers, had eventually managed to escape 'by a miracle' from a

---

[20] Bobrovnikov, 'Abreki i gosudarstvo', 36.
[21] Valerii Dzidzoev, 'Abrechestvo kak forma sotsial'nogo soprotivleniia na Kavkaze vo vtoroi polovine XIX veka', *Dar'ial* 3 (2011), available at: http://www.darial-online.ru/2011_3/dzidzoev.shtml, last accessed 12 August 2019.
[22] Rebecca Gould, 'Transgressive Sanctity: The Abrek in Chechen Culture', *Kritika* 8(2) (2007): 271–306, at 281.
[23] Further reading, see Rebecca Gould, *Writers and Rebels: The Literature of Insurgency in the Caucasus* (New Haven, CT: Yale University Press, 2016).

seemingly hopeless situation. This followed the reports of his death that had been circulating in the media just a few days earlier.[24] On another occasion, rumours appeared in the media claiming that the deposed Shah of Persia, Mohammed Ali, had sent envoys to Zelimkhan seeking his support in his struggle to regain power. Zelimkhan had supposedly declined to offer his support, since he had no wish to help the shah restore his repressive regime; on the contrary, if he, Zelimkhan, came to Persia, it would be to fight for the liberation of the people from the shah.[25]

Rather than helping to discredit banditry, this kind of reporting tended to make the phenomenon more attractive. Accordingly, at this time, the police repeatedly detained young men who had come from other parts of the Russian Empire to join Zelimkhan's band of rogues.[26] Revolutionary students also sought to harness Zelimkhan for their cause. One group consisting mainly of Armenian students, for example, sent five delegates to Chechnya to make contact with Zelimkhan to discuss the possibility of joint terrorist attacks.[27] Even during his own lifetime, Zelimkhan's reputation spread far beyond Russia, with newspapers in Europe and the United States publishing detailed reports about him.[28]

In this context, the Russian administration in the Caucasus was confronting not only Zelimkhan as an individual but a form of banditry that was increasingly coming to be associated with his name. Every successful attack, whether carried out directly by him or under his name, increased his aura of invincibility and prepared the ground for ever more exaggerated rumours. According to one rumour, for example, Zelimkhan had had himself appointed as an imam, and, as Shamil's successor, he was planning to lead the

---

[24] *Novoe vremia*, 18 October 1911; 'Slukh ob ubiistve Zelim-khana', *Russkoe slovo*, 2 October 1911.

[25] 'Eks-shakh i Zelimkhan', *Moskovskaia gazeta kopeika*, 30 August 1911.

[26] 'Vorozhenskie "abreki"', *Russkoe slovo*, 3 November 1911.

[27] This emerges from the letter of 4 May 1911, signed by the head of the Terek *oblast'* and the Cossack ataman to the deputy for the civil administration of the Caucasian Governorate (*namestnichestvo*), contained in L. R. Gudaev, *Abrek Zelimkhan: Fakty i dokumenty* (Groznyi: GUP 'Knizhnoe izdatel'stvo', 2010), 415–16.

[28] The *Los Angeles Times*, for example, devoted several articles to Zelimkhan, including a long report on the occasion of his death: 'Caucasian Brigand Killed by Soldiers', *Los Angeles Times*, 14 December 1913, SN3.

people out of Russian rule. This story was prevalent not only among the local population but also in conservative Russian political and academic circles as well as in the army leadership. In their often Islamophobic conceptions, these circles saw in Zelimkhan an outgrowth of backwardness, religious fanaticism and primitiveness, and thus the confirmation of all those negative attributes that were commonly ascribed to the North Caucasian 'mountaineer' (*gorets*).[29] However, Zelimkhan projected a rather different image in social-democratic-oriented circles. In their view, he fitted the profile of a rebel fighting for the demands of an oppressed people who were protesting against arbitrary acts of state repression.[30]

The topos of the *abrek* was examined particularly closely in the twilight of the tsarist era by social-revolutionary-aligned intellectuals from the North Caucasus as a good fit with their perception of the legitimate aspirations of the people against the injustices of repressive tsarist policy. The social-democrat Akhmet Tembulatovich Tsalikov (1882–1928), for example, attempted to counter negative images of Caucasian bandits as 'beasts in human form' by explaining the cultural and social factors that caused a young man to become an *abrek*.[31] His book *Kavkaz i Povolzh'e*, published in 1913, tells the story of a young man, who, in order to be able to pay the high bride price required for his wedding, is drawn into nocturnal stealing raids but kills a man in the heat of the moment. He then has to take flight to escape the blood feud started by the victim's relatives, and so, without any intention of doing so, he becomes an *abrek*.[32] While regretting the existence of such customs, Tsalikov, himself an ethnic Ossetian from the North Caucasus, saw the central problem not in these traditions as such but in how the Russian imperial state was dealing with them:

> If the Russian authorities in the Caucasus would make the effort to understand the social nature or even the psychology of the Caucasian bandit, they

---

[29] P. I. Kovalevskii, *Vostanie Chechni i Dagestana v 1877–1878 gg.: Zelim-Khan* (St Petersburg: Typografiia M. I. Akhinfieva, 1912), especially 94–5.
[30] Akhmet Tsalikov, *Kavkaz i Povolzh'e: Ocherki inogorodicheskoi politiki i kul'turno-khoziaistvennogo byta* (Moscow: M. Mukhtarov, 1913).
[31] Tsalikov, *Kavkaz i Povolzh'e*, 102.
[32] Ibid., 102–3.

would decisively, once and for all, desist from punitive measures against the [innocent] indigenous population.[33]

It is this perception that prevailed in the early Soviet period following the Bolsheviks' seizure of power and has continued to define the historical portrayal of Zelimkhan and Caucasian *abrechestvo*.[34] In fact, similar arguments were advanced by the Chechen intellectual Aslanbek Dzhemaldinovich Sheripov (1897–1919) in his notes to a collection of Chechen songs, which was published in 1918.[35] Sheripov, who would later become a significant and well-known figure as a leader of Chechens fighting on the side of the Bolsheviks in the Russian Civil War, summarised the significance of the *abrek* as follows, in a passage often cited in Soviet literature:

> State power terrorised the peaceful population, and the *abrek*s terrorised those in power. So naturally, the people came to view the *abrek*s as fighters against suppression and measures carried out by the state. The Chechens used other, more pejorative terms to denote common thieves and bandits ... But *abrek* became a term of respect, and the people did not grant this [honourable] appellation to just anyone. The most highly respected and successful *abrek*s were the object of fascination for the Chechens, who saw them as continuing the struggle [against the Russians] started by Shamil and his *murid*s [i.e., the adepts of a Sufi brotherhood].[36]

This line of thinking became still further accentuated in the Soviet era. In his early writings, for example, Chechen historian (and later dissident) Abdurakhman Avtorkhanov (1908/10–1997) rejects any connection between banditry and *abrechestvo*, instead seeing the latter as a legitimate form of revolutionary struggle, supported by the masses. In his view, therefore, *abrechestvo* and banditry were 'two diametrically opposed currents', seen as 'fundamen-

---

[33] Ibid., 120.
[34] N. I. Pokrovskii, 'Obzor istochnikov po istorii imamata', *Problemy istochnikovedeniia: Vypusk II* (Moscow: n.p., 1936), 187–234, at 188. On the treatment of *abrechestvo* in Russian and Soviet historiography, see Bobrovnikov, 'Abreki i gosudarstvo', 20–4.
[35] Aslanbek Sheripov, *Stati i rechi: Sbornik*, 2nd, extended edn, ed. E. P. Kireev and M. N. Muzaev (Groznyi: Checheno-Ingushskoe knizhnoe izdatel'stvo, 1972), 65–9; the poems are at ibid., 157–72.
[36] Ibid., 67.

tally different' from each other.³⁷ In the second half of the 1920s, a tendency to praise Zelimkhan and *abrechestvo* can be seen throughout Soviet literature in an attempt to harness them for the Bolsheviks' agenda of social transformation. In 1926, the Ossetian poet Dzakho Gatuev (1892–1938) published the first historical novel on Zelimkhan, in which he succeeds in creating an astonishingly authentic-sounding narrative.³⁸ In the 1920s, Soviet cinema produced a series of dramas on *abrechestvo*, including the film *Abrek Zaur* (1926) by Boris Mikhin and *Zelimkhan* by director Oleg Frelikh, which was first screened in 1929 and went on to become a major success.³⁹ The film script for Frelikh's film was by none other than Gatuev, whose version was subsequently adopted by others and had a lasting impact in terms of defining Zelimkhan's public image.⁴⁰

The line of narrative advanced in the early Soviet period, which portrayed Zelimkhan's actions as a form of 'revolutionary struggle', brought *abrechestvo* into close proximity with Imam Shamil's resistance to Russia's colonial war of conquest in the nineteenth century; in fact, already the early Bolsheviks during the Russian Civil War (1918–1920/1) sought to adopt Imam Shamil in a similar way to Zelimkhan, as a symbol for the decades of resistance of the 'mountaineer proletariat' against tsarism and foreign oppression. Iosif Vissarionovich Stalin (real name Dzhugashvili, 1878–1953), in his role as the people's commissar for nationality affairs (a post he held officially from 1917 to 1924), ordered that portraits of the legendary Imam Shamil be put up in the buildings of all official institutions of

---

[37] A. Avtorkhanov, *K osnovnym voprosam istorii Chechni (k desiatiletiiu Sovetskoi Chechni)* (Groznyi: n.p., 1930), 36.

[38] Konst. Gatuev, *Zelimkhan: Iz istorii natsional'no-osvoboditel'nykh dvizhenii na Severnom Kavkaze* (Rostov-on-Don: Severo-Kavkazskoe kraevoe izdatel'stvo 'Sevkavkniga', 1926).

[39] V. I. Fomin, A. S. Deriabin and V. E. Vishnevskii (eds), *Letopis' rossiiskogo kino, 1863–1929* (Moscow: Materik, 2004), 520, 669. In issue 10 (1929), the magazine *Revoliutsiia i gorets* reported on the 'great success' of a film about Zelimkhan that had been screened at cinemas 'in Moscow, Rostov and other cities of the Soviet Union'. According to *Revoliutsiia i gorets*, the film had already been running for two months in Rostov-on-Don and 'every evening in front of a large audience' who would fight for seats. Quotations from V. O. Bobrovnikov, *Musul'mane Severnogo Kavkaza: Obychai, pravo, nasilie; Ocherki po istorii i etnografii prava Nagornogo Dagestana* (Moscow: Vostochnaia literatura RAN, 2002), 14.

[40] Gatuev delivered the script in cooperation with I. Trabskii: 'Zelim-khan', *KinoPoisk*, available at: http://www.kinopoisk.ru/film/596172, last accessed 12 August 2019.

the North Caucasian peoples. Even after the Bolsheviks began consolidating their power during the 1920s and 1930s, and in order to gain sympathies among the indigenous peoples, portraits of Shamil would hang next to, or even replace, the images of Lenin.[41]

All this changed abruptly in 1943/4 when the Chechens and other North Caucasian peoples were declared 'enemies of the people' for their alleged collaboration with Nazi Germany and deported to Central Asia. Following the return of the Chechens from their exile under Khrushchev, however, the cult around the figure of Zelimkhan was renewed and reached a new high point in the late 1960s. It was in this period that the Chechen writer Magomet Mamakaev published his well-known works on *abrechestvo* and Zelimkhan.[42] In the mid-1970s, a monument to Zelimkhan was erected in his home district of Vedeno.[43]

In more recent times, following the collapse of the Soviet Union and the upheavals of the two Chechen wars, a revitalisation of the Zelimkhan cult can be observed. During the First Chechen War of independence of the 1990s, figures such as Shamil or Zelimkhan, who were seen as symbols of resistance to outside attempts of conquest, rose in popularity. This involved occasional reinterpretations of the figure of the *abrek*. The Chechen interim president, Zelimkhan Iandarbiev, claimed in an interview in the mid-1990s that '[e]ven the *abrek*s . . . fought in the name of God'.[44] Caucasian jihadists must also have been well aware of the *abrek* as role models. Not only were many Chechen children born in deportation named after famous *abrek*s, some later-born 'Zelimkhans' were also among the later jihadi Chechen fighters.[45]

The cult of Zelimkhan is still visible in today's Chechnya under its

---

[41] Perović, *From Conquest to Deportation*, 143.

[42] The most prominent of these works is M. A. Mamakaev, *Zelimkhan: Roman* (Groznyi: Checheno-Ingushskoe knizhnoe izdatel'stvo, 1971). This is a Russian translation of the book originally published in Chechen in 1968.

[43] 'Vozvrashchenie abreka', *Checheninfo*, 8 July 2009, available at: http://www.checheninfo.ru/2478-Возвращение абрека.html, last accessed 30 November 2012. A photograph of the monument can be found in Gudaev, *Abrek Zelimkhan*, 507.

[44] Quoted in Florian Mühlfried, 'Don't Trust, Don't Fear, Don't Ask', in Florian Mühlfried (ed.), *Mistrust – Ethnographic Approximations* (Bielefeld; transcript, 2018), 179–200, at 182.

[45] Ibid.

pro-Russian president Ramzan Kadyrov. In 2009, the Soviet monument to Zelimkhan that had been completely destroyed during the Russian–Chechen War of the 1990s, was re-erected.[46] Chechen television produced a major documentary on Zelimkhan and *abrechestvo*,[47] and the *abrek* phenomenon began to attract renewed interest from Chechen historians and the Chechen public in general.[48] Yet, even today, there is considerable divergence in historians' treatment of Zelimkhan. Those who espouse the notion of a national history and construct Chechnya's history in contrast to Russia's history, portray Zelimkhan primarily as a freedom fighter and an early protagonist of Chechen nation-building. Others clearly find it more expedient, in the current political climate, mainly defined by a Russia-friendly orientation under Chechen President Kadyrov, to highlight the social rather than the political aspects of *abrechestvo*, portraying Zelimkhan as a fighter for justice and as a Caucasian version of a 'noble and righteous bandits similar to Robin Hood', as suggested by Chechen historian Lema Gudaev.[49]

This latter view of Zelimkhan is very much in line with Western Marxist writings on socio-economic banditry understood as an expression of social protest and viewed as a 'universal social phenomenon', occurring at different times but in similar forms all over the world.[50] According to this reading, the mythical status attributed to such bandits by the peasant population was often not too far removed from the 'reality of banditry' as described by Eric Hobsbawm, the founder of this historiographic tradition, in his well-known work *Bandits*.[51] In this work, Hobsbawm explicitly refers to Zelimkhan as

---

[46] 'Vozvrashchenie abreka'.
[47] 'Abrek Zelimkhan: Iz glubiny vekov', documentary movie produced by 'ChGTRK Groznyi' (n.d.), available at: http://www.checheninfo.ru/12167-abrek-zelimhan-iz-glubiny-vekov.html, last accessed 12 August 2019.
[48] There is even a web project titled Portal 'Abrek', available at: http://abrek.org, last accessed 12 August 2019, which is run in partnership with the Chechen news agency *Checheninfo*, available at: http://checheninfo.ru, last accessed 12 August 2019, and is dedicated to the memory of Zelimkhan and other *abrek*s.
[49] Gudaev, *Abrek Zelimkhan*, 3.
[50] The concept of 'social banditry' goes back to the British historian Eric J. Hobsbawm, who developed it in 1959 in *Primitive Rebels* and expanded it in his 1969 book *Bandits*. I am drawing here on his revised edition, published in 2000, Hobsbawm, *Bandits*, 21.
[51] See Hobsbawm's reply to his critics in Eric Hobsbawm, 'Social Bandits: Reply', *Comparative Studies in Society and History* 14(4) (1972): 503–5, at 504.

the 'Robin Hood of early twentieth-century Daghestan',[52] and his 'resistance' as continuation of Shamil's battle against Russian conquest.[53] Hobsbawm moreover (and erroneously) asserts that Shamil's war against the Russians was based on the development of '*muridism*' among the local Muslim population, and that this Muslim 'sect', surviving into the early twentieth century, provided 'the celebrated bandit-patriot' with 'aid, immunity and ideology'.[54]

The figure of Zelimkhan has experienced many different uses and interpretations in the course of history. Depending on these specific uses, *abrek*s like Zelimkhan have taken on specific purposes in historiography and the political imaginary – be it as role models of masculine identity for a rebellious youth, or as inspiration for the fearless freedom fighter; the modern jihadists may identify with the *abrek* as a representative of 'the lonely hero', striving to achieve eternal glory through a courageous death. Against this background, the following will try to discover the myth behind the legend by discussing key aspects of Zelimkhan's life and deeds, showing which realities about him were constructed in the past.

The Genesis of an *Abrek*

Zelimkhan's decision to take to the hills as an *abrek* was motivated by a specific incident in his home village. According to a Russian police report of 1911, Zelimkhan Gushmazukaev (sometimes also referred to as Zelimkhan Kharachoevskii) was a 'peaceful and relatively prosperous' inhabitant of the village of Kharachoi in the district of Vedeno until 1894, when a blood feud started with someone from the same village, and Zelimkhan killed his enemy in self-defence. He was then imprisoned by Chernov, the deputy captain in the Vedeno district, acting as prosecutor in the matter. Zelimkhan broke out of prison, however, and planned to take revenge on Chernov. When

---

[52] Hobsbawm, *Bandits*, 49. However, Zelimkhan's equation with Robin Hood is not first found in Hobsbawm, but goes back to (Western) interpretations at the time. The *Los Angeles Times*, for example, in its edition of 10 November 1912, dedicated a detailed report to Zelimkhan, in which he is described as a 'modern Robin Hood' loved by the poor: 'Handsome Highwayman, A Modern Robin Hood', *Los Angeles Times*, 10 November 1912, III26.

[53] Hobsbawm, *Bandits*, 112.

[54] Ibid.

Chernov learned of this, he sent a message to Zelimkhan to the effect that he, Chernov, had been wrong in accusing him of a crime, sought his forgiveness and promised not to continue the prosecution. Chernov was subsequently replaced by Captain Dobrovol'skii, who refused to abide by this agreement. To protect himself from prosecution by Dobrovol'skii, Zelimkhan then went underground as an *abrek*, whereupon Dobrovol'skii also began to persecute Zelimkhan's relatives, forcing them to go into hiding as well. The male members of the family joined Zelimkhan's gang. Zelimkhan is subsequently reputed to have finally succeeded in assassinating Dobrovol'skii in an act of revenge in 1906, setting the final seal on his outlaw status. There was now no way back for him.[55]

This is just one of many versions of the beginning of Zelimkhan's career, but it contains all the main elements required to understand his path to becoming an *abrek* and his subsequent resistance to the Russian imperial authorities. At the root of the tragedy stands a blood feud between two Chechen families.[56] The very first publications on Zelimkhan agree that the blood feud started over a young woman desired by both Zelimkhan's brother, Zoltamurad, and a man from the same village or a neighbouring village. Whether she was actually kidnapped and raped by Zoltamurad's rival or willingly accepted him remains unclear – both scenarios appear in the literature.[57] But at least since the appearance of Gatuev's book, the prevailing view has been that of a love affair between Zoltamurad and the young woman (named as Zezyk by Gatuev), and of the rival's family as standing in the way of the young couple's happiness.[58]

A love story is also the starting point of the tragedy as portrayed by Lieutenant-General Count Dmitrii Petrovich Bagration (1863–1919) in his

---

[55] This passage refers to a police report authored by S. N. Rukavishnikov, which was written no later than 3 November 1911. The report is contained in Kozlov et al., *Vainakhi i imperskaia vlast'*, 246–50, at 246–7. The report does not explicitly mention 1906 as the date of the assassination of Dobrovol'skii. However, this date is found in other reports on Zelimkhan, and is also mentioned in Tsalikov, *Kavkaz i Povolzh'e*, 112.

[56] It is unclear when exactly the blood feud took place. The sources give different dates, but the date 1894, which is also mentioned in the police report from 1911 by Rukavishnikov (see n. 55), seems very early. Gatuev states in his novel that Zelimkhan was arrested and imprisoned as a result of the family feud in 1901, Gatuev, *Zelimkhan*, 48.

[57] Bagration, *Podvig Terskago Kazaka*, 14–15.

[58] Gatuev, *Zelimkhan*, 43.

publication on Zelimkhan, which appeared in 1914.[59] Contrary to Gatuev's version of events, according to Bagration's account the young woman (named by him as Khadyzhat) preferred the rival from the outset, and Zelimkhan, who was himself 'not entirely indifferent to her charms', saw it as his duty to kidnap her and hand her over to his brother.[60]

The various accounts are largely in agreement that members of the Zelimkhan family set out to recapture the girl to restore the family's honour. When a relation of Zelimkhan was killed during the action, it was incumbent on the victim's family to take revenge. There is again a divergence between the sources over the manner in which this was done. According to Gatuev, it was Zelimkhan's father Gushmazuko who killed Zoltamurad's rival.[61] In any event, the young woman was freed from her captors and handed over to Zoltamurad. Given that each of the two families now had one death to mourn, it could perhaps have been possible to bring the blood feud to an end and restore peace between the families, particularly since the Russian state authorities had not at this point intervened in this local dispute. Events took a different turn, however. The other family appealed to the Russian authorities in the person of Chernov. It may well have been the case, as Gatuev claims, that this took place through the village elder who had been on the other family's side (opposed to Zelimkhan) from the outset.[62]

This account of the circumstances is generally consistent with the contents of a letter supposedly written by Zelimkhan that was delivered to the Speaker of the Russian State Duma on 15 January 1909. Zelimkhan did not know Russian, and could neither read nor write, but during his years as an *abrek* he did indeed on several occasions arrange for letters to be written and sent to officials he personally detested.[63] The letter to the Duma, which was

---

[59] Bagration, who at the outbreak of the First World War was to take over the supreme command of a brigade of the newly created Caucasian native equestrian division, based his report essentially on a conversation with Colonel Kibirov, who had led the special operation leading to the killing of Zelimkhan in September 1913, Bagration, *Podvig Terskago Kazaka*, 14.

[60] Ibid., 13–15.

[61] Gatuev, *Zelimkhan*, 41–7.

[62] Ibid., 46.

[63] The *abrek* allegedly sent fourteen letters to the head of the Vedeno district, Colonel Galaev, whom Zelimkhan killed in 1908, in the run-up to the assassination. According to the

first published in February 1909 in the social-democrat-aligned *Golos pravdy* newspaper in St Petersburg, is highly unlikely to have been from Zelimkhan, however.[64] This would have been clear to any impartial observer from a passage at the beginning of the document where the writer emphasises that the letter is being sent to the Duma because its members are about to discuss a question on banditry in the Caucasus. Zelimkhan could scarcely have had any knowledge of such political events taking place in far-off St Petersburg. The main aim of the writer, who as claimed by Gatuev may well have been an oil industrialist and member of the Chechen intelligentsia,[65] would appear to have been to denounce the ruthless attitude of the Russian authorities in the Caucasus, and to make public opinion aware of the nature of banditry in the area.

Essentially, this letter, which the Chechen literature on Zelimkhan continues to treat as an authentic ego-document,[66] is just one more politically motivated communication denouncing Russia's ruthless treatment of non-Russians and alien cultures. Nonetheless, given that the writer discusses in detail the reasons for Zelimkhan having become the 'most prominent *abrek* in Terek and Dagestan', this is still an 'extremely characteristic' record, as Tsalikov calls it, since it sheds light on the 'habitual paths' by which a 'law-abiding citizen' in the Caucasus became an *abrek*.[67] So that the letter would not be seen as a justification or plea for Zelimkhan personally, the writer makes it clear at the beginning of the text that he, Zelimkhan, is well aware that the actions he has committed exclude any possibility of his 'return to peaceful life', and he does not expect anyone's 'mercy or compassion'. It would, however, give him great 'moral satisfaction', as he puts it,

> if the Duma representatives would realise that [he was] not born an *abrek*, any more than his father, brothers and others [were]. Most of them choose

---

memoirs of S. Berdiaev, who was serving under Galaev as administrator of a district in Chechnya from 1908 to 1911, these letters were written in Arabic and by Zelimkhan's father, Gushmazuko, S. Berdiaev, *Chechnia i razboinik Zelimkhan (iz dalekikh vospominanii)* (Paris: n.p., 1931), 39.

[64] Tsalikov, *Kavkaz i Povolzh'e*, 117. The letter can be found in ibid., 112–17.
[65] Gatuev, *Zelimkhan*, 174.
[66] For example, A. Avtorkhanov, *Memuary* (Frankfurt am Main: Possev-Verlag, 1983), 46.
[67] Tsalikov, *Kavkaz i Povolzh'e*, 117.

this path as a result of the unjust behaviour of state authorities, or because of some kind of criminal offence or other unfortunate conjunction of external circumstances.[68]

The writer is clearly at pains to show that the transition to illegality and resistance was not preordained. At the start of Zelimkhan's trajectory, which rapidly saw him caught up in a maelstrom of violence and counter-violence, was the incompatibility between Russian and customary law. Zelimkhan explains in the letter that by killing his brother's rival, whom he had killed himself, 'without accomplices', he had fulfilled the 'sacred duty' that it was incumbent on every Chechen to uphold. Through this action, the writer says, the affair would have been settled for everyone involved, had a person inimically disposed towards him not informed the Russian authorities, whereupon a murder investigation had been initiated.[69] If it had been possible to keep the blood feud a secret from the authorities, the opposing families could have been reconciled, and his family could have continued to live a respectable life. The writer's explicit emphasis on the fact that it was Zelimkhan alone who had killed the rival, and subsequently also committed the murders of state officials, expresses another central concern: rather than minimising the actions committed by Zelimkhan, the writer is clearly looking to remove the blame from other members of his family and the general population and to expose the attitude taken by the authorities, who clearly find it 'much easier to fight peaceful people than *abreks*'.[70]

The fact of innocent people being punished for offences committed by bandits was indeed manifestly unjust, and to be condemned. Yet the writer of the letter had no answer to the question of how *abrechestvo*, which he himself portrays as a phenomenon inherent in the social structure, could be combated without negative consequences for other members of the surrounding community. This perspective on the issue, as the view prevalent in circles supporting social-democratic ideas, also offered no clear indication as to what approach should be taken towards blood feud and other customary legal practices of the peoples of the North Caucasus. It was therefore not

[68] Ibid., 112.
[69] Ibid., 113.
[70] Ibid., 116.

particularly surprising that this form of criticism of Russian policy in the Caucasus found little response in the Duma, where conservative views dominated at this time.

'Imam' Zelimkhan and the Religious Dimension

The Russian perspective, particularly among conservative members of the Russian elite and representatives of the imperial administration, was to a considerable extent based on the assumption that 'Zelimkhan [intended] to declare himself an imam and eradicate tsarist rule',[71] and on his supposed links to 'Islamic fanatics' and external forces hostile towards Russia. An internal report from the autumn of 1912 written by the head of the Russian intelligence department in Constantinople, citing 'various confidential sources', described as reliable, states that in 1909, at a 'great meeting of elders from settlements in the Terek *oblast'* and Dagestan in a mountain *aul* or a historic place in a remote part of Dagestan', Zelimkhan had been 'publicly declared a holy man and a grand imam for the fight against the infidel'. After this, the report continued, he had travelled to Mecca in May 1909, and then to Medina and Istanbul. The attacks carried out in the Caucasus in his absence had been conducted on Zelimkhan's behalf by 'Turkish officers and emissaries of the *Ittihad*'. Finally, we are told that, in the end, Zelimkhan did not, however, go to Mecca to attend the opening of a pan-Islamist congress because he was not an official delegate and was not sufficiently well educated.[72]

This source, on the one hand, puts Zelimkhan in the camp of the Young Turks (the term *ittihad* refers to the Young Turks, a political movement within the Ottoman Empire seeking to set up a greater Turkish state on a secular basis); on the other hand, it puts him in the pan-Islamic camp, an essentially religious movement whose aim was to unify all Muslim settlement areas into a single state. The extent to which the report's author was even aware of this distinction is unclear, but he must have perceived a threat for Russia in both movements. Another Russian secret report from the same period admittedly argued against the opinion that Zelimkhan had had

---

[71] Aslanbek Sheripov formulated this as early as 1918 in Sheripov, *Stati i rechi*, 67.
[72] The document dates from 25 September 1912 and can be found in Kozlov et al., *Vainakhi i imperskaia vlast'*, 250–1.

himself elected an imam, but also had no doubt that Zelimkhan was going to plan an uprising against Russia. In preparation for this, he had supposedly written to various spiritual leaders in Chechnya and Dagestan to encourage them to accept the title of imam, whereas he would restrict himself to organising the armed resistance for the struggle against the Russian state.[73]

There clearly were contacts between the North Caucasus, as a region with a Muslim population, and the Ottoman Empire. However, these primarily took place via high-ranking Islamic scholars from Dagestan, with a far lower level of exchanges with Chechnya. Following the attack on the treasury office in Kizlyar, the imperial authorities initiated an investigation into pan-Islamist tendencies in Islamic schools in the Terek *oblast'*. The report, however, could not confirm previously held assumptions that there was indeed widespread 'pan-Islamist propaganda', or that education was largely 'in the hands of immigrants from Persia and Turkey'.[74] Yet such connections continued to exist in the Russian mind, and personalities such as Zelimkhan were seen as pivotal elements in the scenario of an invasion by the Ottoman Empire. As well as being expressed in internal reports, this view was also trumpeted by conservative commentators. A good example of this can be seen in the statements made by the academician Pavel Ivanovich Kovalevskii (1850–1930), a well-known figure at the time (actually a psychiatrist by profession), who, in October 1912, during a lecture to the Society of Zealots of History (*Obshchestvo revnitelei istorii*) on the topic of 'Zelimkhan and the Caucasus', stated that:

> Even though Russia has conquered the Caucasus, the region has not been fully pacified. All the Muslim peoples of the Caucasus, in their remote *auls*, breathe in an atmosphere of irreconcilable hatred of Russia, and await only the opportunity to rise up together with Turkey in the defence of Islam . . . [T]he barbaric state of affairs prevailing in Chechnya will always represent a danger to Russia, since in the event of a war with Turkey, 250,000 Chechens will be a ready fighting force available to the enemy, penetrating into the most remote corners of the Caucasus.[75]

---

[73] Gudaev, *Abrek Zelimkhan*, 420.
[74] Pastriulin report (see n. 6), contained in Kozlov et al., *Vainakhi i imperskaia vlast'*, 238–9.
[75] Kovalevskii delivered his lecture on 10 October 1912. The text of the lecture is available as a copy of a police report dated 11 October 1912, and contained in ibid., 251–4, at 253.

The idea that Islamist fanatics, with the help of the Ottoman Empire, might aspire to separate the North Caucasus from Russia was not only a cause of deep anxiety, but also a strong argument for advocating a return to the firm-handed approach that many saw as necessary 'when dealing with Asiatic peoples'. This was the line taken by Kovalevskii:

> Zelimkhan is the product of an enormous mistake by the administration [of the Caucasus], which has not been willing to devote the required attention to promoting civilisation in Chechnya and wiping out the fanatical mentality of these peoples.[76]

Zelimkhan's exploits caused a considerable stir in Russia, with commensurately wild speculation on the background and context of the events taking place. All the parties involved had their own reasons for giving credence to or spreading particular rumours. Zelimkhan (or people sympathising with his cause) was well aware of the Russians' fears of another jihad in the Caucasus and in some cases may even have found it expedient to spread reports to this effect. For example, as early as 1908, in a letter sent by him (or in his name) to the then administrator of the Terek *oblast'*, General Aleksandr Stepanovich Mikheev (1853–1914), he informed him of his intention to have himself elected as imam.[77]

In the light of all this, it is scarcely surprising that on the Russian side, following the spectacular attack on the treasury office in Kizlyar, some were ready to see Zelimkhan's action as based not just on pecuniary motives, but also on religious and political grounds as a specific act of revenge. The perceived revenge motive referred to an event that had taken place one year earlier in the town of Gudermes. In March 1909, there had been a bloodbath in Gudermes when a military unit under the command of the ataman of Kizlyar, First Lieutenant Verbitskii, tried to conduct an operation to disarm the local Chechens. When the latter refused to surrender their weapons, the situation escalated and Verbitskii's troops opened fire. The Russian press later reported three deaths and eight wounded, with no mention of their

---

[76] Ibid., 253.
[77] Zelimkhan's letter to Mikheev from 1908 is probably lost; an explicit reference to it can be found in Rukavishnikov's report (see n. 55), contained in ibid., 250.

ethnicity.[78] According to Russian internal reports, however, it is possible that more than thirty were killed in the confrontation, most of whom were presumably Chechens.[79]

It therefore now appeared logical to see Zelimkhan's attack on the treasury office in Kizlyar as an act of revenge for the Chechens killed in Gudermes, particularly given the large number of victims resulting from the attack; and this would not have been the first instance of such motives playing a part in Zelimkhan's actions. Probably in revenge for the seventeen Chechens shot and killed by soldiers of the Shirvanskii regiment on 10 October 1905 at a bazaar in Groznyi, one week later a band of men thought to have been led by Zelimkhan ambushed a passenger train at the Kadi-Iurt station, killing the same number of Russian passengers.[80]

The suggestion frequently advanced at this time that religious motives might also have played a part in the attack on the Kizlyar treasury office again referred back to the incident in Gudermes. The killing of so many people was an event that would obviously also have had an impact on Chechen religious leaders. The then most influential sheikh on the Chechen plain, Bamat Girei Khadzhi Mitaev (*c.* 1838–1914), was reported to have become an advocate for the Chechens and to have sanctioned acts of revenge against Russians. In his younger years, Bamat Girei Khadzhi had been a follower of the well-known sheikh Kunta-Khadzhi. After the death of Kunta-Khadzhi, Bamat Girei Khadzhi became one of the most prominent leaders of the Sufi order of the Qādiriyya. He was revered as a 'holy man', and there were consistent reports of his having a following of hundreds, perhaps even thousands, of *murid*s (in Sufism, the term *murid* refers to an adept of a *tariqa*, an Islamic (Sufi) brotherhood).[81]

---

[78] *Russkoe slovo*, 18 March 1909.
[79] Pastriulin report (see n. 6), contained in Kozlov et al., *Vainakhi i imperskaia vlast'*, 242.
[80] It is unclear whether these were passengers or Russian soldiers, and it is also unclear how many were killed. A Russian newspaper report writes that fifteen passengers were killed and twenty wounded: 'Ubiistvo razboinika', *Russkoe slovo*, 11 September 1908. Rukavishnikov's report (see n. 55) mentions nineteen murdered passengers: Kozlov et al., *Vainakhi i imperskaia vlast'*, 247.
[81] Pastriulin report (see n. 6), contained in Kozlov et al., *Vainakhi i imperskaia vlast'*, 243–4; M. D. Zaurbekov, *Sheikh Ali Mitaev: Patriot, mirotvorets, politik, genii; Etalon spravedlivosti i chesti* (Groznyi: Zori Islama, 2008), 15, 26–7, 38.

The allegation whereby Bamat Girei Khadzhi had actually sent out his *murid*s under the leadership of his eldest son Ali to take revenge for the killed Chechens following the crime in Gudermes, and that Zelimkhan and other *abrek*s had joined ranks with this force, as also reflected in contemporary agency reports and internal Russian reports, is unlikely to be accurate, however. The investigations carried out following the attack on the Kizlyar treasury office were unable to confirm that Ali had been among the attackers. None of the eyewitnesses were able to identify Ali, who was briefly detained after the attack, as a participant.[82]

Verbitskii was undoubtedly detested by the Chechens, and it has to be assumed that animosity on Zelimkhan's part towards the Cossack ataman played its part in the attack. This is corroborated by the letter left behind by Zelimkhan on one of the desks in the treasury office during the attack, in which he directly addressed the Cossack ataman. In the letter, Zelimkhan explicitly condemns the manner in which the ataman has been exercising his official function and accuses him of having deceived the tsar himself with his boastful claims, put about in newspaper articles, that he will soon capture Zelimkhan. Not having found the ataman in Kizlyar, Zelimkhan promises in this letter that he will track him down later.[83]

The view that the attack was an act of revenge for the incident at Gudermes, and had even been carried out with the blessing of a sheikh, was clearly not shared by Colonel I. I. Pastriulin, the head of the gendarmerie of the Tiflis (Tbilisi) Governorate, who had been commissioned by Vorontsov-Dashkov to head the investigation into the Kizlyar attack, and in December 1910 had prepared a detailed report on the background to the attack on the Kizlyar treasury office.[84] Even though the large number of deaths in the attack naturally gave the appearance of a major act of revenge, the conclusion reached by Pastriulin in the report, after interviewing eyewitnesses,

---

[82] *Russkoe slovo*, 25 June 1910.
[83] Count Vorontsov-Dashkov writes in his report to the tsar of 29 April 1910 that on one of the tables in the treasury, a letter was found in the name of Zelimkhan Gushmazukaev, with three of his seals; a summary of this letter is contained in Vorontsov-Dashkov's report: GARF, f. 543, op. 1, d. 462, l. 5.
[84] GARF, f. 543, op. 1, d. 462, l. 1ob; Pastriulin report (see n. 6), contained in Kozlov et al., *Vainakhi i imperskaia vlast'*, 236–46.

was that Zelimkhan had probably not planned in advance to kill so many people. He believed that the bloodbath had in fact resulted from the unexpected resistance encountered by Zelimkhan and his accomplices from the officials and guards inside and in front of the building, to which they had then responded. He argued that this was supported by the fact that in his letter left in the treasury office, Zelimkhan had expressed only his personal suspicion of Verbitskii, without any mention of other motives or any link to Bamat Girei Khadzhi.[85]

It is, however, clear that Zelimkhan and Bamat Girei Khadzhi knew one another, as documented by a photograph from 1904, showing Zelimkhan together with Bamat Girei Khadzhi and his son Ali, in their home village of Avtury.[86] This is hardly surprising, however, since Bamat Girei and Zelimkhan came from the same district of Vedeno, and there would have been almost no prominent figure in the district that the sheikh did not know and almost no event occurring there of which he was not aware. It would, however, have been contrary to Bamat Girei Khadzhi's understanding of his role as a sheikh and to the nature of *muridism* to call for a campaign of revenge, or even to give his consent to a joint campaign between *murid*s and *abrek*s.

Muridism was a term generally applied by the Russian conquerors to denote Shamil's resistance, but persisted also in later times. The prevalent notion was that these brotherhoods were obscure secret societies clandestinely organised by Sufi sheikhs in order to stir up popular anger against Russia. Even after the end of the Russian military conquest, adherents of Sufi brotherhoods were still viewed with suspicion. Recent research shows that while the Sufi brotherhoods were important socially and politically, they did not form the backbone of military resistance against Russia's conquest during the time of Shamil;[87] also, there is no firm evidence that later rebellions such

---

[85] Kozlov et al., *Vainakhi i imperskaia vlast'*, 244.
[86] The photograph is reproduced in Gudaev, *Abrek Zelimkhan*, 495.
[87] See Alexander Knysh, 'Sufism as an Explanatory Paradigm: The Issue of the Motivations of Sufi Movements in Russian and Western Historiography', *Die Welt des Islams* 42(2) (2002): 139–73; Michael Kemper, 'Khālidiyya Networks in Daghestan and the Question of Jihād', *Die Welt des Islams* 42(1) (2002): 41–71; Clemens Sidorko, *Dschihad im Kaukasus: Antikolonialer Widerstand der Dagestaner und Tschetschenen gegen das Zarenreich (18. Jahrhundert bis 1859)* (Wiesbaden: Reichert, 2007), 403–4.

as the one in 1877 were organised by the Sufi brotherhood of the Qādiriyya, as some post-Soviet historians claim.[88]

Holy men such as Bamat Girei Khadzhi were highly regarded by the local population, who turned to them as judges and concilators in order to solve disputes or crimes. In the Sufi tradition, a 'holy man' was one who was able to perform miracles and make prophecies. People turned to them for advice and consolation.[89] In addition, sheikhs always also had a function in terms of power politics, not least due to their often large group of followers, who were totally devoted to them. According to Pastriulin, in Chechnya at that time, there were dozens of sheikhs vying for power and influence. The greater the number of *murid*s a sheikh was able to muster, the richer and more powerful he supposedly became. Whether there were also among their numbers sheikhs who commissioned robbery raids as a source of income, as claimed in Pastriulin's report, is not clear. Pastriulin saw the status of 'holy man' as a function that could be used to elevate the holder's power against other competitors and that was relatively easy to obtain. As he writes in dismissive tones, 'the person merely has to have been to Mecca, and must pray to God and make two or three correct prophecies'.[90] In this context, Pastriulin's report cites various conflicts he says were primarily between sheikhs of long-standing and upstarts.[91]

In his function as a peace-maker, however, Bamat Girei Khadzhi was seeking to arrive at an arrangement with the Russian authorities and definitely not get into conflict with them, as indicated by the fact that, in contrast to some other sheikhs, he never allowed himself to be drawn into a conflict with the authorities, at least up until his deportation in April 1912.[92] When the Russian state authorities exiled him and six other sheikhs to Kaluga, this was for the accusation of having protected Zelimkhan and not having done

---

[88] The best known representative of this problematic thesis is Russian historian Anna Zelkina, who claims that all rebellions after the end of the Great Caucasus War were led by Sufi sheikhs: Anna Zelkina, *In Quest for God and Freedom: The Sufi Response to the Russian Advance in the North Caucasus* (London: Hurst, 2000), 247.
[89] Zaurbekov, *Sheikh Ali Mitaev*, 36.
[90] Kozlov et al., *Vainakhi i imperskaia vlast'*, 243.
[91] Ibid.
[92] GARF, f. 102, op. 146, d. 635-2, l. 92ob.

anything to help the authorities to capture him.[93] It is unlikely that Bamat Girei Khadzhi had actively assisted Zelimkhan in his actions. Quite the contrary: at the end of 1911, he sought to convince the Russian authorities of his good faith and willingness to cooperate, for example, by instructing his second son, Omar, to form a unit consisting of *murid*s in the Vedeno district for the capture of Zelimkhan. According to a newspaper report, up to 1,000 *murid*s were brought together for this purpose.[94]

Yet the accusation that he had done little if anything to assist in the capture of Zelimkhan cannot be dismissed out of hand. As claimed by Russian newspaper reports, the formation of *murid* units for the pursuit of Zelimkhan was merely an exercise in deception, designed to dissuade the Russian authorities from deporting him.[95] Meanwhile, the fact that Zelimkhan and his followers had been able to withdraw towards Vedeno unhindered after the attack on Kizlyar was probably not only attributable to the protection afforded by Chechen elders and locals, but also because Bamat Girei Khadzhi had allowed this to happen given that his influence was predominant specifically in Vedeno. Whereas some Chechen Islamic scholars, probably under direct pressure from the Russian authorities, issued an appeal to the local population at the beginning of 1912 denouncing Zelimkhan's actions as shameful and contrary to sharia, thereby giving permission for him to be killed, Bamat Girei Khadzhi and other influential sheikhs in Chechnya never agreed to put out a statement publicly shaming Zelimkhan.[96] Such a declaration would, however, probably have been essential in order to convince the local population to deny the *abrek* protection.

The ability of Zelimkhan and other *abrek*s to pass unimpeded through Chechen villages did not necessarily reflect positive sentiments towards them, however. This is rather to be understood as a typically Chechen form of passive resistance to the state, whose authority they did not recognise. It

---

[93] Zaurbekov, *Sheikh Ali Mitaev*, 26.
[94] In the newspaper article, he is called 'Umar': 'Presledovanie Zelim-khana', *Russkoe slovo*, 22 December 1911.
[95] Ibid.
[96] The appeal of the sheikhs is contained in 'Neulovimyi Zelim-khan', *Moskovskaia gazeta kopeika*, 1 February 1912. Because the article does not mention any names, it remains unclear which sheikhs specifically called for the killing of Zelimkhan. Thus, it cannot be verified whether sheikhs from Chechnya had ever actually issued such an appeal.

also reflects the fact that North Caucasian culture generally prohibited the betrayal of anyone seeking their protection. Last but not least, protecting the bandits can also be seen as an expression of the very specific fear of provoking a blood feud, since the betrayal of a fugitive could be expected to prompt revenge by the person's family members. The authorities did, however, receive covert assistance, which ultimately played a crucial role in their success in finally tracking down and killing Zelimkhan in September 1913.

Zelimkhan's Death

Not all Chechens saw Zelimkhan as a hero and liberator. For many, he was an irritation, since all too often the punitive policies prompted by Zelimkhan's operations also had negative consequences for those who had played no part in them. So it was that, already in 1908, delegates from a number of Chechen towns in the Vedeno district, following the assassination of the district administrator Galaev, agreed to assist the authorities in the *abrek*'s capture. For this purpose, as well as providing units of horsemen, the various villages in the Vedeno district were required to pay a tax to fund a suitable price on the heads of Zelimkhan and his *abrek*s for anyone who killed the bandits or gave the authorities information on where they were. In the event of any of the relevant individuals being killed in the operation, the money was to go to their family. A total of 16,426 roubles was reportedly provided in this manner, of which 8,000 roubles was allocated solely for the head of Zelimkhan. Because of fears of blood feuds, the authorities were, however, asked to preserve the anonymity of those involved.[97]

There can be little doubt that the Russian administration placed the village elders under pressure to accede to such requests, through the threat of monetary fines, for example. Yet there does not appear to have been major resistance to the plan. On the contrary, the required funds were levied without any great difficulty, and the formation of the required militia units was also completed rapidly. The initial results were not successful, however, as exemplified by the unit formed in July 1908 for the liquidation of Zelimkhan and his followers. Indeed, it was a unit of Chechens from the town of Benoi that in September 1908, in a clash with Zelimkhan's gang, succeeded in killing the *abrek*'s father

---

[97] Kozlov et al., *Vainakhi i imperskaia vlast'*, 247.

Gushmazuko, his brother Zoltamurad and other members of the group. The report that Zelimkhan himself had also perished, which appeared in the *Russkoe slovo* newspaper in its edition of 11 September 1908, proved to be yet another of the false reports appearing in the Russian press on Zelimkhan.[98]

Further evidence that Zelimkhan did not have the undiluted support of the local population can be seen in the fact that the special unit formed for the capture of Zelimkhan following the attack on the treasury office in Kizlyar consisted of Dagestanis, and that the authorities repeatedly relied on Chechen informants in their efforts to capture Zelimkhan.[99] It was no accident that the Dagestanis played a decisive role in Zelimkhan's capture in 1913, because they, too, like the Chechens of Zelimkhan's home village of Kharachoi and of the village of Benoi, had unresolved blood feuds with Zelimkhan. The Dagestanis had suffered losses at his hands in a clash in September 1910 near the Assa ravine, and again one year later during an attack by Zelimkhan on a commission of engineers, in which the entire unit of horsemen escorting the commission, comprising over a dozen Dagestanis under the command of Cavalry Captain Dolidze, was wiped out. Two engineers were also killed, and a third was taken hostage.[100] After this brutal ambush, the Russian administration imposed a fine of 100,000 roubles, to be paid within one month by all mountain *auls* in Chechnya, with the exception of the anti-Zelimkhan town of Benoi.[101]

Along with the blood feud motive, it was the specific prospect of payment of a reward that resulted in Zelimkhan's capture. The telegram received by the police director of the Vladikavkaz unit of the gendarmerie from the Terek *oblast'* on 30 September 1913, announcing that Zelimkhan had been killed, contained a request for payment of 7,000 roubles to Chechens for services ren-

---

[98] 'Ubiistvo razboinika', *Russkoe slovo*, 11 September 1908. Zelimkhan himself was only injured. See also the memoirs of Berdiaev, who claims to have been involved in this action, Berdiaev, *Chechnia i razboinik Zelimkhan*.

[99] The help of 'loyal Chechens' is also emphasised by the head of the Vedeno district, K. N. Karalov, in his report on the death of Zelimkhan, dated 30 September 1913, and contained in Gudaev, *Abrek Zelimkhan*, 424–5.

[100] 'Novoe krovavoe delo Zelim-khana', *Russkoe slovo*, 17 September 1911.

[101] '100-tysiachnyi shtraf', *Russkoe slovo*, 10 November 1911; 'Krovniki Zelim-khana', *Russkoe slovo*, 8 November 1911.

dered. An agreement to this effect had been signed by the group of Chechens, whose names are not revealed, in April of that year.[102] It was significant that the Chechens, probably to forestall the possibility of future acts of revenge, did not kill Zelimkhan themselves, but only provided intelligence about his whereabouts. The operation had been carried out a few days before the date of the telegram by troops of the Dagestani cavalry regiment, under the command of Lieutenant Georgii Alekseevich Kibirov, a Cossack from the Terek *oblast'*.[103] Even though the attack, which took place on 25 September 1913 at 10 pm near the town of Shali, must have taken Zelimkhan by surprise, he managed to wound Kibirov and three of the Dagestanis before dying the following morning from serious wounds. Kibirov reportedly later claimed that there were thirty-two gunshot wounds in Zelimkhan's body (Figure 3.2).[104]

The death of Zelimkhan would later become the subject of numerous legends in Chechen historiography and literature. For example, Chechen historian Avtorkhanov writes in his memoirs that Zelimkhan had already fallen ill in 1911 and had therefore deliberately sought a heroic death in battle with his adversaries. He wanted to die with his enemies in the *gazavat*, in the 'holy war', and, singing prayers, had gone to his death. The many gunshot wounds are said to have been caused by the fact that the soldiers had been firing for a 'long, long' time into the corpse of the *abrek* after his death.[105] This corresponds very much with popular representations of *abrek*s in Chechen ballads (*illi*), where the *abrek* is often portrayed as the 'lonely hero' who remains victorious over his enemies even in death, meeting his fate courageously, and in a beautiful and most dignified way.[106] The fact that the Cossacks and Dagestanis

---

[102] This information can be found in the telegram of 30 September 1913, sent by the head of the Vladikavkaz gendarmerie to the director of the police department reporting on the liquidation of Zelimkhan. The telegram is published in Kozlov et al., *Vainakhi i imperskaia vlast'*, 254. See also the report on the liquidation of Zelimkhan prepared by the head of the Terek *oblast'*, 10–18 October 1913, contained in Gudaev, *Abrek Zelimkhan*, 426–33, at 433.

[103] Bagration, *Podvig Terskago Kazaka*, 3–4. In other sources, Kibirov is referred to as an ethnic Ossetian, Gudaev, *Abrek Zelimkhan*, 427.

[104] Bagration, *Podvig Terskago Kazaka*, 42.

[105] Avtorkhanov, *Memuary*, 68–9.

[106] Rebecca Gould, 'The Lonely Hero and Chechen Modernity: Interpreting the Story of Gekha the Abrek', *Journal of Folklore Research* 51(2) (2014), 199–222.

Figure 3.2 Photograph on the front page of the Russian weekly magazine *Iskry*, No. 40, 13 October 1913. The picture shows the detachment of mountaineers responsible for the capture and killing of Zelimkhan, as well as the family of Zelimkhan. Standing behind the *abrek*'s murdered body are (1) the daughter of Zelimkhan; (2) his daughter-in-law; (3) his son; and (4) the commander of the unit. Available at: http://history-foto.livejournal.com/361128.html#cutid1, last accessed 16 July 2020.

hunting down Zelimkhan fired dozens of bullets into the *abrek*'s body may be seen as an indication that they indeed feared him even when he was dead.

Zelimkhan, like other famous *abrek*s of his time, rose to legendary status and became the topics of songs and stories already during their lifetime. Yet contrary to what one could expect from reading (later) interpretations, which put the phenomenon of *abrechestvo* very much in the context of an anti-colonial struggle, depicting the *abrek* as a fighter for justice and freedom from state oppression, large parts of the indigenous population seem not to have held Zelimkhan in high esteem. In fact, from reading contemporary reports, it becomes quite clear that the *abrek*'s death did not trigger a large outpouring of grief among the local population. According to Kibirov's account, as recorded by Count Bagration in his publication of 1914, the mood among the Chechens in the town of Shali, where Zelimkhan's corpse was taken, was one of celebration. Inhabitants of Zelimkhan's home village of Kharachoi who travelled to Shali together with the administrator of the Vedeno district, First Lieutenant K. N. Karalov, to identify the body, are reported to have been happy that he had been killed. One of those present even wanted to decapitate the body as revenge for the death of his father, which he blamed on Zelimkhan. Lieutenant Kibirov is reported to have been acclaimed as a hero by the crowd gathered for the occasion. As a sign of gratitude for his services, Karalov is reported to have presented Kibirov on behalf of the Chechens with the sword that had once belonged to Shamil, and had been kept by one of his former commanders, the Chechen Talkhikov.[107] When the sword was later delivered to the hospital in Vladikavkaz, where Kibirov was recuperating, it is reported to have been accompanied by a testimony of gratitude bearing 612 signatures of selected representatives from various Chechen *auls*.[108]

Many were clearly relieved that Zelimkhan had been liquidated. The reactions of delight at the news and the gratitude expressed to Kibirov as described by Bagration appear to have been sincere, and definitely not just propaganda on the Russians' part. But Bagration's claim that with this achievement, the Russian state, after having been 'virtually paralysed' for so long by the persistently elusive figure of Zelimkhan, was now able to

---

[107] Bagration, *Podvig Terskago Kazaka*, 47.
[108] Ibid., 48.

significantly boost its authority and credibility, seems exaggerated.[109] The Russian imperial state had shown itself to be incapable of controlling the phenomenon of *abrechestvo*, and through the clumsy operations it carried out against the local population had discredited itself to such an extent that even this late success against Zelimkhan could not restore its tarnished image.

Neither Social Bandit, Freedom Fighter nor Holy Man

The goal of this chapter was to get a better understanding of Caucasian banditry as a historical phenomenon. Investigating the case of Zelimkhan and *abrechestvo* on the basis of contemporary accounts – including Russian newspaper articles, publications from the time and secret police reports – it becomes evident that the meanings attached to *abrek*s and *abrechestvo* varied and very much depended on the type of source and the specific perspective of the observers. Without aspiring to resolve these ambiguities, embedding the figure of Zelimkhan into a historical context has allowed the deconstruction of some of the myths surrounding this *abrek*, and to gain insight into the complex social realities of the Chechen and Ingush inhabited parts of the North Caucasus in the early twentieth century – clearly one of the most difficult to control areas from the perspective of the Russian imperial state.

For one thing, the idea that Zelimkhan and his gang were 'noble bandits' can be dismissed. The Zelimkhan phenomenon cannot be regarded either as an expression of social protest or the continuation of an 'anti-colonial liberation struggle' against Russia. Hobsbawm's notion of Zelimkhan as some kind of modern 'Robin Hood' is as far away from reality as the Bolshevik's attempts to portray this figure as being in line with Shamil or other anti-colonial resistance fighters. It is true that Zelimkhan and other *abrek*s mostly targeted representatives of the state or people seen as being associated with this state, but they did not always kill for 'apparently righteous reasons', as suggested also by more recent Western scholarship;[110] Zelimkhan and his companions were driven mainly by the quest for booty, and they also murdered people arbitrarily, as emerges from the report on the attack in Kizlyar. It was often not clear whether Zelimkhan himself was behind such operations, or if they

---

[109] Ibid.
[110] Mühlfried, 'Don't Trust, Don't Fear, Don't Ask', 183.

were carried out by young men opportunistically forming gangs for robbery raids, and perhaps also to prove their courage and manhood, which was also part of long-standing North Caucasian traditions. Therefore, the Zelimkhan phenomenon has to be viewed first and foremost as part of a specific 'culture of violence', widespread among the mountain peoples of the North Caucasus, in which blood feuds and revenge were prominent motives.[111]

Also, the theme of 'rebellion' does not really capture the essence of the phenomenon of *abrechestvo* at the time, as it would be misleading to see Zelimkhan's actions as being motivated by a desire to organise an anti-Russian uprising. The North Caucasus had a long history of uprisings against Russian imperial rule, and would see several more uprisings in the early Soviet period; but none of these were led by *abrek*s or had anything to do with *abrechestvo* (which did not exclude that individual *abrek*s would take part in such uprisings). Among the most significant rebellions during early Soviet times were the large-scale uprising in the mountains of Chechnya and Dagestan led by imam Gotskinskii in 1920/21, and the massive revolts during collectivisation in the late 1920s and early 1930s.[112] These rebellions resembled other armed uprisings in non-Russian populated parts of the Soviet Union, namely, the Basmachi armed movement in Central Asia, which was put down by the Red Army in the early 1920s.[113]

Zelimkhan should not to be seen as the representative of 'the people' in opposition to a hostile 'state' either. This is already indicated by the circumstances that prompted Zelimkhan to become an *abrek*. In fact, in the initial phase, the state does not appear in the role of a remote alien power. Apart from Zelimkhan's main adversaries – which comprised those Chechens with whom he had an ongoing blood feud – the main actors representing the state were local Cossack officers of the Terek *oblast'*, later also joined by units made up by neighbouring Dagestanis. In this sense, the state was to some extent part of an intra-societal struggle. Zelimkhan's actions were directed against the members

---

[111] Bobrovnikov, 'Abreki i gosudarstvo', 19.
[112] On the Gotskinskii rebellion and the upheavals during collectivisation: Perović, *From Conquest to Deportation*, 152–4, 227–54.
[113] On the Basmachi movement, see H. B. Paksoy, 'Basmachi Movement from Within: Account of Zeki Velidi Togan', *Nationalities Papers* 23(2) (1995): 373–99.

of the Chechen family on the opposing side, and then specifically at those representatives of the local state administration who involved themselves in this societal conflict on the side of Zelimkhan's blood enemies. Only when the scope of the dispute widened did this intra-societal conflict develop into a larger confrontation, with negative consequences for wider sections of the indigenous Chechen and Ingush populations. It was the state's harsh punitive measures which brought back memories from a not-so-distant past of Russian colonial conquest and Cossack oppression. Zelimkhan thus found himself at the centre of a conflict that had deep historical roots, and, consequently, it was easy for social-democrats and the later Bolsheviks to interpret his actions in the context of a continuous struggle of 'the people' against an oppressive tsarist regime.

Zelimkhan's *abrechestvo* is also not to be seen as a further development of *muridism* in the sense of a continuation of resistance to Russian rule based on networks and ideas of the Chechen Sufi brotherhood. The yearning of broad sections of the population for a new imam, as manifested in connection with the elevated status given to Zelimkhan, was not necessarily an expression of affinity for Zelimkhan as an individual or a wish to separate from Russia. Rather, this sort of emotion resulted from a complex of the fears and concerns of a population that longed for a better life and the restoration of law and order – a situation that they perceived as having existed sometime in the past, before the arrival of the Russians. Accordingly, it is not surprising that, in the North Caucasus, the revolution of 1917 was not driven primarily by demands for national independence, but by the individual interests of specific peoples and social groups, who, from a political perspective, had never formed a unity.

While *abrechestvo* was an essentially Caucasian social institution that existed independently from empire, the meanings attached to this phenomenon changed after the Russian military conquest. 'Archaic' practices like blood feuds, raiding and pillaging could ultimately be seen as old Caucasian traditions, but these traditions came into increasing conflict with a modernising state trying to enforce imperial legal norms and practices. Against the background of often deep-seated prejudice and mistrust, Russian officials tended to interpret such acts of violence as being an expression of general dissatisfaction with Russian rule, and feared the potential for rebellion and conspiracy with outside enemies. In this context of perceived danger and increased Russian military oppression, the actions of a figure like Zelimkhan, even though he was neither a 'noble bandit' nor a patriotic freedom-fighter, were therefore automatically viewed with great suspicion. The harsh and at times disproportionate punitive measures undertaken by the Russian state, which for a long time failed to put an end to the activities of Zelimkhan and other *abrek*s, produced headlines and made the Caucasian phenomenon of *abrechestvo* a topic of controversial political debate on the essence of imperial power and state–society relation. In the light of the scarcity of sources pertaining directly to Zelimkhan, it is difficult to arrive at a definite conclusion as to how Zelimkhan himself was aware of the different meanings ascribed to him. However, we can say with some certainty that the dominant (Soviet) interpretations transformed him in ways that did not correspond to the actual role and place of *abrek*s in Chechen and North Caucasian society; also, such interpretations were only partly congruent with perceptions that existed among the native population at the time.

Chechens and other indigenous peoples were the victims of Russia's brutal policies, but, at the same time, they were their own worst enemy in dealing with internal issues. Disputes over land and honour, often degenerating into highly complex blood feuds, paint a picture of a society that was suffering from its own traditions. Clearly, this was also a strife-ridden society, still trying to find a way forward after the wars and uprisings of the nineteenth century. Around the turn of the century, a small proportion of this society chose a path of closer integration in the Russian-defined environment of cities such as Vladikavkaz and Groznyi. In these cities, a thin layer of a North Caucasian intelligentsia began to emerge which included teachers, legal practitioners, businesspeople and officers. Wealthy Chechen families such as the Chermoevs or the Kurumovs whom the Russian imperial state had already in the mid-nineteenth allocated large estates and titles in return for their loyalty and military services in the Caucasian wars, formed an increasingly powerful business elite with strong links to the booming oil industry around Groznyi. However, most of the population remained caught in the environment of their *aul*s, where they lived according to their traditional customs and mores. Their identity was focused on the village and the village community, or individual figures such as the sheikhs mentioned above. The divide, therefore, was increasingly not between Russians and Chechens, but between the developing cities and industries and the vast countryside. For the people living in the more remote areas, the tsar and St Petersburg were a very long way off.

4

Racketeers in Politics: Theoretical Reflections on Strong-man Performances in Late Qajar Iran

Olmo Gölz

During the Constitutional Revolution in Iran between 1906 and 1911, the horse dealer Sattar Khan[1] (1868–1914) and the bricklayer Baqer Khan[2] (1861–1916) from Tabriz became, in all likelihood, the most famous heroes of their country. When the leading revolutionary intellectuals had been executed or were forced into hiding or to flee Tehran and go into exile, the opposition to Mohammad Ali Shah's (1872–1925) dictatorship entrenched itself in Tabriz. In this phase, Sattar Khan and Baqer Khan were crucial in organising the Tabriz resistance, so that eventually heterogeneous groups of revolutionaries could march towards Tehran, with the result that the shah was forced to abdicate in July 1909. To this day, the two men from humble backgrounds are not only honoured as central actors of the Constitutional Revolution, but are even revered as national heroes. It is attributed to their resistance that the cause of the constitutionalist faction did not die in darkness but was kept alive and that the revolution was finally successful. Insofar as they are heroes and representatives of a prominent interpretation of the

---

[1] Anja Pistor-Hatam, 'Sattār Khan', *Encyclopaedia Iranica* (online), accessed 5 November 2019, available at: http://www.iranicaonline.org/articles/sattar-khan-one-of-the-most-popular-heroes-from-tabriz-who-defended-the-town-during-the-lesser-autocracy-in-1908-09.

[2] Abbas Amanat, 'Bāqer Khan Sālār-e Mellī', *Encyclopaedia Iranica* (online), accessed 5 November 2019, available at: http://www.iranicaonline.org/articles/baqer-khan-salar-melli.

revolution, Satter Khan and Baqer Khan are figures of collective memories that stand for a certain perspective on the historical processes themselves, in which the 'simple man' is held responsible for political action.

This chapter will focus on the heroic representations of the two revolutionary actors and will pay special attention to the discursive effects of their heroisation. I argue that in modern Iran they are presented as ideal types who combine three important messages: first, by dint of the constant references to their traditional background – hence, their *luti* status, as will be discussed – the Constitutional Revolution is discursively 'Iranised' and detached from regional and global dynamics and influences. Second, through their heroised example, political–patriotic activity was integrated as a central component into notions of masculinity of the time and in the following decades. This had distinct consequences for the history of twentieth-century Iran, as the analysis of some of Sattar Khan and Baqer Khan's epigones will show. However, and this is the third message, there is a dialectical aspect to it as well: in presenting Sattar Khan and Baqer Khan, a horse dealer and a bricklayer, as the saviours of the *mashruteh* (Constitution), the 'simple man's' obligation to contribute to national politics is valorised – an obviously ambivalent ramification, which sometimes demands explicitly *questioning* the state. The historical example of the role of the *lutis* in the 1953 coup d'état illustrate this effect.[3]

Basically, the success story of the two revolutionary leaders forged a masculinity ethos that put strong emphasis on political action and 'tough-guy' performances at the same time. In effect, their example has had a deep impact on the history of twentieth-century Iran not only because it triggered actions of some prominent epigones, but also because their example has led to a reinterpretation of the *luti* ethos of masculinity itself – a crucial term for the understanding of Iranian history that will be clarified in this chapter. By the same token, even during the Iranian revolutionary movement in the end of the 1970s in Iran, the models of the 'simple men' Sattar Khan and Baqer

---

[3] See also Olmo Gölz, 'The Dangerous Classes and the 1953 Coup in Iran: On the Decline of "lutigari" Masculinities', in Stephanie Cronin (ed.), *Crime, Poverty and Survival in the Middle East and North Africa: The 'Dangerous Classes' since 1800* (London: I. B. Tauris, 2019), 177–90.

Khan were reaffirmed,[4] both in Islamist as well as in leftist discourses, when they were reinvented as idealised *mostazzafin* ('the oppressed' in Islamist parlance) who took matters in their own hands or proletarian leaders of the urban poor, respectively.[5]

In order to discuss the emergence of new configurations of masculinity and their impact on Iranian society, I will first discuss the ambiguous perceptions of the two national heroes against the backdrop of the *luti* ethos in twentieth-century Iran. Here, I shall draw on the racket theory of Max Horkheimer and Theodor W. Adorno for the generalised theoretical classification of an allegedly specifically Iranian phenomenon. Then, I will provide a brief history of the Constitutional Revolution with a special focus on the Tabriz resistance and the significance of the two racketeers Sattar Khan and Baqer Khan. In conclusion, the sociological and historical significance of the heroic pre-figurations of the Constitutional Revolution will be evaluated.

Ambiguous Heroes in Collective Memory

The story of Satter Khan and Baqer Khan during the phase of the Constitutional Revolution was not at all undisputed. Rather, their status dynamically developed towards the heroic posture that both men could take up in Iranian collective memory. Accordingly, in his 1914 book *The Orient Express*, the Irish journalist William Arthur Moore (1880–1962), who was an eyewitness (and actually an occasional combatant) of the Constitutional Revolution in Qajar Iran, remembered the siege of Tabriz by royalist forces in early 1909 as 'certainly one of the oddest' in history and it 'is fortunate that there is always laughter in Persia, for if the laughter stopped there would be room for tears'.[6] With an Orientalist undertone, he claims it to be beyond 'doubt that the townsmen made a better show than their besiegers', but concludes nevertheless that the battle was 'essentially a contest between two sets of inef-

---

[4] Stephanie Cronin, 'Noble Robbers, Avengers and Entrepreneurs: Eric Hobsbawm and Banditry in Iran, the Middle East and North Africa', in Stephanie Cronin (ed.), *Crime, Poverty and Survival in the Middle East and North Africa: The 'Dangerous Classes' since 1800* (London: I. B. Tauris, 2019), 102.

[5] Reza M. Afshari, 'The Historians of the Constitutional Movement and the Making of the Iranian Populist Tradition', *International Journal of Middle East Studies* 25(3) (1993): 481.

[6] Arthur Moore, *The Orient Express* (London: Constable, 1914), 2.

ficients and incapables, each of which feared the other'.[7] Thus, in his memoirs, Moore presents the Tabriz resistance as a ridiculous episode, marked by coincidences and contingencies, wherein Iranian actors like Sattar Khan and Baqer Khan are at best given the role of courageous clowns. According to the Irish journalist, both men's reputations among the inhabitants of Tabriz had suffered immensely by end of March 1909, when 'the town was in the last extremity of starvation'.[8] He reports in the last days before the Russians set Tabriz free that especially the women of the town 'were openly rioting in the streets, and spat when they uttered the names of Sattar Khan, Bakir Khan, the Anjoman, and the *Meshruteh* (Constitution)'.[9]

However, this pejorative evaluation of Sattar Khan and Baqer Khan radically contradicts their appreciation beyond Tabriz and throughout Iran, where they were celebrated as national heroes, appeared on numerous images and photographs,[10] and were cheerfully greeted by the people and local nobility alike as they marched towards Teheran in summer 1909.[11] Furthermore, it also contradicts their status in the dominant Iranian historiography of the Constitutional Revolution, where both men are still presented as unquestionable national heroes and icons of the Tabriz resistance. In Iranian collective memory, these men are the key actors that kept the constitutionalist cause breathing. Accordingly, nowadays middle-school pupils in Iran learn from their textbooks that Sattar Khan and Baqer Khan were the 'brave defenders of Tabriz' against the 'huge army of Mohammad Ali Shah during the period of the *estebdad-e saghir* [lesser despotism]'.[12] Anja Pistor-Hatam concludes that

---

[7] Ibid., 4.
[8] Ibid., 14.
[9] Ibid., 15.
[10] Elahe Helbig, 'From Narrating History to Constructing Memory: The Role of Photography in the Iranian Constitutional Revolution', in Ali Ansari (ed.), *Iran's Constitutional Revolution of 1906 and Narratives of the Enlightenment* (London: Gingko Library, 2016) 64–5
[11] Anja Pistor-Hatam, 'The Iranian Constitutional Revolution as *lieu(x) de mémoire*: Sattar Khan', in Houchang E. Chehabi and Vanessa Martin (eds), *Iran's Constitutional Revolution: Popular Politics, Cultural Transformations and Transnational Connections* (London: I. B. Tauris, 2010), 38–9.
[12] Vezarat-e amuzesh va parvaresh, *Tarikh-e mo'aser-e Iran (kolli-ye reshtehā): Sal-e sevvom-e amuzesh-e mutawasseṭe* (Tehran: Sherkat-e Chap va Nashr-e Ketabha-ye Darsi-ye Iran, 1390 [2011]), 65.

especially the name of Sattar Khan suggested itself immediately when thinking of the Constitutional Revolution, for he even became the embodiment of the revolutionary phase after the coup d'état of 1908.[13]

This observation is remarkable not only in juxtaposition to his and his comrade-in-arms' clownish depiction by the eyewitness Arthur Moore, but also when taking the personal history of the two revolutionaries into account. It is sufficient to say that in the run-up to the Constitutional Revolution, Sattar Khan and Baqer Khan had been strong-men of late Qajar Iran – with no political involvement whatsoever. They both had a record of loutishness, banditry and criminal behaviour, as well as a reputation for being local strong-men in northern Iran prior to the revolution. This means that they were already well-known representatives of the *luti* ethos of masculinity, which could be found among the urban lower classes and leaders of Tabriz rackets. The term 'racket' is to be understood here as a theoretical term that refers to the racket theory of the Frankfurt school,[14] which determines the perspective of this chapter. Against the background of the racket theory and its ideas on the social–theoretical significance of clique formation and racketeering, which will be discussed below, Satter Khan and Baqer Khan can be described as dubious racketeers in the run-up to the revolution.[15]

However, their status changed during and after the revolution when they became the figureheads of the constitutionalist cause. In collective memory,

---

[13] Pistor-Hatam, 'The Iranian Constitutional Revolution as *lieu(x) de mémoire*: Sattar Khan', 35: 'His is one of the names, his is one of the faces, his posture with his comrades and their rifles is one of the images that come to mind most easily. Sattar Khan has impressed himself on the minds of all those who, in one way or another, are connected with the Constitutional Revolution. One might even say that he gives a face to that particular event, that Sattar Khan embodies the revolution, at least after the coup d'état of 1908.'

[14] See Max Horkheimer, 'Die Rackets und der Geist [1943]', in Gunzelin Schmid Noerr (ed.), *Gesammelte Schriften: Band 12: Nachgelassene Schriften 1931–1949* (Frankfurt am Main: Fischer, 1985); Max Horkheimer, 'Zur Soziologie der Klassenverhältnisse [1943]', in Gunzelin Schmid Noerr (ed.), *Gesammelte Schriften: Band 12: Nachgelassene Schriften 1931–1949* (Frankfurt am Main: Fischer, 1985); Theodor W. Adorno, 'Reflexionenen zur Klassentheorie [1942]', in *Gesellschaftstheorie und Kulturkritik* (Frankfurt am Main: Suhrkamp, 1975).

[15] For the application of the terms 'rackets' and 'racketeers' to the Iranian context (here in reference to the *luti*-leaders Tayyeb Hajj Rezai and Shaban Jafari), see Gölz, 'The Dangerous Classes and the 1953 Coup in Iran', 187–9.

the modes of remembrance of the Constitutional Revolution of 1906–1911 in contemporary Iran are bound, on the one hand, to the terminology and institutions of the revolutionary period, which became public symbols for Iran's modern history. These symbols are paradigmatically represented by terms like *mashrutheh* (constitution),[16] *demokrasi* (democracy) or *vatan* (homeland),[17] and institutions like the parliament (*majles*), specific forms of political secret societies (*anjomans*) or the 'house of justice' (*edalat khaneh*), whose establishment became one of the main demands of the constitutionalists. On the other hand, the stories of individual actors and revolutionaries are of tremendous importance for discourses on the character of the revolution itself. These actors included secular intellectuals, tribesmen, members of the urban poor, clerics and armed transnational combatants. In any case, as individualised representatives for the different interpretations of the revolutionary period, the levels of appreciation for the respective actors tells us much about the discourses on the essence of Iranian modernity.[18] They function as representatives for the different strata of society engaged in the constitutionalist cause and compete with each other on the imaginative level, so that the question of who is remembered by whom becomes a matter of political self-positioning in the field of power. In this regard, Reza Afshari identified three tendencies – *populist*, *elitist* and *traditionalist* – among historians of the constitutional movement that correspond to different phases of national historiography and are marked by a fixation on the reconstructed biographies of a certain set of heroic figures that contributed to the invention of different traditions.[19]

In effect, they are not only called heroes for no reason, rather these figures have to be regarded as heroes in an analytical sense as well. In the modes of

---

[16] On the significance of the word *mashruteh* for the early historiography of the Constitutional Revolution, see Joanna de Groot, 'Whose Revolution? Stakeholders and Stories of the "Constitutional Movement" in Iran, 1905–11', in Houchang E. Chehabi and Vanessa Martin (eds), *Iran's Constitutional Revolution: Popular Politics, Cultural Transformations and Transnational Connections* (London: I. B. Tauris, 2010), 17.

[17] Arshin Adib-Moghaddam, 'What is Radicalism? Power and Resitance in Iran', *Middle East Critique* 21(3) (2012): 275

[18] See on the political importance of the historiography of the Constitutional Revolution, Afshari, 'The Historians of the Constitutional Movement and the Making of the Iranian Populist Tradition', 477.

[19] Ibid., 479

a society's boundary construction the stories of heroes symbolise boundaries that structure societies and define their cosmology.[20] Thus, through processes of heroisation and de-heroisation discourses on Sattar Khan and Baqer Kahn were and are used to construct a national identity – or vice versa to discredit an assumed collective identity. Therefore, the answer to the question of what kind of identity would that be that is represented through heroic figures becomes of great importance. In the case of the protagonists discussed here: is it one of backwardness and ludicrousness, as depicted by Arthur Moore, or one of a confident nation standing their ground against imperialism and tyranny? The example of the usage of references to the two 'larger-than-life heroes' showcases that in collective memory figures of boundary work are perpetually under contention, so that, on the one hand, their positions are constantly renegotiated and rearranged,[21] while, on the other hand, the place and posture of these figures in collective memory tells us a lot about the self-perception of a society – and just as much about the perception of the corresponding community by outsiders like Moore.

The *Luti* Phenomenon and the Racket Theory

Against the backdrop of the significance of Sattar Khan and Baqer Khan both for the history of the Constitutional Revolution and for the place of this revolution in collective memory due to their heroisation in Iranian historiography, a word must be said on the socio-economic origins of the two revolutionaries. As has been mentioned, both had rather humble backgrounds. Baqer Khan was born in Tabriz in 1879 and was a bricklayer by profession before he could establish himself as the leading racketeer of the *lutis* in Khiyaban, one of the city's largest quarters located in the eastern part of town.[22] While Baqer Khan was probably just the most efficient bully of his quarter,[23] Sattar Khan, on the other hand, had a more criminal background. Born in the late 1860s

---

[20] Olmo Gölz, 'The Imaginary Field of the Heroic: On the Contention between Heroes, Martyrs, Victims and Villains in Collective Memory' *helden.heroes.héros*, SI 'Analyzing Processes of Heroization: Theories, Methods, Histories' 5 (2019): 27.

[21] Cf. ibid.

[22] Amanat, 'Bāqer Khan Sālār-e Melli'; for a historical map of Tabriz, see Edward G. Brown, *The Persian Revolution of 1905–1909* (London: Cambridge University Press, 1910), 248ff.

[23] Cf. ibid., 442

in Qaradagh, his family moved to Tabriz after his older brother was executed as a highway robber – and Sattar Khan came into conflict with the law very early, too.[24] Accordingly, before the revolution he had already walked through a dazzling criminal career that included mercenary services as well as periods of imprisonment or life as a mugger and bandit in different regions of Iran.[25] In 1906, he returned to Tabriz, joined the local horse dealers and became the leading *luti* of his quarter, Amirkhiz. In the spring of 1907, Baqer Khan and Sattar Khan signed up for the constitutionalist police force of Tabriz, and Sattar Khan additionally joined the constitutionalist secret society of his quarter (*anjoman-e haqiqat*, lit. 'The Truth Association'), later the centre of his political and military activity.[26]

In reference to the life stories of these two constitutionalist celebrities, it seems impossible to ignore the specifically Iranian phenomenon of the *luti*. However, despite the significance of the term for the most emblematic moments in twentieth-century Iran, there is no consensus about all the meanings, layers and connotations of the concept itself. For example, in his evaluation of the *luti* phenomenon in Qajar Iran, Willem Floor focuses on the 'group of acrobats, buffoons and artists', on the one hand, and 'the group of hooligans', on the other hand.[27] Thus, in order to define a set of Weberian ideal type *lutis*, one would have to consider entertainers, bandits, ruffians, knife-wielders and the like, with the common denominator being that the concept of the *luti* refers first and foremost to male members of the lower strata of society.[28] The most convincing synopsis regarding a typological frame of the concept so far has been proposed by Vanessa Martin, who – again with reference to Qajar Iran – defines it as follows:

> The name *lūṭī* was given to people in a variety of occupations in urban centres for many centuries in Iran. It could indicate their cultural values,

---

[24] Pistor-Hatam, 'The Iranian Constitutional Revolution as *lieu(x) de mémoire*: Sattar Khan', 36.
[25] Pistor-Hatam, 'Sattār Khan'; Pistor-Hatam, 'The Iranian Constitutional Revolution as *lieu(x) de mémoire*: Sattar Khan', 37.
[26] Ibid.
[27] Willem M. Floor, 'The *lūṭīs*: A Social Phenomenon in Qājār Persia: A Reappraisal', *Die Welt des Islams* 13(1/2) (1971): 103.
[28] Gölz, 'The Dangerous Classes and the 1953 Coup in Iran', 179.

their economic standing, usually among the poorer social groups, and their political role. In a word, *lūṭīs* could be the socially conscious leaders of the poor, whose heroic values inspired them, and they could be every sort of thug, rogue and thief.[29]

By the same token, the ambiguity of the term not only pertains to the life stories of individuals and their social roles, but rather expands to include configurations of masculinity, for the term must be seen as a relatively flexible concept that floats between the positive and the negative poles of tough manliness.[30] Here, it stands in relation to positively connoted terms like *javanmardi* (i.e., young-manliness)[31] or *pahlevani* (i.e., heroism), as well as negatively connoted terms like *jaheli* (i.e., ignorant) or *gardan koloft* (i.e., unabashed). However, the lowest common denominator of all definitions lies in the assertion that the *luti* represents a social configuration of the *urban poor* deeply ingrained in Iranian traditions. Thus, in contrast to Hobsbawm's rural *social bandit*, which has often been used to frame the term, the *luti* is associated precisely with the urban centres of Iran. Therefore, we have to speak of the *luti* as a man perceived by the community to be living his life according to a traditional configuration of masculinity that champions the enforcement of an alternative order on the local level in an urban environment.[32] Accordingly, the term *lutigari* defines this specific configuration of masculinity that idealises strength, honour, action, and the capability to protect areas, families or disciples – in short, being able to stand one's ground.

Hence, the concept of the *luti* is rich in ambiguities and the perception of a *luti* depends on one's viewpoint: the term can both glorify and condemn. In

---

[29] Vanessa Martin, 'The *Lutis* – The Turbulent Urban Poor', in *The Qajar Pact: Bargaining, Protest and the State in Nineteenth-Century Persia* (London: I. B. Tauris, 2005), 113.

[30] Cf. M. C. Bateson et al., 'Ṣafā-yi Bāṭin: A Study of the Interrelations of a Set of Iranian Ideal Character Types', in Leon C. Brown and Norman Itzkowitz (eds), *Psychological Dimensions of Near Eastern Studies* (Princeton, NJ: Darwin Press, 1977), 266.

[31] See on the ambiguity of the term *javanmardi* itself: Lloyd Ridgeon, 'The Felon, the Faithful and the Fighter: The Protean Face of the Chivalric Man (Javanmard) in the Medieval Persianate and Modern Iranian Worlds', in Lloyd Ridgeon, ed., *Javanmardi: The Ethics and Practice of Persianate Perfection* (Berkeley, CA: Ginkgo Press, 2018), 1-27.

[32] Cf. Willem M. Floor, 'The Political Role of the *Lutis* in Iran', in Michael E. Bonine and Nikki R. Keddie (eds), *Modern Iran: The Dialectics of Continuity and Change* (Albany, NY: State University of New York Press, 1981), 88.

turn, this viewpoint is not to be detached from historical dynamics since positively or negatively perceived protagonists might function as triggers for the discursive perception of the *luti*. This corresponds with the theoretical reflections on the heroic, which point out that individual figures must be regarded as ambiguous tilting figures, whose assessment is ultimately determined by the viewer's standpoint. At the same time, statements about the assessment of representatives of a certain historical episode are also statements about the valuation of this particular episode itself. I have argued elsewhere that the role of prominent *luti* figures in the widely negatively perceived processes of the 1953 coup in Iran have led to a pejorative perception of the concept as a whole,[33] whereas I argue in this chapter that for the Constitutional Revolution it was the other way around: due to the active part of the *lutis* in this mostly positively perceived historical process, the concept itself has been valorised in its aftermath.

However, it is (among other things) due to this ambiguity that we have a hard time framing the *luti* phenomenon theoretically, and accordingly might fall into the traps of overemphasising Iranian cultural exceptionalism and underestimating the historical dynamics of Iran's global and regional entanglements. In this regard, Homa Katouzian goes as far as to state that 'historically, Iran has been an arbitrary state and society where there has been no state, social class, law, politics, and so on, as they have been observed in European history and explained and analysed by European theorists'.[34] Here, I beg to differ. I argue, on the contrary, that the Iranian case in general and the *luti* phenomenon in particular is paradigmatically suited to test and verify the racket theory of Max Horkheimer and Theodor W. Adorno, which formed the intellectual basis of the two authors' seminal *Dialectic of Enlightenment*[35] and thus the key text of critical theory.

The starting point of my application of the racket theory to the Iranian case is built upon the observation that the *lutis* defy 'straightforward class

---

[33] Gölz, 'The Dangerous Classes and the 1953 Coup in Iran', 179.
[34] Homa Katouzian, 'Arbitrary Rule: A Comparative Theory of State, Politics and Society in Iran', *British Journal of Middle Eastern Studies* 24(1) (1997): 53.
[35] Max Horkheimer and Theodor W. Adorno, *Dialektik der Aufklärung: Philosophische Fragmente*, 21st edn (Frankfurt am Main: Fischer Taschenbuch Verlag, 2013).

analysis since their connections with a powerful and "respectable" urban notable often took precedence over solidarity with members of the same group within a given city'.[36] In essence, this is, of course, the same observation that leads Katouzian to assume the impossibility of transferring generalised concepts like social class onto the Iranian case. However, this observation might also lead in the opposite direction: Horkheimer and Adorno have already criticised the classical Marxian class theory for not taking the interests of the individual into account, for belonging to the same class does not by any means translate into equality of interest and action.[37] Considering Sattar Khan and Baqer Khan's position prior to the siege of Tabriz might help to exemplify this proposition: first, they themselves and their disciples form the lower classes, their allies among the clergy as well as their allies among the local nobles clearly had mutual interests that reached far beyond those of the classes to which each of the respective protagonists belonged. In effect, it was these common interests that translated into action and not any given class consciousness. Second, although both actors came from the lower classes and for sure never managed to fully cross the invisible boundaries of their class, they probably were the most powerful men in Tabriz for some years – or as Arthur Moore puts it, 'the de facto governors' of the town 'were the two generalissimos'.[38]

Thus, it is obviously not convincing to categorise these men as merely members of the *lumpenproletariat* in the classical Marxian sense – a concept from which the *luti* is inseparable[39] – since they were not thrown 'hither and thither',[40] but were rather influential members of society. At this point, I suggest bringing the racket theory into play.[41] By reference to the example

---

[36] Farzin Vejdani, 'Urban Violence and Space: *Lutis*, Seminarians, and Sayyids in Late Qajar Iran', *Journal of Social History* 52(4) (2019): 1186.
[37] Adorno, 'Reflexionenen zur Klassentheorie [1942]', 11.
[38] Moore, *The Orient Express*, 22.
[39] See my thorough discussion on the connection of the Marxian concept of the *lumpenproletariat* and the *lutis* in Gölz, 'The Dangerous Classes and the 1953 Coup in Iran'.
[40] Karl Marx, *The Eighteenth Brumaire of Louis Bonaparte*, with the assistance of Alek Blain and Mark Harris (Marx/Engels Internet Archive, 2010), first published: 1st issue of *Die Revolution*, 1852, New York, available at: https://www.marxists.org/archive/marx/works/download/pdf/18th-Brumaire.pdf, 38
[41] I have already proposed racket theory as a theoretical corrective in order to deal with the *luti*

of Nazi Germany, the exiled members of the *Institut für Sozialforschung* developed a theory of domination based on protection. The core of this theoretical perspective lies in the idea that the racket is the basic principle of domination.[42] Horkheimer defines rackets as a conspiratorial group that enforces its collective interests at the expense of the society.[43] Therefore, the term characterises a 'privileged complicity' whose stability is conditioned by the informal ties and the intensity of the linkages to state structures as well as economic, legal *and illicit* structures of the society.[44] By the same token, the racket functions as a form of protection. It protects its members in return for their respect for internal hierarchies, driving out internal competitors as well as fighting external threats.[45] In this regard, the racketeer works in the way Charles Tilly pointed out some decades later: 'Someone who produces both the danger and, at a price, the shield against it is a racketeer.'[46] Consequently, cliquishness defines the actions of individuals, and competing rackets are always struggling to achieve a monopoly in their respective fields of interest.

However, the purpose in formulating the racket theory was not to replace the Marxian class theory, but to refine it. The racket theory provides a more particularistic reflection on group loyalties than classical Marxian class theory while at the same time retaining the close ties to material interests. Hence, the emphasis on the importance of racketeering and cliquishness accompanies the class theory and enriches its strict 'horizontal' thinking with a 'vertical' element: 'The point of referring to rackets, and not just to ruling classes, was

---

racketeers of the 1953 coup in Iran. See Gölz, 'The Dangerous Classes and the 1953 Coup in Iran', 187–9.

[42] Horkheimer, 'Die Rackets und der Geist [1943]', 287.

[43] Max Horkheimer, 'Herrschende Klasse, die von den Rackets beherrschte Klasse und die Rolle der Fachleute: [Späne. 1957–1967]', in Alfred Schmidt and Gunzelin Schmid Noerr (eds), *Gesammelte Schriften: Band 14: Nachgelassene Schriften 1949–1972* (Frankfurt am Main: Fischer, 1988), 334

[44] Kai Lindemann, 'Der Racketbegriff als Herrschaftskritik', in Ulrich Ruschig and Hans-Ernst Schiller (eds), *Staat und Politik bei Horkheimer und Adorno* (Baden-Baden: Nomos, 2014), 118.

[45] Horkheimer, 'Die Rackets und der Geist [1943]', 290.

[46] Charles Tilly, 'War-Making and State-Making as Organized Crime', in Peter B. Evans, Dietrich Rueschemeyer and Theda Skocpol (eds), *Bringing the State Back In* (Cambridge: Cambridge University Press, 1985), 170–1.

that the idea of a racket contains the suggestion of coercion and coercion was the common denominator of domination. From this perspective, history, which Marx had described as the history of classes, was a history of domination.'[47] Accordingly, Horkheimer also transfers the racket principle to state structures and concludes (many years before Charles Tilly termed the state a protection racket with the advantage of legitimacy[48]): 'If an organization is so powerful that it can maintain its will in a geographical area as a permanent rule of conduct for all inhabitants, the rule of persons takes the form of law. This fixes the relative power relations.'[49]

The Constitutional Revolution and the Tabriz Resistance

This observation leads back to the *luti* rackets of Tabriz and the case of the two racketeers Sattar Khan and Baqer Khan, who not only successfully managed to rise through the ranks of the Tabriz rackets, but could also impose their rule on the late Qajar state itself for a time, as will be shown below. In retrospect they paradigmatically showcase the mechanics of the racket theory – not only due to their position in the field of power, but rather due to their political techniques, which were closely related to the logics of the protection racket.[50] In accordance with this observation, Arthur Moore describes Sattar Khan and Baqer Khan's relations with the people and the ruling elites as an extensive system of blackmail:

> The town was theoretically governed by an Anjuman, a miscellaneous collection of mullahs and other notables, who sat on the floor of a large room and spake such wisdom as the spirit prompted them. The de facto governors were the two generalissimos, Sattar Khan and Bakir Khan, whose relations with the Anjuman were of the politest and most ceremonious

---

[47] Peter M. R. Stirk, *Max Horkheimer: A New Interpretation* (Lanham, MD: Harvester Wheatsheaf, 1992), 143; see Adorno, 'Reflexionenen zur Klassentheorie [1942].' 15: 'Die Geschichte ist, nach dem Bilde der letzten ökonomischen Phase, die Geschichte von Monopolen. Nach dem Bilde der manifesten Usurpation, die von den einträchtigen Führern von Kapital und Arbeit heute verübt wird, ist sie die Geschichte von Bandenkämpfen, Gangs und Rackets.'

[48] Tilly, 'War-Making and State-Making as Organized Crime', 169.

[49] Horkheimer, 'Die Rackets und der Geist [1943]', 289.

[50] Tilly, 'War-Making and State-Making as Organized Crime', 170.

kind. But this smooth exterior was a cloak for an extensive system of blackmail.[51]

This phenomenon is, in turn, applicable to the *luti* phenomenon in general, as Varzin Vejdani points out when he describes the socio-economic universe of the *lutis* as 'a liminal zone between licit and illicit forms of work. In many cases, they generated income through violence or the threat of violence when employed as muscle for extortion rackets.'[52] In the 1940s and early 1950s in Iran, the exact same system was revived so that 'tough guys' like Tayyeb Hajj Rezai and Shaban Jafari acted as brutal and illegal racketeers, but were also in close contact with the political elites and even the shah himself.[53]

Thus, while drawing on the racket theory, it is precisely *not* the question if, for example, 'Sattar Khan was in reality only a simple *luti* (social bandit or rascal) and *rahzan* (highway robber), who by chance was drawn into the revolution, or whether he was the "bravest of the brave men of Iran" (*shoja'-e shoja'an-e Iran*), who saved the revolution.'[54] On the contrary, theoretically speaking, he is an archetypal racketeer representing both sides of the coin – the opportunist and the protector, the criminal and the hero. Thus, his as well as Baqer Khan's example is paradigmatically suited to explicitly *not* giving rise to an exceptionalist understanding of the Constitutional Revolution in a Katouzianian fashion. On the contrary: by dint of the constant reference to local traditions,[55] the role of the *lutis* in the revolutionary process showcases the nationalised manifestation of a general social–theoretical phenomenon, that is, the principles of the Frankfurt School's racket theory. This is what Floor observes when he remarks with regard to *luti* rackets in Iran:

---

[51] Moore, *The Orient Express*, 21–2.
[52] Vejdani, 'Urban Violence and Space', 1199.
[53] Olmo Gölz, 'Gewaltakteure in Iran: Rackets, Racketeers und der Kampf um das Gewaltmonopol in Teheran 1941–1963',(PhD thesis, University of Freiburg, 2016).
[54] Pistor-Hatam, 'The Iranian Constitutional Revolution as *lieu(x) de mémoire*: Sattar Khan', 36.
[55] Cf. Mansour Bonakdarian, 'A World Born through the Chamber of a Revolver: Revolutionary Violence, Culture, and Modernity in Iran, 1906–1911', *Comparative Studies of South Asia, Africa and the Middle East* 25(2) (2005): 334

The occurrence of the *lūṭīgars* was an urban phenomenon. They had specific ties with certain city quarters. They were characterized by a strong esprit de corps and notwithstanding the social ideas which prevailed among them, they were essentially a 'we-group'. Their loyalties were first with the group then the quarter and the city and what was beyond that did not count much.[56]

Nevertheless, with reference to the theoretical elaboration, we can add a less orientalist corrective to the last sentence: the racket *per se* contains a dynamic drive towards power, and the narrow focus on one's own quarter or city may well change. This is precisely what happened during the Constitutional Revolution in Tabriz and beyond.

The Constitutional Revolution in Iran is to be understood against the historical background of the Tobacco Revolt in 1890–2,[57] which in many aspects can be seen as a rehearsal for the processes of 1905–11[58] – not because it was the first political act in Iranian history, as Katouzian claims,[59] but rather because it led to a break-up of the long-standing hostility between secular as well as religious reformers on one side and conservative members of the Shiite religious establishment (*ulama*) on the other.[60] This specifically Iranian configuration of a 'religious–radical alliance' was formed during the 1890s in a local response to global challenges and was strengthened in the first years of the twentieth century, when the effects of the Russian

---

[56] Floor, 'The *lūṭīs*', 109.

[57] See for an early evaluation of the connection between the tobacco crisis and the revolution Ervand Abrahamian, 'The Causes of the Constitutional Revolution in Iran', *International Journal of Middle East Studies* 10(3) (1979): 399–404.

[58] Ervand Abrahamian, *A History of Modern Iran* (Cambridge: Cambridge University Press, 2008), 39; Adib-Moghaddam, 'What is Radicalism? 274.

[59] Homa Katouzian, 'The Revolution for Law: A Chronographic Analysis of the Constitutional Revolution of Iran', *Middle Eastern Studies* 47(5) (2011): 759.

[60] Janet Afary, 'Social Democracy and the Iranian Constitutional Revolution of 1906–11', in John Foran (ed.), *A Century of Revolution: Social Movements in Iran* (London: UCL Press, 1994), 21; Esfandyar Batmanghelidj, 'From Tobacco Revolt to Youth Rebellion: A Social History of the Cigarette in Iran', *Iranian Studies* 49(1) (2015): 111; Stephanie Cronin, *Soldiers, Shahs and Subalterns in Iran: Opposition, Protest and Revolt, 1921–1941* (Basingstoke: Palgrave Macmillan, 2010), 9; Nikki R. Keddie, 'The Origins of the Religious-Radical Alliance in Iran', *Past & Present* 34 (1966): 77; Nikki R. Keddie, *Religion and Rebellion in Iran: The Tobacco Protest of 1891–1892* (London: Cass, 1966), 1.

Revolution of 1905, the Ottoman Revolution of 1908 and effectively the Iranian Constitutional Revolution itself reached the Middle East. The causes and effects of the first Iranian revolution cannot be analysed separately from the events of the other two revolutions – and can even be considered to be entangled with other events in faraway places like the Mexican Revolution of 1910–14 and the Chinese Revolution of 1911, as has previously been argued by Joanna de Groot.[61] In effect, one can speak of a connected history of these revolutions due to their shared ideologies and methods,[62] as well as to the contribution of trans-local actors and groups, predominantly of Caucasian origin.[63] Therefore, the Iranian Constitutional Revolution is to be viewed against the background of a local history of the alliance of intellectual forces, religious actors and economic interest groups,[64] the influence of regional developments, their actors and ideologies, as well as the impact of global powers representing the imperial order, first and foremost Russia and Great Britain.

The Constitutional Revolution had been triggered by an economic crisis in 1904/5 that led the bankrupt Mozaffar ad-Din Shah (1896–1907) to ask British and Russian banks for new loans, which they provided under the condition that the shah hand over the entire customs system to the Belgian official Joseph Nauss,[65] who had already held key positions in the Qajar administration in the years before. Basically, it was his customs, trade and tariff reforms against which merchants and clerics protested between 1900 and 1905.[66] Consequently, demands regarding his dismissal became one of

---

[61] Joanna de Groot, 'Whose Revolution?'
[62] Nader Sohrabi, 'Historicizing Revolutions: Constitutional Revolutions in the Ottoman Empire, Iran, and Russia, 1905–1908', *American Journal of Sociology* 100(6) (1995): 1383
[63] Cf. Janet Afary, *The Iranian Constitutional Revolution, 1906–1911: Grassroots Democracy, Social Democracy, & the Origins of Feminism* (New York: Columbia University Press, 1996), 212; Houri Berberian, 'The Dashnaktsutiun and the Iranian Constitutional Revolution, 1905–1911', *Iranian Studies* 29(1/2) (1996): 7–33; Houri Berberian, 'Connected Revolutions: Armenians and the Russian, Ottoman, and Iranian Revolution in the Early Twentieth Century', in François Georgeon (ed.), *'L'ivresse de la liberté': La révolution de 1908 dans l'Empire ottoman* (Paris: Peeters, 2012); Cosroe Chaquéri, *The Russo-Caucasian Origins of the Iranian Left: Social Democracy in Modern Iran* (Richmond: Curzon, 2001).
[64] Afary, 'Social Democracy and the Iranian Constitutional Revolution of 1906–11', 21.
[65] Abrahamian, *A History of Modern Iran*, 41.
[66] Helbig, 'From Narrating History to Constructing Memory', 67.

the main requests of the protesters in spring and summer 1905. This year was also characterised by numerous unfavourable circumstances, which led to inflation, bread riots and the bastinadoing of a highly respected merchant, which caused the whole bazar in Teheran to shut down in protest.[67] As social unrest and dissatisfaction[68] spread all over the country, Tehran witnessed major protests headed by the leading clerics Behbehani and Tabatabai. This finally led to the establishment of a constitutional monarchy by the end of 1906. It is to these events that the neo-mystical terms *mashruteh*, *majles* and *edalat khaneh* owe their existence, just like the veneration of the intellectual constitutionalists can be traced back to them.

This somehow romanticised phase in modern Iranian history did not last long due to the unfortunate circumstance that Mozaffar ad-Din Shah, who at least did not muster all that much resistance to the demands of the protesters, died on 7 January 1907 – only ten days after signing the constitution. His successor Mohammad Ali Shah was not eager to bow to the new conditions and restraints on the throne. Biding his time, he saw his chance in the summer of 1908 after Iran was divided into 'spheres of influence' by the Anglo-Russian Convention of 1907. The two powers agreed to respect each other's turf and not to interfere in the affairs of the other and mostly left the constitutionalist of the *majles* – who themselves had made some serious mistakes in their first attempts at democracy and governance[69] – to their own devices. Finally, in June 1908, the shah staged a coup with the help of the Persian Cossack Brigade. In effect, most of the intellectuals among the constitutionalists and the parliamentary leaders fled the country or took sanctuary in foreign embassies, while Mohammad Ali Shah was able to establish the *estebdad-e saghir*.[70]

Precisely at this point, the opposition to Mohammad Ali Shah's dictatorship entrenched itself in Tabriz, the city at the crossroads between Caucasia, Iran and the Ottoman Empire that became the new centre of national

---

[67] Abrahamian, *A History of Modern Iran*, 42.
[68] Adib-Moghaddam, 'What is Radicalism?' 275.
[69] Abrahamian, *A History of Modern Iran*, 50.
[70] Kamran Matin, 'The Enlightenment and Historical Difference: The Case of Iran's Constitutional Revolution', in Ali Ansari (ed.), *Iran's Constitutional Revolution of 1906 and Narratives of the Enlightenment* (London: Gingko Library, 2016), 92.

resistance.[71] The leaders of the Tabriz uprising organised themselves with the help of secret political societies (*anjoman*s) formed during the constitutionalist period. Due to the influences of social democratic ideas from the Russian Caucasus, the powerful Tabriz *anjoman* known as the 'Secret Centre' (*markaz-e gheybi*) was more liberal and left-wing than its counterparts in other regions of Iran.[72] The Azerbaijan province and its main city had already become a spot of Transcaucasian revolutionary activity since the 1890s.[73] The Iranian northwest functioned as operation base for Armenian political parties so that Persian soil became a revolutionary hotspot.[74] Furthermore, the volunteer army raised by Sattar Khan included Azeri, Armenian and Georgian revolutionaries, veterans from Transcaucasia,[75] as well as Muslim intellectuals and *mujahidin* or *feda'i*.[76] Effectively, with the aid of the Transcaucasian actors – predominantly Armenian social-democrats, but also other people of Caucasian and Ottoman origin[77] – the Tabriz racketeers organised a heterogeneous force across class boundaries composed of *lutis*, peasants, theology students, tribesmen and others.[78]

For the following months, Tabriz resisted the royalist forces, which initially were able to take over parts of the city, but were forced out of town by local rackets headed by the racketeers Sattar Khan and Baqer Khan, who unified the quarters in the city's defence and built up a considerable force.[79] The

---

[71] Afary, *The Iranian Constitutional Revolution, 1906–1911*, 6.
[72] Afary, 'Social Democracy and the Iranian Constitutional Revolution of 1906–11', 26.
[73] Edward J. Erickson, *Ottomans and Armenians: A Study in Counterinsurgency* (New York: Palgrave Macmillan, 2013), 17.
[74] Berberian, 'The Dashnaktsutiun and the Iranian Constitutional Revolution, 1905–1911', 10.
[75] Afary, *The Iranian Constitutional Revolution, 1906–1911*, 6.
[76] Ibid., 211.
[77] See for a critical discussion Moritz Deutschmann, 'Cultures of Statehood, Cultures of Revolution: Caucasian Revolutionaries in the Iranian Constitutional Movement, 1906–1911', *Ab Imperio* 2 (2013): 175. On the relationship between Ottoman revolutionaries and the Tabriz resistance in particular, see Farzin Vejdani, 'Crafting Constitutional Narratives: Iranian and Young Turk Solidarity 1907–9', in Houchang E. Chehabi and Vanessa Martin (eds), *Iran's Constitutional Revolution: Popular Politics, Cultural Transformations and Transnational Connections* (London: I. B. Tauris, 2010), 331.
[78] Cf. Afary, *The Iranian Constitutional Revolution, 1906–1911*, 212.
[79] Moore, *The Orient Express*, 3: 'After the expulsion of the militant Royalists in the previous

resistance in Tabriz started with a remarkable heroic act of Sattar Khan: when fighting broke out, his men went to protect their quarter, Amirkhiz, against the government troops. In contrast to Baqer Khan who, after nearly two weeks of heavy fighting, hoisted a white flag to signal his surrender, Sattar Khan held his ground. It is told that he personally rode through the streets on 17 July 1908 and tore down all the white flags hoisted by the people.[80] After this heroic act, the people of Tabriz were encouraged to reorganise their resistance and stand their ground against the shah's troops.

The following siege was brought to an end by Russian intervention and occupation of Tabriz in April 1909.[81] However, as Asghar Fathi puts it vividly, 'it was owing to the courage, sacrifice, and sincere effort of . . . [a] socially insignificant group of men' like Sattar Khan and Baqer Khan that the royalists failed to capture Tabriz and stifle the constitutionalist cause.[82] Regardless of the 'social insignificancy' of its leaders – which is, of course, to be questioned against the backdrop of the racket theory – the Tabriz resistance was considered a beacon of hope for the constitutionalists and, thus, the city's stubborn opposition to the shah triggered a series of uprisings throughout the country, particularly in Gilan and Isfahan.[83] Edward G. Brown, another contemporary of the Constitutional Revolution, wrote in 1910:

> But it was Tabriz the second city of the Kingdom, the great industrial centre of the north-west, the Manchester of Persia, which best knew and

---

autumn, Tabriz was in the hands of the Constitutionalist party. Their resources were considerable. The population is always estimated by Persians as 300,000. There is no census, but there is said to be a register showing 60,000 inhabited houses; and if this be so, the average rough European conjecture of 200,000 may be under the mark. Including their own smuggled arms, the defenders had at their disposal 20,000 rifles, an adequate supply of ammunition, three mountain-guns, and some old muzzle-loading cannon, as well as mortars. The great majority of the rifles and all their bayonets remained undisturbed in the Government arsenal. The nominal fighting force at the disposal of Sattar Khan and Bakir Khan, the two Constitutionalist leaders, was less than 2,000.'

[80] Pistor-Hatam, 'Sattār Khan'; Pistor-Hatam, 'The Iranian Constitutional Revolution as *lieu(x) de mémoire*', 38.
[81] Afary, *The Iranian Constitutional Revolution, 1906–1911*, 6.
[82] Asghar Fathi, 'The Role of the "Rebels" in the Constitutional Movement in Iran', *International Journal of Middle East Studies* 10(1) (1979): 56.
[83] Afary, *The Iranian Constitutional Revolution, 1906–1911*, 212.

least liked Muhammad Ali Shah, and best understood and most loved freedom and independence, which 'kept the flag flying' for nearly ten months while Tihran [sic] lay prostrate under the iron heel of Colonel Liakhoff and his Cossacks, and which, ere it finally succumbed to the stress of hunger, gave to Isfahan, Rasht and other cities the encouragement and the time which they needed to rally to the popular cause.[84]

Sattar Khan and Baqer Khan, who left Tabriz and resumed their revolutionary activities in Rasht, were instrumental in the spread of the resistance movement. Eventually, larger heterogeneous groups of revolutionaries composed of *lutis*, tribesmen and the part of the Cossacks led by Tonekaboni, who had switched sides after the failed siege of Tabriz, marched from the west, the north and the south towards Tehran and managed to retake the capital in the name of the *mashruteh*. Therefore, there is no doubt that Sattar Khan's activities were crucial to the survival of the Constitutional Revolution, for had he surrendered, the *estebdad-e saghir* of Muhammad Ali Shah would surely have prevailed. To put it bluntly, it was his actions that encouraged constitutionalists all over the country to keep up the struggle.[85] His resistance turned him into 'a national icon, his image [became] emblematic of a nation's hopes and aspirations. His photographs, moving from hand to hand, evoked a sense of belonging and identification with the resistance so much so that, for fear of their power, they were forbidden.'[86] The former *lutis* Baqer Khan and Sattar Khan eventually emerged as the military leaders and icons of the constitutionalist cause.[87] This veneration was reflected in the titles that the two resistance fighters received for their efforts: while Sattar Khan was given

---

[84] Brown, *The Persian Revolution of 1905–1909*, 248.
[85] Pistor-Hatam, 'Sattār Khān'; see also Moore, *The Orient Express*, 20–1. At least regarding the outcome of the Tabriz resistance, the eyewitness agrees – although he interprets the events totally differently: 'Tabriz was ultimately saved by the coming of the Russians. Their entry into the town was the direct cause of the opening of the roads, the dispersal of the disappointed armies of the Shah, the promulgation of the Constitution, and the appointment of a Constitutionalist Ministry. It saved Tabriz from a surrender which could not otherwise have been delayed for three days longer, and thereby it averted the complete collapse of the Constitutional movement.'
[86] Helbig, 'From Narrating History to Constructing Memory', 69.
[87] Bonakdarian, 'A World Born through the Chamber of a Revolver', 330.

the honorific *sardar-e melli* (the people's commander), Baqer Khan received the epithet *salar-e melli* (national chieftain).

Theoretical Reflections

Against the background of the racket theory, on the one hand, and the events during and after the Tabriz resistance, on the other hand, some theoretical reflections can be drawn that might help to shed light on the role of the *luti* masculinity ethos, embodied by Sattar Khan and Baqer Khan, during the Constitutional Revolution, as well as its reverberations on other significant episodes of Iranian history in the twentieth century. I have argued at the beginning that: (1) the constant references to the *luti* status of the two racketeers Sattar Khan and Baqer Khan helped to 'Iranise' the Constitutional Revolution and obfuscate its transnational entanglements; (2) their example helped to reshape gender discourses in general and notions of hegemonic masculinity in particular; and (3) this had distinct consequences for Iran's history in the course of the century, for the 'simple man's' obligation to contribute to national politics is valorised.

(1) The discussion about the *luti* status of central actors of the Constitutional Revolution and the resulting question about the Iranisation of the Islamic Revolution consists of two levels: the first is historiographic, the second historic. The historiographic level refers to the significance of the social background of Sattar Khan and Baqer Khan in Iranian historiography. Anja Pistor-Hatam has already shown how the fixation on the *luti* Sattar Khan left an imprint on the eyewitnesses of the first Iranian revolution, that is, Kasravi, Malekzadeh and Amirkhizi, which is reflected in their writings on these events.[88] This, however, influenced following scholarly discussions on the *luti* phenomenon in Qajar Iran,[89] as well as leaving a deep impact on the perception of the Constitutional Revolution. The constant discussion

---

[88] Pistor-Hatam, 'The Iranian Constitutional Revolution as *lieu(x) de mémoire*', 42.
[89] Reza Arasteh, 'The Character, Organization and Social Role of the Lutis (Javan-Mardan) in the Traditional Society of the Nineteenth Century', *Journal of the Economic and Social History of the Orient* 4:1 (1961), 47–52; Bateson et al., 'Ṣafā-yi Bāṭin'; Fathi, 'The Role of the "Rebels" in the Constitutional Movement in Iran'; Floor, 'The *lūṭīs*'; Floor, 'The Political Role of the *Lutis* in Iran'; Martin, 'The *Lutis* – The Turbulent Urban Poor'; Vejdani, 'Urban Violence and Space'.

about the respective actors' *luti* status (a concept that is deeply anchored in Iranian history) and thus the fixation on the *lutis* as a social group[90] ultimately distracts from the entangled history of the Constitutional Revolution – although for example, due to the important involvement of Caucasian political figures and racketeers like the Armenian Yeprem Khan (1868–1912) in the processes of the Constitutional Revolution, the Iranian case had a prominent place in Soviet historical narratives.[91] In Iranian historiography however, it is discussed where the *lutis* come from, what their traditions are, whether they could be explained by the concept of social bandits, and so on and so forth. What is either not explicitly asked or even ridiculed is the question about the interests of these actors. What agendas do they pursue? And most importantly: how do they use local, regional and global political and economic dynamics for their purposes? The representation of Sattar Khan and Baqer Khan, despite their entanglement with politics in Tabriz and northern Iran as well as trans-local actors, is an excellent example of this, for they not only managed to gain influence in their local rackets beyond class boundaries, rather they also crossed the logics of the *luti* ethos in a spatial aspect when they engaged in the uprising of Rasht and appeared in Tehran in 1909.[92] Here, the racket theory helps to clarify: although the *luti* ethos is a distinctively Iranian phenomenon, the logic of cliquishness and racketeering is a universal one. In turn, the *luti* ethos helped to historiographically nationalise the functioning principle of the racket. With reference to the racket theory for the case of the *luti,* it is sufficient to follow Stephanie Cronin's synopsis on the Constitutional Revolution:

---

[90] Cf. Fathi, 'The Role of the "Rebels" in the Constitutional Movement in Iran', 58.
[91] Deutschmann, 'Cultures of Statehood, Cultures of Revolution', 166–7: 'Apart from its relevance for Iran, the Constitutional Movement marked the first case in which a significant number of revolutionary activists from the Russian Empire became involved in a revolution outside of Europe. Most of these activists were from the South Caucasus, and some of them, for example, the Georgian Sergo Ordzhonikidze, would later rise to important positions in Soviet politics; beyond the Constitutional Revolution, they would continue to influence Russian and Soviet engagements with Iran, for example, the Gilan Republic, the attempt to create a Soviet republic in northern Iran, in 1921. In Soviet historical narratives, the connections of the Constitutional Movement to the Caucasus therefore had a prominent place.'
[92] Cf. Bonakdarian, 'A World Born through the Chamber of a Revolver', 321–2, n. 12.

The constitutional revolution may best be understood when it is placed within its historical and global context. It was an Iranian manifestation of an international trend, part of a wave of such movements and upheavals which swept across much of the world, including southern Europe, the Middle East and Asia, in the late nineteenth–early twentieth centuries. At the same time, its precise character, the social forces which it mobilized, its leadership and its agenda were conditioned by the specific circumstances of Iranian history. The methods employed by the revolutionaries drew on a deep indigenous tradition of urban protest. Their objectives, however, were no longer localized grievances but, in an illustration of the growth of a modern political consciousness, national demands focused on the state.[93]

This leads to the second level of the representation of the Constitutional Revolution's heroes' *luti* status, the historical one. Bonakdarian observes that already during the constitutional period, the examples of the revolutionaries of Tabriz had the effect that 'the *culturally naturalized* masculine cult of the *luti* was now overladen with a *nationalized* attribute.'[94] An effect which could be observed in the historical moment itself, when images of Sattar Khan and Baqer Khan circulated in the public sphere and stories about the both strongmen's bravery became common knowledge so that their examples were used to construct a national identity.[95]

(2) However, their examples not only helped to mobilise for the constitutionalist cause but also had lasting impact on the gender order through reshaping notions of masculinity in Iran – so that patriotism became a character trait inseparable from masculinity, as Sivan Balslev puts it.[96] This is of

---

[93] Cronin, *Soldiers, Shahs and Subalterns in Iran*, 12.
[94] Bonakdarian, 'A World Born through the Chamber of a Revolver', 335.
[95] Helbig, 'From Narrating History to Constructing Memory', 63–4; see also Bonakdarian, 'A World Born through the Chamber of a Revolver', 335: 'As has been mentioned in reference to Sattar Khan, masculinity and national heroism were recorded for posterity through both biographic and autobiographic oral, textual, and visual inscriptions, including oral narratives, poetry, memoirs, press reports, photography, and tombstone inscriptions. Yet the concept of masculinity (in both its former culturally naturalized and recently nationalized attributes) was by no means a stable or uncontested category. "Emasculation," both physical and metaphoric, continuously threatened and destabilized existing and changing definitions of masculinity.'
[96] Sivan Balslev, *Iranian Masculinities: Gender and Sexuality in Late Qajar and Early Pahlavi Iran* (Cambridge: Cambridge University Press, 2019), 92–3.

course not to be isolated from the discursive developments regarding the gendering of the nation in the context of European Imperialism. Najmabadi convincingly shows how the discursive production of Iran as a female body was achieved by intellectualist discourses taking classical literature into account,[97] and how this discourse was maintained during the Constitutional Revolution.[98] This gave way for notions of masculinity that valorise patriotism in the context of the regional processes and the global entanglements that led to the Constitutional Revolution. In short, if it is a man's duty to protect women, in an analogous logic it also becomes his duty to defend the country's honor against foreign intrusion and penetration. Thus, the homeland was not only scripted 'as a female figure of male desire but [as] subject to his possession and protection'.[99] Although the making and remaking of masculinities has to be seen in the context of the intellectualist discourses at the turn of the century which included the engagement in political activities and the valorisation of 'modern' and 'rational' masculinities,[100] the success of the two strong-men in the Constitutional Revolution leads to a paradoxical effect, i.e. the exaltation of non-intellectualist masculinities which were integrated into the new discourses and performative practices of the nation and her honor.[101]

In effect, I argue that the actual argument to call the Constitutional Revolution a distinct Iranian phenomenon – hence, the exaggeration of the importance of the *luti* ethos for the constitutionalist cause – leads to a discursive inversion of the outcomes of the revolution itself, for the strongman habitus in politics as a decisively Iranian configuration is eventually

---

[97] Afsaneh Najmabadi, 'The Erotic Vatan [Homeland] as Beloved and Mother: To Love, to Possess, and To Protect', *Comparative Studies in Society and History* 39:3 (1997), 445.

[98] Ibid., 461: 'Particularly during the politically crucial years of the Constitutional Revolution, the civil war, and restoration of the parliament (1906–09), the recitation of the suffering of the mother's fevered and tormented body was employed to incite fear and panic over the loss of the mother, thus arousing her uncaring children out of their slumber. The threat of the mother's death was invoked as a reason for political action.'

[99] Ibid., 446.

[100] Joanna de Groot, '"Brothers of the Iranian Race": Manhood, Nationhood, and Modernity in Iran c. 1870–1914', in Stefan Dudink, Karen Hagemann, and John Tosh, eds., *Masculinities in Politics and War: Gendering Modern History* (Manchester: Manchester University Press, 2004), 151–2.

[101] Bonakdarian, 'A World Born through the Chamber of a Revolver', 334.

an invention of tradition and an outcome of the revolution. This was triggered by traditional Iranian perceptions of manhood, the politicisation of the public sphere in the face of global tendencies, and the amalgamation of these phenomena with the revolutionary ethos of the time that cannot be detached from regional developments. In effect, patriotism as well as the capability to *protect* infused dominantly the hegemonic masculinity back then, so that the racket principles in general and the *luti* ethos in particular had been romanticised in the aftermath of the revolution.

(3) This in turn have had distinct repercussions for the history of twentieth-century Iran due to the fact that not only discourses on ideal manhood had been reshaped by the successful racketeers in politics, but also that numerous epigones actually grasped on the same logics. Moritz Deutschmann has argued that bandits in the Russio-Iranian borderlands left their traces in the popular culture on both sides of the border and that not only Stalin was influenced by romantic tales of Georgian resistance to Russian rule, but also Sattar Khan's brother was considered to have had connections to prominent robbers and bandits of the region.[102] In the Iranian case however, it was the example of Sattar Khan and Baqer Khan themselves which shaped future generations of strong-men as well as 'simple men' in politics. The first and one of the most important epigones is represented by Mirza Kuchek Khan (1880–1921) who himself was a combatant of the Constitutional Revolution, founded the Jangal movement in 1915 and announced the Socialist Republic of Gilan in northern Iran in 1920.[103] The discursive connection of Mirza Kuchek Khan, Satter Khan and Baqer Khan can be witnessed in contemporary Iran when all these actors are linked to each other via the masculinity ethos of *javanmardi* which is closely related to the *luti*. Consequently, Iranian students learn from the same textbook series that exalts Sattar Khan's and Baqer Khan's role in the Constitutional Revolution that 'Mirza's name and his manly resistance to tyranny and aggression remained permanently alive in the memory of the Iranian people and was a role model for the fighters who followed him.'[104]

---

[102] Deutschmann, 'Cultures of Statehood, Cultures of Revolution', 171.
[103] Chaqueri, Cosroe. *Soviet Socialist Republic of Iran, 1920–1921: Birth of the Trauma* (Pittsburgh: University of Pittsburgh Press, 1995), 188ff.
[104] Vezarat-e amuzesh va parvaresh, *Tarikh-e Iran va jahan (reshte-ye adabiyat va 'olum-e*

Furthermore, as Stephanie Cronin concludes, Reza Khan had on the one hand to deploy the discourse of the 'man of order' and thus a strong-man appearance in politics. On the other hand only the emergence and success of alternative local rulers gave him the opportunity to project an image of such a 'man of order' with the aim 'to establish the new state's physical control throughout the countryside, over rural criminals of all sorts, bandits, highway robbers and nomadic raiders, but also, and as part of the same process and often using the same justificatory vocabulary, over tribal khans and semi-autonomous local rulers and their agricultural-pastoralist populations.'[105]

The hefty outreach of the influence of the historic prefigures might best be shown by the examples of the two famous *lutis* and powerful racketeers of the 1940s and 50s in Tehran, Shaban Jafari and Tayyeb Hajj Rezai. Both played important roles during the Coup d'état in 1953 when they helped to bring down the government of Mohammad Mosaddeq on behalf of the Mohammad Reza Shah Pahlavi – the son of the strong-man whose face was tattooed on Tayyeb Hajj Rezai's belly.[106] I have argued that the example of the two revolutionary heroes Sattar Khan and Baqer Khan, originating from the lower classes and adhering to the *luti* values and virtues, forged a notion of masculinity which put strong emphasis on political action and legitimised questioning the state – and actually opposing it when the community under the *lutis'* protection is endangered.[107] In the post-war period, it can be witnessed that these exact heroic examples offered an image of ideal manhood that does not encourage respect for the state in general but rather for ad hoc political action in the form of transgressive politics on the streets. Accordingly, the political performances of Shaban Jafari and Tayyeb Hajj Rezai relied in great part on the discourses shaped by the examples from the

---

ensani): Sal-e sevvom-e amuzesh-e muṭawasseṭe (Tehran: Sherkat-e Chap va Nashr-e Ketabha-ye Darsi-ye Iran, 2009), 184.

[105] Stephanie Cronin, 'Noble Robbers, Avengers and Entrepreneurs: Eric Hobsbawm and Banditry in Iran, the Middle East and North Africa', *Middle Eastern Studies* 52(5) (2016): 854.

[106] Geruh-e farhangi-ye Shahid-e Ibrahim Hadi. *Ṭayyeb: Zendeginameh va khaterat-e Horr-e nehzat-e Imam Khomeyni Shahid-e Ṭayyeb-e Ḥajj Reza'i* (Tehran: Nashr-e Aminan, 1392 [2013]), 21.

[107] Gölz, 'The Dangerous Classes and the 1953 Coup in Iran', 181–2.

Constitutional Revolution.[108] A performance which is – at least in respect to Tayyeb Hajj Rezai – exalted and romanticised even in present discourses on the *lutis* in the Islamic Republic of Iran in which the simple man's contribution to politics makes up an important part of the Islamic Revolutionary discourse. Consequently, the *lutis* are retrospectively presented as those 'in whose hands the safety of the people lay, especially in times of weakness of the central state'.[109]

Conclusion

To conclude, by referencing to the *luti* status – and therefore to an allegedly traditional concept – of the national heroes who function as figures of boundary work in Iran, the Constitutional Revolution gets historiographically detached from global entanglements and regional developments. However, the Iranization of the revolution and the surrounding process comes at a price, for the *luti* status of the two racketeers leads two a form of self-exotization in which the racket-principle of domination gets downgraded from a generalizable social-theoretical phenomenon to an Iranian specifity.

However, their example helped to reshape notions of masculinity which put emphasis on political action so that effectively these role models had a deep impact on the history of 20th century Iran, for in the course of the century, numerous other individuals and local leaders adopted the logic of political action couched in strong-man behaviour and participated in the competition for power and influence, first in the fragile political system of late Qajar Iran and later in the Pahlavi period. These behavioural patterns were both locally rooted and at the same time under the influence of transnational discourses, as can be observed using the example of the local leader Mirza Kuchek Khan (1880–1921), who managed to build up a quasi-state in northern Iran, the Armenian Revolutionary Yeprem Khan (1868–1912), the short-time police president of Tehran, or even Reza Khan (1878–1944), who later became the founder of the Pahlavi dynasty. Furthermore, the examples of the Tabriz resistance fighters were reactivated in the processes of the 1953 coup, when famous 'tough guys' like Shaban Jafari (1921–2006)

---

[108] Ibid., 182.
[109] Geruh-e farhangi-ye Shahid-e Ibrahim Hadi. *Tayyeb*, 21.

or Tayyeb Hajj Rezai (1911–63) emerged as epigones of the Tabrizi *luti*, acted as having a political agenda while simultaneously pushing to enforce their own order and rejecting the state order. What is more, the idea of the 'simple man's' obligation to contribute to national politics had also mobilising effects throughout the 20th century that reached far beyond identifiable political leaders or gang-bosses who acted as epigones of the national heroes of the Constitutional Revolution in Iran. These mobilising effects of the heroic example of the two *luti* leaders culminated in the Islamic Revolution of 1978/79 when the urban poor had been caught up in the revolutionary discourse. Satter Khan and Baqer Khan provided the perfect foil here, not only presenting *ideal men* from humble backgrounds opposing the state who are addressed by the communist *and* Islamist discourses on the suppressed, but also ideal *Iranian* men who supposedly adhered to the *luti* tradition of the country – a tradition which their example helped to invent in the first place.

PART II
ROGUES AND REGIMES

5

Conspiracy under Trial: Christian Brigands, Rebels and Activists in Bosnia during the Tanzimat

Anna Vakali[1]

> Have you ever heard of a land the subjects of which don't pay taxes? ...
> In which law and in which book is it written that more
> than a thousand people rise up and send a representative to the officials,
> saying 'we don't pay the tithe and the tax anymore'?[2]

The Ottoman nineteenth century witnessed increased levels of mobilisation among ordinary Christians throughout the Balkans. Preceded by the Greek and Serbian revolutions and the establishment of autonomous Serbia (1830) and the Greek kingdom (1832), the onset of the Ottoman centralising and modernising reform programme known as the Tanzimat (1839–76) was followed by consecutive tax revolts, local uprisings connected with intense smuggling of weaponry, as well as the formation of networks, (secret) societies and clubs facilitated by the dissemination of printed material. National teleology though that presents such revolts 'as a final stage and logical outcome of a multi-centuries-long struggle for independence'

---

[1] I would like to thank the editors and the external reviewers of this volume, as well as Ebru Aykut, Yonca Köksal and Çiğdem Oğuz for valuable feedback on this chapter.
[2] The question was addressed in court to Ottoman peasants in Ostrožac (northwest Bosnia) who had denied paying their taxes, see BOA (*Başbakanlık Osmanlı Arşivi*, Prime Ministry Ottoman Archive, Istanbul), I.MVL. 467 21167, 2 July 1862. The assigned date of the BOA files is the date of the file's final document. All translations from the Ottoman documents into English belong to the author.

has long since lost its analytical strength.[3] Revisionist approaches propose that local economic factors, and the failure of the imperial regime to uphold basic standards of justice during the implementation of centralising reforms regarding state finances and military conscription, prepared the ground for such insurrections-turned-wars of national liberation.[4] During this process, activists put a different notion of consciousness into currency, conceiving of it as a susceptible, variable matter that is subject to countless influences, including kinship relations, local rivalries, education, wages, peer pressure, rhetoric, symbols, gifts and so on.[5] As Sohrabi has noted when tracing the evolution of Albanian nationalism, '. . . like all social movements . . . there was a convergence between the local more immediate concerns on the ground, and the larger, global frames put forth by the intelligentsia, such as nationalism, autonomy, and independence'.[6]

The mobilisation described in this chapter formed part of a 'wide variety of revolutionary, reformist, autonomist and defensive mobilising projects', which contributed to the lengthy crisis of the dynastic and Islamic state during the long nineteenth century.[7] From a global perspective, during the period between 1848 and 1865 uneven economic growth, and the associated questioning of the legitimacy of all forms of power, formed the crucible

---

[3] Hannes Grandits, Nathalie Clayer and Robert Pichler, 'Social (Dis-)Integration and the National Turn in the Late- and Post-Ottoman Balkans: Towards an Analytical Framework', in Hannes Grandits, Nathalie Clayer and Robert Pichler (eds), *Conflicting Loyalties in the Balkans: The Great Powers, the Ottoman Empire and Nation-Building* (London: I. B. Tauris, 2011), 5.

[4] Frederick F. Anscombe, 'The Balkan Revolutionary Age', *Journal of Modern History* 84(3) (2012): 572; Ramazan Hakkı Öztan, 'Nationalism in Function: "Rebellions" in the Ottoman Empire and Narratives in its Absence', in M. Hakan Yavuz and Feroz Ahmad (eds), *War and Collapse: World War I and the Ottoman State* (Salt Lake City: University of Utah Press, 2016), 168.

[5] Edin Hajdarpasic, *Whose Bosnia? Nationalism and Political Imagination in the Balkans, 1840–1914* (Ithaca, NY: Cornell University Press, 2015), 112.

[6] Nader Sohrabi, 'Reluctant Nationalists, Imperial Nation-State, and Neo-Ottomanism: Turks, Albanians, and the Antinomies of the End of Empire', *Social Science History* 42(4) (2018): 27.

[7] John Chalcraft, *Popular Politics in the Making of the Modern Middle East* (Cambridge: Cambridge University Press, 2016), 529.

of conflict worldwide.⁸ The revolutionary outbreaks of the mid-1850s in Europe occurred at the same time as widespread movements of rural protest. Movements of rural protest and no-rent campaigns endangered those old-style landlords who had survived, particularly in eastern and southern Europe, and continued to levy their seigneurial dues. In addition, urban discontent in Europe had already turned into urban, nationalist revolt. Forcible peasant occupations of land and attacks on cloth merchants aside, the revolutions in Italy, for example, were revolutions of patriotic lawyers, merchants and liberal landowners against the domination of Austria, which had been re-imposed following the defeat of Napoleon.⁹ Indeed, the world crises between 1848 and 1865 gave great impetus to different projects of nation-states within and outside Europe, whereas 'the form of national community remained highly contested and ambiguous in almost every case and there was no consensus about whom the nation belonged to, and what the nation was'.[10]

Tax-related uprisings swept all over the Balkans from the 1840s on, following the promulgation of the first reform edict in 1839. Tanzimat reformers' attempts aimed at coupling increased fiscal and military exigencies with a more standardised and just tax system, based not on collective but individual distribution. The expectations of peasants though that their tax burden would be reduced soon proved to be futile. Wealthier social segments, who were now subjected to heavier taxes, often incited the local population against the authorities.[11] The ensuing tax revolts spanned from Niš (1841), to Vidin (1849) and Bosnia (1857–62), up to the uprisings in Herzegovina (1875–7) and to the Bulgarians' April Uprising (1876), which led to the Ottoman–Russian war, ending with the establishment of a Bulgarian autonomous state and the occupation of Bosnia by Austria, both in 1878. Literature suggests that, while driven by economic demands, such uprisings soon mutated into nationalist revolutions.[12] In this sense, social conflicts were instrumentalised

---

[8] Christopher A. Bayly, *The Birth of the Modern World 1780–1914: Global Connections and Comparisons* (Malden, MA: Blackwell, 2004), 168.
[9] Ibid., 156–8.
[10] Ibid., 199–207.
[11] Ahmet Uzun, *Tanzimat ve Sosyal Direnişler: Niş İsyanı Üzerine Ayrıntılı bir İnceleme (1841)* (Istanbul: Eren, 2002), 56–7.
[12] Donald Quataert, 'Rural Unrest in the Ottoman Empire, 1830–1914', in Farhad Kazemi

for political interests with competing (also nationalist) goals.[13] Secession took place, ultimately, because the central Ottoman state was unwilling to confront and dismantle the forms of decentralised class and political power against which peasants and their allies were above all pressing.[14]

While aiming at refuting teleological narratives on the formation of nationalist projects, such explanations run the risk of falling into similar pitfalls. Accordingly, nationalist feelings, even when evolving out of everyday grievances, were transferred to the people by 'elite mediums', implying an agency deficit in this metaphor of 'transplantation'.[15] Instead of viewing these uprisings as a linear chain of events, during which specific demands of the population were manipulated by external and internal agents having a nationalist agenda, this chapter aims to approach them in their full complexity, without the hindsight of the ensuing events. By focusing on a series of local uprisings in Ottoman Bosnia during the late 1850s and early 1860s, and utilising hitherto unearthed archival material including the interrogation protocols of their protagonists when tried in the Ottoman courts, I argue that the process of 'nationalisation' was less linear and reductionist than has been accepted; various social groups posing different demands operated simultaneously; agency belonged not (only) to 'elite mediums', like educated elites, teachers or merchants, but was exercised by such diverse local actors as peasants, village priests, brigands and jobless wanderers, motivated and mobilised by different agendas. Peasants utilised rumours in order to defend their refusal to pay taxes; village priests played a leading part in investing in such rumours, distributing smuggled weapons and inciting the peasants to rebel; while jobless wanderers were roaming the countryside disseminating rumours and distributing letters and pamphlets containing nationalist calls. In interpreting these relations, it is important to remember the key question: not whether the activists failed or achieved in their desired aims (liberation,

---

and John Waterbury (eds), *Peasants and Politics in the Middle East* (Miami: Florida International University Press, 1991), 41.

[13] Hannes Grandits, *Herrschaft und Loyalität in der spätosmanischen Gesellschaft: Das Beispiel der multikonfessionellen Herzegowina* (Vienna: Böhlau, 2008), 683.

[14] Chalcraft, *Popular Politics in the Making of the Modern Middle East*, 92.

[15] Andreas Lyberatos, 'Through Nation and State: Reform and Nationalism "From Below" in the Late Ottoman Balkans: Introduction', *Turkish Historical Review* 7(2) (2016): 121–2.

mobilisation, etc.), nor whether a well-paid teacher, well-decorated revolver or a well-heeled pair of shoes was too little or just enough to win over the local populace, but what these relations signified and made possible in the first place.[16]

Situated at the northern Balkan fringe of the Ottoman Empire, the geographical position of the province of Bosnia posed 'administrative and financial' challenges for the authorities.[17] Permanent tensions existed between sharecroppers and landowners. According to the Ottoman Yearbook of 1870, 49.8 per cent of the population were Muslims, 36.4 per cent Orthodox Christians and 12.6 per cent Catholics.[18] While at first the landholders could be either Christians or Muslims, and the peasants who worked their estates (*çiftliks*) were also of both religions, by the nineteenth century all major landholders were Muslims and the vast majority of the non-landowning peasants, called *kmets*, were Christians.[19] Sharecroppers had to deliver the *üçleme* tax (one-third) of their produce to their landowners. Together with the state tithe, a money payment equivalent to one-tenth of the crop and given to the tax-collectors, they accounted for 40 per cent of the peasants' total product; and there were other state taxes of various kinds, such as the new tax in lieu of military service, on top of that.[20] Moreover, sharecroppers complained that the landowners were taking half and not one-third of their produce, that they purchased their animals at a very low price, and that they were coerced into forced labour in the land estates.[21] However, instructions sent to the province in 1847 stated, among others, that a 'special way' had to be found in the application of the Tanzimat in the province of Bosnia, without affecting the old order.[22] While the Muslim

---

[16] Hajdarpasic, *Whose Bosnia?*, 111.
[17] BOA, A.DVN. 31 29, 8 December 1847.
[18] Zafer Gölen, *Tanzimat Döneminde Bosna Hersek: Siyasi, Idari, Sosyal ve Ekonomik Durum* (Ankara: Türk Tarih Kurumu, 2010), 26, 31.
[19] Fatma Sel Turhan, *The Ottoman Empire and the Bosnian Uprising: Janissaries, Modernisation and Rebellion in the Nineteenth Century* (London: I. B. Tauris, 2014), 57–8.
[20] Noel Malcolm, *Bosnia: A Short History* (London: Macmillan, 1996), 129.
[21] Zafer Gölen, *Tanzimat Dönemi Bosna İsyanları (1839–1878)* (Ankara: Alter, 2009), 30–3.
[22] BOA, A.DVN. 31 29, 8 December 1847.

nobility lost their previous political power, they continued to dominate economically the rural areas.[23]

The uprisings in Bosnia started in 1857, one year after the promulgation of the second reform edict, and lasted for five years. They started in the sub-province of Zvornik, located in the east, at the border with Serbia, and soon spilled over to the sub-provinces of Banja Luka, Bihać and Herzegovina. Peasants were refusing to pay their taxes, weapons were smuggled in from Serbia and Austria, while Christians were migrating to the latter two countries. In 1861, for example, the governor of Banja Luka confiscated 2,042 weapons from the Serbian *millet* of his district.[24] In 1855, 400 subjects were reported as having fled to Austria due to the usurpations of the tax-collectors and the oppression of the officials, and some dozens to Serbia.[25] According to the governor of Bosnia, in 1865, 2,200 people had left the sub-provinces of Bihać and Banja Luka, and 500 had left Zvornik, migrating to Serbia.[26] Bandits from Serbia and Austria were constantly crossing the borders into Bosnia.[27] The remainder of this chapter elaborates on the quotidian protagonists of these uprisings.

Tax Refusals

While the Tanzimat reforms aimed at a better distribution of taxes, state revenue between the 1780s and the First World War increased by more than fifteenfold due to growth in the state's tax-levying capacity.[28] Next to this, a Land Code was promulgated in 1858, requiring landowners to register ownership. While large, commercialised estates had been established in many parts of the empire from the eighteenth century on, the Ottoman land laws of 1858 'did ultimately contribute to consolidating property rights, but with differential consequences. In Anatolia and parts of Rumelia, consistent with

---

[23] Grandits, *Herrschaft und Loyalität in der spätosmanischen Gesellschaft*, 674.
[24] BOA, A.MKT.UM. 525 67, 17 December 1861; A.MKT.UM. 530 7, 4 January 1862.
[25] BOA, HR.MKT. 124 2, 17 October 1855.
[26] BOA, A.MKT.MHM. 336 64, 5 July 1865.
[27] BOA, A.MKT.MHM. 761 57, 25 June 1862.
[28] Nadir Özbek, 'The Politics of Taxation and the "Armenian Question" during the Late Ottoman Empire, 1876–1908', *Comparative Studies in Society and History* 54(4) (2012): 775.

historic Ottoman policy, the law consolidated the predominance of peasant family farms.'[29] In Bosnia and Herzegovina however, Muslim holders of privatised military land grants and tax farms urged Muslim and Christian peasants to revolt against Ottoman land-registration measures in 1858–9. The peasants rose up, hoping to expropriate their landlords. However, the landlords maintained their holdings, their domination of the peasantry and their control over a majority of the agricultural surplus.[30] Resistance though on the part of the groups excluded by claims of private ownership accounted for the highly fluid character of property relations in the 'age of property', as the nineteenth century has been succinctly described.[31] The cultivators resisted what amounted to the establishment of singular and absolute ownership rights by the estate holders and the redefinition of their own use rights in terms of restricted tenancy rights. Following, for example, a land dispute in the province of Ioannina in today's northern Greece in 1875, tenants called for adherence to local customary practices, and achieved the position wherein holders of title to the land could not revoke a tenancy, evict a tenant or raise the amount of rent.[32]

From the onset of the Tanzimat, peasants often refused to pay taxes, especially the *üçleme* tax which was paid to the landowners. Peasant avoidance certainly was the most common form of protest, a refusal to perform duties, or pay taxes, or enter the military, a posture that might end in flight.[33] As Aytekin has argued, 'the refusal to pay tax had important implications for the ownership of the land, because the local magnates' claims for rents and taxes were based on their claims of ownership. When the peasants refused to pay the tax, they rejected such claims by landlords and asserted their own ownership of the land in question.'[34] There is evidence that even before the

---

[29] Joel Beinin, *Workers and Peasants in the Middle East* (Cambridge: Cambridge University Press, 2001), 51.

[30] Ibid., 58.

[31] Huri Islamoglu, 'Property as a Contested Domain: A Re-evaluation of the Ottoman Land Code of 1858', in Roger Owen (ed.), *New Perspectives on Property and Land in the Middle East* (Cambridge, MA: Harvard University Press, 2000), 7.

[32] Ibid., 37–8.

[33] Quataert, 'Rural Unrest in the Ottoman Empire, 1830–1914', 40.

[34] E. Atilla Aytekin, 'Peasant Protest in the Late Ottoman Empire: Moral Economy, Revolt, and the *Tanzimat* Reforms', *International Review of Social History* 57(2) (2012): 216.

break out of the uprisings, non-Muslim tenant farmers (*müstecir*) had been refusing to pay their taxes. In a document addressed to the governor of Bosnia in 1857, it was stated that non-Muslim sharecroppers of the sub-province of Zvornik, who had been paying the *üçleme* to the landlords (*ashab-ı alaka*), as well as the *aşar* (tithe) for the provisions they have been harvesting from the land around their houses, were now opposing the payment of their taxes. The situation alarmed the authorities, which attributed this refusal to seduction (*iğfalat*), while the landlords were not stepping back. The issue was finally delegated to the religious officials (bishops and metropolitans) of the region, and a thorough examination was ordered.[35]

Similar to other places, it was mainly the spread of rumours in Bosnia in the late 1850s that enabled peasants to mobilise around the issue of taxation. Rumours constitute 'both a universal and necessary carrier of insurgency in any pre-industrial, pre-literate society'.[36] They 'serve as a vehicle for anxieties and aspirations that may not be openly acknowledged by its propagators'.[37] If the message of dissent is too explicit, its bearers risk open retaliation; if it is too vague, it passes unnoticed altogether. Accordingly, the realities of power require that the 'hidden transcript'[38] either be spoken by anonymous subordinates or be protected by disguise as rumour, gossip, euphemism or grumbling that dares not speak in its own name.[39] Peasant 'misunderstandings' of the reforms through rumour did not stem from ignorance or lack of access, but were intentional acts intended to reinterpret and radicalise the Tanzimat in accordance with peasant aspirations.[40] Rumours played a decisive role in such tax revolts: they filled the vacuum created by relations between illiterate and literate peasants, enabled the peasants to agree on common demands in situation of crisis and helped them to bypass local authority by appealing

---

[35] BOA, A.MKT.UM. 296 89, 8 November 1857.
[36] Ranajit Guha, *Elementary Aspects of Peasant Insurgency in Colonial India* (Durham, NC: Duke University Press, 1999), 251.
[37] James C. Scott, *Domination and the Arts of Resistance: Hidden Transcripts* (New Haven, CT: Yale University Press, 1990), 145.
[38] The term belongs to James C. Scott, and defines forms of resistance and dissent that are kept out of the sight of those in power.
[39] Scott, *Domination and the Arts of Resistance*, 156.
[40] Aytekin, 'Peasant Protest in the Late Ottoman Empire', 196.

to the justness of the sultan.[41] During the uprisings in Bosnia at the end of the 1850s, peasants utilised a variety of rumours, including that the *üçleme* had been abolished, that the peasants of neighbouring districts were not paying the tax, or that no respective decree of the sultan existed. Authorities were alarmed and proclamations (*ilannames*) were disseminated to the people stating that similar rumours were fabricated by Montenegrin and Serbian bandits.[42]

In 1859, for example, eight men were reported to wander around the villages of the district of Zvornik and Gradačac, escorted by bandits, trying to persuade the peasants not to pay the *üçleme* tax by spreading the rumour that nearby districts were not paying it either. In fact, one of the bandits, named Vasil Milenković, had gone several times to Serbia and had allegedly spread several rumours among the peasants of the district of Brčko in the sub-province of Zvornik upon his return.[43] In the same district, a disagreement unfolded between the peasants and the tax collectors (*mültezim*) of the tithe regarding the transport of the tithe provisions. When state officials were sent from the province's capital in order to solve the issue, the peasants gathered seventy to eighty bandits as their heads and appeared at the local council stating that either they should be provided with a decree that stipulated that the peasants were obliged to pay the *üçleme*, or they would refuse to pay it. When the landowners attempted to collect the tax based on a directive (*talimat*) they had received from the inspector of the province Aziz Paşa, they failed. Some representatives of the non-Muslims were summoned to the district council in order to be warned about their behaviour. They arrived again in the company of some dozens of bandits, this time stating that they would not pay the tax as long as the peasants of the neighbouring Bijeljina district were not paying it either. Nevertheless, when the men were tried in the council of the province's capital, they denied their actions.

Finally, in spring 1859 the investigative council of the province of Bosna reported that three peasants had been wandering from village to village in the district of Bijeljina, intimidating their residents with the threat that were

---

[41] Ibid., 224–5.
[42] BOA, A.MKT.UM. 525 67, 17 December 1861.
[43] BOA, MVL. 897 55, 16 April 1859, A.MKT.MVL. 107 12, 30 April 1859.

anyone to pay the *üçleme* they would burn down his hayloft, together with his house, and kill him. One of these three non-Muslims burned the grass which another non-Muslim had stored for his own animals, because he had delivered two carriages of hay in order to pay his tax debt. When he was called to the house of the governor, he appeared in companion of sixty bandits, resorting to 'improper behaviour' and stating that nobody had to the right to collect the *üçleme* from the peasants.[44]

Activist Clergy and 'Bandit' Priests

Despite a significant volume of literature on nation-state-building in southeastern Europe, there exists little analysis of the way in which churches participated in this process. The actions of Orthodox churches in the nineteenth century oscillated between the four main paradigms of nationalism, namely, modernism, ethno-symbolism, perennialism and primordialism.[45] Similarly, in nineteenth-century Europe, religious sentiments and symbols could nearly always be drawn upon by nationalist orators and organisers, while priests and pastors were often strongly influenced by nationalist ideas and gave them influential support through sermons, 'national' hymns, the teaching in church schools and Christian youth organisations.[46] Even if nineteenth-century nationalism is often seen as essentially secular, local Orthodox village priests appear in the Ottoman archives as one of the main pillars behind the revolts in Bosnia, similar to the Niš uprising in 1841.[47]

The upper levels of the clerical hierarchy in Bosnia were dominated mostly by Greek-speaking Phanariot bishops, while the Orthodox Church insisted on a Greek liturgy to the exclusion of Slavic varieties, and de facto, only Greek priests could obtain higher positions in the hierarchy.[48] Yet it

---

[44] BOA, MVL. 897 55, 16 April 1859; A.MKT.MVL. 107 12, 30 April 1859. All defendants in these cases received five years of hard labour at the Imperial Arsenal in Istanbul as a punishment.

[45] Lucian N. Leustean, 'Introduction', in Lucian N. Leustean (ed.), *Orthodox Christianity and Nationalism in Nineteenth-Century Southeastern Europe* (New York: Fordham University Press, 2014), 7.

[46] Hugh MacLeod, 'Christianity and Nationalism in Nineteenth-Century Europe', *International Journal for the Study of the Christian Church* 15(1) (2015): 12–14.

[47] Uzun, *Tanzimat ve Sosyal Direnişler*, 53–4.

[48] Suraiya Faroqhi and Fikret Adanir, 'Introduction', in Fikret Adanir and Suraiya Faroqhi

would be an anachronism to ascribe to the Patriarchate of Constantinople a conscious policy designed to promote the 'hellenisation' of the Balkans before the nineteenth century. Conflicts between the clergy and the laity did exist, but were mainly social and economic, not ethnic, something which changed radically when nationalism became a major factor in Balkan politics.[49] Moreover, Serbian monks had been travelling to Russia from the sixteenth century; the Balkan monks, as they came to rely on Russia for both material support and philosophical direction, were bound to be affected by the fundamental transformations Russia was going through pertaining to modernisation and secularisation.[50] While 'national' perception did emerge among the regional clergy and relations to Serbia and Russia were cultivated, it is argued here that it was mainly the issue of taxation and land ownership through which priests tried to mobilise their flock.

In the uprisings of the late 1850s, priests secured communication, smuggled in weapons and authorised men to incite the Christians. At the end of 1858, it was reported that priest Proto,[51] together with Luka, had dared to incite (*tahrik*) 'orally' the inhabitants of several villages of the sub-province of Bihać. Consequently, the two men were sentenced to five years' hard labour at the Imperial Arsenal in Istanbul.[52] Priest David, from a village in the district of Bihać, had participated in a gathering of bandits, and was arrested on his way to some villages to incite the Christians.[53] Sedition, however, took mostly more violent forms. Take the story of priest Ivan, for example, who was responsible for two villages in the Bijeljina district of the sub-province of

---

(eds), *The Ottomans and the Balkans* (Leiden: Brill, 2002), 29; Grandits, *Herrschaft und Loyalität in der spätosmanischen Gesellschaft*, 443.

[49] Paschalis M. Kitromilides, 'Orthodox Cultures and Collective Identity in the Ottoman Balkans during the Eighteenth Century', *Oriente Moderno* 18(79):1 (1999): 140–2.

[50] Carole Rogel, 'The Wandering Monk and the Balkan National Awakening', in William W. Haddad and William Ochsenwald (eds), *Nationalism in a Non-National State: The Dissolution of the Ottoman Empire* (Columbus: Ohio State University Press, 1977), 88.

[51] Based on their village of origin, this Proto was different from the Proto described below. In Serbian, *prota* is not actually a name, but a title for the Orthodox clergy, meaning priest. In the Ottoman documents though it is also used as a name, for example, in the expression 'papas Proto', which could be translated as 'priest Proto'.

[52] BOA, MVL. 891 57, 6 November 1858; A.MKT.MVL. 103 26, 22 November 1858.

[53] BOA, MVL. 891 73, 22 February 1859.

Zvornik. In the summer of 1859, he was accused of visiting, together with two other men, all armed, nearby villages and inviting their Christian inhabitants to participate in the rebellion. Given that Ivan was a clergyman, he did not receive the same punishment as the others: he was exiled to Kütahya in Anatolia for five years, while the other two men served five years' hard labour at the Imperial Arsenal in Istanbul.[54] One year before, two Christian peasants testified[55] in front of the local court of Zvornik as being in the house of the priest Haci Petkov when shooting took place with the gendarmerie. The peasants denied any implication and accused Haci Petkov of visiting various villages for the last two years, inciting the people not to pay the *üçleme* tax. He had managed to form a group (*cemiyet*) comprising one hundred people, had gathered them in front of his church, provided them with gunpowder he had brought from Austria, and advised them to fight against the Muslims soldiers.[56] Haci Petkov, whose interrogation was still ongoing, was labelled a 'bandit' (*şaki*) by the Supreme Court, while the two defendants received five years' hard labour at the Imperial Arsenal. Other priests had fled to Serbia and were active from there, such as the priest Ilya, originally from the district of Sjenica in the sub-province of Yenipazar. He had been arrested and sent to Istanbul but had managed to flee on the way and had passed over to Serbia. In spring 1861, information arrived that Ilya was gathering a group of people in a village near the Bosnian–Serbian border, providing them with a salary of 250 *kuruş* (piaster) per person.[57]

It is the story of Proto which is most indicative for the decisive and long-term leadership provided by local priests to the uprisings in Bosnia. On 29 August 1858, a Christian defendant named Blagoje was called to testify in front of the local court of the sub-province of Zvornik situated in the northeast of the province of Bosnia. Blagoje was accused of inciting the Christian

---

[54] BOA, MVL. 899 8, 5 June 1859; A.MKT.MVL. 108 79, 9 July 1859.
[55] The interrogation protocols were written in Ottoman Turkish. In some cases, it was stated that a translator facilitated the dialogues. Süleyman *ağa*, for example, was promoted to district governor in the sub-province of Mostar as a reward for the long-term services he had provided in local Bosnian courts translating for Christians who could not speak Turkish, see BOA, A.MKT.UM. 369 78, 4 October 1859.
[56] BOA, A.MKT.MVL. 108 25, 1 June 1859.
[57] BOA, I.DH. 471 31583, 3 May 1861.

peasants of the vicinity by spreading the news that the *üçleme* tax had been lifted and that they should refrain from paying their taxes. Blagoje for his part argued in court that he had received this information from a certain Ostojanaç and the priest Proto, who had returned from a trip to Austria and had been spreading rumours that an imperial decree had been issued stipulating that the *üçleme* would no longer be collected. Proto had also managed to gather a group of 'stupid' people (*sebük-mağzan*), urging them to burn down a house in which gendarmeries had been staying.[58] Proto reappears in the archives organising uprisings from Serbia, where he had fled in order to avoid his arrest.

In May 1860, the council of Zvornik reported that three priests from the district of Gračanica, together with some other men, had been inciting the Christian people with seditious news they had received from the 'famous priest Proto' from Serbia. As a result of this news spread among the people, the state had encountered difficulties in the collection of the vicinity's taxes.[59] In the following year, in January 1861, the priest Proto, who was now coined a 'bandit' (*şaki*), was accused of gathering thirty-six vagabonds (*serseri*), providing them with weapons and sending them to Zvornik to seduce the Christians.[60] Some of these men had been arrested and were sentenced to seven years' hard labour in Vidin. Moreover, it was ordered that Proto should be arrested the moment he crossed the borders. The priest, though, continued his activities. In May 1862, a report of the Supreme Court in Istanbul stated that Proto, now coined the 'leader of bandits' (*reis-i eşkiya*), had sent the priest Teodosije Şenkil, originally from Bihać in Bosnia, to supervise the uprising around the townships of Livno and Glamoč. Teodosije was arrested and exiled together with his family to Bolu in Anatolia.[61]

---

[58] BOA, A.MKT.MVL. 108 25, 1 June 1859. Blagoje received five years' hard labour at the Imperial Arsenal in Istanbul.
[59] BOA, I.MVL. 424 18584, 26 October 1860; A.MKT.MVL. 122 14, 8 November 1860.
[60] BOA, A.MKT.MVL. 413 79, 2 January 1861.
[61] BOA, I.MVL. 466 21099, 1 May 1862; A.MKT.MVL. 146 88, 24 May 1862.

Wandering Rebels and Suspicious Documents

Rumours were not the only means through which rebels in Bosnia communicated with each other. While imperial decrees forbade the smuggling into the country of any material that would 'incite the minds of the non-Muslim subjects',[62] dozens of Christian rebels, often jobless persons, were crossing the countryside transporting seditious printed documents and handwritten letters. On behalf of the government, such documents were described as comprising false rumours (*eracif*), inciting (*tahrik*) or causing the subversion of the minds of the people (*ifsad-ı/tağlit-i ezhan-ı ahaliye*). In fact, in 1854 it was forbidden by decree that any newspaper, book or document with political implications could enter the province of Bosnia.[63]

Neighbouring Serbia played a distinct role in mobilising ordinary Christians to roam the Bosnian countryside, travelling back and forth between Serbia and Bosnia. The father of Serbian nationalism and statesman, Ilija Garašanin, had been organising a growing network of 'secret agents' dedicated to the nationalisation of the multi-confessional Bosnia since the 1840s.[64] Nationalist organisation expanded in the 1860s and 1870s, when the earlier stands of Romantic nationalism entwined with the more militant revolution-making of the 1860s. Examples like the one of Bojo the son of Sava Rusić are abundant in the Ottoman archives: originally from the Ihlevne district in the sub-province of Travnik, he was caught while wandering around in the villages of the sub-province of Bihać. In court he testified that he had been sent together with a hundred more men by Serbian officials. He had been given the monthly salary of two Hungarian silver coins, on condition that he would 'incite the minds of the Bosnian people'. Following his trial, Bojo was sentenced to lifelong exile to Trablus.[65]

Several such men were tried in the Ottoman courts for travelling between Serbia and Bosnia with seditious documents in their possession. Juro was

---

[62] Anna Vakali, 'A Christian Printer on Trial in the Tanzimat Council of Selanik, Early 1850s: Kiriakos Darzilovitis and His Seditious Books', *Cihannüma* 1(2) (2015): 29–30.
[63] Gölen, *Tanzimat Döneminde Bosna Hersek*, 102.
[64] Hajdarpasic, *Whose Bosnia?*, 97.
[65] BOA, I.MVL. 473 21432, 15 September 1862.

arrested in a village near Bihać in 1858, with documents hidden among the double cloth of this coat, predicting an uprising in Bihać and Banja Luka. Juro, however, stated in court that he was a merchant returning from a business trip to Serbia, where he had bought the coat, unaware of the documents hidden in it.[66] Three other armed men were arrested while wandering (*geşt-ü güzar*) in the sub-provinces of Travnik and Bihać and inciting (*ifsad*) their Christian residents.[67] Their leader, Budo, was killed in ensuing fighting with the gendarmerie, but his weapons, money, horse and saddlebag were sent to the council of Travnik. Suspicious documents were found hidden inside his saddlebag, urging banditry and uprising (*şekavet ve cumhuriyete*[68] *takviyet üzere taahhüdü*), written in Serbian, signed and sealed. The two companions of Budo were tried at the council in Travnik, where they testified that they had succeeded in inciting seventy to eighty Christians in the villages of the district of Jezero, by using as a pretext of their travelling that they were collecting money to build a church in the same district. In another example, in the district of Ostrožac, a Christian, dressed in the clothes of a beggar, was sent by bandits to transport documents inciting the Christians of the districts of Livno and Novo Selo.[69]

Destojić and Petro were tried in 1860 at the council of Zvornik for wandering around the villages near Zvornik and inciting the Christians.[70] During their arrest, shots were exchanged with the gendarmerie, and a soldier, named Ali, was killed. In court, the two men admitted that they had fled Bosnia during the 1858 uprising and had now returned in order to 'understand the relations between Christians and Muslims (*muamele-i haliye*) in Zvornik',

---

[66] BOA, A.MKT.UM. 326 56, 22 September 1858.

[67] BOA, MVL. 891 57, 6 November 1858.

[68] The word '*cumhur*' carried the meaning both of 'the people', as well as of 'a mob', see J. W. Redhouse, *New Redhouse Turkish–English Dictionary*, 8th edn (Istanbul: Redhouse Yayınevi, 1986), 232; Uğur Bayraktar, 'From Salary to Resistance: Mobility, Employment, and Violence in Dibra, 1792–1826', *Middle Eastern Studies* 54(6) (2018): 887. The derived word '*cumhuriyet*' was understood as republicanism towards the end of the nineteenth century, but here its meaning relates to 'collective insurrection'. I thank Alp Eren Topal for the latter information.

[69] BOA, MVL. 895 73, 22 February 1859. The men in both cases were punished with five years' hard labour at the Imperial Dockyard in Istanbul.

[70] BOA, I.MVL. 424 18584, 26 October 1860; A.MKT.MVL. 122 14, 8 November 1860.

and were disseminating seditious letters and rumours (*fesadamir mektuplar ve eracif-i neşr*) among the peasants. Aware though that the murder of Ali, which would be adjudicated separately at a *şer'i* court, could result in capital punishment, they denied it. The Supreme Court further accused them of organising meetings during which groups of 200–250 men would practise shootings at night, and of working towards an uprising (*cumhuriyet-i ilka' çalışmaları*). Destojić and Petro were sentenced to lifelong hard labour in Vidin,[71] while the people who were hiding them were exiled for five years to Kütahya and Karahisar.

In the same year, nineteen men were arrested in the Zvornik sub-province in a destitute situation, having not eaten for days. Eight of them were tried at the council of Herzegovina, as the rest had managed to escape.[72] While the accusation included inciting Christian peasants, all defendants insisted in court that mundane reasons had brought them back to Bosnia. They had initially left Bosnia for Serbia in search of a better life, but, in time, their expectations had proved to be futile. Bankrupt businesses, debts, crimes committed in Serbia, as well as soldier recruitments in the neighbouring country were mentioned by the defendants in court as the main reasons of their migrating back, in search of a better life.[73]

Nevertheless, documents found in the bag of one of them, named Deste, revealed different intentions. They included four handwritten letters, one addressed to Deste and three written by himself. The first one expressed deep regret about the separation of Serbs living in Serbia and Bosnia, and placed hope in Milos, the Serbian prince, to save Serbian co-religionists (*din karındaşlarımız*) in Bosnia.[74] The letters written by Deste himself, addressed

---

[71] The men who had been hiding them were sentenced to temporary hard labour, according to Article 63. Nevertheless, it was acknowledged by the Supreme Court that it was difficult to resist the 'bandits', and therefore they were exiled for five years each to the provinces of Kütahya and Karahisar.

[72] BOA, I.HR. 182 10124, 25 February 1861.

[73] They used similar expression for this: '*geçinmek/idare olmak için çıktık/bir kapı aramak üzere/orada geçinmek güç olduğundan*'.

[74] BOA, I.HR. 182 10124, 25 February 1861: '. . . it is not possible to express with words the wounds in our hearts, the separation [between Christians in Serbia and Bosnia] is a very evil thing . . . My brother, we will not abandon you, as we will not abandon our co-religionists . . .'

to various Bosnians, informed them that 400 people were coming from Serbia, divided into gangs (*çete*), fighting against oppression, and counting on the help of the locals.[75] When Deste was asked in court to comment on the content of the letters, he chose to remain silent. In his writing, the governor of Bosnia assured the Supreme Court that these men had been among the bandits (*eşkıya çetelerinden*) who had fled from Bosnia to Serbia and were working towards a general sedition. Their leader, Deste, was expelled by the Austrian consul on account of holding an Austrian passport, while the rest of the men, since they denied their deeds and thus could not be punished with hard labour, were expelled for an indefinite period to Kütahya.

A New Political Imaginary?

Promises to peasants concerning the abolition of taxes were often coupled with political ones, referring to a new order or the establishment of a 'state of Christians', as the protagonist of this section, priest Simo, was heralding to his fellow Christians. The following story of the village priest Simo illustrates how the abolition of taxes depended upon a new political order, in which Christians would be governing themselves. Peasants were attracted to this new idea not through cultural or ethnical references, but through the promise of the fulfilment of their main concern, the abolition of taxes and the ownership of the lands they were cultivating. In this sense, priest Simo acted differently than nationalists like the teacher at the Orthodox school in Sarajevo in the 1860s, Teofil Petranović, who organised a group of people to go out into the villages and tell the Orthodox peasants that they should stop calling themselves '*hriscani*' (the local term for 'Orthodox') and should instead self-define themselves as 'Serbs'.[76]

In 1861, weapons were smuggled by priest Simo and some village men from Serbia to the Banja Luka sub-province.[77] Thirty defendants were tried

---

[75] Ibid.: 'My brother Vasilice, we inform you that we have arrived from Serbia. The moment you receive my letter . . . inform our coreligionists, that they should prepare themselves right away . . . We are sending *çete* from four directions . . . We have experienced numerous oppressions by our enemies. If it is necessary, we will inform Europe about our situation . . .'
[76] Malcolm, *Bosnia*, 126.
[77] BOA, I.MVL. 459 20664, 30 December 1861; I.MVL. 493 22328, 22 September 1863. All footnotes in this section are based on these two folders.

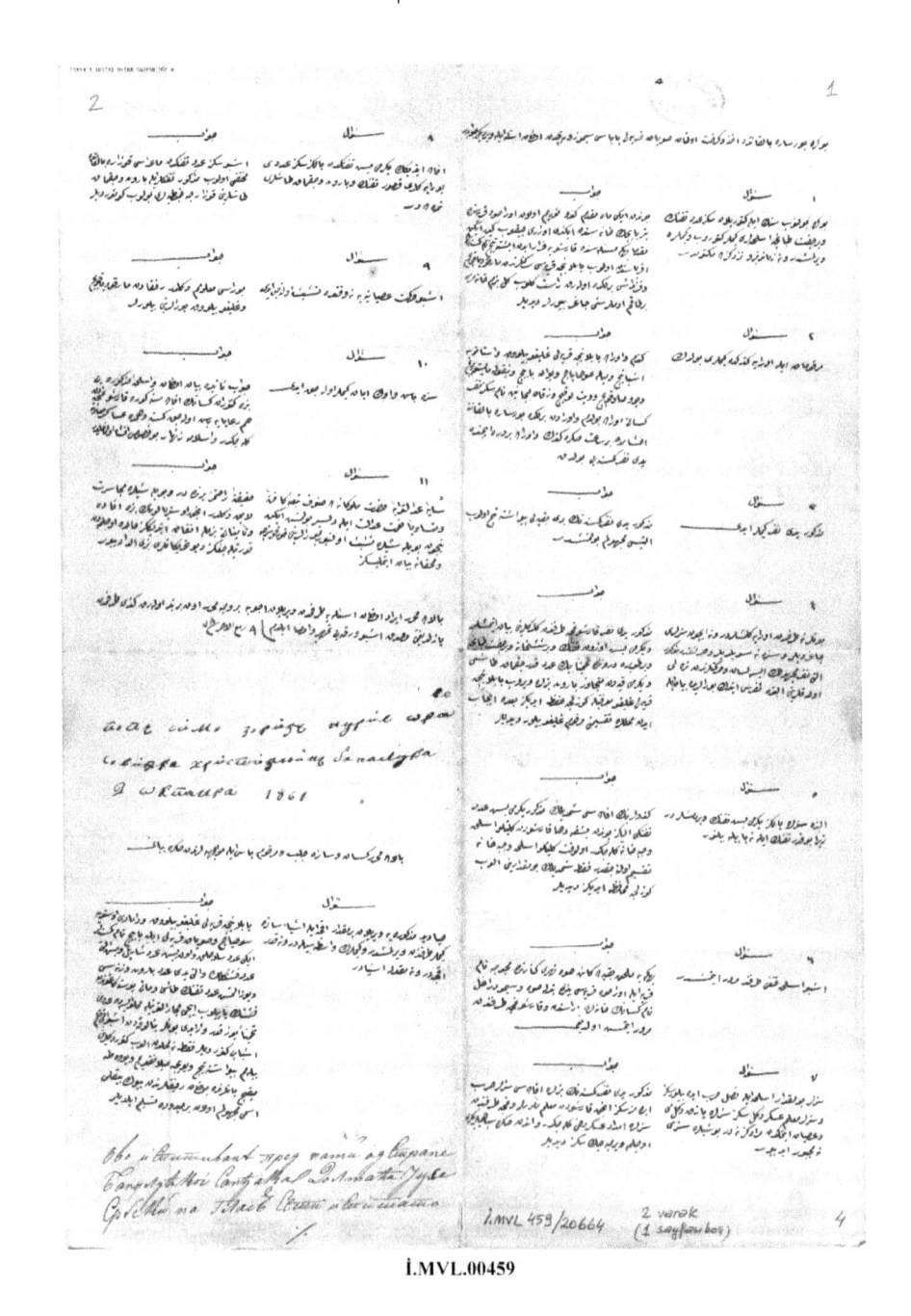

Figure 5.1 Example of an Ottoman interrogation protocol. BOA, I.MVL. 459 20664, 30 December 1861.

in the framework of this case for having received and smuggled the weapons (Figure 5.1).[78] The peasants, interrogated one by one, stated in court that they had received the weapons, gunpowder and military tools from bandits, who had invited them to the mountains. The latter were among the 'famous bandits', who had fled to Serbia after the first uprisings, and priest Simo was the main contact person to them. Upon meeting with the bandits, the peasants were each given three to four rifles and pistols, gunpowder and some flints. According to some defendants, 600 guns had arrived from Serbia and Moscow. The defendants argued that they were forced to hide the guns, until an uprising would take place up to six months later.[79]

According to the defendants' statements in court, while connecting them to the bandits in the mountains, Simo promised them that many soldiers were about to come from Serbia and Austria in order to support the uprising; soldiers would 'fall like rain' (*yağmur nasıl yağarsa öyle buraya çok asker gelecektir*), and all Christians were about to rise up (*bütün hristiyan ayaklanacağını*). Nevertheless, Simo was careful in pinpointing that the fight would not be with the sultan's soldiers (*padişah ile gavga olmayacak*), but with the fief-holders (*fakat sipahiler ile gavga edecekler*).[80] Both the Austrian emperor and the Turks had no knowledge of the smuggling of guns. In this sense, Simo conformed to the common discourse of peasants, who used to 'formulate their demands in the language of allegiance to the Ottoman state, positioning

---

[78] The defendants were tried at the local council of Banja Luka, which, according to the regulations of the Tanzimat, comprised twelve members, one of whom was an Orthodox notable and one a Catholic. This was similar in all councils which adjudicated the cases presented in this chapter.

[79] Particularly, defendants argued that the bandits would have killed their families – as they had witnessed in similar cases – if they had refused to accept the guns. One defendant had hidden the gunpowder he had been given in the ceiling of his house; when it accidentally fell on the ground and exploded, two of his younger sisters (two and three years old) were burnt and died some days later. The Supreme Court though interpreted the peasants' actions as part of 'a contemplated and decided sedition'; accordingly, their acceptance of the guns signalled their agreement to the uprising against the state.

[80] It is interesting that Simo did not use the word *ağa* (local big landowner), but *sipahi* (cavalry soldier, holder of fiefdom). In fact, Muslim lords, descendants of *sipahis*, and urban notables became the true owners of state land during the eighteenth century, see Quataert, 'Rural Unrest in the Ottoman Empire, 1830–1914', 42.

themselves as antagonists to local authorities, but not to that in Istanbul'.[81] Their aim thereby was to 'evade some of the possible consequences of a failed insurrection, but also to increase their chances of success'.[82] Priest Simo though did not refrain from polarising his flock: a fight would be started with the Turks/Muslims – both terms used – and the peasants had to keep pace, as well as provide the soldiers with animals and grain provisions. The use of violence was often a strategic weapon on behalf of smaller or even 'political' groups or, in our case, Simo, in order to create loyalties despite resistance. As Grandits has observed in his study on late Ottoman Herzegovina, during the dynamics of war, uprisings and organised violence, people were urged to 'clear assignments', loyalty on the basis of confession was asked, and the multi-layered loyalties – related to the *çiftlik*, family, as well as confession – were negated.[83]

Simo's main promises to the peasants pertained to the issue of taxation and land ownership. Analysing the rise of nationalism in the European parts of the Ottoman Empire, Bayly has argued that 'the main force aiding the intelligentsia in fragmenting the empire was the practical calculation of the peasantry that it would gain more secure property rights after national independence from the Ottomans'.[84] In addition, Hajdarpasic has underlined the importance of neighbouring Serbia, 'due to the existence of [which], notions of statehood – even then declared unattainable or rejected by many patriots – were nonetheless present as organizational templates that helped generate in the early nineteenth century new political positions and relations across eastern Europe'.[85] Thus, according to priest Simo, the peasants' main concerns would be fulfilled in a new political order: if they would rise up, they would not be obliged anymore to pay the *üçleme* to the landlords (*ondan sonra sipahilerinize üçleme vermeyeceksiniz*); the landlords' stewards would be expelled from the villages (*subaşıları köylerden ihraç edeceğiz*); the peasants would become owners of their own property (*kalktığınız vakitte mülke malik*

---

[81] Aytekin, 'Peasant Protest in the Late Ottoman Empire', 219.
[82] Ibid., 221.
[83] Grandits, *Herrschaft und Loyalität in der spätosmanischen Gesellschaft*, 665–6, 675.
[84] Bayly, *The Birth of the Modern World 1780–1914*, 213.
[85] Hajdarpasic, *Whose Bosnia?*, 93.

olacağınız); and, finally, 'Turks would rule over Turks and Christians over Christians, like it was the case in Serbia' (*bundan böyle Türklere Türkler ve hristiyanlara hristiyan Sirbya gibi hükm edecek*). Simo was sentenced for his inciting behaviour to exile to Amasya, and the rest of the men to five years' imprisonment in Diyarbakir.[86]

By the mid-nineteenth century, notions of statehood had spread not only in Bosnia, but throughout the Balkans. The promises of Simo and their adoption by peasants in front of the court echoed the statements made by Bulgarian priests, artisans and peasants in the courts of the Tuna province, following local uprisings they had organised in the same period, that is, the early 1860s.[87] When asked to account for their actions, Bulgarians referred to mundane intentions like 'making money', but mainly to political promises that had been made to them, including seizing/conquering territories (*istediğiniz mahalleleri/vilayetleri/yerleri alıp zapt/istila edeceğiniz*), putting a flag on the mountains (*bayrak dikeceğiz*), establishing a Bulgarian government (*Bulgar hükümeti teşkil edeceğiz*), up to bringing a king to Bulgaria (*Bulgaristan'a krallık kazandırmak için*). In fact, between the uprisings in the early and late 1860s, the aspirations of Bulgarians as stated in court increasingly homogenised around the goal of establishing a Bulgarian state, with all defendants providing identical statements to their interrogators by the late 1860s. The establishment of the Serbian Principality and the Greek kingdom had highly affected the political imaginary of non-Muslims throughout the Balkans, 'a collective structure that organizes the imagination and the symbolism of the capital';[88] ordinary non-Muslims saw that the possible fulfilment of their quotidian demands relied upon a new, self-governing political order.

---

[86] Simo had confided to the defendants that the metropolitan was also after him. Nevertheless, when he himself was interrogated in court, he stated that he had been incited by Austrians, who had promised to free them from taxation were they to ally with Austria.

[87] Anna Vakali, 'Tanzimat in the Province: Nationalist Sedition (*fesat*), Banditry (*eşkiya*) and Local Councils in the Ottoman Southern Balkans (1840s to 1860s)', PhD thesis, University of Basel, 2017, 132–6.

[88] Craig Browne and Paula Diehl, 'Conceptualising the Political Imaginary: An Introduction to the Special Issue', *Social Epistemology: A Journal of Knowledge, Culture and Policy* 33(5) (2019): 393.

The State's Reaction

While the state labelled and punished the protagonists of this widespread mobilisation among the non-Muslims of Bosnia, it was hardly able to tackle the main reasons that engendered it. Local courts, as well as the Supreme Court in Istanbul and the sultanic decrees, employed a standardised language in order to describe the protagonists of the cases described above: they were organised by 'bandits' (*eşkıya*), who were seducing (*tahrik, iğfal*) the people, organising secret committees (*ittifak-ı hafi*) and were thus committing sedition (*fesat*) and violating (*ihlal*) the public order (*asayiş-i umumi*). The standardised and repetitive usage of legal terms such as '*fesad*' and '*tahrik*' reveals little about the exact content of such terms, and especially the meanings they acquired for the Ottoman authorities. The term 'bandit' is of particular interest as its ubiquitous use in official correspondence seems to empty it of any specific meaning. In fact, even before the Tanzimat, the term 'bandit' had been used in order 'not to refer to a certain or fixed group of people identified as bandits in that locality, but as a sort of generic term to emphasize the "outlaw" or "criminal" character of the accused'.[89]

In the examples provided here we have seen the term used for local priests, for people delivering suspicious documents, for groups supporting in court peasants who were refusing to pay their taxes, or for men who smuggled in weapons from Serbia into Bosnia. Reports like this from Bihać in February 1859 further corroborate this point: 'bandits' had used two Christian men as their 'secret agents', while another man in Novo Selo had incited the bandits of his own village.[90] Recent historiography on Ottoman banditry in the eighteenth century has widened the spectrum of banditry, arguing that 'there was more to banditry than material gains; a complex "economy of violence" entailed exchanges of resources, prestige, symbolic capital and promotion'.[91] The widespread use by the Ottoman authorities of the word 'bandit' aimed at

---

[89] Basak Tuğ, *Politics of Honour in Ottoman Anatolia: Sexual Violence and Socio-Legal Surveillance in the Eighteenth Century* (Leiden: Brill, 2017), 129.
[90] BOA, MVL. 895 73, 22 February 1859.
[91] Tolga U. Esmer, 'Economics of Violence, Banditry and Governance in the Ottoman Empire around 1800', *Past and Present* 224(1) (2014): 164.

'play[ing] down the political intention of the various plotters and treat[ing] them as mere criminals'.[92] Ottomans used precisely the same language of 'bandits' or 'conspirators' for the Greek and, later, for all the other nationalist, revolutionary, irredentist or secessionist movements, and did not identify them as 'nationalists' or 'revolutionaries'.[93]

The Supreme Court and the sultanic decrees were judging the culprits according to the Penal Codes of 1840, 1851 and 1858. In cases where the offences had been committed before the issuing of the Penal Code of 1858, the crimes were adjudicated according to the previous Penal Code. Depending on the severity of the deeds, culprits could be punished by three to fifteen years' hard labour as well as by capital punishment. In the cases discussed here, the most usual punishment was either exile to an Anatolian province or hard labour at the Imperial Dockyard in Istanbul. Even after having completed their terms, the culprits were often not allowed to return to their homes. A decree issued in September and October 1861 ordered that the participants of the Zvornik uprisings, who had completed their terms of hard labour, should now be exiled to Kütahya for an indefinite period, as it would not be safe to allow them to return to their places of birth.[94]

During and after the uprisings, the state was unable to mitigate the three main issues connected to them: owning and smuggling guns, migration and, above all, taxation. The Ottoman Balkans had never been a society without guns, but, by the late nineteenth and early twentieth century, the region truly became what might be called a 'gun society' when its inhabitants increasingly connected themselves with the illicit circuits of the global marketplace of revolution.[95] Efforts to collect the guns from non-Muslims had taken place as early as the 1850s, but fright and panic among the population obliged the

---

[92] Florian Rieder, *Opposition and Legitimacy in the Ottoman Empire: Conspiracies and Political Cultures* (London: SOAS, Routledge, 2011), 68.

[93] Hakan Erdem, '"Perfidious Albanians" and "Zealous Governors": Ottomans, Albanians, and Turks in the Greek War of Independence', in Antonis Anastastopoulos and Elias Kolovos (eds), *Ottoman Rule and the Balkans, 1760–1850: Conflict, Transformation, Adaptation* (Rethymno: University of Crete, 2007), 236.

[94] BOA, I.MVL. 454 20320, 2 October 1861; A.MKT.MVL. 133 79, 14 October 1861.

[95] Ramazan Hakkı Öztan, 'Tools of Revolution: Global Military Surplus, Arms Dealers and Smugglers in the Late Ottoman Balkans, 1878–1908', *Past and Present* 237(1) (2017): 193.

authorities to postpone the measures.[96] In December 1861, the governor of Banja Luka reported that Serbian bandits were secretly importing guns and disseminating them to the people. Nevertheless, the people should not be pressured to deliver the weapons to the authorities, as this could cause fright and their flight to Austria. Instead, proclamations (*ilanname*) in the Serbian language were disseminated to the villages, asking the people to give up their weapons of their own will, for their protection from the bandits.[97] Later, in 1868, the governor of Bosnia, Osman Paşa, informed the sultan that he had received information that the committee (*cemiyet*) of Bucharest was about to send weapons to Travnik, calling for respective measures to be taken.[98]

Christians continued to migrate between Bosnia and Serbia. A few years after the uprisings, in 1865, the governor of Bosnia reported that seditious people had entered his province, holding Serbian passports, on the pretext of selling agricultural products.[99] Their actual intention had been to provide promises to non-Muslims pertaining to the services they would enjoy from the Serbian government should they migrate to Serbia: land, animals, agricultural tools and housing were promised; in addition, no taxes would be collected for five years and no military conscription would take place for ten years. Secret agents had also been sent to Serbia in order to convince the people who had already migrated to return: they reported that the fugitives regretted their migration, were not able to make ends meet in Serbia, and neither did they possess the necessary resources to pay for their expenditures to come back. In fact, they were on the verge of starvation. The governor of Bosnia visited the sub-provinces of Zvornik, Banja Luka and Bihać himself in April 1865 in order to 'reform' the minds of the people (*islah-ı efkarları*), leading to 2,004 fugitives returning to their homeland.

Examination of the successive tax regulations reveals a government earnestly trying to resolve the dilemma between its desire for a civil tax collection system and the financial challenges it faced.[100] Tanzimat bureaucrats were

---

[96] BOA, I.HR. 86 4197, 20 April 1852.
[97] BOA, A.MKT.UM. 529 29, 2 January 1862; A.MKT.UM. 528 74, 31 December 1861.
[98] Gölen, *Tanzimat Döneminde Bosna Hersek*, 122.
[99] BOA, A.MKT.MHM. 336 64, 5 July 1865.
[100] Özbek, 'The Politics of Taxation and the "Armenian Question"', 779.

aware that their failure to create a more humane system threatened to erode taxpaying subjects' loyalty to the government.[101] During the uprisings of the late 1850s two tax directives were issued, albeit their actual implementation seemed problematic. According to the one of 1857, forced labour (*angarya*) was forbidden, while the process of tax collection was described in detail.[102] Nevertheless, in the following years complaints of the peasants continued, including that their animals were being bought at very low prices, that they paid for the transport of the products to the landlord, and that the houses they built were taken by the landlords.[103] The most encompassing directive, the Safer Decree, was issued in September 1859, but could not be enforced.[104] Following the gathering of a commission in Istanbul comprising landowners, *kmets* and free peasants, it was decided that *angarya* would be limited, the peasants were free to leave the landlord, while the latter was allowed to evict them only on grounds of unsatisfactory work or non-payment of dues; finally, an upper limit on the products delivered to the landowner was determined.[105] Overall, while the rights of the landlords over the peasants were narrowed with the Safer Decree of 1859, the actual abolition of landowners' rights did not take place and the tributes paid by the peasants were not reduced. Nevertheless, the Safer Decree brought peasant families more legal protection and more security in settling on a plot of land. Peasants could not be sent away any more by the landowner, bigger villages and settlements evolved, and peasants were eager to buy land from the landowners.[106] Measures for a better distribution of taxes continued in the 1860s,[107] while taxation continued to be the main plague of Ottoman subjects. A bigger uprising broke out in 1875, leading to the occupation of Bosnia by the Habsburg Empire.

---

[101] Ibid., 779.
[102] Gölen, *Tanzimat Döneminde Bosna Hersek*, 36–9.
[103] BOA, A.MKT.NZD. 281 57, 16 May 1859.
[104] Gölen, *Tanzimat Dönemi Bosna İsyanları (1839–1878)*, 32.
[105] Malcolm, *Bosnia*, 129.
[106] Grandits, *Herrschaft und Loyalität in der spätosmanischen Gesellschaft*, 175–8.
[107] BOA, MKT.MHM. 336 64, 5 July 1865. Starting from the district of Derbend, and then proceeding also to other districts of Banja Luka, councils comprising twenty-nine Muslim and non-Muslim notables, as well as peasants, were established in order to correct the tax registries.

Conclusion

The uprisings unfolding around the 1860s left their imprint on the population: at the outset of Habsburg rule in Bosnia in 1879, imperial officials already observed that the turmoil of the past uprisings made 'the population warlike, in recent years often forced to ... protect their interest by arms, [and] easily accessible to foreign "agitators" and "agents"'.[108] Max Bergholz has argued that in analysing violence we should better 'appreciate the power of violence not simply as a destructive force, but also as a highly generative one in radically shaping the limits and possibilities for individual and group identification'.[109] Violence, in short, is a generative force in shaping forms of ethnic identification and social relations.

Yet this chapter argues that both the actors as well as the demands of the early violent uprisings of the late 1850s to early 1860s were very much diverse; indeed, the agency which these actors displayed refutes any linear explanation of the culmination of ethnic violence that followed in the Balkans during the late nineteenth century. Local village priests appear as the main forerunners of social mobilisation, authorising individuals and gangs to incite fellow Christians – often in lieu of material gains – securing communication between people over wider areas, and smuggling and distributing weapons. A combination of factors such as their position in local communities, as well as their opposition to the higher echelons of the Orthodox Church and the Patriarchate in Istanbul – dominated by Greek-speaking Phanariotes, who demonstrated a higher allegiance to the Ottoman Empire – positioned these priests at the forefront of the uprisings. Peasants, on the other hand, were not passive recipients of inciting messages, but took the initiative of refusing the payment of taxes, providing, moreover, a thorough argumentation in front of the Ottoman courts. Messages of an uprising and the allegiance to Serbia made it to the countryside not through educated elites like teachers, but via jobless wanderers and 'bandits', who travelled around, often in a destitute situation, with letters and pamphlets

---

[108] Hajdarpasic, *Whose Bosnia?* 99.
[109] Max Bergholz, *Violence as a Generative Force: Identity, Nationalism, and Memory in a Balkan Community* (Ithaca, NY: Cornell University Press, 2016), 16.

addressed to the people. The mobilisation and gradual 'nationalisation' of the people was based not on references to cultural or ethnical allegiances, but on the abolition of the heavy tax burden which had been loaded on the peasant population. The promise of the abolition of the *üçleme*, the main tax paid by Christian peasants to their Muslim landowners, carried important implications for the ownership of the lands Christians were cultivating; a refusal to pay the *üçleme* implied the questioning of the Muslim landowners' rights over their lands and opened the way for the appropriation of the land by the peasants. Indeed, promises made to the peasants by local priests equated tax abolition with the establishment of 'a state of Christians': it was only in such a state that peasants could become the true owners of the lands they were cultivating.

The protagonists of this chapter can be understood as early examples of the 'Age of Rogues' (1880s–1920s), to which this volume is dedicated. In fact, while research has mainly focused on the culmination of ethnic violence towards the late nineteenth and early twentieth century, during which 'rogues' or '*komitadjis*' decisively determined social mobilisation in what had remained of the Ottoman Balkans, the present chapter argues that the 'Age of Rogues' carries a longer history than has been generally assumed. For sure, in comparison with later rogues, the protagonists of this chapter were more loosely organised than later examples; their mobility was rather local, covering the immediate frontier regions of the empire and neighbouring countries; the smuggling of weapons entailed smaller quantities. Yet the 'Age of Rogues' inherited certain experiences and practices from these earlier examples described in this chapter: the utilisation of rumours in order to mobilise people; the transfer of handwritten and printed material in order to incite the people; the organisation of people throughout wider geographies; and, most importantly, paramilitarism, banditry and guerrilla warfare as the main codes and strategies which the 'rogues' of the mid-nineteenth century passed over to their successors. Without a 'genealogy' of the rogues throughout the nineteenth century, the depiction of a sudden eruption of inter-ethnic violence at the turn of the twentieth century remains problematic and incomplete.

6

The Abode of Sedition: Resistance, Repression and Revolution in Sasun, 1891–1904

Toygun Altıntaş

In autumn 1904, the governor of Bitlis dispatched a coded telegram to the Yıldız Palace, the seat of the Ottoman sultan, regarding the completion of the construction of military installations in Sasun, a remote and mountainous region of the province. The report also included a detailed description of the opening ceremony. The governor stated that he had accompanied an assortment of government officials and local Muslim notables to the villages and wards where a network of military outposts and a barracks had been constructed. The notables, the officials and the accompanying troops prayed for the health of the sultan against an assembly of local Armenians – including those who worked in the construction (*kariyan ve asakir-i şahane tarafından haffar-ı kesire ve mahalli kurra Ermeni ahali-i müctemasına karşı padişahım çok yaşa dua-ı maruzu ile çıkarılan avaz ve sedalar*). On the other hand, the local Muslims, the governor reported, were immensely relieved and grateful that the construction was finally completed. It would prevent further sedition and rebellion in the region, which had turned into a centre for the organisation of such acts.[1]

The claim and bravado of the governor's report echoed another memorandum that had been submitted to the palace a decade ago. In autumn

---

[1] Devlet Başkanlığı Osmanlı Arşivi (Prime Ministry's Ottoman Archives, BOA hereafter), Yıldız Perakende Evrak-ı Umum Vilayet (Y. PRK. UM.) 71/49, 2 October 1904.

1894, the commander of the Ottoman Fourth Army had informed the palace that the military expedition to Sasun, which he personally concluded, had resulted in the death of approximately a thousand rebels, and had decisively stopped the process of its transformation into an 'abode of sedition' (*darü'l-fesad*).[2] This chapter will explore how and why this remote and mountainous region came to acquire such political significance that local and imperial officials of rank and status expressed such interest in its subjugation or even conquest at the turn of the twentieth century. It will also explore how Armenian revolutionaries utilised transgressive politics and propagated its use in order to further their goals.

In the last quarter of the nineteenth century, Sasun was home to a mixed population of Armenian and Muslim peasants and pastoralists.[3] The former grew grains and maintained herds of sheep and goats. Most paid tribute in kind to a Muslim lord, and expected protection from outsiders in return. On the one hand, such 'traditional' tributary payments constituted a heavy burden on Armenian peasants, some of whom also paid tithes and the sheep tax to official tax-collectors or tax-farmers. On the other hand, bonds of clientage and patronage could produce stronger solidarity than religious or ethnic affiliation in armed disputes. The regional demographics underwent seasonal changes as Kurdish pastoralists from the southwest and the southeast arrived in increasing numbers in the summer to graze their flocks in the highlands.

For most of the nineteenth century, Sasun lay outside the direct reach of Ottoman modernisation. However, the state's failure to reach the highlands of Sasun does not suggest that the inhabitants of the region were isolated from the transformations of the long nineteenth century. On the contrary,

---

[2] BOA, Yıldız Esas Evrak (Y. EE.) 158/8, 6 October 1894.
[3] Reliable estimates for the historic region of Sasun list some 40,000 Armenian inhabitants to a roughly equal number of Kurds. The particular section of Sasun, which would witness the most severe bouts of mass violence in 1894 and 1904, was home to roughly 10,000 Armenians. For a detailed outline of Armenian villages and corresponding estimates for their populations, see Garo Sasuni, *Patmut'iwn Taroni Ashkharhi* (Ant'ilias: Mets Tann Kilikiyo Kat'oghikosut'iwn, 2013) 328–39. Sasuni reworked figures from the works of the Soviet Armenian scholar, Vartan Bedoian. Also see Raymond Kevorkian, 'The Armenian Population of Sassoun and the Demographic Consequences of the 1894 Massacres', *Armenian Review* 47(1/2) (2001): 41–53.

the Armenians of Sasun maintained close cultural and economic connections with the lowlands, the towns of Muş and Aleppo, and the imperial capital among other places through trade, education, pilgrimage and seasonal migration.[4] The latter was a particularly contested issue: the increase in the number of pastoralists who arrived in Sasun to graze their animals increased in the last decades of the nineteenth century. The Ottoman district governor of Genc attributed this increase to the wretched conditions of their wintering grounds.[5] Zozan Pehlivan has pointed to the intermittent waves of drought in the nineteenth century and the profound crisis in which they placed the pastoralists of Ottoman Kurdistan, particularly with regard to the scarcity of available pastures and the mass starvation of herd animals.[6] The use of pastures in Sasun quickly became a source of dispute between Armenian peasants and Kurdish pastoralists. The Armenian peasants requested the intervention of the state to prevent their arrival. While a ban was in place for several years, it was no longer in effect by the 1890s both in order to address the pastoralists' desperate need for alternative pastures and to place the Sasun Armenians under the pastoralists' dominance. In a region where the inhabitants – Muslim and Armenian alike – possessed firearms, disputes over the use of pastures escalated to armed clashes. Cattle rustling also took place with increasing frequency.

Between 1891 and 1904, Sasun and its inhabitants came to occupy a central position in the articulation of Ottoman policies of ethnic exclusion and hierarchisation, and Armenian revolutionary plans to organise an armed rebellion and attract international attention. Yet the existing literature has paid little attention to the dynamics of these policies of exclusion, with the notable exception of the Hamidian massacres of 1895/6.[7] Scholars have out-

---

[4] For Sasuntsi migrant-labour in Aleppo, for example, see Vahram L. Shemassian, 'The Sasun Pandukhts in Nineteenth-Century Aleppo', in R. Hovannisian (ed.), *Armenian Baghesh/Bitlis and Taron/Mush* (Costa Mesa, CA: Mazda, 2001), 175–89.

[5] BOA, Y. EE. 172/10, 8 August 1893.

[6] Zozan Pehlivan, 'El Niño and the Nomads: Global Climate, Local Environment, and the Crisis of Pastoralism in Late Ottoman Kurdistan', *Journal of the Economic and Social History of the Orient*, forthcoming. I am grateful to the article's author for sharing it with me before publication.

[7] This is also true in relation to Sasun: most recent research focuses on the massacre of 1894. For a study of the 1894 massacre based primarily on diplomatic, journalistic and mission-

lined the economic and demographic impact of the large wave of pogroms and massacres against Armenians, and discussed the indirect influence of government policy in exacerbating the scale of the violence.[8] Nevertheless, the singular focus on that episode of mass violence needs to be supplemented with studies which outline the dynamic processes by which a combination of Hamidian policy, Great Power posturing, Armenian revolutionary agitation, and the initiatives of local actors transformed ethno-confessional hierarchies over the course of the reign of Sultan Abdülhamid II.[9]

At the turn of the twentieth century Sasun became one of the most important testing grounds and showcases for Ottoman policy regarding Armenians. Mobilisation of local Muslims in the policing and suppression

---

ary accounts, see Owen Miller, 'Sasun 1894: Mountains, Missionaries, and Massacres at the end of the Ottoman Empire', PhD thesis, Columbia University, 2015. For a study that primarily utilises the Ottoman archives, see Mehmet Polatel, 'The Complete Ruin of a District: The Sasun Massacre of 1894', in Yasar Tolga Cora, Dzovinar Derderian and Ali Sipahi (eds), *The Ottoman East in the Nineteenth Century: Societies, Identities and Politics* (London: I. B. Tauris, 2016), 179–98. For an apologetic account that seeks to whitewash mass violence, see Justin McCarthy, Ömer Turan and Cemalettin Taşkıran, *Sasun: The History of an 1890s Armenian Revolt* (Salt Lake City: University of Utah Press, 2014).

[8] Robert Melson, 'A Theoretical Inquiry into the Armenian Massacres of 1894–1896', *Comparative Studies in Society and History* 24(3) (1982): 481–509; Selim Deringil, 'Abdülhamid Döneminde Ermeni Meselesi' ('The Armenian Question during the Period of Abdülhamid') in Fikret Adanır and Oktay Özel (eds), *1915: Siyaset, Tehcir, Soykırım*. (Istanbul: Tarih Vakfı, 2015), 95–108; Edip Gölbaşı, 'The Official Conceptualization of the anti-Armenian Riots of 1895–1897', *Études arméniennes contemporaines* 10 (2018): 33–62. For an examination of mass conversions during the Hamidian massacres, see Selim Deringil, '"The Armenian Question is Finally Closed": Mass Conversions of Armenians in Anatolia during the Hamidian Massacres of 1895–1897', *Comparative Studies in Society and History* 51(2) (2009): 344–71.

[9] Two important works on the revolutionary parties include Gerard Libaridian, 'What was Revolutionary About Armenian Revolutionary Parties in the Ottoman Empire?' in Ronald G. Suny, Fatma M. Göçek and Norman M. Neimark (eds), *A Question of Genocide: Armenians and Turks at the end of the Ottoman Empire* (Oxford: Oxford University Press, 2011), 82–112; Louise Nalbandian, *The Armenian Revolutionary Movement: The Development of Armenian Political Parties in the Nineteenth Century* (Los Angeles: University of California Press, 1963). For a recent study of the Hunchakian Social Democratic Party's attentats against Armenian notables in the imperial capital, see Varak Ketsemanian, 'The Hunchakian Revolutionary Party and the Assassination Attempts against Patriarch Khoren Ashekian and Maksudzade Simon Bey in 1894', *International Journal of Middle Eastern Studies* 50(4) (2018): 730–55.

of Armenian dissent, discriminatory utilisation of the law against Armenians, and the withholding of punishment from official and civilian Muslims – sometimes even rewarding them – for their offences against Armenians in Sasun constituted some of the most influential, if not the earliest, precedents of Hamidian policy against Armenians. Sasun was also an important and early zone of contention for Armenian revolutionaries, who sought to assume the mantle of self-defence against the depredations of local actors such as landlords, gendarme officers and tax-collectors. They attempted to reorient localised Armenian grievances against these individuals to the Ottoman state writ large. Finally, the revolutionaries attracted the attention of foreign diplomats and international public opinion by fostering armed confrontations between themselves and the Armenian peasantry, on the one hand, and the Ottoman state, on the other.

The Hamidian State, the Hunchakian Social Democratic Party and Sasun

The central government's early interest in Sasun was primarily related to securing the allegiance of the Kurdish tribes, who resided in the region or travelled there to graze their flocks in the late spring and summer. A joint expedition under the leadership of a colonel and the former district governor of Siird was dispatched in 1889 to survey Sasun, its Kurdish inhabitants and have them submit to imperial authority. Mehmed Safi Bey, the former district governor, penned a report and a policy paper to present the conduct of the expedition, its findings and recommendations. According to the district governor, the pastoralist tribes that wanted to use the Sasun pastures had submitted to imperial authority at the first sign of overwhelming force. Without bloodshed, the military expedition had secured their allegiance, received promises from them for orderly conduct and loyalty to the sultan.[10]

However, the sedentary Kurds of Sasun raised the district governor's concern. During his travels between Muslim villages in the region over a period of twenty-five days, Mehmed Safi Bey had observed serious deficiencies in the religious orthodoxy of their inhabitants. He stated that the peasants displayed a remarkable ignorance of Sunni law and practice, did not allow the settle-

---

[10] BOA, Y.PRK.UM. 19/64, Mehmed Safi Bey's Memorandum, 13 November 1890.

ment of Sunni clerics among them, and freely engaged in extramarital sex. Moreover, they freely mingled with their Armenian neighbours, and adopted their language and cultural practices.[11]

In order to minimise Armenian influence in the region, Mehmed Safi Bey advised the expansion of a network of religious and educational institutions in the region to bolster orthodoxy among the sedentary Kurds. More importantly, however, the palace was not to pay much heed to Armenian complaints about raids by Kurdish tribes. He accepted that Armenian complaints needed to be contained, but added that reliance on Armenian accounts in the settlements of the inter-confessional conflicts would reduce the influence of Kurds in the region. If Kurdish tribal leaders felt that their authority was wavering, they might make common cause with the Armenians or openly revolt against the government.[12] Therefore, the preservation of Muslim primacy in the region would be beneficial to the government, and act as a bulwark against any future Armenian attempt at a rebellion.

Sasun was also one of the first regions in which Armenian revolutionaries sought to organise in large numbers. Its location in mountainous terrain afforded valuable shelter to small armed bands, while allowing access to the Muş plain and the town when they needed. The relative scarcity of gendarmes and soldiers in the region also drew the interest of early revolutionary organisers. Perhaps more important than both, however, was the established prevalence of the possession and utilisation of firearms among the peasants of the region. The Armenians of Sasun were known to have clashed with pastoralist Kurds over access to their pastures, and participated in the inter-tribal disputes of their Muslim lords and neighbours. Many revolutionaries viewed the presence of such a martial culture among Armenian peasants as a blessing and an opportunity: the extant truculence and experience were to be refocused and redirected against the state.

Mihran Damadian (1863–1945) was one of the first revolutionaries to arrive in Sasun. He was an Armenian Catholic from the imperial capital and worked as a primary school teacher in Muş between 1884 and 1888. He joined the nascent Hunchakian Party in the late 1880s and participated

---

[11] Ibid.
[12] BOA, Yıldız Perakende Arzuhaller ve Jurnallar (Y.PRK.AZJ.) 17/116, 13 November 1890.

in one of their first mass demonstrations in Kumkapı in 1890. He fled to Athens to avoid capture during the ensuing investigation. The Hunchakian central committee, located in Athens at the time, tasked him with travel to and organisation in Sasun. In late 1891, he entered the empire clandestinely, and travelled to Muş through Diyarbakır in a long and arduous journey.[13]

Damadian was a frequent contributor during 1892 and 1893 to the official organ of the Hunchakian Party. Writing under the pen-name Scourge (*Mdrag*), he wrote on the socio-economic difficulties faced by the Armenian peasants of Sasun as well as the Muş plain.[14] He wrote about the increasing frequency of pastoralist incursions to the Armenians pastures in the highlands, as well as the pastoralist lords' attempts to extract tributes from the peasants.[15] In addition to his journalistic reports, Damadian penned a monograph of poetry and songs while he was residing in Sasun. The subject matter ranged from episodes of violence against Armenians to a list of regulations and rules for the revolutionary written in verse. His literary production was a central component of his revolutionary activism. Every piece was accompanied by a list of annotations, which explicated the specific geographical locations, people and events that were mentioned. The literary body was organised in a manuscript, which Damadian probably planned to smuggle out of Sasun and have published abroad for Armenians throughout the world.[16]

In *The Gallantry of the Permtsis*, one of the longest poems in the manuscript, Damadian recounted an encounter with a young Armenian peasant from the village of Perm. The youth told Damadian of his armed exploits against Muslims – from clashes against gendarmes to assisting their Kurdish

---

[13] Some of this biographical information was compiled by his fellow revolutionary Hampartsum Boyajian in a biographical note, which was later confiscated by the authorities. BOA, Y.EE 175/10. Also see Ara Aharonian, *Heroic Figures of A.D.L.* (Los Angeles: Nor-or Publications, 2006).

[14] For some examples, see 'Namakner T'urk'iyayits'', *Hnch'ak* 3 (1892), 21 December 1891, 'Namakner Daronits'', *Hnch'ak*, 6 (1892), 20 April 1892, 15–27 April 1892, 22 April 1892 O.S. (3 May 1892).

[15] 'Namakner Daronits'', *Hnch'ak* 6 (1892), 20 April 1892.

[16] BOA, Y. EE. 175/10, 'Permts'ots' K'achut'iwn'. The manuscript was confiscated by the Ottoman authorities during the capture of some revolutionaries in 1894. I am grateful to Melissa Bilal for her comments and assistance in surveying the material. Needless to say, all errors are my own.

allies against their tribal opponents. He boasted at having killed a gendarme corporal and witnessed the killing of a sheikh at the hands of an Armenian. Damadian expressed surprise and admiration for his young narrator.[17] It is impossible to determine how much of the narrative was Damadian's invention. Nevertheless, his unmistakably positive portrayal of the young peasant and his violent encounters explicated the moral of the story: Armenian salvation could be realised only by turning the tables on Muslim oppressors and militarily overwhelming them. Armed struggle, even without sufficient political articulation, was among the most important components of the Armenian national cause.

Damadian and his revolutionary band did not hesitate to put their rhetoric into practice. In 1892 and 1893, they assisted the Sasun peasants in their clashes against Kurdish pastoralists, who came to Sasun to use their pastures and extract tributary payments from them.[18] Moreover, they assassinated several Muslims, whom they accused of exploiting the peasantry or cooperating with the government against Armenians.[19] When the gendarmes investigated one of the assassinations, it ended in failure. Armenian peasants from the region denied any knowledge, simply stating 'We know nothing. We will abide by the legal ruling.'[20] It is highly unlikely that the peasants did not know the circumstances of these attacks; their reluctance to assist the investigators stemmed from their sympathy for the revolutionaries.

That is not to suggest, however, that the Sasun Armenians' sympathy for the revolutionaries was perfectly consistent or unequivocal. Damadian was captured while traveling in Sasun in June 1893. An article in *Droshak* stated that it was not only the government's persistent efforts that had led to the detention of the famed revolutionary, but also the actions of some local Armenians.[21] The priest of Semal and his brother had informed on the whereabouts of Damadian and his companion. Another revolutionary source claimed that the priest had denied them lodging, which facilitated

---

[17] BOA, Y. EE. 175/10, 'Permts'ots' K'achut'iwn'.
[18] 'Daroni Sharzhumnerĕ', *Hnch'ak*, addendum to 6 (1892), 16 May 1892 O.S. (28 May 1892).
[19] 'Namakner T'urk'iyayits'', *Hnch'ak*, 6 (1892), 29 April 1892 O.S. (11 May 1892).
[20] BOA. Y. EE. 175/20, 1 November 1892.
[21] 'Sasuni Teghekagrut'iwn', *Droshak*, 5 (1893).

his capture.[22] Notwithstanding the exact circumstances of his detention, Ottoman gendarmes and their Kurdish allies placed Damadian under arrest, and immediately arranged for his transfer to Muş. On the road, he was tortured and injured.[23]

Damadian's capture heightened the palace's fears and anxieties regarding Armenian dissent in general, and tensions in Sasun in particular.[24] When clashes between pastoralists and Sasun Armenians began later in June, officers were dispatched from the palace to determine the cause and consequences of these intercommunal tensions.[25] The governor of the province, Tahsin Paşa, also travelled to the region to report on the violence. He claimed that the Armenian peasants had killed several pastoralists in brutal fashion, after which their fellow tribesmen attacked the Armenians.[26] The Armenians retreated to the safety of the mountains, at which point the governor arrived. A few days later, Tahsin Paşa reported that the Armenians had been compelled to return to their villages, while the pastoralists had been convinced to return to their wintering grounds. The governor claimed that Armenian truculence could be explained only by the presence of foreigners and instigators among the peasants.[27] The officers from the palace confirmed his observations.[28]

What they did not report was equally as important. Neither report mentioned the fact that the pastoralists had looted the villages after the Armenians withdrew to the mountains. Moreover, the pastoralists had previously been barred from accessing the pastures of Sasun. The ban had eroded over the course of the late 1880s, so that by the summer of 1893 several pastoralist tribes summered in Sasun and attempted to extract tributes from Armenian villages. The district governor of Genc justified the

---

[22] BOA, Y.EE. 175/10.
[23] 'Sasuni Teghekagrut'iwn', *Droshak*, 5 (1893); Aharonian, *Heroic Figures*, 36.
[24] Damadian's interrogation at Bitlis can be found in Y. EE. 172/10; his memorandum on revolutionary societies, which he submitted to the palace in return for his release, was published in Haluk Selvi, *Mihran Damadyan: Bir Ermeni Komitecinin İtirafları* (Istanbul: Timaş, 2009).
[25] BOA, Y.EE. 97/53.
[26] BOA, Y. EE. 155/22, 8 July 1893.
[27] BOA, Yıldız Sadaret Hususi (Y. A. HUS.) 277/141, 13 July 1893.
[28] BOA, Y. EE. 97/53, 17 July 1893.

erosion of the ban by drawing attention to the impoverished conditions of the pastoralists, who needed access to more pastures to sustain their flocks.

As imperial attention focused on Sasun, the material circumstances and hierarchies of exploitation in the region disappeared from official accounts. It was replaced by a simple narrative of increasing Armenian aggression against innocent Muslims. Despite evidence of extensive looting by the pastoralists, which was provided by two officers on the ground,[29] for example, the affair was reframed as a violent episode of Armenian aggression. Over the course of the next year, the designations of 'evildoer' (*müfsid, fâsid, fesede* (pl.)) and rebel (*şâki, eşkıyâ* (pl.)) were extended from the small band of revolutionaries to the entire Armenian male population of Sasun capable of bearing arms.[30] Thus, a local struggle over resources and tributary arrangements had gained imperial significance by the summer of 1894.

The Massacre of 1894

In June 1894, a company of imperial troops was dispatched to Sasun with instructions to pursue rebels. Yet the official designation of several thousand Armenian peasants as rebels and evildoers suggests that a mere company of troops was not sufficient to execute the orders. In the meantime, the pastoralists started to arrive in some numbers from the southeast and southwest, encircling the aforementioned settlements and creating a virtual state of siege as one letter stated in *Hnch'ak*.[31] The large group of pastoralists from different tribes appears to have been motivated by a combination of the organising work of an influential sheikh, rewards for their behaviour

---

[29] BOA, Y. EE. 172/10, 7 July 1893.

[30] The governor of Bitlis demanded an investigation into Armenian sedition in late April 1894 at the beginning of which he prescriptively stated that 'it was clear that the Talorians' reluctance to pay taxes and wander about with weapons stemmed from their intent to start a rebellion'. BOA, Y. EE. 172/16, 23 April 1894. He demanded more information on the Armenians so that imperial orders could be secured to dispatch soldiers. The subsequent correspondence between the governor of Bitlis and the district governor of Genc affirmed the designation of all male peasants in the Shadakh, Dzovasar, Dalvorig and Geliguzan regions of Sasun as rebels. BOA, Y. EE. 172/16.

[31] 'Namakner T'urk'iyayits", *Hnch'ak*, 2 (1894), 25 November 1893; 'Namakner T'urk'iyayits", *Hnch'ak*, 8 (1894).

by the governor of Bitlis, and a general sense of rage against openly defiant Armenian behaviour.[32]

On the other hand, some of the Sasun Kurds, who viewed themselves as the rightful lords of the Armenian peasants, continued to trade with them. Local officials expressed concern over the leaders of these tribes – namely, Hişman Ağa of Sasun and Hüseyin Ağa of Hiyan – who refused to isolate the Armenians. Allegedly, the ağas reacted with disdain to official instructions that they refrain from associating with the Armenians. They stated that the Armenians were their subjects/clients under protection, and hence would not pay taxes to the state (*bu Ermeniler bizim re'aya ve himayemizdedirler devlete akça vermeyeceklerdir*).[33] However, government policy during and after the summer of 1894 would make such a position untenable for Kurdish notables in the region.

The contours of government policy become clearer when the utter neglect of local officials to pastoralist attacks against the Sasun Armenians is taken into account. There was no effort to reinstate the ban on pastoralist access to the pastures of Sasun despite the bloody clashes of summer 1893. In fact, the former ban would later be listed as one of the reasons why the Armenians dared to engage in sedition, the implication being that the pastoralists' extortionary demands had kept the Armenians pliant (*tertib-i mefsedete cüreti Bekran aşiretinin Talori içinden memnu'iyet-i mürurlarından neş'et eylediği*).[34] In July, the pastoralists started attacking the Armenians, who retreated to the safety of the mountains. The band of revolutionaries and armed peasants engaged in several clashes against the pastoralists, which left several dead and wounded on both sides. Unlike the previous year, however, the pastoralists failed to make substantial advances.[35] The pastoralists were irked by the army's passivity at this point, and took their dead to the encamp-

---

[32] Sheikh Mehmed of Zilan was listed as one of the main culprits for pastoralist incursions into Sasun on the pages of *Hnch'ak*. 'Namakner T'urk'iyayits'', *Hnch'ak*, 1 (1894). The governor of Diyarbekir reported that the same sheikh had claimed that he would lead a large number of his men to avenge the killings of his kinsmen in 1893. BOA, Y. EE. 155/21, 29 June 1893.
[33] BOA, Y. EE. 172/8, 22 July 1894.
[34] BOA, Y. EE. 172/8, 5 August 1894.
[35] BOA, Y. EE. 153/5, 23 August 1894.

ment of the military nearby.[36] Armenian peasants and later revolutionary accounts would claim that some soldiers joined the pastoralists in Kurdish garb to assist them in their assaults.[37]

It was only in late August, however, that the company in the region was bolstered with two additional companies and mountain guns. Under the leadership of Colonel Tevfik Bey, the troops advanced against the Armenians with orders to destroy all the rebels in the region with the pastoralists in their tow. The military force maintained constant communication with the command in Muş, which, in turn, reported its correspondence to the Fourth Army command. Imperial aides-de-camp were also dispatched to maintain an alternative line of communication.[38] The palace received frequent, almost daily, updates on the status of the military expedition. Early reports were enthusiastic: Colonel Tevfik Bey reported that the majority of the Armenians had fled en masse at the sight of advancing imperial troops to nearby Mount Antok.[39]

Two days later, the commander of the Fourth Army reported that the troops had not encountered any resistance in their ascent to the mountain. Aside from a small band of foreigners in military garb – undoubtedly a reference to the band of revolutionaries – the overwhelming majority of Armenians in flight were peasants.[40] The palace's response to this piece of information was quite telling of its expectation from this expedition. The original orders to destroy all rebels were reiterated with deliberate and cynical ambiguity: 'All of the rebels are to be destroyed without giving them the opportunity to surrender and seek clemency. They are to be ruined and eradicated so as to teach Armenian evildoers a powerful lesson' ('*bu eşkıyanın iltica ve istimanlarına mahal ve meydan verilmeksizin hem'en ve seri'en cümlesinin mahv edilmesi . . . cümlesinin Ermeni erbab-ı mefsedetine ibret-i müessire olacak suretde mahv ve izalesi*'). The only exception were the 'foreigners' (*ecnebi*), or the band of revolutionaries, whom the palace ordered to be

---

[36] The National Archives (TNA hereafter), Foreign Office (FO), 424/178, No. 339, Inc. 1.
[37] 'Namakner T'urk'iyayits'', *Hnch'ak*, 1 (1895).
[38] BOA, Y. EE. 97/53; BOA, Y. EE. 153/115.
[39] BOA, Y. EE. 153/115, 8 August 1894.
[40] Reports from the ground had referred to these 'black-hats' (*siyah kalpaklılar*) in early July. BOA, Y. EE. 172/16, 1 July 1894.

captured alive, presumably for the purpose of extracting information from them.[41]

After the troops surveyed the Antok heights and pursued and killed a large number of Armenians, they proceeded to the larger villages of Geliguzan and Dalvorig. Before they shelled the villages, a number of peasants – men, women and children – sought clemency from the imperial troops. They were led by the priest of Semal. Colonel Tevfik Bey interviewed some of the peasants on the number and condition of the other Armenians in the region.[42] He informed his superior, Zeki Paşa, of what had happened and his plan to order the execution of the prisoners. Lieutenant General Edhem Paşa, who oversaw the transfer of information from the mountains in Sasun through the telegraph office of the Muş command to Zeki Paşa, attempted to intervene. He argued that Tevfik Bey's course of action would tarnish the reputation of the Ottoman state. The colonel and the commandant insisted; and the male peasants were executed that night.[43]

The execution of the peasants was a turning point for the military expedition. Edhem Paşa informed the palace of what had transpired. Although the palace had insisted on the destruction of the rebels to the last man until that point, a discernible shift took place after Edhem Paşa's report. The following day, orders were dispatched to make a clear distinction between insurgents and civilians.[44] Officials who disregarded these orders were to be held accountable for their actions. The governor of Bitlis wrote that he had no knowledge of the mass execution of Armenian peasants.[45] Zeki Paşa left his post in Erzurum to personally lead the conclusion of the military expedition and oversee the capture of the revolutionaries.[46] Hampartsum Boyajian, who had assumed the leadership of the revolutionaries in Sasun after Damadian's arrest, and his comrades were captured on 6 September, some two weeks after the imperial troops had commenced their attacks.[47]

---

[41] BOA, Y. EE. 153/142, 30 August 1894; BOA, Y. EE. 97/53, 30 August 1894.
[42] BOA, Y. EE. 153/147, 31 August 1894.
[43] BOA, Y. EE. 155/14, undated.
[44] BOA, Y. EE. 156/7, 1 September 1894.
[45] BOA, Y.EE. 156/1, 2 September 1894.
[46] BOA, Y. EE. 156/4, 2 September 1894.
[47] BOA, Y. EE. 156/57, 6 September 1894; BOA, Y. EE. 97/53, 8 September 1894.

What explains the shift in the tone of the official orders emanating from the palace after the mass execution of the peasants? It is clear that the palace was aware that the overwhelming majority of the Armenians in Sasun were peasants before the attack began. Its entire conduct from the beginning of summer 1894, its insistence on the destruction of the 'rebels' to the last man, while simultaneously calling for the capture of the 'black-hats', suggest that the killing of Armenian male peasants was a central component of the military expedition. It is possible that the colonel's earlier decision to accept the surrender of the peasants, *then* order their execution was seen as a violation of proper conduct, even against rebels. It is more likely, however, that the intervention and opposition of a high-ranking military officer like Edhem Paşa, irked the palace. A few more similar leaks had the potential to transform Sasun from an internal issue into an internationalised crisis. Therefore, the operation was to be concluded before news of Ottoman atrocities was made public.

By the time the small revolutionary band was captured in a cave on 6 September, over a thousand Armenians had been killed, and several villages had been torched. Official Ottoman reports stated that the troops faced very little resistance throughout the operation.[48] The destruction of the villages was attributed to the fleeing Armenians, who wished to deny shelter to the imperial troops. The 'rebels' had been destroyed in large numbers, and order had been restored. The women and children, according to the reports, had been given the necessary treatment as dictated by Islam and humanitarianism (*İslam ve İnsaniyet icab ettirdiği*). There was no mention of the mass execution of surrendered peasants.[49]

However, the palace soon found that it was impossible to contain the flow of information regarding the details of the massacre. By mid-October, the British ambassador had compiled a preliminary report of what had happened. Unlike official Ottoman reports, which were silent on the clashes between the pastoralists and the peasants, the British report included detailed information on the demographics of Sasun, as well as the web of relationships

---

[48] BOA, Y. EE. 172/16, 7 September 1894.
[49] Ibid.

between pastoralist Kurds, Armenian peasants and their sedentary lords.[50] On 1 November, the British Embassy requested an independent inquiry into allegations of official participation in the massacre as well as the recruitment of pastoralists in the attack. Sultan Abdülhamid II claimed he had no knowledge of the events, and would order an internal inquiry.[51]

In the next few weeks British pressure mounted. The palace was forced to accede to British demands regarding an official inquiry, and the inclusion of international observers from Russia, France and Britain to attend the hearings and question witnesses. While the British delegate was tasked with compiling a separate report to determine the extent to which Ottoman officials were implicated in the massacre of Armenian peasants,[52] the Ottoman members of the commission of inquiry were given a very different set of instructions.[53] For the palace, the primary function of the commission was the reiteration of the fiction that Sasun Armenians had engaged in armed rebellion and massacred their Muslim neighbours, that they burned their own villages upon the arrival of the imperial troops, and that the Ottoman army had acted with perfect discipline in quelling the rebellion and restoring order.

From the end of January until early May 1895, the Ottoman commission of inquiry heard witnesses and attempted to formulate a narrative explaining the Sasun 'affair' in Muş. The palace maintained direct contact with members of the commission of inquiry and called for the 'preservation of the interests of the imperial throne, the sacred rights of the Caliphate, and the honour of the military'.[54] One of the methods the commission employed was the compilation of new official reports in accordance with the wishes of the palace. Colonel Tevfik Bey's initial report to the commission, which had mentioned the presence of Kurdish pastoralists among the troops and their involvement in the burning of Armenian villages, was changed.[55] Another method the commission employed was the coaching of witnesses in order to bolster the government's narrative. Hişman Agha, who was listed among

[50] TNA, FO, 424/178, No. 260, 15 October 1894.
[51] TNA, FO, 424/178, No. 278, 3 November 1894.
[52] TNA, FO, 424/178, No. 538.
[53] BOA, Y. EE. 66/8, 6 January 1895.
[54] BOA, Y. EE. 66/8, 12 February 1895.
[55] BOA, Y. EE 66/8, 16 March 1895; 17 March 1895; 18 March 1895.

the unruly Kurdish notables of Sasun before the beginning of the military attacks, had been detained since the summer. His testimony in front of the commission, in which he claimed that the pastoralist tribes had done no wrong to the peasants and that Armenians had been preparing for a rebellion against the state and their Muslim neighbours, was a direct rejection of his established relationship with the Sasun Armenians.[56]

Nevertheless, the inquiry also provided the Sasun Armenians with a unique opportunity to get their voices heard in a semi-public setting. From late January until early May, Armenian survivors of the massacre and a few revolutionaries testified in front of the commission. The survivors provided first-hand accounts of massacre, mass execution,[57] wanton destruction[58] and rape,[59] while Ottoman officials attempted to produce excuses to invalidate their accounts.[60] Their testimonies derailed Ottoman efforts in producing a Manichean narrative of order versus rebellion. The revolutionaries downplayed their political agenda, and drew attention to the worsening conditions in which the Armenian peasantry of the region found itself.[61] When the inquiry concluded its report in May 1895, it had become increasingly clear that a massacre had taken place, and that the Ottoman government continued to protect its perpetrators.

---

[56] TNA, FO, Correspondence Relating to the Asiatic Provinces of Turkey: Turkey, No. 1 (1895), Part 2: Commission of Inquiry at Moush: Procés-Verbaux and Separate Depositions. London: 1895, P-V. 41, 13 March 1895; BOA, Y. EE. 168/4, İctima' 41, 13 March 1895. The British Vice-Consul had also reported on Hişman Ağa's imprisonment for his refusal to participate in the assault; TNA, FO, 424/178, No. 390, inc., Vice-Consul Boyajian to Ambassador Currie.

[57] BOA, Y. EE. 168/2, İctima' 19, 15 February 1895; TNA, FO, *Proces-Verbaux*, P-V. 17, 15 February 1895.

[58] BOA, Y. EE. 168/2, İctima' 19, 15 February 1895.

[59] BOA, Y. EE. 168/5, İctima' 61, 8 April 1895; TNA, FO, *Proces-Verbaux*, P-V. 61, 8 April 1895.

[60] A cynical example was the swift compilation of a medical report by doctors in the employ of the Muş municipality that the wound of the witness, who had claimed to be bayoneted by soldiers, had in fact been caused by a searing metal object. TNA, FO, *Proces-Verbaux*, P-V. 22, 19 February 1895.

[61] BOA, Y. EE. 168/9, İctima' 86, 14 May 1895; TNA, FO, *Proces-Verbaux*, P-V. 86, 14 May 1895.

Fomenting and Settling Disputes

In summer 1895, the Ottoman government found itself in a precarious position regarding the question of Armenian reforms. It had failed to pacify diplomatic pressures regarding the recent massacre of Sasun Armenians. Moreover, the Great Powers had presented the Porte with a reform plan in May. The Hunchakian Party organised a demonstration in the imperial capital at the end of September to protest the government's reluctance to implement the plan, during which several revolutionaries and policemen were killed. In October, Abdülhamid II announced his intention to implement the aforementioned reforms.[62]

The empire-wide wave of anti-Armenian violence that which followed this announcement has been the subject of numerous studies.[63] Between autumn 1895 and early 1897, mobs, gendarmes and armed militias killed and wounded thousands of Ottoman Armenians in pogroms and massacres. Armenian property was looted and expropriated. In the countryside, many Armenians were forced to convert to Islam.[64] It is not within the scope of the current chapter to provide a comprehensive analysis of what came to be known as the Hamidian massacres. Nevertheless, their impact in Muş and Sasun would prove significant.

In spring 1895, Protestant missionaries and British diplomatic representatives had established a basic system of delivering aid to the Sasun Armenians to help them in their reconstruction of their villages and their resettlement in the region.[65] When the wave of anti-Armenian violence hit the province of Bitlis in autumn 1895 shortly after the announcement of the sultan's reform plan, the tide began to turn against the Sasun Armenians once again. Resembling many other pogroms during the Hamidian massacres, a Muslim mob attacked Armenian shops and homes after the Friday prayer in Bitlis

---

[62] Nalbandian, *The Armenian Revolutionary Movement*, 122–6.
[63] For a representative sample, see Melson 'A Theoretical Inquiry into the Armenian Massacres of 1894–1896'; Gölbaşı, 'The Official Conceptualization of the anti-Armenian Riots of 1895–1897'; Deringil, 'Abdülhamid Döneminde Ermeni Meselesi'.
[64] Deringil, '"The Armenian Question is Finally Closed"'.
[65] For assistance in kind, see TNA, FO, 424/187, No. 108, inc. 2, 13 May 1896; for assistance in cash, see TNA, FO, 424/189, No. 229, inc., 4 November 1896.

in late October. Hundreds of Armenians were killed, while others were left destitute as a result of the attack.[66]

As the wave of anti-Armenian violence spread to the rest of the province, the aid programme to Sasun was left in a difficult position. According to the British vice-consul, the efforts of the district governor of Muş had prevented the occurrence of a similar pogrom in the town. Nevertheless, relative peace and order had come at a price: the Muslim notables of the city called for a meeting with Ottoman officials and Armenian notables and intimated the likelihood of a similar attack on Muş Armenians unless the missionaries and their aid workers helping Sasun left the city. The British vice-consul advised that the missionaries accede to these demands to preserve intercommunal peace.[67] The British aid relief programme persevered in a limited manner despite these pressures, entrusting the task of distribution to Ottoman officials, who were occasionally accused of confiscating the relief.[68]

It was within this atmosphere of international and imperial neglect that Armenian revolutionaries resumed their efforts to arm Armenian peasants in Sasun, and turn them against the Ottoman government, while assisting them in their disputes with sedentary and pastoralist Muslims. The massacre of Sasun Armenians by the army, and government officials' obvious partiality motivated many local Armenians to join armed bands under the leadership of revolutionary leaders such as Serob Vartanian, Andranig Ozanian, Armenak Ghazarian and others. Unlike the earlier bout of revolutionary activism in the region, however, it was the Armenian Revolutionary Federation (ARF) that drew the Sasun revolutionaries to its ranks. It is likely that local recruits turned away from the Hunchakian Party in the midst of the organisation's internal turmoil in the aftermath of the Hamidian massacres, while the ARF succeeded in establishing a clandestine traffic of arms and people across the Russian and Iranian borderlands.[69] At least at the local level, organisational

---

[66] TNA, FO, 424/184, No. 731, 7 December 1895, inc., 2, 6 November 1895; the Ottoman acting governor blamed the missionaries and Armenian notables for having conspired to provoke Muslims to attack Armenians. BOA, Yıldız Perakende Askeri Maruzat (Y. PRK. ASK.) 108/103, 22 October 1895.
[67] TNA, FO, 424/182, inc., 11 November 1895.
[68] For assistance in cash, see TNA, FO, 424/189, No. 229, inc., 4 November 1896.
[69] Sasuni, *Patmut'iwn Taroni Ashkharhi*, 538–41, 551–2.

ethno-religious conflicts and the acts of propaganda by deed. In the 1890s, the violence became more intense, and in addition ordinary state violence accelerated and improved its organisational capacity, which changed the level of penetration of violence into daily life.[9] Violent acts, which were deployed as a strategy of resistance by the revolutionary circles, also became a form of political communication and were performed to claim an alternative political legitimacy.[10]

Different revolutionary groups with different ideological backgrounds began to organise as secret societies in the nineteenth century[11]; the members of revolutionary circles could reach guns, dynamite or the ingredients for explosives more easily in line with the Ottoman Empire's integration in the world economy.[12] Furthermore, the relation between secret societies explores the ties between nationalist, socialist and anarchist groups in the Ottoman Empire, and also their transnational networks with Persian, Russian and European revolutionary circles.[13] There were some anarchist

---

[9] This does not mean that violence is a natural outcome of high-level politics, but rather is a process that also played an important role in building boundaries, belongings and ethno-religious consciousness, as well as a constitutive part of the state formation. Stathis N. Kalyvas, *The Logic of Violence in Civil War* (Cambridge: Cambridge University Press, 2006), 21; Keith Brown, *Loyal unto Death: Trust and Terror in Revolutionary Macedonia* (Bloomington: Indiana University Press, 2013); Yosmaoğlu, *Blood Ties*, 217.

[10] Nelida Fuccaro, 'Urban Life and Questions of Violence', in Nelida Fuccaro (ed.), *Violence and the City in the Modern Middle East* (Stanford, CA: Stanford University Press, 2016), 13; Rasmus Christian Elling, 'The Semantics of Violence and Space', in Nelida Fuccaro (ed.), *Violence and the City in the Modern Middle East* (Stanford, CA: Stanford University Press, 2016), 24; Varak Ketsemanian, 'The Hunchakian Revolutionary Party and the Assassination Attempts against Patriarch Khoren Ashekian and Maksudzade Simon Bey in 1894', *International Journal of Middle East Studies* 50(4) (2018): 735–55.

[11] The revolutionary secret societies date back to the early nineteenth century with Greek revolutionaries. See Douglas Dakin, *The Greek Struggle for Independence, 1821–1833* (Berkley:University of California Press, 1973).

[12] Ramazan Hakkı Öztan, 'Tools of Revolution: Global Military Surplus, Arms Dealers, and Smugglers in the Late Ottoman Balkans, 1878–1908', *Past & Present* 237(1) (2017): 167–95.

[13] Duncan M. Perry, *The Politics of Terror: The Macedonian Liberation Movements 1893–1903*, (Durham, NC: Duke University Press, 1988); M. Şükrü Hanioğlu, *Preparation for a Revolution: The Young Turks, 1902–1908* (New York: Oxford University Press, 2001). For a connected revolutions approach in the case of Armenian revolutionaries, see Houri Berberian, *Roving Revolutionaries, Armenians and the Connected Revolutions in the Russian, Iranian, and Ottoman Worlds* (Oakland, CA: University of California Press, 2019).

infrastructure appeared to be the main determinant as to which revolutionary party would be ascendant.

By the turn of the century, Sasun had become an important node in the network of revolutionary bands in a larger geography, which encompassed the Muş plain, the towns of Muş and Bitlis, and the districts of Ahlat and Kulp. Revolutionaries continued to assist Armenian peasants and organise targeted attacks against government officials, Muslim lords, whom they accused of oppressing the peasantry, and Armenian informers, whom they accused of cooperating with the Ottoman government. Their actions influenced the political atmosphere of the entire region. Raids by revolutionary bands under the leadership of Serob Vartanian, and the imperial troops' search for them heightened tensions in towns like Muş and Bitlis.[70]

The government relied heavily on Muslim proxies on the ground in its pursuit of revolutionaries and terrorisation of Armenian peasants so that they would deny shelter and support. Kurdish lords and religious leaders were able to collect intelligence on which villages and which homes the revolutionary leaders frequented, which Armenians were sympathetic to the revolutionaries, and what the number of recruits was. Moreover, Kurdish lords and their retinues inflicted 'punishments' on Armenian villages suspected of aiding and abetting, and responded with greater alacrity than the authorities when they received reports of nearby revolutionaries. In return, they faced virtual immunity from discipline and punishment.

In autumn 1899, the aforementioned Halil Beşar Ağa cooperated with military authorities to trap and besiege Serob Vartanian in the village of Geliguzan in Sasun. Vartanian and most of his family were killed during the attack. The officer in charge of the attack dispatched his severed head to the centre of the province in Bitlis for public display.[71] The palace awarded decorations and promotions to the soldiers, gendarmes and others who had shown their loyalty.[72] What the government viewed as a definitive victory over the

---

[70] BOA, Dahiliye Tesri-i Islahat ve Muamelat Komisyonu Muamelat (DH. TMIK. M.) 69/62, 25 May 1899.
[71] BOA, Y. PRK. UM. 48/82, 7 November 1889; Sasuni, *Patmut'iwn Taroni Ashkharhi*, 557–60.
[72] BOA, Y. PRK. UM. 48/82, 7 November 1889.

revolutionaries – much as they had done at the conclusion of the massacre in 1894 – would be a turning point in the escalation of internecine violence among Muslims and Armenians in the region, and the participation of the government in the further marginalisation of Sasun Armenians.

The following summer, the British Embassy approached the Porte with a request for an inquiry regarding allegations of mass violence against Armenians in Sasun. According to British reports, a joint group of gendarmes and local Kurds had arrived at the village of Sbghank in pursuit of revolutionaries, pillaged it, killed dozens of peasants and torched a number of buildings.[73] The sultan acceded to the British request and dispatched two high-ranking officials – Brigadier General Enver Paşa from the General Council of Military Inspection (*Teftiş-i Umumi-i Askeri Komisyon-ı Alisi*) and Mehmed Efendi from the Constantinople Court of Second Instance.[74]

Two separate sets of instructions are on file for the officials. The first, undated set of instructions contains a brief summary of the allegations reported by the British Embassy, the military officer's denial, and strict orders for the conduct of a just and impartial inquiry (*Esas vazife bu Sbğank karyesi hadisesi hakkında tahkikat-ı adilane ve bi tarafane icra olunduğundan*).[75] The second set of instructions clarified the true expectations of the palace. The officials were ordered to tell foreign consuls in the region that their only interest was in the discovery of the truth. In fact, however, they were ordered to exert all necessary efforts to disprove the slander of the foreigners (*ecnebilerin şu iftiralarını haksız bırakacak mesai ve ikdamattan geri durmamaları*).[76] In other words, the officials were instructed to make an appearance of an impartial inquiry while compiling a simple refutation of all allegations, and acquiring a collective signed statement from local Armenian priests which attested to their refutation.

Unsurprisingly, Enver Paşa and Mehmed Efendi submitted an official report exactly to that effect. They stated that Ali Paşa had personally led a detachment of imperial troops to the village of Sbghank after receiving

---

[73] TNA, FO, 424/200, No. 81, 31 July 1900.
[74] BOA, Y. EE. 6/23, 23 August 1900.
[75] Ibid.
[76] BOA, Y. EE. 6/23, 23 August 1900.

reports of revolutionary presence in the village. He enlisted the assistance of Halil Beşar Ağa and his men as guides in order to move efficiently on the difficult terrain. Upon their arrival in the village, the revolutionaries opened fire from the village church. Despite several attempts by the troops to convince the revolutionaries to surrender, they refused at the loud encouragement of one of them. An attempt was made to smoke them out. Sixteen revolutionaries were killed during the operation. It was discovered at the end that a woman, a child and a priest had also been hiding in the church and had been killed because of the smoke. The rest of the report was a virtual indictment of the Armenians of Sasun, who had time and again showed their affinity with rebels and evildoers.[77]

What was surprising, however, was the officials' submission of a second, unofficial report in addition to the first one in order to explain what really happened. They stated in the second report that Ali Paşa had delegated the task of finding and killing revolutionaries in Sbghank to the chief of police Hüsnü Efendi and the Kurdish lord Halil Beşar Ağa. The first was untrustworthy, and the second, an ignorant Kurd, famous for his hatred of Armenians. The latter had garnered a special vendetta against the peasants of Sbghank because they had defeated his men in battle in 1899, killing four of them in the process. As a result, Halil Beşar Ağa did not wait for the arrival of imperial troops, and set upon the village under cover of night. His men overpowered their opponents, killing sixteen of them in the process, and torching nine buildings in the village. Furthermore, two women and four children were killed during the fire at the church. The officials described the grave markers made for the women, with crosses made of flowers on top of which the murdered women's hair was affixed. They added that the charred remains of a person were discovered among the ruins of another house. At the conclusion of the second report, the officials recommended the construction of a network of defensive structures and the permanent presence of a unit in the region. This would decrease the reliance of military authorities on local Kurds on both matters of intelligence-gathering and counter-insurgency. Nevertheless, they exculpated Ali Paşa of any wrongdoing, and laid the blame on the 'natural savagery and barbarity

---

[77] BOA, Yıldız Perakende Komisyon (Y.PRK. KOM.) 10/65, 11 October 1900.

of the men whom he trusted' (*emniyet eylediği adamların vahşet ve huşunet-i tabiiine mebni*).[78]

The palace did nothing to punish Halil Beşar Ağa for what was, in the view of Ottoman officials, a vile act contrary to imperial will. In autumn 1900, however, the revolutionaries in Sasun waylaid Halil Beşar Ağa and killed him. Andranig Ozanian, who was one of the rising figures within the ARF, led the attack and cut off the Kurdish lord's head. The act was a deliberate response to both the killing of Serob Vartanian the previous year and the recent sack of the village of Sbghank.[79] The governor of Bitlis informed his superiors that the lord's assassination had caused a furore among the Kurds, and that orders had been dispatched to local civilian and military authorities to prevent a general Kurdish attack on the Armenians.[80]

The palace's cover-up of the Sbghank massacre and its protection of the perpetrators echoed its actions after the Sasun massacre in 1894. The continuity in the government's marginalisation of Sasun Armenians was contemporaneous with a marked exacerbation of relations between the Armenians and Kurds of the region. Hişman Ağa, who had tried to shield 'his' Armenians from the government and pastoralists, had lost his influence in the region after his detention in 1894. Halil Beşar Ağa, whom *Droshak* had called an opportunist leader in 1894, had become one of the chief auxiliaries of government policy.[81] Moreover, he had used his newly expanded power and influence to extort and kill.

The revolutionaries inserted themselves at the centre of the growing conflict between Kurdish lords with a licence to extort and punish, and the Sasun Armenians, for whom armed clashes became an increasingly frequent occurrence. They went further than their predecessors before the 1894 massacre; they targeted gendarmes and soldiers as well as the likes of Halil Beşar Ağa. The latter was not only a powerful Kurdish lord, but also one of the most important agents of the government in pursuing revolutionaries and consolidating the marginalisation of the Sasun Armenians by force

---

[78] BOA, Y.PRK. KOM. 10/65, 11 October 1900.
[79] Sasuni, *Patmut'iwn Taroni Ashkharhi*, 573–5.
[80] BOA, DH. TMIK. M. 95/48, 16 October 1900.
[81] 'Sasuni Abstamput'ean Arach'', *Droshak*, No. 14, December 1894.

and intimidation. It is clear that both the peasants and the revolutionaries cultivated better relations with other Kurds outside Sasun; some assisted them in the procurement of weapons and ammunition. Nevertheless, a state of perpetual unease, if not outright hostility, between the Armenians and Kurds of Sasun had come about by the turn of the twentieth century.

The 1904 Uprising

The revolutionaries also sought to expand the impact of their activities in Sasun and Muş at an international level. Although the reform plans of 1895 had proven a dead letter, the ARF leadership outside the Ottoman Empire as well as the militants on the ground believed that Great Power intervention was crucial for the realisation of their goals. In autumn 1901, some twenty-five revolutionaries under the leadership of Andranig Ozanian descended from Sasun to occupy the Holy Apostles Monastery on the Muş plain. The Ottoman authorities promptly ordered a siege.[82]

While some clashes took place in the first few days, the crisis assumed international import due to the historic and regional significance of the monastery and the presence of priests and students inside. A frontal assault was likely to result in many Ottoman casualties, while the bombardment of the monastery with priests and students inside was not a feasible solution. With representatives of the Great Powers as well as the Apostolic Patriarchate present within the vicinity of the monastery, the commanding officer Ali Paşa was compelled to negotiate with the revolutionaries to arrange a peaceful conclusion to the affair. The revolutionaries demanded imperial pardons and guarantees of safe passage across the Ottoman borders. Moreover they submitted a list of more general demands, which included the immediate release of political prisoners as well as the punishment of the perpetrators of the Sbghank massacre and the plunder of villages on the Muş plain.[83] Unsurprisingly, the authorities refused these demands and continued the siege. Ozanian organised a daring escape from

---

[82] Sasuni, *Patmut'iwn Taroni Ashkharhi*, 580–3; Dahiliye Şifre Kalemi (DH. ŞFR.) 271/26, 1 December 1901.
[83] Ibid., 585–7.

the monastery under cover of night in order to avoid capture or death along with his comrades.[84]

Although the revolutionaries' successful escape was an embarrassment for the authorities, they still failed to attract international attention to their cause. In 1904, the revolutionary groups in Sasun received orders from the ARF congress to prepare for an armed rebellion against the state. They were to invite additional fighters from surrounding areas, and collect weapons and ammunition.[85] It is likely that the timing of this call for a rebellion was deliberate: the Ottoman government had recently succumbed to international pressure regarding the administration of political reforms in Macedonia after a failed rebellion in 1903.[86] Even if the armed rebellion in Sasun were to fail, the international pressure which would come to bear on the Ottoman government would facilitate reforms.

In order to sustain an armed rebellion for an extended period of time, the revolutionaries sought to draw fighters, produce, and import weapons and ammunition from across the border with mixed success. Of the 200 ARF fighters in Sasun in early 1904, the overwhelming majority still hailed from the Daron region, which included the districts of Kulp, Bulanık, Genc and Sasun, with only fifteen fighters from Transcaucasia.[87] For ammunition, they established makeshift workshops to produce gunpowder within Sasun. Their efforts to import weapons were sometimes cut short by the joint actions of Ottoman and Russian authorities. In early 1904, the Russian police confiscated 120 chests of ammunition and seventy-eight modern rifles in response to a tip from the Ottoman authorities to the Russian consul in Erzurum.[88]

The first stage of the rebellion was marked by two developments: first, revolutionaries killed several Muslims from the mixed villages of Tapik and

---

[84] BOA, DH. ŞFR., 272/18, 16 December 1901.
[85] Hratch Dasnabedian, *History of the Armenian Revolutionary Federation: Dashnaktsutiun 1890/1924* (Oemme Edizioni: Milan, 1990), 72.
[86] For a comprehensive overview of the background to the Ilinden Uprising and its subsequent 'settlement' through the Mürzsteg Protocol, see İpek Yosmaoğlu, *Blood Ties: Religion, Violence, and the Politics of Nationhood in Ottoman Macedonia, 1878–1908*, (Ithaca, NY: Cornell University Press, 2013), 19–47.
[87] Sasuni, *Patmut'iwn Taroni Ashkharhi*, 615.
[88] BOA, Y. PRK. ASK. 213/99, 22 February 1904.

Laçkan, whom they viewed as agents of the state, and expelled the rest after torching their homes.[89] According to Ottoman reports, they also took hostages from the Muslim populace.[90] Second, several revolutionary bands travelled across Sasun to escort the Armenian inhabitants of the outlying villages to the heights of Antok, where they would be safe from the advancing troops and pastoralists. They torched Armenian villages in order to deny food and lodging to the advancing Ottoman troops.[91]

Many male peasants from the districts of Sasun, which became the centre of the rebellion, also joined the revolutionaries' armed rebellion. According to Garo Sasuni's estimates, some thousand peasants fought against the imperial troops.[92] The governor of Bitlis stated that a local Muslim preacher in Sasun estimated that 2,000 peasants had joined the revolutionaries.[93] The contrast with 1894 is clear: whereas peasants had been reluctant to fight against imperial troops a decade before, they were willing to attempt a defence of their villages in 1904. The experience of the 1894 massacre obviously motivated many Armenian peasants to join the revolutionaries. Moreover, the revolutionaries had succeeded in cultivating a network of supporters in the Armenian villages, who had provided them with food and shelter in the previous years. Finally, the chances of success – if not of outright victory over the Ottoman troops, then a prolonged defence until the mediation of the Great Powers – must have seemed higher with the presence of some 200 experienced fighters.

When news of these developments reached the palace, the Fourth Army command was ordered to organise an offensive against the revolutionaries before they could seek the intermediacy of foreign missionaries or diplomats. The palace also sent clear instructions not to involve the Muslim population in the military offensive; the sultan feared the involvement of the Great Powers.[94] Despite the efforts of the Fourth Army command and the local authorities, however, the bulk of the troops only reached the villages under the revolutionaries' control by late March due in part to the hostile climate.

[89] Sasuni, *Patmut'iwn Taroni Ashkharhi*, 612–13; Y. A. HUS. 470/98, 14 April 1904.
[90] BOA, Y. PRK. ASK. 213/99, 28 February 1904.
[91] Sasuni, *Patmut'iwn Taroni Ashkharhi*, 618.
[92] Ibid., 615.
[93] BOA, Y. A. HUS. 470/16, 4 April 1904.
[94] BOA, Y. PRK. ASK. 213/99, 28 February 1904.

Several skirmishes took place between imperial patrols and the revolutionaries at the villages of Shenik and Semal at the bottom of the valleys, ascending up to the heights around Mount Antok and the populous settlements of Geliguzan and Dalvorig.

The governor and the military commandant of Bitlis arrived in the region with the priest of the Holy Apostles Monastery and the Muş prelate in late April. The clerics were given 12 hours to convince the revolutionaries to surrender to the authorities to avoid bloodshed, which mostly was a formality (or a ploy according to revolutionary accounts).[95] Clashes began shortly thereafter on 27 April. The revolutionaries were entrenched at and around the village of Geliguzan. In addition to a well-prepared defence, the Ottoman troops were faced with hostile weather in early April with frequent bouts of rain, sleet and snow in their attempts to advance.[96] The governor and the military commandant of Bitlis were on location, providing updates on the status of the Ottoman advance. On the first day of the clashes, they reported twenty-one dead, three missing and twenty-five wounded. They stated that they would resume their offensive upon the arrival of 800 troops in reinforcements.[97]

The revolutionaries held the village for a week against the army, which then utilised its mountain guns to force them to retreat or submit. After several more days of fighting around Geliguzan, the surviving revolutionaries succeeded in wedging through Ottoman lines to the Muş plain and beyond. Garo Sasuni estimated approximately 1,000 Sasun Armenians were killed during the rebellion. Thousands of survivors became refugees in Muş, Bitlis and the Muş plain.[98] Women and children had started arriving at military camps in early May after the revolutionaries were pushed out of Geliguzan. By the end of the month, many more had surrendered to the troops or sought protection and food elsewhere.[99]

After the rebellion was put down, the Ottoman government developed

---

[95] 'Her'agirnerê', 17 May 1904, *Droshak*, Nos 4–5, April–May 1904; BOA, Y. A. HUS. 470/16, 4 April 1904.
[96] BOA, Y. A. HUS. 471/71, 23 April 1904.
[97] BOA, Y.A.HUS. 471/110, 27 April 1904.
[98] 'Her'agirnerê', 25 May 1904, *Droshak*, Nos 4–5, April–May 1904.
[99] BOA, Y. A. HUS. 472/48, 7 May 1904; TNA, FO, 424/216, No. 81, 1 June 1904.

two alternative plans to settle the Sasun 'problem' once and for all. The first option was to expel all Armenians from the areas in Sasun where the revolutionaries had established control earlier. As early as 7 May, the palace informed the governor of Bitlis that women and children were to be given 'appropriate lodging' – implying that they were not to be sent back to their villages – while officials at the palace and the Ministry of the Interior discussed the feasibility of resettling the Armenian peasants on the Muş plain.[100] The second option was to realise a plan which had been proposed before: the construction of a network of military sentry towers with a barracks at the village of Geliguzan so that Ottoman troops could be present in the region throughout the year.[101]

In the end, the authorities adopted the latter solution. In addition to extending the reach of the Fourth Army further into the region, an important reason for their choice was British opposition to the scheme of mass deportations.[102] After a summer of extensive efforts to complete the construction of the military installations, the governor of Bitlis proudly informed the palace that the project was nearing completion at the end of September. He requested the approval of the sultan to travel to Sasun and conduct the opening ceremony to showcase the glory and grandeur of the caliphate against the residents of the mountains, and all Armenians (*umum Ermenilere ve cebel sekenesine karşı*).[103]

Conclusion

The multipolar set of struggles between Armenian peasants, Kurdish pastoralists, Muslim lords, Armenian revolutionaries and the Ottoman state in Sasun captures some of the most crucial facets of the 'Armenian Question' in the *fin de siècle*. First, the state's intent and methods of asserting and reshaping Muslim primacy vis-à-vis Armenians are perceptible. From the late 1880s onwards, the Ottoman government's civilian and military officials sought willing partners among the Muslim notability to police and marginalise

---

[100] BOA, Y. A. HUS. 472/48, 8 May 1904.
[101] This plan had been proposed as early as 1896. BOA, DH. TMIK. M. 10/22, 9 July 1896.
[102] TNA, FO, 424/216, No. 95, inc., 4, 14 July 1904.
[103] BOA, Y.PRK.UM. 71/22, 21 September 1904.

Armenian populations. In return, pastoralist and sedentary lords were given a free licence to extort Armenians. The state reinforced this strategy by extending rewards, withholding privileges and occasionally enforcing direct punishments. The contrast between the government's relations with two Sasun Muslim lords is illustrative in this sense. While Hişman Ağa, who attempted to preserve his established relations of patronage with the Sasun Armenians, faced imprisonment, Halil Beşar Ağa, who enthusiastically assumed responsibility for pursuing revolutionaries and policing Armenians, received rewards and decorations. Moreover, the latter enjoyed de facto legal immunity for his brutal conduct against Armenians.

The officials' reliance on local auxiliaries in the enforcement of their policies is connected to the second facet. The government's only means of projecting direct power and influence in the region was through the Fourth Army. The deployment of imperial troops against the Armenian population, however, was a double-edged sword. Not only did it attract unwanted international attention, but it also necessitated a substantial mobilisation of material and human resources, which the empire lacked. In 1894, this took the form of a general massacre of Sasun Armenians' male peasants, and the destruction of several villages. In 1904, it took the form of a sustained military assault and the subsequent construction of a network of military installations, which afforded the military a permanent presence in the region.

The third facet of the Armenian question most clearly illustrated in Sasun relates to the Armenian revolutionary movement. The initial reception of the revolutionaries among Sasun Armenians was equivocal: while some supported the revolutionaries, others remained indifferent (or according to some, participated in their capture). The peasants refused to clash with imperial troops in 1894. It was only within the context of pressures and atrocities from an increasingly hostile government and local Muslim notability that the Armenian peasantry started extending shelter and protection to the revolutionary bands. The revolutionaries succeeded in drawing greater support by assisting the peasants in their local disputes, delivering them modern arms and ammunition, and targeting notables and government officials. It was the revolutionaries' close engagement with the socio-ethnic conflicts of the peasants that made their call for a general rebellion in the spring of 1904 more popular than it had been in 1894.

Finally, the state and the revolutionaries sought to engage with a multitude of audiences through their actions in Sasun. These were not limited to the Armenian and Muslim inhabitants of Sasun, but extended to the Muslims and Armenians of the empire writ large as well as the governments of the Great Powers and Western public opinion. After the recent experience of the Russo-Ottoman War and the subsequent transformation of Ottoman Europe, the Ottoman government feared Great Power intervention in favour of the Armenians. Therefore, it attempted to portray any and all expression of Armenian dissent and resistance in Sasun, and conflict between Sasun Muslims and Armenians as the nefarious product of Armenian revolutionism.

For the revolutionaries, Great Power interest and intervention in Sasun were crucial for the realisation of their goals. They consciously attempted to replicate the feats of Bulgarian revolutionaries, which had earned them a considerable degree of autonomy despite military defeats in 1877 and 1904. In order to do so, they needed spectacular confrontations against the Ottoman army which would draw the eyes of diplomatic observers. They succeeded in publicising the 'Armenian Question' at the international level several times: the massacre of 1894, the siege of the Holy Apostles Monastery in 1901, and the rebellion in 1904. However, the translation of international and public attention into action and intervention relied on many other factors, over which the revolutionaries had little influence.

The waves of violence in Sasun at the turn of the nineteenth century also merit attention because of their place in the context of the general history of Ottoman and global armed revolutionism, insurgency and repression, particularly in the countryside. The Armenian revolutionaries' focus on the recruitment, mobilisation and arming of peasants as the ultimate agents of political change echoes the large-scale campaign of Macedonian revolutionaries.[104] The Ottoman officials' totalising conflation of Armenian dissent with Armenian sedition, and the criminalisation of the former is contemporaneous with British policies of suspending civil and political rights in the face

---

[104] Keith Brown, *Loyal unto Death: Trust and Terror in Revolutionary Macedonia* (Bloomington: Indiana University Press, 2013).

of revolutionary terrorism in colonial India.[105] One of the important effects of the criminalisation of dissent writ large was the gradual normalisation of revolutionary violence along with other modes of political opposition – in the Ottoman East and in colonial Bengal.[106]

The failure of Ottoman efforts to put down the Zaydi rebellion in Yemen at the turn of the nineteenth century, on the other hand, presents an interesting point of comparison: the collective punishment of suspect rural communities by the military did not result in their submission. The Ottoman authorities' heavy reliance on the use of what Vincent Wilhite calls 'punitive repression' could not compensate for the scarcity of Ottoman manpower and materiel on the ground. Instead, the absence of a permanent policing presence resulted in the further alienation of the local populace.[107] In Sasun, the Ottoman state's careful cultivation of a working relationship with willing Kurdish notables in the collective punishment and terrorisation of the local Armenians can be understood as an attempt to 'outsource' this task. Nevertheless, a common result in both cases was the alienation of the suspect rural communities – Zaydi or Armenian – and an increase in their sympathy for the revolutionaries/rebels.

---

[105] Kim A. Wagner, *Amritsar 1919: An Empire of Fear and the Making of a Massacre* (New Haven, CT: Yale University Press, 2019). Wagner's meticulous analysis of how the memory of the Indian Rebellion of 1857 influenced British officialdom's interpretation of political opposition in the early twentieth century is also relevant; the Bosnian–Bulgarian crisis, the subsequent Russo-Ottoman War, and the collapse of Ottoman rule in a large section of its European holdings in the 1870s would influence Ottoman thinking about and suspicion of its Armenian population.

[106] Durba Ghosh, *Gentlemanly Terrorists: Political Violence and the Colonial State in India, 1919–1947* (Cambridge: Cambridge University Press, 2017).

[107] Vincent Steven Wilhite, 'Guerrilla War, Counterinsurgency, and State Formation in Ottoman Yemen', PhD thesis, Ohio State University, 2003.

7

Conspiracy, International Police Cooperation and the Fight against Anarchism in the Late Ottoman Empire, 1878–1908

İlkay Yılmaz

Security implications had a long-term impact that created routinised and ordinary forms of violence, which not only affected the provinces but also transformed the state centre in the late Ottoman Empire. This chapter is an introduction that explores how perceptions of security developed with routinised practices of discourse and administration, and how these perceptions were tied into politics. In doing so, the chapter draws on political science, specifically the model of securitisation. According to securitisation theory, by placing a topic in the area of security by a 'speech act' – that follows a specific grammatical and rhetorical structure – an actor moves the topic from politics into an area of security concern, which also creates the grounds for legitimating extraordinary means against the constructed threat.[1] However, the speech act is not sufficient in analysing how security operates, and security discourses have to be analysed in the context of the security practices and the conditions of these practices.[2] While different types of political violence were

---

[1] According to the securitisation theory the players (mostly politicians), use linguistic representations to prepare the audience to take action in the direction of the player and could position a particular issue to an existential threat. Barry Buzan, Ole Wæver and Jaap de Wilde, *Security: A New Framework for Analysis* (Boulder, CO: Lynne Rienner, 1998); Matt McDonald, 'Securitization and the Construction of Security', *European Journal of International Relations* 14(4) (2008): 563–87.

[2] Didier Bigo, 'Globalized (In)Security: The Field and the Ban-Opticon', in Didier Bigo and

one of the main characteristics of the Hamidian era and was mainly discussed with regard to Armenians, Bulgarians and anarchism, this chapter will mostly focus on the ways in which the Ottoman bureaucracy securitised them, with a special focus on the Armenian question. This case study will discuss how the Ottoman government framed political problems as a 'security' issue with reference to anarchism; to do so, daily bureaucratic discourse (specifically regarding Armenians), administrative regulations and their practices will be examined with the Ottoman involvement in anti-anarchist inter-imperial police cooperation. While the changes in security definitions, concepts and new methods of policing triggered structural changes in state apparatus in the nineteenth century, the Ottoman Empire was also part of this process in the European context.

It is evident that after Congress of Vienna (1815), several inter-imperial coalitions emerged between European powers in some specific areas such as anti-smuggling, anti-piracy and anti-anarchism, or to fight uprisings in colonies and nationalism in imperial settings.[3] The Vienna System and these imperial coalitions then not only created systematic structures such as permanent diplomatic representation, international police cooperation (which led to Interpol) and an international legal framework against specific security problems, but also left its mark on the mentality of state elites, and thus on security perceptions and norms. Controlling geographical mobility and cross-border activities of political groups, refugees and migrants were also part of the new security regimes, which also dealt with cross-border political crime.[4] Acting transnationally the political opposition, revolutionaries and

---

Anastassia Tsoukala (eds), *Terror, Insecurity and Liberty: Illiberal Practices of Liberal Regimes after 9/11* (Abingdon: Routledge, 2008), 10–48. For a detailed discussion on history of security, see Eckart Conze, *Geschichte der Sicherheit: Entwicklung-Themen-Perspektiven* (Göttingen: Vandenhoeck & Ruprecht, 2017).

[3] Beatrice De Graaf, Ido de Haan and Brian Vick (eds), *Securing Europe after Napoleon* (Cambridge: Cambridge University Press, 2019); Karl Härter, 'The Transnationalisation of Criminal Law in the Nineteenth and Twentieth Century: Political Crime, Police Cooperation, Security Regimes and Normative Orders – an Introduction', in Karl Härter, Tina Hannappel and Conrad Tyrichter (eds), *The Transnationalisation of Criminal Law in the Nineteenth and Twentieth Century: Political Crime, Police Cooperation, Security Regimes and Normative Orders* (Frankfurt am Main: Vittorio Klostermann, 2019), 1–20.

[4] Tina Hanneppel, 'Extradition and Expulsion as Instruments of Transnational Security

other dissident groups had cross-border effects, and, furthermore, starting with the French revolution European governments identified and labelled these groups as security threats referring to transnational or international conspiracies.[5] Accordingly, this approach influenced the security regimes which operated in an international setting and functioned with actors like diplomats, intelligence agents, military personnel, police and even civilians that enabled the creation of an international security network as well as international conferences. As part of this process, routinised bureaucratic decisions and acts created the normalisation of internal security measures. The Ottoman Empire was also part of the new security regimes and was interested in international law mostly to ensure the 'survival of the empire', even before the Treaty of Paris (1856).[6] This chapter paves the way for discussing the dynamic relationship between the security politics of Ottoman government during the Hamidian era and the larger international context of security. While the conflict between the international context of empire and imperialism was undeniable, this study focuses on how they also interacted in shaping a security regime.

Threat Perceptions and the Ottoman Government

After the Ottoman–Russian War, a new era that began with the Berlin Treaty (1878) came to deeply dominate the security perceptions and practices of the Ottoman Empire, especially in two frontier regions: Macedonia and six provinces in the Ottoman East. In line with the Berlin Treaty, in the wake of the loss of eastern European territory, the Ottoman Empire was forced to enact administrative and security reforms under Great Power surveillance in

---

Regimes against Anarchism in the Late Nineteenth Century', in Karl Härter, Tina Hannappel and Conrad Tyrichter (eds), *The Transnationalisation of Criminal Law in the Nineteenth and Twentieth Century: Political Crime, Police Cooperation, Security Regimes and Normative Orders* (Frankfurt am Main: Vittorio Klostermann, 2019), 65–98.

[5] Karl Härter, 'Security and Transnational Policing of Political Subversion and International Crime in the German Confederation after 1815', in Beatrice De Graaf, Ido de Haan and Brian Vick (eds), *Securing Europe after Napoleon* (Cambridge: Cambridge University Press, 2019), 193–213.

[6] See Mustafa Serdar Palabıyık, 'The Emergence of the Idea of "International Law" in the Ottoman Empire before the Treaty of Paris (1856)', *Middle Eastern Studies* 50(2) (2014): 233–51.

Macedonia to improve living conditions for the Christian population,[7] as well as in six provinces of Eastern Anatolia to protect the Armenian population from the exactions and attacks of Kurdish and Circassian tribes.[8]

During the 1890s, the threat perception of Ottoman political elites was strongly influenced by the Armenian and the Macedonian questions, either of which could be used as a pretext for foreign intervention according to the Ottoman Government. As new diplomatic interventions in Ottoman domestic policies occurred, the fear of losing territory, which had come to reshape the threat perception, became greater for Ottoman state elites. In the 1890s, the Ottoman state elites' security policies focused on the Macedonian and Armenian questions, while 'anarchism', which state elites identified as the propaganda of the deed, came to be largely associated with these two questions in Ottoman diplomacy.

The Hamidian era was marked with both state oppression and political violence, which was evident with popular uprisings, guerrilla warfare,

---

[7] For Macedonian question, see Fikret Adanır, *Die Makedonische Frage. Ihre Entstehung und Entwicklung bis 1908* (Wiesbaden: Franz Steiner, 1979); İpek K. Yosmaoğlu, *Blood Ties: Religion, Violence, and the Politics of Nationhood in Ottoman Macedonia, 1878–1908* (Ithaca, NY: Cornell University Press, 2014.

[8] For detailed analyses and different perspectives on the Armenian question, see Robert Farrer Zeidner, 'Britain and the Launching of the Armenian Question', *International Journal of Middle East Studies* 7(4) (1976): 465–83; Stephen Duguid, 'The Politics of Unity: Hamidian Policy in Eastern Anatolia', *Middle Eastern Studies* 9(2) (1973): 139–55; Stephan H. Astourian, 'The Silence of the Land: Agrarian Relations, Ethnicity, and Power', in Ronald G. Suny, Fatma Müge Göçek, and Norman M. Naimark (eds), *A Question of Genocide: Armenians and Turks at the End of the Ottoman Empire* (Oxford: Oxford University Press, 2011), 55–81; Janet Klein, *The Margins of Empire: Kurdish Militias in the Ottoman Tribal Zone* (Stanford, CA: Stanford University Press, 2011); Jelle Verheij, 'Diyarbekir and the Armenian Crisis of 1895', in Jelle Verheij and Joost Jongerden (eds), *Social Relations in Ottoman Diyarbekir, 1870–1915* (Leiden: Brill, 2012), 85–142; Owen Miller, 'Sasun 1894: Mountains, Missionaries and Massacres at the End of the Ottoman Empire', PhD thesis, Columbia University, 2015; Robert Melson, 'A Theoretical Inquiry into the Armenian Massacres of 1894–1896', *Comparative Studies in Society and History* 24(3) (1982): 481–509; Hans-Lukas Kieser, *Der verpasste Friede. Mission, Ethnie und Staat in den Ostprovinzen der Türkei 1839–1938* (Zürich: Chronos, 2000); Selim Deringil, 'The "Armenian Question is Finally Closed": Mass Conversions of Armenians in Anatolia during the Hamidian Massacres of 1895–1897', *Comparative Studies in Society and History* 51(2) (2009): 344–71; Ruben Safrastyan, *Ottoman Empire: the Genesis of the Program of Genocide, 1876–1920*, trans. Svetlana Mardanyan (Yerevan: Zangak, 2011).

groups and individuals in the empire, however, most of them did not get very involved in propaganda by deed style political violence.[14] Nonetheless, the ideology and the discussions on propaganda by deed were also spreading with mobile groups and individuals as well as with the printed media.[15] Thus, some revolutionary and nationalist organisations deployed violent propaganda techniques borrowed from anarchist organisations and ideologies. The demonstrations, bombings and assassination attempts were also significant acts that reveal the context for the emergence of new political actors who challenged the status quo.

This is the same period that Macedonian and Armenian revolutionary groups, who were active in the Ottoman Empire, were already established inside and outside the Ottoman Empire.[16] These organisations introduced socialism into the Macedonian and Armenian questions; furthermore, their political programmes were mostly in line with a political agenda that aimed to reach political freedoms through revolutionary action. However, the

---

[14] The Italian presence in the Ottoman anarchist scene is strikingly visible in the Ottoman security reports. Most of these people were exiles, workers or had family ties with Levantine community in the empire. Although there were Jewish and Greek anarchists in the empire, Hamidian bureaucracy was not alerted by their very existence. Axel Çorlu, 'Anarchists and Anarchism in the Ottoman Empire, 1850–1917', in Selim Karahasanoğlu and Deniz C. Demir (eds), *History from Below: A Tribute in Memory of Donald Quataert* (Istanbul: Istanbul Bilgi Üniversitesi Yayınları, 2016), 551–83; Avraam Benaroya, 'A Note on the Socialist Federation of Saloniki', *Jewish Social Studies* 11(1) (1949): 69–72; James Sotros, *The Greek-Speaking Anarchist and Revolutionary Movement (1830–1940): Writings for a History* (n.p.: No Gods-No Masters, 2004).

[15] Toygun Altıntaş, 'The Ottoman War on "Anarchism" and Revolutionary Violence', in Houssine Alloul, Edhem Eldem and Henk de Smaele (eds), *To Kill a Sultan* (Basingstoke: Palgrave Macmillan, 2018), 99–128. For a detailed analysis of leftist radicalism spanning four continents and linking Beirut, Cairo and Alexandria, see Ilham Khoury-Makdisi, *The Eastern Mediterranean and the Making of Global Radicalism, 1860–1914* (Oakland, CA: University of California Press, 2013).

[16] One of the Armenian revolutionary organisations, Armenakan, was established in Van in the 1880s; the Internal Macedonian Revolutionary Organization in 1893 in Thessaloniki; and the External Macedonian Organization in 1895. However, the Social Democrat Hunchakian Party, founded outside the empire in Geneva in 1887, and the Dashnaktsutyun (Dashnak) in Tiflis in 1890, were composed of well-educated revolutionaries from the Armenian population of the Russian Empire. The Committee of Union and Progress was also founded as a secret society in 1889 and had a complicated relationship and network with other revolutionary groups in the Ottoman Empire. Hanioğlu, *Preparation for a Revolution*.

political actors involved in these organisations were not only revolutionaries by definition, the actors were more diverse in their ideological tendencies, personal interests, and they had complex positions in transgressive politics that also makes it easier to define them as rogues.[17] By the early 1890s, the situation had grown increasingly tense, both in Istanbul and the eastern provinces, and Hamidian massacres of Armenians in 1894–1897 generated a new level of violence. The Hunchakian Party and Dashnaksutyun sought to use violence as a revolutionary method and as a strategy of resistance to change the status quo for the Armenian poor during the 1890s.[18] The Hunchaks recruited members from among the Armenian seasonal workers who came to Istanbul from the provinces, and the first armed Hunchakian groups emerged in the provinces in the early 1890s. Although the guerrilla warfare was continuing in the Balkans, the Serres Revolutionary District of the Internal Macedonian Revolutionary Organization (IMRO) decided to practise the methods of propaganda by deed, to weaken the Ottoman government and to attract international attention to the Macedonian question.

Various actions in the Ottoman Empire were inspired by the Russian revolutionary organisation, *Narodnaya Volia*.[19] Such instances which attracted international attention included the occupation of the Ottoman Bank,[20]

---

[17] For a detailed discussion, see in this volume, Alp Yenen and Ramazan Hakkı Öztan, 'Age of Rogues: Transgressive Politics at the Frontiers of the Ottoman Empire', Chapter 1.

[18] Regarding the fact that the Ottoman government postponed and never implemented the promised reforms in the eastern provinces, the Armenian peasantry needed protection against Kurdish warlords and later on Hamidian cavalry. The Ottoman government tried to organise Kurds into light cavalry units which were actively involved in the Hamidian massacres of Armenians in 1894–1897. The local villagers' need for protection was then solved with their support of the local bandits to protect them from the attacks of the Kurdish landlords. Later on these bandits turned out to be the roots of the *fedayi* movement. *Fedayi* were the bands that were emerged in second half of the 1880s and were ethnically segmented collectives, who aimed at protecting the Armenian villagers, then revolutionise with the effect of revolutionary parties mostly their time in the Ottoman prisons. For the *fedayi* movement, see Miller, 'Sasun 1894', 45 and 113.

[19] Manoug Joseph Somakian, *Empires in Conflict: Armenia and the Great Powers, 1895–1920* (London: I. B. Tauris, 1995), 16.

[20] Edhem Eldem, '26 Ağustos 1896 "Banka Vak'ası" ve "Ermeni Olayları"', *Tarih ve Toplum Yeni Yaklaşımlar* 1(5) (2007): 114–15.

the attempted assassination of Armenian Patriarch Ashikian on 25 March 1894,[21] the Kumkapı Demonstration,[22] the Thessaloniki assassinations[23] and the assassination attempt on Abdülhamid II.[24] There were also several railway bombings, targeted killings of high-level civil servants and police officers which did not receive international interest. These actions emerged amid popular demands for justice and a constitution that would grant greater scope for public involvement and national autonomy, and also deeply affected the threat perception of the Ottoman government.

Anti-anarchism, Surveillance and International Cooperation in Policing

Considering international dynamics, the extant threat perceptions and the resultant security policies can be analysed on two transitional levels: one *administrative* and the other *discursive*. The administrative level can be examined by investigating anti-anarchist policies and policing techniques that emerged with the establishment of modern police institutions. In response to domestic and international developments, these policies resulted in the formation of an 'administrative network', whose scope was widened by data-gathering – using documents for identifying, registering and classifying personal identity to the utilisation of photographs and the *portrait parlé*

---

[21] See Hüseyin Nazım Paşa, *Ermeni Olayları Tarihi*, vol. 1 (Ankara: T. C. Başbakanlık Devlet Arşivleri Genel Müdürlüğü Osmanlı Arşivi Daire Başkanlığı, 1994), 13–21; Hüseyin Nazım Paşa, *Hatıralarım: Ermeni Olaylarının İçyüzü* (Istanbul: Selis Kitaplar, 2007). Başkanlığı Osmanlı Arşivi (Prime Ministry's Ottoman Archives, hereafter BOA), BEO, 381/28512, 13 Mart 1310 (25 March 1894); BOA, BEO, 382/28612, 13 Mart 1310 (25 March 1894); BOA, Y.A.HUS., 292/82, 14 Mart 1310 (26 March 1894).

[22] Louis Nalbandian, *The Armenian Revolutionary Movement: The Development of Armenian Political Parties through the Nineteenth Century* (Berkeley: University of California Press, 1963), 119.

[23] Mark Mazower, *Salonica, City of Ghosts: Christians, Muslims and Jews, 1430–1950* (London: HarperCollins, 2004); Meropi Anastasiadou, *Salonique 1830–1912: Une Ville Ottomane à l'âge des Réformes* (Leiden: Brill, 1997); Orhan Türker, 'Selanik'te 28–29 Nisan 1903 Olayları', *Tarih ve Toplum* 31(182) (1999): 27–30 ; Misha Glenny, *Balkans 1804–1999: Nationalism, War and the Great Powers* (London: Granta, 1999), 202.

[24] İlkay Yılmaz, 'Propaganda by the Deed and Hotel Registration in the Late Ottoman Empire', *Journal of Ottoman and Turkish Studies Association* 4(1) (2017): 137–56; Houssine Alloul, Edhem Eldem and Henk de Smaele (eds), *To Kill a Sultan* (Basingstoke: Palgrave Macmillan, 2018).

as criminal investigation methods. Other security reforms during the era, including the foundation of a new police institution and reforms within the gendarmerie,[25] can be understood as aspects of the foundation of a modern state apparatus. While this process was part of the standardisation of information relating to personal identity, the classification and codification of this information with new filing techniques created a detailed mechanism for the security apparatus in the long term.

The effects of anti-anarchist policies and regulations in Europe are evident from the Ottoman administrative and security reforms in the late nineteenth century. In particular, the Rome Conference in 1898 and the protocol of St Petersburg in 1904 can be considered important components of the security strategies and techniques of the Ottoman Empire. These two developments not only affected Ottoman policing techniques and strategies, but also provide us with insights into the Ottoman politics of legitimising threat perceptions using diplomatic tools in the international arena.[26]

As police institutions began to employ new techniques during the 1850s, state elites, ministers and high-level civil servants attempted to standardise different policing practices.[27] While new concepts of threat and security emerged in international relations after the Congress of Vienna in 1815, new tactics on borders, the fight against revolutionaries and imperial interventions were also developed in the inter-imperial setting. This process continued with new techniques in state surveillance on criminal activities; however, these new techniques were mostly experimental in the beginning.[28] While the Ottoman Empire was involved in new systems of criminal justice and surveillance, it also benefitted from the new security implications in the context of

---

[25] Nair Özbek, 'Policing the Countryside: Gendarmes of the Late-Nineteenth-Century Ottoman Empire (1876–1908)', *International Journal of Middle East Studies* 40(1) (2008): 47–67.

[26] All kinds of opposition could easily be labelled as 'anarchism', including the Young Turks by the Ottoman government; see Françoise Georgeon, *Abdülhamid II. Le Sultan Calife (1876–1909)* (Paris: Fayard, 2003), 380–3.

[27] Mathieu Deflem, *Policing World Society: Historical Foundations of International Police Cooperation* (New York: Oxford University Press, 2012), 12–34.

[28] Jens Jäger, 'Photography: A Means of Surveillance? Judicial Photography, 1850 to 1900', *Crime, Histoire & Sociétés/Crime, History & Societies* 5(1) (2001): 27–51; İlkay Yılmaz, 'The Ottoman State, Police Photographs and Anthropometry', *Photoresearcher: European Society for History of Photography* 31 (2019): 90–100.

geopolitics, while at the same time suffering from them as part of the imperial interventions by the Great Powers.

During the 1880s, the police institutions of various states began to form formal alliances to develop more effective mechanisms to fight against the violent methods of propaganda by deed and to ensure border security.[29] Incidents such as bombings, explosions and assassinations were usually associated with the anarchist movement.[30] This tendency of the police and other state institutions to identify anyone who used violence as a method of propaganda by deed with anarchism meant that the ideology became pejoratively linked with terror attacks.[31] One of the major steps towards standardisation and the creation of an international police alliance was the Anti-Anarchist Conference in Rome three months after the assassination of Empress Elizabeth of Austria-Hungary.[32]

The Ottomans decided to send representatives to the conference due to the empire's understanding of 'humanity' and 'benevolence'. Internal Ottoman correspondence relating to the conference invitation indicates that there were some anarchists – mostly workers – in the Ottoman Empire, but that they did not seek involvement in criminal activities against the empire since the state had surprisingly taken no action against them.[33] In actuality, the Ottoman government had begun employing the term 'anarchist' in diplomatic correspondence relating to Armenians and Bulgarians long before

---

[29] Mathieu Deflem, 'Wild Beasts without Nationality: The Uncertain Origins of Interpol, 1889–1910', in Philip Reichel (ed.), *Handbook of Transnational Crime and Justice* (Thousand Oaks, CA: Sage, 2005), 276; Richard Bach Jensen, 'The International Campaign against Anarchist Terrorism, 1880–1930s', *Terrorism and Political Violence* 21(1) (2009): 92; Richard Bach Jensen, *The Battle against Anarchist Terrorism: An International History (1878–1934)* (Cambridge: Cambridge University Press, 2014).

[30] Richard Bach Jensen, 'The International Anti-Anarchist Conference of 1898 and the Origins of Interpol', *Journal of Contemporary History* 16(2) (1981): 323–47.

[31] Propaganda by deed was one of the key issues at the Anarchist Congress in 1881, and the use of such violence created an atmosphere of fear and suspicion that resulted in the imposition of repressive policing measures. For example, the surveillance and policies of repression against labour organisations and secret societies that increased in the aftermath of the Paris Commune in 1871 were implemented, at least in part, because of the wave of attacks against high-level civil servants and members of dynasties in the 1880s.

[32] Jensen, 'The International Anti-Anarchist Conference', 323–47.

[33] BOA, İ.HUS 69/66, 24 C. Ahir 1316, 10 October 1898.

the conference, not only because this provided a legitimate reason for the empire's security policies in the international arena, but also because Police Minister Hüseyin Nazım Paşa had started associating revolutionary movements with anarchism in the 1890s.[34] On the other hand, the conference was also perceived as an opportunity to roll back some of the purview of the capitulations and to monitor not only the actions of foreigners, but also the products and publications they were delivering to the Ottoman Empire.[35] The conference was also important for the government in terms of fostering international cooperation to limit the production and export of explosives.[36] After considering the possible ramifications of the conference, the Ottoman Empire accepted the invitation and dispatched a delegation to Rome under Consul Mustafa Reşit Efendi, which included representatives of the legal adviser of the Bab-ı Ali, Hakkı Bey and the clerk of foreign affairs, Nuri Bey.[37] Nuri Bey represented the Ottomans on the administrative committee, while Hakkı Bey was placed on the judicial committee.[38] They subsequently reported back to the Ottoman government regarding various policing techniques employed by different states, including better record-keeping methods for storing intelligence on individuals and creating an effective administrative network for investigations.

The main topics of the conference were the identification of anarchists and their activities; the creation of new policing procedures, practices and techniques to prevent anarchist actions and publications; and the drafting of extradition procedures. An 'anarchist act' was defined as 'having as its aim the destruction through violent means of all social organisation', while an anarchist was simply one who committed such an act.[39] This definition of an

---

[34] Hüseyin Nazım Paşa's report and memoirs are two important sources for understanding the Ottoman government's perspective on these incidents. His report was mainly on the Armenian question during the 1890s and was prepared in 1907. His memoir was also mainly about the Armenian question and was first published in 1924. Hüseyin Nazım Paşa, *Ermeni Olayları Tarihi*, vols 1–2; Hüseyin Nazım Paşa, *Hatıralarım*.

[35] BOA, İ.HR 24/1316.B.3, 18 November 1898.

[36] BOA, İ.HR 24/ 1316.B.3, 18 November 1898.

[37] BOA, İ.HUS 49/13 Şaban 1316, 27 December 1898. B.O.A.-İ.HR 24/1316.B.3, 18 November 1898.

[38] BOA, Y.PRK.EŞA. 31/136, 6 Kanun-u Sani 1899.

[39] Jensen, 'The International Anti-Anarchist Conference', 327; Adil Baktıaya, '19. Yüzyıl

anarchist act conceptualised anarchism as a criminal act rather than a political phenomenon that could easily be managed with the administrative measures and practices of police institutions.[40]

The representatives of the police departments of the participating states agreed to adopt the same control and surveillance methods as France, Germany and Russia. This required the preparation of key information for each deported anarchist in a standard format, including a photograph, a certificate of identity, information about appearance based on a *portrait parlé*, and information about the individual's arrival, departure and intended destination. This was then to be distributed among police forces in other states. The central police departments of all states would share such documented information about anarchists internationally. The *portrait parlé* was accepted as an international criminal identification method in line with an Ottoman proposal, which had also been discussed at a previous commission meeting without the Ottoman Empire, at which the French representative conducted a briefing on the system.[41] To expand the usage of the *portrait parlé*, every state was required to send a police officer to France for training in the method.[42] The Ottoman Empire declared that a police officer would be appointed to learn the technique and would practise the *portrait parlé* in the empire.[43] After the conference, a French expert on the method came to the Ottoman Empire to teach new biometric criminal identification techniques,[44] even though archival documents indicate that the Ottoman state had already been interested in the technique, imported the tools and arranged to invite a French expert before the conference.[45] Because the Ottoman police did not have the

---

Sonunda Anarşist Terör, "Toplumun Anarşistlerden Korunması Konferansı (1898)" ve Osmanlı Devleti', *Bilgi ve Bellek* 4(8) (2007): 65–6; BOA, Y.A.RES., 101/31, 12 S 1317 (22 June 1899) and 'Hariciye Nezareti'ne 3 Kanunusani 1899 tarihinde Roma Sefaret-i Seniyesi'nden varid olan 2 numerolu mahremane tahriratın tecümesi suretidir', in BOA, Y.PRK.EŞA., 31/136, 20 Ş 1316, 3 January 1899.

[40] Deflem, 'Wild Beasts', 279.
[41] BOA, Y.PRK.EŞA, 31/136, 6 Kanun-u Sani 1899.
[42] BOA, Y.PRK.EŞA, 31/136, 20 Ş 1316, 3 January 1899.
[43] BOA, Y.PRK.HR, 27/31, 10 May 1899.
[44] BOA, İ.HUS, 8, 27.R.1318, 23 August 1900, and BOA, ZB, 45/27, 24 August 1898. Baktıaya, '19. Yüzyıl Sonunda Anarşist Terör', 71.
[45] BOA, ZB, 45/27, 24 August 1898.

knowledge to use the *portrait parlé* method with imported tools, authorities moved to prepare a regulation on the description of how to use the tools. According to a further note in the same document, a new regulation was prepared concerning the issue.[46]

During discussions of extradition procedures for anarchists, the Ottoman Empire supported a German proposal that anarchists be deported, irrespective of their crimes, within the scope of extradition agreements. Ottoman representatives supported the German and Russian delegations' proposals and objections on eliminating restrictions on the extradition agreements. Ottoman and Russian delegates presented the Russian proposal as a joint suggestion advocating the extension of extradition procedures to include political crimes.[47]

Ottoman delegates supported the extradition procedures for perpetrators of assassination attempts against monarchs and dynastic families, and even submitted a proposal to extend the scope of the article so that actions leading to extradition should not be limited to these groups, but would also apply to any initiative, alliance, provocation, encouragement or proposition that could be tied to an assassination plan. But after this proposal was rejected, the Ottoman Empire sent a note to the Italian government emphasising that the Ottoman government insisted on the regulation and that the Ottomans would defend the same position in further meetings regarding international cooperation.[48]

After the conference, the Ottoman Empire drafted an anti-anarchist bill that was passed in the House of Representatives (*Meclis-i Vükela*) but rejected by the Prime Minister's Office (*Grand Vizierate*), primarily because, in contrast to the widespread 'trouble of anarchism' in the United States and Europe, only Armenians and a few Bulgarians were implicated in anarchism in the Ottoman Empire. The Prime Ministry, therefore, decided that the penal code was adequate and capable of dealing with such crimes. This meant that the Ottoman Empire would define such crimes as 'crimes against the state', which were already enshrined in the penal code, without specifically

---

[46] BOA, İ.HUS, 8, 1318.R.27, 23 August 1900, and BOA, ZB, 45/27, 24 August 1898.
[47] BOA, Y.PRK.HR, 27/31, 10 May 1899.
[48] BOA, İ.HR, 18/1317 Ra 29, 6 August 1899.

defining anarchist acts themselves.[49] Consequently, the Ottoman Empire, while using international cooperation to fight against anarchism, sought to avoid de-politicising it by declaring it a political crime.

Although the Ottomans refrained from enshrining the internationally accepted definition of anarchist actions in its laws, attending the conference was important for the empire, as it entailed participation in international police cooperation and was a possible first step towards the standardisation and global integration of police institutions. The Ottoman Empire's delegates to the Rome Conference also gathered information about the police departments and policing methods of various states, while the empire itself found an opportunity to obtain international support to legitimise its policing methods against anarchist actions, mainly defined as crimes against the state. In addition to these measures, collaboration in sharing information about anarchists also began between the empire and Belgium.

The Ottoman police force was organised based on the French model.[50] In 1884, the Parisian police officers, Inspector Bonin and Inspector Lefoulon, a specialist in anti-anarchist policing techniques, were invited to Istanbul to share their expertise on policing techniques and investigation methods for ordinary criminal activities and political opposition. The two prominent inspectors were hired to reorganise the Ottoman police in accordance with the institutionalisation of the police in France.[51] Lefoulon was also responsible for dealing with anarchists from foreign countries. For example, in 1896, he was appointed to track down Armenian anarchists in Marseille and Geneva.[52] As

---

[49] BOA, Y.A.RES, 116/23, 6 S 1320, 15 May 1902.

[50] For a detailed discussion on Ottoman police, public order and urban transformation, see Noémi Lévy-Aksu, *Ordre et désordres dans l'Istanbul ottomane (1879–1909): de l'État au quartier* (Paris, Karthala: 2013); Nurçin İleri, 'A Nocturnal History of Fin de Siecle Istanbul', PhD thesis, Binghampton University, 2015.

[51] Roger Deal, 'Celestin Bonnin and the Creation of a Modern Ottoman Police Force', in Marinos Sariyannis (ed.), *New Trends in Ottoman Studies: Papers Presented at the 20th CIÉPO symposium* (Rethymno: Department of History and Archaeology, University of Crete and Institute for Mediterranean Studies of the Foundation for Research and Technology, 2014), 166–75.

[52] Noémi Levy, 'Polislikle İlgili Bilgilerin Dolaşım Tarzları: Osmanlı Polisi için Fransız Modeli mi?', in Noémi Levy, Nadir Özbek, Alexandre Toumarkine (eds), *Jandarma ve Polis Osmanlı Tarihçiliğine Çapraz Bakışlar*, trans. Deniz Öztürk and Burak Onaran (IIstanbul: Tarih Vakfı Yurt Yayınları, 2009), 154–6.

a result of the inspectors' influence, the Ottomans developed anti-anarchist policing techniques that were very similar to the French model.

On 14 March 1904, Russia, Romania, Serbia, Bulgaria, Austria-Hungary, Germany, Denmark, Sweden, Norway, Spain, Portugal and the Ottoman Empire signed a further protocol in St Petersburg on expanding the practical details on expulsion, the structure of police institutions and international police collaboration – all topics which had received the attention of the administrative committee at the Rome Conference. The Ottoman government stated that the extradition procedures that acted as a catalyst for the St Petersburg protocol would not affect the agreement between Russia and the Ottoman Empire regarding Armenian migrants.[53] The Ottoman government ratified the protocol on 9 April 1904.[54]

Fesad, Vagrant and Anarchist

On the administrative level, the Ottoman Empire practised traditional and modern policing techniques side-by-side. The Ottoman bureaucracy started to deploy the concept of 'vagrant' in parallel to concepts such as 'anarchist' and '*fesad*',[55] which had acquired a pejorative connotation in an era of guerrilla warfare in the provinces, railway bombings, assassination attempts and ethnic conflicts. This, ultimately, was the terrain of the *discursive* level of the security policies.

The discursive strategies that the state was constituting as conceptualisations of threat had historical continuity. One of the significant concepts in these historical vocabularies was *fesad*, which can be translated as 'evildoer', 'seditious', 'conspirator' or 'villain'.[56] *Fesad* referred to the disturbance of order and public peace, which Islamic thought discusses in terms of natural

---

[53] BOA, İ.HUS, 115/89, 24 M 1322, 10 April 1904; BOA, Y.A.HUS, 469/36, 8 M 1322, 25 March 1904.

[54] BOA, İ.HR, 388/14, 5 S 1322, 21 April 1904.

[55] *Fesad* does not have a clear translation in English. It can be translated as evildoer, seditious, villain or conspirator. Instead of choosing one of the English words, the original version of the word will be used in this chapter.

[56] For use of *fesad* as nationalist sedition between 1840 and 1860, see Anna Vakali, 'Tanzimat in the Province: Nationalist Sedition (*Fesat*), Banditry (*Eşkiya*) and Local Councils in the Ottoman Southern Balkans (1840s to 1860s)', PhD thesis, University of Basel, 2017.

balance. The decline of order was commonly interpreted in a framework that related to the disobedience to God, which caused destruction of land and society. This destruction was caused by infringing legal or moral rules, contravening the religious way of living in daily life, or destroying the political order that was constituted as God's order. The scope of the concept was very extensive and can be associated with petty crimes, robbery, assault, rape, banditry, murder, mutiny and rebellion against the political order.[57] *Fesad* was the term used in state correspondence to refer to people who contravened the law, who rebelled against the state or who tried to change the political order.[58] *Fesad* was also an important concept in the Ottoman Panel Code (*Ceza Kanunname-i Hümayün*, 1858).[59] Although the concept can be traced in the articles under the section on crimes against the state, in the correspondence from a high level to the lower ranks of the bureaucracy, the administrative language used *fesad* to refer to every act or person that could potentially violate the social order. Thus, the use of the term in state documents was applied

---

[57] İlhan Kutluer, 'Fesad', *Türkiye Diyanet Vakfı İslam Ansiklopedisi*, vol. 12 (Istanbul: Diyanet Vakfı Yayınları, 1995), 421.

[58] Mustafa Akdağ, *Türk Halkının Dirlik ve Düzenlik Kavgası* (Ankara: Bilgi Yayınevi, 1975), 163–78; Engin Deniz Akarlı, 'Maslaha from "Common Good" to "Raison d'Etat" in the Experience of Istanbul Artisans, 1730–1840', in Kaan Durukan, Robert W. Zens and Akile Zorlu-Durukan (eds), *Hoca, 'Allame, Puits de Science: Essays in Honor of Kemal H. Karpat* (Istanbul: ISIS Press, 2010).

[59] In the Ottoman legal system before the Panel Code of 1858, the defendant or suspect was classified in one of three categories. The first category was modest persons (*kendi halinde kimseler*), who were known for their honesty and had not been convicted of any crime. As these persons had no criminal records, the authorities acted towards them on the presumption of their innocence. The second category was suspected persons (*mazanne* or *müttehem*) who had criminal records. If they faced any accusations, they could not benefit from the presumption of innocence; the burden of proof was on their shoulders and they could be arrested immediately. The third category was people of unknown circumstances (*meçhul'ül ahval*) who had no guarantors from the local community or had no proof that they earned their livelihoods by legal means. They could be arrested until the authorities obtained sufficient information on them. People of unknown circumstances were generally associated with *fesad*, without investigation of the person's reason for leaving their residence. Ahmet Akgündüz, *Osmanlı Kanunnameleri ve Hukuki Tahlilleri: Kanuni Sultan Süleyman Devri Kanunnameleri: I. Kısım Merkezi ve Umumi Kanunnameler*, vol. 4 (Istanbul: Fey Vakfı, 1992), 157; Mehmet Akman, *Osmanlı Devletinde Ceza Yargılaması* (Istanbul: Eren Yay, 2004), 51–52; Betül Başaran, *Selim III, Social Control and Policing in Istanbul at the End of the Eighteenth Century* (Leiden: Brill, 2014), 161–7.

to some groups as a label, like 'vagrant', and had an extensive and arbitrary area of discursive practice. The extent and arbitrariness of its usage made it one of the components of security discourse used when defining facts, events or persons in the context of political fear, threat and danger.

The Ottoman political centre used a surety system to control its settlement policy, public order, security and tax system. If someone left their residence for an 'acceptable reason', the person was obliged to find a guarantor to ensure that they would continue to fulfil their duties and pay their taxes.[60] Ultimately, the Ottoman Empire's guarantor system was designed as a social control system to prevent the disruption of public peace. The authorities generally perceived migrants and seasonal workers without guarantors to be highly suspect and potential criminals, as the labels 'suspect' (*ahvali mechul*, *mazanne* or *mütehhem*) or *fesad* prove. Thus, the authorities regularly checked seasonal workers staying in bachelor rooms or inns, deporting those migrants who had no guarantors from the city.[61] The Ottoman Empire in the Hamidian era (1876–1908) employed the surety system in combination with modern surveillance techniques. Identity cards, international and internal passports, and hotel registration systems must be understood within this framework.[62]

One significant aspect of policing was anti-vagrancy regulations.[63] Vagrancy and other public order offences did not constitute crimes in and of themselves. Instead, what constituted an offence was the involvement of a

---

[60] Ahmet Saydam, 'Kamu Hizmeti Yaptırma ve Suçu Önleme Yöntemi Olarak Osmanlılarda Kefalet Usulü', *Tarih ve Toplum* 28(164) (1997): 5.

[61] See Başaran, *Selim III, Social Control and Policing*. Numerous imperial decrees regarding the surety system were issued during the upheavals. The specific ethnic or religious origin of the rebels was the most significant factor affecting their perception as a threat. This pattern can be observed with the Albanians in the Patrona Halil Rebellion and with Muslim students during the Celali Rebellion, which caused Ottoman authorities to issue special orders regarding these groups.

[62] For a detailed discussion, see İlkay Yılmaz, *Serseri, Anarşist ve Fesadın Peşinde, II. Abdülhamid Döneminde Güvenlik Politikaları Ekseninde Pasaport, Mürür Tezkeresi ve Otel Kayıtları* (Istanbul: Tarih Vakfı Yurt Yayınları, 2014).

[63] The Ottoman regulations on vagrancy can be detected during times of rebellion or simple political events of the opposition in different historical periods. See Akdağ, *Türk Halkının Dirlik ve Düzenlik Kavgası*; Başaran, *Selim III, Social Control and Policing*.

certain kind of person, rather than any specific action or lack thereof.[64] The definition itself widened the scope of police intervention in daily life. The Vagrancy Act described vagrants as those who lacked legitimate work and either possessed no affiliation or registered residence or were deemed to be travelling without specific departure and arrival dates; they were identified as vagrants (*serseri*) and people of unknown circumstances (*meçhul'ül ahval*).[65] According to the Internal Passport Regulation of September 1887, every person travelling in the Ottoman Empire was required to carry an internal passport specifying his or her departure and arrival dates.[66] As far as the police were concerned, travelling without an internal passport was a criminal act, so labelling somebody a vagrant or suspicious person was the natural result of their travelling without an internal passport.[67] Laws against public order crimes and the Vagrancy Act can also be seen as instruments to control the population. However, in the Hamidian era, this manner of control was related not only to public order issues, but also to perceptions of threats to security. Given the local upheavals and guerrilla warfare occurring in the provinces, the railway bombings, and the assassination attempts in the city centre, the state elites' use of the concept interwove with other pejorative categories, such as 'anarchist'. In their internal correspondence, Ottoman state elites applied this discourse to anarchists, vagrants and seasonal workers. This link raises the issue of the filing and classification processes of the modern state and the flexibility of the concepts used in this process. These discursive strategies also restricted the extent of legitimate public spheres and marginalised certain identities, making it easier to side-line the poor, especially those who were politically mobilised, on a discursive level.

This process featured a discriminative discourse in administrative mechanisms that frequently used the terms '*fesad*', 'anarchist' and 'vagrant',

---

[64] Ferdan Ergut, 'Policing the Poor in the Late Ottoman Empire', *Middle Eastern Studies* 38(2) (2002): 150; R. Quinney, *The Social Reality of Crime* (Boston, MA: Little Brown, 1970).

[65] Serseri ve Mazanna-i Su' olan Eşhas Hakkında Nizamname, 3 Sefer 1308, 6 September 1306, 18 September 1890, *Düstur*, 1. Tertip 6, 748.

[66] *Düstur*, 1. Tertip, vol. 5:223, 861–5.

[67] See İlkay Yılmaz, 'Governing the Armenian Question through Passports in the Late Ottoman Empire (1876–1908)', *Journal of Historical Sociology* 32(4) (2019): 388–403.

especially for lower-class Armenians, Bulgarians and foreigners. This further marginalised, and even criminalised, them. The new usages of 'vagrant' and '*fesad*' created a discursive link to 'anarchism' and 'anarchist' in their pejorative meanings.[68] These all served as crucial discursive tropes for the security discourse of the state, which claimed to be keeping the country unified against its 'internal and external enemies'. This discourse is also important due to its effects on administrative activities. By using these terms, the state also constructed and widened a sphere of security, meaning that the other issues faced by Armenians and Macedonians were narrowly perceived in terms of threats and defence, to the exclusion of their socio-economic aspects. Therefore, the modernisation of security techniques and anti-anarchist regulations can also be analysed in terms of the discursive strategies.

Although there were some incidents of propaganda by deed, the conspiracy theories of the era also served to legitimise rebuilding and internationalising police institutions.[69] This discursive link exposes the ambiguity and arbitrariness of the classification of administrative information and the issues surrounding its administrative filing. By limiting the public sphere, such discursive strategies targeted and marginalised certain identities, ultimately resulting in the criminalisation of the poor – especially the politicised poor. During the Hamidian period, the use of 'anarchist', 'vagrant' and '*fesad*' in correspondence to refer to Armenians, Bulgarians and (mostly foreign) seasonal workers, served not only to marginalise these groups, but also criminalise them, as these labels were also legal concepts. This labelling process addresses the discursive level of Ottoman security policies. This kind of marginality was not based on exclusion by society, but by state rationality, which also shaped the relationship between public order and security, and shaped the compo-

---

[68] The Armenian community wrote a report and a petition demanding the elimination of the widespread use of the terms *fesad* and *şaki* (bandit, rebel) to refer to Armenians in daily bureaucratic correspondence and in newspapers. Later, the Ottoman government issued an *irade* (decree) ordering the removal of the cause of complaint, but even in daily correspondence, the term *fesad* continued to be used to refer to the Armenians. BOA, DH.TMIK.M., 26/ 57, 15 Ş 1314, 18 January 1897; and BOA, DH.TMIK.M, 26/88, 20 Ş 1314, 24 January 1897. See, Yılmaz, *Serseri, Anarşist ve Fesadın Peşinde*.

[69] Karl Harter, 'Security and Cross-Border Political Crime: The Formation of Transnational Security Regimes in 18th and 19th Century Europe', *Historical Social Research*, SI 'Security and Conspiracy in History, 16th to 21st Century' 38(1) (2013): 96–106.

sition of administrative practices by extending the limits of administrative discretion. As a result, the political, social or economic aspects of problematic questions became invisible, while these questions, which were framed as security issues, paved the way for securitisation; anti-anarchism and the regulations referring to it were also critical aspects of this. Even if there were attacks of propaganda by deed, the extension of police discretion and police activity were legitimised by the state's indulgence in conspiracy theories.

Threat Elements, Anti-anarchism and the Ottoman Empire

The anti-anarchist policies of European states were also practised in the Ottoman Empire, to the degree that its infrastructure permitted such action and was mostly directed against Bulgarians, Italians and, specifically, Armenian seasonal workers. This was especially after the 1890s when the Ottoman government's Armenian policy became harsher and Armenian revolutionaries started to use the propaganda of deed. Striving to deploy the latest policing techniques, the Ottoman Empire took extensive measures against Armenian revolutionaries and implemented new practices against seasonal workers from the Armenian community. This tendency suggests that state elites viewed lower-class Armenians as a potential threat. New policing measures, however, targeted not only the Armenian poor but also foreign workers with new security investigations and practices in different regions of the empire. The security rationale thereby maintained class distinctions with discursive links in a fashion similar to what was also occurring in Prussia, France, Austria-Hungary and other states.

Exploring the correspondence in the Police Ministry and the memoir and report on the Armenian question of Hüseyin Nazım Paşa, the police minister (*Zaptiye Nazırı*) and head of the security apparatus, reveals how the higher and lower ranks of the Ottoman bureaucracy perceived the Armenian question at the intersection of the administrative and discursive levels in 1890s.[70] In the report, which was written amid the anti-anarchist policies while conspiracy theories were being peddled in Europe, the expressions referring to Armenian revolutionary organisations display an overriding tenor of anti-anarchism.

[70] Hüseyin Nazım Paşa, *Ermeni Olayları Tarihi*; Hüseyin Nazım Paşa, *Hatıralarım*.

In his report, Hüseyin Nazım Paşa identified the Armenian movement as '*Ermeni fesadı nâmı verilen şekavetler*' ('banditry called Armenian conspiracy').[71] According to the police minister, Ottoman Armenians had encountered no difficulties living on Ottoman soil, in contrast to the claims of Armenian revolutionaries. However, the revolutionary organisation had two goals that used these claims as legitimising tools; the first was to set off political upheaval in the places inhabited by Armenians to establish an independent government through revolution. The second and longer-term goal was developed from anarchist ideas and featured multiple components, including the establishment of equality between rich and poor by sharing public and private property, self-government, and the abolishment of the state, religion, marriage, and other such trappings of the state and tradition. Hüseyin Nazım Paşa viewed the second goal through the prism of anarchism and emphasised that no European state practised any of these proposed goals. Thus, state elites characterised the Armenian revolutionary movement as a threat that could shake the foundations of society by seeking to create a new order. According to different sections of the report, the threat relating to the second goal concerned not merely the Ottoman Empire, but also overlapped with the goal of European nihilists and anarchists to unite and destroy monarchic governments. The report identified actions such as assassinations, threats and other destruction as *fesad*, while also linking them to anarchist ideas. Considering the allegations of a joint conspiracy among Armenian revolutionaries, European anarchists and Russian nihilists to collaborate against the Ottoman Empire – something that naturally must be prevented, according to the report – the importance of the relationship between violent political actions and anarchism was paramount for Hüseyin Nazım Paşa.

For Ottoman state elites, the fear of anarchism and its political consequences raised the spectre of an international anarchist network organised against the empire. But the elites also realised that tying this conspiracy to the Armenian revolutionary movement could be useful, as it could legitimise its measures against Armenians on the international stage while also ensuring that sympathy for Armenian revolutionaries would fall sharply in Europe.

---

[71] For the response of the Armenian Patriarch, see BOA, DH.TMIK.M, 26/ 57, 15 Ş 1314, 18 January 1897; and BOA, DH.TMIK.M, 26/88, 20 Ş 1314, 24 January 1897.

The document's reports of incidents, some of which were linked to anarchism on the basis of the demonstrations and flyers of the Hunchakian Party, were ultimately all tied to *raison d'état*.

Another significant narrative in the report was the distrust of poor Armenians. Armenian peasants were depicted as 'naive' and 'ingenuous' people who, as passive subjects, were easily deceived by revolutionary organisations – although the report also emphasised that propaganda by the groups would foster popular support for an independent Armenia among the Armenian poor. According to Hüseyin Nazım Paşa, the Armenian poor, working as porters, day labourers, firemen and the like, ignored the police's punitive measures and continued to support revolutionary ideas, making them threat elements. Without discussing the socio-political causes of the Armenian question, the main tendency of the report was to securitise the Armenian question by associating it with anarchism.

The anti-anarchist policies affected Armenian seasonal workers the most. The police administration argued that Armenian organisations were rousing public opinion for an independent Armenia, a dream supported by Armenian seasonal workers in Istanbul. The state elites categorised the Armenian poor as a potential threat.[72] This approach also allowed the Ottoman bureaucrats to perceive Armenian seasonal workers as the ones who transferred the Armenian question from the provinces to the capital city. During the Bab-ı Ali demonstration, the police ordered the Beyoğlu governor to arrest Armenian seasonal workers who came from other provinces and 'loafed about the streets like vagrants'.[73] Another document reports how Armenians associated with '*fesad*' were arrested, while others who were known to be associated with '*fesad*' were not, but sent back to their home towns due to lack of evidence. After the Bab-ı Ali demonstration, the sultan ordered that 'poor and unemployed Armenians in Istanbul should be returned to their homelands and the entry of the vagabonds coming from the countryside to Istanbul should be

---

[72] Zabtiye Nezâreti'nden Makâm-ı Sadâret-Penâhîye 16 Haziran Sene 1311 Târihiyle Yazılan Tezkirenin Sûretidir, Hüseyin Nazım Paşa, *Ermeni Olayları Tarihi*, vol. 1, 64–7.

[73] '17 Haziran Sene 1311 Târih ve İki Yüz Yirmi Üç Numara ile Beyoğlu Mutasarrıflığı'na Yazılan Müzekkirenin Sûretidir', in Hüseyin Nazım Paşa, *Ermeni Olayları Tarihi*, vol. 1, 74.

prevented'.[74] In addition, seasonal workers living in bachelor rooms and hostels were expelled from the city and returned to their home towns.[75] The most frequently applied measure against seasonal workers deemed to be 'dangerous' or 'suspicious' was deportation. When workers without jobs or regular pay left the city, their travel document stated that it had been prepared only on the condition that they did not return to Istanbul.[76]

The state not only expelled vagrants and mischievous or suspicious people, but also kept records on them,[77] especially seasonal workers. Armenian porters, bricklayers, boatmen and others were all recorded in a special register.[78] In order to investigate 'vagrant Armenians', a special commission was formed under the Ministry of Interior Affairs before being transferred to the Police Ministry.[79]

After the Thessaloniki bombings by a Bulgarian anarchist group, state elites received intelligence that a further series of bombings had been planned for Istanbul.[80] Accordingly, an order was sent to the Bulgarian Exarchate to identify suspicious Bulgarians residing in the city.[81] Extra security measures were also implemented due to information about a plan by Bulgarians to assassinate the Russian consul.[82] The measures included police patrols in Galata and Beyoğlu, identity checks, and tax registrations of tenants, shopkeepers and artisans in order to obtain intelligence about suspicious and foreign individuals.[83] To prevent any attack on the Ottoman Bank in Istanbul,

---

[74] BOA, İ.HUS, 85, 19 R 1313, quoted in Vahdettin Engin, *Sultan Abdülhamid ve İstanbul'u* (Istanbul: Simurg, 2001), 60.

[75] 'Dâhiliye Nezâret-i Celîlesi'ne Vârid Olan 30 Haziran Sene 1312 Târih ve İki Yüz Seksen Numara ile Yazılan Tezkire Sûretidir', in Hüseyin Nazım Paşa, *Ermeni Olayları Tarihi*, vol. 2, 282–4 and 'Dâhiliye Nezâret-i Celîlesi'ne Yazılan 23 Mayıs Sene 1312 Târihli Tezkire Sûretidir', in Hüseyin Nazım Paşa, ibid., vol. 2, 244–5.

[76] BOA,BEO, 2249/168648, 19 L 1321, 7 January 1904.

[77] The documents include lists of the Armenians who were sent to their home towns by the police. BOA, Y.PRK.ZB, 18/34, 25 Ra 1314, 3 September 1896.

[78] BOA, ZB, 30/26, 21 May 1316, 3 June 1900.

[79] BOA, İ.ZB, 1/1314-B-1, 01 B 1314, 6 December 1896.

[80] BOA, Y.A.HUS, 448/64, 20 S 1321, 18 May 1903.

[81] BOA, Y.A.HUS, 448/77, 21 S 1321, 19 May 1903.

[82] BOA, Y.A.HUS, 448/99, 23 S 1321, 21 May 1905; and BOA, Y.A.HUS, 448/135, 27 S 1321, 25 May 1903.

[83] BOA, Y.A.HUS, 448/111, 24 S 1321, 22 May 1903.

all streets and locations around the bank were checked, while the police and municipality collaborated to record on a map the names of all those working or living in the area. In addition, those working in the bank had to find a guarantor, while anyone entering the bank was also obliged to register with the police.[84]

The authorities attempted to prevent 'anarchists' from entering Ottoman territory by subjecting people arriving to various procedures.[85] The security practices imposed on Armenians were also applied to other foreign lower-class groups, particularly Italians. Like many European states, including Russia, the Ottoman Empire tried to prevent anarchists from entering, as noted in various documents in the Ottoman archives that are directly concerned with foreign anarchists. All foreign travellers had to carry a passport with a visa, an internal passport, and another document issued by their consulate that contained details of the holder's identity, residence, purpose of travel and duration of visit. Police checks also became a routine part of procedures aimed at foreigners. Regulations prohibited visitors to Ottoman territory from involvement in politics, while 'revolutionaries like anarchists' had to be stopped.[86] If any socialists or anarchists managed to enter, they were to be deported after their photograph was taken and their identity details were recorded in special registers.[87] For example, one Greek citizen, Rano son of Rusi, was expelled on suspicion of being a socialist from France, having already been rejected by Russia and Romania before coming to Istanbul. According to the official report, he was unemployed and involved in politics, and 'he was even expelled from a republican country like France'.[88] Another practice was to gain intelligence about anarchists before their arrival and send photographs to other departments in order to prevent their arrival.[89]

After an Italian anarchist assassinated France's president in Lyon on 25

---

[84] BOA, A.MKT.MHM., 731/4, 3 S 1321, 1 May 1903.
[85] BOA, A.MKT.MHM, 541/ 20, 18 R 1315, 15 September 1897.
[86] BOA, DH.MKT, 2131/14, 24 C 1316, 9 November 1898; and BOA, DH.TMIK.M, 71/46, 3 S 1317, 11 June 1899.
[87] BOA, DH.MKT, 2068/45, 27 M 1312, 30 July 1894.
[88] BOA, DH.MKT, 267/30, 29 M 1312, 1 August 1894; and BOA, DH.MKT, 2068/45, 27 M 1312, 30 July 1894.
[89] BOA, Y.PRK.ZB, 29/26, 03 Ca 1319, 18 August 1901.

June 1894, French state elites began to view all Italians as potential anarchists and criminals, resulting in the deportation of many, although some managed to escape from France. In the meantime, Ottoman state elites urgently banned Italians from entering,[90] including those who had been deported from other countries.[91] Italian ferry companies were warned not to permit anarchists to travel to Ottoman ports.[92] Other measures included an order to deport Italian anarchists after taking their photographs,[93] the arrest and deportation to Italy of three Italian anarchists,[94] and the refusal to issue visas to Italian workers in order to avoid difficulties with their deportation.[95] Other policies that can be analysed as anti-anarchist included the investigation of thirty Italian workers without visas who had arrived in Istanbul on the ferry Taormina,[96] as well as the refusal to grant visas to other Italian workers and miners.[97] The stricter procedures for Italians were also evident in the case of Italian Rayak-Hama railway workers.[98] These Italians had asked to travel from Romania to Beirut to work on railway construction. However, before they could be issued visas, an investigation took place with the cooperation of the Italian consulate.[99] In 1902, after King Leopold II of Belgium was targeted in an assassination attempt by the Italian anarchist Gennaro Rubino, controls on Italians became even tougher.

Despite all the measures, some Italian anarchists in the Ottoman Empire managed to stay in the Ottoman territories, even with the strict procedures, passport regime and the incriminating information regarding them.[100] Although the Ottoman government did conduct surveillance and engage in

---

[90] BOA, İ.HUS, 25/1311 Z-102, 22 Z 1311, 26 June 1894.
[91] BOA, MV, 96/59, 23 B 1316, 8 December 1898.
[92] BOA, Y.A.HUS, 524/25, 04 B 1326, 2 August 1908.
[93] BOA, Y.PRK.ZB, 32/43, 26 M 1320, 5 May 1902.
[94] BOA, Y.PRK.ŞH, 12/2, 16 M 1320, 25 April 1902.
[95] BOA, Y.PRK.ZB, 25/107, 16 R 1318, 12 August 1900.
[96] BOA, DH.MKT, 1770/25 29 S 1308, 14 October 1890; BOA, HR.TO, 345/48, 18 September 1890.
[97] BOA, DH.MKT, 2512/109, 12 R 1319, 29 July 1901.
[98] BOA, BEO, 1696/127178, 13 R 1319, 30 July 1901.
[99] BOA, DH.TMIK.M, 119/13, 15 Za 1319, 24 February 1902.
[100] Makdisi, *The Eastern Mediterranean and the Making of Global Radicalism*, 227–37; Çorlu, 'Anarchists and Anarchism in the Ottoman Empire'.

record-keeping on Italian anarchists since their relations and networking with other Ottoman political groups were known, the main factor was that the state lacked the infrastructural capacity necessary to exert control throughout the Ottoman Empire's extensive territory.

The Italian government also informed the Ottoman Empire about Italians heading to Istanbul without visas and asked the Ottoman Empire to intercept them.[101] After the assassination of Empress Elizabeth, Italy sought to demonstrate that the Italian state did not support anarchism and was open to international collaboration. In another case, the consulates of Russia, France, Germany and Austria-Hungary collaborated to investigate the identities of anarchists going to Istanbul,[102] and such joint anti-anarchist policies continued with the signing of the 1904 St Petersburg Protocol.[103]

Conclusion

As an administrative body, the Ottoman Empire began to use modern techniques against political threats or actions disrupting public order in the late nineteenth century. This process occurred as an aspect of the larger internationalisation of police departments in Europe and against the backdrop of Ottoman cooperation with other countries against anarchists. The Ottoman state was actively using international police cooperation and new techniques for identifying criminals, especially during the investigations of violent acts.[104] However, the Ottoman state elites focused on both political threats and actions against public order, resulting primarily in the marginalisation of specific groups in the empire. Although administrative regulations and the bureaucracy are central to the infrastructural power of the modern state,[105] policing practices in the Ottoman Empire show us that the daily practices of state security can also make such regulations the basis for a political threat. The

---

[101] BOA, HR.TO, 345/ 48, 18 September 1898.
[102] BOA, Y.PRK.HR, 30/54, 11 M 1319, 30 April 1901.
[103] BOA, İ.HUS, 115/89, 24 M 1322, 10 April 1904.
[104] For an example, see Raşit Gündoğdu and Ömer Faruk Yılmaz (eds), *Sultan İkinci Abdülhamid Han'a Yapılan Suikastin Tahkikat Raporu* (Istanbul: Çamlıca Basım Yayın, 2007).
[105] Michael Mann, 'The Autonomous Power of the State: Its Origins, Mechanisms and Results', *European Journal of Sociology* 25(2) (1984): 185–213.

politics of fear and the process of identifying these threats can also be discussed as political tools that were employed for the state elites' political strategies.

The history of security opens a space for wide-ranging discussion on policing reforms and how state elites defined threat elements.[106] Naturally, conspiracies and deeds were also useful in legitimising[107] the new policing techniques and directly affected the administrative process, especially for Armenians, Italians and Bulgarians. In the Ottoman case, the internationalisation of the Armenian question must be considered in the context of internal security measures, as must the process of labelling social groups that state elites inevitably associated with revolutionary or nationalist organisations. While trying to analyse the security implementations, another significant point is how the Police Minister Hüseyin Nazım Paşa regularly referred to concepts of 'conscience', 'justice' and 'truth' in explaining the position of the Ottoman government in his report. While he constantly referred to these concepts as discursive tools to point out the 'propaganda of Armenian revolutionary (*fesad*) organisations which were [in] contrast [to] the truth (*muhalif-i hakikat*)', this very narrative, based on a security mentality, created 'the provocation thesis'.[108] This kind of securitisation paved the way for an impunity regime towards the Armenian community, and unpunished crimes against humanity in the long term, from Ottoman to post-Ottoman Turkey.

---

[106] Cornel Zwierlein and Beatrice de Graaf, 'Security and Conspiracy in Modern History', *Historical Social Research* 38(1) (2013): 7–45; Cornell Zwierlein and Beatrice de Graaf, 'Historicizing Security – Entering the Conspiracy Dispositive', *Historical Social Research* 38(1) (2013): 46–65.

[107] Legitimisation in terms of acceptance of the system's norms and values. David Easton, *A Systems Analysis of Political Life* (New York: John Wiley, 1965); S. M. Lipset, 'Some Social Requisites of Democracy: Economic Development and Political Legitimacy', *American Political Science Review* 53(1) (1959): 69–105.

[108] The Ottoman bureaucrats developed a narrative on 'sedition' that blamed Armenian radicals by inciting the 'naive' and 'poor' Armenian peasants and workers to commit violence against the state with the aim of attracting the attention of foreign countries. State elites have also used the provocation thesis as one of the main discursive strategies for the genocide denial during the republican era.

8

Between Ruler and Rogue: Sayyid Talib al-Naqib and the British in Early Twentieth-century Basra

Aline Schlaepfer

Sayyid Talib al-Naqib was born in Basra in the late 1860s to a family of *nuqabā'* (pl. *naqīb*), traditional leaders and marshals of the *ashrāf* (descendants of the Prophet, pl. *sharīf*). Since the Ottoman victory against the Mamluks and their subsequent reconquest of the Iraqi provinces, the last three generations of *nuqabā'* held important positions both locally in Basra, and had good relations with the Ottoman authorities in Istanbul. Talib al-Naqib became a member of the Ottoman parliament, but like many other Ottoman officials from Arab provinces, he soon began to express opposition against the Committee of Union and Progress' (*İttihad ve Terakki Cemiyeti*, CUP) policies and drew closer to the British. After they occupied Basra, however, Talib's presence there was deemed undesirable and he was exiled to India. While for a short time, Talib was considered a serious candidate for the crown of Iraq, his candidacy was eventually rejected in favour of Faysal, son of Husayn of Mecca. Despite a few attempts to play a key role in the provisional government, most notably as Minister of Interior, his aspirations to rule failed, and resulted in his banishment. He was again exiled, this time to Ceylon. Finally, after repeatedly trying to resettle in Syria, Egypt and later Iraq, he died in Germany in 1929.

Talib al-Naqib's trajectory is, *a posteriori*, one of failure. Consequently, his story has often been relegated to the margins of national and colonial histories, with the exception of two monographs – one by Haifa Ahmed al-Nakib, who wrote a Master's thesis at the University of Leeds in 1973, and another one by Husayn Shallah, who published a political biography in 2002.[1] British sources, however, give a stunning impression of the complexity of Talib's strategies, as well as the challenges his political moves presented for British administrations in Iraq, Egypt and India in particular. Because of his influence in the region – mainly around Basra, Kuwait and Muhammara – as well as his defiant behaviour, British officials expressed both great mistrust vis-à-vis Talib, and the will to maintain him as a political ally in the region. In fact, the British could not decide whether to maintain the man they considered a 'rogue' as far away from Iraqi politics as possible, or to keep him on their side as a local ruler. A generous monthly allowance, as well as repeated forced exiles, was deemed to be the best solution to keep things on hold. By exploring mainly British correspondence and reports on Talib – from Basra, Baghdad, Istanbul, Cairo, Damascus, Delhi and Bombay between 1904 and 1929 – but also Iraqi historiography, press and memoirs, I show how Talib's deliberate use of his liminal position – between rogue and ruler – proved to be an effective tool that brought him to the bargaining table and at times kept the balance of power in his favour. Ultimately, I intend to use Talib's story to show how the presumably clear-cut distinction between rogue and ruler – or the law and the outlaw – can prove to be problematic.

The Office of the *Naqīb al-Ashrāf* in Basra at the Turn of the Twentieth Century: Between the Law and the Outlaw

In Eric Hobsbawm's reading of the opposition between rebel and ruler, the 'social bandit', who emerges at the margins of and in reaction to the state's control, is considered a criminal by the state.[2] In the historian's interpretation, the frontier between the law and the outlaw is therefore clear, as the outlaw

---

[1] Haifa Ahmed al-Nakib, 'A Critical Study of Saiyyid Talib Pasha al-Nakib in the Setting of his Time and Environment, on the Basis of Arabic and Foreign Documents', MA thesis, University of Leeds, 1973; Husayn Shallah, *Talib Basha al-Naqib al-Basri wa Dawruhu fi al-Ta'rikh al-'Iraq al-Siyasi al-Hadith* (Beirut: al-Dar al-'arabiyya lil-mawsu'at). In 1989, Eliezer Tauber also contributed with an article about Talib's early political career. Eliezer Tauber, 'Sayyid Talib and the Young Turks in Basra', *Middle Eastern Studies* 25(1) (1989): 3–22.

[2] Eric Hobsbawm, *Bandits* (New York: Pantheon, [1969] 1981).

needs to show clean rupture with the state apparatus in order to meet the definition of a bandit. But, in order to clearly identify the boundary between the law and the outlaw, the very nature of the state and the extent of its power need to be defined first. However, this task can become difficult. Following the definition given by the editors of this volume in the Introduction, an age of rogues is made possible in a specific geopolitical context characterised by strong inter- and intra-imperial rivalries, thus allowing conflicting voices not only to emerge more easily, but also to blur the boundary between the law and the outlaw. As the story of Talib al-Naqib will illustrate, the context of Basra at the turn of the twentieth century is one of complex rivalry and transition between the Ottoman Empire, British occupation and later mandate. Multiple attempts to establish or maintain separate political entities in the Gulf, such as emirates in al-Muhammara, Kuwait and Basra, also further complicated matters. Because various forms of states co-existed and often overlapped over a significant period of time, rulers were many and the state cannot be considered a clear and monolithic institution. It is therefore problematic to think in terms similar to the Hobsbawmian reading of social banditry in total disconnect from the state.

Also, it could be useful to investigate the historical origins of the function held by Talib through the office of *naqīb al-ashrāf*, the marshal of the nobility in Basra, in order to materialise the problematic distinction between ruler and rebel. Although the exact roots of the *naqīb al-ashrāf* office are unknown, it was most certainly established during the Abbasid period for the first time. Abbasid caliphs needed to prove their lineage to the Prophet Muhammad – their *sharaf* – to be acknowledged and legitimised at the top levels of the political institution. Large towns of the empire had their own *nuqabā'* who were supervised by one chief *naqīb* originally based in Baghdad. The *naqīb* – literally the 'syndic' or 'chief' – was in charge of preserving the nobility of the Prophet's lineage, mostly by keeping records of the death of each *sharaf*, and by checking that marriages were kept within the community of *ashrāf*.[3]

---

[3] The nobility was divided between two main branches of the family, the *Talibiyyin* and the *'Abbassiyyin*. Axel Havemann, 'Naķīb al-Ashrāf', *Encyclopaedia of Islam*, 2nd edn, Brill online, 2012, last accessed 4 November 2019. See also Vanessa Van Renterghem, *Élites bagdadiennes au temps des Seldjoukides* (Beirut: Presses de l'Ifpo, 2015), 474–80.

According to the eleventh-century Shafi'i jurist Abu al-Hasan al-Mawardi, the *naqīb* was also responsible for the financial revenue of the Sharifian community. He was supposed to supervise the *waqf* management for the *ashrāf* and ensure all those entitled to its revenue should benefit from it. The *naqīb* was, therefore, also responsible for the distribution of profits within the community.[4]

The office of the *naqīb al-ashrāf* was, nevertheless, malleable in nature and, therefore, evolved over time. When the office of *naqīb al-ashrāf* was reactivated by the Ottoman sultan Bayazid II, it reflected a will to reassert Sunni legitimacy by bringing the *ashrāf* from the Hashemite branch of the Prophet's family closer to power. From then on, the *ashrāf* benefited from their own judicial system and from the financial protection offered to them by their provincial *naqīb*, who was appointed by the *naqīb al-ashrāf* in Istanbul.[5] Over the course of the eighteenth and nineteenth centuries, the *nuqabā'* seemed to have gained more political power at the scale of the provinces.[6] In the case of the province of Baghdad, the office of *naqīb al-ashrāf* survived the collapse of the Ottoman Empire and lasted until well into the twentieth century. In fact, the founder of the Republic of Iraq 'Abd al-Karim Qasim officially abolished the office as late as 1962, when the *naqīb* of Baghdad Ibrahim Sayf al-Din al-Gaylani died. Until his death, the *naqīb* of Baghdad al-Gaylani was in charge of supervising the *awqāf* for the Qadiriyya order.[7]

In Basra, the office of the *naqīb al-ashrāf* was held by Talib al-Naqib's family from the 1870s. As land owners around the city of Basra, the family became particularly powerful after the introduction of the Ottoman Land Law of 1858. They imposed extensive influence over town, country and tribes, which enabled them to help the *vali* Midhat Paşa gain control over the region. Sayyid Muhammad Sa'id, Talib al-Naqib's grandfather, was

---

[4] Mawardi (al-), 'Ali Ibn-Muhammad (974–1058), *Al-Ahkam al-Sultaniyya*, 3rd edn (Cairo: Mustafa al-Babi al-Halabi, 1973), 144–9.

[5] Technically, the provincial *naqīb* was a 'deputy *naqīb*' (*naqīb al-ashrāf qā'im-maqām*, or *naqīb al-ashrāf wākilī*).

[6] Herbert Bodman, *Political Factions in Aleppo, 1760–1826* (Chapel Hill: University of North Carolina Press, 1963), 79–102.

[7] Meir Basri, *Al-'Iraq al-hurr*, s.l.: 25 August 1999.

appointed *naqīb al-ashrāf* in 1874, and his son Sayyid Rajab followed in his father's political footsteps. Rajab officially became *naqīb* himself when his father died in 1896, although his father had already nominated his son to act as *naqīb* on health grounds a few years earlier. For similar reasons, Rajab transferred the *niqāba* to his brother Hashim. Technically, Talib should have officially inherited the title after his father's death, but this did not happen. In practice, Talib's uncle Hashim kept the title, while Talib remained a '*naqīb* without the *niqāba*', even after his father's death.[8] In addition to their administrative tasks pertaining to genealogical supervision and control over the supervision of the *ashrāf*'s finances, the Naqib family in Basra held strategic political positions, mostly acting as political mediators for the southern Gulf region. First, they mediated between the Porte and the al-Sabah family of Kuwait, and, later, in the context of mounting tensions in the Najd, between the Al Sa'ud and the Al Rashid. Thus, given the financial, judicial and political power that Talib inherited from his father, and despite multiple regime changes, he maintained social, political and financial control over the region until his death in 1929, not only in the province of Basra, but also in northern parts of the Gulf as a whole.

Thus, the man whom the British called a 'villain', 'ruffian' or 'rogue', as I will show further in the chapter, was actually part of an order existing well before the British presence and that continued to exist after that. And the Basrawi Robin Hood figure – which I will also examine in greater detail – based on distribution of wealth in the community appears to have stemmed from a tax practice originally rooted in the historical function of *naqīb*, although with abusive interpretations. In other words, in the context of numerous rivalries between various forms of states, on the one hand, and given the very nature of *naqīb*'s function, on the other hand, Talib al-Naqib found himself in a position of in-betweenness, between the law and the

---

[8] Reasons for this are unclear. Some claim that Talib himself chose not to become the official *naqīb*, while others maintain that he was in exile in India at the time his father passed away and could not therefore officially become *naqīb*. Talib's biographer Husayn Shallah, however, insists that the first explanation is more likely than the second. Shallah, *Talib Basha al-Naqib al-Basri*, 75–6.

outlaw. He did not emerge as either a fully rebellious figure against a disputed order or as the undisputed ruler himself.

Talib al-Naqib's Ottoman Début in Istanbul and Basra: Birth of the Iraqi Hero

Sayyid Talib b. Rajab b. Muhammad Saʻid b. Talib al-Naqib al-Rifaʻi was born between 1868 and 1870.[9] Talib al-Naqib made his political début in the Ottoman political arena in 1899, when he came sent to Istanbul to make a complaint about the *vali* of Basra Hamdi Paşa. A conflict had occurred between the latter and Sheikh Mubarak of Kuwait, an ally of Talib's family. The *vali* was subsequently ousted and replaced with one who was on friendlier terms with the sheikh and Talib.[10] Three years later, in June 1902, Talib was appointed *mutasarrıf* for the *sancak* of Najd, in order to act as mediator between Ibn Rashid and Ibn Saʻud.[11] However, Talib's presence was requested in Istanbul as he was suspected of murdering the *vali* of Qatar Hacı Mansur Paşa. He therefore resigned in 1904 and settled in Istanbul.[12] There, two men offered protection to Talib. First, Sheikh Abu al-Huda al-Sayyadi, *naqīb al-ashrāf* in Aleppo and a Sufi from the same Rifaʻiyya order as Talib, was very influential in the sultan's entourage, and, second Ahmad ʻIzzat al-ʻAbid Paşa, the sultan's Second Palace Secretary.[13] With their support, he managed to join the Council of State. In 1904, a collection of poems was published in Cairo in Talib's honour, celebrating the man 'devoted to the Ottoman Sultan'.[14]

A report written in August 1904 by the British ambassador in Istanbul Sir Nicholas O'Conor shows that Talib's activities in Istanbul attracted the

---

[9] Sayyid (pl. *sāda*) is the title used by acknowledged descendants of the Prophet (*ashrāf*).

[10] Tauber, 'Sayyid Talib and the Young Turks in Basra', 3.

[11] He became governor for the *sancak of* al-Ahsa, which was part of the *vilayat* of Basra, located in the Najd.

[12] Gökhan Çetinsaya, *Ottoman Administration of Iraq, 1890–1908* (New York: Routledge, 2006), 20.

[13] Butrus Abu-Manneh, 'Sultan Abdulhamid II and Shaikh Abulhuda Al-Sayyadi', *Middle Eastern Studies* 15(2) (1979): 131–53; Thomas Eich, 'The Forgotten Salafi. Abu al-Huda al-Sayyadi', *Die Welt des Islams* 43(1) (2003): 61–87.

[14] Reidar Visser, *Basra, the Failed Gulf State: Separatism and Nationalism in Southern Iraq* (Münster: Lit Verlag, 2006), 34.

attention of the British. Because of their ambitions in the region, they were interested in particular in his connections with Istanbul and in the Gulf region with sheikhs Khaz'al of Muhammara and Mubarak of Kuwait. Also, his mediation experience in the Najd would make Talib a valuable partner in the future, as the Gulf, located at the southeast end of the Ottoman Empire, had long been considered a contentious frontier. They had managed to get their hands on a detailed report that Talib al-Naqib had written to the Grand Vizier about a strategy to adopt in order to avoid British influence in the Gulf and 'to gain the sympathy of the Arabs', which sparked their interest. The report included a number of recommendations for reform – according to the English translation thirty-three – in the legal, political and social fields from Syria to Yemen, in order to ensure Arabs' loyalty towards Istanbul and avoid British interference.[15] O'Conor wrote: 'Talib Bey's views are of some interest . . . His opinions are doubtless colored by his sense of the most favourable light in which to present them to the Porte and the palace, but I have nevertheless thought it worth while to send direct to the acting consul at Bussorah'. In order to gain Talib's attention in return, O'Conor proposed to use Talib's ambitions to obtain the position of *vali* in Basra, 'which will make him a likely candidate for the post . . . at next vacancy'.[16]

After the Young Turk Revolution of July 1908, new political forces began to attract individuals in Istanbul and elsewhere. A few politicians from Iraqi provinces (Baghdad and Basra), such as 'Abd al-Muhsin al-Sa'dun, remained loyal Unionists until very late; but, similarly to other Arab provinces, a great number of Iraqi deputies rapidly joined the opposition against the Committee of Union and Progress' policies.[17] According to Sulayman Faydi, lawyer, founder of the Basrawi reformist newspaper *al-Iqaz* and close friend of Talib, the Iraqi 'liberals' (*al-aḥrār*) – as they were called – often

---

[15] Nakib Zade Talib Bey, 'Report on Arabia', enclosed to letter from O'Conor, Constantinople, 3 August 1904, The National Archives (hereafter TNA) FO 416/20, File E 109.

[16] N. R. O'Conor, Constantinople, 3 August 1904, TNA: FO 416/20, File E 109.

[17] Bedross Der Matossian, *Shattered Dreams of Revolution: From Liberty to Violence in the Late Ottoman Empire* (Stanford, CA: Stanford University Press, 2014). See also 'Abdallah, *'Abd al-Muhsin al-Sa'dun wa Dawruhu fi al-'Iraq al-siyasi al-mu'asir* (Beirut: Jadawel, 2011), 42. Arab Bureau, Basra Branch, 'The Muntafik', printed in Calcutta, 1917, 4, TNA: CO 1073/53/11947895.

spoke highly of the Ottoman *millet* and defended territorial integrity, which they perceived as threatened by the CUP policies. They also favoured a decentralisation policy (*al-lā-markaziyya*), by advocating for the free use of the Arabic language in schools, in response to the attempt to 'turkify the Arabs' (*tatrīk al-'Arab*).[18] In 1911, the Freedom and Accord Party (*Hürriyet ve Itilaf Fırkası*) was established in Istanbul, and many branches were created locally in, for example, Beirut, Baghdad and Basra.[19]

Talib al-Naqib had strong connections with the Hamidian *ancien régime*, which earned him the description of being 'a hater of the Young Turk and a Turk of the old school' by the British.[20] He nevertheless managed to become member of the Ottoman parliament, representing Basra in December 1908,[21] and was re-elected twice after that. In 1909, when Süleyman Nazif, a leading Unionist, was appointed *vali* of Basra, Sayyid Talib incited a number of notables from Basra to sign a petition against Nazif who attempted to limit the influence of the *nuqabā' al-ashrāf* in provincial politics, and the *vali* was eventually dismissed. Despite Talib's pressure, however, a few signatories chose to personally accompany the *vali* to the port of Basra to say farewell, in secret from Talib. In his memoirs, Sulayman Faydi explains that he was the only one who later confessed the secret to Talib, and thus gained his trust. The two men became 'like father and son'. Talib al-Naqib and Sulayman Faydi later founded the Basrawi branch of the Party of Freedom and Understanding, named the Free and Moderate Party (*al-Hizb al-Hurr al-Mu'tadil*), in early August 1911, together with other notables from the city. The same year, in the name of the party, Talib al-Naqib addressed a

---

[18] Sulayman Faydi, *Mudhakkirat Sulayman Faydi* (London: Al-Saqi, [1952] 1998), 117. Hasan Kayalı shows that the notion of 'turkification' of empire resulted less from an active discrimination towards Arabs (as non-Turks) than from a systematic and despotic centralisation policy, subsequently leading to the under-representation of Arabs. Hasan Kayalı, *Arabs and Young Turks: Ottomanism, Arabism, and Islamism in the Ottoman Empire (1908–1918)* (Berkeley: University of California Press, 1997), 82–96.

[19] 'Ali al-Wardi, *Lamahat Ijtima'iyya min Ta'rikh al-'Iraq al-Hadith*, vol. 3, 2nd edn (s.l.: s.n.), 211. Alternatively, *al-Hizb al-hurr al-mu'tadil*, literally the Free and Moderate Party.

[20] Telegram from Bombay to Delhi, 28 January 1915, 163, TNA: IOR/L/PS/10/535, File 94/1915.

[21] British consulate in Basra to Ambassador Gerard Lowther, Constantinople, 4 December 1908, 552, TNA: FO 195/2275.

call for support to the Sharif Husayn of Mecca, 'for us, Arab deputies', together with a declaration acknowledging the deputies' loyalty to Husayn as the leader of a 'caliphate attending to the interests of all Arab countries'.[22] According to Eliezer Tauber, Talib's prestige increased significantly in Basra after his successful political move against the *vali* and after the founding of his party.[23]

On 28 February 1913, the Free and Moderate Party was dissolved and renamed the Reform Society in Basra (*al-Jam'iyya al-Islahiyya fi al-Basra*) by Talib al-Naqib in his own home with the help of Sulayman Faydi. Local notables gathered and wrote a *mazbata* composed of 300 signatures, claiming that Arabs sided with neither the CUP nor the Liberals, but 'will devote their efforts to the cause of Turkey as a whole without party distinction'.[24] In the text, the society insisted on preserving Ottoman territory and sanctioning concessions granted to foreigners in Iraq. As Mahmoud Haddad notes, this request particularly confirmed Talib al-Naqib's fierce opposition, which he had already expressed in the Chamber of Deputies in 1909, against the concession given to the British Lynch Brothers Company.[25] The second priority pertained to the promotion of the Arabic language at various administrative, judicial and educative levels of the province.[26] Finally, the Reform Society also used an Islamic tone to denounce the 'heretical' drift of the Young Turks' policies. In the media favourable to Talib al-Naqib, emphasis was put on his 'intense love for Ottoman and Islamic unity'.[27] During the same period, Talib al-Naqib visited the British Consul in Basra. In essence, Talib told him that he rejected state control while still claiming Ottoman identity: They were 'anxious to uphold the constitution as faithful Ottoman subjects'.[28]

---

[22] Exact date of the letter unknown. Reprinted in Faydi, *Mudhakkirat*, 89–92, 100–1, 122.
[23] Tauber, 'Sayyid Talib and the Young Turks in Basra', 4.
[24] Consul Crowe to Gerard Lowther, Basra, 1 February 1913. Reprinted in *Records of Iraq (1914–1966)*, vol. 1, ed. Alan de Rush (Slough: Archives Ed., 2001), 61.
[25] Mahmoud Haddad, 'Iraq before World War I: A Case of Anti-European Arab Ottomanism', in Rashid Khalidi (ed.), *The Origins of Arab Nationalism* (New York: Columbia University Press, 1991), 128–40.
[26] See al-Nakib, 'A Critical Study of Saiyyid Talib Pasha al-Nakib', app. D, 125–8.
[27] *Sada Babil*, quoting *al-Ra'y al-'amm*, Baghdad: 16 March 1913.
[28] Lowther to Edward Grey, Constantinople, 28 January 1913. Reprinted in *Records of Iraq (1914–1966)*, 60.

Overall, while the party's new direction echoed the decentralisation policies (*al-lā-markaziyya*) articulated in the Syrian provinces of the empire, it also reflected Talib's own ambitions to rule over an independent emirate in Basra, similar to that of Kuwait and Muhammara.[29]

In June 1913, suspicions rose about Talib al-Naqib's implication in the murder of Farid Bey – former *mutasarrıf* for the Muntafiq known for his anti-Arab feelings. According to the Iraqi historian and sociologist 'Ali al-Wardi, four men were seen leaving Talib al-Naqib's house carrying mattresses in which they had concealed the rifles. The four men hid and waited in an abandoned house until Farid's boat arrived in the port. Farid and Badi' Nuri (Sati' al-Husri's brother) were both shot dead right after they got off the boat. The assassination, notes al-Wardi, consolidated Talib's nascent popularity. In the eyes of many, Talib had become the 'chief of Iraq' (*'amīd al-'Irāq*).[30] Talib's fame even reached Damascus, where the French consul described him as the 'hero of the day' for many Arabs.[31] The Lebanese traveller and fervent Arab nationalist Amin al-Rihani similarly described him as 'half lion, half fox' (*shay' min al-asad, shay' min al-tha'lab*), while in the *Who Is Who in Mesopotamia* 1915 issue, Talib is named as 'The Lion of Iraq'.[32] While Talib owned or directly controlled some of the newspapers covering his story, like the journal *al-Dustur*, which described him as a 'reformer',[33] or *al-Iqaz*, others expressed similar enthusiasm and praise for Talib's actions. For a few examples, the well-known Baghdadi National Scientific Club asked Talib

---

[29] Pierre-Jean Luizard, *La formation de l'Irak contemporain: le rôle politique des ulémas chiites à la fin de la domination ottomane et au moment de la construction de l'Etat irakien* (Paris: Editions du CNRS, 1991), 103.

[30] 'Ali al-Wardi, *Lamahat*, 215–16.

[31] 'Le héros du jour parmi eux semble être en ce moment Seyid Taleb de Bassorah', M. Ottavi, consul général, Damas, à M. Pichon, ministre des Affaires étrangères, 19 September 1913. Reprinted in *Documents diplomatiques et consulaires relatifs à l'histoire du Liban et des pays du Proche-Orient du XVII siècle à nos jours*, Tome 20, documents recueillis sous l'égide de Maurice Chéhab, ed Adel Ismail (Beirut: Éditions des œuvres politiques et historiques, 1979), 315.

[32] Amin al-Rihani, *Muluk al-'Arab* (Beirut: Al-Matba'a al-'ilmiyya, 1925), 341; *Who Is Who in Mesopotamia of 1915* (Simla: Government Central Branch Press, 1915), 342.

[33] *Al-Dustur*, Basra, 25 April 1915, quoted by Tauber, 'Sayyid Talib and the Young Turks in Basra', 9. The journal *al-Dustur* was the mouthpiece for the Basrawi branch of the Freedom and Accord Party (*Hürriyet ve İtilaf Fırkası*) opposed to the CUP.

al-Naqib to become its president. Famous poets like Kadhim al-Dujayli, 'Abd al-Rahman al-Bana' and Khayri al-Hindawi wrote poems in his honour. The Baghdadi journal *al-Nahda* spoke in the name of Talib, and considered him the founder of a rising Iraqi national movement. *Sada Babil*, also based in Baghdad, called Talib the 'hero of Iraq' (*baṭal al-'Irāq*).[34]

The wave of trans-regional support for Talib also came with its lot of rivalry among actors of the nascent nationalist movement in Iraq. The Baghdadis who took part in the first Arab Congress in Paris in June 1913 and formed the Arab nationalist *al-'Ahd* movement, kept a suspicious eye on Talib al-Naqib's activities, which they considered a threat. Tawfiq al-Suwaydi, future prime minister of Iraq, suspected Talib al-Naqib of spying on the activities of *al-'Ahd*.[35] Despite an ever-growing number of enemies, however, Talib's first steps in regional politics were marked by a successful process of heroisation. The *naqīb* made use of his socio-political status in order to exert influence – and pressure – over local notables, managed to gain control over party politics, and won popular support among parts of public opinion in Basra and beyond. With this, on the eve of British occupation of Basra, Talib al-Naqib had become extremely powerful in Basra, in the midst of an imperial crisis between the Ottomans and the British.

Talib al-Naqib and the British: Transgressive Dynamics of Inclusion and Exclusion

By mid-1914, an intense process of negotiation about the future of Basra took place between the British and Talib. While British relations with local figures from the Gulf region dated back to the seventeenth century, first and most notably through the East India Company, they materialised later, with the establishment of a legation in Basra in the late eighteenth century.[36] The Acting British Consul in Basra, R. W. Bullard wrote that 'there has

---

[34] 'Ali al-Wardi, *Lamahat*, 214–16; Lutfi 'Abdallah, *'Abd al-Muhsin al-Sa'dun*, 54; *Sada Babil*, Baghdad: 16 March 1913.

[35] Suwaydi (al-), Tawfiq, *Mudhakkirat Nisf Qarn min Ta'rikh al-'Iraq w-al-Qadiyya al-'Arabiyya* (Beirut: Dar al-Kutub, 1969), 82.

[36] Matthieu Rey, 'The British, the Hashemites and Monarchies in the Middle East', in Robert Aldrich and Cindy McCreery (eds), *Crowns and Colonies: European Monarchies and Overseas Empires* (Manchester: Manchester University Press, 2016), 228–30.

been a remarkable improvement in Talib's position here during the last few months ... and has impressed the [Turkish] Government with the extent of his authority'.[37] In comparison, the *vali* of Basra appeared to the consul as 'weak and incompetent ... he speedily became a mere factotum to Sayyid Talib'.[38] The Minister of Interior in Istanbul reportedly offered Talib al-Naqib three positions: ambassador, *vali* of Basra or member of the Senate, but later withdrew the proposition entirely.[39] In the eyes of the British, Talib would from then on be more easily accessible for new discussions with them.

In October 1914, Sayyid Talib paid a visit to the British political resident in Basra, in order to discuss his position. He reminded his interlocutor of a meeting he had with Lord Kitchener in Egypt in 1912, where the latter had proposed cooperation.[40] The time for collaboration had come, Talib concluded, as he wanted to be 'recognised as Ruler of Basrah under the protection [of the British]'.[41] The British official wrote that he found the proposition to be 'preposterous' and that Talib could not be trusted, as he 'has been too much in both camps to justify any confidence with him'.[42] But on 30 November 1914, a few days after the British occupation of Basra, Istanbul announced Talib al-Naqib's defection and declared him a 'traitor' on the grounds that he had helped the British troops to capture Basra.[43] In return for the services he would offer, and for his guarantee of protection for European

---

[37] R.W. Bullard, Acting British Consul in Basra, to the Ambassador in Constantinople, Basra, 20 June 1914, 328–30, TNA: IOR/L/PS/10462, File 3136/1914.
[38] R.W. Bullard, Acting Consul in Basra, to Sir L. Mallet, Constantinople, 25 July 1914, FO 371/3403. Reprinted in *Records of Iraq (1914–1966)*, 127.
[39] Erskine, Acting Consul-General, Baghdad, to British Ambassador, Constantinople, 15 April 1914, summaries of events in Turkish Iraq during the period February–July 1914, FO 371/3403. Reprinted in *Records of Iraq (1914–1966)*, 123.
[40] L. Mallet to Edward Grey, Constantinople, 7 October 1914, 82, TNA: IOR/L/PS/10462, File 3136/1914.
[41] Telegram from the political resident in the Persian Gulf to the Secretary to the Government of India, 30 October 1914, 205–6, TNA: IOR/L/PS/10/535, File 94/1915.
[42] L. Mallet to Edward Grey, Constantinople, 7 October 1914, 82, TNA: IOR/L/PS/10462, File 3136/1914.
[43] Telegram from 30 November 1914, 21, TNA: IOR/L/PS/10/463, File 3136/1914. Telegram by Turkish consular at Lingeh to Tehran, 392, TNA: IOR/L/PS/10/535, File 94/1915.

merchants in the region, the British then offered the *naqīb* their preservation of rights and privileges of the *nuqabā'*, among other conditions. Basra would never again be subject to authority in Istanbul and the British would protect him against reprisal.[44] Thus, during the first stage of negotiations with Talib al-Naqib in Basra under British occupation, they expressed intentions to include him – as the *naqīb* – in the new regional order.

A few months later, however, in January 1915, the British decided that Talib al-Naqib's presence in the south of Iraq had become undesirable. Sir Percy Cox – then political resident in the Persian Gulf – sent him a passport urging him to proceed to India.[45] Talib was consequently sent to Bombay, with a monthly allowance of 1,200 Rs.[46] He resided there as a 'state guest' for a short time, but, according to a note from Cairo about the possibility of sending Talib to Egypt, in early 1915 the police in Bombay delivered a memorandum describing Talib as a 'dangerous character'. His conduct would threaten the good relations with the local Muslim community – who otherwise 'behave with great discretion' – and the rest of the population. The police investigation, describing Talib as a 'first-class badmash', revealed many complaints about him, mainly concerning his 'heavy drinking' and womanising habits.[47] Talib al-Naqib was reportedly seen visiting a religious figure (Pir of Baghdad) while drunk, at any time during day or night.[48] He was consequently asked to move to Bellary (Madras) due to bad conduct.[49] When in Madras, excluded from politics, Talib al-Naqib addressed many demands and petitions to the British government, including ones for 'the restoration of the liberty of which [he has] been deprived', and to be allowed to leave Bellary.[50]

---

[44] Political resident in the Persian Gulf to Talib al-Naqib, 14 September 1914, 211, TNA: IOR/L/PS/10/535, File 94/1915.
[45] Percy Cox to Talib al-Naqib, 12 January 1915, 119–20, TNA: IOR/L/PS/10/535, File 94/1915.
[46] From Viceroy to London, 25 January 1915, 174, TNA: IOR/L/PS/10/535, File 94/1915.
[47] Memorandum by the Commissioner of Police, Bombay, 5 February 1915, 158, TNA: IOR/L/PS/10/535, File 94/1915.
[48] Bombay, 11 February 1915; 13 February, 158–60, TNA: IOR/L/PS/10/535, File 94/1915.
[49] From Viceroy to London, 26 February 1915, 170, TNA: IOR/L/PS/10/535, File 94/1915.
[50] Talib al-Naqib to Viceroy, Bellary, 24 November 1915, 119, TNA: IOR/L/PS/10/535, File 94/1915.

In early 1916, after a few months of repeated changes in Talib al-Naqib's whereabouts in India, a long discussion took place within the British administration on what to do with him. In an attempt to get rid of Talib, the British government in India tried to negotiate with the High Commissioner in Egypt for them to host him and provide education for two of his sons.[51] Cairo first refused, arguing that Talib could 'lead to intrigue about Syria' from Egypt,[52] but later agreed to host him 'in purely private capacity',[53] and under certain circumstances. Talib al-Naqib should in return renounce any travel to Basra and 'serve the British government well and loyally'.[54] In addition, he accepted that he must write an 'appeal to the Muslim World', to be published in Egyptian newspapers, in which he was to emphasise how the Young Turks, by destroying the legacy of Adbülhamid, were ruining the life of Muslims. The only solution to rescuing the Muslim world was to elect the only true caliph, the Sharif Husayn of Mecca.[55] Thus, Talib's voice was considered to be influential enough to condition public opinion in Egypt in favour of Husayn on the eve of the Arab revolt. In Egypt, Talib al-Naqib's situation stabilised for a few years, but new suspicions against him quickly rose again, leading the British to decide to send him away again in 1920. He would be allowed to return to Iraq once a peace treaty was signed. He arrived in Basra on 8 February 1920.[56]

It is interesting to note here that when Talib was in India he was officially invited as a 'state guest', and although he was regularly threatened with having his allowance reduced, he was continuously assured that he 'should be treated as such'.[57] However, in British internal bureaucratic language, Talib was referred to as an 'Arab deportee' or 'prisoner' and his stay in India as

---

[51] Talib al-Naqib had seven children; some were in Basra with his father, some in Beirut and others in Egypt. Delhi, 20 February 1917, TNA: FO 141/607.
[52] Note on Talib enclosed with letter from Arab Bureau (Cairo) to Delhi, 5 March 1917, 2, TNA: FO 141/607.
[53] Delhi to Cairo, 5 March 1917, TNA: FO 141/607.
[54] Talib al-Naqib, Torquilstone, Bangalore, 28 October 1916, TNA: FO 141/607.
[55] Talib Nakib Zadeh of Basra, 'Appeal to the Muslim World', March 1916, exact date unknown, TNA: FO 141/607.
[56] Civil Commissioner, Baghdad, 25 February 1920, 9, TNA: IOR/L/PS/10/535, File 94/1915.
[57] Bombay, 19 February 1915, 159, TNA: IOR/L/PS/10/535, File 94/1915.

'detention'.[58] During the war in fact, thousands of Ottoman prisoners were interned by the British in Indian and Burmese camps.[59] In some instances, Talib appears to be considered one of them. Officially, then, the British kept friendly and diplomatic relations with him – responding to some of his demands and even supporting him financially – while at the same time considering him a criminal, and even at times a prisoner. Therefore, the British treated Talib both as a threat to be contained and as a possible ally for the future of their presence in Iraq, whom they needed to treat as such. Because the British were not ready to settle on one solution or the other, they kept Talib in a liminal position; he was both excluded from and part of power.

At this point in the history of the relations between the British and Talib al-Naqib, the British administration could not decide what to do with him and, arguably, what to think of him. In fact, reports often reflect British officials' doubts about their own judgement of Talib. For example, the consul in Basra Francis Crow, on the eve of his departure from the city after almost twelve years of service in 1915, described Talib – a man he had known personally for years – as the 'most interesting personality' who 'has undoubted intelligence'. But Crow also feared that he might have been tricked by Talib as he was unsure of his intentions and real influence: 'Sometimes I have doubted whether he possessed as much real influence as he led me to suppose'. The consul believed that 'his energies, if rightly redirected might . . . prove a valuable asset in . . . the development of Mesopotamia . . . I admire him'.[60] Like Francis Crow, Oriental Secretary Gertrude Bell was rather unsure of what to think of him. She wrote to her father that he was 'as sharp as a needle', 'entirely unscrupulous . . . but he is the ablest man in the country'.[61] When her father came to visit her in

---

[58] Titles of various reports from the government of India to London between 1915 and 1916 (10 September–4 October 1915, 128; 14 April–8 May 1916, 115; 16 June–15 July 1916, 107), TNA: IOR/L/PS/10/535, File 94/1915.
[59] See, for example, TNA: FO 383/88, File 16900/121.
[60] Consul F. E. Crow, Memo on Seyyid Talib Bey, Basra, 5 January 1915, 180–5, TNA: IOR/L/PS/10/535, File 94/1915.
[61] Gertrude Bell, *Letters to her Father*, 29 February 1920, 26 July 1920 (Gertrude Bell Archive: Newcastle University), available at: http://gertrudebell.ncl.ac.uk, last accessed 4 November 2019.

Baghdad, she insisted that he met Talib 'amongst other Schenswurdigkeiten (sic)'.[62] And she adds: 'I like the rogue – I can't help liking him; but a rogue he is and there are no two opinions about it.'[63] Other reports also stress their difficulties in trying to identify Talib's intentions, emphasising the man's complex 'duplicity' and 'versatility'.[64] At times, some even spoke very highly of him, like Harry St John Philby who long supported Talib: a 'vigorous personality, of great charm and dignity'.[65] Observers also describe his strong and 'magnetic personality',[66] a '*deus ex machina*' and 'solver of all local ills in Arabia and Mesopotamia'.[67]

In addition to that, the British considered Sayyid Talib to be a threat against their territorial ambitions. Separatist movements were widespread in the Gulf region and, as Reidar Visser has shown in *Basra, the Failed Gulf State*, Basra was no exception. Although direct connections between the separatist movements in Basra and Talib al-Naqib's activities are not always clear, the public more often than not associated separatism with the possibility of a 'Talibian State' (*al-dawla al-ṭālibiyya*), named after Talib al-Naqib's struggle to establish an independent emirate already prior to the British presence, and which continued after that.[68] As an experienced politician, with great influence in the region, and a leading actor in a potentially additional division of territories in British-controlled areas, Talib al-Naqib could become an important threat to British political ambitions in the region. For all these reasons, they chose to maintain him as a political interlocutor on friendly terms.

Nevertheless, British intentions to exclude the *naqīb* from power were also saliently expressed in the vocabulary they used to describe him. The most

---

[62] Gertrude Bell, *Letters to her Stepmother*, 29 February1920 (the correct spelling is Sehenswürdigkeiten, meaning 'attractions').
[63] Bell, *Letters to her Father*, 22 January 1921.
[64] Consul F. E. Crow, Memo on Seyyid Talib Bey, Basra, 5 January 1915, 184, TNA: IOR/L/PS/10/535, File 94/1915.
[65] Philip Ireland, *Iraq: A Study in Political Development* (New York: Russell & Russell, 1970), 231–2.
[66] Philip Graves, *The Life of Sir Percy Cox* (London: Hutchinson, 2008), 269. Quoted by al-Nakib, 'A Critical Study of Saiyyid Talib Pasha al-Nakib', 38.
[67] W. H. T. Shakespear to Arthur Hirtzel, Kuwait, 26 June 1914, 90. TNA: IOR/L/PS/10/535, File 94/1915.
[68] Visser, *Basra, the Failed Gulf State*, 73–86, 132–3.

recurring term is that of 'rogue': a 'leading rogue'[69] 'unscrupulous rogue',[70] 'the greatest rogue unhung'.[71] The concept of 'villain' is also frequent: an 'accomplished villain',[72] 'a savage villain'[73] or an 'unscrupulous villain'.[74] He is also described as 'a vicious man . . . a bad man', who 'terrorised the town',[75] 'redoubtable'[76] and a 'professional blackmailer'.[77] 'Notoriously untrustworthy and slippery',[78] he is described as 'a dangerous scoundrel',[79] 'treacherous and cruel', 'a source of embarrassment' and a 'first-class badmash'.[80] His entourage is also strongly depreciated. Talib is described as an 'extravagant' man, who manages to gather around him 'a band of ruffians'[81] or, alternatively, 'a band of cut-throats'.[82] But as Nathan Brown argues in relation to the Egyptian peasantry at the turn of the twentieth century, it is less important to prove whether rogues exist or not than the question of how, when and why the category emerges in the sources. Brown stresses that the category of bandit was invented and produced by Egyptian and British elites in order to justify their attempts to suppress social unrest. The bandit category, therefore, constitutes a useful tool for asserting authority against dissidence.[83] The same can

---

[69] Bell, *Letters to her Stepmother*, 29 February 1920.
[70] Bell, *Letters to her Father*, 10 January 1921.
[71] Bell, *Letters to her Stepmother*, 23 February 1920.
[72] H. St John Philby, *Heart of Arabia: A Record of Travel and Exploration*, vol. 1 (London: Constable, 1922), 240–1.
[73] Bell, *Letters to her Father*, 24 July 1921.
[74] Telegram from Bombay to Delhi, 28 January 1915, 163, TNA: IOR/L/PS/10/535, File 94/1915.
[75] India Office, Mesopotamia: Review of Civil Administration, Baghdad, 24 June 1920, 2, TNA: IOR E12569/13/44.
[76] St John Philby, *Heart of Arabia*, 240–1.
[77] Telegram, 2 November 1914, 177, TNA: IOR/L/PS/10/463, File 3136/1914.
[78] Telegram from Ambassador, Constantinople, to Simla, 29 October 1914, TNA: IOR/L/PS/10/535, File 94/1915.
[79] Telegram, 30 November 1914, 21, TNA: IOR/L/PS/10/463, File 3136/1914.
[80] Memorandum by the Commissioner of Police, Bombay, 5 February 1915, 158, TNA: IOR/L/PS/10/535, File 94/1915.
[81] India Office, Mesopotamia: Review of Civil Administration, Baghdad, 24 June 1920, 2, TNA: IOR E12569/13/44.
[82] Telegram from Bombay to Delhi, 28 January 1915, 163, TNA: IOR/L/PS/10/535, File 94/1915.
[83] Nathan Brown, 'Brigands and State Building: The Invention of Banditry in Modern Egypt', *Comparative Studies in Society and History* 32(2) (1990): 281.

be argued for Talib al-Naqib: the British fabricated the rogue/villain figure in order to criminalise his actions and in an attempt to undermine his influence.

The British also took the rogue category a step further by comparing Talib with other historical or legendary figures, like 'the John Wilkes of the Arab movement'.[84] But the most frequent comparison related to Robin Hood. 'His generosity to the poor was proverbial, but it was the liberality of a Robin Hood.'[85] They insist, however, that Talib's Robin Hood reputation was not built on genuine selflessness: 'He is a comparatively poor man and can only meet the expense of his Robin Hood generosity to the poor . . . by levying blackmail on all his wealthy compatriots in Basra.'[86] Interestingly, Talib al-Naqib somehow reclaimed the category for himself. During his exile in Bangalore, he used the name 'Torquilstone' for his own house, certainly after the castle of Lord Torquilstone that Robin Hood besieges in Walter Scott's novel *Ivanhoe*. In his correspondence headings with both friends and foes, Talib wrote: 'Torquilstone, 15 Infantry Road, Bangalore'.[87] In a similar vein, Gertrude Bell remembers a conversation in which Talib openly reclaimed his criminal actions, paradoxically in order to persuade the British that he himself was the most fit to be king: 'What's needed in this administration . . . is experience. I've got it. A doctor before he learns his trade will kill at least 200 people. I've killed my 200 – no one knows it better than yourself.'[88] The mobilisation of the rogue category, Robin Hood or criminal figure was therefore not restricted to colonial discourse: Talib himself reused it by self-appropriation.

In Hobsbawm's reading of social banditry, the legendary Robin Hood embodies the 'noble robber' par excellence. And the more the state regards bandits as criminals, Hobsbawm argues, the more likely they are to become 'heroes, champions, avengers, fighters for justice, perhaps even leaders of liberation' in the eyes of public opinion in opposition to state oppression.[89]

---

[84] T. E. Lawrence, *Seven Pillars of Wisdom: A Triumph* (London: Cape, 1963), 45.
[85] Ireland, *Iraq*, 231–2.
[86] R.W. Bullard, acting British Consul in Basra, to the Ambassador in Constantinople, Basra, 20 June 1914, 328–30, TNA: IOR/L/PS/10462, File 3136/1914.
[87] Faydi, *Mudhakkirat*, 317; Talib al-Naqib, Bangalore, 28 October 1916, TNA: FO 141/607.
[88] Bell, *Letters to her Father*, 16 August 1920.
[89] Hobsbawm, *Bandits*, 17.

On this, Talib al-Naqib's consent to playing the criminal certainly echoes Hobsbawm's conclusions. For some in Basra, Baghdad and beyond, Talib's criminal activities against the state were what made him a hero in the first place, as I have shown. Similarly to what Alex Winder notes in the case of the famous Palestinian bandit Abu Jilda – also compared with Robin Hood in later literature – at the turn of the twentieth century, Talib's popularity as a hero stemmed from his very transgressive activities.[90] To put it differently, Talib needed to be the rogue in order to stay the hero, and the British *rogue narrative* served to fuel the *hero narrative*. Dynamics of exclusion and inclusion therefore worked both ways. As much as the British worked on criminalising Talib's activities in order to demean his power, self-exclusion from British power allowed Talib to maintain influence in the region. This statement of mutual dependency somehow echoes Karen Barkey's argument on the co-option of bandits by the Ottoman state as part of the centralisation process.[91] The *naqīb* too had no interest in completely challenging imperial power because he depended on it. Talib could maintain his position by being transgressive, but moderately so. Here again, with the rogue being part of the social order and the state part of a form of 'organised crime',[92] the dividing line between the law and the outlaw becomes blurred.

The *Naqīb*'s Final Years

Dynamics of inclusion and exclusion as well as Talib's moderately transgressive attitude continued after the establishment of the British mandate in 1920, but for a short time only. Upon his return, Talib made his intentions clear regarding his will to rule the new country.[93] At first, the British asked him to put together a constituent assembly.[94] He was also elected

---

[90] Alex Winder, 'Abu Jilda, Anti-Imperial Antihero: Banditry and Popular Rebellion in Palestine', in Cyrus Schayegh and Andrew Arsan (eds), *The Routledge Handbook of the History of the Middle East Mandates* (New York: Routledge, 2015), 309.
[91] Karen Barkey, *Bandits and Bureaucrats: The Ottoman Route to State Centralization* (Ithaca, NY: Cornell University Press, 1994), 141–88.
[92] Charles Tilly, 'War Making and State Making as Organized Crime', in Peter B. Evans, Dietrich Rueschemeyer and Theda Skocpol (eds), *Bringing the State Back In* (Cambridge: Cambridge University Press, 1985), 169–91.
[93] Civil Commissioner, Baghdad, 25 July 1920, 6, TNA: IOR/L/PS/10/535, File 94/1915.
[94] Bell, *Letters to her Father*, 26 July 1920, 8 August 1920.

president – by obtaining two-thirds of the votes – of a committee composed of former Ottoman deputies, responsible for organising Iraqi elections.[95] In October 1920, Talib al-Naqib was invited to accept office in the provisional government as the Minister of Interior. He then famously declared that 'by autumn he'll be King of Iraq'.[96] In fact, until the Cairo Conference in March 1921, Talib al-Naqib was still considered to be a serious candidate to the throne, and benefited from the support of some British officials.[97] Ministers Ja'far al-'Askari and Sasun Hasqail, who were invited as experts to the Cairo Conference, shortlisted three names out of the six discussed as the most suitable candidates, and Talib al-Naqib was one of them (the two others were Faysal and the *naqīb* of Baghdad).[98]

In *Muluk al-'Arab*, Amin al-Rihani claims that after the Cairo Conference, the wind had turned for good for Talib al-Naqib. When Faysal was chosen to be king, Talib's situation deteriorated rapidly. Talib gave a heated speech against the British during a dinner at his house on 14 April 1921, announcing his intention to gather an army of 20,000 tribesmen if Britain failed to accept Iraqi demands for self-determination. According to al-Rihani, the *naqīb* threatened his British audience with these words: 'The mandatory government has declared its intention to respect the will of the Iraqi people, and we will respect the government in return. But if it fails to do so, here are 20,000 rifles.'[99] Gertrude Bell – who was not present at the party – sent a report to the High Commissioner Percy Cox based on the statement of two witnesses.[100] The British used Talib's heated speech against them as a pretext to expel him for fomenting civil disturbances. Two days after the scandal

---

[95] Faydi, *Mudhakkirat*, 426; Naji Shawkat, *Sira wa Dhikrayat* (Baghdad: Matba'at Salman al-A'dhami, 1990), 52; see also Ireland, *Iraq*, 291.
[96] Bell, *Letters to her Father*, 13 February 1921.
[97] Harry St John Philby initially offered support but later retracted. Faydi, *Mudhakkirat*, 297; H. St John Philby, *Arabian Days: An Autobiography* (London: Hale, 1948), 189–99.
[98] First meeting of political committee in Mesopotamia, 'Report on Middle East Conference held in Cairo and Jerusalem', 12 March 1921, 44, TNA: CO 935/1/1.
[99] al-Rihani, *Muluk al-'Arab*, 341–2.
[100] Bell, *Letters to her Father*, 17 April 1921.

took place, Talib al-Naqib was arrested in a Baghdad street and ordered to leave the country immediately, for a second exile this time in Ceylon.[101]

At this stage, the British did not need Talib as a political strongman any more, but he nevertheless remained a threat due to his influence in Basra and Baghdad, as well as in other Arab cities. To begin with, a separatist movement in Basra was reinitiated at the same time as Talib's departure to Ceylon, with a petition signed by 4,500 individuals. Although Talib was not actively involved in this scheme, rumours spread that Talib prepared a new secret separatist movement this time together with 'Abd al-Muhsin al-Sa'dun, in order to weaken the central government in Baghdad led by King Faysal.[102]

Sayyid Talib was not welcome in Egypt and in the Bilad al-Sham either. His family joined him in Ceylon a few weeks after his banishment, but he was sent to Italy for treatment a year later.[103] The Governor General of Ceylon gave strict orders that Talib al-Naqib should 'on no account be allowed to disembark' in Port Said while travelling.[104] During the next couple of years, Talib al-Naqib tried to return to Iraq on several occasions, but orders came from Baghdad not to accept him until the Organic Law was promulgated. All consular offices in the region, whether in Amman, Jerusalem, Cairo, Beirut, Damascus or Aleppo, were informed and forbidden to issue a visa for him.[105] He nevertheless managed to go to Amman in September 1924, and later to Damascus where the British consulate wrote that Talib al-Naqib's presence was not desirable, as his arrival was received with great enthusiasm by parts of the local population.[106] After a short time spent in Palestine and Egypt, Talib was again invited in November 1924 to travel to Jeddah by King 'Ali of

---

[101] Bell, *Letters to her Father*, 17 April 1921; Percy Cox, Report on the Finances, Administration and Condition of Iraq, for the period from 1 October 1920 to 31 March 1922, FO 371/9004. Reprinted in *Records of Iraq (1914–1966)*, 813.
[102] Visser, *Basra, the Failed Gulf State*, 73–86, 132–3.
[103] al-Nakib, 'A Critical Study of Saiyyid Talib Pasha al-Nakib', 110–17.
[104] Confirmation was given a few days later that Talib al-Naqib received one visit on board, by Naim Effendi Sulayman Shubli (Soleiman Choubli). Governor General of Ceylon to High Commissioner for Egypt, Cairo, 2 March 1922, and other correspondence between 2 and 6 March 1922, TNA: FO 141/607.
[105] Baghdad to Cairo, 22 September 1924, TNA: FO 141/607.
[106] British consulate, Damascus, 25 September 1924, TNA: FO 141/607.

Hijaz, in order to act as a mediator between him and Ibn Saʻud.[107] The British gave him authorisation because the travel could 'conveniently delay his return to Iraq', and because he was then considered a 'would-be peace negotiator'. But the negotiation failed.[108]

Talib al-Naqib finally managed to return to Iraq in May 1925 and spent the last years of his life there, before moving to Germany. A note on Talib's Egyptian file suggests that he had been living in Germany for a long time when he died in Munich on 14 June 1929.[109] But Haifa Ahmed al-Nakib writes that he stayed in Basra and avoided political activities until he moved to Munich for health reasons and died there.[110] A letter heading, adressed to Naji Shawkat – who called Talib *ʻamm* (uncle) as he was a very close friend of his father – indicates that, in June 1928, Talib was still based in Basra.[111] Immense public gatherings took place in Basra and its surrounds when his body was returned for burial a few weeks later. In Arnold Wilson's interpretation, the demonstration that took place on this occasion was 'unique in the history of 'Iraq'.[112] When the news of his death was dispatched from the Foreign Office in London to the office in Cairo, an unidentified handwritten note on the last page of Talib al-Naqib's file from the Consulate in Egypt read: 'This man, the Naqib of Basra, should, in the opinion of many, have been our candidate for the throne of Iraq. He has been killing himself in wine and women in Germany for the last few years.'[113]

Bandits, Anton Blok argues against Hobsbawm, are not heroes voicing the claims of the poor against social injustice. Rather, they make use

---

[107] British Consulate, Alexandria, to Cairo, 7 November 1924, TNA: FO 141/607.
[108] Correspondence between Cairo and Alexandria, 11 and 20 November 1924, TNA: FO 141/607.
[109] British Consulate, Munich, 18 June 1929, TNA: FO 141/607.
[110] al-Nakib, 'A Critical Study of Saiyyid Talib Pasha al-Nakib', 117.
[111] The exact date is 9 June 1928. Shawkat, *Sira wa Dhikrayat*, 119.
[112] A. T. Wilson, *Loyalties: Mesopotamia (1914–1917)* (Oxford: Oxford University Press, 1930), 18, quoted by al-Nakib, 'A Critical Study of Saiyyid Talib Pasha al-Nakib', 117. See also Visser, *Basra, the Failed Gulf State*, 142.
[113] Foreign Office, London to Cairo, 9 July 1929 (handwritten note 18 July 1929), TNA: FO 141/607.

of social disparities in order to reclaim these voices in their own name.[114] In my analysis, I focused on the strategies Talib put in place in order to reclaim the various forms of discontent in his name, and what he obtained with it. Pursing his political ambitions, Talib al-Naqib made use of preexisting structures of authority pertaining to his own social background (the *niqāba*) in order to gain support locally. He also took advantage of his liminal position between empires (Ottoman and British) in order to negotiate his political status. And, finally, he reclaimed for himself the 'rogue' category produced by the British, hoping his moderately transgressive attitude would preserve the 'hero' standards on the long run. By doing this, Talib brought together rogue and ruler, thus blurring the dividing line between the law and the outlaw. Talib was partly successful: he did not become either the ruler of Basra under British occupation or king of Iraq as he had hoped, but he accessed a privileged position within the spheres of imperial as well as local politics, maintained his influence in Basra and elsewhere in the region, and even ensured an income.

---

[114] Anton Blok, 'The Peasant and the Brigand: Social Banditry Reconsidered', *Comparative Studies in Society and History* 14(4) (1972): 494–503.

PART III
ROGUE TRAJECTORIES

9

Chemistry of Revolution: Naum Tyufekchiev and the Trajectories of Revolutionary Violence in the Late Ottoman Europe

Ramazan Hakkı Öztan[1]

The late nineteenth-century revolutionaries operated at a time of grand structural transformations that had been rapidly changing states and societies alike. This was when increasing interstate rivalries manifested themselves in the growing frequency of conventional warfare which, more often than not, translated into massive displacement of civilian populations. In the absence of wars, irregular conflicts perpetuated the cycle of violence, institutionalised by secret revolutionary societies that began to mushroom across the frontiers of empires. These organisations controlled a string of armed bands operating in rural zones which were becoming increasingly difficult to govern for central authorities. In urban theatres of operation, the cells of conspirators were actively plotting to carry out high-profile assassinations and stage bomb attacks. For these rogues, individual motivations such as access to wealth and power co-existed with deeply-held ideological convictions, all of which were fuelled by personal vendettas, informed by cultures of youth and masculinity, and shaped by ritualised ties of intragroup trust. Their emerging

---

[1] For their generous help in the course of this research, I would like to single out Cengiz Yolcu, Anke Hilbrenner, Dimitar Popov, Erik Jan Zürcher, Rossitsa Gradeva, Nadejda Vasileva, Sinan Kuneralp, Orçun Can Okan, Neriman Ersoy-Hacısalihoğlu, Chris Moffat, Mehmet Hacısalihoğlu, Ana-Teodora Kurkina, Divna Manolova, Alp Yenen, Alptuğ Güney, Slavi Mitkov Slavov, Hakan Erdagoz, Murat Kaya, Sevinç Küçükoğlu, Houssine Alloul and Alexandra Trifonova.

rogue conduct took place against the backdrop of systemic changes, where war made the state and the state made war, while, at the same time, the state made refugees, and refugees made the state.

This chapter charts the life of one such rogue – Naum Tyufekchiev – and unpacks the story of this refugee chemist-cum-bomb-maker and arms merchant who provides us with a window to peek into this complex world of contentious politics. As a professional revolutionary, Tyufekchiev's skills in bomb-making turned him into an indispensable figure for the turn-of-the-century revolutionary organisations active from the Balkans to the Caucasus. A prominent revolutionary figure with crucial know-how, Tyufekchiev had gained transnational notoriety since the early 1890s, when he began to become involved in a range of high-scale assassinations, bombing campaigns and arms transfers, all of which kept the Russian, Ottoman and Bulgarian authorities on their toes. Yet this chapter is less a biography of Naum A. Tyufekchiev than the biography of transgressive politics in the frontiers of empires, where business, politics, ideology, violence and diplomacy all intersected in the personalities of such rogues as Tyufekchiev. After all, individuals like him were as much products of these complex late nineteenth-century transformations as they were also instrumental in shaping them.

Tyufekchiev's story provides the narrative perspective away from the usual suspects such as ideologues and the high-profile politician, and instead focuses on the middlemen whose stories, albeit difficult to trace, illustrate individual agencies in a world of revolutionary politics riven by factionalism and conspiracy. The microcosm provided by his story illustrates the connectedness and intertwinement of personal networks, such as those of friends, relatives and compatriots, in shaping a complex world of contentious politics on the path to the First World War. His story does not mesh well, either, with the existing biographical approaches to the history of revolutions which often come from nationalist scholars who had the ulterior motive of reconstructing either the biographies of 'traitors' or those of the 'standard-bearers' in nationalist historiographies. After all, Tyufekchiev is neither. Having left behind a mixed historical legacy, he presents us with a case which is resistant to any attempts to categorise him into clearly defined ideological boxes. His case similarly challenges the standard ideological determinism of intellectual histories, since discussing Tyufekchiev is charting the significance of technical know-how and the historical roles played by illicit commodities, not those of revolutionary ideas. All in all, Tyufekchiev as a trans-imperial subject embodies diverse socio-economic and political agendas, which makes his biography as well as that of late Ottoman Europe attractively layered and complex.

Early Life, Education and Immigration to Bulgaria

Naum Andreev Tyufekchiev (25 July 1863–26 February 1916, Figure 9.1) was born in Resne (modern Resen), a town located in Ottoman Macedonia, where he grew up with his brothers, that is, Dencho, Nikola and Dimitri. Their last name instantly betrayed their familial profession: *tüfekçi* means gunsmith in Turkish, *tüfek*, rifle. André and Anastasié were the proud father and mother of these boys (and however many daughters). The exact circumstances that led to this family's scattering across diverse geographies is not immediately clear. While the father Andrea died in Vidin in 1874, the two oldest brothers decided to seek their fortune after the mid-1870s somewhere other than the Ottoman domains.[2] The Tyufekchiev brothers accordingly left behind the provincial town of Resne – not to step foot back in it until 1908 – and chose to settle in Bulgaria, a country that had emerged as an autonomous entity after the Russo-Ottoman War of 1877–8.

The war with Russia had deeply devastated the Ottoman Balkans, with a string of massacres that turned over a million of the local population into refugees. The ensuing diplomatic negotiations, which eventually culminated in the Treaty of Berlin (1878), introduced new border arrangements that featured significant minorities in each state, only facilitating further rounds of population movements and interstate conflicts. The flight of Tyufekchiev and his brothers from Resne took place within this context of warfare and displacement. They were among the thousands of Macedonians who left Ottoman lands to settle in Bulgaria, a land that offered as much a refuge as a range of opportunities for socio-political and economic upward mobility.[3]

The Bulgaria where the Macedonians like Tyufekchiev found themselves,

---

[2] I complied the personal information of the family from two separate forms Tyufekchiev provided to the Belgian authorities in 1886 and 1894. See Archives Générales du Royaume Bruxelles (AGR hereafter), 444.432, ff. 3 and 9.

[3] Here I use 'Macedonians' as a term that denotes a place of origin rather than a fixed identity.

Figure 9.1   Naum Tyufekchiev, *Servet-i Fünun*, 17 Eylül 1331, 309.

however, was a country in flux, with a range of uncertainties due to a highly factionalised political scene, divided between a strong pro-Russian faction and a more independently minded revolutionary elite who wanted to keep Russia at bay. After the Treaty of Berlin, the Bulgarian National Assembly elected Alexander of Battenberg, a German prince, as the first Bulgarian head of state. Having fought in the war against the Ottomans and with personal connections to the tsar, he enjoyed a good reputation both in St Petersburg and among the Bulgarians. Yet the new prince soon revealed his intentions to be more than a figurehead, with a readiness to clash with the existing factions in Bulgaria, while leveraging Russian support in the process. His aspiration to do so only became more urgent after the assassination of the Russian tsar on 1 March 1881. His return to Sofia from the tsar's funeral marked his crackdown on the liberal opposition and the start of his direct rule that would last for two years.[4]

Part of Alexander Battenberg's attempt to consolidate his power in Sofia

[4] R. J. Crampton, *Bulgaria* (Oxford: Oxford University Press, 2007), 102–7.

included a programme to send students abroad to train a new generation of technocrats and officers loyal to himself. Naum Tyufekchiev was one such student.[5] Sent to the University of Liège, Belgium, in summer 1885, he was to study general sciences and chemistry at the Special School of Mechanics and then become an armament officer upon his return to Sofia.[6] Tyufekchiev spent five years in Liège where he cultivated strong links both with officers from the Belgian army as well as other Ottoman Macedonian émigrés living in the city, such as Dimitar Rizov.[7] The city of Liège as an important centre of weapon manufacturing in Europe was a fitting context for the upbringing of this cadre of political radicals.[8] The experiences of bonding among these Macedonian students must have been profound, crucial to the formation of trust and comradery, as they observed the plight of their Macedonian compatriots under Ottoman rule.[9]

This latter attachment to the Macedonian cause was most probably the strongest characteristic that defined Tyufekchiev and his generation of likeminded Macedonians. For the realisation of this ideological constant, many of them felt closest to Russia, seeing it as the most important powerhouse to keep the Ottomans and, if need be, the Bulgarians in line.[10] Macedonians therefore continued to maintain their allegiance to St Petersburg, even well after the Bulgarian Prince Alexander of Battenberg moved away from the Russian orbit in the mid-1880s. When Russia prepared a plot in late 1890 in collaboration with the Bulgarian officer Major Panitza, the Macedonians

---

[5] Başbakanlık Osmanlı Arşivi, Prime Ministry's Ottoman Archives (BOA hereafter), Y.PRK. MŞ. 4-2, 21, 14 Mart 1308.

[6] AGR. 444.432, ff. 9–10.

[7] 'L'Attentat de Sofia: Conversation avec le frère de Naoum Tufekchiew', *Le Figaro*, 21 Juillet 1895, 1; Süleyman Kâni İrtem, *Ermeni Meselesinin İçyüzü: Ermeni İsyanları Tarihi, Bomba Hâdisesi, Adana Vak'ası. Meclis-i Mebusan Zabıtları*, ed. Osman Selim Kocahanoğlu (Istanbul: Temel Yayınları, 2004), 107.

[8] Michael George Kort, 'Leonid Krasin: Engineer of Revolution, 1870–1908', PhD thesis, New York University, 1973, 245–46.

[9] One must note that the Ottoman immigrant communities in Europe, even if they shared the same place of origin, often maintained varied and contradictory agendas. For an argument along these lines, see Isa Blumi, 'Publishers, Hitmen, Diplomats, and Dreamers: Switzerland's Ottoman–Albanian Diaspora, 1899–1920', *Schweizerische Zeitschrift für Geschichte = Revue suisse d'histoire = Rivista storica svizzera* 52 (2002): 309–20.

[10] Crampton, *Bulgaria*, 121.

stood solidly behind the putsch. In supporting the latter, 'Tyufekchiev was just like all other Macedonians of Sofia'.[11] The quelling of the coup, however, meant the start of the purge and the exodus of all the Russophiles, including Macedonian immigrants from Sofia.[12] Even though Tyufekchiev was in Liège when the abortive coup took place, Stefan Stambolov, the Bulgarian prime minister, had firm beliefs that the Macedonian émigrés in Liège were in communication with Major Panitza, and denied them access to Sofia.[13]

Russian Meddling

The expulsion of Russophile Macedonians from Sofia concentrated them largely in three spots abroad, Belgrade, Odessa and Constantinople. It was in this triangle that Tyufekchiev would play major roles in the organisation of a number of well-planned attacks against Bulgarian politicians throughout the early 1890s through exploiting the existing interstate rivalries. Because Stefan Stambolov maintained warm relations with the Ottoman sultan, it was not Constantinople but rather Belgrade and Odessa that provided Tyufekchiev with the greatest room for manoeuvre. In the end, Serbia had been at odds with Bulgaria since the Serbo-Bulgarian War of 1885, while Russia had grown bitter towards Sofia, the proxy it had failed to control fully since the mid-1880s.

Benefiting from such existing geopolitical competition, the Macedonian cell in Belgrade began to lay the groundwork for the assassination of Stambolov, whom they saw as a collaborator with the Ottomans. The mastermind of the plan was Dimitar Rizov who had teamed up with the Tyufekchiev brothers Naum and Nikola in Belgrade. As they hatched their plans, the plot also involved the youngest of the Tyufekchiev brothers, namely, Dencho who had recently arrived in Sofia to attend the high school.[14] Seventeen at the time, Dencho was given the task of keeping an eye on Stambolov in Sofia to try to establish a routine in his behaviour so that they could strike him in a

---

[11] 'L'Attentat de Sofia', *Le Figaro*, 21 Juillet 1895, 2.
[12] Duncan M. Perry, *Stefan Stambolov and the Emergence of Modern Bulgaria, 1870–1895* (Durham, NC: Duke University Press, 1993), 87–9.
[13] 'L'Attentat de Sofia', *Le Figaro*, 21 Juillet 1895, 2.
[14] Ibid.

predictable fashion.[15] The long-awaited moment came on 15 March 1891 when four hit men, including Dencho and Mikhail Stavrev (alias Haliu) – Tyufekchiev's cousin from Resne – cornered Stambolov as he stepped out of his favourite coffee shop in Sofia. In the utter darkness of the evening, Dencho fired his pistol but accidentally shot and killed Hristo Belchev, the finance minister, mistaking him for Stambolov. The latter went unharmed – they indeed looked alike.[16] While the other three hit men had already managed to run away abroad, Dencho was arrested in Sofia shortly thereafter, but long before he confessed anything he died in custody. Even though he had probably been tortured and beaten to death, the official cause of death was phthisis.[17] One thing was certain, though, Dencho's death would give the Tyufekchiev brothers a more personal reason to seek revenge in the upcoming years on Stambolov.[18]

The murder of Belchev also had broader consequences. As the Stambolov government tried to save face, it immediately began to mount pressure on Serbia, asking the latter to cease its support for the Macedonian émigrés, if not to dissolve the cell in Belgrade completely. This was particularly urgent as Sofia traced indications of other plots, complete with intelligence briefs that reported the shipment of dynamite bombs from Galati across the Danube into Bulgaria.[19] Yet this pressure on Serbia yielded very little. Similar overtures to Constantinople fell on sympathetic ears, however, whereby the Porte (aka Ottoman central government) agreed to extradite to Sofia Stanchiev and Popov, two suspects implicated in Belchev's murder.[20]

Such plots and rumours of conspiracies were so many that they sustained a constant diplomatic tension among Bulgaria, Serbia and Russia.[21] In late January 1892, Count Gustav Kálnoky, the Austria-Hungarian Minister of

---

[15] Duncan M. Perry, *The Politics of Terror: The Macedonian Liberation Movements, 1893–1903* (Durham, NC: Duke University Press, 1988), 32–4.
[16] BOA. Y.A.HUS. 245–58, 4, 18 Şaban 1308; Perry, *Stefan Stambolov*, 171–2, 232.
[17] 'Bulletin de l'étranger: Bulgarie', *Le Temps*, 25 Décembre 1891, 2.
[18] Perry, *The Politics of Terror*, 34.
[19] BOA. Y.A.HUS. 255–24, 6, 10 Cemaziyelahir 1309. For the intelligence on the shipment of bombs, see BOA, Y.A.HUS. 253–72, 2, 4 Teşrinisani 1307.
[20] BOA. Y.A.HUS. 252–99, 25 Rebiülevvel 1309; BOA. A.} MTZ. (04) 23–70, 18 Rebiülahir 1309.
[21] Perry, *Stefan Stambolov*, 176.

Foreign Affairs, responded and assured all the parties that both Belgrade and Sofia had already taken some steps, and that 'the danger of an[other] assassination seemed to have been averted for the time being'.[22] Indeed, that was the case for Ferdinand I and Stambolov, but not for other Bulgarian politicians. By December 1891, Sofia had already unearthed one conspiracy after its agents intercepted a letter sent by Nikola Tyufekchiev from Odessa to Bone Georgiev, a Bulgarian nationalist in Belgrade. Once the letter was deciphered, it was clear that the Tyufekchiev brothers had invited a certain Hristo Stefkov from Constantinople to Odessa so that they could explore the possibilities for the assassination of the Bulgarian diplomatic representative to Istanbul, Dr Georgi Vulkovich,[23] who was seen as responsible for playing an important role in monitoring the constant flow of exiled Macedonian émigrés.[24]

When Hristo arrived in Odessa in September 1891, Naum Tyufekchiev inquired about a possible hit man to carry out the assassination, and Hristo assured him that he could find the right person in Istanbul. A few months later in mid-December 1891, Tyufekchiev took a Russian steamer to Istanbul to meet Hristo's candidate, Yorgi Merdzhan(ov) who hailed from Kalkandelen but lived in Istanbul's district of Kasımpaşa. It was Vladimir Shismanov, an employee of the Russian postal office, who oversaw Tyufekchiev's clearance through the Ottoman customs in Galata. Shismanov then got him settled in the nearby Russian Orthodox Aya Panteleimon Church, which extended extraterritorial protection over Tyufekchiev. Shismanov then contacted Hristo announcing Tyufekchiev's arrival. Few days later, Tyufekchiev went to the house of Dimitri Filippov, where he met Hristo and Merdzhan(ov) to discuss the details of the plot. A few more meetings took place until Tyufekchiev left Constantinople, having met up with his mother who had arrived from Resne.[25]

---

[22] BOA. Y.A.HUS. 256–1, 2, 26 Kanunisani 1892.
[23] BOA. Y.A.HUS. 256–104, 25 Şubat 1892.
[24] Perry, *Stefan Stambolov*, 116.
[25] Compiled from the Ottoman interrogation reports, the written judicial decree, as well as the notes sent in by the Bulgarian Ministry of Foreign Affairs: BOA. Y.MTV. 60–79, 2, 11 Mart 1308; BOA. Y.A.HUS. 262–14, 4 Zilhicce 1309; BOA. Y.A.HUS. 258–67, 3, 31 Mart 1891.

On 24 February 1892, at around 1 am, when Dr Vulkovich was returning from a visit, he was fatally stabbed in his abdomen near Kabristan Street, a wound from which he died two days later.[26] The exact identities of the murderers are a point of debate. Hristo told the authorities that Merdzhan(ov) had actually rejected Tyufekchiev's offer to be the hit man. Hristo also maintained that Tyufekchiev told them before he left Istanbul that two other assassins had arrived from Odessa to carry out the murder. While Hristo's account sounds like too convenient an alibi, the Ottoman authorities managed to implicate Merdzhan(ov) in the murder after a knife master identified him as one of his earlier customers. Merdzhan(ov)'s claim that he did not have good enough night vision and that he was physically impaired to carry out the deed was also proven wrong by expert opinion. The authorities brought the case to completion after a number of individuals came out and testified to seeing both Hristo and Merdzhan(ov) with Tyufekchiev and Shismanov.[27] As for the verdict, both Merdzhan(ov) and Hristo were given death penalties, while Naum and Nikola Tyufekchiev were sentenced to fifteen years in absentia.[28] Shismanov had already been freed after giving a brief testimony, on the grounds that he was a Russian subject.[29]

Who were all these operatives that Tyufekchiev was able to summon for such a high-profile murder? Hristo Stefkov, Dimitri Filippov, the butcher, as well as the barkeeper Kalchov hailed from the Macedonian town of Resne, that is, Tyufekchiev's home town. Their point of origin certainly highlights the significance of networks of expatriates. As for Vlad Dimitri Shismanov, he did not hail from the same home town but rather embodied a similar political destiny with Tyufekchiev. He was born in the Ottoman province of Edirne (Adrianople), and after the Russo-Ottoman War of 1877–8 he began to work in the government of Eastern Rumelia up until the Russia-backed coup of 1886, after which he moved to Istanbul.[30] Thus, Shismanov was also a Russophile just like Tyufekchiev, kicked out of Bulgaria on conspiracy

---

[26] BOA. Y.PRK.MŞ. 4–2, 1, 13 Şubat 1307.
[27] BOA. Y.MTV. 60–79, 2, 11 Mart 1308.
[28] 'Dr. Vulkovitch's Assassins: Convicted by a Turkish Court and Sentenced to Death', *The New York Times*, 11 May 1892, 2.
[29] BOA. Y.MTV. 62–42, 12 Şevval 1309.
[30] BOA. Y.A.HUS. 258–67, 3, 31 Mart 1891.

charges. It was this historical conjuncture that placed him in the same camp as Tyufekchiev.

The assassination of Vulkovich brought to the fore a number of issues. It first and foremost illustrated the Ottoman inability to make even the most lawful of demands from a Great Power, that is Russia. All the suspects in the murder such as Shismanov and Tyufekchiev were Ottoman citizens born in the empire. Contrary to the Ottoman Nationality Law (1869), however, they also held Russian citizenship, having assumed another nationality without the Porte's approval.[31] In addition to being unable to bring Shismanov to justice, Constantinople failed to present a strong case for the extradition of Tyufekchiev, letting down Bulgaria in the face of Russia. The Porte indeed found itself in a difficult position.[32] It did not want to alienate Bulgaria, fearing that it would declare independence, while it did not want to tackle St Petersburg head-on, afraid of unintended consequences. The Porte's unwillingness to do so led to unsolicited publicity in Europe which Constantinople watched out insecurely.[33] The assassination ultimately damaged Ottoman standing in Sofia and its claims of suzerainty over Bulgaria, while it made Stambolov more relentless in his crackdown and less tolerant of the opposition, leaving him fewer friends.

As diplomatic repercussions from the assassination were steadily unfolding, Tyufekchiev's threats took more direct forms. Few weeks after Vulkovich's murder, he sent a concise but clearly worded letter to the Ottoman General Consul in Odessa (Hocabey). Signed 'Bulgarian Underground', the letter warned that the general consul could share a similar destiny with Dr Vulkovich if the Porte continued to take steps benefiting the government of Stambolov.[34] Based in Odessa, a port city with perfect maritime connections to many major urban centres on the Black Sea, Tyufekchiev must have appreciated the gradually developing populist social revolutionary scene in his immediate surroundings in southwestern Russia, particularly in Jewish

[31] Ibid.
[32] BOA. Y.A.HUS. 257–46, 2, 9 Şaban 1309.
[33] BOA. Y.A.HUS. 257–155, 2, 29 Şaban 1309; BOA. Y.PRK.TKM. 25–2, 3 Zilkade 1309; BOA. HR.SYS. 2824–26, 12 Mayıs 1892.
[34] BOA. Y.A.HUS. 257–82, 2, 12 Mart 1892.

quarters that had suffered tremendous economic destitution and political oppression.[35] Tyufekchiev must also have felt at home in Odessa, which not only 'produced and attracted radical intellectuals' but was also characterised by a tough class of immigrants who, like Tyufekchiev, 'were male, young, adventurous, and disdainful of laws and rules'.[36] But the developments in Sofia were soon to clear the way for Tyufekchiev to return home.

Fall of Stefan Stambolov and Tyufekchiev's Comeback

With his major allies assassinated, Stambolov's power back in Sofia had been eroding since the early 1890s. As it did, Prince Ferdinand began to consolidate his own position. In a sense, the prince gradually felt powerful enough to afford a fallout with Stambolov, the person who brought him to power in the first place. The competition between the two came to a close in May 1894 when Stambolov felt compelled to resign from his position as the prime minister. The upcoming months saw the dismantling of the Stambolovist powerbase by the opposition, facilitated by a gradual rapprochement between Bulgaria and Russia. In order to facilitate the reconciliation, the new cabinet in Sofia was quick to offer a number of symbolic gestures, such as the release from prison of a number of Russophiles, including even 'those accused of participation in the Belchev murder'.[37]

It is within this context that Tyufekchiev also returned to Sofia in November 1894 after 'four years of emigrant suffering' in Russia.[38] Even though Tyufekchiev was arrested right after his arrival, his custody lasted only briefly as he was released on a bail. Upon hearing of Tyufekchiev's return to Sofia, the Porte immediately asked for his extradition to Istanbul, but Konstantin Stoilov's government, busy trying to mend relations with St Petersburg, opted to retain Tyufekchiev.[39] After all, as Stoilov argued, because

---

[35] Paul Avrich, *Russian Anarchists* (Princeton, NJ: Princeton University Press, 2015), 17–18.
[36] Patricia Herlihy, *Odessa: A History, 1794–1914* (Cambridge, MA: Harvard University Press, 1986), 283, 281.
[37] Perry, *Stefan Stambolov*, 218; Crampton, *Bulgaria*, 138–44.
[38] Bulgarian National Archives (hereafter DAA), ф. 600К, оп. 3, а.е. 964, л. 4–5, 'Letter from N. Tufekchiev to K. Stoilov', 30 October 1895. The dates cited from the DAA reflect the Julian calendar which was 12 to 13 days shorter than the Gregorian calendar.
[39] BOA. A.} MTZ. (04) 176–58, 2, 15 Kanunisani 1310.

Tyufekchiev's citizenship was a matter of dispute, they 'cannot hand him over to the Ottoman government or try him' until the matter got solved.[40] Later on, the Bulgarian authorities would ask for the dispatch of relevant court files so that charges could actually be brought against Tyufekchiev in Sofia, an offer the Porte rejected readily since Istanbul deemed him an Ottoman subject beyond Bulgarian jurisdiction.[41]

As Tyufekchiev settled back in Sofia, he became an active member of the Macedonian cause and began to work in the Ministry of Public Works, 'appointed to the departmental section for the study of the Central Railway'.[42] Tyufekchiev then teamed up with Dimitar Rizov to set their legal record straight.[43] In late 1894, the case on the assassination of Belchev was accordingly brought back to the Court of Appeal for reconsideration, whereby both Dimitar Rizov and Naum Tyufekchiev were let out on bail. In turn, Stambolov was ridiculously framed as one of the perpetrators of the murder, the harbinger of what was to come as his opponents sought to corner Stambolov legally.[44]

Tyufekchiev's comeback, however, was part of the process where there was a clear shift in policy from the times of Stambolov who 'had always nipped any movement in the bud by imprisoning the leaders and hotter-headed partisans'.[45] While the rapprochement with Russia accentuated this policy change, there were significant domestic factors that the new government took into account. After all, around 26–29 per cent of Sofia's population was made up of Macedonian immigrants, 33 per cent of Bulgarian military officers were born in Macedonia, and 43 per cent of the civilian bureaucracy hailed from the imperial territories.[46] In the words of Nachovich, the Bulgarian Minister of Foreign Affairs, 'this formed a body of people with whom it was necessary to count, especially when they were advocating a

---

[40] Perry, *Stefan Stambolov*, 227.
[41] BOA. A.} MTZ. (04) 181–21, 2, 7 Kanunievvel 1311.
[42] The National Archives (TNA hereafter), Foreign Office (FO hereafter) 78/4662/101, Sofia, 18 July 1895, f. 140; TNA. FO 78/4853/10, Sofia, 18 January 1897, enclosure 2: Stamboloff's Letter dated 16 March 1895, titled 'The Plan for my Assassination', f. 25.
[43] BOA. A.} MTZ. (04) 607–9, 15 Kanunievvel 1310.
[44] TNA. FO 78/4661/1, Sofia, 1 January 1895, ff. 2–4.
[45] TNA. FO 78/4661/41, Sofia, 25 March 1895, f. 147.
[46] Perry, *Politics of Terror*, 35.

cause which was a patriotic one, and close to the heart of every Bulgarian'.[47] Accordingly, much to the annoyance of the Ottomans, both the Macedonian and Armenian organisations had become active, organising public meetings where they voiced grievances over the status of non-Muslims and called for reform in the empire.[48]

It was within this context that Tyufekchiev began to assume positions of leadership within the expanding Macedonian movement. In late December 1894, Tyufekchiev, together with Dimitar Rizov and the Ivanov brothers, a prominent merchant family, established the Fraternal Union, a small clique that began to promote more radical solutions.[49] Tyufekchiev's inner circle was in fact one of the most vocal to advocate violent means in Ottoman Macedonia, arguing that it would be useless to expect a foreign intervention to change the status quo in the empire, unless armed action was taken up. That Tyufekchiev and the Ivanov brothers traded arms, weapons and bombs certainly played into these tactics.[50]

By February 1895, in pursuit of these tactics, the Fraternal Union began to organise concert nights and staged plays to raise funding for the Macedonian cause, attracting Macedonian students.[51] According to the Union's newspaper *Pravo*, the organisation was able to raise 800 francs within a short period of time and expanded its body to 300 active members. Even though the Union competed with other Macedonian activists over tactics, resources and membership, campaigns to reconcile the two soon bore fruit. Kitanchev, the chairman of the Union (also from Resne), was a popular figure in both camps, and he managed to convince both the radicals and the moderates to merge into a single Macedonian Committee where Tyufekchiev was elected to be the vice president.[52]

---

[47] TNA. FO 78/4662/72, Sofia, ff. 19–20, 7 June 1895.
[48] TNA. FO 78/4661/12, Sofia, 19 January 1895.
[49] Mercia MacDermott, *Freedom or Death: The Life of Gotsé Delchev* (London: Journeyman, 1978), 124.
[50] Ramazan Hakkı Öztan, 'Tools of Revolution: Global Military Surplus, Arms Dealers, and Smugglers in the Late Ottoman Balkans, 1878–1908', *Past & Present* 237(1) (2017): 167–95.
[51] BOA. A.} MTZ. (04) 27–26, 7 Şubat 1310. BOA. Y.A.HUS. 323-1, 15 Mart 1311.
[52] Perry, *Politics of Terror*, 45–6.

While Tyufekchiev continued to consolidate his position within the Macedonian movement, his plans to take revenge on Stambolov also became more concrete. Together with a gang of ten to fifteen people, Tyufekchiev lived in a Sofia hotel owned by the Ivanov brothers, where they hatched plans and weighed alternatives for the murder of Stambolov.[53] Apparently, Tyufekchiev enjoyed regular meetings with Grigor Nachovich, then the foreign minister, who had reportedly relayed him his tacit support.[54] Meanwhile, Stambolov continued to receive threats, with one letter he received in June telling him that 'he would die by the knife that killed Vulkovich'.[55] That was not a bluff. On 15 July 1895, Stambolov left the Union Club at around 8 pm and took a carriage to go home. Shortly thereafter, shots were heard and Stambolov, who got out of the carriage with his pistol, was knocked down by three individuals who literally hacked him in the street, leaving him in a critical condition with terrible wounds.[56] When asked who attacked him, Stambolov, half conscious, uttered the names of 'Haliu and Tyufekchiev'.[57] He died few days later. His funeral service, well attended by foreign representations, also saw the coming together all of Stambolov's enemies 'who collected at the grave-side to indulge in blasphemous exultation'.[58]

Less public was the hit squad involved in the assassination, who were in fact hand-picked by three families who shared a common hatred towards Stambolov.[59] One of them was Bone Georgiev with whom the Tyufekchiev brothers had kept in contact since their stint in Belgrade. Georgiev was the secretary and close friend of Major Panitza who was executed after his failed coup plot. Others included Haliu Stavrev – Tyufekchiev's cousin from Resne who also participated in the killing of Belchev. The final hit man was Taliu Tsvetkov, a Macedonian émigré who also lived in Sofia. Among those impli-

[53] Perry, *Stefan Stambolov*, 224–5.
[54] TNA. FO 78/4662/101, Sofia, 18 July 1895, f. 140.
[55] Perry, *Stefan Stambolov*, 229.
[56] TNA. FO 78/4662/100, Sofia, 15 July 1895, ff. 132–5.
[57] TNA. FO 78/4853/10, Sofia, 18 January 1897, enclosure 1: 'Report on the Trial of the Persons Accused of the Murder of Mr. Stamboloff', f. 16; 'Revue des Journaux', *Le Figaro*, 9 Aout 1895, 2.
[58] Hans Roger Madol, *Ferdinand of Bulgaria: The Dream of Byzantium*, trans. Kenneth Kirkness (London: Hurst & Blackett, 1933), 82.
[59] 'L'Assassinat de M. Stamboulof', *Journal des Débats Politiques et Littéraires*, 6 Aout 1895, 1.

cated in the broader plot was the carriage driver, Mircho Atsov, as well as the Ivanov brothers.[60] As Stambolov clearly implicated Naum Tyufekchiev on his deathbed, he was quickly arrested but was soon released on bail 'because his judges and several ministers received threatening letters' from the Macedonian quarters.[61]

While Tyufekchiev finally succeeded in taking revenge for his dead brother by murdering Stambolov, the Macedonian Committee he led together with Kitanchev also kept the promises made earlier in the year by dispatching armed bands (*cheta*s) into Ottoman Macedonia in late June 1895.[62] These bands acted under the leadership of experienced officers such as Boris Sarafov, but they were far from inciting a local uprising successfully, suffering from a lack of local support. The fact that some of them chose to plunder instead of sticking to their political agenda certainly did not help the cause, which strengthened the Ottoman position. The failure of the uprising created a backlash against those who had promoted the tactic of armed intervention in Macedonia, which certainly included Tyufekchiev, and would eventually increase the popularity of moderates.[63]

It was the crisis of leadership that brought these existing issues to the fore. When Kitanchev died on 15 August, there were rumours that Tyufekchiev was going to take over.[64] The internal strife among the revolutionaries in Sofia became all the more apparent when a congress gathered in December, 1895 to discuss the policy options in Ottoman Macedonia. Lasting for thirteen days, the congress resulted in the victory of the moderate faction over the radicals whereby the likes of Tyufekchiev were side-lined.[65] His earlier involvement in a number of assassinations was a regular point of contention in Sofia. In the midst of the December Congress, Dimitar Rizov, one of Tyufekchiev's oldest allies, openly blackmailed and silenced Tyufekchiev by threatening to divulge what he knew about the assassination of Stambolov.[66]

---

[60] Perry, *Stefan Stambolov*, 231–2.
[61] TNA. FO 78/4663/141, Sofia, 4 September 1895, f. 21.
[62] BOA. A.} MTZ. (04) 177–25, 2, 6 Muharrem 313.
[63] MacDermott, *Freedom or Death*, 123.
[64] TNA. FO 78/4662/120, Sofia, 15 August 1895, ff. 233–4.
[65] TNA. FO 78/4663/219, Sofia, 31 December 1895, ff. 325–6.
[66] MacDermott, *Freedom or Death*, 123.

With the fallout, the Macedonian Committee in Sofia was divided into two factions, with Tyufekchiev representing the radicals, while Toma Karaiovov (1868–1951), the editor of *Pravo*, stood for the moderates. The brewing conflicts inside the committee meetings were soon divulged out into the open as both factions began to publish incriminating attacks against one another throughout January 1896.[67] However, these speculative attacks pointed to the rapprochement between the government and the Tyufekchiev faction. The op-eds in *Pravo* openly accused Tyufekchiev and Ivanov of being on the payroll of the Bulgarian government and functioning as its agents, thereby allowing Sofia to exploit the Macedonian question as political expediencies demanded it.[68] The Bulgarian government became increasingly supportive of Tyufekchiev and wary of the newly emerging leaders of the Macedonian Committee who were seen as being eager to focus more on 'internal politics' in Bulgaria than on the developments in Ottoman Macedonia.[69] By choosing to support the radical faction, Sofia essentially wanted to keep the option of armed incursions and planned attacks as a way of reminding the Porte of what could go wrong in Macedonia, in case the reforms beneficial to Sofia were not forthcoming.

Getting Down to Business: Manufacture of Hand Bombs

Enjoying the direct support of the government, Tyufekchiev opened a bomb factory in Sofia at some time in early 1896 and began to manufacture hand bombs to be used in Ottoman Macedonia. The factory remained operational only for few months until March 1896, but it still managed to manufacture 300 hand bombs.[70] Tyufekchiev had already enjoyed good relations with the Internal Macedonian Revolutionary Organization (IMRO), that is, the committee that operated underground in Ottoman Macedonia, which remained

---

[67] BOA. A.} MTZ. (04) 181–51, 10, 'Le Journal *Progrès* du 13 Janvier 1896 by N. Tufektchieff'; BOA. A.} MTZ. (04) 181–51, 10, 'Le Journal *Pravo* du 21 Janvier 1896, la Réponse de Karayovoff'.
[68] BOA. A.} MTZ. (04) 181–51, 9, 'Le Journal *Pravo* du 21 Janvier 1896'; BOA. A.} MTZ. (04) 181–41, 1, 12 Kanunisani 1311.
[69] TNA. FO 78/4753/5, Sofia, 8 January 1896, f. 19.
[70] MacDermott, *Freedom or Death*, 123.

distinct and organisationally independent from the revolutionary committees in Sofia. After the ascendancy of the moderate faction in Sofia at the expense of Tyufekchiev, the relations between IMRO and the Supremists had already begun to falter. The latter wanted to exercise full control over the internal organisation which it saw as subordinate to Sofia, while the IMRO wanted to keep its organisational independence intact. Transfer of arms from Sofia had always come with strings attached. The break-away of Tyufekchiev was therefore an opportunity for the IMRO to get supplies into Macedonia without compromising their standing. For Tyufekchiev, in turn, delivering bombs and dynamite into Macedonia was a way of strengthening his own position which had suffered greatly from the intra-organisational strife since the late 1895. The downside for the IMRO, however, was that Tyufekchiev was a businessman, so they actually had to pay to acquire supplies through him. This they did. One of the shipments by Tyufekchiev in early 1896, for instance, included '100 bombs, three boxes of dynamite, forty-one rifles, two swords and several revolvers'.[71] By spring 1896, he was rumoured to have begun showing 'signs of a sudden accession of wealth'.[72]

Not all transfers went through seamlessly, though. One batch of supplies by Tyufekchiev was intercepted on 7 April 1896, when a certain Done Stoyanov was stopped by the Ottoman authorities as he was entering Manastır (Bitola) with sacks of rice loaded on pack animals. The authorities, eager to find contraband tobacco, pierced the sacks with needles, only to hit the casings of empty bombs. Stoyanov was tortured but did not confess a word.[73] The smuggling of dynamite bombs into Ottoman Macedonia by Tyufekchiev caused the Ottoman authorities to renew their efforts to extradite him to Istanbul where he could serve his fifteen-year punishment but Sofia did not budge an inch. By July 1896, in describing Tyufekchiev, the Ottoman commissioner declared that 'the influence of this wicked guy was due to his skills in manufacturing dynamite and delivering it to the bandits in Macedonia . . .

---

[71] Ibid., 136.
[72] The British authorities traced the source of his wealth to an alleged payment of 50,000 francs for his role in the Stambolov assassination. TNA. FO 78/4754/74, Sofia, 30 April 1896, ff. 39, 43.
[73] Perry, *Politics of Terror*, 61–2; MacDermott, *Freedom or Death*, 140–1.

if we manage to put this individual into prison, that means we have destroyed 40% of the strength of the Macedonian Committee'.[74]

While the Ottoman authorities sought ways to contain Tyufekchiev, a set of developments had already started to damage his influence in Sofia. In March 1896, the factory that he ran in Sofia was closed down by the Bulgarian authorities as a gesture to extract more privileges from Constantinople.[75] Within the same month, the Supreme Committee created a bureau of military affairs which was tasked with planning armed solutions to the Macedonian question. Because this bureau advocated a position comparable with Tyufekchiev's faction, some officers who had sided with Tyufekchiev were also attracted to the Supremists, further facilitating an organisational fallout.[76]

Tyufekchiev's dwindling popularity was also related in part to the ongoing trial in Sofia for Stambolov's assassination, which challenged him financially and forced him to keep a low profile.[77] Several people came out as witnesses and testified to seeing Tyufekchiev coming out the Ivanov's shop on the day of the murder with packages that matched with the evidence at hand.[78] During the trials in late December 1896, Tyufekchiev was also put in prison after it became apparent that he had been sending threatening letters to the prosecutor, the jurors and witnesses.[79] In a more amicable letter he sent to Stoilov, the prime minister, from the Black Mosque where he was kept in custody, Tyufekchiev highlighted his economic difficulties, with his 'unfortunate 70-year-old mother living on the streets' in addition to his inability to support Nikola who was at the time pursuing an engineering degree in Liège. Suggesting to Stoilov that he would change his ways, Naum declared that he would put his 'stormy and miserable' life in order by marrying a girl from Resen, Olga, while repeating his belief in a favourable outcome of the

---

[74] BOA. HR.SFR.04. 351–62, 1 (2), 15 Temmuz 1896.
[75] MacDermott, *Freedom or Death*, 123; Perry, *Politics of Terror*, 68–9.
[76] Perry, *Politics of Terror*, 54.
[77] DAA. ф. 600K, оп. 3, а.е. 964, л. 21–2, 'Letter from N. Tufekchiev to Stanchev', 31 August 1898.
[78] TNA. FO 78/4853/10, Sofia, 18 January 1897, enclosure 1: 'Report on the Trial of the Persons Accused of the Murder of Mr. Stamboloff', f. 21.
[79] TNA. FO 78/4755/245, Sofia, 24 December 1896, f. 327.

case.[80] Yet the case against him would remain over his head like the sword of Damocles for few more years.

Such legal troubles, coupled with his dwindling influence among the revolutionaries in Sofia, was in contrast to his continued relevance for the revolutionary groups active in Ottoman Macedonia. The latter depended on Tyufekchiev's networks for the purchase and transfer of supplies from Sofia. Even though he was known to have overcharged his customers, he did not mind if payments were in arrears.[81] The leaders of IMRO such as Gotse Delchev were in constant contact with Tyufekchiev, discussing issues of supply and outlining further collaboration. After the Bulgarian Government closed down his bomb factory in Sofia, Tyufekchiev was instrumental in establishing contacts between the leaders of IMRO such as Gyorche Petrov and Armenian revolutionaries. In the end, the Armenian operatives had become notorious for their capability in carrying out high-scale attacks, particularly after the successful invasion of the Ottoman Bank in Constantinople in August of 1896.[82] One such contact that Tyufekchiev facilitated involved an Armenian bomb master named Grigor who was convinced to establish a bomb factory in Sofia in 1897. Too close to the Bulgarian surveillance, however, the operatives decided to move the factory to a village in Köstendil (Kyustendil), where they were able to manufacture around a thousand hand bombs until the plant got closed down by the Bulgarian authorities in late 1898.[83]

While relations with the Supremists continued to be strained throughout 1897, the Tyufekchiev faction was able to expand the business of arms trade in favourable ways and further develop relations with the IMRO.[84] This took place within the context of the Ottoman–Greek War of 1897, which began to brew in late January as a question over the future of Crete. Concurrently, rumours began to circulate in diplomatic circles to the effect that 150,000

---

[80] DAA. ф. 600К, оп. 3, а.е. 964, л. 15–16, 'Letter from N. Tufekchiev to K. Stoilov', 22 December 1896.
[81] MacDermott, *Freedom or Death*, 171; Perry, *Politics of Terror*, 166.
[82] BOA. Y.PRK.ZB. 18-13, 2, 4 Eylül 1312.
[83] Perry M. Duncan, 'The Macedonian Revolutionary Organization's Armenian Connection', *Armenian Review* 42(5) (1989): 61–70, 64–5; Perry, *Politics of Terror*, 168.
[84] Perry, *Politics of Terror*, 74.

rifles and 50 million cartridges had been sold to the Ivanov brothers, 'who were deeply implicated in the murder of Mr. Stamboloff, and who are members of the extreme party of action in the Macedonian Society'.[85] Indeed, the news that Tyufekchiev's strongest allies had just acquired weapons was correct, but the number of weapons was not. Later reports established the number to be '14,800 infantry rifles, and 24,000 cavalry carbines', which were mostly obsolete Krinka models that were largely not serviceable without repair.[86] Even though the Bulgarian officials defended the transaction by arguing that the Ivanov brothers would send them to Belgium for recycling, the Ottoman authorities were afraid that Sofia sought to take advantage of the unfolding conflict with Greece in order to arm civilians in Bulgaria and transfer supplies into Macedonia.[87] The Ottoman fears were spot on, as the later intelligence indicated the shipment of these weapons in smaller batches across the border.[88]

While the Tyufekchiev faction had access to a considerable number of second-hand weapons and cartridges, their shipment into the Ottoman interior was wrought with a number of challenges. First, the IMRO did not have the necessary funds to purchase weapons. Nor did they have Sofia's backing, since the Bulgarian officials were afraid of a possible backlash from the Ottomans if such shipments were to be intercepted. Such issues, among others, plunged the Supremist organisation into a crisis of leadership where no one credible stepped in to take charge. Accordingly, Gotse Delchev and Gyorche Petrov, the representatives of the IMRO to Sofia, first convinced Boris Sarafov, an experienced Bulgarian officer known for his activist outlook, and then began to campaign for his election. By 1899, they indeed managed to get him elected as the Supremist leader.[89]

From his election in 1899 to his fall from leadership in 1901, Sarafov's activist agenda provided a window of opportunity for the Sofia arms dealers

---

[85] TNA. FO 78/4853/25, Sofia, 28 January 1897, f. 57.
[86] TNA. FO 78/4853/35, Sofia, 11 February 1897, ff. 78–9.
[87] BOA. HR.SFR.04. 757–5, 1(1–2), 9 Muharrem 1315.
[88] TNA. FO 78/4853/96, Sofia, 21 April 1897, ff. 253–4; TNA. FO. 78/5017/78, Sofia, 3 June 1899, ff. 9–10; TNA. FO. 78/5017/84, Sofia, 14 June 1899, f. 65.
[89] Perry, *Politics of Terror*, 82–3.

such as Tyufekchiev and the Ivanov brothers who began to be paid handsomely for the purchase of thousands of rifles, bombs and other military hardware destined for Ottoman Macedonia.[90] When the Supremist aid declined from late 1900 onwards, the IMRO was able raise funds through other means, such as the kidnapping in September 1901 of an American missionary, Ellen Stone, which provided much needed ransom money that funded further purchases of arms.[91] Therefore, Tyufekchiev continued to secure supplies for the IMRO regardless of the developments in Sofia. Correspondence intercepted by the Ottoman authorities in spring 1903 noted how Tyufekchiev purchased and shipped 300 hand bombs, 192 kilos of dynamite, 200 hundred primers, and fifty revolvers across the border.[92]

Even though Tyufekchiev lost his broader influence in the revolutionary politics in Sofia by his late thirties, he had emerged as a successful arms dealer, supplying the IMRO together with the Ivanov brothers. A range of transactions that Tyufekchiev's faction concluded with the government in a sense illustrate the greater range of support he enjoyed within the bureaucracy at this period. As a result of such 'powerful influences', Tyufekchiev was even acquitted from the Stambolov case by March 1898.[93] Yet his past continued to haunt him. Particularly, it was his cousin, Haliu, whose repeated appearances in Sofia continued to complicate things. Haliu frequently visited the Ivanov brothers and asked them for his share from the proceeds for the murder of Stambolov. After one such confrontation, Haliu was briefly detained in December 1900 but released after Vasil Radoslavov, the Minister of Interior, intervened on his behalf.[94] Tyufekchiev seems to have cultivated a working relationship with Radoslavov, as he repeatedly asked for favours

---

[90] Ibid., 166–7.
[91] Charles M. Dickinson, Consul General in Istanbul, to David J. Hill, Assistant Secretary of State, No. 19, 4 December 1901, in *Despatches from United States Consuls in Sofia, 1901–1904* (National Archives Microcopy T-682, Roll 1, 3 July 1901–26 August 1904); Perry, *Politics of Terror*, 103–5.
[92] BOA. BEO. 2078-155845, 2 and 4, 10 Mayıs 1319. There were also other reports that suggested that Tufekchiev sent packages of dynamite via the employees of the Orient Express, an intelligence I was not able to corroborate. BOA. HR.SFR.04. 222–31, 1, 10 Nisan 1319.
[93] TNA. FO 78/4851/32, Sofia, 11 March 1898, f. 86.
[94] TNA. FO 78/5080/90, Sofia, 13 August 1900, f. 3; TNA. FO 78/5080/150, Sofia, 8 December 1900, ff. 213–14.

from the minister, ranging from appointments for his own to scholarship awards for his brother Nikola.[95]

Haliu was not as lucky few months later when he was arrested in the midst of a broader crackdown by the Bulgarian government on the revolutionary committees – a scheme to appease Russia in return for financial aid.[96] In late October 1902, after few days on trial, Haliu was sentenced to death for his involvement in Stambolov's murder.[97] This was more than enough to make Tyufekchiev furious, particularly towards the Ministry of Interior, A. Lyudskanov. Tyufekchiev began to leak his correspondence with the latter dating back to 1892, thus implicating the minister in the murder of Dr Vulkovich. In doing so, Tyufekchiev pointed fingers at others, too, such as Nikolay Ignatyev, Dimitar Rizov, P. Stanciov, the Prefect of Varna and Vladimir Shismanov, the Director of the National Library. As Tyufekchiev assumed the role of a whistle-blower, his revenge letters created a good shake-up in Sofia, where Prince Ferdinand was expressly upset with the existing cabinet members.[98] The prince's view of Tyufekchiev was much worse: 'a proven killer is walking around my capital', he said, which, 'I must admit, just frightens me'.[99]

Arming the Bolsheviks: Tyufekchiev as a Transnational Actor

In late 1903 and early 1904, Tyufekchiev spent a few months in Paris where he used the false name Ivanov as he stayed at 17 Rue Montmartre.[100] The Ottoman reports on Tyufekchiev were more than eager to pass on to Istanbul

---

[95] DAA. ф. 313K, оп. 1, а.е. 1109, л. 1, 'N. Tufekchiev to V. Radoslavov', 13 March 1899; DAA, ф. 313K, оп. 1, а.е. 1109, л. 2–3, 'N. Tufekchiev to V. Radoslavov', 17 January 1900.

[96] Perry, *Politics of Terror*, 108–9.

[97] TNA. FO 78/5219/158, Sofia, 25 October 1902. Within a year and half, however, Haliu's sentence was commuted into fifteen years' hard labour. TNA. FO 78/5360/61, Sofia, 4 April 1904, f. 225.

[98] TNA. FO 78/5219/171, Sofia, 18 November 1902; A. G. Drandar, *La Bulgarie sous le Prince Ferdinand, 1887–1908* (Brussels: Etablissement Généraux D'Imprimerie, 1909), 132–3.

[99] DAA. ф. 600K, оп. 3, а.е. 318, л. 19, 'Letter from Prince Ferdinand to K. Stoilov', 20 April 1902.

[100] BOA. Y.A.HUS. 465–73, 2, 15 Kanunisani 904.

the rumours occasioned by his presence in the city. The first intelligence suggested that Tyufekchiev had purchased weapons and dynamite in Paris for the use of Macedonian revolutionaries.[101] He was then reported to have tried to raise money from the Red Cross on behalf of the Macedonian refugees.[102] This genre of intelligence reports around Tyufekchiev often recycled rumours mixed with reality. Tyufekchiev indeed exchanged letters with Boris Sarafov in early January 1904, informing him of the possibility of purchasing 3,000 Mannlicher rifles.[103] In another letter few days later, Tyufekchiev also told Sarafov about a map of treasure, complete with instructions, sketches and secret symbols leading to a Venetian dowry worth 40 million francs buried back in 1473.[104] Individuals like Tyufekchiev, with dubious connections and characteristically adventurous lives, made any story line sound credible and suspicious at the same time.

The events that transpired throughout 1905 confirmed this thin line between rumours and complex reality,[105] illustrating that Tyufekchiev began to emerge as an important revolutionary with undertakings beyond Macedonia. This was when Tsarist Russia began to experience revolutionary upheavals in what is known as the Constitutional Revolution of 1905. Even though the Russian Social Democrats – both the Bolsheviks and Mensheviks – characteristically renounced terrorism and the use of violence, this did not mean that theory was always put into practice.[106] Particularly from 1905 onwards when Russia was seething with revolution, different factions in the Social Democrats began to resort to terrorist tactics, particularly in places such as the Caucasus where the bottom-up push for calculated use of terror

---

[101] BOA. A.} MTZ. (04) 112–33, 3, 27 Şubat 1903.

[102] BOA. Y.A.HUS. 465–73, 2, 15 Kanunisani 1904.

[103] DAA. ф. 1947K, оп. 1, a.e. 84, л. 3, 'Letter from N. Tufekchiev to B. Sarafov', 5 January 1904.

[104] DAA. ф. 1947K, оп. 1, a.e. 84, л. 5–6, 'Letter from N. Tufekchiev to B. Sarafov', 10 January 1904.

[105] For an attempt where I tried to expand upon this argument in the context of interwar Turkey, see Ramazan Hakkı Öztan, 'Republic of Conspiracies: Cross-Border Plots and the Making of Modern Turkey', *Journal of Contemporary History*, available at: https://doi.org/10.1177/0022009419884627.

[106] Anna Geifman, *Death Orders: The Vanguard of Modern Terrorism in Revolutionary Russia* (Santa Barbara, CA: Praeger, 2010), 62–3.

tactics often found practitioners in the name of self-defence, even among the more moderate Mensheviks.[107] It was in the charged atmosphere of the 1905 Revolution that the Bolsheviks also began to make preparations for an armed uprising in support of the mass political movement, in line with the resolutions adopted by the Third Congress of the Russian Social Democratic Labour Party in late April.[108]

As the Bolsheviks began to make preparations for an armed rising in St Petersburg, their effort was largely coordinated by N. E. Burenin, the experienced Bolshevik smuggler, and Leonid Krasin, the famous Bolshevik engineer. Burenin's group actively experimented with the development of bombs and Finland was used as a gateway for smuggling the supplies into nearby St Petersburg, including two hand grenades destined for the St Petersburg Soviet led by Leon Trotsky.[109] Active in the Burenin group was M. P. Skosarevskii, with the codename Omega, who had been a student of the famous Russian chemist Alexey Favorsky.[110] Omega was sent by the Bolsheviks to Sofia where he stayed for three months from February to April 1905 and imported the technical know-how from Tyufekchiev in building hand grenades.[111] Skosarevskii also made a stop in Geneva where he most probably discussed the initiative with Lenin. After a three-month stay in Sofia, he came back to St Petersburg 'loaded with blueprint, contacts, and other information germane to the manufacture of cast iron encased bombs', followed by the establishment of 'St Peterburg's first underground bomb factory' where bombs were produced based on Tyufekchiev's designs. This small workshop manufactured bombs for several months until police surveillance soon forced it out of business.[112]

---

[107] Erik van Ree, 'Reluctant Terrorists? Transcaucasian Social-Democracy, 1901–1909', *Europe–Asia Studies* 60(1) (2008), 127–54.

[108] V. I. Lenin, *Collected Works, vol. 8: January–July 1905* (Moscow: Progress Publishers, 1962), 368–74.

[109] Michael Futrell, *Northern Underground: Episodes of Russian Revolutionary Transport and Communications through Scandinavia and Finland, 1863–1917* (London: Faber & Faber, 1963), 59–61.

[110] David Lewis, *Early Russian Organic Chemists and their Legacy* (Heidelberg: Springer, 2012), 126.

[111] Kort, 'Leonid Krasin', 226.

[112] Ibid., 227. Timothy Edward O'Connor, *The Engineer of Revolution: L. B. Krasin and the*

Omega was not the only one to visit Tyufekchiev in Sofia, however. A few months later, Burenin himself came to Sofia to purchase primers and fuses, since the ones previously acquired did not work well. Tyufekchiev and Burenin later met in Paris in summer 1905 to purchase reliable and technologically advanced fuses for the Bolsheviks. When Burenin went to Tyufekchiev's room in the Savoy Hotel, Tyufekchiev put on a live experiment with 'capsules of fulminate of mercury and rolls of bickford fuses ... to show how well the fuses burned and in a few seconds the room was filled with smoke'. After Tyufekchiev calmly lied to the hotel staff who rushed to his room, he managed to purchase the necessary material for a much-impressed Burenin.[113] Armed with new fuses, the Bolshevik chemists back in St Petersburg improved Tyufekchiev's hand bomb designs, and bragged that 'the new fuses were as professional as those of the Tsarist government issued for its forces'.[114]

Purchasing arms and transferring know-how was not the only trick up Tyufekchiev's sleeve, however, as he would play similarly important roles in the later Bolshevik attempts to prepare for an armed uprising. In summer 1906, Maxim Litvinov was tasked with acquiring military hardware, ranging from machine guns to ammunition, from multiple suppliers in different European cities. It was then planned that they would be shipped to the Caucasus via the Black Sea in order to be used in guerrilla warfare. Litvinov was accordingly able to amass thousands of cartridges and rifles in Europe. Shipping them to Batumi, however, was particularly troublesome, since the authorities throughout Europe tightened their grip on customs and shipments, alerted by the reliable Russian counter-intelligence.[115] The only option that Litvinov was able to come up with was to transfer the goods through a German company to Varna, a Bulgarian port city where Naum Tyufekchiev, 'a person without fear', came forward and promised to arrange the

---

Bolsheviks, 1870–1926 (Boulder, CO: Westview, 1992), 71. Anna Geifman, *Thou Shalt Kill: Revolutionary Terrorism in Russia, 1894–1917* (Princeton, NJ: Princeton University Press, 1993), 201.

[113] Kort, 'Leonid Krasin', 244–5.
[114] O'Connor, *The Engineer of Revolution*, 73.
[115] Zinovy Sheinis, *Maxim Litvinov*, trans. Vic Schneierson (Moscow: Progress Publishers, 1990), 46–7.

rest.[116] Litvinov described Tyufekchiev as a very good intermediary 'but by no means an unselfish' one, since he agreed to arrange the necessary permits and secure the goodwill of the port authorities for a handsome fee.[117]

Litvinov (aka Felix) first secured the cooperation of the Bulgarian minister of war, General Savov, during a private meeting held in Paris, whereby he managed to convince the latter to help transfer the arms 'in sealed boxcars'.[118] Indeed, Tyufekchiev's correspondence in September and October 1906 illustrate all the troubles Litvinov ran into while arranging the logistics of intra-European transport. By mid-October, for instance, Felix told Tyufekchiev he was still trying to secure funds, while also looking for crew members for the locomotives involved in the transport of the supplies.[119] While doing so, Felix continued to send letters to Tyufekchiev from Trieste. Felix also spotted a yacht in nearby Fiume, one that was small enough to avoid detection by the Russian patrol boats but also fast enough to avoid the Ottoman steamers. Pretending to be the brother of Tyufekchiev, Felix paid 30,000 francs for the yacht and named it *Zora*, thereby registering it under the name of Nikola Tyufekchiev.[120]

Yet the money necessary for the final transport was not forthcoming from St Petersburg as the Mensheviks gained the upper hand in the Central Committee. Eager to have a personal audience with the leadership of the Social Democrats, Litvinov travelled to St Petersburg under the watchful gaze of the Tsarist authorities who allowed him to proceed in the hope of trailing his contacts in St Petersburg, but Litvinov 'vanished into thin air'.[121] Much to his surprise, he managed to convince the Mensheviks to release funds to complete the operation, possibly due to the bottom-up pressures from 'the more radical party elements from the Caucasus, for whom the weapons were intended'.[122] As Litvinov was leaving St Petersburg, he sent

[116] 'M. Litvinov raconte son passé révolutionnaire', *Le Temps*, 25 Septembre 1934, 2.
[117] Kort, 'Leonid Krasin', 305–12.
[118] Sheinis, *Maxim Litvinov*, 49.
[119] DAA. ф. 213Б, оп. 1, а.е. 58, 'Letter from N. Tufekchiev to N. Vladikin', 10 October 1906; DAA. ф. 213Б, оп. 1, а.е. 59, 'Letter from N. Tufekchiev to N. Vladikin', 21 October 1906.
[120] 'M. Litvinov raconte son passé revolutionnaire', 2.
[121] Sheinis, *Maxim Litvinov*, 52.
[122] Hugh D. Phillips, *Between the Revolution and the West: A Political Biography of Maxim M. Litvinov* (London: Routledge, 1992), 9–11.

a letter to Tyufekchiev, noting his prolonged absence in Paris and stating that he would come to Sofia in few days, asking whether 'he could do his job safely'.[123]

While Litvinov was safely in Bulgaria, the delays in funding meant that the stormy season of the Black Sea was near. Only in the very last days of 1906 did the *Zora* finally manage to set sail from Varna, fully loaded, but 'with a crew from Odessa who did not inspire much faith'.[124] In ways somewhat similar to the 1905 John Grafton Affair in Finland, the storms made the *Zora* run aground onto a sandbar in early January 1907 off the coast of Romania. The wreckage was spotted late in the evening by Romanian officials and local fishermen who were reported to have heard gunshots and then seen the crew clinging to the funnel of the ship. Despite the roughness of the sea, the fishermen brought the crew to shore the next day. They conversed in Russian, and asked about the whereabouts of the gendarmerie in order to avoid them. As the *Zora* was sinking, the crew apparently threw out the boxes of rifles and ammunition and tried to get rid of some of the illicit cargo on board. The officials spotted many of these boxes scattered across the shoreline.[125]

The crew were later taken into custody and the Romanian officials were able to retrieve around 300 boxes from the ship, which included 2,000 rifles and 600,000 cartridges in addition to seditious print literature.[126] Litvinov quickly left for Bucharest in the hope of salvaging the situation, but he was too late as the Russian Legation in the city had already taken the necessary measures.[127] While the Romanian authorities noted that the freight was destined for the use of Russian revolutionaries, which the crew also confirmed, the Ottoman authorities doubted this claim. By pointing out Tyufekchiev's direct involvement, they argued that the weapons were to be used by the Bulgarian revolutionaries.[128] After all, Tyufekchiev was not shy about his role in the affair. He had even paid a visit to the Bulgarian Ministry of

---

[123] DAA. ф. 213Б, оп. 1, а.е. 69, 'Letter from N. Tufekchiev to N. Vladikin'.
[124] Sheinis, *Maxim Litvinov*, 53.
[125] BOA. A.} MTZ. (04) 153–5, 10 (1–2), 19 Kanunisani 1907.
[126] BOA. A.} MTZ. (04) 153–5, 4, 7, 25 Kanunisani 1907 and 9 Şubat 1907.
[127] 'M. Litvinov raconte son passé revolutionnaire', 2.
[128] BOA. A.}MTZ.(04) 152–1, 28 Kanunievvel 1322.

Foreign Affairs to ask for the release of the illicit merchandise confiscated by Romania, but to no avail.[129]

This expensive fiasco was not where Tyufekchiev's involvement with the Bolsheviks came to a halt, however. The crew members who were arrested in Romania included Semen Ter-Petrosiyan, codename Kamo, who was known as 'the idealistic robber who worshipped Lenin'.[130] Russia had already filed a request to extradite him as well as others who were held in the prison of Constanta, but the Romanian authorities decided to set him loose.[131] Once freed, Kamo left for Berlin where, in April, he consulted with Lenin, Litvinov and Krasin, and decided to add to carry out a massive armed robbery in Tbilisi in order to make up the financial losses incurred as a result of the *Zora* running aground.[132] Since 1905, both Kamo and Stalin had gained experience in carrying out 'expropriations', whereby they robbed banks, stagecoaches and trains throughout Georgia in support of the Bolshevik purse.[133] This they did few months later, on 13 June 1907, when Stalin and Kamo staged a successful attack against the money courier of the Russian Imperial Bank in Tbilisi's Erevan Square, stealing a total of 341,000 rubles. Kamo managed to escape to Finland, and the stolen cash was smuggled into Europe. The problem, however, was that the majority of the money – 250,000 rubles to be exact – was in 500-ruble notes whose serial numbers were shared with the authorities, which certainly made it difficult to cash in the money. In response, Lenin planned to exchange the money simultaneously in various European cities from early 1908 onwards.[134] A number of Bolsheviks were arrested during this operation across Europe from Paris to Stockholm, Munich to Rotterdam to Geneva.[135]

Right after the failure of this operation, Tyufekchiev was spotted in

---

[129] BOA. HR.SFR.04. 457–53, 5 (1), 15 Avril 1908.
[130] Geifman, *Death Orders*, 65–6.
[131] Jacques Baynac, *Lenin'in Fedaisi Kamo*, trans. Selim Sezer (Ankara: Sınırsız, 2015), 85.
[132] Roman Brackman, *The Secret File of Joseph Stalin: A Hidden Life* (London: Frank Cass, 2001), 47.
[133] Helen Rappaport, *Conspirator: Lenin in Exile* (New York: Basic Books, 2012), 234–6.
[134] Brackman, *The Secret File*, 47–52.
[135] See 'Held as Tiflis Robbers: Russian Woman and Two Men Caught', *The New York Times*, 19 January 1908; ProQuest Historical Newspapers, 9.

France, where he spent a month visiting Paris and Nice from mid-March to mid-April 1908.[136] By the time Tyufekchiev returned to Sofia, the authorities in Sofia had already tipped off the banks in the city to be careful with transactions involving Russian rubles.[137] That is why the bank officials quickly became suspicious on 25 April 1908 when Tyufekchiev sent a certain Dimitar Sotirov to the Bank Générale to exchange rubles for 15,000 francs. Tyufekchiev also arrived in the bank where he vouched for Sotirov whom he said was 'a good man'. Soon afterward the money exchange the bank contacted the city police and asked for their money back. The police went to the house of Tyufekchiev to do so. A thorough search of his house yielded few other bundles of rubles posted to a certain Lovosfanov in Sofia – probably a pseudonym for Tyufekchiev – and the authorities thought the money had originated from the bank robbery in Tbilisi.[138] The search of his house on 23 Regentska St, near the Church of Sveta Sofia, further uncovered a small workshop in the attic where the authorities discovered eight sacks of bombs, *machine infernale* and dynamite.[139]

During his interrogation in late April 1908, Tyufekchiev argued that he had received the money as a payment for the bombs he manufactured for the Armenian revolutionaries, which the authorities in Sofia found hard to believe, since they continued to suspect that the brand-new ruble banknotes had originating from the Tbilisi robbery earlier in the year.[140] Even though the Armenian connection was most probably just an alibi to cover up his involvement with the Bolsheviks, it still piqued the interest of Ottoman intelligence which was eager to associate Tyufekchiev with the Armenians in any possible fashion.[141] As for Tyufekchiev, the incident contributed to the bad publicity surrounding him, as many press articles began to question

---

[136] DAA. ф. 176К, оп. 2, а.е. 268, л. 2, 'An Application by Naum Tufekchiev to the Ministry of Foreign Affairs', 9 May 1908.
[137] DAA. ф. 176К, оп. 2, а.е. 268, л. 11-12, 'Letter from the Prosecutor's Office at the Sofia Regional Court to the Ministry of Foreign Affairs', 26 August 1908.
[138] BOA. A.} MTZ. (04) 166–7, 2, 13 Nisan 1324.
[139] BOA. Y.A.HUS. 521–3, 3, 16 Nisan 1324. Today this address corresponds to 29 Moskovska St.
[140] DAA. ф. 176К, оп. 2, а.е. 268, л. 11–12, 'Letter from the Prosecutor's Office at the Sofia Regional Court to the Ministry of Foreign Affairs', 26 August 1908.
[141] BOA. HR.SFR.04. 457–53, 3, 5, 15–16 Avril 1908. DAA.

what he was up to during the one-month period he spent in France. While Tyufekchiev sought legal ways to clear his name, the Bulgarian authorities were under a different sort of pressure. The Prefect of Police who questioned Tyufekchiev, for example, received many anonymous letters that threatened him, asking for Tyufekchiev's release, which eventually happened on bail of 15,000 francs.[142] The ongoing investigation in the following months failed to produce enough evidence to press charges against Tyufekchiev, however. Even though the Russian authorities produced supporting documents from the local Tbilisi authorities, the case came to a close with his acquittal.[143]

After all, by 1908, Tyufekchiev had grown all the more connected to government circles which not only provided him with legal backing in such cases, but also continued to award him hefty contracts. In accessing government circles, Tyufekchiev seems to have used the channels of Nikola Yonkov-Vladikin, an important scholarly figure and political activist with whom Tyufekchiev had kept in close contact. Their correspondence reflects this complex world of political influence, corruption and crime, where the information revealing Tyufekchiev's relations with the Bolsheviks conjoined his broader conduct of business with the government. In many of his letters, Tyufekchiev presses Vladikin to use the latter's existing contacts in the Ministry of War to conclude contracts with the government to purchase his bombs, while suggesting that he could always sell 'his inventions to the Armenians'.[144] In return, Vladikin quickly asks for a loan from Tyufekchiev, but the latter seems to have been hard-pressed for cash throughout the first half of 1906.[145] After all, Tyufekchiev's path to becoming a government contractor was not so straightforward as he often had to compete with other suppliers while also trying to balance a steady flow of supplies from European factories, for which he often lacked the capital. In late June, for instance, Tyufekchiev complained about a competitor who had better contacts at the Ministry of War and was therefore poised to undercut him, even if

[142] BOA. HR.SFR.04. 457–53, 3, 5, 15–16 Avril 1908.
[143] DAA. ф. 176К, оп. 2, а.е. 268, л. 15–16, October 1908.
[144] DAA. ф. 213Б, оп. 1, а.е. 4, 'Letter from Tufekchiev to N. Vladikin', 15 January 1906.
[145] DAA. ф. 213Б, оп. 1, а.е. 11 and 14, 'Letters from Tufekchiev to N. Vladikin', 5 and 18 March 1906.

Tyufekchiev had arranged the supply of 15 tons of pyroxylin with the Nobel brothers from their factories in Hamburg.[146]

Indeed, by mid-September, the Ministry of War awarded the contract for the supply of pyroxylin to a well-connected supplier named Kiselov, even though Tyufekchiev's offer was lower. Yet, at the same time, Tyufekchiev reported the successful test of his bomb design, noting that 'the bomb was accepted, tested, analysed, and produced wonderful results, even better than the initial trials'.[147] In the coming months, Tyufekchiev managed to conclude similar deals supplying the Ministry of War, even though the process was laden with difficulties in overcoming competitors and expanding his political influence at home. A year later, in June 1907, for instance, Tyufekchiev was reported to have received a concession to manufacture the smokeless powder as well as other chemical substances such as melinite, trotyl and carbonite. The deal was complete with a public relations campaign, whereby the concession was hailed by the Bulgarian media as a victory of Bulgarian businesses and a rejection of foreign capital – particularly Jewish.[148] As Tyufekchiev continued to build on his growing prominence within the government and cultivate lucrative political and financial ties, his business prospects took an unexpected turn after summer 1908.

'Turning Turk': Tyufekchiev on the Path to the First World War

By 1908, Tyufekchiev had cultivated a strong record of transnational cooperation with a range of revolutionary organisations, including the Macedonians/Bulgarians, Armenians and the Bolsheviks, which often took the form of providing technical know-how or the direct transfer of supplies.[149] The Young Turk Revolution on 23 July 1908, however, only expanded

---

[146] DAA. ф. 213Б, оп. 1, а.е. 17 and 26, 'Letters from Tufekchiev to N. Vladikin', 17 June and 7 August 1906.

[147] DAA. ф. 213Б, оп. 1, а.е. 41, 'Letters from Tufekchiev to N. Vladikin', 8 September 1906. By the end of the month, Tufekchiev received the first instalment of his payment from the ministry, with which he ended up paying his standing debt. DAA. ф. 213Б, оп. 1, а.е. 47, 'Letters from Tufekchiev to N. Vladikin', 14 September 1906.

[148] BOA. HR.SFR.04. 241–30, 1, 2, 29 Mayıs 1323.

[149] İrtem, *Ermeni Meselesinin İçyüzü*, 107; Vartkes Yeghiayan, *The Armenians and the Okhrana, 1907–1915: Documents from the Russian Department of Police Archives* (Los Angeles: Center for Armenian Remembrance, 2016), 55.

Tyufekchiev's network further and cemented his status as a transnational revolutionary-cum-businessman. This was when the Young Turks managed to force the Ottoman sultan Abdülhamid II to reinstate the Ottoman Constitution of 1876 and bring the revolutionaries across Ottoman Europe into the fold of legal politics. The armed revolutionaries descended down the mountains and a sense of revolutionary brotherhood dominated the sociopolitical atmosphere across the empire. Tyufekchiev also left Sofia to visit his home town, Resne, for the first time since he left it more than thirty years before. Tyufekchiev also visited Ohrid, where Süleyman Kani (later İrtem) was serving as the district governor. There Tyufekchiev was initiated into the Committee of Union and Progress and became an active Young Turk. He paid his membership dues to the organisation's Ohrid branch until the Bulgarian declaration of independence in October 1908.[150] Even though Tyufekchiev's stint as a Young Turk was brief, the later political developments would provide him with opportunities to cooperate with the Young Turks once again.

Since late 1908, Russia had sought a Balkan alliance as a measure against the growing influence of Austria-Hungary after the latter had annexed Bosnia-Herzegovina. This Russia did by courting a Serbian–Bulgarian rapprochement, which, over the course of 1912, turned into a Balkan League with the addition of Greece and Montenegro. By early October, the Alliance declared war upon the Ottomans, which resulted in a decisive Ottoman defeat.[151] Yet the victors, unable to divide the spoils of the war and jealous of Bulgaria's territorial gains in Macedonia, grew anxious of each other, with the radicals in Sofia such as Tyufekchiev demanding a pre-emptive attack against Serbia to consolidate Bulgaria's position in Macedonia.[152] This second round of the conflict resulted in a catastrophe for Bulgaria, as it reversed nearly all of the Bulgaria's initial gains.

The Bulgarian defeat had radically shifted the calculations in the Balkans

---

[150] Süleyman Kani Irtem, *Yıldız ve Jön Türkler: İttihat-Terakki Cemiyeti ve Gizli Tarihi*, ed. Osman Selim Kocahanoğlu (Istanbul: Temel Yayınları, 1999), 422.

[151] For the war's impact on the Ottoman Empire, see Ramazan Hakkı Öztan, 'Point of No Return? Prospects of Empire after the Ottoman Defeat in the Balkan Wars (1912–1913)', *International Journal of Middle East Studies* 50(1) (2018): 65–84.

[152] Crampton, *Bulgaria*, 198–201.

by late 1913, paving the way for an unlikely rapprochement of the defeated between Bulgaria and Ottoman Empire. After all, Bulgaria suddenly found itself in need of Ottoman leverage to counter-balance the growing influence of Greece and Serbia in the region. As for Constantinople, an alliance with Bulgaria seemed equally promising, first, because it was Greece, not Bulgaria, that began to pose the greatest risk for the Ottomans in the aftermath of the Balkan Wars. Second, an alliance with Bulgaria would create a land corridor connecting the Ottoman Empire to Berlin and Vienna. It was this effort to seek an alliance between Bulgaria and the Ottoman Empire that provided a range of non-state actors with new opportunities.[153] Vasil Radoslavov, the new Germanophile Bulgarian prime minister, first contacted Ethem Ruhi, a prominent Young Turk living in Bulgaria, so that he could broach the topic of the necessity of improved relations with the leaders in Istanbul.[154] The Young Turks in turn decided to send two of its important members to Sofia, that is, Fethi Bey (Okyar) as the ambassador and Mustafa Kemal (Atatürk) as the military attaché, both of whom were tasked with securing Bulgaria's goodwill in negotiations.[155]

These Ottoman manoeuvres were complete with the later dispatch of intelligence agents and funds from Istanbul to Sofia, where they were ordered to carry out acts of sabotage in order to shape public opinion for an alliance with Germany and the Ottoman Empire.[156] One such plot was the bombing in mid-February 1915 of Sofia's city casino. The explosion at midnight killed four during a masked ball.[157] The operation was funded and masterminded by the Ottoman intelligence, with the local set-up provided by

---

[153] See Sinan Kuneralp, 'Osmanlı İmparatorluğu ve Müttefikleri: Yumuşak Güç Diplomasisi Örneği" in Edhem Eldem, Sinan Kuneralp, and Bahattin Öztuncay (eds), *I. Dünya Savaşı'nda İttifak Cephesinde Savaş ve Propaganda* (Istanbul: Koç Üniversitesi ANAMED, 2014), 40–67.

[154] Ethem Ruhi Balkan, *Hatıraları*, Canlı Tarihler series (Istanbul: Türkiye Yayınevi, 1947), 51–2.

[155] Andrew Mango, *Atatürk: The Biography of the Founder of Modern Turkey* (New York: Overlook Press, 2002), 123–4.

[156] Hasan İzzettin Dinamo, *Kutsal İsyan: Milli Kurtuluş Savaşının Gerçek Hikayesi*, vol. 2 (Istanbul: May Yayınları, 1966), 122–5.

[157] 'Bomb at Sofia Ball', *The New York Times*, 17 February 1915; ProQuest Historical Newspapers, 4.

Naum Tyufekchiev.[158] Unsurprisingly, the Bulgarian government announced the attack to be the work of Serbian and Russian partisans, an occasion Radoslavov used to attack his domestic opponents.[159] The Bulgarian Court Martials passed sentences regarding the plot in July 1915, but Tyufekchiev and the Ottoman connection was not spelled out in any fashion.[160]

In addition to such violent means, Tyufekchiev also began to play the unlikely role of a mediator brokering the alliance through diplomatic talks with the Ottomans. First, he came to Istanbul as a member of a three-man delegation, and on 10 June 1915 attended a purposefully visible banquet organised by Talat Paşa, the Ottoman minister of interior. A few days later on 18 June, Tyufekchiev visited the printing house of *Tanin* newspaper, the semi-official mouthpiece of the Young Turks, where he donated money for the Ottoman martyrs in the Dardanelles front.[161] Positing himself 'as a well-known benefactor and friend' of the Young Turks, Tyufekchiev asked for a concession in return for Bulgarian commitment to the alliance, which was a strip of land that would secure better access for Sofia to the Black Sea.[162] Tyufekchiev trusted his relations with the top Turkish officials, particularly highlighting 'the great affection and unlimited trust of Enver Pasha'.[163] As these negotiations for an alliance continued uninterrupted amidst such gestures of friendship, Tyufekchiev visited Istanbul once again in August (Figure 9.2).[164] It was in that meeting that both parties were able to agree on the

---

[158] Пантев and Гаврилов, *100-те най-влиятелни българи в нашата история със 121 илюстрации* (София: Репортер 7, 2014), 276–7.

[159] BOA. DH.EUM.5.Şb. 9–37, 1, 14 Şubat 1915.

[160] BOA. HR.SFR.04. 885–116, 3, 12 Juillet 1915.

[161] Yusuf Hikmet Bayur, *Türk İnkilabı Tarihi: 1914–1918 Genel Savaşı*, vol. 3 (Ankara: Türk Tarih Kurumu Basımevi, 1955), 476–7.

[162] DAA. ф. 313К, оп. 1, а.е. 1109, л. 5–6, 'Letter from N. Tufekchiev and Dr. G. Nikolov to V. Radoslavov', 31 May 1915.

[163] DAA. ф. 313К, оп. 1, а.е. 1109, л. 9–10, 'N. Tufekchiev to V. Radoslavov', 31 May 1915.

[164] Most recently, Hans-Lukas Kieser used this photograph in his biography of Talat Paşa, but he misidentified Tyufekchiev as Alfred Nossig, buying into the latter's attempts to present himself as more important than he actually was. See Hans-Lukas Kieser, *Talaat Pasha: Father of Modern Turkey, Architect of Genocide* (Princeton, NJ: Princeton University Press, 2018), 23.

Figure 9.2 Naum Tyufekchiev in the Ottoman Ministry of War with Enver and Talat Paşas and Halil Bey, from Alfred Nossig, *Die Türkei und ihre Führer* (Halle: Otto Hendel, 1916).

details of the alliance which was then signed in Sofia in early September.[165] Bulgaria declared war a month later on 14 October.

Yet what explains Tyufekchiev's sudden transformation into such a crucial figure who managed to broker an alliance between two powers on the eve of the First World War? According to Muhittin Birgen, a prominent Young Turk journalist in *Tanin*, Tyufekchiev was 'a friend of Turks who frequented Istanbul back and forth', where he was 'not only engaged in politics but also in business'.[166] He was so close to the Young Turks that he functioned as a reliable courier for the Armenian revolutionaries by relaying their messages personally to Talat Paşa.[167] His growing prominence, however, seems

---

[165] Bayur, *Türk İnkilabı Tarihi*, 480.
[166] Muhittin Birgen, *İttihat ve Terakki'de On Sene: İttihat ve Terakki Neydi?* ed. Zeki Arıkan, vol. 1 (Istanbul: Kitap Yayınevi, 2006), 247–8.
[167] Ahmet Emin Yalman, *Turkey in the World War* (New Haven, CT: Yale University Press, 1930), 218.

Figure 9.3 Tyufekchiev together with the members of the CUP and select journalists from Constantinople, *L'Illustration Contemporaine*, No. 17 (October 1915), 7.

to be closely related to the necessities of a bourgeoning war economy. When the Ottoman Empire joined the First World War on 1 November 1914, it largely depended on German aid for the conduct of the war. Because the naval blockades of the Straits paralysed the traditional supply lines, Bulgaria emerged as a crucial supply corridor, both for the Central and Entente powers (Figure 9.3).[168]

In ways similar to the Marxist revolutionary Alexander Parvus, Tyufekchiev's importance grew within the context of the burgeoning war economy.[169] In early May 1915, Tyufekchiev notified the Ottoman embassy in Sofia that he had convinced Prime Minister Radoslavov to the effect that ammunition would be imported from Romania into Bulgaria as if it was intended for the Bulgarian army, but would then be secretly shipped into the Ottoman Empire.[170] The trade of goods was not limited to ammunition. As

---

[168] Anne Christine Holden, 'Bulgaria's Entry into the First World War: A Diplomatic Study, 1913–1915', PhD thesis, University of Illinois at Urbana-Champaign, 1976, 118.
[169] M. Asım Karaömerlioğlu, 'Rusya, Almanya ve Türkiye'de Büyük bir Kozmopolit Entelektüel ve Eylemci: Helphand-Parvus', *Doğu Batı*, no. Entellektüeller-3 (2006), 157–79, at 177–9.
[170] BOA. HR.SFR.04. 281–3, 1, 9 Mai 1915.

Bulgaria had been a traditional supplier of wool cloth (*aba*) for the Ottoman army since the early nineteenth century, Tyufekchiev was also able to tap into its wartime trade.[171] He did so by supplying Istanbul with 150,000 metres of thick wool cloth and 2,000 pairs of trousers in August 1915.[172] In exchange for such useful services, the Ottomans allowed Tyufekchiev to import 400,000 kilos of sheep's wool (*yapağı*) into Bulgaria despite the existing bans on exports in general.[173]

Yet the most important merchandise that Tyufekchiev was able to sell to the Ottomans was what he was known for the most, namely, explosives. In April 1915, he sent 31,000 bombs which were designed to be deployed from airplanes.[174] He then made a deal for the sale of 100,000 hand bombs, which he began to ship to the Ottomans from late September 1915 onwards.[175] It is clear that as Tyufekchiev strengthened his political and economic position in Bulgaria and received concessions from Sofia, his merchandise only became more professional, attracting interstate customers such as the Ottomans. While the previous hand grenades used in the empire were mounted on a wooden stick and featured a fuse, Tyufekchiev's bombs were round and could be carried on a belt across the chest, with firing mechanism that could be activated with a match.[176]

It was the booming wartime trade in such commodities that made

---

[171] Neriman Ersoy-Hacısalihoğlu, 'Textile Trade in Bulgaria in the mid-19th Century and the Gümüşgerdan Family', in Vera Constantini and Markus Koller (eds), *Living in the Ottoman Ecumenical Community: Essays in Honour of Suraiya Faroqhi* (Leiden: Brill, 2008), 181–99; Andreas Lyberatos, 'State and Economy in Late Ottoman Thrace: Mihalaki Gümüşgerdan and the "Woollens of the State"', *Turcica* 46 (2015): 205–36.

[172] BOA. HR.SFR.04. 690–10, 7, 11 Şevval 1333.

[173] BOA. MV. 199–27, 17 Zilkade 1333. There seems to have been some contractual problems with the payments and indemnities about this transaction, however, that occasioned a second round of communication between Turkey and Bulgaria in 1925. See BOA. HR.İM. 63-2, 1–2, 14 Teşrinievvel 1341.

[174] BOA. HR.SFR.04. 690–24, 3, 29 Avril 1915.

[175] BOA. HR.SFR.04. 687–28, 26, 16 Septembre 1915, and 28, 29 Septembre 1915; BOA. HR.SFR.04. 694–23, 1, 8 Janvier 1916.

[176] T. Nejat Eralp, *Tarih Boyunca Türk Toplumunda Silah Kavramı ve Osmanlı İmparatorluğu'nda Kullanılan Silahlar* (Ankara: Türk Tarih Kurumu Basımevi, 1993), 139; Arif Hikmet Koyunoğlu, *Osmanlı'dan Cumhuriyet'e Bir Mimar: Anılar, Yazılar, Mektuplar, Belgeler* (Istanbul: Yapı Kredi Yayınları, 2008), 189.

Tyufekchiev increasingly powerful and rich, with strong connections in Istanbul and Sofia. Some Macedonian revolutionaries, however, began to perceive his wealth and influence as more of a threat, if not a vulnerability, that could make Tyufekchiev care more for his personal interests than revolutionary ideals. Tyufekchiev must have known how serious these threats were, as he sought the protection of three personal guards.[177] The latter were unable to protect him, though, as on 9 March 1916 he was shot to death at around 7.30 pm.[178] He died in front of his own apartment. Tyufekchiev's funeral took place at the St Nedelya Church; he was survived by his wife Olga, their newly born son, their daughter Margarita and son-in-law Nikolai.[179] It was perhaps unthinkable that Tyufekchiev, the organiser of so many assassinations himself, could have passed away in any other fashion. Strong evidence indicates that he was killed on the orders of Todor Alexandrov, an important Macedonian revolutionary.[180] His execution was in line with the wartime practice of Bulgarian nationalists targeting the left-wing revolutionaries who had aligned with the Young Turks after 1908, as it was most prominently the case with the assassination of Yane Sandanski in 1915.[181] According to Fuat Balkan, a famous Young Turk revolutionary, Tyufekchiev was killed by the operatives of the pro-Russia faction in Sofia in order to put an end to his shipment of bombs to Constantinople.[182] While it is not immediately clear how his murder actually affected the existing contractual obligations, Tyufekchiev's afterlife continued to illustrate interesting biographical twists, as his grenades continued to see service as late as 1922 during the Greco-Turkish War.[183]

---

[177] DAA. ф. 313K, оп. 1, a.e. 1343, 'Anonymous Letter to Prime Minister V. Radoslavov', 12–15 March 1916.
[178] BOA. HR.SFR.04. 274–46, 10 Mars 1916 and BOA. DH.EUM.1 Şb. 14–24, 29 Şubat 1331.
[179] Information taken from his obituary published in *Mir*, Sofia, No. 4808, 28.02.1916, available at: https://commons.wikimedia.org/wiki/File:Naum_Tyufekchiev_necrologue.jpg.
[180] DAA. ф. 313K, оп. 1, a.e. 1343, 'Anonymous Letter to Prime Minister V. Radoslavov', 12–15 March 1916.
[181] Mehmet Hacısalihoğlu, 'Yane Sandanski as a Political Leader in Macedonia in the Era of the Young Turks', *Cahiers Balkaniques* 40 (2012): § 32.
[182] Turgut Gürer (ed.), *Komitacı: BJK'nin Kurucusu Fuat Balkan'ın Anıları* (Istanbul: Gürer Yayıncılık, 2008), 27.
[183] Cemal Karabekir, *Maçka Silahhanesi Hatıraları, İstiklal Harbi Kahramanları* (Istanbul: Nehir Yayınları, 1991), 56.

Conclusion

Tracing the stories of complex figures such as Tyufekchiev requires a careful engagement with different historical trajectories that co-shape the careers of such rogues. My pursuit of his biography as a window to understanding the revolutionary politics in late Ottoman Europe reveals four scales that are mutually constitutive. First is the primacy of interstate conflict and the foundational impact of war and displacement on the formation of late nineteenth-century transgressive politics. The generation of the Tyufekchiev brothers and their radical political ethos was shaped by the refugee-generating processes of warfare that caused havoc to much of the imperial frontiers of the Balkans and Caucasus throughout the second half of the nineteenth century. Just like the rest of Macedonian refugees, Naum Tyufekchiev, too, found shelter in the newly autonomous Bulgaria after the ravages brought about by the Russo-Ottoman War of 1877–8. It did not take long before this sizeable Macedonian community turned political. Organised along the lines of associations and secret societies, the Macedonian diaspora quickly emerged as a powerful constituency that began to assert greater influence upon the course of politics in Sofia. The formation of ties of trust among these refugees was shaped through a shared notion of belonging to a homeland from which they were uprooted. Resne, as we have seen, features prominently in the biographies of Tyufekchiev's inner circle of associates, playing a key role in the formation of their networks. Indeed, it is difficult to overstate the significance of late nineteenth-century refugeedom and the massive human displacement across the Ottoman domains and beyond. Tyufekchiev, too, was part of this refugee generation whose life was defined by precariousness from the very start.

It was not the first time in history that wars generated refugees, however. Nor was it the case that all refugees sought political mobility through recourse to transgressive actions. In this sense, there was something peculiar to the political careers of non-state actors such as Tyufekchiev that begs further explanation. While non-state actors have long wielded influence on interstate politics, the ways in which interstate relations operated in the late nineteenth century favoured and promoted a certain class of political entrepreneurs who did not shy away from radical means, and could therefore serve as useful proxies. After all, the equilibrium of power in Europe which sought to minimise interstate conflicts required the expansion of the field of non-state politics, where interstate rivalries could continue to play out. The changing patterns of interstate competition is therefore the second theme that stands out in Tyufekchiev's biography, whereby state actors needed his generation of precarious refugees as much as the latter needed states for sovereign protection. Accordingly, non-state actors such as Tyufekchiev managed to play central roles in how interstate rivalries came to unfold. In this sense, the trajectory of Naum Tyufekchiev from his modest beginnings as a refugee hailing from Ottoman Macedonia to his transformation into a go-between during the alliance negotiations between Bulgaria and the Ottoman Empire illustrate how non-state actors could thrive in the expanding political field of interstate relations. Indeed, Tyufekchiev, too, was part of this larger generation of revolutionaries-turned-statesmen that characterised many other post-Ottoman states.

Tyufekchiev's path to do so was determined soon after he arrived in Bulgaria and was sent to Europe in pursuit of Sofia's goal in shaping a loyal generation of technocrats. Indeed, the upward social mobility afforded by professional specialisation was a characteristic of Tyufekchiev's generation of refugees who were living in an age of greater mobility – the third theme that emerges so forcefully in his biography. Much like in the rest of the world where careers in the military led to greater social mobility for those coming from lower classes in the nineteenth century, Tyufekchiev also began to receive technical schooling in Belgium on behalf of the Bulgarian military. His acquisition of technical know-how in chemistry and explosives would make him indispensable to a range of revolutionary organisations always interested in his services. He would accordingly emerge as a reliable partner who could fulfil the revolutionary demand for new technologies of violence by tapping into illicit flows so characteristic of the late nineteenth century. Even when Tyufekchiev suffered strategic miscalculations and unavoidable setbacks, his technical background and experience in navigating the black markets was an asset that helped him to survive the ups-and-downs. As Tyufekchiev gradually emerged more as a business entrepreneur than a revolutionary broker by the *fin de siècle*, the mobility that defined his earlier life also began to shape his business prospects. By mobilising his earlier networks, he managed to secure governmental contracts that positioned him as the supplier of European war material as well as his own bomb designs. By 1914, the booming war economy only consolidated those who could trade means of violence across the globe. Tyufekchiev, too, was one such entrepreneur who thrived in the dark nexus between business and politics, enabled in part by better prospects of upward social mobility in the second part of the nineteenth century.

His business ventures were not the only way Tyufekchiev wielded influence on politics, however. As we have seen, his involvement in conspiracies and other forms of violent political action allowed non-state actors like him to brutalise politics in formative ways – the last theme that defines the biography of Tyufekchiev. As we have seen, each cycle of violence that served the interests of interstate actors such as Russia or Serbia had in fact explosive potential to strain relations with neighbouring powers such as the Ottoman Empire and Bulgaria. To be sure, such conspiratorial acts that became so characteristic of his biography also helped to facilitate the formation of international system and law out of the sheer necessity to cope with such individuals as Tyufekchiev. Yet, just like many other members of his generation who were involved in acts of violence, Tyufekchiev, too, was one such revolutionary conspirator who managed to switch to more formal avenues of politics in his later years. This trajectory certainly tells us something about the masculine youth cultures that dominated the revolutionary politics in the frontiers of the Ottoman Empire. Tyufekchiev was a figure charismatic enough to peer pressure not only his brothers into acts of violence, but also to mobilise others whom he came across and shared similar political trajectories. In this sense, much like the rest of his generation, Tyufekchiev, too, was a political entrepreneur with an immense individual agency who charted a course of precarious life that typify so well the violent age of rogues.

10

Late-Ottoman 'Rogues' and their Paths to Power: A Prosopographic Study

Benjamin C. Fortna

This contribution addresses the relationship between men of violence and the centres of power in the late Ottoman Empire through a prosopographic study of Unionist *komitacı*s (also known as *komitadji*), that is, militant partisans of the organisation known as the Committee of Union and Progress (CUP) in the years before the First World War. Choosing a selection of activist officers who identified themselves as *fedaî*s, or self-sacrificing agents, the chapter examines their career paths in order to disentangle the various ways in which affective affinity, personal allegiance, opportunism, serendipity and structural change in the empire's military combined to shape their formation. Taking as its focus a core group of middle-ranking officers from different ethnic and geographical backgrounds who came together to serve in the key battles of the 'Young Turk' era, including the Ottoman–Italian War in Tripolitania (modern Libya) of 1911–12, the Balkan Wars of 1912–13, the First World War and the 'National Forces period, the study analyses their education, early careers, and patronage links to ascertain patterns and divergences. This group, including but not limited to such individuals as İzmitli Mümtaz, Kuşçubaşı Eşref, Selim Sami, Süleyman Askerî, Ja'far al-'Askari, 'Aziz 'Ali al-Misri, Sapancalı Hakkı and Yakup Cemil, features men who rose to certain degrees of prominence – and often notoriety – due to their service for and loyalty to those at the upper echelons of the military establishment, including most prominently İsmail Enver, a key leader of the 'Young Turk'

Revolution of 1908. Relying in no small part on the support and physical intimidation supplied by these men, Enver rose rapidly to become the leading military figure of the empire's final years. Throughout, the chapter attempts to assess the tensions between the network of personal and patronage-based connections linking the late-Ottoman *komitacı*s and the broader but increasingly volatile structural dynamics of the period that brought these men to the fore, with dramatic consequences for the empire, its fragile demographic and social patterns, and the individuals' post-imperial histories.

The long history of the Ottoman Empire was hardly devoid of violence. The initial waves of Ottoman territorial expansion in the late twelfth and thirteenth centuries were, of course, effected by military conquest, while subsequent centuries saw a seemingly unending series of wars, insurrections and political infighting that was often spectacularly violent. Most infamously, the Ottoman dynasty turned to fratricide to preserve the unity of the imperial line. A recent study of the office of the chief eunuch in the institution of the imperial harem reveals such a steady diet of violent deaths that when an official's death is described as a mere execution, the reader is almost relieved. In fact, as Hathaway describes it, by the middle of the seventeenth century, 'violence had become a normative part of factional politics, even inside the residential sections of the palace'.[1] The combination of 'factionalism, militarisation, ethno-regional rivalries and friction' between internal intergovernmental power blocks that Hathaway describes for the pre-modern Ottoman era very well applies, *mutatis mutandis*, to the period under discussion here.

Violence continued to be an important element of Ottoman politics in the transition from the pre-modern to the modern era. At the turn of the nineteenth century the relationship between outlaws of various stripes and the state was a perennial feature shaping Ottoman governance, especially in the provinces. Istanbul relied on both irregular forces for its military campaigns and paramilitary forces – and their perpetration of acts of violence against local populations – when not in full campaign mode.[2] Interestingly

---

[1] Jane Hathaway, *The Chief Eunuch of the Ottoman Harem: From African Slave to Power-Broker* (Cambridge: Cambridge University Press, 2018), 104.
[2] Tolga Esmer, 'Economies of Violence, Banditry and Governance in the Ottoman Empire around 1800', *Past & Present* 224(1) (2014): 174.

for our purposes, Tolga Esmer notes that the bandits at the centre of his study of Ottoman Balkan violence in this earlier period 'exhibited behaviour that is generally associated with twentieth-century paramilitary groups', including widespread networks that turned around multiple loyalties, 'intimate yet clandestine ties with high-ranking state officials', the use of violence and coercion to 'discipline' populations in parallel with the state's own processes of governing, and the use of 'state-sanctioned terror to intimidate specific confessional and ethnic groups'.[3] The same violent measures found in the late eighteenth- and early nineteenth-century provinces, such as kidnapping, ransom, intimidation, pillaging, extortion and extra-judicial killing, would persist well into the twentieth century, as the exploits of some of the individuals considered in this chapter will show. So, also, would the late Ottoman state at times display a distinctly ambivalent attitude towards this violent behaviour. Despite its drive to modernise, the Ottoman state continued to rely on the services of mobile populations, including bandits, usually associated with its pre-modern governing and martial modes, well into its final decades.[4]

By the late nineteenth century, ethnic tensions had become inflamed, fanned by the upsurge in nationalism and frequently encouraged by foreign powers. The situation became especially complicated from the 1890s onwards due to the founding of several societies devoted to clandestine, revolutionary aims among both the Muslim and non-Muslim populations of the empire. The main such 'komite' structures were that of the Armenian Hunchak (founded in 1887) and Dashnaksutyun (1890) organisations, the majoritarian Committee of Union and Progress (1889), and both the Internal and External Macedonian Revolutionary Organisations (1893 and 1895, respectively).[5] The Ottoman government of Sultan Abdülhamid II (r. 1876–

---

[3] Ibid., n. 24. See also his reference to bandits and the *Teşkilat-ı Mahsusa* and the *Kuva-yı Milliye*, 199.

[4] Reşat Kasaba, *A Moveable Empire: Ottoman Nomads, Migrants, and Refugees* (Seattle: University of Washington Press, 2009).

[5] Ramazan Hakkı Öztan, 'Tools of Revolution: Global Military Surplus, Arms Dealers and Smugglers in the Late Ottoman Balkans, 1878–1908', *Past & Present* 237(1) (2017): 167–8. The term '*çete*', meaning 'gang' or 'crew', was frequently used by the Ottoman *fedai*s themselves.

1909) was thus increasingly drawn into unwanted violent confrontations that disturbed its preference for avoiding flashpoints that would further complicate its relations with both the various constituent demographic groups inside the empire and the Great Powers who frequently used any such episodes as pretexts to interfere. Abdülhamid II soon nevertheless became a byword for violence, especially in the West where he was known in anti-Turkish propaganda as the 'Red Sultan' due to the violence perpetrated against Armenians during his reign, especially in the 1890s. Given the sultan's reluctance to avoid armed conflict, the emergence of the appellation is somewhat ironic. The Hamidian reign's main approach to its domestic adversaries, at least among the elite or proto-elite, was to send them into exile, either internal or external. As a result, those individuals who crossed the sultan ended up in relatively pleasant places, such as Rhodes, Bursa or Paris. The noted exception to this pattern of relatively benign, even paternalistic, punishment is the case of the key Ottoman reformer Midhat Paşa, who died in highly suspicious circumstances while imprisoned in Arabia.[6]

After the Young Turk revolutionaries ousted Sultan Abdülhamid II and exacted revenge by sending him into exile in Salonica, the tenor of Ottoman politics changed abruptly; a sudden sharp escalation in political violence ensued. The Young Turks were in a hurry to effect a style of politics that would be purposeful and direct, shedding the studied, cautious style of their predecessor. They were young men in a hurry who reflected the frustrations of what they considered the old way of doing things. There is a deep irony in the fact that while in opposition the Young Turks had carried out a sustained criticism of Abdülhamid's regime as one of violence and decay, their path to power via the revolution of 1908 and subsequent rule saw a rapid acceleration in violent conduct, both internally and externally, that ended with the empire's collapse after the First World War. In retrospect, they made the previous era of Ottoman politics seem relatively mild, an era of careful equivocation, playing for time, and avoiding extreme reactions whenever possible. By the crudest of measures, namely, the body count, the Young Turks rapidly

---

[6] For the most recent and most thorough account of Midhat Paşa's trial and subsequent death, see Avi Rubin, *Ottoman Rule of Law and the Modern Political Trial: The Yıldız Case* (Syracuse, NY: Syracuse University Press, 2018).

outdid their predecessor's long reign in a very short time. Their approach to politics, both international and domestic, had been forged in Macedonia. It was both the fierce fighting against the separatist nationalist '*komitacıs*' and the deeply resented irritant of Great Power intervention that spurred the activist officers to join the opposition Unionist movement before 1908.[7]

After the revolution of 1908 brought them to power, the change they represented was immediately – and disastrously – apparent. In the first few years of Unionist control, the empire lurched into a series of conflicts that were increasingly large in scale and destabilising in effect. Although in the first two conflicts the Ottomans came under unprovoked attack, the Unionist government was up for the fight. First, in 1911 against the Italian invasion of the Ottoman province of Tripoli in Libya (Trablusgarb), then in the two vicious Balkan Wars (1912–13), and finally with the First World War (1914–18), the Ottomans staggered from one conflict to another, each time finding themselves in a position for which the empire's armed forces were severely underprepared. Within a decade of the Young Turks' seizure of power, the empire had all but ceased to exist. A violent end, effected by the Ottoman's entering the First World War on what turned out to be the losing side, was the outcome of a style of politics and an approach to imperial problems that relied increasingly on physical violence, intimidation and assassination.

This study explores the men of violence who made possible this rapid turn of events in late Ottoman history. These men formed a group that was used by their more senior colleagues as a kind of human lever to influence the course of imperial politics. They were deployed to embody the notion that, 'Violence is primarily a resource rather than the final product; it is intended to shape the behaviour of a targeted audience by altering the expected value of particular actions.'[8] Wittingly or not, they were used to enforce the programme of a certain faction of military officers over whoever

---

[7] Erik Jan Zürcher, 'Macedonians in Anatolia: The Importance of the Macedonian Roots of the Unionists for their Policies in Anatolia after 1914', *Middle Eastern Studies* 50(6) (2014): 962–3.
[8] Stathis N. Kalyvas, *The Logic of Violence in Civil War* (Cambridge: Cambridge University Press, 2006), 100.

stood in their way, whether civilian politicians or other military men. Using force or often simply the threat of violence, they were actors in a larger political game. By looking at those individuals who operated at the sharp end of the late Ottoman era, in particular the middle-level operatives of the political organisation called the Committee of Union and Progress (CUP), this chapter aims to identify the patterns by which these men, both individually and collectively, came to leave such a dramatic mark on the history of empire and its people. The men under consideration here are thus the men who served directly under the more prominent Unionist figures, drawing inspiration from them but clearly subordinate to them.[9] The aim here is to complement, however modestly, the path-breaking work of Erik Zürcher and Şükrü Hanioğlu in identifying and analysing the senior Unionist figures, their *modus operandi* and their worldview.[10]

Selection

Identifying the individuals to include in this study was not a straightforward task. The solution I chose here is one that incorporates the actors' own self-selection, reflecting one participant's view of the men who volunteered to form the inner core of a larger group of 'self-sacrificing officers' (*fedaî zabitan*),[11] and

---

[9] On the distinction between the two levels of Unionist organisation, namely, the popular organisers at the local level and that of the higher officers, see Nader Sohrabi, 'Illiberal Constitutionalism: The Committee of Union and Progress as Clandestine Network and the Purges', in François Georgeon (ed.), *'L'ivresse de la liberté': La Révolution de 1908 dans l'Empire Ottoman* (Paris: Peeters, 2012), 110–11.

[10] Erik Jan Zürcher, *The Unionist Factor: The Rôle of the Committee of Union and Progress in the Turkish National Movement* (Leiden: Brill, 1984); Erik Jan Zürcher, 'Who Were the Young Turks?' in *The Young Turk Legacy and Nation Building: From the Ottoman Empire to the Atatürk's Turkey* (London: I. B. Tauris, 2010), 95–109; Erik Jan Zürcher, 'The Balkan Wars and the Refugee Leadership of the Early Turkish Republic', in M. Hakan Yavuz and Isa Blumi (eds), *War and Nationalism: The Balkan Wars, 1912–1913, and their Sociopolitical Implications* (Salt Lake City: University of Utah Press, 2014), 665–78. See also M. Şükrü Hanioğlu, *The Young Turks in Opposition* (New York: Oxford University Press, 1995); M. Şükrü Hanioğlu, *Preparation for a Revolution: The Young Turks, 1902–1908* (New York: Oxford University Press, 2000).

[11] The term stems from the officers who volunteered to fight under Enver against the Italians in Tripolitania. Stanford J. Shaw, *The Ottoman Empire in World War I* (Ankara: Türk Tarih Kurumu, 2008), 1746. The term '*fedaî*' was not a common or popular appellation but rather reflected the fact that the men so named had all formally enlisted as *fedaî*s prior to

then expanding their number slightly so as to include those who became separated from the group by later developments. Specifically, I begin with the self-anointed group drawn up by one of these individuals, namely, Kuşçubaşı Eşref, who named as its inner core the 'ten promised paradise' (*aşere-i mübeşşere*), a term drawn from early Islamic history to denote those early Muslims who fought alongside the Prophet Muhammad at the Battle of Badr in 624 CE, a crucial early test for the young community of believers. These ten were promised paradise by the Prophet, to whom the members were personally loyal.[12] The term is admittedly problematic in the late Ottoman context in the sense that apart from Eşref's own writings and a few sources that derive from them, it is not widely attested in the sources from this period.[13] Yet it neatly captures the self-sacralisation and self-valorisation of the men with whom we are concerned here. Linking the late Ottoman activist officers with the earliest Muslim protagonists (and doing so in ranked fashion), the term conveys both the sense of camaraderie and competitiveness that was typical of the group. It clearly carries the sense of self-importance that underpinned their bravado and, at times, their excess. It also echoes the term used by the Unionists to sacralise their organisation: *cemiyet-i mukaddes* (the holy committee).[14]

More important than the term itself is the fact that its membership matches closely that of a group described by Şevket Süreyya Aydemir in his three-volume biography of Enver. Aydemir, also the biographer of Mustafa Kemal Atatürk and İsmet İnönü as well as the author of an atmospheric memoir of this period, refers to the members of the group photographed together in the period after the Revolution of 1908, as the '*ünlü silâhsörlar*',

---

the 1908 Revolution. Afterwards they were those who volunteered for the most dangerous assignments, including assassinations.

[12] M. Naim Turfan, *Rise of the Young Turks: Politics, the Military and Ottoman Collapse* (London: I. B. Tauris, 2000), 346ff.; Benjamin C. Fortna, *The Circassian: A Life of Eşref Bey, Late Ottoman Insurgent and Special Agent* (London and New York: Hurst and Oxford University Press, 2016), 19.

[13] For example, Mustafa Kemal's longtime friend Ali Fethi (Okyar) (1880–1943) uses the term '*aşere-i mübeşşere*' in his memoir, but this work was edited by Cemal Kutay who was Kuşçubaşı Eşref's literary executor and had access to his memoirs before they were apparently destroyed by a fire in Kutay's house. Fethi Okyar, *Üç Devirde Bir Adam*, ed. Cemal Kutay (Istanbul: Tercüman, 1980), 201.

[14] I thank the editors for highlighting these parallels.

which could be translated as 'famous men-at-arms', or perhaps more apposite here, 'famous gunslingers'.[15] The composition of Aydemir's group differs from Eşref's in that it names only eight gunmen who follow after the mention of two other well-known figures, the poet, orator, Unionist propagandist, and Special Organization member Ömer Naci and the writer, poet, and Unionist official Mehmed Emin (Yurdakul). Of these eight, six are common to both groups. One of the exceptions, Yenibahçeli Şükrü, is one we will include in our study. The other, a certain Erzurumlu Dadaş Salim, is one about whom I could find no further information. Another difference between the groups is that Eşref lists himself and his brother Sami as the first and second members, while Aydemir places them last. Otherwise, Aydemir largely corroborates Eşref's choices for the men who formed the core of this group of men of violence.

We do not know the timing or context that shaped the forming of Eşref's list, but we can suspect that it was drawn up or possibly re-imagined considerably after the break-up of the empire. It is therefore not surprising that it contains few whose ethnic origins were not Turkish or Circassian. The prominence of Circassians among the group – easily over half of its number – is one of its most notable features and speaks to their strong representation in the growing ranks of the late Ottoman paramilitary forces, the result of their arrival in Ottoman lands as refugees from Russian expansion in the Caucasus in the late nineteenth century.[16] The lack of Arab participants is the most glaring omission, one doubtless explained by the defection of several Arab members of the *fedaî zabitan* in the wake of the 'Arab Revolt', Cemal Paşa's wartime policies in Syria, and the emergence of separate Arab polities after the First World War. But we know that several Ottoman officers of Arab

---

[15] Şevket Süreyya Aydemir, *Makedonya'dan Orta Asya'ya Enver Paşa* (Istanbul: Remzi, 1970) vol. 2, 118–19. He also describes them as 'young, mobile, daredevils, powerful, handsome men'.

[16] The prominence of the Circassians in the paramilitary forces of the late Ottoman Empire has been frequently noted. In particular, see Ryan Gingeras, *Sorrowful Shores: Violence, Ethnicity, and the End of the Ottoman Empire, 1912–1923* (New York: Oxford University Press, 2009). On the longer arc of the Circassians in the empire and the Turkish Republic, see Zeynel Abidin Besleney, *The Circassian Diaspora in Turkey: A Political History* (London: Routledge, 2014) and Caner Yelbaşı, *The Circassians of Turkey: War, Violence and Nationalism from the Ottomans to Atatürk* (London: I. B. Tauris, 2019).

origin had originally formed part of this group. A number of Arab officers fought in the Ottoman–Italian War over Tripolitania in 1911–1912 and others fought in the Balkan Wars in the following years. The reduction from the collective of 'Ottoman Muslims', a term that included Turks, Arabs, Kurds, Albanians, Circassians and so on, to a number of supposedly primordial, distinct ethno-nationalities is one of the more insidious but frequently accepted historiographical problems of the post-Ottoman era. So, I have adopted a form of self-selection for this group and then adapted it to include a few others from the same orbit in order to allow for a broader intake, especially where ethnicity is concerned. A particular issue to take into consideration in this piece of history that was so marked by the break-up of the multi-ethnic Ottoman Empire into a number of nationally defined successor states is that of subsequent splits and the divergence of political or national affiliation. Remembered afterwards, the grouping of activists tends to appear rather more coherently homogeneous in ethno-national terms than as actually occurred during the historical period in question. In order to correct for the subsequent tendency to focus on the late Ottoman era as a pre-history for the national eras that followed, I have included a few representatives not named by the participants themselves, presumably due to the parting of the ways that occurred during wartime. The most significant group here is that of the Arab members of the CUP, most of whom defected to join the 'Arab Revolt' during the war. In addition, it was also not uncommon for actors in this period to be retrospectively characterised as belonging to different ethno-political groups as political affiliations shifted and international borders were redrawn.

An illustrative case is that of the Circassian–Ottoman military officer named 'Aziz 'Ali 'al-Misri' ('the Egyptian') (1879–1959), or Aziz Ali Bey, as he was more simply known in an Ottoman context. Descendant of immigrants to the Ottoman Empire from the Caucasus of the Ubih (Ubykh/Vubıh) ethnic group, 'Aziz 'Ali was born in Egypt, home to a large number of Circassian *émigrés*. He was educated at the Imperial War College (*Mekteb-i Harbiye-i Şahane*, or *Harbiye* for short) in Istanbul, graduating at the top of his class and therefore selected for the General Staff. Like many of the young officers of his generation, 'Aziz 'Ali was assigned to late Ottoman flashpoints such as Macedonia and Yemen, before serving in the Tripolitanian and Balkan wars. During the early years of the First World War, he seems to have transferred his primary political allegiance from that of the Ottoman state to the nascent Arab independence movement and thus attracted the suspicions of the military leadership. He was arrested, tried and sentenced to death by the imperial authorities, but saw his sentence commuted on the condition that he leave the empire. He returned to Egypt and joined the 'Arab Revolt' against the Ottoman army in Arabia, ending up on the opposite side of many of his former classmates and colleagues. Subsequently, he is referred to as an 'Arab nationalist exemplar'.[17] Yet for 'Aziz 'Ali and a not a few others who served the empire in its final decades, the boundaries between Circassian, Ottoman and Arab must have been remarkably fluid. As a result, subsequent writers have claimed individuals like 'Aziz 'Ali for different sides and for correspondingly different doses of historical treatment. Ultimately, assigning a primary designation such as 'Ottoman', 'Circassian' or 'Arab' to an individual like 'Aziz 'Ali reveals more about a particular historian's focus than it explains about the man himself, reflecting a problem that hovers over the history of this period which is so steeped in nationalist projection.[18]

Another, more basic problem confronting this study is one of evidence, reflecting the varying amount of information available concerning the individuals selected. Almost by definition, an inquiry into men of violence turns up widely different individual life trajectories that make a consistent ground for comparison difficult and sometimes even impossible. For example, as might be expected from such a martial group, several of the men under study here met an early death. As we shall see, two died during the First World War, one executed by the CUP government for planning a *coup d'état*, and another who took his own life after being wounded in a failed attempt to stop the advance of

---

[17] Michael Provence, *The Last Ottoman Generation and the Making of the Modern Middle East* (Cambridge: Cambridge University Press, 2017), 33.

[18] Some works highlight 'Aziz 'Ali's 'Arabness', often omitting his Circassian origins entirely, while others foreground his Circassian identity, for example, by providing his Circassian family name (Şaplı, in 'Aziz 'Ali's case) and sub-Circassian ethno-linguistic identification (Ubıh). A further symptom of the problem inherent in such an individual's multiple identities: those focusing on his Arab identity naturally tend to transliterate his name with Arabic diacritical marks, thus 'Aziz 'Ali. And, of course, the label 'al-Misri' (the Egyptian), indicating the land of his birth, seems to have been used throughout his career and afterwards as a way of cementing his serendipitous 'Arab' *bona fides*.

the British army in Mesopotamia. Another was killed in an apparent attempt to infiltrate the Turkish Republic in order to assassinate Mustafa Kemal (later Atatürk) in 1927. Others were put to death as a result of the 'Independence Tribunals', a series of Soviet-style show trials intended to weed out men not sufficiently loyal to the young Turkish Republic and its leader Mustafa Kemal. Some stayed out of the public eye while others became relatively well known. Quite apart from the issue of the widely variant life trajectories of the individuals under discussion here is the equally important question of the extent to which their different *vitae* are supported by documentation. For some of them we have sheaves of material and in some cases even autobiographies, while for others we are left with little in the way of accessible information, sometimes even basic facts.[19] Nevertheless, working with the material we have, we can discern the broad lines of both the shared and the divergent aspects of their lives.

Below is the list of the activist officers under scrutiny here, indicating their names,[20] their birth and death dates, and their ethnicity:[21]

Kuşçubaşı Eşref (Sencer)	(1883–1964)	Circassian
Kuşçubaşı Selim 'Hacı' Sami	(1885–1927)	Circassian
Süleyman Askerî	(1884–1915)	Circassian(?)[22]
Yakup Cemil	(1883–1916)	Circassian
Sapancalı Hakkı	(1882–1937)	Circassian[23]

---

[19] On the problem of sources for the Unionist officers, see Zürcher, 'Who Were the Young Turks?', 96–7, 102, where he specifically mentions the lower-ranking officers, the *fedaîs*, as particularly problematic in terms of sources. Ironically, the two surviving memoirs written by members of this group, Jafar al-Askari's, *A Soldier's Story: From Ottoman Rule to Independent Iraq. The Memoirs of Jafar Pasha Al-Askari* (London: Arabian Publishing, 2003) and *Yenibahçeli Şükrü Bey'in Hatıraları* (Konya: Çizgi Kitabevi, 2009), offer very little information about the early periods of their lives.

[20] Names in parentheses indicate the surnames adopted in Turkey after the promulgation of the Surname Law (*soyadı kanunu*) of 1934.

[21] Since officials of the Ottoman Empire did not generally record the ethnicity of its subjects, information about ethnic origins should be considered with caution. I include it here to suggest both the diversity of the group under consideration and the complexity of the question of ethnicity in this period.

[22] Gingeras, *Sorrowful Shores*, 58, 180, identifies him as a Circassian, as do Eşref's descendants, but he is not listed in Sefer E. Berzeg's compendium of Circassian biographies and the one book-length study of his life makes no mention of his ethnicity.

[23] Sefer E. Berzeg, *Çerkes-Vubıhlar: Soçi'nin İnsanları* (Ankara: Kurban, 2013), identifies him

Çanakkaleli Atıf (Kamçıl)	(1880–1947)	Turk
Abdulkadir Antepli	(1881–1926)	Turk
Topçu Mehmed İhsan (Eryavuz)	(1877–1947)	Turk
Filibeli Hilmi[24]	(1885–1926)	Turk
İzmitli Mümtaz	(188–1936)	Circassian
Ja'far al-'Askari	(1885–1936)	Arab[25]
'Aziz 'Ali 'al-Misri'	(1879–1959)	Circassian
Yenibahçeli Mehmed Şükrü (Oğuz)	(1881–1953)	Circassian

With two exceptions, they were all born in the early-mid 1880s and thus formed a generational group in the Mannheimian sense that they experienced roughly the same historical events together. As a chronologically defined cohort, they were for the most part a few years younger than such key figures as Ahmed Cemal (1872–1922), Ahmed Niyazi (1873–1913), Mehmed Talât (1874–1921), Eyüp Sabri (1876–1950) and İsmail Enver (1881–1922) who were the most prominent members of the CUP. That even very basic biographical information is lacking for a few of them reflects the fact that for the most part they were figures who worked outside the public eye for the period under examination here, an issue to be discussed below in more detail. Nevertheless, as a more or less cohesive unit with a strong sense of self-identification as 'self-sacrificing officers', they together played an important if somewhat overlooked role in the Young Turk era.

To the extent that this group of individualistic, combative men exhibited a shared cohesiveness beyond their shared Turkish and Circassian roots and

---

as Circassian (*Ubıh*), but Seydi Vakkas Toprak, 'Teşkilat-ı Mahsusa Komitacılığından İzmit Mebusluğuna: Sapancalı Hakkı Bey', available at: http://www.kocaelitarihisempozyumu.com/bildiriler4/60.pdf, last accessed 26 August 2019, (p. 1135), states that he came from a Turcoman family from the Aleppo region.

[24] Not to be confused with writer Şehbenderzâde Ahmed Hilmi (1865–1914), also from Filibe (Plovdiv), who was a critic of the CUP.

[25] The future Iraqi prime minister is generally considered to have been an 'Arab' officer and politician, but his family was from a Kurdish region in what later became northern Iraq. While most classify him as an ethnic Arab, others have noted his Kurdish background. On the problems of identifying the ethnic origins of late Ottoman officers, see Mesut Uyar, 'Ottoman Arab Officers between Nationalism and Loyalty during the First World War', *War in History* 20(4) (2013): 530.

experience as military school students, it was to be found in their loyalty to its central figure and leader, İsmail Enver, later Enver Paşa. Even though Enver was not much older, with one or two exceptions the men in this group revered him as a leader – for many he was *the* leader – to whom they were passionately committed. Enver's role *vis-à-vis* the men who served under him was at once both personal and structural. His character and charisma played a vital role in bringing these men into his orbit and forming them into a force that was uniquely loyal to him. There was something about him that seems to have produced strong bonds of affection, even devotion verging on hero-worship. While we lack detailed information about how Enver attracted these men into his circle in most cases, the materials preserved by Kuşçubaşı Eşref suggest a few points to consider. First, although the details are sketchy, it seems clear that Eşref had begun working for Enver in the Balkans as early January 1908, that is, importantly, before the revolution that brought the CUP to power. Eşref is identified in an internal Ottoman document as a gendarmerie lieutenant who had uncovered a cache of important papers while conducting a house search in Kosovo under Enver's orders.[26] Subsequently Eşref seems to have worked as a Unionist organiser in the Izmir area. Eşref and Enver then came into repeated contact in the Tripolitanian War against the Italians. There Eşref worked under Enver to handle relations with the tribal forces with whom the Ottomans were allied in the fight to repel the Italian invasion. With time Eşref appears to have become a trusted operative, available for a variety of assignments, particularly in liaising with the local tribes. Second, Enver's personal touch seems to have played a role in cementing the relationship. Eşref describes a number of one-on-one meetings with Enver, some in the thick of operational decision-making, others more relaxed. A note from Enver to Eşref, written on the back of Enver's *carte visite*, probably when Eşref had returned to Istanbul from one of his missions to Arabia, reveals Enver's direct, unpretentious style: 'Eşref, Welcome back. We're thankful for your services. Come to dinner and let's talk openly. [signed] Enver.'[27] Eşref would later praise Enver's generosity, fidelity and valour, as well as his

---

[26] Fortna, *The Circassian*, 42.
[27] I thank Dr Philip Stoddard for sharing this source, which he obtained from Eşref in the early 1960s.

unpretentiousness.[28] By contrast, the two cases in which the relationship with Enver ruptured, namely, 'Aziz 'Ali's and Yakup Cemil's high-profile breaks with Enver and with the Unionists, are exceptions that prove the importance of the personal links in this highly volatile mix of personalities.

Complementing such personal relations and 'man-management' in creating the constellation of 'self-sacrificing officers' around Enver was undoubtedly the structure and authority supplied by his positions with the CUP and the Ottoman military. As a key Unionist figure who had established his *bona fides* in the revolution of 1908 and as a rapidly rising star in the Ottoman military, Enver used his positions to create his network of followers. As he advanced through the ranks, Enver was increasingly well placed to recruit lower-ranking officers. In turn, these acolytes were often tasked with carrying out their own recruitment of fighting men, expanding the pyramid of personal connections downward and outward. In doing so, Enver and his subordinates were effectively bolstering the Enverist faction within the CUP and the Ottoman government. As Talha Çiçek has recently shown, despite their name, the Unionists were riven by factions that were ultimately linked to the dominant individuals. The CUP was less of a unified triumvirate than a competing combination of cliques.[29] As we will see, Enver's activist officer faction increased their leverage *vis-à-vis* both those opposing the CUP in general and their internal Unionist rivals, most notably the factions dedicated to Talât and Cemal paşas, by pursuing a politics of *fait accompli*, almost always effected through violence or the threat of violence. Such tactics resulted in Enver forcing through his appointment as minister of war at the beginning of 1914.

It is precisely this interplay between Enver's personal connections and

---

[28] Another aspect of Enver's persona which may have attracted some of the *fedaîs* and distinguished him from the other leading Unionists was his apparent religiosity. Eşref lists Enver's avoidance of alcohol, card-playing and womanising among his many virtues, and recounted that he never abandoned the practice of praying five times a day or carrying Qur'anic verses in his field jacket. EK Papers. Resim 006. Likewise, Enver's engagement and subsequent marriage to the Ottoman princess Naciye Sultan would have played well to those who were loyal to the Ottoman dynasty.

[29] Talha Çiçek, 'Myth of the Unionist Triumvirate: The Formation of the CUP Factions and Their Impact in Syria during the Great War', in Talha Çiçek (ed.), *Syria in World War I: Politics, Economy, and Society* (New York: Routledge, 2016), 9–10.

official capacities that seem to have been responsible for the extraordinary attachments he built around him, attachments that allowed him to carry out an extremely aggressive style of politics. Crucially, the structural and personal dimensions of the relationship were mutually reinforcing. Enver could draw on the individually inspired devotion of these men of action as the spring that propelled his drive to power.

Education

The men whose lives are explored here came from across the breadth of the Ottoman lands. Their geographical origins range from Prizren (Kosovo) in the west to Baghdad in the east. Most were born in Istanbul and its environs. Two were born in Eastern Anatolia and one in Cairo. In ethnic terms, the clear majority (seven or eight out of thirteen) were from families of Circassian background, four or five were Turks, and one was an Arab. All were Muslims and all attended the educational institutions of the late Ottoman Empire. These schools, some civil but mostly military, were relatively recent innovations that emerged across the empire's provinces during the latter decades of the nineteenth century as the state's expansion demanded greater numbers of graduates to fill its burgeoning personnel needs. The students of the new schools thus embodied a newly institutionalised version of older patterns of recruitment and training that featured in earlier periods of the empire's history. They provided avenues for both social mobility and regional and ethno-regional mixing that was unprecedented in Ottoman history. What was perhaps unexpected for Ottoman educationalists was that some of the older patterns of allegiance, such as common regional or ethnic background, would persist in the modern-style schools.

Almost all of these individuals began their education in Qur'anic primary schools before continuing on to the new state offerings, whether civil or military, and then going on to continue their education in military schools. The normal pattern for becoming a school-trained (*mektepli*) officer was to attend a middle or advanced-primary military school (*askeri rüşdiye*) before continuing on to a military preparatory school (*askeri idadî*) in a provincial capital before entry to the Imperial Military Academy (*Harbiye*) in Istanbul.[30]

---

[30] Uyar, 'Ottoman Arab Officers', 529.

The top 5–10 per cent of these cadets were selected for additional training to become officers of the General Staff. While this was the expected career path for an Ottoman officer, we have remarkably little information about how these individuals or perhaps their families made the choices necessary to navigate such a system.[31] Some made remarkable efforts to advance their education. Ja'far al-'Askari travelled for forty-four days to reach Aleppo en route to Istanbul, which he eventually reached by ship, to study at *Harbiye*.[32] Others had to overcome obstacles closer to home. A well-known incident in the life story of a key colleague of the men in this group, namely, Mustafa Kemal, later Atatürk, reveals that such choices were often fraught with difficulty and involved strongly held family views. Growing up in Salonica, so the story goes, young Mustafa had admired the sharp uniforms worn by the students at the local military academy and was determined to join them. However, he was aware that his mother was against her only son joining the military and thus secretly took the entrance examination, presenting her with a *fait accompli* once he had been admitted.[33] Unlike Atatürk, whose life has to be the most well-researched, if not always well-attested, of all historical actors in this period, key turning points in the lives of the officers under consideration here remain far more obscure.

However their life decisions were made and wherever their education began, most of the men under consideration here attended *Harbiye*, as it was more commonly known, the empire's elite military institution in Istanbul. Some, like 'Aziz 'Ali, finished at or near the top of their graduating class, while others, such as Kuşçubaşı Eşref, did not graduate at all. Two names on the list, Süleyman Askerî and 'Aziz 'Ali, were selected for the Ottoman General Staff (*Erkân-ı Harbiye*), which required a further three years of training. But none of these men reached the highest military ranks; they were mostly middle-ranking officers, many of whom appear to have

---

[31] On the question of educational trajectories in this period, see Benjamin C. Fortna, 'Education and Autobiography at the End of the Ottoman Empire', *Die Welt des Islams* 41(1) (2001): 1–31.

[32] Provence, *The Last Ottoman Generation*, 43.

[33] Andrew Mango, *Atatürk* (London: John Murray, 1999), 34. It is important to note that this story derives from anecdotes that Atatürk told only later in life; there is little independent evidence for his early years.

benefited from being outside the established command structure of the Ottoman military, often relying on 'pull' when they collided with the chain of command. Most of the men, therefore, were not household names in their period of activity. There were, however, a few exceptions. 'Aziz 'Ali Bey was well known and became even more newsworthy when he was arrested as part of a purge of Arab officers suspected of disloyalty. 'Aziz 'Ali was ostensibly on trial for malfeasance during the war with Italy, but this was probably the result of his falling out with Enver and suspicions that he had engaged in Arab anti-Ottoman political intrigues with acquaintances in Egypt and Iraq.[34] In any event, he was correctly suspected of a leading role in organising an Arab separatist movement and for entering into discussions with the British in the early years of the First World War; he had founded a secret organisation for Arab officers called Al-'Ahd (The Covenant) in Istanbul in 1913.[35] Court-martialled and tried, 'Aziz 'Ali was condemned to death but eventually acquitted on the condition that he leave the empire. The case became sufficiently discussed that popular opinion apparently played a role in his acquittal, much to the frustration of Enver, as did the intervention of the British Ambassador Louis Mallet.[36]

The common career path was overwhelmingly a military one. All the men considered here obtained at least some military education and became officers of one rank or another. A comparison with the career path of the key Unionist Mehmed Talât is instructive for identifying the key attributes of the self-sacrificing officers. Thanks to Hans-Lukas Kieser's recent biography, we now have considerable information to consider Talât's path to power alongside those of the cohort considered here. Talât was born in 1874 to a

---

[34] Feroz Ahmad, *The Young Turks and the Ottoman Nationalities: Armenians, Greeks, Albanians, Jews, and Arabs, 1908–1918* (Salt Lake City: Utah University Press, 2014), 124.

[35] Hasan Kayalı, *Arabs and Young Turks: Ottomanism, Arabism, and Islamism in the Ottoman Empire, 1908–1918* (Berkeley: University of California Press, 1997), 178.

[36] Murat R. Şiviloğlu, *The Emergence of Public Opinion; State and Society in the Late Ottoman Empire* (Cambridge: Cambridge University Press, 2018), 2–3; G. P. Gooch and Harold Temperley (eds), *The Last Years of Peace, vol. 10, Pt II: British Documents on the Origins of the War, 1898–1914*, with the assistance of Lillian M. Penson, PhD (London: His Majesty's Stationery Office, 1938), 824–38, available at: https://wwi.lib.byu.edu/index.php/British_Imperial_Connexions_to_the_Arab_National_Movement, last accessed 28 August 2019.

middle-class family in Edirne. His father died when he was eleven years old, leaving Talât as the family's only male. Talât attended the military *rüşdiye* in Edirne but, like a number of the future self-sacrificing officers, was expelled for an act of violence, in his case for assaulting a teacher-officer. Here his path diverged from that of the self-sacrificing officers. He subsequently worked for the post office, and taught Turkish in one of the schools run by the Alliance Universelle Israélite, the progressive Jewish organisation.[37] When freed after being arrested as part of the opposition to Sultan Abdülhamid II, he was exiled to Salonica where he resumed working for the postal service, eventually being promoted to head clerk. Thus, while he fits much of the pattern that produced the self-sacrificing officers, the path he took towards a civil and not a military career stands out as the crucial difference. Talât was not therefore one of those men, to use the words of Çerkes Edhem, another important *fedaî*, 'who could live with weapons in their hands'.[38]

Perhaps expectedly, some of the men in this group became known for their quarrelsome behaviour. Their involvement in various violent incidents led to fights, disciplinary cases and school expulsions, a pattern that followed them in subsequent assignments. Several of the men here were involved in some of the most notorious acts of violence associated with the Unionists and their coming to power in 1908 and the returning to power in 1913. Çanakkaleli Atıf assassinated Şemsi Paşa, the Ottoman general sent to Manastır (today's Bitola) in the summer of 1908 to suppress the nascent rebellion of Unionist officers. Five years later, Yakup Cemil assassinated Hüseyin Nâzım Paşa, the minister of war, as part of the 'Raid on the Sublime Porte', the *coup d'état* of January 1913 that brought the CUP back to power. That such violence could be contemplated against the group itself is demonstrated a few years later; Yakup Cemil was hanged in 1916 for plotting a *coup d'état* against the wartime CUP government. Also arrested in the subsequent investigation was Sapancalı Hakkı. Using violence against the group's own members was a perhaps a logical outcome of a system that, despite its military rigour, gave a remarkable degree of leeway to unpredictable behaviour. Acts of violence,

---

[37] Hans-Lukas Kieser, *Talaat Pasha: Father of Modern Turkey, Architect of Genocide* (Princeton, NJ: Princeton University Press, 2018), 41–2.
[38] Gingeras, *Sorrowful Shores*, 63.

insubordination and, indeed, criminal activity earlier in these men's careers had frequently been forgiven, with subsequent rehabilitation justified by the incessant military demands of the Unionists' foreign policy. As Eşref said when discussing his early career during the Hamidian era, one filled with a long list of extra-legal conduct both as a student and as an officer, 'There was always "one last pardon".'[39] The Unionist era was far less forgiving unless, like Eşref and other *fedaî*s, one could rely on personal connections at the very top of the 'Young Turk' hierarchy.

That was fortunate because collectively these men had much to be excused. To take only a few examples, İzmitli Mümtaz had apparently killed a fellow officer in Salonica in 1904, been sentenced to prison in Jaffa, escaped and was on the lam until an amnesty was proclaimed after the 1908 Revolution;[40] Eşref was known to have engaged in a long list of violent incidents which, by his own telling, lasted until he was an old man living a civilian life; Yakup Cemil, perhaps the wildest of the bunch, apparently once killed a black (*zenci*) officer named Bandırmalı Şükrü at Tobruk in North Africa because he suspected him of being a spy.[41] In 1916, Yakup Cemil attempted to carry out his own *coup d'état* against the wartime Unionist government but was apprehended and executed.

Indeed, there was a degree of restlessness, perhaps even what we would today refer to as 'hyperactivity', that was a common feature in the lives of many of these men. In a sense, they might be considered to have personified the antithesis of what the modernising Ottoman administration had expected its schools and military institutions to produce. The diagrams of the educational reformers of the late Ottoman era were predicated upon a steady flow of obedient, pliable students who would pass seamlessly from one level of schooling to the next, absorbing the lessons of the curricula and the textbooks on which they depended. They were to have internalised the lessons of quietism, respect for authority, obedience and so on. Doubtless such was the result for many, perhaps even the majority, of the students who peopled the new schools and advanced into the ranks of the bureaucracy. But the men con-

---

[39] Fortna, *The Circassian*, 36.
[40] Berzeg, *Çerkes-Vubıhlar*, 402.
[41] EK Papers, EK2 Scans 36–7.

sidered here represented something altogether different. Instead of respecting authority, they seemed to relish almost any opportunity to challenge and, if possible, thwart it. Incidents involving school fights, insubordination and expulsion figured fairly often in their *vitae*. As a result, they represented a very different profile from the more public Unionist officials under whom they served. The latter could appear more statesmanlike while delegating some of the more unseemly and often violent tasks to the *fedaî*s, which preserved for them the possibility of plausible deniability.

And yet such seemingly disruptive events could also be creative or constructive in the sense that they could be formative for the interpersonal connections between and among the men considered here. While we know instinctively that friendships and personal alliances are crucial to the creation and functioning of any group, such relationships are the most difficult to uncover and assess. Occasionally, we can catch glimpses of the ways in which such relationships were formed. For example, Kuşçubaşı Eşref appears to have formed lasting friendships with both Süleyman Askerî and Yenibahçeli Şükrü while he was a student at the military preparatory school in Edirne.[42] But Eşref was only in Edirne in the first place because he had been expelled from the Kuleli military academy in Istanbul due to his role in a fight among two factions of cadets that seem to have formed along ethnic lines.[43] Clearly, an element of unpredictability or serendipity played a role in the formation of attachments of the group, even if most of these connections remain impossible to discern due to the limited nature of the sources available.

Warfare

After the friendships created during their school years, it was serving together in combat or other missions that forged or further cemented most of the personal relationships among this group of military men. For them, it was usually postings to the Balkan provinces that provided the first combat opportunity. The late Ottoman military was trying to combat a series of ostensibly irredentist insurrections – that of the Internal Macedonian Revolutionary

---

[42] Nurettin Şimşek, *Teşkilat-ı Mahsusa'nın Reisi Süleyman Askerî Bey: Hayatı, Siyasi ve Askeri Faaliyetleri* (Istanbul: IQ Kültür Sanat Yayıncılık, 2008), 28.
[43] Fortna, *The Circassian*, 26–8.

Organisation (IMRO) was the most persistent and best organised – in the Balkans and that is where most young officers were sent to cut their teeth in the first years of the twentieth century. The *komitaci* tactics they encountered played a crucial role in changing the way the Ottoman officers, and especially its younger members, approached counter-insurgency. According to a leading expert on the late Ottoman military, *komitaci* tactics 'came to dominate the collective Ottoman military mind'.[44] Along with the effectiveness of *komitaci* tactics on display, the sheer number of different conflicts in which the Ottoman army was involved in its final decades and the general consensus that its levels of preparedness were wanting encouraged the adoption of similarly unconventional tactics by the Ottoman military. Many of the men considered here fit the bill for this kind of paramilitary service.

The military history of the late Ottoman Empire ensured that they would have plenty of opportunity to fight; the *fedaî*s were usually given the most dangerous assignments.[45] From the counter-insurgency operations already mentioned to the formally declared conflicts in North Africa, the Balkans, and then the many theatres of the First World War, there would be no shortage of opportunity for these volunteers to make their mark. Before they reached the combat zones, travelling there seems to have been important for strengthening bonds of camaraderie. For example, in 1911 Sapancalı Hakkı and Yakup Cemil travelled together from Istanbul to Egypt, the first stage on their route to fight the Italians in Tripolitania. In their company were the friends Mustafa Kemal and Ömer Naci, fellow Unionists. (Later when Yakup Cemil was interrogated about the coup he was planning during the First World War, he reportedly said that he had intended to replace Enver with Mustafa Kemal as minister of war.[46]) It seems clear that the experience of fighting in North Africa, in which the lessons learned from the Ottoman military's anti-insurgency experience in the Balkans were put into practice against the Italian army of invasion, had a notable effect on these men.

---

[44] Edward J. Erickson, *Ottomans and Armenians: A Study in Counterinsurgency* (New York: Palgrave Macmillan, 2013), 36.
[45] Erik Jan Zürcher, 'Atatürk as a Unionist', in *The Young Turk Legacy and Nation Building*, 127.
[46] Ibid., 132.

The successes recorded while fighting alongside the Sanusi fighters left them with the impression that it was a conflict that they would have won had the Balkan Wars not intervened. It served to vindicate the unconventional, asymmetrical tactics adopted out of necessity by the Ottomans, given that they were prevented from sending large numbers of troops there by British and Italian control of the sea lanes. Echoes of the tactics adopted against the Italians in Tripolitania can be seen in later Ottoman efforts in the Balkan Wars, the First World War and in the fighting in the Caucasus. A degree of Muslim anti-colonialism or Muslim nationalism was evident in Enver's efforts to include fighters, propagandists and notable figures from across the Muslim Mediterranean, such as Sheikh Salih of Tunisia, the sons of 'Abd al-Qadir, hero of the resistance against the French occupation of Algeria who later resettled in Ottoman Syria, and, of course, the Sanusiyya order in North Africa.[47] The Tripolitanian experience also seems to have been a time of camaraderie and bonding among the volunteer officers, some of whom had made extraordinary efforts to reach the front, travelling undercover either through France and Tunisia, as in the case of Enver's brother Nuri and uncle Halil, or Egypt,[48] in the case of Eşref, Süleyman Askerî, İzmitli Mümtaz and Mustafa Kemal.

Almost all of the men considered here began their actual combat experience in the Balkans. For example, after graduating from *Harbiye* in 1905, Süleyman Askerî was assigned to the Ottoman Third Army in Manastır.[49] It was there that he joined the CUP, taking part in the organisation's rapid expansion in the face of the Macedonian insurgency and the young officers' perceptions that the Hamidian regime and, in their view, its overly obsequious officers were failing to rise to the challenges confronting the empire.

---

[47] Jonathan Claymore McCollum, 'The Anti-Colonial Empire: Ottoman Mobilization and Resistance in the Italo-Turkish War', PhD thesis, University of California Los Angeles, 2018, 121–3; Fortna, *The Circassian*, 80–1.

[48] Alp Yenen, 'Nuri Killigil', in *1914–1918 Online: International Encycloedia of the First World War*, available at: https://encyclopedia.1914-1918-online.net/article/killigil_nuri. Nuri later returned to Tripolitania with Ja'far al-'Askari during the First World War. Ja'far was subsequently captured by British forces in 1916 and joined the 'Arab Revolt' againt the Ottomans after his release.

[49] Şimşek, *Teşkilat-ı Mahsusa'nın Reisi Süleyman Askeri Bey*, 34.

(CUP organisers among the group also include Sapancalı Hakkı, who played an active role in Salonica and İşkodra (Shkodër in today's Albania); İzmitli Mümtaz organised in Syria between the 1908 Revolution and the war in Tripolitania; 'Aziz 'Ali played a similar role in Ohrid, and so on.) Serving in the Balkans appears to have enhanced Süleyman Askerî's connections with the other members of the group. He already knew Eşref from his school days in Edirne; now Eşref was working for Enver and coming into contact with the other key leaders of the organisation. Eventually, Süleyman Askerî and his militant colleagues formed the group that called themselves the self-sacrificing officers (*fedaî zabitan*). This included İzmitli Mümtaz, Çanakkaleli Atıf, Sapancalı Hakkı, Topcu İhsan, Yakup Cemil and Yenibahçeli Şükrü, together with a few others such as Ali Çetinkaya and the aforementioned poet, orator and Unionist propagandist Ömer Naci.[50] The group's members did not move in lock step – and did not always see eye-to-eye – but various combinations would come together in several different contexts.

The first such common cause was the war in Tripolitania. When the Italian army invaded the last remaining Ottoman territory in Africa in 1911, the Unionist government felt compelled to launch a defence. Given Britain's occupation of Egypt and the Italians' naval superiority in the Mediterranean, the Ottoman military was unable to send the forces necessary to try to repulse the invasion. There was also considerable opposition within the upper echelons of the military to participating in this adventure. Senior officers accepted that the Ottomans had little chance of defeating the numerically superior Italians.[51] The solution was to rely on a small number of younger volunteers who would work with and train the men of the local Sanusi order. The *fedaî*s formed a key component of the Ottoman group; many had to overcome considerable difficulties in getting to the front, most sneaking through British-controlled Egypt in disguise. At least eight of the cohort under consideration here rushed to North Africa from various parts of the empire when they heard the news of the Italian invasion. Kuşçubaşı Eşref, Süleyman Askerî, İzmitli Mümtaz, 'Aziz 'Ali, Yakup Cemil, Sapancalı Hakkı, Çanakkaleli Atıf and

---

[50] Ibid., 36.
[51] Rachel Simon, *Libya between Ottomanism and Nationalism: The Ottoman Involvement in Libya during the War with Italy (1911–1919)* (Berlin: Klaus Schwarz Verlag, 1987), 93.

Ja'far al-'Askari all took part in the Tripolitanian War. They did not always get along – 'Aziz 'Ali's feud with Enver, referred to above, seems to have begun in Tripolitania and Süleyman Askerî, initially assigned to serve under the command of 'Aziz 'Ali, soon fell out with him and had to be reassigned – but, as indicated above, it seems to have been an important period of bonding for many in the group. The fact that the Ottoman–Sanusi alliance was inflicting some defeats on the Italians, forcing them to reorganise their strategy, seems to have played an important role in creating a positive group feeling. This was only reinforced when the First Balkan War broke out in early 1912, forcing the Ottomans to recall most of the officers in North Africa. 'Aziz 'Ali stayed behind to oversee the skeleton force.

The Balkan Wars offered another opportunity for the cohort to prove their mettle. The fact that both conflicts were bruising, vicious encounters with many civilian atrocities made the preceding Tripolitanian War seem like a much more enjoyable adventure. The seriousness of that conflict for Istanbul meant that most of the group who had volunteered to fight in Tripolitania were withdrawn and redeployed to the Balkans, familiar territory for many of them. At least seven of them served in the Balkan Wars, with the Kuşçubaşı brothers, Eşref and Sami (together with their younger brother Ahmed), Süleyman Askerî, Topcu İhsan, Çanakaleli Atıf, Yakup Cemil and Filebeli Hilmi all seeing action between autumn 1912 and autumn 1913. The First Balkan War was an unmitigated disaster for the Ottomans. The coalition of Greece, Bulgaria, Serbia and Montenegro put aside their considerable political and territorial differences and united to drive the Ottomans from all but their last territory in Europe. When the self-sacrificing officers redeployed from North Africa to the Balkan fronts, the Young Turks were not in power. Politically, the disastrous losses that the Ottoman army experienced at the hands of the Serbian and Bulgarian armies in the First Balkan War became an opportunity for the Unionists to recapture the Ottoman government. The Bâb-ı Âli Coup of 23 January 1913, to be discussed below, in which several of the *fedaî*s played an active part, restored Unionist control of the Ottoman government. The Second Balkan War provided some modest reversals in the Ottomans' favour. Taking advantage of the rancour among the new-found allies, the Ottomans went on the offensive. Ottoman forces, with Enver at their head, recaptured Edirne, symbolically important due to its status as a former imperial capital. Several of the *fedaî*s played key roles in a telling episode that followed the recapture of Edirne. The mini-state they created in Western Thrace, first called the Provisional and then the Independent Government of Western Thrace, exemplified the Unionist politics of *fait accompli* on the international stage. Süleyman Askerî, Eşref, Selim Sami and Sapancalı Hakkı featured in the offices of the short-lived entity before its territory was ceded to Bulgaria in the Treaty of Constantinople in 1913. These symbolically important gestures provided a kind of vindication for the politics of violence that had returned the Unionist to power.

Collective Instrument

After being brought together in the fields of education and warfare, the third area where members of the cohort intersected was in the decisive political events of the late Ottoman period. And it is here that they may be said to have changed the face of Ottoman political history, serving as a blunt instrument in the hands of their leaders. As previously mentioned, the first such prominent role for the self-sacrificing volunteers occurred during the events of the 1908 Revolution. In particular, Çanakkaleli Atıf's assassination of Şemsi Paşa served as a turning point for the revolution. Şemsi was the Ottoman general sent by Istanbul to Manastır (today's Bitola) to suppress the rebellion launched by the CUP officers in response to the meeting in Reval (today's Talinn) between the British and Russian monarchs who agreed on a plan for foreign intervention to resolve the Macedonian conflict. For the super-patriotic officers, this unwanted outcome was their pre-arranged sign to act. One faction of the activist officers under Ahmed Niyazi took to the hills, an action that caused the government both to send a force from Anatolia to counter the rebels and to dispatch a senior officer, the aforementioned Şemsi Paşa to lead them.[52] Carrying out a plan that he had apparently arranged ahead of time with Süleyman Askerî, by then leader of the CUP's branch in Manastır,[53] Atıf's violent act proved to be a crucial moment in the chain of events that culminated in the revolution that eventually restored the Ottoman Constitution, suspended since 1878, and brought the Unionists to

---

[52] Hanioğlu, *Preparation for a Revolution*, 266–8.
[53] Ibid., 472.

power. Although hardly the revolution's only momentous event, Atıf's decisive intervention was both 'a decisive blow to the palace' and indicative of the lengths to which the *fedaî*s would go to carry out their aims.[54]

Subsequently, there followed other noteworthy events in which members of the cohort were engaged. For example, several of them served in the 'Action Army' (*Hareket Ordusu*) that marched on Istanbul from Salonica to put down the conservative counter-revolution of 1909. Meanwhile in Izmir, where the CUP propaganda effort had been led by the infamous Dr Nazım, Eşref was engaged in suppressing the local manifestations of the anti-Unionist uprising. By his own account, he, together with his brother Selim Sami and their frequent accomplice Çerkes Reşid, 'took matters into their own hands' and 'gave no quarter'.[55] Eşref also captured the key figure in this counter-revolutionary movement, namely, the Nakşibendi Sufi sheikh and journalist Derviş Vahdeti when the ship on which he was escaping from Istanbul entered Izmir harbour. Derviş Vahdeti was subsequently hanged, adding to the rising body count of the period.

But even more dramatic actions involving the *fedaî*s were yet to come, perhaps none more so than the infamous 'Raid on the Sublime Porte' of January 1913. This *coup d'état* or, more accurately, *putsch* bore all the fingerprints of the activist officers. Once again, quite a few of the cohort were involved. The context for the *coup* involved the accumulation of bad news for the Unionists, including the disastrous results of the First Balkan War, the rise of opposition to CUP rule both in the provinces and in Istanbul, the creation of a national unity cabinet that was determined to limit the power of the Unionist officers, and the dissolution of parliament. The key Unionist leaders, increasingly alarmed by what they felt to be persecution of their number, had decided that decisive action was required and were determined to proceed, even over the objections of colleagues, such as Ali Fethi (Okyar) who had urged moderation and was subsequently side-lined. With the peace negotiations demanding, and the Ottoman government appearing ready to yield, the Ottoman loss of Edirne, an emotional issue for the Unionists, they

---

[54] Ibid., 268.
[55] Eşref Kuşçubaşı papers, EK2, Picture 012.

had the pretext they wanted to intervene.[56] Working to a plan organised by Talât Paşa,[57] they gathered a crowd of activist officers, including among others İzmitli Mümtaz, Sapancalı Hakkı, Filibeli Hilmi and Yakup Cemil, and marched towards the Sublime Porte alongside Enver where they forced their way inside. According to several reports, Sapancalı Hakkı and İzmitli Mümtaz were at the forefront of planning the violence that followed, including the death of War Minister Nazım Paşa. In all likelihood, it was Yakup Cemil who assassinated the minister. According to Eşref's account, Sapancalı Hakkı had fortified himself for the intervention with ample amounts of cognac.[58] The plotters forced the Grand Vizier to resign and installed a new, more pliable government.

The activities of the *fedaî zabitan* were not limited to such spectacular and public political theatre. Their presence was perhaps equally felt in the less visible but no less important internal decision-making processes of the late Ottoman period. Their ability to enforce their will over civilian politicians, even those within the CUP, using violence and coercion when they deemed it necessary, was often critical. A telling episode in this regard is that by which the volunteers managed to help elevate their leader Enver to the highest position in the Ottoman military. As late as December 1913, Enver had still only reached the rank of colonel despite his ambitions to play the leading role among his fellow officers. The *fedaî zabitan* helped to ensure that Enver was not only promoted but also became the leading figure in the politics of the period. Appearing before no less an imposing and influential figure than Mehmet Talât on 25 December 1913, four members of the *aşere-i mübeşşere* made it clear that Enver 'would be the moving power in both politics and war'.[59] Similarly, the way in which Ahmet İzzet Paşa subsequently yielded his position as minister of war to Enver, who had in the meantime been rapidly promoted to brigadier-general, contains more than a whiff of coercion, with

---

[56] Erik Jan Zürcher, *Turkey: A Modern History*, 2nd edn (London: I. B. Tauris, 1998), 112–13.
[57] Kieser, *Talaat Pasha*, 133.
[58] Taha Toros papers DSC00250.
[59] Naim Tufan, *The Rise of the Young Turks: Politics, the Military and Ottoman Collapse* (London: I. B. Tauris, 2000), 352.

the deposed paşa later indicating that he had been forced to resign.[60] The following year Enver was appointed to three key positions, namely, vice-commander-in-chief (the sultan was nominally the commander-in-chief), minister of war, and chief of the general staff.[61] On the way to such a consolidation of power, Enver could rely on a political instrument that others could not; in the 'desperadoes' of the *fedaî zabitan* he possessed a trump card that could be played to decisive effect. To quote Tufan at length:

> Nevertheless, revolutionary, far-flung and influential as the *Aşere-i Mübeşşere* soon became, by itself it represented merely an instrument, not a driving force. As matters stood, such a force could only come from one source – from Enver Bey himself . . . Enver Bey appears to have believed that he would not be able to increase his impact on Ottoman political life without calling upon revolutionaries more revolutionary than himself.[62]

Talât, for all of his wily organisational and strategic nous, had to give way in the face of physical intimidation that worked in Enver's favour.

Likewise, an incident from summer 1914 offers another example of how the men of violence could be used to silence a Unionist insider. Evranoszâde Rahmi (Arslan) was a lawyer and large landowner from Salonica who was a member of the CUP's Central Committee. Appointed governor of Aydın province, which contained the important city of Izmir, in 1913, he would become popularly known as 'Governor (Vali) Rahmi'. The area to which he was appointed had become even more important in the period immediately after the Balkan Wars when its large Greek Orthodox (Rum) population was increasingly seen as a provocation by Unionist hardliners; thoughts of revenge were increasingly focused on the Rum population. Enver had sent Kuşçubaşı Eşref to the region to establish a branch of the Special Organisation in early 1914. Soon thereafter Eşref and his brother Selim Sami were working on Enver's orders to expel the Rum from areas considered strategic and possibly vulnerable in the event of further warfare with

---

[60] Ibid., 353.
[61] Erik Jan Zürcher, 'Young Turk Governance in the Ottoman Empire during the First World War', *Middle Eastern Studies* 55(6) (2019): 898.
[62] Tufan, *Rise of the Young Turks*, 346.

Greece.[63] Vali Rahmi told British officials in Izmir that he was aware of Eşref and Sami's activities, including gathering arms and armed men in Eşref's house in the Cordelio (Karşıyaka) neighbourhood of Izmir, and was perturbed by them. But, he said, since Eşref enjoyed the strong protection of Enver, there was nothing that the governor could do.[64] High-profile Unionist and Central Committee member though he was, Governor Rahmi was clearly not completely trusted by Enver. He thus understandably claimed to be powerless against the armed instrument of Enver. It seems clear that Rahmi had been excluded from key, behind-the-scenes decision-making concerning the province over which he was nominally in charge, part of a pattern that was becoming increasingly apparent in the period between the Balkan Wars and the First World War.[65] Indeed, Rahmi's dismay at the power of the activist agents would take a personal turn when in early 1919 the brothers Çerkes Edhem and Reşid kidnapped Rahmi's son and transported him to Eşref's farm at Salihli while Eşref was a British prisoner-of-war on Malta.[66] The boy was later returned unharmed, but the incident highlights both the acute differences between and among even the top-ranking Unionists and the distinctive role that banditry and violence played in the *modus operandi* of the *fedai*s.

Conclusion

While space does not allow for a detailed discussion of the ways in which transgressive politics played out in the First World War years, it is clear that the trend continued and was heightened by the increasingly high-stakes nature of the Ottoman fight for survival. As Erik Jan Zürcher has shown, the key turning point in this development was the Bab-ı Ali coup of 1913. Thereafter, an increasingly 'makeshift, informal' style of decision-making was adopted that consistently excluded those colleagues, even prominent Unionists, known or suspected to be against the most radical action. A good example, as we've seen, was CUP Central Committee member Vali Rahmi,

---

[63] Fortna, *The Circassian*, 131.
[64] Ibid., 131–2.
[65] Erik Jan Zürcher, 'Young Turk Decision Making Patterns 1913–1915', 12, available at: https://www.academia.edu/12486176/Young_Turk_decision_making_patterns_1913-1915?auto=download.
[66] Fortna, *The Circassian*, 225–7.

who had shown signs of ambivalence towards the Ottoman Rum and was close to many of the prominent Levantine families in and around Izmir.[67] The Raid on the Sublime Porte paved the way for an increasingly 'drastic and radical' series of decisions that bypassed such individuals and ultimately proved fateful for the empire and its inhabitants, none more so than the Armenians.

These desperadoes, whose actions have often been dismissed as outmoded or, indeed, déclassé, nevertheless had an outsized impact on the course of events of the late Ottoman Empire. Although we have not had the scope to consider it here, many of them (including Süleyman Askerî, Kuşçubaşı Eşref, Selim Sami, Topcu İhsan, Çanakkaleli Atıf, Yakup Cemil and Filebeli Hilmi), were members of the Special Organisation (*Teşkilat-ı Mahsusa*) that was established by Enver as a multifaceted special operations and intelligence unit after the Tripolitanian War; Süleyman Askerî served as its head. Their names thus appear again and again in various accounts of this period. The end of the empire saw their paths diverge. The departure of Enver, first to Berlin and eventually to Central Asia where he died fighting the Red Army in 1922, left many of the cohort without the leader to whom they were fervently devoted. A few made their peace with his internal rivals and went on to prominence – and sometimes notoriety – in the Turkish Republic and other post-war states, such as Iraq where Jafar al-'Askari twice served as prime minister or Egypt where 'Aziz 'Ali became a general. In Turkey, where the majority of those still living after the First World War resided,[68] some cast their lot with first the movement established by Mustafa Kemal in defiance of both the last Ottoman government and the Allies and then the Republic which that movement created in 1923. A few, like Çanakkaleli Atıf and Filebeli Hilmi, became members of parliament in the new Turkey; Topcu İhsan rose to prominence as the minister of the navy, but also became the first minister of the young republic to be forced to resign as a result of a kickback scandal involving a French company.

Others, however, took against the Kemalist state. The Kuşçubaşı brothers

---

[67] Zürcher, 'Young Turk Decision Making Patterns 1913–1915', 12.
[68] Süleyman Askerî committed suicide in 1915 in what is today Iraq after his mission to organise tribal fighters to repulse the British Mesopotamian advance ended in failure. Yakup Cemil was hanged for having planned a *coup d'état* against the CUP government in 1916.

fought against Ankara, Selim Sami meeting his end in an apparent effort to infiltrate the Western Anatolian coastline on a mission to assassinate Mustafa Kemal. Eşref went into exile for many years, only returning in the 1950s as an old man. The 'dangerous' Abdülkadir Antepli served as governor of Ankara during the 'Independence War', but was suspected of involvement in an attempt to eliminate Mustafa Kemal in 1926 and was eventually caught while trying to flee the country and hanged. Yenibahçeli Şükrü, having served as a member of the Ankara parliament, seems to have turned against the Kemalists and was sentenced to death for his role in an earlier plot to assassinate Kemal in 1926. While his sentence was lifted, his brother Nail, another militant CUP officer, was executed. Sapancalı Hakkı was arrested as part of the same investigation but eventually released. Interestingly, Topcu İhsan had earlier served as president of the same Independence Tribunal (*İstiklâl Mahkemesi*) that passed judgement on Şükrü, Nail and a number of other former late Ottoman militants, reflecting the varying pathways that the former militants took in the new political context.

When in action as a mostly coherent group in the late Ottoman period, the parapolitical and paramilitary 'rogues' considered here certainly affected the course of history. The structures and context of the late nineteenth- and early twentieth-century empire provided the pathways that allowed them to come to the fore. The new educational system drew them into the orbit of the state, turning them into officers. The combination of the empire's seemingly endless conflicts, the shortage of qualified personnel, and the tendency towards relying on unconventional and often paramilitary tactics created considerable opportunity for men of violence in this era. As we have seen, the change to an increasingly transgressive politics effected by the Young Turk leadership encouraged and, indeed, frequently relied upon the self-sacrificing officers to an unprecedented degree. Zealously loyal to their leader Enver, they together served as the instrument that brought him to power and reinforced his bellicose responses to both domestic and international politics, with devastating and long-lasting consequences.

11

A Man of the Frontier: Ramadan Shallash and the Making of the Post-Ottoman Arab East

Michael Provence[1]

Nineteenth-century state education meant acculturation. State modernisers sought to mould loyal, productive citizens and state servants through a process of initiation, education and association. The goal was compliant modern citizens who appreciated the state and acknowledged its opportunities and increasing domination over their lives, choices and options. Some would-be modern citizens were more easily persuaded than others. In capitals, big cities and growing towns, the benefits of the modern state were more obvious, and alternative possibilities increasingly inconceivable. In frontier zones, places without government offices, and only sporadic, and generally unwelcome contact with state officials, the effort to persuade compliance was more difficult, and more likely to require compulsion, threats and violence.

Histories of Ottoman modernisation have usually focused on the region surrounding Istanbul and the Balkans. Important scholarly studies of the past couple decades centred on the men who challenged the monarchy and state system in 1908, bent it to their collective will before 1914, and lost the war in 1918. Their post-war insurgency campaign, from which emerged

---

[1] The author wishes to express his deep thanks to the editors, Ramazan Hakkı Öztan and Alp Yenen, and to Dr Talal Chlach and Laith Chelache, son and great-grandson of Ramadan, for their help and encouragement, without which this chapter would not have been possible.

the Turkish Republic, was understood as a singular experience in which the 'Turkish homeland' loomed large. Their collective ideology and shared habitus was believed to have been formed in the crucible of Great Power proxy wars, nationalist movements and guerrilla struggles in the Balkans during the tumultuous decades preceding the First World War.[2] But the Ottoman state was far more than its 'European' provinces, and in the decades after 1876 the focus of Ottoman resources and efforts was increasingly Anatolia and the Kurdish and Arab regions. Arguably late Ottoman Damascus received more state funding and attention than any other city apart from Istanbul in the late nineteenth century. Similarly, ex-Ottoman soldiers challenged the post-war settlement in distant places like Iraq, Syria and Palestine into the 1940s. Anatolia was far from the only site of post-Ottoman resistance. Perhaps adopting the biases of their elite Ottoman protagonists, historians have often ignored these frontier regions.

The mythic American frontier, its outlaws, sheriffs, nomads, indigenous people, heroes and villains is a commonplace. Stories of frontier drama and struggles, highly fictionalised, have featured in North America myth-making for a century. Hollywood movies spread the legend of the frontier around the globe. In other places the collective memory of the frontier is different, and potentially more interesting. Ottoman frontiers in Eastern Anatolia, today's Iraq, and the Syrian desert experienced state expansion, persuasion and compulsion in ways both familiar and unique. In the Middle East, where traditions of city life and urban high culture are more ancient than anywhere on earth, the frontier remains a place disdained for its lack of refinement, feared for its perceived lawlessness and rebellion, and sometimes romanticised as the fount of mythical tribal or ancestral authenticity. Urban folk rarely knew

---

[2] See, for example, M. Şükrü Hanioğlu, *The Young Turks in Opposition* (Oxford: Oxford University Press, 1995), and M. Şükrü Hanioğlu, *Preparation for a Revolution: The Young Turks, 1902–1908* (Oxford: Oxford University Press, 2001). See also Erik-Jan Zürcher, *The Unionist Factor: The Role of the Committee of Union and Progress in the Turkish National Movement (1905–1926)* (Leiden: Brill, 1984); and especially for the purposes of this chapter, Erik-Jan Zürcher, 'The Young Turks: Children of the Borderlands?' *International Journal of Turkish Studies* 9(1/2) (2003): 275–86. For an outstanding recent corrective, see Alp Yenen, 'The "Young Turk Zeitgeist" in The Middle Eastern Uprisings in the Aftermath of World War I', in Hakan Yavuz and Feroz Ahmed (eds), *War and Collapse: World War I and the Ottoman State* (Salt Lake City: University of Utah Press, 2016), 1181–216.

the frontier first-hand and such regions were usually left to the inhabitants; those who remained outside the realms of cultured society and the reach of the state.[3]

Ottoman Modernisation and the Making of a Frontier Man

Far-flung late nineteenth-century modernising states, possessed of vast steppe land, mountain pastures and deserts, sought to assert control over their frontiers. In Russia, North America, Iran and the Ottoman realms, resource-strapped states devoted scarce revenues and signed concessions to build communication networks of telegraphs, roads and railways. The concessions helped to build lasting private fortunes in the vacuum left by an absent state authority. Government offices, outposts, barracks and schools followed.[4] In the mid-1890s, Ottoman Sultan Abdülhamid II, whose telegraph, road, railway and clock-tower memorials remain to this day in a dozen Ottoman successor states, decided to build a centralised boarding school for prominent boys from the frontiers. Most of his late Ottoman innovations are forgotten today, but few are more obscure than the Imperial Tribal School, or *Aşiret Mekteb-i Humayun*.

In 1892, an adolescent boy from the upper Euphrates region of the Ottoman Zur Sanjaq, today's Syrian, Turkish and Iraqi border zone, entered the first class of the new school. School officials enrolled him as Ramadan Shallash 'Abdallah, of the Zur Sanjaq, student ID No. 23. He was born in 1882, a son of Shallash al-'Abdallah, the sheikh of the upper

---

[3] For Ottoman frontiers, see Cem Emrence, *Remaping the Ottoman Middle East: Modernity Imperial Bureaucracy and Islam* (London: I. B. Tauris, 2012); Eugene Rogan, *Frontiers of the State in the Late Ottoman Empire: Transjordan, 1850–1921* (Cambridge: Cambridge University Press, 2002); and Selim Deringil, *The Well-Protected Domains: Ideology and the Legitimation of Power in the Ottoman Empire, 1876–1909* (London: I. B. Tauris, 1998). The literature on the North American frontier is vast, and usually starts with Frederick Jackson Turner. The best recent work is Pekka Hämäläinen, *The Comanche Empire* (New Haven, CT: Yale University Press 2009).

[4] The two most important books on late Ottoman education are Benjamin Fortna, *Imperial Classroom: Islam, the State, and Education in the Late Ottoman Empire* (Oxford: Oxford University Press, 2002); and Selçuk Akşin Somel, *The Modernization of Public Education in the Ottoman Empire, 1839–1908: Islamization, Autocracy and Discipline* (Leiden: Brill, 2001).

Euphrates tribe al-Bu-Saraya, which today numbers 250,000 members in ten villages spread along the Euphrates. In the early-1890s an emissary from Ottoman Sultan Abdülhamid II had visited their village of al-Shumaytiyya and invited the leading sheikh to send sons for education and board at the expense of the sultan himself in the imperial capital. Family members were leaders among the regional Bedouin tribes, and were related by kinship and marriage to most of the leading local clans. Leading families in other Ottoman frontier regions, including those that eventually furnished the rulers of Kuwait and Saudi Arabia, accepted similar invitations and sent sons also, but school recruiters were not always able to convince parents of the value of distant state education, and the recruiting targets were rarely met. Sheikh Shallash was among those who understood the value of education and the opportunity at hand, and so he sent Ramadan and his brother Ahmad to the imperial capital at government expense to attend the recently conceived special boarding school, known as *Aşiret Mekteb-i Humayun*.[5]

Young Ramadan and Ahmad would have travelled up river to al-Raqqa and onward on foot or horseback to Aleppo, and its port of Iskenderun, from which they would embark by steamship for a journey of a week or so to the imperial capital. Istanbul, then, as now, would have been an awe-inspiring sight coming into view from the deck of a ship, as the great city, its hills ringed with imposing walls, palaces, domes and slender minarets, rose from the sea. It is easy to imagine the excitement and wonder such a journey would inspire in a promising boy from the distant frontier.

The Imperial Tribal School opened in 1892, just up the hill from the sprawling seaside Dolmabahçe Palace, which Sultan Abdülmecid I built in the 1850s. The school and student dormitories had a sweeping view of the Bosporus. In its first year the school enrolled about fifty boys from what Ottoman elites considered their wild imperial frontier.[6] It is unlikely that

---

[5] Eugene Rogan, 'Aşiret Mektebi: Abdülhamid II's School for Tribes (1892–1907)', *International Journal of Middle East Studies* 28(1) (1996): 83–107. Rogan's article is the best investigation of the Tribal School. According to the table Rogan compiled, Sheikh Shallash sent another son, Ahmad Tawfiq also.

[6] Rogan, 'Aşiret Mektebi', 90–1.

the boys had received much formal schooling before their selection and journey to Istanbul, at between ten and thirteen years of age.[7]

Ramadan, like most of the boys, would have needed the specialised elementary curriculum of the Tribal School. Ottoman reformers designed the school to introduce the governing culture and potential benefits of the state to influential rural and frontier families. Instructors taught Ottoman Turkish; a language to which none of the boys would likely have been exposed, and doubly difficult since while most of the boys probably spoke the varying Arabic dialects of their regions, few would have been literate, and they were expected to learn to read and write Arabic at the same time. Eventually they learned French as well. The school was envisioned as the first of a network of regional schools for prominent rural youth, but the other schools were never built. The state was committed to the success of students like Ramadan, but the training was rigorous and sizeable percentages of students washed out of the Tribal School and Imperial Military Academy that followed it.[8] Ramadan graduated in the first class in 1898, and entered the military academy the same year.

Ottoman education officials intended the Tribal School to furnish equal numbers of students to the Military Academy (*Mekteb-i Ulum-i Harbiye*) and high Civil Service Academy (*Mekteb-i Mülkiye*). In the event, due to reasons of academics, culture or interest, students far favoured martial vocations and the Military Academy. Officials organised special classes and curricula for the tribal school graduates, and upon graduation from their respective service

---

[7] According to Ramadan Basha Shallash's youngest son, Dr Talal R. Chlach, his father was born in 1882, though some records list 1879. Much of this reconstruction is based on interviews generously conducted with Dr Talal and his father's unpublished manuscript memoirs in his possession. Talal Chlach graciously reviewed several drafts. Other sources are confused. Jurj Faris, *Man hum fi 'alam al-'Arabi* (Damascus: Maktab al-Dirasat al-Suriyya wa-al-'arabiyya, 1957), 344, records Shallash's birth date in 1869, which is surely an error. Khayr ad-Din Al-Zirkili, *al-A'lam qamus tarajim li-ashar ar-rijal wa'n-nisa min 'arab a'l-musta'ribin al-mustastriqin*, 8 vols (reprint of c. 1950) (Beirut: Dar al-'Ilm lil-Malayin 1990), vol. III, 32, has the same mistaken birth date. Rogan notes in his article that most students entered the Tribal School between the ages of twelve and sixteen, in Rogan, 'Aşiret Mektebi', 86. Ramadan's entry in the first class of 1892 confirms his later birth date.

[8] Istanbul University, archival section (hereafter IU), Mekatıb-ı Askeriyye, h1318 (1901). Seventy-four out of a class of 811 entering students failed and washed out.

academies, officials attempted to arrange both special honours and special postings for them; a goal that apparently met resistance from those accustomed to the more common, and perhaps more meritocratic, path to state employment.

After the five-year course of study, with its emphasis on religion, Ottoman history and culture, and basic reading and writing skills, Tribal School graduates probably still had difficulty competing on an equal footing with military academy students, most of whom were younger urban youth who had already received eight or nine years of intensive elite schooling in one of the empire's larger cities against five years for Tribal School students.

For Ramadan Shallash, eight years in the Tribal School and military academy was good preparation for his career as an officer in the Ottoman army. He graduated a captain of cavalry from the *Harbiye* in 1902, and served in the Ottoman army for the next fifteen years and well into the First World War. Officers originating in the Tribal School usually received special decorations and honours and promotion to captain (*Yüzbaşı*) upon graduation, while the usual *Harbiye* graduate was a third or second lieutenant (*Piyade Mülazım*). Tribal School graduates seem to have always entered the cavalry or infantry, and none seem ever to have ascended the lofty academic heights of the Ottoman Staff College (*Erkan-i Harbiye Askeriye*), or further study in Germany, which was a distinction for the top 10 per cent of *Harbiye* graduates, among whom were Mustafa Kemal (Atatürk), future Iraqi prime minister Yasin al-Hashimi, and Syrian national icon Yusuf al-'Azma, among a handful of others, who graduated staff captains after a further three years of study. It is ironic that the favoured tribal school graduates obtained the same initial rank as those selected for the most rigorous, selective and elite officer training available. Ramadan Shallash became an honorary military attaché to Sultan Abdülhamid; an honour that seems to have been shared with other Tribal School graduates.

Five decades later Ramadan Shallash composed an autobiographical entry and continued to use by then deeply unfashionable lofty titles to refer to the Ottoman state and its sultan, indicating the pride his Ottoman education and service instilled. Information on his decades of Ottoman army service is spotty, and his family had little knowledge of what must surely have been an adventurous and tumultuous period. His Ottoman education and vocation as an army officer made him a prolific letter writer, and he wrote hundreds of letters to friends, comrades and enemies over this long career. His sons relate that he served in his upper Euphrates region either in the regular army or the special Hamidiye Cavalry Brigade, members of which considered themselves an irregular sultanic guard. The Hamidiye brigade comprised mostly Kurdish units, but there were a few Arab Bedouin units, the area of operation of which included the Zur Sanjaq.[9]

The Hamidiye Cavalry or regular army cavalry comprised a mobile state police force in the frontier zones. Duties included providing muscle for revenue collection, tribal revolt suppression, and pursuit of bandits and Bedouin raiders. Association with the Hamidiye brigades began with an alliance between individual sheikhs and the state, but the association usually came to include the entire tribe, and brought a number of benefits to favoured tribes. With the power and prestige of the state behind them, they enjoyed wealth and privilege in the frontier regions that was otherwise difficult to obtain, and could be used for advantage against local political and economic rivals. Arguably the state benefited from the visible presence and nominal law and order an associated tribe, and its uniformed brigades, could provide. If deficits outweighed benefits of a particular alliance, the more formal state officials had means, through manipulation of alliances, withholding favour, encouraging rivals or, finally, sending the army, to discipline its more unruly tribal and *Hamidiye* deputies. Whatever his official position, this is the world Captain Ramadan Shallash worked within in the first decade of the twentieth century.

Wars of the New Century

Ramadan Shallash spent the next years in regular Ottoman army service in the Balkans. It is likely that he commanded some special cavalry or counter-insurgency unit made up of tribal or rural troops. In 1911, he volunteered to go to Libya to fight the Italian invasion of that Ottoman province. There he met, or become re-acquainted with, the three most prominent commanders of the defence; all provincial products of the Ottoman education system,

---

[9] Janet Klein, *The Margins of Empire: Kurdish Militias in the Ottoman Tribal Zone* (Stanford, CA: Stanford University Press 2011), 185.

'Aziz 'Ali al-Misri, İsmail Enver (later Enver Paşa) and Mustafa Kemal (Atatürk). Other young Arab Ottoman officers like Sa'id al-'As, Fawzi al-Qawuqji, Yasin al-Hashimi and Ja'far al-'Askari also saw action in Libya. The Libya campaign is forgotten today, but in the following years it was widely linked to the outbreak of the Balkan wars in 1912 and 1913, and the First World War in summer 1914. The Libya and the Balkan wars were arguably the first salvos in the First World War, and, similarly, part of the so-called Eastern Question; the debate and struggle, with its origins in nineteenth-century European diplomacy, over the disposition and eventual partition of the Ottoman Empire in the Balkans and the Middle East.[10] Ramadan Shallash and his brother officers, Ottoman statesmen and engaged citizens, knew of the covert designs on Ottoman territory and shared a deep and durable mistrust of the ostensibly Christian Great Powers, which underlay their political outlook to the end of their lives. He, like those of his generation, was immersed in an atmosphere of life or death struggle over the survival of the Ottoman homeland they had been trained to defend. Like the First World War it preceded, the Italian invasion of Libya was accompanied by a long series of secret negotiations and agreements between Britain, France and the Italian kingdom. Despite the supposed secrecy, Ottoman citizens knew their collective destiny was subject to tectonic Great Power forces outside their control.

The Ottoman defenders in Libya fought a guerrilla war in which tribal irregulars collaborated with Ottoman officers. Ottoman views on insurgency and mobile asymmetrical war were shaped in Libya and the Balkans in the first decade of the twentieth century. Tribal School-trained officers and military operatives like Ramadan Shallash were invaluable in such efforts to bridge the gap of understanding and foster cooperation between tribal fighters and an elite Ottoman officer corps, most of whom had little in common with, or ability to understand, the empire's rural and nomadic majority.

The Libyan campaign, formative though it was, ended in defeat for the Ottomans, and, in 1912, Ramadan Shallash was sent to Medina to join

---

[10] Ramazan Hakkı Öztan, 'Point of No Return? Prospects of Empire after the Ottoman Defeat in the Balkan Wars (1912–13)', *International Journal of Middle East Studies* 50(1) (2018): 65–84.

the Ottoman garrison there. The Islamic holy cities of Mecca and Medina and their Red Sea port of Jeddah in the Hijaz had become increasingly important to Ottoman legitimacy and diplomacy. The storied Hijaz railway reached Medina in 1908, at about the same time as Sultan Abdülhamid II appointed al-Sharif al-Husayn the Amir of Hijaz.[11] With the constitutional restoration the same year, Abdülhamid's authority faded until he abdicated after the failed counter-revolution in 1909. His partisans, including Husayn, felt themselves under threat from the new government and particularly Unionist military officers in the ascendance. While Husayn enjoyed prestige as the religious amir, and local delegate of the sultan/caliph, not to mention direct descendant of the Prophet Muhammad, political power lay with the Ottoman political *wali* or governor, who exercised political authority directly under the central state interior ministry, increasingly linked by telegraph, rail and the Ottoman military garrison.[12] Husayn's relations with the new government deteriorated in the years between 1908 and the outbreak of the First World War.

According to his family, Ramadan Shallash enjoyed close and intimate relations with Husayn.[13] Perhaps in contrast to the majority of Ottoman officers, he seems to have sympathised with the local perspective of Husayn and the Hijazis, rather than with the central state and its new leaders. Owing to his background he served as a liaison between local and Bedouin elements, Husayn and the Ottoman command. At the outbreak of war in late 1914 in Medina, he remained in Ottoman service among the sizeable army contingent stationed there.

In 1916, leading Ottoman statesmen Enver and Cemal paşas made a visit to Hijaz and to Husayn himself. Noted Damascene journalist and chronicler Muhammad Kurd 'Ali accompanied them. Surely, they hoped to cement Husayn's association with the state, convince him to organise tribal levies for the war effort, and cease exploring other alliances, about which whispers

---

[11] Hasan Kayalı, *Arabs and Young Turks: Ottomanism, Arabism, and Islamism in the Ottoman Empire, 1908–1918* (Berkeley: University of California Press, 1997), 148–9.
[12] Martin Strohmeier, 'Fakhri (Fahrettin) Paşa and the End of Ottoman rule in Medina (1916–1919)', *Turkish Historical Review* 4(2) (2013): 195.
[13] Interview, Dr Talal Chalch, August 2019.

circulated, but they were disappointed, and as historian Martin Strohmeir notes, deeply suspicious of what they experienced as visitors to the Hijaz. Within a couple of months, in May 1916, the high command dispatched an enlarged Ottoman force under the command of Fahri Paşa, which ultimately defended the besieged city from Husayn's Arab Revolt and the British Army until after the armistice of Mudros in October 1918. Medina was the last Ottoman stronghold to surrender.

Husayn, having concluded his secret negotiations with Henry McMahon, British High Commissioner in Egypt, chose Fahri Paşa's arrival as the signal to defect from the Ottoman order. Ramadan Shallash soon joined Husayn, probably before there was much in the way of any organised Arab Revolt forces, and thus became one of the only Ottoman officers to freely defect to the Arab Revolt.[14] The better-known Sharifian officers like Nuri al-Said, Ja'far al-'Askari, and Mawlud Mukhlis, were recruited from prison camps by British intelligence officers. Ramadan's family makes clear that he based his choice on his personal connection and loyalty to Husayn, not on ideological or nationalistic grounds. Other evidence suggests his choice did not really curtail his Ottoman allegiances, and was thus probably a matter of personal loyalty and conviction, and wartime exigencies.

Ramadan Shallash considered himself personally close to Husayn more than to his sons, who he considered too ambitious and too subservient to British officials in the region. He spent the years 1916–18 as a military adviser to Husayn owing to his training, intimate knowledge of the Ottoman army and tribal pedigree.[15] Ramadan remained with Husayn and his son Sharif 'Abdallah in the Hijaz between 1916 and 1918, rather than joining Sharif Faysal in the Palestine campaign. In later life his connection with 'Abdallah and Arabia returned to provide him with an intermittent refuge from French and British mandate martial law, though Ramadan fell afoul of both Faysal and 'Abdallah for his relentless opposition to British occupation in the region.

The battle of Khaybar was one of the most significant engagements

---

[14] Mesut Uyar, 'Ottoman Arab Officers between Nationalism and Loyalty', *War in History* 20(4) (2013): 538.

[15] Interview, Dr Talal Chalch, August 2019, and Ramadan Shallash memoirs.

between Sharif 'Abdallah's forces and Ottoman forces. Ramadan Shallash was probably there, and with his cavalry training and experience would have contributed to the victory. 'Abdallah's forces came upon a small Ottoman column led by the famous special operator, Eşref Kuşçubaşı transporting a fortune in Ottoman gold to relieve the garrison in Yemen. 'Abdallah captured a hand full of Ottoman soldiers and 20,000 gold Ottoman lira.[16] He packed the Ottoman captives, including Eşref Kuşçubaşı, off to British prison camps.

According to his manuscript memoirs, Husayn sent Ramadan Shallash to assist Faysal after the capture of Aqaba in July 1917. Faysal and his forces prepared to embark by the Royal Navy ship HMS *Hardinge* from Jeddah. Ramadan served as Faysal's honour guard, and supervised the loading of the ship with men and their mounts. When British Arab Bureau intelligence officer Lieutenant Colonel John Bassett, frustrated with the loading progress, demanded that they 'get those dogs off the ship and load the horses first', Ramadan took offence at the insult against the Arab soldiers and struck Bassett. Egyptian officers detailed to Faysal separated them as they fought. Bassett and the British command demanded that Faysal dismiss Ramadan Shallash. Husayn learned of the situation, reassured Ramadan, called him back to Mecca, and appointed him part of his personal escort.

A few months later, in November 1917, the new Bolshevik government published the secret Sykes–Picot accord between Britain and France partitioning Ottoman greater Syria, Iraq and Arabia. Ottoman military governor of Syria, Cemal Paşa publicised the accord and wrote to Faysal and Ja'far al-'Askari to alert them to the fact that the British authorities had lied and intended to cheat them out of the promised independence. When Husayn learned of the British double-dealing he demanded a response, and noted the exchange of letters between himself and MacMahon promising British recognition of Arab independence in return for the Arab Revolt against the Ottoman army. Lieutenant Colonel Bassett, then British acting agent at Jeddah, hand delivered an official letter in Arabic to Husayn claiming that the Sykes–Picot accord was an Ottoman forgery aimed at the rebellious Arabs:

---

[16] Benjamin Fortna, *The Circassian: A Life of Eşref Bey, Late Ottoman Insurgent and Special Agent* (Oxford: Oxford University Press, 2017), 195–6.

It would be superfluous to point out that the object aimed at by Turkey is to sow doubt and suspicion between the Allied Powers and those Arabs who, under Your Majesty's leadership and guidance, are striving nobly to recover their ancient freedom. The Turkish policy is to create dissension by luring the Arabs into believing that the Allied Powers have designs on the Arab countries, and by represent to the Allies that the Arabs might be made to renounce their aspirations. But such intrigues cannot succeed in sowing dissension among those whose minds are directed by a common purpose to a common end.

His Majesty's Government and their allies stand steadfastly by every cause aiming at the liberation of the oppressed nations, and they are determined to stand by the Arab peoples in their struggle for the establishment of an Arab world in which law shall replace Ottoman injustice, and in which unity shall prevail over the rivalries artificially provoked by the policy of Turkish officials. His Majesty's Government re-affirm their former pledge in regard to the liberation of the Arab peoples.[17]

Struggle at the Frontiers of Empires

Ramadan was with Husayn at Jeddah when British and Arab forces occupied Damascus on 1 October 1918. He was useful to Husayn, who needed experienced military men capable of bringing discipline to his mostly nomadic troops, but Ramadan was eager to return to Syria and take part in events unfolding there. Husayn provided him with a letter to Faysal. Ramadan rode north to Damascus across the devastated post-war landscape of Palestine. In Damascus he sought out ex-Ottoman officers Yusuf al-'Azma and Yasin al-Hashimi and offered to join Amir Faysal's forces. Ramadan had special skills and connections, not least his tribal pedigree, and by February 1919 he had visited his upper Euphrates region to garner support and collect pledges of loyalty to Faysal's Damascus government.[18]

In November 1919, Chief-of-Staff Yasin al-Hashim sent Ramadan

[17] George Antonius, *The Arab Awakening: The Story of the Arab National Movement* (London: Hamish Hamilton, 1938), app. C, 431–2.
[18] Eliezer Tauber, 'The Struggle for Dayr al-Zur: The Determination of the Borders between Syria and Iraq', *International Journal of Middle East Studies* 23(3) (1991): 365.

Shallash with a small camel-mounted military force to assume the district governorship of the region of Raqqa near his native region along the Euphrates. On his way north from Damascus, Shallash met with Ibrahim al-Hananu in the countryside of Aleppo, where Hananu was fighting French forces.[19] Soon after, in December 1919, Shallash issued a revolutionary proclamation directed at the people the region, opposing the Sykes–Picot accord and calling for the expulsion of the British and French occupation forces and their allies. The proclamation constitutes the opening statement of what came to be called the Iraqi Revolt of 1920. The next month, in December 1919, his now larger force defeated a British garrison and occupied Dayr al-Zur. He captured and held eighteen British personnel, including the district civil affairs officer, and forced a general British retreat towards Iraq.[20] When Faysal, then seeking diplomatic support in Europe for his tottering government, was informed that the town had been captured in the name of the Arab government, he disavowed the action, and instructed his brother Zayd in Damascus to repudiate and arrest the 'rebels'.[21] Zayd sent a letter to Ramadan instructing him that British forces were the allies of the Arab government and he must cease operations against them. Ramadan declared his intention to defend Arab land for the Arabs. 'Neither the British nor Faysal had the right to give away our lands.'[22]

Shallash's capture of the garrison and the threat of a wider uprising led British authorities to arrest Faysal's chief-of-staff, Yasin al-Hashimi. General Allenby ordered that al-Hashimi be imprisoned at Ramla in the British-occupied zone in Palestine. British officials feared that al-Hashimi could become the leader of an insurgency on the model of and in collaboration with Mustafa Kemal, but when the French refused to take custody of al-Hashimi, Allenby ordered his release, noting publicly that he was complying with

---

[19] For Hananu and the region of Aleppo, see Michael Provence, *The Last Ottoman Generation and the Making of the Modern Middle East* (Cambridge: Cambridge University Press, 2017), 110–22.
[20] Interview with Dr Talal R. Chalch, 21 August 2019.
[21] British Government, *Review of the Civil Administration of Mesopotamia* (London: HM Stationary Office, 1920), 135.
[22] Dr Talal Chlach correspondence, and Shallash memoirs, 20 August 2020.

Figure 11.1 Ramadan Shallash (centre right) at the Arab Officer's Club Damascus, c 1920, courtesy of Dr Talal Chlach.

a French request.[23] Both al-Hashimi and Yusuf al-'Azma criticised bitterly Faysal's refusal to seriously prepare for military confrontation with France as the British withdrew into the zones allotted in Sykes–Picot and at the San Remo conference.[24] RAF aircraft dropped a letter from Faysal on Ramadan's camp, asking him to release his British prisoners. Ramadan had the prisoners escorted east of Abu-Kamal and released. In the next months the Iraq Revolt took on a momentum of its own and spread to the towns along the great rivers, threatening Britain's hold on the region.

In spring 1920, Ramadan travelled briefly to Damascus. It is easy to imagine his discussions with other ex-Ottoman officers about the need to confront British and French designs on the region, the news from Anatolia and the prospects of region-wide armed struggle (Figure 11.1). The officers shared a frustration with Faysal's effort, ultimately futile, to conciliate France. Ramadan resolved to return to Dayr al-Zur and organise an armed defence

---

[23] The National Archives (TNA), FO 371/5033 Allenby to FO, 14 March 1920.
[24] Sati' Al-Husri, *Yawm al-Maysalun: Safahat min Tarikh al-'Arab al-Hadith* (Beirut: Maktabat al-Kishaf, n.d. c. 1947), 123.

against the French forces. Faysal again summoned him and informed him that armed action against France was contrary to the interests of the Arab government, and he should cease war preparations. Faysal had already delivered the same message to Yasin al-Hashimi and Yusuf al-'Azma. Ramadan was more obstinate than some, however, and he returned to the countryside to gather men and weapons and carry on an unsuccessful, shoe-string, insurgency against Britain and France.

During the early 1920s he made many visits to Transjordan where he offered his unique skills and was welcomed by Amir 'Abdallah, the new prince that Colonial Secretary Winston Churchill had installed to rule the region east of the Jordan. Amir 'Abdallah received him cordially, but withheld support. Ramadan suspected that 'Abdallah reported their meetings to British officials. He eventually received a message from 'Abdallah threatening dire consequence if he continued to threaten disorder and refused to lay down his arms.

While 'Abdallah had come to terms with the British forces, Faysal had bigger problems, and with the withdrawal of British support, he was unable to satisfy French ultimatums. When French forces marched on Damascus from Beirut, Faysal fled, first to Amman, and eventually to Cairo where he took up residence in a hotel supported by a meagre British Foreign Office subsidy. France defeated the Arab forces at Maysalun and occupied Damascus in July 1920. French colonial officials favoured rural elites, and Damascus military governor Georges Catroux invited Ramadan to discuss his grievances and meet at Dar'a on the newly drawn Syrian–Tranjordanian frontier. Ramadan Shallash requested that Catroux appoint him governor of Dayr al-Zur in return for recognising the French mandate. Catroux stalled, but finally refused on the grounds that Ramadan was untrustworthy from the perspective of the French authorities.

Ramadan Shallash returned to his region, since Syria had been claimed by France, and France had no grievance with him. He assumed a temporarily tranquil existence in his village of al-Shumatiyya. Like other ex-officers and revolutionary figures, he found that men wanted by one mandate power could live freely in another, and while the British surely wished to imprison him, the French authorities allowed him to live openly near Dayr al-Zur. He attended to family and tribal matters and stayed out of Damascus- or

Aleppo-centred politics. His oldest son, Muhammad Amir Shallash, born in 1910, was ten years old as they settled into village life, and his family remember Ramadan as a loving and attentive father to all his children. His family was happy to have him back after years of distant adventures from one end of the Ottoman realms to the other. In 1920 he was thirty-eight years old.

Like thousands of other unemployed Ottoman veterans, Ramadan Shallash cast about for a course of action. He stayed in contact with Anatolian insurgents and followers of ex-Ottoman general Mustafa Kemal, and like every ex-Ottoman soldier, he followed the exciting news from Anatolia. In 1922 or 1923 he travelled to Mecca to visit his old patron Sharif Husayn. In Mecca, Husayn honoured Ramadan Shallash lavishly, promoted him to paşa, promised money and weapons, and asked him to return to Syria and lead a revolution against France. He gave Ramadan a letter to Amir 'Abdallah directing him to support Ramadan's mission in Syria. Ramadan returned to Amman, where he found 'Abdallah had a more finely tuned sense of the emerging balance of power and regional scene than his father. 'Abdallah again received him cordially, but advised him to mobilise a tribal military force, return south to Hijaz and take the field for Husayn's Hijazi kingdom against the forces of al-Sa'ud.

During the course of the early 1920s Ramadan travelled repeatedly between Syria, Transjordan and Hijaz. He wrote dozens of letters and made scores of visits to old comrades and tribal leaders seeking to support Arab independence and the Hashemite position in the Hijaz. He stayed one step ahead of British intelligence, and seems to have survived as a permanent fugitive. In 1924, he went by sea to Yemen to seek the support of the Imam Yahya as King Husayn's envoy in his battle against al-Sa'ud. His efforts and adventures were ultimately futile, and King Husayn was forced to flee al-Sa'ud's forces, first from Mecca, and finally from Jeddah, from which he became a refugee king and guest of his son 'Abdallah in Amman.[25]

In 1925, Syrian national politics beckoned and Ramadan Shallash left Hijaz to join the Syrian Revolt alongside his comrades from the Ottoman army, Arab Revolt and Tribal School. In early October, he gathered a group of armed men and participated in the seizure and short-lived occupation of

---

[25] Dr Talal Chlach correspondence, and Shallash memoirs, 20 August 2020.

Hama, with his Ottoman army comrade Fawzi al-Qawuqji. Out of international view, and with limited occupation forces, French officials ordered a devastating artillery bombardment of Hama, ending the uprising there. Ten days later, Ramadan Shallash and several former Ottoman officers led the ill-fated assault on Damascus. Many Damascenes welcomed the insurgents and celebrated their arrival, but French forces had other ideas. The garrison commander had been heard to wish 'the Damascenes would give France a chance of dealing with them as the Hama rebels had been dealt with'.[26] The barrage began with no warning and lasted two full days. Unlike Hama, international newspaper coverage was intense and brought withering criticism of France and its mandate policy. Damascus was probably the first major city in history to be intensely bombed by airplanes. Several square blocks of the old city were destroyed so thoroughly that the streets were redrawn when it was rebuilt.

In the days before the barrage, French authorities had publicly hanged a number of rural Syrians in the central Marja square. The bodies were left hanging for hours. Signboards around the necks of the corpses described their alleged crimes. French columns had failed to engage insurgents from the dense gardens around Damascus, but an infantry patrol had returned with a donkey train loaded with twenty-six dead rebels, who were laid out in the square for public viewing. A large crowd gathered and the Damascenes claimed the dead had been ordinary peasants murdered in their fields, since mandate forces had been unable to engage any actual insurgents.[27]

That autumn and early winter 1925, Ramadan Shallash became one of the most effective rebel leaders in the insurgent battles of the Damascus countryside. He was both famous and feared for his denunciations of rich landlords, collaborators and the colonial government. French mandate intelligence officers collected and preserved in their archives a series of demands for revolt taxes, men, weapons and money. Ramadan Shallash mobilised and led poorly armed villagers from the mountain region west and north

---

[26] TNA, FO 371/10835, 10 October 1925.
[27] *La Syrie*, 8 October 1925, quoted in Alice Poulleau, *À Damas sous les bombes: Journal d'une Française pendant la révolte Syrienne, 1924–1926* (Yvetot: Bretteville, 1926), 80–1; *The Times*, 'Parade of Corpses', 27 October 1925; *Le Temps*, 24 October 1925.

of Damascus. Shallash called himself a commander of the National Army, which evoked dreaded French memories of the defeat at the hands of the Anatolian insurgency four years earlier in the Cilicia campaign. According to French intelligence, Shallash's call to arms appropriated the Anatolian example of Mustafa Kemal, and claimed each village was like Ankara in 1920. It was a potent argument and served to mobilise villagers of all sects, including Uniate Christians, against the mandate authorities. Ramadan had learned to read and write in Ottoman schools, and used his skills in letters to the leading rural landlords demanding their contribution to the 'national struggle'. Shallash's appeal to villagers mixed patriotism, popular religion and class warfare against landlords. He routinely threatened prominent Syrians with violence, and his missives resemble strongly the calls-to-arms signed by Mustafa Kemal a few years earlier. He was enormously popular as a revolt leader and national hero.

> To the mukhtars and sheikhs of the village of Qutayfa,
>
> Greetings and blessings of God.
>
> We need you to gather your mujahidin and leave one part to guard your village from the [French] troops and bring the other part to Yabrud tomorrow for the greater glory of the religion of Islam. If you bring them late, you will be responsible before God and before the partisans. If you do not respond to this appeal, and assemble [the mujahidin] today, we will come and take them tomorrow.
>
> 14 October 1925
>
> General Ramadan Shallash[28]

After the bombardment of Damascus, insurgents and their ex-Ottoman officer leaders returned to the orchards and villages of the Damascus countryside. In the hamlets of rural Syria, they preserved an advantage and continued to engage the colonial army with guerrilla tactics innovated in Ottoman

---

[28] Centre des Archives Diplomatiques de Nantes (CADN), carton 1704, Bulletin de Reseingnements, (BR) 241, 5 December 1925, annexe 1. French translation of an Arabic original.

army engagements of the previous decades. Each night insurgents fought mandate forces in the Damascus neighbourhood of Maydan and the surrounding orchards and gardens. Many villages joined the uprising. But the tide gradually turned against them as thousands of French troops, airplanes and heavy weapons arrived.

In December, a faction within the revolt's leadership targeted Ramadan. He was summoned, arrested, and tried in a hasty and improvised 'trial' in a village in the Damascus countryside. His many supporters among the rebels were not present and heard of the proceedings after the events. Evidence suggests he transgressed by extorting money from well-connected landlords, who had refused to support the uprising but who had allies among some rebel leaders. The debate over his expulsion split the rebel ranks and damaged the prospects for revolt. Ramadan escaped his would-be prosecutors when French airplanes bombed the village in which they were hiding.[29]

Ill-provisioned and hungry in the snow-covered mountains north and west of Damascus, Ramadan Shallash headed towards Dayr al-Zur. Traversing the mountains west of Hama, he called on some Ismaili sheikhs for support. French colonial policy centred on attracting Syrian minorities to support France, and mandate intelligence officers had recruited counter-insurgency forces from among the religious minorities, including young Ismaili men. Ramadan tried to appeal to the patriotic feelings of the sheikhs and encourage their young men to defect from French service. In the event, the villagers identified their interests differently, and alerted the French authorities to his presence. The villagers detained Ramadan Shallash near Masyaf. The Ismaili sheikhs conveyed a message from High Commissioner de Jouvenel, promising amnesty and protection for his family if he surrendered. He asked for and received written confirmation and the Ismaili sheikhs agreed to accompany him to Beirut, where he surrendered.[30] He was made to visit High Commissioner de Jouvenel in Beirut where he denounced his comrades who had expelled him and was photographed in the office of the High Commissioner. In later years he attributed his surrender to the tricks

---

[29] I covered the trial of Ramadan Shallash in detail in Michael Provence *The Great Syrian Revolt and the Rise of Arab Nationalism* (Austin: University of Texas Press, 2005), 133–9.

[30] Dr Talal Chlach correspondence, and Shallash memoirs, 20 August 2020.

of his enemies. Several of his former comrades wrote memoirs in which they bitterly denounced the injustice Ramadan had suffered. He spent the next twenty years under French house arrest in Beirut.

Exile, Resistance and Return

In a modern version of an old French practice, Ramadan and his family lived in modest comfort at French expense in Beirut. Earlier privileged captives had included people like Emir Abdelkader, the nineteenth-century resistance leader of Algeria. Beirut was far from the upper Euphrates, and Ramadan apparently much preferred life in his region and among his relatives. His children, including Muhammad Amir, received elite French education at state expense. Muhammad Amir continued to the Syrian military academy, which remained in the Damascus Ottoman *Mekteb-i Askeri İdadi* in the Tankiz Mosque complex on Jamal Basha Street (today's al-Nasr Street). After Syrian independence he eventually became a major general and chief-of-staff to Adib Shishakli, and, finally, chief military adviser to the Kuwaiti government commissioned to form the police force, army and national guard.[31]

In 1939, an incident near Dayr al-Zur drew Ramadan Shallash's attention. French forces engaged some village men in fighting, and when a larger punitive force entered their village, they fled into the safety of the desert. The French force harassed and detained women who stayed in the village, and the village men in turn ambushed and killed some French soldiers. The village mukhtar, one of a Ramadan's brothers, was called upon to turn over the guilty men, which he refused. French forces detained and tortured some among the village men, and killed at least one man in the process, dismissed the mukhtar and appointed a distant Shallash cousin to the post.

Ramadan Shallash, still under house arrest in Beirut, heard the news and eventually received an emissary. He somehow escaped his confinement in Beirut, and travelled across the country via Hums and Tadmur (Palmyra) to his village of al-Shumaytiyya. Upon his arrival, Ramadan assumed the command of what became minor armed uprising. He was a vigorous fifty-seven years old, and led a spirited defence, but was eventually captured and returned to house arrest in Beirut.

---

[31] Interview, Dr Talal Chalch, August 2019

After the fall of France the next year, in 1940, the Lebanese and Syrian mandates came under the control of Vichy French officers. In 1941, British and Free French forces invaded and defeated the Vichy mandate. Between 1941 and independence in 1946 a British and French general, in tense cooperation, ruled Syria and Lebanon under allied military occupation. In 1944, British General Spears overruled his French counterpart General Catroux, who bitterly remembered fighting against Ramadan Shallash as a young intelligence officer during the Great Syrian Revolt in 1925, and finally allowed Ramadan to return to his village.

In 1946, retreating French forces offered to take Ramadan Shallash and his family to France but he refused the invitation. Political action spanned a wide spectrum for the men and women of the last Ottoman and mandate generation. Insurgent revolutionaries like Shallash occupied one pole, while far more compromised and compromising figures like former Prime Minister Jamil Mardam-Bey occupied another. In the independence era new states celebrated the martyrs of the struggle, but the living heroes of armed resistance movements, simply by their presence, raised troublesome questions for the legitimacy of the post-colonial state and its leaders. In many cases they were pushed aside and sent into exile either inside or outside the country.[32]

Shallash, like his friend Sultan al-Atrash and a number of other heroic figures of the armed struggle against France, expected to be feted and to claim their rightful place at the centre of national politics. Syria's immediate post-independence leaders, like President Shukri al-Quwwatli, had other ideas, however, and did not wish to be shadowed by heroic figures, their auras undimmed by compromise with the former colonial power. Ramadan Shallash was unwelcome in national politics, and perhaps even unwelcome in Damascus, and so he, like others of his generation, retired to their villages. Back in al-Shumaytiyya, he threw himself into local affairs, the care of his family and the raising of his children. His youngest son Dr Talal Chalch remembers that Ramadan secured government electrical service for the village and area in the 1950s, and had a kind word for everyone. He was beloved by his family and neighbours. In 1961, Ramadan Shallash moved his family to

---

[32] Benjamin Fortna makes this point about Eşref Kuşçubaşı, and his exile from the new Turkish Republic. See Fortna, *The Circassian*, 229–58.

Damascus to receive medical care. The family rented a furnished house, and it was there, on the morning of 21 August 1961, that he died at the age of about seventy-nine. He was buried in Damascus.

Conclusions

The late Ottoman state, like other continent-spanning empires, developed new means to claim, control and exploit frontier zones. Education, indoctrination and temporary social or commercial alliances, either in the form of concessions, or in the form of land grants to companies, tribes, families and groups, helped to advance the interests of the state. Over the course of the twentieth century and its many upheavals, things changed and states could revoke or advance privileges over time. In 1910, men like Ramadan Shallash appeared to be crucial to the survival of the state, but a couple decades later, such men had become less useful and more dangerous. His life is thus a vivid and poignant illustration of the shattering changes of his times.

12

The Last Ottoman Rogues: The Kurdish–Armenian Alliance in Syria and the New State System in the Interwar Middle East

Jordi Tejel[1]

The Paris Peace Conference of 1919 paved the way for the emergence of new modern states in the Middle East, whether as fully independent entities or under mandatory oversight, by granting them sovereign powers within new 'national' territories. Paradoxically, however, as Bradley Miller puts it, the 'same sovereignty that empowered states also undermined them by limiting the reach of their authority in a world in which people crossed borders, with much more dexterity than law'.[2] Just as borders emerged as a resource for many to secure new economic avenues, sustain trans-border family connections or simply escape the law – criminals and smugglers[3] – the

---

[1] This chapter has received funding from the European Research Council (ERC) under the European Union's Horizon 2020 research and innovation approval (Grant Agreement No. 725269).

[2] Bradley Miller, *Borderline Crime: Fugitive Criminals and the Challenge of the Border, 1819–1914* (Toronto: Toronto University Press, 2016), 6.

[3] On smuggling activities across the Middle Easter borders in the early twentieth century, see Cyrus Schayegh, 'The Many Worlds of 'Abud Yasin; or, What Narcotics Trafficking in the Interwar Middle East Can Tell Us about Territorialization', *American Historical Review* 116(2) (2011): 273–306; Liat Kozma, 'White Drugs in Interwar Egypt: Decadent Pleasures, Emaciated Fellahin, and the Campaign against Drugs', *Comparative Studies of South Asia, Africa and the Middle East* 33(1) (2013): 89–101; Ryan Gingeras, *Heroin, Organized Crime, and the Making of Modern Turkey* (Oxford: Oxford University Press, 2014); Haggai Ram, 'Hashish Traffickers, Hashish Consumers, and Colonial Knowledge in Mandatory Palestine', *Middle Eastern Studies* 52(3) (2016): 546–63; Mitchell Alan

new borders brought about disconnected jurisdictions that provided 'old' political actors with new opportunities, too.

Diverse ex-Ottoman revolutionary groups in particular tapped into the cracks of the emerging international system in the Middle East to pursue their political goals, taking advantage of a context still marked by instability and uncertainty. For one, although the First World War formally ended in 1918, it left behind several zones of post-war violence, as the disappearance of imperial borders – from Eastern Europe to the Caucasus and the Middle East – created spaces without order or a definite state authority.[4] Among these 'shatter zones',[5] the provisional frontier between Turkey and Syria holds an important place, since it 'proved more contentious and even more complicated to manage' for Turkish and French authorities alike.[6] Turkish and French authorities sought to cope with cross-border mobility, on the one hand, and insecurity and the lack of definition of the new international borders, on the other, by resorting to a delicate, albeit not always effective, act of balance, from co-opting armed irregular bands (*çetes*) and/or revolutionary groups to state violence, diplomatic manoeuvres, propaganda, security cooperation and informal agreements between low-level border officials.[7]

Bacci, 'Smugglers and State Builders: Opiate Trafficking and Institutional Development in Interwar Egypt and Turkey', MA thesis, University of Texas, 2017; Ramazan Hakkı Öztan, 'The Great Depression and the Making of the Turkish–Syrian Border, 1921–1939', *International Journal of Middle East Studies* 52(2) (2020): 311–26.

[4] Robert Gerwarth and John Horne (eds), *War in Peace: Paramilitary Violence in Europe after the Great War* (Oxford: Oxford University Press, 2012).

[5] Omer Bartov and Eric D. Weitz (eds), *Shatterzone of Empires: Coexistence and Violence in the German, Habsburg, Russian, and Ottoman Borderlands* (Bloomington: Indiana University Press, 2013).

[6] Amit Bein, *Kemalist Turkey and the Middle East: International Relations in the Interwar Period* (Cambridge: Cambridge University Press, 2017), 42. See also Christian Velud, 'Une expérience d'administration régionale en Syrie durant le mandat français: conquête, colonisation et mise en valeur de la Gazîra, 1920–1936', unpublished dissertation, University of Lyon 2, 1991; Jean-David Mizrahi, *Genèse de l'Etat mandataire. Service des Renseignements et bandes armées en Syrie et au Liban dans les années 1920* (Paris: Publications de la Sorbonne, 2003); Sarah D. Shields, *Fezzes in the River: Identity Politics and European Diplomacy in the Middle East on the Eve of World War II* (Oxford: Oxford University Press, 2011).

[7] Jean-David Mizrahi, 'La répression du banditisme sur les confins de la Syrie mandataire: nouveaux Etats et nouvelles frontières dans le Moyen-Orient des années 1920', *Relations*

This chapter explores how and to what extent the new borders in the region created opportunities and constraints to ex-Ottoman clandestine political groups in this rapidly changing historical context. Drawing from Turkish, British and French Mandate archival sources as well as Kurdish and Armenian activists' pamphlets and memoirs, the chapter focuses on the Khoybun League which, in 1927, brought together the formerly Istanbul-based Kurdish activists with the Armenians of the Dashnak Party into a revolutionary organisation active in French Syria and Lebanon with the aim of 'liberating' Armenia and Kurdistan from the Republic of Turkey.[8]

The chapter first analyses the factors that led to this alliance as well as the roles assigned to each group. While the Khoybun League sought to secure the allegiance of irregular armed bands on the slopes of Mount Ararat (1927–32), an area stretching between contemporary Turkey and Iran, the Dashnak militants committed themselves to providing their Kurdish counterpart with weapons, money and a solid transnational network of Armenian cells. Admittedly, the propagandists of the revolt took benefit from the increasing speed of travel and transportation facilities available in cities such as Aleppo, Cairo, Beirut or Alexandretta to disseminate their political goals with relative ease and to collect funds in places as far as Detroit, Rome and Nice. Notwithstanding this, while the region indeed witnessed an unprecedented intensification of the movement of people, goods and ideas,[9] the acceleration of speed and time compression that characterised the incipient

---

Internationales 114 (2003): 173–87; Yücel Güçlü, *Question of the Sanjak of Alexandretta: A Study in Turkish–French–Syrian Relations* (Ankara: Türk Tarih Kurumu, 2001).

[8] The Armenian Revolutionary Federation (ARF), also known as Dashnaktsutyun (in short form Dashnak), was established in Tbilisi in 1890. On the Armenian activities in the late Ottoman period, see for a Unionist perspective Şükrü Hanioğlu, *Preparation of a Revolution: The Young Turks, 1902–1908* (Oxford: Oxford University Press, 2001), 94–129. For an Armenian viewpoint, see Dikran Mesrob Kaligian, *Armenian Organization and Ideology under Ottoman Rule, 1908–1914* (New Brunswick, NJ: Transaction Publishers, 2008); For a transnational study on the Armenian political parties, see Houri Berberian, *Roving Revolutionaries: Armenians and the Connected Revolutions in the Russian, Iranian, and Ottoman Worlds* (Berkeley: University of California Press, 2019).

[9] James L. Gelvin and Nile Green (eds), *Global Muslims in the Age of Steam and Print* (Berkeley: University of California Press, 2014); Liat Kozma, Cyrus Schayegh and Avner Wishnitzer (eds), *A Global Middle East: Mobility, Materiality and Culture in the Modern Age, 1880–1940* (London: I. B. Tauris, 2015).

modern globalisation outspread in a rather uneven manner. For one, armed rebels in Mount Ararat travelled with great difficulty across this mountainous region. More significantly, couriers and weapons deliveries by and large failed to reach the 'liberated area', thereby further increasing the experience of isolation among the former.

Of course, these activities did not go unnoticed. The chapter shows in its second section that the transnational networks mobilised by Kurdish and Armenian rebels to fight the Turkish regime contrasted against a backdrop of interstate cooperation to deal with this challenge. For different reasons, Turkey, British Iraq, French Syria and, ultimately, Persia concluded that the Kurdish–Armenian alliance was not beneficial for a region where stability was necessary for the consolidation of newly established states. Consequently, state authorities attempted to curtail revolutionaries' mobility in different ways, including border controls and the pervasive use of visas as a key device to channel cross-border movements. Although documentation of status was not completely new in the region, passports together with visas became tools of securitisation widely used after the First World War.[10] Several members of the Khoybun League and Dashnak were arrested, banished or expelled by the state authorities on such legal grounds. I argue thus that while the disruption of territorial sovereignty offered unprecedented political opportunities to former 'Ottoman' transnational revolutionary networks, the new emerging international system imposed new realities that, for them, also turned out to be insurmountable.[11]

---

[10] See Will Hanley, *Identifying with Nationality: Europeans, Ottomans, and Egyptians in Alexandria* (New York: Columbia University Press, 2017), 70–4. See also John Torpey, *The Invention of the Passport: Surveillance, Citizenship, and the State* (Cambridge: Cambridge University Press, 2000); Mark B. Salter, *Rights of Passage: The Passport in International Relations* (Boulder, CO: Lynne Rienner, 2003).

[11] For a critical assessment of the new international system and its contradictions, see Mark Mazower, *No Enchanted Palace: The End of Empire and the Ideological Origins of the United Nations* (Princeton, NJ: Princeton University Press, 2009); Laura Robson, *States of Separation: Transfer, Partition, and the Making of the Modern Middle East* (Berkeley: University of California Press, 2017).

The Rugged Path towards the Kurdish–Armenian Alliance

At the end of the First World War, the Ottoman government accepted the conditions imposed by the victorious Allied powers at the Paris Peace Conference. Among the post-war accords, the Treaty of Sèvres (1920) holds an important place with regard to the international relations between Turkey and its southern neighbours throughout the interwar period. The treaty stipulated partitioning of the Ottoman Empire and obliged Turkey to renounce all its claims over the Arab provinces of the empire. In addition, the pact provided for an independent Armenia as well as an autonomous Kurdistan in contemporary northeastern and southeastern Turkey, respectively.

However, the resistance movement led by Mustafa Kemal – an Ottoman brigadier general – rejected the treaty altogether, and carried out a successful struggle that mixed paramilitary and conventional means of warfare. As Mustafa Kemal and other ex-Ottoman officers obtained a series of significant military victories in the Caucasus and southeastern Anatolia, the resistance movement made its territorial ambitions clear through what was called the *Misak-ı Milli* (the National Pact) which laid claim over Mosul province as well northern Syria, including Alexandretta and Aleppo.[12] The Pact of January 1920 rejected any division of territories populated by those Ottoman Muslims who were 'united in religion, culture, and aim' and, consequently, served as basis for cooperation between different anti-colonial fronts.[13] After the collapse of Faysal's kingdom (1918–20) in Syria, however, France officially received from the League of Nations its mandate over Syria and Lebanon. Likewise, the mandate for Iraq was awarded to Great Britain in 1920, while the political status of Mosul province was left open for negotiations between the Turkish and British governments.

---

[12] Bein, *Kemalist Turkey and the Middle East*, 10.
[13] For some comprehensive accounts on the anti-colonial fronts along the present Turkish–Syrian and Turkish–Iraqi borders, see Ahmet H. Saral, *Türk İstiklal Harbi Cilt IV: Güney Cephesi: İngiliz ve Fransızların Güney-Doğu Anadolu'yu İşgal Etmeleri Milli Mücadele Hareketleri, Bu Bölgede Yapılan Muharebeler ve Revandiz Harekatı* (Ankara: Genelkurmay Başkanlığı Harp Tarihi Dairesi, 1966), 265–78; Oktay Bozan, *Milli Mücadele Döneminde Diyarbakır, 1918–1923* (Konya: Çizgi Kitabevi, 2016), 255–312; Enes Demir, *Vazgeçilmeyen Topraklar Misak-ı Milli* (Istanbul: Post, 2017).

These international arrangements failed to bring stability to the region. A coalition of Turkish, Arab and Kurdish bands succeeded in repelling French advances in Cilicia and pushing the front line southwards, and, significantly, imposing new peace negotiations on France. Subsequently, after the Ankara agreement of October 1921 with the French, the Turkish government severed its links with Arab armed bands north of Aleppo, which allowed for the delimitation of the temporary boundary between Turkey and Syria.[14] This bilateral accord in addition to the French evacuation of Cilicia further isolated Great Britain in the face of anti-colonial unrest across Mesopotamia. By 1922, France and Great Britain were thus ready to open negotiations with the new leaders of Turkey.[15] The subsequent treaty of Lausanne of 24 July 1923 buried the perspectives of the Armenian and Kurdish states altogether.

Turkish–French relations nevertheless remained contentious along the common frontier. Particularly, Turkish propaganda in northeastern Syria proved to be extremely effective in hindering the advance of French troops up until 1926. Meanwhile, several French voices (unions, parties, anti-colonial committees) raised concerns about the financial viability as well as the political prospects of French mandate over Syria and Lebanon.[16] It is within this context, marked by both external and internal constraints, that the French high commissioner saw the launch of a profitable economic programme in Syrian as a tool that could serve to justify its 'civilising' mission in the Levant.[17]

However, the local populations that included both Kurdish and Arab elements were deemed insufficiently large and 'unprepared' to undertake a potential increase in arable lands. French authorities accordingly began to settle Christian migrants and refugees – Armenians and Syriacs – from south-

[14] Mizrahi, 'La répression du banditisme sur les confins de la Syrie mandataire', 173–87.
[15] Peter Sluglett, *Britain in Iraq: Contriving King and Country* (London: I. B. Tauris, 2007).
[16] Paul Huvelin, *Que vaut la Syrie?* (Marseille: Chambre de Commerce de Marseille, 1919); Alice Poulleau, *À Damas sous les bombes: journal d'une française pendant la révolution syrienne, 1924–1926* (Yvetot: Imprimerie Bretteville, s.d.); Pierre Bonnardi, *L'Imbroglio syrien* (Paris: Rieder, 1927).
[17] Christian Velud, 'La politique mandataire française à l'égard des tribus et des zones de steppe en Syrie: L'exemple de la Djézireh', in Riccardo Bocco, Ronald Jaubert and Françoise Métral (eds), *Steppes d'Arabie: Etats, pasteurs, agriculteurs et commerçants: le devenir des zones sèches* (Paris: PUF, 1993), 70–1.

ern Anatolia into the region.[18] This wave of rural Armenian settlement in northern Syria took a further twist with the arrival of politicised Armenian refugees fleeing from the Caucasus after the collapse in 1921 of the Dashnak-led Democratic Republic of Armenia.[19]

By 1925, as French troops and Christian settlers were still being attacked by irregular forces, the high commissioner encouraged Kurdish tribes fleeing repression from the Turkish government after the collapse of the Sheikh Said revolt to settle in northern Syria.[20] These refugees were supposed to serve two complementary goals: stabilising the frontier and increasing the agricultural production of the Upper Jazira. Yet among the newcomers there were not only tribal groups, but also members of Istanbul's Kurdish nationalist clubs that had been banished after the establishment of the Turkish Republic in 1923. Whereas some of these intellectuals and diverse members of the late Sheikh Said's family found refuge in Iraq, most of them looked to France for protection in the Levant.[21]

Although one could assume that the shared experience of exile and the existence of a 'common enemy' – that is, Turkey – could explain the later collaboration between the Kurdish and Armenian activists, the pre-existing Ottoman networks and contacts turned out to be equally important, if not more decisive. In that regard, the presence in Syria of some members of the Badirkhan family was key not only for the establishment of the Khoybun League, but also for its subsequent evolution, including its political alliance with the Dashnak Party.

---

[18] Christian Velud, 'L'émergence et l'organisation sociales des petites villes de Jézireh, en Syrie, sous le mandat français', *URBAMA* 16/17 (1986): 85–103; Vahé Tatchijan, *La France en Cilicie et en Haute-Mésopotamie: Aux confins de la Turquie, de la Syrie et de l'Irak* (Paris: Karthala, 2004).

[19] The return of some Dashnak members to the Levant was not surprising, for many of them had fought in Cilicia until 1920 when they decided to go to the Caucasus to back the short-lived Armenian Republic. Tatchijan, *La France en Cilicie et en Haute-Mésopotamie*, 100.

[20] The Ankara government deported some Kurdish tribal chieftains towards the west of the country as a means of clearing the eastern provinces of its more rebellious elements. Robert Olson, *The Emergence of Kurdish Nationalism and the Sheikh Said Rebellion, 1880–1925* (Austin: University of Texas Press, 1989).

[21] Jordi Tejel, *Le mouvement kurde de Turquie en exil. Continuités et discontinuités du nationalisme kurde sous le mandat français en Syrie et au Liban, 1925–1946* (Bern: Peter Lang, 2007), 115–44.

Badirkhan Paşa had succeeded in creating a dynasty and ruled the semi-independent Bohtan emirate until 1847 when the Ottoman government crushed the short-lived rebellion. Most members of the Badirkhan family were forcibly exiled (*sürgün*) throughout the Ottoman territories while working for the empire at different administrative levels.[22] Although the majority of the Badirkhanis accommodated with the new situation, others such as Miqdad Midhat – editor of the first Kurdish newspaper *Kurdistan* (1898) – and Sureya opposed first the rule of Abdülhamid II and then the Unionist regime.[23]

In the last Ottoman years, the Kurdish clubs in Istanbul were torn down by two competing leaderships: Sayyid Abdulkadir (1851–1925), hailing from a Naqishbandi family of the Hakkari region, on the one hand; and Amin Ali Badirkhan (1851–1926), on the other. Although the two blocs were active within the *Kürdistan Teali Cemiyeti* (KTC), founded on 17 December 1918,[24] tensions between the two families led to a split in 1920 when the Badirkhanis created a committee with the aim of gaining Western support to create an independent Kurdistan.[25] After the establishment of the Republic of Turkey in 1923 and the suppression of the Sheikh Said rebellion two years later, all members of this society settled in the former Arab provinces of the empire. In the Levant, Jaladat, Kamuran and Sureya Badirkhan mobilised their family connections across the region to reorganise the Kurdish movement under their leadership.[26]

Apart from the Kurdish networks, the Armenian political movement

---

[22] See Malmîsanij, *Cizira Botanlı Bedirhaniler ve Bedirhan Ailesi Derneğinin Tutanakları* (Spanga: APEC, 1994).

[23] Sureya Badirkhan established a secret society in 1912 and made arrangements to assassinate Unionist leaders. Despite his capture, a year later Sureya escaped to Egypt where he kept publishing *Kurdistan* until 1917. See Basile Nikitine, 'Badrkhani, Thurayya (1883–1938) et Djaladat (1893–1951)', *Encyclopédie de l'Islam*, vol. 1 (Leiden: Brill, 1960), 895.

[24] For a comprehensive analysis of the tensions and debates within the KTC, see Martin Strohmeier, *Crucial Images in the Presentation of a Kurdish National Identity* (Leiden: Brill, 2003), 36–74.

[25] Centre d'Archives diplomatiques de Nantes (CADN hereafter), Fonds Ankara, 36PO/1/92. 'Letter by the Ligue Sociale kurde', Istanbul, 18 May 1920.

[26] Barbara Henning, *Narratives of the History of the Ottoman–Kurdish Bedirhani Family in Imperial and post-Imperial Contexts: Continuities and Changes* (Bamberg: University of Bamberg Press, 2018), 509.

was not completely foreign to the Badirkhani.[27] In particular, Abdurrahman Badirkhan – via the journal *Kurdistan*[28] – as well as Armenian intellectuals had called for a decentralisation policy in order to keep together the different ethnic and religious groups inhabiting the Ottoman Empire.

In the aftermath of the Armenian Genocide, however, there seemed to be no reason to expect a renewal of contacts. Several Kurdish tribes had played a crucial role in the massacres and confiscation of property during the First World War.[29] Unexpectedly, however, the former Ottoman-Kurdish diplomat Sharif Paşa and the Armenian representative Boghos Nubar attempted a rapprochement in order to gain Western support at the Paris Peace Conference in 1919.[30] Thus, while Sharif Paşa's memorandum distilled anti-Armenian rhetoric, the accompanying map acknowledged Armenian territorial claims in northeastern Anatolia. Notwithstanding this, as Kurdish and Armenian delegates at the Conference partly laid claims over the same territories in Eastern Anatolia, mistrust rather than solidarity seemed to prevail.[31] The rapprochement therefore occurred against all expectations. According to Garo Sasuni, president of the Dashnak section in Beirut, the *Kürt Millet Fırkası* and Dashnak reached a provisional agreement that opened the door for a united action against the Turkish Republic in 1924.[32] However, in spring 1925 the

---

[27] See, for instance, the Dashnak call for friendship in its official journal *Troshak*, 'Kürtlere çağrı' 6 (8 June 1898), 5.

[28] Abdurrahman Badirkhan published a call to the Kurdish people in 1901 in which he asked the Kurds to stop attacking the Armenians and claimed unity between the two peoples. Garo Sasuni, *Kürt Ulusal Hareketleri ve 15. YY'dan Günümüze Ermeni Kürt İlişkileri* (Istanbul: Med Yayinevi, 1992), 130.

[29] For a long durée perspective, see Tessa Hofman and Gerayer Koutcharian, 'The History of Armenian–Kurdish Relations in the Ottoman Empire', *Armenian Review* 39(4) (1986): 1–45. For a comprehensive study of the role played by Kurdish tribes in the Armenian genocide, see Janet Klein, *The Margins of Empire: Kurdish Militias in the Ottoman Tribal Zone* (Stanford, CT: Stanford University Press, 2011).

[30] Tejel, *Le mouvement kurde de Turquie en exil*, 196–8.

[31] Diverse Kurdish members of the KTC published a series of articles in the official journal *Jîn* ('Life') in which they contested Armenian aspirations in Eastern Anatolia using quantitative arguments. In addition, they argued that the Armenians were not the only Ottoman nation to have suffered in the war. See Memduh Selim, 'Bir harikati tenvir', *Jîn* 15 (27 March 1919), 100–1.

[32] Sasuni, *Kürt Ulusal Hareketleri*, 184.

Sheikh Said revolt unpredictably erupted without any coordination with the Armenian revolutionaries. The channel of communication between the two parties was not completely disrupted, though. In Paris, during summer 1927, 'several Armenians and Kurdish nationalists met together and resolved to unite their endeavours to establish the political freedom of the Kurdish and Armenian nations'.[33] The last and definite shape of the alliance was nevertheless given in the Levant, once more under the Badirkhan leadership.

The formation of the Khoybun League (*Xwebûn* in Kurdish-Kurmanji, lit. translated as 'Be yourself') or 'Independence League' was the result of a series of meetings held between September and October 1927 in Lebanon, which brought together seventeen representatives from several Kurdish organisations as well as tribal chiefs to discuss the political future of the Kurds in Turkey.[34] The goals of the new organisation included: to fight the Turks in order to create a Kurdish entity; collaborating with the Armenians; refusing to comply with the anti-Kemalist caliphate partisans (as a successful collaboration with this group offered insufficient guarantee of Kurdish independence);[35] friendly relations with the USSR, Persia and Iraq; and seeking support from a Great Power (France or, if necessary, Great Britain). Officially, however, the organisation simply sought to collect funds for the Kurdish refugees originating from Turkey and aimed to publish a newspaper in Kurdish and French.[36]

---

[33] The National Archives (TNA hereafter), CO 730/133/1. Confidential. The Residency in Baghdad to the Secretary of state for the Colonies, 14 July 1928.

[34] CADN, Fonds Syrie et Liban (1SL hereafter) /1/V/569, Report on the Kurds and Kurdistan. Beirut, 1 February 1929.

[35] The anti-Kemalist opposition was not limited to the Kurds and Armenians, though. While in the early 1920s, the Circassian irregular forces fought the Greeks and the royalists in Anatolia, the consolidation of Mustafa Kemal's authority soon brought about rifts between the new Turkish authorities and the Circassian leaders who commanded the formerly useful armed bands. In addition, Circassians were over-represented among the anti-Kemalist opposition, also known as the '150 undesirables' or *persona non grata* in Turkey. See Sedat Bingöl, *150'likler Meselesi: Bir İhanetin Anatomisi* (Istanbul: Bengi Yayınları, 2010). On the role played by Circassians in political conspiracies against the Kemalist leadership, see Ramazan Hakki Öztan, 'Republic of Conspiracies: Cross-Border Plots and the Making of Modern Turkey', *Journal of Contemporary History* (April 2020), available at: https://doi.org/10.1177%2F0022009419884627.

[36] CADN, 1SL/1/V/1055. Intelligence from Aleppo, Aleppo, 19 November 1927.

From the beginning, the Badirkhanis opened the door of the organisation to the Dashnak party. Furthermore, the first congress of the Khoybun League was held at the summer residence of Vahan Papazian, ex-Ottoman deputy for Van, in Behamdun (Lebanon). Thereafter, Papazian also participated, along with Ador Levonian, in the subsequent congress in Aleppo on 29 March 1928. In addition, other Dashnak members worked in close cooperation with the Kurdish committee. This collaboration was sealed when the treaty of October 1927 was signed in Beirut between the Dashnak and the Khoybun League, advocating the liberation of the two 'brother states'. According to the agreement, the two parties would recognise the right to independence of Kurdistan and United Armenia, while the delimitation of the border between the two states was to be decided according to the pre-war indigenous Kurdish and Armenian populations and as per the legal framework of the Treaty of Sèvres.[37]

For Yves Ternon, the alliance between the two parties was strategically 'natural'; even though the Dashnak lost any presence in Turkey in the aftermath of the Armenian Genocide and the fall of the Democratic Republic of Armenia in the Caucasus, the party still possessed a solid revolutionary experience and material resources that the Kurds lacked. In turn, the Kurds had the potential capacity to recruit and mobilise thousands of fighters against the Turkish Republic in Eastern Anatolia.[38] Although some Kurds were more doubtful of the prospects of an alliance,[39] previous intellectual relations together with pressing financial constraints led the Badirkhani to resist all critiques and actively collaborate with the Dashnak Party; a cooperation that bore some significant results between 1927 and 1932.

---

[37] See the agreement in Hamit Bozarslan, 'Histoire des relations kurdo-arméniennes', in Hans-Lukas Kieser (ed.), *Kurdistan und Europa* (Zurich: Chronos, 1997), 182–6.
[38] Yves Ternon, *La cause arménienne* (Paris: Seuil, 1983), 118.
[39] In May 1928, a number of Kurds published in the Damascus newspaper *Fatât al Arab* a proclamation openly repudiating the Khoybun League and stigmatising it as a plot to cheat the simple-minded Kurds into making war against the Turks, 'so that on their dead bodies the Armenians might create a national home in which the Kurds would be their slaves'. TNA, CO 730/133/1. Confidential. The Residency in Baghdad to the Secretary of state for the Colonies, 14 July 1928.

Khoybun's Activities under Dashnak Influence

The Khoybun League rapidly succeeded in creating a transnational network of branches across the Middle East in cities such as Aleppo, Damascus, Antioch, Hama, Jarablus and Hasaka (Syria); Baghdad, Mosul and Zakho (Iraq); Beirut (Lebanon); Cairo (Egypt); and Amman (Jordan) and beyond (Paris, Detroit). The committee, however, embodied a sort of 'unnatural marriage' between a Westernised intelligentsia – namely, intellectuals and ex-Ottoman officers – and representatives of traditional Kurdish society; that is, aghas, sheikhs and tribal leaders.[40] However, this alliance was not self-evident. A substantial effort on the part of Kurdish intellectuals was needed to adapt the modernist discourse on nationalism to the tribal social relations. The following oath formulated by the Khoybun constitutes a striking example:

> I do hereby swear on my honour and religion that from the date of my signing this promise for a period of two years . . . I will postpone until the expiration of these two years, all blood feuds and other disputes, and do my utmost to prevent bloodshed between two Kurds on private matters. Any Kurd who attempts to contravene this undertaking is regarded a traitor of his nation, and the murder of every traitor is a duty.[41]

Under Dashnak influence, the Khoybun League insisted on the importance of maintaining a tight internal structure and organisational discipline. In particular, Vahan Papazian monitored its formative period, imposing the Dashnak model on Khoybun thanks to Armenian financial leverage over its Kurdish counterpart.[42] Thus, according to the fundamen-

---

[40] The core of the Khoybun League at the time of its creation was made up of Jaladat Badirkhan (1893–1951), Kamuran Badirkhan (1895–1978), Sureya Badirkhan (1883–1938), Memduh Selim (1897–1976), Mehmed Şükrü Sekban (1881–1960), Ihsan Nuri (1893–1976), Bozan Shahin Beg (1895–1968), Mustafa Shahin Beg (?–1953), Sheikh Abdul Rahman Garisi (1869–1932), Hajo Agha (?–1940) and Rifat Mevlanzade (1869–1930). By 1929, the arrival of new Kurdish refugees strengthened the organisation. Among them were Akram Cemil Paşa (1891–1974), Kadri Cemil Paşa (1892–1973), Osman Sabri (1905–93), Ahmad Nafiz (1902–68) and Arif Abbas (1900–84).

[41] TNA, AIR 23/416, 'Kurdish nationalism. The Khoybun society', Special service officer, Mosul, 26 February 1930.

[42] FONDS RONDOT, Dossier Comités kurdes, 'Kurdes', 13 February 1940.

tal regulations, 'every member is to carry out any given order without raising objections'.[43] The society similarly underscored the responsibility of its members to induce 'every Kurd' to join the League. To do so, the committee charged its members with 'the duty of spreading propaganda for Kurdish independence and against the Turkish oppression and atrocities'.[44]

Khoybun's propaganda was, however, of variable geometry, as the themes put forth and the vocabulary used changed depending on the audience. This is perfectly illustrated by a letter written by Sureya Badirkhan to his brother Kamuran as the former was completing the publication of a propaganda brochure. Sureya Badirkhan explained that 'the brochure in the Persian language will deal with the weakening of the Aryan race . . .' In order to counter this danger, there should be an 'Aryan Confederation' led by Iran and uniting the Kurds, Armenians and Persians.[45] However, the Arab brochure was to deal with 'our numerous services rendered to the Islamic and Arab causes'. Finally, the French brochure would deal with 'the history of our revolutions and insurrections . . . foreigners' opinions of us and the duties incumbent on civilized Europe'.[46]

In addition to organisational inspiration, the Dashnaks also provided an ideological back-up to Kurdish propaganda. Roupen Ter Minassian (1882–1951), a long-time member of the ARF Bureau and a member of the short-lived Parliament of Yerevan, heralded the Aryan unity as a counterweight in the face of the pan-Turkism in the Caucasus and Central Asia.[47] The Armenian party also justified cooperation with the Khoybun League before Western public opinion and international forums such as the Second Socialist International. Thus, for instance, Armenian-American lawyer and

---

[43] TNA, AIR 23/414. 'The Khoybun Society: The Kurdish Race and Country', Special Service Officer, Sulaymaniyya, 10 September 1928.
[44] Ibid.
[45] The alleged Aryan character of the Armenians could also be read as a response to the anti-Armenian discourse in Germany based on a theory that did not include the Armenians in the Aryan race. See Stefan Ihrig, *Justifying Genocide: Germany and the Armenians from Bismarck to Hitler* (Cambridge, MA: Harvard University Press, 2015).
[46] CADN, 1SL/1/V/1055, Sûreté Générale, Information No. 1985, Beirut, 22 August 1930.
[47] Roupen Ter Minassian, 'Iran yév Touran', *Troshak* 4 (1927).

activist Vahan Cardashian (1883–1934) published a couple of articles in support of the Ararat revolt in the *New York Times*.[48]

In a joint effort, Khoybun and Dashnak representatives sought to establish 'diplomatic' alliances with all powers that could help the two parties to reach their political aims – from the USSR to Great Britain, France, Italy, Greece and Persia. Although the results were not as expected, the Kurdish and Armenian representatives were received by state officials, thereby gaining in political legitimacy. Such diplomatic initiatives were topped off with further collaboration on tactics of violence that were tightly connected to earlier Ottoman practices; the organisation of armed bands on the slopes of Mount Ararat closely followed the *çete* model,[49] on the one hand, and the orchestration of assassination plots against the Turkish leadership, on the other.[50]

The continuity of such practices was hardly surprising. Several representatives of the 'last Ottoman generation' played crucial roles in the rebellions that sparked across the Levant and Anatolia in the 1920s.[51] As Michael Provence has observed 'abundant evidence . . . suggests that rebel participants – collective veterans of wars to save the Ottoman state – did not view the

---

[48] Vahan Cardashian, 'Kurds Fight for Freedom', 6 June 1930, and 'Assert Kurds are Winning', 18 October 1930, *New York Times*.

[49] Jean-David Mizrahi, 'Un nationalisme de la frontière: bandes armées et sociabilités politiques sur la frontière turco-syrienne au début des années 1920', *Vingtième Siècle: Revue d'histoire* 78 (2003): 19–34; Nadine Méouchy, 'Rural Resistance and the Introduction of Modern Forms of Consciousness in the Syrian Countryside, 1918–1926', in Thomas Philipp and Christoph Schumann (eds), *From the Syrian Land to the States of Syria and Lebanon* (Beirut: Orient-Institut, 2004), 275–90; Laila Parsons, *The Commander: Fawzi al-Qawuqji and the Fight for Arab Independence, 1914–1948* (New York: Farrar Straus & Giroux, 2016).

[50] On conspiracies in the Ottoman period, see Florian Riedler, *Opposition and Legitimacy in the Ottoman Empire: Conspiracies and Political Cultures* (London: Routledge, 2011); Gwynne Dyer, 'The Origins of the "Nationalist" Group of Officers in Turkey, 1908–1918', *Journal of Contemporary History* 8(4) (1973): 121–64; Erik Jan Zürcher, 'Macedonians in Anatolia: The Importance of the Macedonian Roots of the Unionists for their Policies in Anatolia after 1914', *Middle Eastern Studies* 50(6) (2014): 960–75. See also Alp Yenen, 'The Young Turk Zeitgeist in the Middle Eastern Uprisings in the Aftermath of World War I', in Hakan Yavuz and Feroz Ahmad (eds), *War and Collapse: World War I and the Ottoman State* (Salt Lake City: University of Utah Press, 2016), 1181–216.

[51] Michael Provence, *The Last Ottoman Generation and the Making of the Modern Middle East* (Cambridge: Cambridge University Press, 2017).

post-Ottoman revolts as separate movements of national liberation but rather as locally conditioned elements of a single, undifferentiated struggle'.[52] Yet while a shared repertoire of *komitadji* – that is, partisans, irregular troops or guerrilla movements[53] – conduct was evident, the former Ottoman officers framed their struggles in a variety of ways, borrowing ideas and discourses from diverse sources and cultural idioms, including Turkish nationalism, 'Ottoman-Muslim solidarity',[54] as well as Arab and Kurdish nationalism.

Such was the case of the military leader of the Ararat revolt. Like many Kurdish officers while declaring himself a 'Kurdish patriot', Ihsan Nuri (1892–1976) did not desert the Ottoman army during the First World War.[55] Subsequently, he joined the KTC and published an article in the association's newspaper *Jîn* where he hailed the Wilsonian principles on self-determination as a solution for the 'Kurdish issue'.[56] By 1922, he founded together with other officers and young intellectuals *Azadî* ('Freedom'), a nationalist organisation that sought to create a Kurdish state as per the Treaty of Sèvres.[57] In the meantime, however, Ihsan Nuri remained in the Turkish army until 1924, when he was sent to Bayt al Shabah – in the Hakkari region – to suppress a Nestorian uprising. After having received, and more likely misinterpreted, a telegram from the *Azadî* headquarters in Istanbul, Ihsan Nuri and his Kurdish comrades mutinied in September 1924.[58] Idly organised, the revolt failed and their leaders had to seek refuge in British Iraq. On their way, diverse Kurdish officers were either imprisoned or

---

[52] Michael Provence, 'Ottoman Modernity, Colonialism, and Insurgency in the Interwar Arab East', *International Journal of Middle East Studies* 43(2) (2011): 207.
[53] See for instance, Uğur Ümit Üngör, 'Paramilitary Violence in the Collapsing Ottoman Empire', in Robert Gerwarth and John Horne (eds), *War in Peace: Paramilitary Violence in Europe after the Great War* (Oxford: Oxford University Press, 2012), 164–83.
[54] Erik Jan Zürcher, 'The Vocabulary of Muslim Nationalism', *International Journal of the Sociology of Language* 137(1) (1999): 81–92.
[55] Born in Bitlis, Ihsan Nuri studied at the Military Academy in Istanbul. During the First World War, Nuri was injured. After his recovery, he was sent to the Russian front where he was in constant contact with Kâzim Karabekir.
[56] Ihsan Nuri, 'Wilson Prensipleri ve Kürtler', *Jîn* 15 (1919).
[57] Nuri Dersimi, *Kürdistan tarihinde Dersim* (Köln: Mezopotamien Verlag, 1999), 177; Zinar Soran, 'Civata Azadiya Kurd', *çira* 1 (1995): 58–60.
[58] Dersimi, *Kürdistan tarihinde Dersim*, 178; Olson, *The Emergence of Kurdish Nationalism*, 43–5.

killed, leaving Ihsan Nuri more isolated from his closest collaborators in the army.[59]

Invited to participate in the foundational congress of the Khoybun League in 1927, Ihsan Nuri rather preferred to move to the slopes of Mount Ararat where Ibrahim Agha of the Jalali tribal confederation had initiated an uprising against the Ankara government. Subsequently, the Khoybun League granted the ex-Ottoman officer the title of General Chief of the Kurdish forces. A Dashnak *komitadji*, Ardashes Mouradian (alias Zeynal Bey), was sent to the Ararat area to serve as a liaison with the Kurdish forces.[60] While Ihsan Nuri tried to disseminate notions of national solidarity and use modern means of propaganda and warfare – the Kurdish flag and a national anthem, the journal *Agri*, and a transitional 'Constitution' – in the 'Republic of Ararat', the Kurdish forces were actually organised along tribal lines and could only conduct raids in small groups against remote Turkish military posts.[61] Like other ex-Ottoman officers engaged in rebellions throughout the 1920s, Ihsan Nuri tried to adjust the national ethos to the rural milieu and guide, unsuccessfully, guerrilla bands that ultimately lacked military discipline and expertise.

Finally, while the Ararat revolt took place in isolation in a peripheral area, the Khoybun and Dashnak operatives resorted to other violent means to reach their goals; that is, assassination plots against the Republic leadership. Thus, for instance, in 1928 Memduh Selim entrusted a Khoybun *fedaî* with the assassination of Mustafa Kemal. However, the plot was uncovered and the Turkish police caught the *fedaî* in Istanbul.[62] As the revolt appeared to collapse, the Dashnak Party allegedly made two new – and ineffective

---

[59] Ihsan Nouri, *Mon destin de Kurde* (*Besar hatimin*, trans. Ayoub Babo Barzani) (Geneva: Editions Orient-Réalités, 2019), 103–5.

[60] Garabet K. Moumdjian, 'Armenian Involvement in the 1925 (Ararat) and 1937 (Dersim) Kurdish Rebellions in Republican Turkey: Mapping the Origins of Hidden Armenians', *International Crimes and History* 19 (2018): 188–9.

[61] Ihsan Nouri, *La révolte de l'Agri Dagh* (Geneva: Editions kurdes, 1986), 129–30. For the regulations issued at Mount Ararat, see CADN, 1SL/1/V/1055, 'Proclamation de l'occupation effective et de l'institution du gouvernement', Services civils du Délégué, Aleppo, 23 May 1933.

[62] TNA, AIR 23/407, 'Turkey and Syria: Anti-Kemalist and Kurdish Activities', Special Service Officer, Mosul, 29 September 1928.

– attempts at assassinating members of the Turkish leadership.[63] Such activities, however, required a completely different context than in Mount Ararat; that is, speed of movement, transport facilities and a solid transnational network of revolutionary cells.

The Benefits of the Disruption of Sovereignty and Mobility

Being a trans-imperial organisation from its inception, the Dashnaks had been involved in the Russian, Persian and Ottoman revolutions in the early twentieth century.[64] As the three empires collapsed between 1917 and 1925, the Dashnaks became a trans-national party with many ramifications in the Middle East and beyond, with several of its militants remaining operational in the interwar years. Kaspar Ipekian, for instance, took an active role in the Persian constitutional revolution of 1905 and in 1931. After becoming director of the tobacco company Matossian in Beirut, he became a go-between between the Dashnaks and the Khoybun League. In particular, he hired some Khoybun members and Dashnak militants as fee collectors and suppliers for the tobacco company in different towns located along the Turkish–Syrian border.[65] As a result, the Khoybun agents benefited from a legal cover to travel throughout the Levant to gather information, distribute funds among the local branches of the respective organisations and coordinate the Khoybun–Dashnak activities.[66]

Khoybun–Dashnak undertakings, however, were not limited to interpersonal relations in the Levant. Actually, the two parties took advantage of a

---

[63] According to the Turkish authorities, Hrant Canikyan, a Dashnak *fedaî*, left Beirut and travelled first to Athens and then to Istanbul to kill certain Turkish elites in 1931. He was caught in Istanbul, but ended up committing suicide. Türk İnkilap Tarihi Enstitüsü (TİTE hereafter), K. 27, G.103, 2 October 1931; TNA, FO 371/16095, 'Alleged Armenian Plot against Leading Kemalists in Turkey', Ankara, 12 August 1932.

[64] Berberian, *Roving Revolutionaries*.

[65] CADN, 1SL/1/V/1/572, Sûreté Générale, 'Note sur le mouvement kurde', Beirut, 4 January 1931; CADN, 1SL/1/V/1/1765, Sûreté Générale, Aleppo, 10 August 1931. See also Vahé Tatchjian, 'Le Khoybun dans la Haute-Mésopotamie syrienne sous mandat français et le rapprochement kurdo-arménien', *Etudes kurdes* 6 (2004): 7–40.

[66] In 1932, Kaspar Ipekian was replaced having been accused of neglecting the tobacco business in favour of his political activities. Thereafter, several Khoybun and Dashnak activists working for the company in northern Syria lost their legal covers. CADN, 1SL/1/V/1/1767, Sûreté Générale, Information No. 578, Beirut, 2 February 1932.

modern world that was increasingly connected and interdependent. Taking a cue from the increasingly robust literature on mobility and globalisation studies,[67] Houri Berberian underlines that already in the early twentieth century non-Western areas witnessed, albeit in an uneven manner, significant shifts in technologies of global communication and transportation such as the railways and telegraph, 'resulting in an important new round of "time–space compression" or the accelerated "shrinking" of the world', thus making the world smaller, time shorter and life faster.[68]

Unsurprisingly, the Khoybun and Dashnak propagandists tapped into the improvement and circulation of new technologies and the consequent 'shrinking of the world' to disseminate their ideas, reach distant locations and collect money to support the military revolt in Mount Ararat. For one, in addition to written propaganda reproduced in different formats – booklets, printed illustrations and postcards – information about Khoybun's aims and activities were also spread verbally through the use of gramophones, which at that time were played in coffeehouses before they became household items.[69] The Sodwa Company of Aleppo, for instance, recorded Kurdish songs with anti-Kemalist sentiments that were then smuggled into Turkey.[70] Likewise, the Khoybun activists used the magic lantern to make short films that were to be screened 'in the United States for propaganda purposes'.[71]

Human mobility became a key factor for Khoybun activities as well. In 1928, Sureya Badirkhan spent seven months in the United States in order to mobilise the Kurdish American community – about 10,000 or 12,000 in number[72] – in favour of the Ararat revolt and attract political support to the

---

[67] Roland Wenzlhuemer, *Connecting the Nineteenth-Century World: The Telegraph and Globalization* (Cambridge, Cambridge University Press, 2015), 47.

[68] Berberian, *Roving Revolutionaries*, 41–2.

[69] Uri M. Kupferschmidt, 'On the Diffusion of "Small" Western Technologies and Consumer Goods in the Middle East during the Era of the First Modern Globalization', in Liat Kozma, Cyrus Schayegh, and Avner Wishnitzer (eds), *A Global Middle East: Mobility, Materiality and Culture in the Modern Age, 1880–1940* (London: I. B. Tauris, 2014), 243–4.

[70] CADN, 1SL/1/V/571, Sûreté Générale, Beirut, 25 November 1936; BCA.030.18.71.8.6, 'Şeyh Said tarafından doldurulmuş Kürtçe plağın, yurda sokulmasının yasaklanması', Ankara, 28 January 1937.

[71] CADN, 1SL/1/V/1055, Sûreté Générale, Beirut, 12 April 1930.

[72] Most Kurds in the United States lived in cities such as Detroit, New York and Philadelphia.

Kurdish cause. Additionally, Sureya published a booklet in Philadelphia on the Kurdish Question (*The Case of Kurdistan against Turkey*), as well as a proclamation to the Kurdish community in America. In the latter, after recalling the sacrifices of Kurdish soldiers for the sake of the Ottoman Empire, Sureya summoned the Kurdish community in America to help the Khoybun: 'Let us prove to the world that a Kurd, although far away from home, is still a Kurd and a true patriot.'[73]

Sureya Badirkhan's manoeuvres turned out to be, at least partly, successful. According to the British Consulate in Detroit, 'the Kurds in this country had been sending $50,000 to $60,000 annually to Mustafa Kemal, but Sureya has converted them to the idea of independence and they have agreed to tax themselves one dollar weekly, which will be sent to the Khoybun' instead.[74] Sureya's journey was not, however, a straightforward one. The same report explains that on his way to the United States, Sureya Badirkhan was invited by Benito Mussolini and 'spent fifteen days as his guest at Rome and came away with the impression that Mussolini was willing to help the Kurds'. When Badirkhan eventually left New York for Paris on 19 April 1929, in the steamboat *Ile-de-France*, he also went to London and the Greek president allegedly invited him 'to visit Athens on his way back'.[75]

Equally, the Khoybun representative in Baghdad, Şükrü (Mehmed) Sekban, travelled to Paris in June 1927, via Beirut and Marseille. In addition to Paris, he visited Berlin, Brussels and London. Upon his return to Baghdad via Cairo and Beirut in November 1927, he brought with him funds said to amount £10,000.[76] Khoybun's allies did not lag behind, either. In 1928, Vahan Papazian was thought to have distributed $20,000 to the Kurdish

---

After Sureya Badirkhan's stay in Detroit, a Khoybun branch made up of 25–30 people was created in that city. Rohat Alakom, 'Ji aliyê kurdan de keşfkirina Amerîkayê (1915–1930)', *Nûdem* 21 (1997): 95–6.

[73] TNA, AIR 23/157, 'Khoybun's Proclamation to the Kurdish Community in America, 20 June 1928'. Qaimaqan Sinjar to Administrative Inspector, Mosul, 28 August 1929.

[74] TNA, AIR 23/415, British Consulate in Detroit, John Cameron to Sir Austen Chamberlain, Detroit, 18 April 1929.

[75] Ibid.

[76] TNA, AIR 23/413, 'Advance Extracts to the Iraq Police', Iraq Police, Criminal Investigation Department, Baghdad, 19 May 1928; TNA, FO 371/13032, 'Kurdish–Armenian collaboration', Air Headquarters, Iraq Command, Baghdad, 14 June 1928.

organisation after an active campaign from diverse Armenian cells in different countries.[77]

Steamboats were not only crucial for the circulation of the Kurdish and Armenian revolutionaries across the seas, they were also important for the shipment of weapons for the Kurdish rebels in Mount Ararat. Thus, for instance, in 1930 several Greek cargos reportedly departed from Nice carrying around 125,000 guns and 50,000 grenades, which were to be delivered at a dock in the Persian Gulf.[78]

Admittedly, the experience of movement was not the same for all Kurdish and Armenian activists. For one, whereas the propagandists of the revolt took benefit from the increasing speed of travel and transportation facilities available in cities such as Aleppo, Cairo, Beirut or Alexandretta, armed rebels in the Ararat travelled with great difficulty across this mountainous region. Incidentally, individuals experienced the tensions between *acceleration* and *deceleration* processes during their long journeys across a region in motion.[79] Such was the case of Yashar Khanum, who by late 1928 left western Turkey to join her husband, Ihsan Nuri, in northeastern Turkey. Drawing on Khanum's memoirs, Kumru Toktamis reports that she 'travelled from Denizli to Izmir by train, from Izmir to Mersin on boat, took another train to Aleppo'. After spending some months in diverse houses of Khoybun members in northern Syria, she travelled on carriages a few times between Kobane and Aleppo, before driving to Mosul via Deir ez-Zor and reached Baghdad. Then, she took a 'train to cross the Iraq–Iran border and arrived in Tabriz by the next fall', from where she arrived at Mount Ararat on horseback.[80]

Individual stories, together with the observation of particular locations, allow us to nuance the narratives of a growing literature in Middle Eastern

---

[77] TNA AIR 23/407, Air Staff Intelligence, Baghdad, 25 May 1928; TNA AIR 23/414, Air Staff Intelligence, Baghdad, 2 November 1928.

[78] There is, however, no evidence that this delivery reached the rebels in Mount Ararat, Archives Nationales, Série F7:13436, Police commissariat, Nice, 25 October 1930.

[79] On this idea, see Huber Valeska, *Channelling Mobilities: Migration and Globalisation in the Suez Canal Region and Beyond, 1869–1914* (Cambridge: Cambridge University Press, 2013).

[80] Kumru Toktamis, 'Yashar Khanum: The Woman for Whom the War never Ended', in Tomasz Pudlocki and Kamil Ruszala (eds), *Intellectuals and World War I: A Central European Perspective* (Krakow: Jagiellonian University Press, 2018), 299.

globalisation that tends to emphasise mobility and integration while neglecting the processes of exclusion as well as the 'limitations and tenuousness of global exchange' in the interwar years.[81] Ultimately, they also point to the existence of multiple mobilities and their interdependence, for despite the expectations of unhampered speed in an increasingly modern world, transnational revolutionaries realised that the traditional forms of mobility – camels, animal transport vehicles and horses – were essential in securing connectivity across the modern Middle East.

Tightening the Rope around Trans-border Activists

Contrary to general assumptions about the eagerness of Middle Eastern states to curtail cross-border movement in the interwar years, a closer observation of the increasing flows of people, ideas and goods across new and old borders, shows that the former, as elsewhere, sought to both facilitate and prevent mobility through different 'channelling processes'.[82] In turn, and as a consequence of this enduring balancing act, human and non-human mobilities played 'a foundational role in both (re)making and empowering states' in these critical years.[83] The facilitation and prevention of circulation of transnational revolutionaries by states was by no means an exception.

Undeniably, the French authorities could have prevented, from the very beginning, all activities by the Khoybun League should they have so wished. Available documentation reveals that the French intelligence services in the Levant were well aware of the Kurdish committee's subversive activities. Furthermore, as Elizabeth Thompson points out, the French authorities imposed on all newly established organisations in Syria and Lebanon a standard procedure to inform them of their minutes and their activities.[84] Although the Khoybun League kept some decisions and plans under the French radar,

---

[81] Nile Green, 'Fordist Connections: The Automotive Integration of the United States and Iran', *Comparative Studies in Society and History* 58(2) (2016): 292.

[82] See Joel Quirk and Darshan Vigneswaran, 'Mobility Makes States', in Darshan Vigneswaran and Joel Quirk (eds), *Mobility Makes States: Migration and Power in Africa* (Philadelphia: University of Pennsylvania Press, 2015), 1–34.

[83] Ibid., 8.

[84] Elizabeth Thompson, *Colonial Citizens: Republican Rights, Paternal Privilege, and Gender in French Syria and Lebanon* (New York: Columbia University Press, 1999), 91–2.

the mandatory authorities had 'official' informers in the Khoybun League itself, notably Memduh Selim and Jaladat Badirkhan, as well as spies within both the Kurdish and Armenian communities.[85]

Against this backdrop, the Turkish government believed that the French authorities were systematically ignoring Khoybun and Dashnak activities in the Levant and, more importantly, Ankara suspected France of exploiting both organisations against Turkey's interests. Turkish concerns were not completely groundless. On the one hand, France relied on Kurdish and Armenian refugees, given their essential role in the stabilisation of the frontier as well as the economic development of Syrian Jazira. Their settlement along the Turkish–Syrian border became thus unquestionable. Turkish–French relations entered a critical phase in the early 1920s due to the contentious demarcation of the common border. Beyond the economic considerations, France aimed at controlling a zone that could ensure various means of communication with the ex-Ottoman province of Mosul.[86] In turn, between 1925 and 1926, Turkish interest in securing control of the Upper Jazira became more marked. The definitive annexation of Mosul province to Iraq, together with the settlement of Kurdish intellectuals and tribal leaders in northern Syria entailed the loss of two predominantly Kurdish territories which Turkey could not effectively control. Crucially, the French could use the Khoybun–Dashnak card if necessary.

In the late 1920s, however, new regional developments brought about a dramatic shift in interstate relations for the two revolutionary organisations. On 29 June 1929, a standing bilateral Frontier Commission began to work on the actual delineation of the Syrian–Turkish boundary between Nusaybin and Jazirat ibn Omar. Thereafter, the Turkish delegation frequently denounced the presence of Kurdish and Armenian cells along the border during the meetings of the Frontier Commission.[87] Although some

---

[85] The Kurdish leaders frequently met the French authorities to explain the evolution of the movement. In return, Jaladat Badirkhan and Memduh Selim could claim to be 'close' to the mandatory power and thus gain in political and social influence among the Kurds. CADN, 1SL/1/V/569, 'Rapport sur les Kurdes et le Kurdistan', Damascus, 1 February 1929.

[86] David McDowall, *A Modern History of the Kurds* (London: I. B. Tauris, 1996), 151–71.

[87] BCA.030.10.230.549.4, 'Türkiye-Suriye Daimi Hudut Komisyonu'nun Halep'teki toplantısında alınan kararla ilişkin Urfa Valisi Ethem Bey'in raporu', Ankara, 24 May 1931.

Turkish claims were simply exaggerated, Turkey succeeded in developing an important intelligence network in northern Syria, and thus came to observe very closely Khoybun's activities.[88]

At first, the French did not undertake any drastic measures against the two committees. However, after the failure of the Khoybun leaders' intervention in July 1930, the mandate authorities took a more negative stance towards the Kurdish organisation.[89] French authorities accordingly began to expel some Khoybun members from the border area and imposed house arrests on others. Although the Dashnak Party did not participate in this military intervention, some of its members were resettled in other cities, while Vahan Papazian, who happened to be in Paris at the time of the Khoybun action, was not allowed to return to Syria.[90]

The cooperation between French mandatory and Turkish authorities to solve 'common security problems' considerably paved the way for a much more thorough surveillance and regulation of mobility across the Syrian–Turkish border and, ultimately, the emergence of a 'boundary regime'.[91] In addition, passports and visas became standard tools to hinder Khoybun–Dashnak activities across the region: 'The French Consulates in Baghdad and Mosul should be advised to refuse any visa application for Syria' to all Dashnak and Khoybun members based in

---

[88] The intelligence network was especially effective in Aleppo, where the Turkish Consulate gathered information from different northern provinces. See, for instance, BCA.030.10.113.771.1, 'Cemil paşazade Ekrem, Kadri, Mehmet, Bedri aileleriyle Halep'te Santral otelinde kalkıkları ve Hoybun üyesi Memduh Selim'in evinde bir toplantı yapılacağı', Aleppo, 4 April 1929.

[89] In 1930, as the Turkish army surrounded the Kurdish rebels in Mount Ararat, the Khoybun leadership in Syria organised a raid in Turkey to divert Turkish attention from the Ararat area. Jaladat Badirkhan and other members of the Kurdish committee crossed the border in small groups and in different directions. However, the lack of local support among the Kurdish populations in Turkey led the raiders to return to Syria immediately. CADN, 1SL/1/V/1055, Sûreté Générale, Beirut, 9 August 1930.

[90] TNA, AIR 23/243, Special Service Officer, Mosul, 9 September 1930; MAE, Quai d'Orsay, Série Levant 1918–1940, sous-série Syrie-Liban, 466. Report by Lieutenant Mortier, director of the Service des renseignements, Beirut, 23 August 1930.

[91] George Gavrilis defines 'boundary regimes' as locally cooperative methods of border control. George Gavrilis, *The Dynamics of Interstate Boundaries* (Cambridge: Cambridge University Press, 2008), 14–15.

Iraq.[92] Although the French authorities continued to ignore and even encourage contraband along the Turkish–Syrian border in order to force Turkey to open its national market to goods produced or circulating through French Syria, they impressed on Jaladat and Kamuran Badirkhan the need to transform their political and military activities into a cultural movement.[93]

Similarly, by the late 1920s, Great Britain had lost interest in allowing cross-border cooperation between the Syrian and Iraqi Kurdish committees. At first, the British government had attempted to reconcile the aspirations of Kurdish nationalists with the objectives of British policy in Iraq; that is, 'the consolidation of King Faysal's government in Baghdad, and the maintenance of the territorial integrity of Iraq so that it would become a viable state'.[94] Yet, after securing control over Mosul in 1926 and despite League of Nations' provisions summoning Great Britain to guarantee cultural rights for the Kurdish populations, the British dismissed the aspirations of the Kurdish nationalist committees for the duration of the Mandate. Stability and the viability of the Iraqi state were perceived as being incompatible with the pervasiveness of trans-border Kurdish connectedness.

When Jaladat Badirkhan established contacts with the Rowanduz Committee in Iraq – led mainly by the exiled family of the late Sheikh Said, British concerns grew further.[95] By 1928, the mandatory authorities in Iraq and the British consulates in the Levant were closely monitoring all moves and exchanges between the two Kurdish committees, for any attack against Turkey from Iraqi territory could have very negative effects on British Iraq. Just as with the French, the meetings of the Turkish–Iraqi Permanent Frontier Commission became a privileged setting for the Turkish delegation to protest against the facilities which were being given to Kurdish and

---

[92] CADN, 1SL/1/V/572, Sûreté Générale, 'Note sur le mouvement kurde', Beirut, 4 January 1931.
[93] CADN, 1SL/1/V/1055, Cabinet Politique to the General Inspector of Customs, Damascus, 28 December 1932.
[94] Othman Ali, 'The Career of Özdemir: A Turkish Bid for Northern Iraq, 1921–1923', *Middle Eastern Studies* 53(6) (2017): 968.
[95] On the Rowanduz Committee and its contacts with the Khoybun League, see CADN, 1SL/1/V/1055, Information No. 345, Beirut, 4 June 1928; TNA, AIR 23/407, 'Anti-Kemalist and Kurdish Activities', Aleppo, 17 June 1929.

Armenian propagandists in Syria to visit Iraq. Anxious to appease diplomatic relations with Turkey, the British paid particular attention to the work of vetting and verification of revolutionary agents entering and crossing Iraqi territory, urging the refusal of visa applications by 'members of the Badirkhan family and any person suspected of being connected with the Kurdish or Armenian nationalist movement'.[96]

As the rope was tightening around Khoybun–Dashnak agents across the region, Persian support for Turkish endeavours in the Ararat area became central. As a matter of fact, between 1928 and 1930 the rebels in Mount Ararat 'received at least tacit and probably some actual support from Iran'.[97] For one, during the revolt, Tehran allowed Kurdish forces to cross freely into its territory; they conducted hit-and-run actions against the Turkish positions and then sought refuge in Persian territory.[98] In addition, Persian authorities temporally allowed Khoybun agents to sustain a channel of communication with the headquarters in Mount Ararat. Thus, for instance, when Jaladat Badirkhan requested a visa to travel to Iraq and Persia in order to meet Ihsan Nuri, the British enquired of the Persian government whether they wished Jaladat to go on to Persia. Although at first the answer was negative, a few hours later a second telegram arrived saying 'that the Persian Government

---

[96] TNA, CO 730/133/1, The Residency in Baghdad to the Secretary of state for the Colonies, 14 July 1928.

[97] Robert Olson, *The Kurdish Question and Turkish–Iranian Relations: from World War I to 1998* (Costa Mesa, CA: Mazda, 1998), 23.

[98] Mount Ararat and its surroundings served for centuries as the frontier region between the Ottoman and Safavid empires. In 1913, Great Britain and Russia mediated between the two powers for a more precise demarcation of the common boundary. It left Mount Ararat on the Turkish side of the border, whereas Little Mount Ararat was recognised as Persian territory, more precisely in (western) Azerbaijan province. Notwithstanding this, Persia was still concerned that Turkey might harbour a pan-Turkish agenda, including territorial ambitions on Persian Azerbaijan. In addition, Simko's relations with Turkey led Reza Shah to consider a wait-and-see strategy with regard to the Kurdish rebels in Mount Ararat. See Bein, *Kemalist Turkey and the Middle East*, 35–41. On Simko, see Martin van Bruinessen, 'A Kurdish Warlord on the Turkish–Persian Frontier in the Early Twentieth Century: Ismail Agha Simko', in Touraj Atabaki (ed.), *Iran and the First World War: Battleground of the Great Powers* (London: I. B. Tauris, 2006), 69–93. For a long-term study on this frontier, see Sabri Ates, *Ottoman–Iranian Borderlands: Making a Boundary, 1843–1914* (Cambridge: Cambridge University Press, 2013).

desired that no obstacle should be put in the way of his going on to Persia, as they wished to see what he was like'.[99]

Nader Entessar argues that Reza Shah 'apparently was intent on using his Kurdish card to force Turkey to settle some of its territorial disputes with Iran'.[100] Yet, as the revolt reached its highest point in the summer of 1930, the Ankara government threatened to bomb Persian's territory if Tehran did not stop supporting the Kurdish rebels and, allegedly, built an airstrip to accommodate 100 aircraft near the border.[101] Importantly, Ankara suggested that modification of the border through territorial exchange – that is, giving Little Mount Ararat to Turkey – was essential to guarantee peace and security along the frontier zone.[102] Thereafter, Reza Shah eventually decided to cooperate with Ankara in a joint military campaign against the Kurdish forces; the Persian army blocked the roads on the eastern slopes and evacuated the whole Persian–Kurdish population from the frontier zone. Interestingly, this dramatic shift was justified by Tehran with reference to the principle of international cooperation between sovereign states enshrined in the post-First World War international system:

> The Persian Government had no direct interest or concern in the annihilation of the Ararat Kurds. But no order-loving state can countenance insurrection even in a foreign country; it is rather in duty bound to assist in stamping it out.[103]

In May 1931, in the face of a new joint military operation the rebels were dispersed with casualties and retreated in the vicinity of the frontier. Helpless, Ihsan Nuri and other leaders of the revolt sought refuge in Persia in small groups. The collapse of the Ararat revolt coincided with the signing of the Turkish–Persian Frontier treaty on 23 January 1932, which by and large satisfied Turkey's requests; namely, full control over Little Mount

---

[99] TNA, CO 730/133/1, Confidential, The Residency in Baghdad to the Secretary of state for the Colonies, 14 July 1928.
[100] Nader Entessar, *Kurdish Ethnonationalism* (London: Lynne Rienner, 1992), 85.
[101] Olson, *The Kurdish Question and Turkish–Iranian Relations*, 23.
[102] 'Mount Ararat: Turkish Offer to Persia', *The Times*, 25 August 1930.
[103] TNA, FO 371/15369, 'Translation from the *Iran* of 15 July 1931', Interview with Colonel Kazem Khan Sayah, Chief of the Turco-Persian Frontier Security Commission.

Ararat. In return, Persia received small strips of land near Kotur and Bazirgan.

Conclusion

While few former 'Ottoman' revolutionaries succeeded in reaching their political goals and securing durability in the interwar years, this chapter has shown that the transnational networks were nevertheless crucial in testing the limits of national sovereignties across the newly established Middle East. In that regard, the study of the Dashnak–Khoybun alliance against the Turkish Republic between 1927 and 1932 allows us to better grasp the contentious processes of state formation and border-making in the interwar Middle East. The emergence of spaces without order or a definite state authority in the aftermath of the First World War, along with the disruption of sovereignty that characterised the post-war international system, allowed revolutionary groups to challenge the newly established states. The room for manoeuvre of the former, however, was subject to a number of conditions; namely, the continuity of interstate rivalry.

Critically, between 1927 and 1930, the Khoybun League and Dashnak benefited from the on-going territorial tensions between Turkey and Syria, on the one hand, and between Turkey and Iran, on the other. This was the time when Great Britain adopted a neutral strategy, while working to avert the consolidation of trans-border relations between the Syrian and Iraqi Kurdish committees, which could threaten the stability of the Iraqi state. As a result, the Kurdish and Armenian rebels were allowed to pursue their revolutionary activities across the region and beyond. In so doing, the two organisations were to some extent garnered with external support to their cause and collected significant financial resources.

At first, these activities further strained regional interstate relations. Yet the failed armed intervention of the Khoybun leaders in 1930, along with the timid improvement of the diplomatic relations between France and Turkey in 1929, struck a powerful blow against the Khoybun–Dashnak alliance. Crucially, several members of the Khoybun League and Dashnaks were removed from the border zone, while others were banished or expelled from the Levant territories by the French authorities on legal grounds. Eager to cooperate with Turkey, Great Britain increasingly denied visas to Khoybun activists, thereby preventing cross-border mobility and, more significantly, the connection between the Khoyboun leaders in Syria and the military headquarters in Mount Ararat. The growing military power of the Turkish army as well as the Turkish–Persian security cooperation along the border did the rest.

Incidentally, the Khoybun League and its fighters in Mount Ararat experienced themselves a ubiquitous characteristic of state borders; that is, depending on the time period and geographic location, borders may be acutely monitored in one instance and neglected the next.[104] While borders remained widely open between 1927 and 1930, interstate cooperation made them less porous in the early 1930s, with dramatic consequences for transborder revolutionaries. Confronted by the failure of the revolt in Ararat and the internal struggles in the Kurdish camp, the 1927 accord that sealed the Khoybun–Dashnak alliance became simply obsolete.

---

[104] Sabine Dullin, 'Des frontières s'ouvrent et se ferment. La mise en place d'un espace socialiste derrière le rideau de fer, 1953–1970', *Relations internationales* 147 (2011): 35–48.

Afterword

Erik Jan Zürcher

Age of Rogues is a collection of case studies and, as in any such collection, the cases selected are intended as so many tools to detect recurrent patterns; to uncover larger historical developments through comparison, even if that comparison is implicit rather than explicit. The larger questions that suggest themselves in the context of this volume, therefore, obviously are: is there an overarching category that can usefully be called 'rogues'? And, is there something that can be meaningfully designated an era in which they were especially prevalent or played an especially important role – an 'age of rogues'?

On the face of it, the cases collected here are extremely diverse: a Chechen bandit, a female Armenian terrorist, a north Syrian tribal chief, a Bulgarian arms trader, and a Muslim notable from Basra, among others. They go by many different descriptors: bandits, militias, paramilitaries, gangs and gangsters, irregulars, guerrillas, and – in the language of the period: *haiduks*, *chetes*, *komitajis*, *fedais* and *lutis*.

So, what connects all or most of these disparate historical figures? In their introduction to the volume, Alp Yenen and Ramazan Hakkı Öztan provide us with an answer. In their view, the key element is that of transgression. The behaviour of the rogues was indeed transgressive in the sense that it overstepped the boundaries set by the state in its laws, particularly where it concerned the use of violence. At one point or another, all of them were criminals in the eyes of one of the states involved. This is, of course, a subjective yardstick and the same behaviour may well have been recognised as being of an acceptable traditional pattern by inhabitants of rural Macedonia, Chechnya or Dagestan, or indeed – in the case of the *lutis* – by the urban population of Tabriz and Tehran. To their fellow partisans, it would of course not have been transgressive at all, but legitimate in their struggle against oppression.

Perhaps it is therefore safer to say that the one factor that connects these rogues is their readiness to use violence to achieve their aims. The character of the violence varied: bomb-maker and arms trader Tyufekchiev mainly visited death and destruction on others indirectly – through the provision of armaments – but he was also directly involved in the very brutal assassination of Prime Minister Stambulov in Sofia. Rubina set the timer for a bomb that killed twenty-six and wounded fifty-eight, as well as many horses. When the band of Zelimkhan tried to rob the treasury office of Kizlyar in the Russian Caucasus they killed guards, clerks and innocent bystanders in cold blood. The *fedais* (volunteers) of the Committee of Union and Progress (CUP), many of whom were themselves refugees or children of refugees from the Caucasus, whose families had fled from extreme Russian brutality, frequently used the method of political assassination, most notably during the 1908 Revolution (with the murder of General Şemsi Paşa), after it (with the murder of liberal journalist Hasan Fehmi), and during the *coup d'état* of January 1913 (with the murder of War Minister Nazım Paşa).[1] In the guise of the Special Organisation (*Teşkilat-ı Mahsusa*), many of these *fedais* were involved in the terror campaign against Greek Orthodoxs on the Anatolian west coast in 1914 and in the Armenian Genocide of 1915–16. Even the individual described in this volume who has the least violent profile and whose transgression seems to have consisted mainly of getting in the way of, first, the Young Turk and then British ambitions, Sayyid Talib, the *naqib al-ashraf* of Basra, was implicated in two political murders.

These, then, were violent men and women, for whom the threshold for using arms was low. It should be remembered, however, that the areas in which they primarily operated, the Ottoman and Russian frontiers, were a

---

[1] Erik Jan Zürcher, 'The Young Turks – Children of the Borderlands?' *International Journal of Turkish Studies* 9(1/2) (2003): 275–86.

geography of endemic violence. In the northern Caucasus, Kurdistan, the Arabian desert and Albanian mountains, this endemic violence was linked to social structures in which tribal affiliation and clans were important and where there were strongly developed traditions of blood feuds. Areas like Macedonia and the Aegean coast of Anatolia had a reputation for widespread brigandage. On the desert fringes in Syria and Iraq, but also in the mixed Kurdish–Armenian areas in eastern Anatolia the age-old competition for resources between sedentary agriculturalists and nomadic pastoralists seems to have grown worse as the nineteenth century wore on. The question of to what extent this was an effect of climatic change still needs further research. What can be argued, however, is that the modernising and centralising ambitions of the Ottoman state since Mahmud II (r. 1808–39), as well as the Russian conquest of the Caucasus led to the destruction of regional power centres that exercised a degree of effective control and thus contained non-state violence such as Ali Paşa of Yanina's rule in the western Balkans, that of the Karaosmanoğlus in western Anatolia, or that of the Kurdish emirates in the east destroyed by Mahmud II. Martin van Bruinessen has shown how this destruction led to the fragmentation of Kurdish society along tribal lines.[2] In the first half of the nineteenth century, the Ottoman Empire managed to destroy the regional power centres, but until the end it lacked the financial and human resources to bring the outlying areas under effective state control and establish a monopoly of violence. The areas where Ottoman (or Russian or Qajar) control was tenuous formed the habitat of the 'rogues'.

Where the violence of the late nineteenth century was different from earlier forms was in its political nature. The guerrilla fighters and terrorists of the Internal Macedonian Revolutionary Organisation (IMRO) and the Supreme Committee of the Armenian Revolutionary Federation (ARF), the Hunchak Social Democratic Party, and the CUP, of the anti-French Arab forces in Syria and of the Khoybun – all of them committed their violence in the name of a nationalist political programme. Some of the means employed seem to have been traditional and it is a moot question as to whether nationalist movements adopted a pre-existing methodology of bandits or whether

---

[2] Martin van Bruinessen, *Agha, Shaikh and State: The Social and Political Structures of Kurdistan* (London: Zed Books, 1992).

possibly the nationalist and – in the case of the Ottoman Empire and Iran – constitutionalist struggle opened up an opportunity space for bandits and legitimised their actions. This volume seems to offer arguments for both points of view.

It is certainly clear that, quite apart from the use of traditional forms of violence of the frontiers, the 'rogues' also learned from each other. It is clear that the 'demonstrative units' of the ARF copied their *modus operandi* from the Russian anarchists. The CUP seems to have copied the creation of a *fedai* wing from the ARF and its actions during the revolution of 1908 were copied from the Bulgarian *komitacis*, with which officers like Enver and Niyazi were intimately familiar after years of counter-insurgency warfare. Khoybun combined Kurdish know-how on guerrilla warfare with international Armenian support networks.

Even if violence on the part of non-state actors was endemic, or even in a sense 'traditional' in these frontiers, it is also true that transgressive politics gained a higher profile in the late nineteenth century. Can we say therefore that there was an 'age of rogues' spanning the late nineteenth and early twentieth century? In a general sense, it is of course true that the rogues of this period were operating in a context of peak inter-imperial rivalry, of modernist state-building, and of the rise of the nation state. All three of these elements certainly played a role in creating the playing field for the rogues. But there is also a more specific way in which the period created the right conditions in southeast Europe and the Middle East. This is linked to the particular constellation that was the result of the Russian–Ottoman conflict of 1876–8.

The importance of this conflict and its outcome, the peace Treaty of Berlin, in the history of the Ottoman Empire and its successor states can hardly be overstated. The peace treaty restored Macedonia and Thrace to the Ottoman Empire after the loss of these areas under the Treaty of San Stefano, but the fact that most of the European provinces had been lost by the Ottoman army and only restored through intervention of European Great Powers, left a profound sense of insecurity among the Muslims of the European provinces. At the Congress of Prizren in June 1878, the Albanian Ottoman Beys concluded that they could no longer rely on Constantinople to safeguard their interests against Serbs, Bulgarians and Greeks. From then on, the idea that the Albanians should be entrusted with the defence of the western Balkans in partnership with the Ottomans gained strength.

The story of the temporary loss of the homeland and the feeling of it being under continuous threat was also one that was still very much alive in the urban Muslim middle-class households in which the 'generation of 1880' grew up. This generation would spawn the second Young Turk movement that started with the Ottoman Liberty Society in Salonica in 1906, and that brought off the Constitutional Revolution of July 1908 (and eventually created the Republic of Turkey in 1923).[3] The main motivation behind their actions was the fear that the Ottoman Empire was about to lose its European provinces.

The Berlin arrangement left deep scars on the other side as well, as both Bulgarians and Bulgaro-Macedonians felt they had been robbed of their rightful prize. Bulgaria did not achieve full formal independence, the area south of the Balkan mountain range remained an Ottoman province (even if run from Sofia) and, of course, Macedonia was completely lost. This gave rise to a strong and increasingly violent irredentist movement, which in turn led to Serbia and Greece inciting and arming their own guerrilla movements in Macedonia. As İpek K. Yosmaoğlu has shown, these movements and the competing Bulgarian ones were much more lethal to each other than to the representatives of the Ottoman state.[4]

In the east, the Berlin Treaty destabilised the situation in two ways. It left Batumi, Kars and Ardahan in Russian hands. This profoundly changed the military situation on the ground and meant that the Ottoman army in eastern Anatolia could easily be exposed to a Russian invasion. But, as is well known, Article 61 of the treaty also stipulated that the sultan's government was bound to execute reforms in the 'provinces inhabited by the Armenians' and that the Great Powers would monitor the execution of these reforms.[5] As

---

[3] Erik Jan Zürcher, 'How Europeans Adopted Anatolia and Created Turkey', *European Review* 13(3) (2005): 379–94.

[4] İpek K. Yosmaoğlu, *Blood Ties: Religion, Violence, and the Politics of Nationhood in Ottoman Macedonia, 1878–1908* (Ithaca, NY: Cornell University Press, 2014).

[5] 'Treaty between Great Britain, Germany, Austria, France, Italy, Russia, and Turkey for the Settlement of Affairs in the East: Signed at Berlin, July 13, 1878', *American Journal of International Law* 2(4) (1908): 401–24, at 422.

social conditions in the east deteriorated and tensions between Armenians, on the one hand, and Kurds and Circassians, on the other, rose, this article would form the basis for Armenian activism designed to provoke the intervention of the Great Powers.

The political situation between 1878 and 1908 was therefore fundamentally unstable. The consensus among the Great Powers was that the Berlin settlement marked a pause rather than a reversal of Ottoman decline, and that was a hope shared by Balkan nationalists as well as a fear felt by the Ottoman Muslims. The Young Turk revolution of July 1908 changed the perceptions and gave the Balkan states and the imperialist rivals alike the idea that they had to strike before there was a chance of a serious regeneration of the Ottoman state such as promised by the Young Turks. The successful land grab by Austria-Hungary and Greece and the proclamation of Bulgarian independence were the first steps, followed by a totally unprovoked Italian invasion of Tripolitania, which formed the beginning of a decade of almost uninterrupted warfare.

For men and women whose stock in trade was violence, war of course created spaces of opportunity. In a sense any war is an 'age of rogues'. In the context of the wars in the Balkans and the Middle East, the rogues gained in importance. Their role as volunteers in organising Arab resistance against the Italians in Tripolitania and Cyrenaica seems to have been particularly important and a formative experience for many of them (whether of Turkish, Albanian, Circassian or Arab extraction). Many of them played an active role in the First World War, be it in the Ottoman army, among the Armenian volunteer units or in the embryonic Arab army of the Hashemites. In the post-war struggles, they continued to play an important role as well. The role of Ottoman Arabs in the resistance against the Mandates regime is referred to in several chapters of this book, but in the early phase of the post-war 'national struggle' in Turkey the rogues were also of great importance. In 1919–20, the irregulars of Circassian Edhem and his brother Reshid were the strongest force of the nationalists in western Anatolia until Edhem fell out with Mustafa Kemal (Atatürk) Paşa and went over to the Greek side. Mustafa Kemal Paşa himself used the band of an archetypal rogue, Topal (Lame) Osman from Giresun, who had built up a particularly gruesome reputation for killing Armenians and Greeks on the Black Sea coast, as his bodyguard (and to intimidate opposition figures in Ankara) from 1919 to 1923.

The 'rogues' thus certainly deserve our attention. They may in one sense have been marginal figures engaging in transgressive politics in the frontiers of empires, but they were not marginal at all in a historical sense. Quite the opposite: they played a pivotal role in the end of empire and in the emergence of a whole series of successor states. In these states, in the Balkans as well as in the Middle East, they often played a significant role in politics until the 1950s. In addition, men of violence of later generations who fitted the archetype of the rogue very well at one point in their lives – Yasser Arafat, Menachem Begin, Yitzhak Shamir, Abdullah Öcalan, Muammar al-Qaddafi, Hashim Thaçi – went on to shape today's world. It is therefore more than timely that this book, which moves the rogues centre-stage, has appeared.

Index

Abbasid caliphate, 237
'Abd al-Qadir (Abdelkader) al-Jazairi
  (Emir), 323, 352
Abdülhamit II, 18, 20, 24, 39, 53, 60, 63,
  66, 75, 181, 192, 194
  assassination attempt (1905), 60, 63, 73,
  215, 248, 292, 304, 305, 319, 335–6,
  338, 341, 362
'Abdallah I bin al-Hussein,
  342–3
Abdülkadir Antepli, 313, 332
Abdülmecid I, 336
abrek(s), 35, 88, 90–1, 93–102, 107–8, 102,
  110–11, 113–17, 119
Abu al-Hasan al-Mawardi, 237–8
Abu Jilda, 253
Abu-Kamal, 346
Action Army (*Hareket Ordusu*), 327
Adib Shishakli, 352
Adil-Iurt, 87
Afshari, Reza, 125
Africa, 24, 320, 322–5
Agri (journal), 370
Aharonian, Avetis, 79
al-'Ahd (society), 245, 318
Ahmad al-'Izzat al-'Abid Paşa, 240
Ahmet İzzet Paşa, 328
Ahlat, 196
Ahrar (Freedom Party), 242 Aknuni
  (Khachatur Malumian), 79
Aksai, 87

Albania, Albanian(s) 12, 24, 36, 152, 310,
  324, 385–7
  Albanian uprising in Firzovik (1908),
  23–4
Aleppo, 180, 240, 256, 317, 336, 345, 348,
  357, 359–60, 365–6, 372, 374
Alexandretta, 357, 359, 374
Alexander II of Russia, 39, 55
Alexander of Battenberg, 264, 265
Alexandrov, Todor, 298
Algeria, 323, 352
Ali (King of Hijaz), 256
Ali Fethi (Okyar), 327
Ali Paşa, 197–8, 200
Ali Paşa of Yanina, 385
Ali Suavi, 20
Allenby, Edmund, 345
Alliance Universelle Israélite, 319
Amasya, 171
Amirkhiz, 127, 138, 140
Amir 'Abdallah, 347–8
Amman, 256, 347–8, 366
Anarchism, 41, 43, 208–9, 211, 215,
  217–21, 225–9, 231–3
Anatolia, 8, 26–9, 36, 40, 48, 156, 162–3,
  173, 211, 316, 326, 332, 334, 346,
  348, 359, 361, 363, 365, 368, 384–5,
  387
Anglo-Russian Convention of 1907, 136
Anjoman, 40–1, 123, 125, 127, 132, 137
Ankara, 29, 332, 350, 370, 376, 380, 389

Antioch, 366
Antok mountain, 189–90, 202–3
Apostolic Patriarchate, 200
Aqaba, 343
Arab(s), Arabia, 27–8, 46, 235, 241–4, 250, 305, 310–11, 314, 316, 334, 342–7, 359–60, 362, 369, 384–5, 388
   Arab Congress in Paris (1913), 245
   Arab Revolt (1916), 38, 248, 309–11, 342–3, 348
Arafat, Yasser, 389
Ararat, 58, 357–8, 368, 370–2, 374, 379, 380–2
   Ararat revolt (1930), 368–70, 372, 380, 382
Araxes valley, 58
Ardahan, 387
Areshian, Mikhail (Misha), 80
   Areshian, Rubina, 82
Arghutian, Hovsep, 79
Armenia, 45, 59, 76, 80, 229, 357, 359, 361, 365
Armenian(s), 2, 26, 27, 40–1, 45–6, 53, 57–61, 64, 75, 80–1, 92, 137, 178–234, 279, 289, 290–1, 295, 305, 331, 357–8, 360–7, 374, 376, 379, 387, 381, 388
   Armenian Genocide, 363, 365, 384
   Armenian question, 26, 204–6, 209, 211, 213, 227, 229, 234
Armolotoi, 36
Aryan Confederation, 367
al-ʻAs, Saʻid, 340
Ashikian (Armenian Patriarch), 214
al-ʻAskari, Jaʻfar, 254, 302, 313, 317, 325, 331, 340, 342–3
Askerî, Süleyman, 302, 312, 317, 321, 323–6, 331
Aşar (tithe), 158
Athens, 60, 184, 373
al-Atrash, Sultan, 353–4
Atsov, Mircho, 275
Austria-Hungary, 11, 153, 156, 162–3, 167, 169, 174, 222, 227, 233, 292, 388
Avtorkhanov, Abdurakhman, 94, 113
Aya Panteleimon Church (Russian Orthodox), 268
Azadi (Society), 369
Azam-Iurt, 87
Azerbaijan, 91, 137
Aziz Paşa, 159
ʻAziz ʻAli al-Misri (Aziz Ali Bey), 302, 310–18, 324, 325, 331, 340
al-ʻAzma, Yusuf, 338, 344, 346, 347

Bâb-ı Âli demonstration, 229
Bâb-ı Âli Coup (1913), 25, 319, 325, 327, 330, 384
Badirkhan, Abdurrahman, 363
Badirkhan, Amin Ali, 362
Badirkhan, Jaladat, 362, 376, 378–9
Badirkhan, Kamuran, 362, 367, 378
Badirkhan, Sureya, 362, 367, 372–3
Badiʻ Nuri, 244
Baghdad, 236, 237–8, 241–2, 245, 247, 250, 253–6, 316, 366, 373–4, 377–8
Bagration, Dmitrii Petrovich, 99, 100, 115
Baku, 28, 58–60
Balkan, Fuat, 298
Balkan(s), 4, 6, 7, 10, 11, 14, 23–4, 33–4, 38–48, 52, 64, 66, 151, 153, 155, 161, 171, 173, 176–7, 214, 262, 263, 292, 299, 304, 314, 321–5, 333–4, 339–40, 385–9
Balkan Wars (1912–13), 25, 28, 41, 293, 302, 306, 310–11, 323, 325–30, 340
al-Bana, ʻAbd al-Rahman, 245
Bandırmalı Şükrü, 320
Bangalore, 252
Banja Luka, 156, 165, 167, 174
Baqer Khan, 120–7, 130–3, 137–47
Basmachi (rebels), 29, 37, 38
Basra, 235–57, 383–4
Bassett, John, 343
Başıbozuk, 36
Batumi, 58, 285, 387
Bayazid II, 238
Bazirgan, 381
Bedouin tribes, 336, 339
Begin, Menachem, 389
Behamdum, 365
Beirut, 232, 242, 256, 347, 351–2, 357, 363–6, 371–4
Belchev, Hristo, 267, 271–4
Belgium, 221, 232, 265, 280, 300
Belgrade, 266–8, 274
Bell, Gertrude, 250, 252, 254
Bengal, 207
Benghazi, 24
Benoi, 111, 112
Berlin, 24, 60, 288, 293, 331, 373
Bestuzhev-Marlinskii, Aleksandr, 91
Beyoğlu, 229–30

Bihać, 156, 161, 163–4, 165, 172, 174
Bijeljina, 159, 161
Bitlis, 178, 188, 190, 194, 196, 199–204
Black Hand Society, 42
Black Mosque, 278
Black Sea, 29, 270, 285, 287, 294, 388
Boghos Nubar, 363
Bohtan emirate, 362
Bolshevik(s), 29, 56, 94–6, 116, 118, 282–91, 343
Bolu, 163
Bombay, 236, 247
Bosnia, 42, 151–67, 171–6, 292
Boyajian, Hampartsum, 190
Britain, British, 11 38, 42, 135, 191–5, 197, 207, 235–57, 312–18, 323–6, 330–48, 353, 357–60, 364, 368, 373, 378–81, 384
Brčko, 159
Brussels, 19, 373
Bucharest, 174, 287
Bulanık, 201
Bulgaria, Bulgarian(s), 12–14, 18, 45, 61, 66, 76, 153, 171, 206, 209, 217, 222, 226–7, 230, 234, 262–82, 287, 290–301, 325–6, 386–7
Bulgarian April Uprising (1876), 153
Bulgarian independence (1908), 292, 388
Burenin, N. E., 284, 285
Bursa, 305
al-Bu-Saraya, 336

Cairo, 19, 80, 236, 240, 247–8, 256–7, 316, 347, 357, 366, 373–4
Cairo Conference (1921), 254
Caliphate, 192, 204, 243, 364
Cardashian, Vahan, 368
Catholics, 155
Catroux, Georges, 347, 353
Caucasus, Caucasian, 4, 6, 7, 26–8, 35, 40, 42, 48, 52–60, 79–93, 96, 101–5, 111, 116–19, 136–7, 141, 201, 233, 262, 283–6, 299, 309–10, 323, 356, 359, 361, 365, 367, 384, 385
(Ahmed) Cemal Paşa, 28, 309, 313, 315, 341, 343
Chechen(s), Chechnya, 83–8, 91–119, 383, 384
Ceylon, 235, 255
Chermoevs, 119
Chernov, Victor, 65, 98, 99, 100

Cheta (çete), 37, 38, 44, 45, 167, 275, 356, 368, 383
Christian(s), 11, 45, 151, 155, 156–7, 160–77, 211, 350, 360–1
Chinese Revolution (1911), 135
Chlach (Shallash), Talal, 346, 353
Churchill, Winston, 347
Cilicia, 80, 350, 360
Circassian(s), 36, 211, 309–13, 316, 388
Civil Service Academy (*Mekteb-i Mülkiye*), 337
Committee of Union and Progress (*İttihad ve Terakki Cemiyeti*, CUP), 18–29, 41, 46–7, 235, 241–3, 292, 296, 302, 304, 307, 310–15, 319, 323–32, 384–6
Congress of Berlin (1878), 11
Congress of Prizren (1878), 386
Congress of Vienna (1815), 209, 216
Constanta, 288
Constitution of 1876 (*Kanun-i Esasi*), 20, 24, 292, 326
Cordelio (Karşıyaka), 330
Cossacks, 83–7, 107, 113, 117–18, 139
Cox, Sir Percy, 247, 254
Crete, 279
Crimea, 19
Crow, Francis, 249, 250
Çanakkaleli Atıf (Kamçıl), 313, 319, 324, 325, 326, 327, 331
Çerkes Edhem, 319, 330, 388
Çerkes Reşid, 327, 330, 388
Çetinkaya, Ali, 324

Dagestan, Dagestani(s), 26, 85, 88, 91, 98, 101–4, 112–13, 117, 384
Dalvorig, 190, 203
Damadian, Mihran, 183–6, 190
Damascus, 236, 244, 256, 334, 344–54, 366
Danube, 267
Darʿa, 347
Dardanelles, 294
Dashnak(s), Dashnaksutyun (ARF), 26, 27, 45, 52, 57–67, 70–2, 76–9, 195, 199–201, 214, 304, 357–61, 363, 365–72, 376–7, 381, 385–6
Dayr al-Zur, 335, 339, 345–7, 351, 352, 374
Delchev, Georgi, 13
Delchev, Gotse, 279, 280
Delhi, 236

Demonstrative Body (also Responsible Body), 61, 67, 71–3, 77, 78
Denizli, 374
Denmark, 222
Dersakissian, Minas, 45
Derviş Vahdeti, 327
Detroit, 357, 366, 373
Diyarbakir, 171, 184
Dolmabahçe Palace, 336
Droshak (journal), 185, 199
Duma, 100–1, 103
Duman, Nikol (Nikoghayos Ter Hovhannisian), 59
al-Dustur (journal), 244
Dr Nazım, 327

Eastern Question, 340
East India Company, 245
Edward VII of the United Kingdom, 23
Edhem Paşa, 190, 191
Edirne, 25, 45, 269, 319, 321, 324, 325, 326, 327
Egypt, Egyptian(s), 235–6, 246–8, 252, 255–7, 310–11, 318, 322–4, 331, 342–3, 366
Elisavetpol, 58
Empress Elisabeth of Austria (Austria-Hungary), 39, 63, 217, 233
(İsmail) Enver Paşa, 10, 19–30, 37, 40, 43, 51, 197, 294, 295, 302–3, 308, 313–18, 322–32, 340–1, 386
Erzurum, 190, 201
Erzurumlu Dadaş Salim, 309
Ethem Ruhi, 293
Euphrates, 335, 336, 339, 344–5, 352
Evranoszâde Rahmi (Arslan), 329–30
Eyüp Sabri, 313

Fain, Samuel, 60
Fahri (Türkkan) Paşa, 342
Farid Bey, 244
Favorsky, Alexey, 284
Faysal I bin al-Hussein, 235, 254–5, 342–7, 359, 378
feda'i, 23, 46, 137, 302, 307, 309, 319, 320–2, 328–9, 324–7, 330, 370, 383–6
Fenerjian, Kris, 73
Ferdinand I, 268, 271, 282
Ferghana, 38
Fethi (Okyar) 293, 327
Figner, Vera, 56

Filibeli (Filebeli) Hilmi, 313, 325, 328, 331
Filippov, Dimitri, 268, 269
Finland, 284, 287, 288
First World War, 6, 8, 25, 28–9, 41–2, 51, 80, 156, 262, 291, 295–6, 302, 305–6, 310–11, 318, 322–3, 330–4, 338, 340–1, 356, 358–9, 363, 369, 380–1, 388
Fiume, 286
France, French, 11, 192, 210, 219–22, 227, 231–3, 289–90, 323, 332, 340–61, 364, 368, 375–8, 381, 385
Fraternal Union, 273
Free and Moderate Party (*al-Hizb al-Hurr al-Mu'tadil*), 243
Freedom and Accord Party (*Hürriyet ve İtilaf Fırkası*), 242–3
Frelikh, Oleg, 95

Galata, 230, 268
Galati, 267
Galaev, 111
Garašanin, Ilija, 164
Garvanov, Ivan, 17
Gatuev, Dzakho, 95, 99–101
Geliguzan, 190, 196, 203–4
Gemidzhii, 17
Genc, 180, 186, 201
Geneva, 19, 71, 79, 221, 284, 288
Georgia, Georgians, 26, 58, 91, 137, 144, 288
Georgiev, Bone, 268, 274
Germany, 26, 28–9, 39, 96, 131, 219–22, 233, 235, 256–7, 285, 293, 296, 338
Ghazarian, Armenak, 195
Gilan, 138
Giresun, 388
Giulk[h]andanian, Abraham, 76, 79
Glamoč, 163
Golos pravdy, 101
Imam Gotskinskii, 117
Gračanica, 163
Gradačac, 159
Great Power(s), 11–12, 23, 181, 194, 200, 202, 206, 210, 217, 270, 305–6, 334, 340, 364, 386–8
Greece, Greek(s) 12, 18, 36, 45, 60, 151, 157, 160, 171, 173, 176, 280, 292–3, 325, 329–31, 368, 373, 384, 386–8
Greek-Orthodox Patriarchate, 12, 161, 176
Groznyi, 106, 119

Gruev, Dame, 13
Gudermes, 87, 105, 106, 107
Gushmazuko, 100, 112
Gushmazukaev, Abrek Zelimkhan, 83–8, 91–119, 384

Habsburg Empire, 4, 33, 51, 175–6
Hacı Mansur Paşa, 240
Haci Petkov, 162
Hadzhinikolov, Ivan, 13
Hakkari, 362, 369
Halil (Kut) Paşa, 323
Halil Beşar Ağa, 196, 198, 199, 205
Halil (Menteşe), 295
hayduk(s), 34, 383
Hama, 349, 351, 366
Hamburg, 291
Hamdi Paşa, 240
Hamidian, 18, 20, 181–2, 209–11, 224–6, 242, 305, 320, 323
  Hamidiye Cavalry Brigade, 339
  Hamidian massacres (1894–6), 60, 180, 187, 194, 195, 202, 214
al-Hananu, Ibrahim, 345
Hasaka, 366
Hasan Fehmi, 384
Hashemite dynasty, 238, 348, 388
al-Hashimi, Yasin, 338, 340, 344–7
Hasqail, Sasun, 254
Herzegovina, 153, 156, 157, 166
  Ottoman Herzegovina, 170
  Bosnia-Herzegovina, 292
Hijaz, 28, 256, 341–2, 348
Hişman Ağa, 188, 192, 199, 205
Holy Apostles Monastery, 200, 203, 206
Hunchakian Social Democratic Party, (Hnchakian) 58, 182–4, 187, 194–5, 214, 229, 304, 385
Husayn bin Ali al-Hashemi (Sharif of Mecca), 243, 248, 341–2, 344, 348
Husayn Shallah, 236
Hüseyin Ağa (of Hiyan), 188
Hüseyin Nazım Paşa (Police Minister), 218, 227, 228, 229, 234, 319
Hüseyin Nazım Paşa (Minister of War), 328, 384
Hüsnü Efendi, 198
al-Husri, Sati', 244

Ibn Rashid, 240
Ibn Sa'ud, 240, 256
Ibrahim Agha, 370

Ibrahim Sayf al-Din al-Gaylani, 238
Ihlevne, 164
İhsan Nuri, 369–70, 374, 379–80
al-Iqaz (newspaper), 242, 244
Ilinden Uprising (1903), 17–18, 20
Imperial Arsenal in Istanbul (*Tersane-i Amire*), 161, 162, 173
Imperial Tribal School (*Aşiret Mekteb-i Humayun*), 335, 336, 337, 338, 340, 348
Imperial War College (*Mekteb-i Harbiye-i Şahane*), 310
Imperial Military Academy (*Mekteb-i Ulum-ı Harbiye*), 316, 317, 323, 337, 338
Independence Tribunal (*İstiklâl Mahkemesi*), 312, 332
India, 207, 235, 236, 247, 248, 249
Ingush, 85, 86, 116, 118
Internal Macedonian Revolutionary Organisation (IMRO), (see Macedonian question)
Internal Passport Regulation (1887), 225
Interpol, 209
Ioannina, 157
Ipekian, Kaspar, 371
Iran, 40, 46, 58, 80, 88, 120–30, 133, 134, 136–7, 140–4, 146–7, 196, 335, 357, 374, 379–81, 386
  Constitutional Revolution of Iran (1906–11), 120–9, 132–5, 138–47, 371
Iraq, Iraqi, 235–6, 238, 241–9, 254, 255–7, 318, 331, 334–5, 343–5, 358–9, 361, 364, 366, 369, 374, 376, 378–9, 381, 385
  Iraqi Revolt of 1920, 345, 346
Irkutsk, 80
Isfahan, 138, 139
Iskenderun, 336
İşkodra (Shkodër), 324
Islam, 91, 93, 103–6, 122, 147, 152, 191, 194, 222, 243, 308, 350, 367
İsmet (İnönü), 308
Istanbul (Constantinople), 13, 19, 25, 56, 60–1, 63, 74, 79, 103, 170, 172, 197, 214, 221, 229, 230–6, 238, 240–2, 247, 266–71, 277–9, 282, 293–8, 303, 314–18, 321–2, 326–7, 333–4, 336–7, 357, 361–2, 369, 386
Italy, Italian(s), 24, 153, 220, 227, 231–4, 255, 314, 318, 322–5, 231–3, 340, 368

Ivanov brothers, 66, 273–5, 280–1
İzmir (Smyrna), 60, 314, 327, 329, 330–1, 374
İzmitli Mümtaz, 302, 313, 320, 323, 324, 328

Jafari, Shaban, 133, 145–6
Jaffa, 320
Jalali tribes, 370
Jamil Mardam Bey, 353
Jarablus, 366
Jazira (Syria), 361, 376
Jazirat ibn Omar, 376
Jeddah, 256, 341, 343–4, 348
Jerusalem, 45, 256
Jews, 11–12
Jezero, 165
Jin (journal), 369
John Grafton Affair in 1905, 287
Jordan, Transjordan, 347–8, 366
Joris, Edward, 76

Kabadayı, 47
Kadhim al-Dujayli, 245
Kadi-Iurt, 87, 106
Kadyrov, Ramzan, 97
Kalkandelen, 268
Kálnoky, Gustav, 267
Kaluga, 109
Karahisar, 166
Karaiovov, Toma, 276
Karalov, K. N., 115
Karaosmanoğlu dynasty, 385
Kars, 58, 387
Kasımpaşa, 268
Kasravi, Ahmad, 140
Kendirian, Vramshapuh, 61, 71, 75, 77–8
Kharachoi, 98, 112, 115
Kharkov, 80
Khasav-Iurt, 84
Khayri al-Hindawi, 245
Khaybar, Battle of, 342
Khaz'al (Sheikh of Muhammara), 241
Khazhak, Garegin, 79
Khrushchev, Nikita, 96
Khiyaban, 126
Khoybun League, 357, 358, 361, 364, 365, 366, 367, 368, 370, 371, 372, 373, 374, 375, 376, 377, 379, 381, 382, 385, 386
Kibirov, Georgii Alekseevich, 113, 115
Kitchener, Lord Herbert, 246

Kizlyar (Terek oblast), 83–8, 104–7, 110, 112, 116, 384
klepht(s), 34
Kobane, 374
komitadji (*komitacı*), 21, 24, 38, 41, 44–6, 177, 302–3, 306, 322, 369–70, 383, 386
Kosovo, 23, 314, 316
Kotur, 381
Kovalevskii, Pavel Ivanovich, 104, 105
Köstendil (Kyustendil), 279
Krasin, Leonid, 284, 288
Krinka rifles, 280
Kuleli military academy, 321
Kulp, 196, 201
Kumkapı, 184, 215
Kunta-Khadzhi, sheikh, 106
Kurd(s), 35–6, 179–80, 182–6, 188, 192–3, 196–200, 204, 207, 211, 310, 339, 355, 357–9, 360–70, 373–82, 385, 388
Kurdistan, 180, 334, 357, 359–60, 362, 365, 369, 376, 385
Kurdistan Teali Cemiyeti (KTC), 362, 369
Kurdistan (newspaper), 362, 363
Kürt Millet Fırkası, 363
Kurumov family, 119
Kuşçubaşı Eşref (Sencer), 302, 308–9, 312, 314, 317, 320–1, 323–32, 343
Kuşçubaşı Selim Hacı Sami, 302, 309, 312, 325–7, 329–32
Kütahya, 162, 166–7, 173
Kuwait, 236, 237, 239–41, 244, 336, 352

Laçkan, 202
Land Code of 1858, 156, 238
Lebanon, 353, 357, 359–60, 364–6, 375
Lenin, Vladimir, 96, 284, 288
Leopold II of Belgium, 232
Lermontov, Mikhail, 91
Levant, 360–2, 364, 368, 371, 375–6, 378, 381
Levantines, 331
Levski, Vasil, 14
Libya (Tripolitania/Trablusgarp), 19, 24, 164, 302, 306, 310, 322–5, 339–40, 388
Liége, 265–6, 278
Litvinov, Maxim (aka Felix), 285–8
Livno, 163, 165
London, 257, 373
Long Depression (1873–96), 39

luti, 47, 121–2, 124, 126–30, 132–4, 137, 139–47, 383–4
Luzhenovskii, Gavriil N., 56
Lynch Brothers Company, 243
Lyon, 231
Lyudskanov, A., 282

Macedonia, Macedonian(s), 10–14, 16–24, 29, 66, 72, 201, 206, 210–11, 213, 226, 263, 265–8, 272–7, 279–81, 283, 290–2, 298–300, 306, 311, 384–6, 387
   Macedonian question, 11, 23, 26, 211, 213–14, 265, 272–4, 276, 278, 323, 326
   Supreme Macedonian Committee, 14, 17, 273–81, 304
   Internal Macedonian Revolutionary Organisation (IMRO), 13–21, 30, 40, 43, 47, 52, 214, 276, 277, 279, 280, 281, 304, 321, 322, 385
MacMahon, Henry, 342, 343
Madras, 247
Mahmud II, 385
Malekzadeh, Mahdi, 140
Mallet, Louis, 318
Malta, 330
Mamakaev, Magomet, 96
Mamluks, 235
Manastır (Bitola), 19–20, 277, 319, 323, 326
Mannlicher rifles, 283
Marseille, 221, 373
Masyaf, 351
Maydan (Damascus), 351
Maysalun, battle of (1920), 347
McKinley, William, 63
Mecca, 103, 109, 235, 243, 248, 341, 343, 348
Medina, 103, 340, 341, 342
Mediterranean, 323–4
Mehmed Safi Bey, 182–3
Memduh Selim, 370, 376
Mensheviks, 283–4, 286
Merdzhan(ov), Yorgi, 268, 269
Mersin, 374
Mesopotamia, 249–50, 312, 360
Midhat Paşa, 238, 305
Middle East, 4, 6, 7, 28, 34, 35, 42, 47, 48, 52, 135, 142, 334, 340, 355, 356, 366, 371, 374, 374–5, 381, 386, 388, 389
Mikayeliyan, Ellen, 77, 78

Mikayeliyan, Kristapor, 59–61, 64, 68–72, 74–9, 82
Mikheev, Aleksandr Stepanovich, 105
Mikhin, Boris, 95
Milenković, Vasil, 159
Milos (Serbian prince), 166
Minasian, Sargis (Aram-Ashot), 67
Miqdad Midhat, 362
Mirza Kuchek Khan, 144, 146
Mitaev, Bamat Girei Khadzhi, 106–10
Mohammed Ali Shah, 92, 120, 123, 136, 139
Mohammad Reza Shah Pahlavi, 145
Montenegro, 11, 159, 292, 325
Montreal, 80
Moore, Arthur William, 122–4, 126, 130, 132
Mosaddeq, Mohammed, 145
Moscow, 80, 169
Mosul, 359, 366, 374, 376–8
Mouradian, Ardashes (alias Zeynal Bey), 370
Mozaffar ad-Din Shah, 135, 136
Mubarak of Kuwait (Sheikh), 240–1
Mudros armistice (1918), 342
Muhammara, 236–7, 241, 244
Muhammad Kurd 'Ali, 341
Muhammad (Prophet), 237, 308, 341
Mukhlis, Mawlud, 342
Munich, 256, 288
Muntafiq, 244
Muridism, 98, 108, 118
Muslim(s), 15, 23, 29, 40, 43, 58, 98, 103–4, 137, 155–7, 162, 165, 170, 177–87, 192–7, 201–2, 204–6, 247–8, 304, 308, 310, 316, 323, 359, 383, 386–8
Mussolini, Benito, 373
Mustafa Kemal (Atatürk) Paşa, 293, 308, 312, 317, 322–3, 331–2, 338, 340, 345, 348–50, 359, 370, 373, 388
Mustafa Reşit Efendi, 218
Muş, 180, 183–4, 186, 189–90, 192, 194–6, 200, 203–4

Nachovich, Grigor, 272, 274
al-Nakib, Haifa Ahmed, 235–6, 256
Naqīb al-Ashrāf, 236, 237–40, 242, 384
Naqib family, 239
al-Naqib, Sayyid Talib, 235–57, 384
al-Naqib, Sayyid Rajab, 239
Najd, 239–41

al-Nahda (journal), 245
Napoleon, 153
Nasser-al-Din Shah, 39, 63
Nauss, Joseph, 135
New York, 373
New York Times (newspaper), 368
Nice, 289, 357, 374
Nicholas II of Russia, 23, 84, 86
Nihilists, 228, 264
Niš, 153, 160
Niyazi (Resneli), 313, 326, 386
Nobel brothers, 291
Norway, 222
Non-Muslim(s), 6, 43, 158–60, 164, 171–4, 273, 304
Novo Selo, 165, 172
Nuri (Killigil), 323
Nusaybin, 376

O'Conor, Sir Nicholas, 241
Odessa, 266, 268–71, 287
Ohanjanian, Hamo, 59, 76–7, 79–80
Ohrid, 292, 324
Ömer Naci, 309, 322, 324
Orthodox Christian(s), 12, 155, 160, 167, 176
Osman Paşa, 174
Ostrožac, 165
Ottoman Bank, 38–9, 214, 230, 279
Ottoman Empire, 3-4, 6, 8–10, 12, 14–21, 25–6, 33, 35–7, 39, 41, 44–5, 51–2, 54, 58–60, 103–5, 136, 154–5, 164, 169–70, 172, 176, 182, 189–90, 192–7, 200–2, 224, 225, 227–8, 231–5, 237–9, 241, 253, 261, 263, 267, 269–72, 277–8, 280, 281, 287, 292, 293, 296–7, 299–304, 307, 309, 310–11, 315–16, 319–20, 322, 325, 327–8, 331, 334, 338, 340, 342, 348–51, 354, 359, 362–3, 368–9, 373, 385–8
Ottoman(s), 16–18, 21, 28, 40, 52, 66, 170, 173, 217–18, 220–2, 241–2, 245, 264–6, 273, 280, 292–4, 297, 306, 314, 317, 322–5, 340–2, 344, 346, 349–50, 359, 366, 369–70, 381, 387
Ottoman General Staff (*Erkân-ı Harbiye*), 317
Ottoman Penal Code, 173, 220, 223
Ottoman Staff College (*Erkan-i Harbiye Askeriye*), 338
Ottoman–Greek War (1897), 279

Ottoman–Italian War (1911–12), 302, 306, 310, 311, 314, 314, 322–5, 331, 339, 340, 388
Ottoman Liberty Society (*Osmanlı Hürriyet Cemiyeti*), 21, 387
Ottoman Nationality Law (1869), 270
Ozanian, Andranig, 195, 199–200
Öcalan, Abdullah, 389

Pahlavi period, 146
Palestine, 28, 256, 334, 342, 344, 345
Panitza, Major, 265, 266, 274
Papazian, Vahan, 365, 366, 373, 377
Paris, 19, 51, 245, 282–3, 285–9, 305, 364, 366, 373, 377
Paris Peace Conference (1919), 355, 359, 363
Parvus, Alexander, 296
Pastriulin, I. I., 107, 109
People's Will (*Narodnaia Volia*), 55, 64–5, 70, 214
Perm, 184
Perovskaia, Sofia, 55–6, 67, 68
Persian Gulf, 237, 239, 241, 245, 247, 250, 374
Persian Cossack Brigade, 136
Petranović, Teofil, 167
Petrov, Giorche, 279, 280
Philadelphia, 373
Philby, Harry St. John, 250
Plovdiv, 12
Pravo (newspaper), 273, 276
Prizren, 316
Port Said, 255
Prussia, 227

al-Qaddafi, Muammar, 389
Qadiriyya sufi order, 106, 109, 238
Qajar Iran, 4, 40, 51, 52, 63, 92, 104, 120, 122, 124, 127, 132, 135, 138, 140, 146, 358, 364, 269, 368, 379, 379–81, 385
Qaradagh, 127
Qasim, 'Abd al-Karim, 238
al-Qawuqji, Fawzi, 340, 349
Qutayfa, 350
al-Quwwatli, Shukri, 353

Radoslavov, Vasil, 281, 293–4, 296
rahzan, 133
Ramla, 345

Raqqa, 336, 345
Al-Rashid dynasty, 239
Rasht, 139, 141
Rayak–Hama railway, 232
Red Army, 29, 117, 331
Red Cross, 283
Red Sea, 341
Reform Society in Basra (*al-Jam'iyya al-Islahiyya fi al-Basra*), 243
Resne (Resen), 263, 267–9, 273–4, 278, 292, 299
Reval conference (1908), 23, 326
Rezai, Tayyeb Hajj, 133, 145–7
Reza Khan (Shah Pahlavi), 145–6, 380
Rifa'iyya sufi order, 240
al-Rihani, Amin, 244, 254–5
Rizov, Dimitar, 265, 266, 272–3, 275, 282
Rhodes, 305
Robin Hood, 88, 97, 98, 116, 239, 252, 253
Romanov dynasty, 4, 51
Romania, 11, 18, 222, 231, 232, 287, 288
Rome, 217–18, 357, 373
Rome Conference (1898), 216, 221, 222
Rostom (Stepan Zorian), 71, 77–8
Rotterdam, 288
Rowanduz Committee in Iraq, 378
Rubina (Sophie Areshian), 53–82, 384
Rubino, Gennaro, 232
Rumelia, 12, 156, 269
Rus (newspaper), 56
Rusić, Sava, 164
Russkoe slovo (newspaper), 112
Russo-Ottoman War (1877–8), 11, 17, 153, 206, 210, 263, 269, 299, 386
Russian Empire, 12–13, 19, 21, 24, 26–7, 35, 55, 58, 64, 79, 80, 83–119, 123, 135, 144, 161, 192, 196, 201, 219, 222, 231, 233, 262–72, 282–3, 286, 288, 290, 292, 301, 309, 326, 335, 385, 387
Russian(s), 55, 65, 85, 87, 91, 94, 98, 101, 105–6, 110, 112, 115–16, 118–19, 123, 135, 212, 214, 220, 270, 283, 287, 294
Russian Civil War, 94–5
Russian Social Democratic Labor Party, 284
Russian Imperial Bank, 288
Russian Constitutional Revolution of 1905, 134–5, 283, 284, 371
Russophile(s), 13, 97, 264, 266, 269, 271, 298

Sada Babil (newspaper), 245
Al-Sabah dynasty of Kuwait, 239
Sa'id, Sayyid Muhammad, 239
al-Sa'dun, 'Abd al-Muhsin, 241, 255
Safo (Martiros Margarian), 59, 62, 67, 70–9
al-Said, Nuri, 342
St Nedelya Church, 298
St Petersburg, 12, 80, 85, 101, 119, 216, 222, 264–5, 270–1, 284–6
St Petersburg Protocol (1904), 233
Salihli, 330
Salonica, 13, 17, 18, 19, 21, 305, 317, 319, 320, 324, 327, 329, 387
Salonica Affair (1901), 16–17
Salonica bombings (1903), 215, 230
San Remo Conference (1920), 346
Sandanski, Yane, 298
Sanusiyya sufi order, 323–5
Sapancalı Hakkı, 302, 312, 319, 322, 324, 326, 328, 332
Sarafov, Boris, 72, 275, 280, 283
Sarajevo, 42, 167
Sasun, 60, 178–207
Sasuni, Garo, 202, 203, 363
Sattar Khan, 12–13, 137–42, 144–5, 147
Saudi Arabia, 336
Al-Sa'ud dynasty, 239, 348
Savov, Mihail, 286
al-Sayyadi, Abu al-Huda, 240
Sayyid Abdulkadir, 362
Sbghank, 197, 198, 199, 200
Scott, Walter, 252
Second Socialist International, 367
Secret Centre (*markaze gheybi*), 137
Semal, 185, 190, 203
Şenkil, Teodosije, 163
Serbia, 12, 18, 42, 151, 156, 159, 161–72, 171, 174, 176, 222, 266–7, 292–3, 301, 325, 387
Serbian Revolution of 1804–17, 151
Serbian(s), 12, 159, 161, 166, 167, 174, 294, 386
Serbo-Bulgarian War of 1885, 266
Servet-i Fünun newspaper, 264
Shali, 88, 113, 115
Shallash, Ahmad, 336
Shallash, Muhammad Amir, 348, 352
Shallash, Ramadan, 333, 335–53
Shamil (Imam), 90, 92–8, 108, 115
Shamir, Yitzhak, 389
Sharif Paşa, 363
Shawkat, Naji, 256

Sheikh Said, 361–2, 364, 378
Sheikh Salih of Tunisia, 323
Shenik, 203
Sheripov, Aslanbek Dzhemaldinovich, 94
Shismanov, Vladimir (Vlad Dimitri), 268, 269, 270, 282
Shumaytiyya, 336, 347, 352, 353
Siberia, 80
Siird, 182
Sinai, 28
Sjenica, 162
Skosarevskii, M. P. (Omega), 284–5
Socialist(s), 41, 55, 56, 57, 64, 65, 212, 231
Socialist Republic of Gilan, 144
Society of Zealots of History (*Obshchestvo revnitelei istorii*), 104
Sofia, 12–14, 17, 63, 264–8, 270–82, 284–5, 287, 289, 292–300, 384, 387
Sotirov, Dimitar, 289
Soviet Russia, 29, 38, 56, 80, 94–6, 117, 364, 368
Spain, 222
Spiridonova, Maria, 56, 57
Stanchiev, Sofia, 267
Stanciov, P., 282
Stalin, Joseph (Iosif Vissarionovich Dzhugashvili), 56, 95, 144, 288
Stambolov, Stefan, 13, 39, 266–8, 270–2, 274–5, 278, 280–2, 384
Stavrev, Haliu, 274, 281, 282
Stavrev, Mikhail, 267
Stefkov, Hristo, 268, 269
Stockholm, 288
Stoilov, Konstantin, 271, 278
Stone, Ellen, 281
Stoyanov, Done, 277
Sufi(s), 94, 106, 108, 109, 118
Sunzha, 85
Sulayman Faydi, 241–3
Süleyman Kani (İrtem), 292
Süleyman Nazif, 242
al-Suwaydi, Tawfik, 24
Sykes-Picot Agreement, 343, 345, 346
Syria, 3, 27–8, 235, 241, 244, 248, 309, 323–4, 334, 343–4, 347–8, 350, 352–3, 355–62, 366, 374–9, 381–2, 385
Syrian(s), 349–51, 378, 381
Syrian revolt (1925–7), 348, 353
Sweden, 222
Şemsi Paşa, 319, 326, 384

Cemaleddin Efendi (Şeyhülislam), 63
Şükrü (Mehmed) Sekban, 373

Tabriz, 120, 122–4, 126, 127, 130, 132, 134, 136–42, 146, 374, 384
Tahsin Paşa, 186
(Mehmed) Talat Paşa, 27, 294, 295, 313, 315, 319, 318, 328, 329
Talkhikov, 115
Tanin (newspaper), 294, 295
Tankiz Mosque, 352
Tanzimat, 151, 153, 155–8, 172, 174
Taormina (ferry), 232
Tapik, 201
Tehran, 120, 136, 139, 141, 145–6, 379–80, 384
Terek region, 83, 85, 101, 103–5, 112–13, 117
Terek River, 84
Ter-Petrosiyan, Semen (Kamo), 288
Ter-Minassian, Roupen, 367
Teşkilat-ı Mahsusa (Special Organisation), 26, 28, 41, 44, 309, 329, 331, 384
Thaçi, Hashim, 389
Thrace, 326, 386
Tiflis (Tbilisi), 57–8, 79–80, 107, 288–9, 290
Tiflis Gymnasium, 58
Tobacco Revolt (1890–2), 40, 134
Tobruk, 320
Topal (Lame) Osman, 388
Topçu Mehmed İhsan (Eryavuz), 313, 324–5, 331, 332
Trabzon, 29
Travnik, 164, 165, 174
Treaty of Berlin (1878), 11, 210, 263, 264, 386–7
Treaty of Constantinople (1913), 326
Treaty of Lausanne (1923), 360
Treaty of Paris (1856), 210
Treaty of San Stefano (1878), 386
Treaty of Sèvres (1920), 359, 365, 369
Trieste, 286
Trotsky, Leon, 41, 284
Tsalikov, Akhmet Tembulatovich, 93, 101
Tsvetkov, Taliu, 274
Tuna province, 171
Tunisia, 323
Turkestan, 29, 37
Turkey, 35, 45, 52, 103–4, 234, 243, 294, 312, 331, 344, 356–82, 387, 388

Turk(s), 26, 46, 169, 170–1, 295, 305, 310, 316, 360, 364, 369
Turkish–French relations, 360, 376
  Ankara agreement (1921), 360
Turkish–Iraqi Permanent Frontier Commission, 379
Turkish–Persian Frontier treaty (1932), 380
Turkish War of Independence, 298, 332, 348, 350, 359
Tyufekchiev brothers, 263, 266–8
Tyufekchiev, Dencho, 263, 266–7
Tyufekchiev, Dimitri, 263
Tyufekchiev, Naum Andreev, 66–7, 261–3, 265–6, 268–301, 384
Tyufekchiev, Nikola, 263, 266, 268–9, 278, 282, 286

Union of Muslim Revolutionary Societies, 29
University of Liège, 265
United States of America, 58, 92, 220, 334, 335, 372, 373
üçleme (one third) tax, 155, 157–60, 162–3, 177

Vagrancy Act, 225
Van, 365
Varna, 61, 282, 285, 287
Vartanian, Serob, 195, 196, 199
Vedeno, 84, 87, 96, 98, 108, 110–11, 115
Vidin, 153, 163, 166, 263
Vienna, 72, 293
Vlachs, 12
Vladikavkaz, 112, 115, 119
Verbitskii, 87, 105, 107, 108
Vorontsov-Dashkov, Illarion, 84–7, 107
Voivode, 44–5
Vulkovich, Dr Georgi, 268–70, 274, 282

Wilkes, John, 252
Wilson, Arnold, 256
Wilsonian principles, 369

Imam Yahya, 348
Yakup Cemil, 302, 312, 315, 319–20, 322, 324–5, 328, 331
Yeghigian, Ashod, 69
Yemen, 207, 241, 311, 343, 348
Yenibahçeli Mehmed Şükrü (Oğuz), 309, 313, 321, 324, 332
Yenipazar, 162
Yeprem Khan, 141, 146
Yerevan, 58, 288, 367
Yıldız Mosque, 61, 63
Yıldız Palace, 178
Yonkov-Vladikin, Nikola, 290
Young Macedonian Literary Society, 13
Young Ottomans, 20
Young Turk(s), 10, 18–19, 21, 25, 29, 40, 103, 242–3, 248, 292–3, 294–5, 298, 302, 305–6, 313, 320, 325, 332, 384, 387–8
Young Turk Revolution of 1908, 24, 135, 241, 291, 302, 303, 305, 306, 309, 315, 320, 324, 326, 387–8
Yurdakul, Mehmed Emin, 309

Zakho, 366
Zavarian, Simon, 78
Zaydi rebellion, 207
Zeki Paşa, 190
Imam Zelimkhan, 103
Zelimkhan (film), 95
Zelimkhan, Iandarbiev, 96
Zheliabov, Andrei, 67
Zeitlian, Sona, 56
Zoltamurad, 99, 100, 112
Zvornik, 156, 158–9, 162–3, 165–6, 173–4